THIS DAY IN AEROSPACE

THIS DAY IN AEROSPACE

A 365-DAY JOURNEY THROUGH AVIATION AND SPACE HISTORY

AMY STAMM, DR. JOSEPH ABEL, AND DR. JENNIFER LEVASSEUR

ABRAMS, NEW YORK

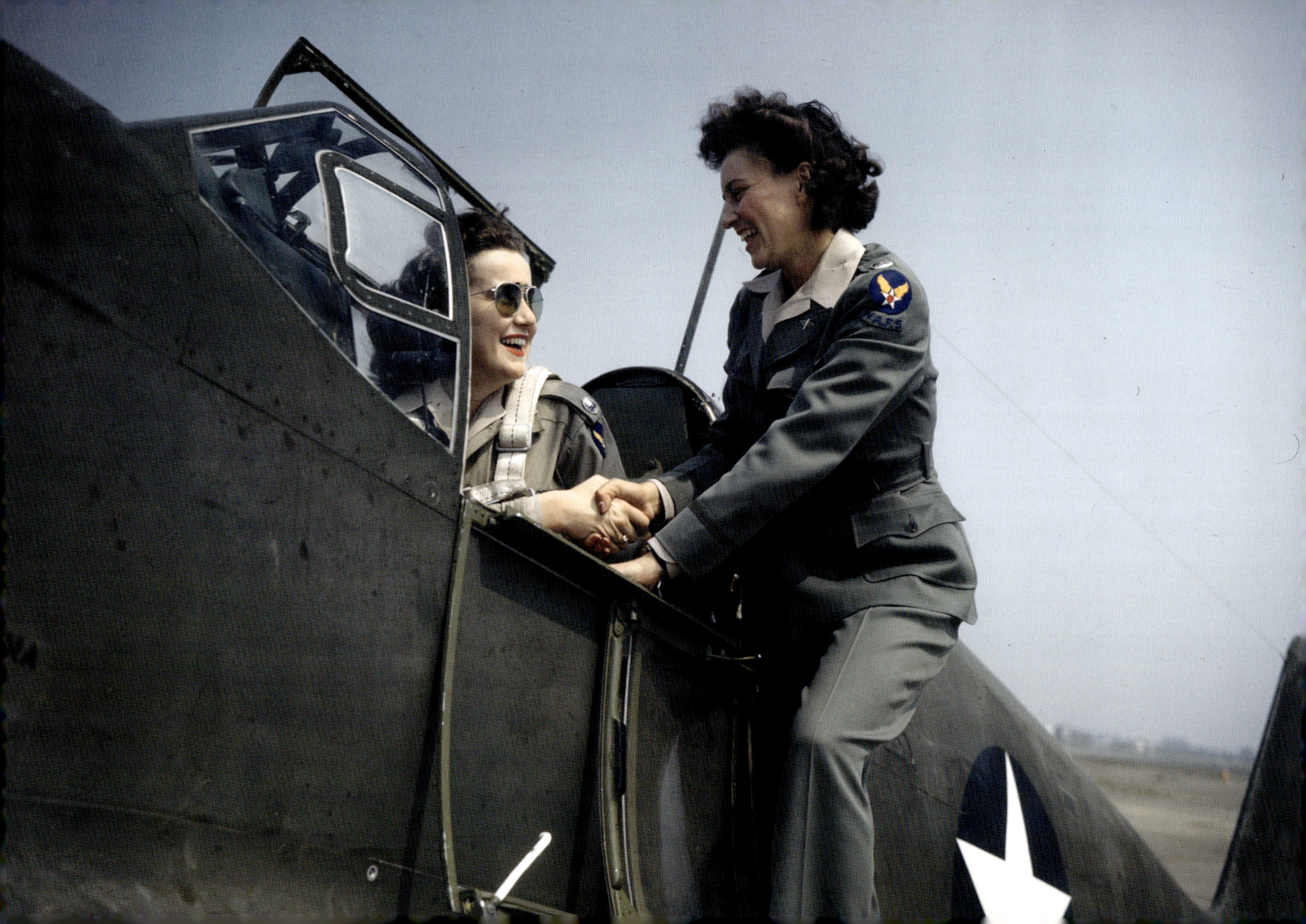

INTRODUCTION

When people think of aviation and space history, monumental moments that changed the world probably come to mind: the Wright brothers making the first flight of a controlled, powered aircraft in 1903; Charles Lindbergh flying solo nonstop across the Atlantic in 1927; or Neil Armstrong and Buzz Aldrin stepping foot on the Moon in 1969. But there are so many other important and intriguing moments worth remembering. More than one every single day of the year, in fact.

Within this book, you will find one moment from the history of aviation or space connected to each day of the year. Some are industry-defining moments, and others represent stepping stones that made aerospace what it is today. Many will be familiar to you, and some you will be learning about for the first time. All have been selected to provide a wide look at the various fields of aviation and spaceflight. You'll find stories about exploring other planets and sending humans to space; about early helicopters and cutting-edge military jets; and about the people who made aerospace breakthroughs possible.

The selection of featured events is also informed by the collection of the Smithsonian's National Air and Space Museum. In fact, most of these events have associated artifacts in the Museum's collection. Representing the world's largest collection of historic aircraft and spacecraft, the Museum's holdings include almost eighty thousand artifacts and an even greater number of archival records, including photographs and documents related to the history of flight.

The Museum's collection contains everything from artifacts from when engineers were just figuring flight out, like early gliders, to objects representing the height of technological achievement, like Saturn V rockets. These artifacts range in size from the very large (think airliners and a Space Shuttle orbiter) to the very small (for example, a half-inch-long chip of wood from the Wright Flyer that traveled to the Moon on Apollo 11). Many of these objects are on display at the Museum's two public locations in Washington, D.C., and Chantilly, Virginia, which together are visited by millions of people each year. Additional artifacts are on loan to other museums around the world, while a large portion of the collection is stored for study, preservation, and future display.

It is through this unparalleled collection and the expertise of its curators and staff that the Museum celebrates, commemorates, and preserves aviation and space history.

The history-making events and people highlighted in this book span centuries—ranging from the years 1452 to 2026—and continents. They also cover numerous aspects of aviation and spaceflight. You may choose to read this book straight through—or perhaps read the corresponding event each day of the year. If you would prefer to jump around and read about the topics that most interest you, you can also explore by color-coded curatorial categories.

With tens of thousands of artifacts to classify and organize, curators from the Museum's Aeronautics and Space History departments established categories for grouping the artifacts in their collections.

Throughout this book, each featured event and personality will be identified with one of seventeen curatorial categories. You can find the event groupings by curatorial category in the index.

These categories are:

AVIATION HISTORY

Commercial Aviation: The business of transporting nonmilitary passengers and cargo, including airlines and airmail

Early Flight: Aircraft, people, and events associated with the years before 1914, including some pre-twentieth-century innovators such as Leonardo da Vinci and Otto Lilienthal

General Aviation: Nonscheduled and nonmilitary civilian aircraft, including private, business, and utility aircraft, as well as gliders, ultralights, and homebuilts

Lighter-Than-Air Flight: Balloons, airships, and other objects that fly because they are buoyant

Modern Military Aviation: Aircraft, people, and events associated with military aviation after World War II, from 1945 to the present

Pioneers of Flight: The men and women who set aviation records, accomplished firsts, and built iconic companies or machines; though these trailblazers are mostly associated with the "golden age" of flight before World War II, pioneering moments continue to occur into the present

Vertical Flight: Helicopters, autogyros, and vertical takeoff and landing (VTOL) aircraft

World War I and Interwar Military Aviation: Aircraft, people, and events associated with military aviation from 1914 to 1939

World War II Military Aviation: Aircraft, people, and events associated with military aviation from 1939 to 1945

SPACE HISTORY

Civilian Applications Satellites: Equipment related to studying Earth, providing communications, and gathering information on weather

Guidance and Navigation: Computers and other equipment used to control a spacecraft's movement through space

Human Spaceflight: Spacecraft and equipment that allow humans to live and work in space

International Space Programs: Space-related artifacts from countries other than the United States

National Security Space: Previously classified and unclassified military and other security mission equipment

Rockets and Missiles: Rockets, missiles, and equipment for military and human spaceflight launches

Social and Cultural Space: Science fiction and memorabilia of actual spaceflight

Space Science: Tools and spacecraft used to study astronomy, geology, the solar system, and other scientific interests in space

HISTORY OF THE NATIONAL AIR AND SPACE MUSEUM

The National Air and Space Museum location in Washington, D.C., officially opened in 1976, but the history of the Museum began long before that.

In 1861, early aeronaut Thaddeus Lowe made a tethered balloon flight from the Columbia Armory grounds in downtown Washington, D.C. One hundred fifteen years later, the National Air and Space Museum opened just a stone's throw away. The Smithsonian's interest in ballooning, and thus aviation, stretches back even earlier.

The Smithsonian Institution was founded in 1846 after English chemist and mineralogist James Smithson left his estate to the United States to found an organization "for the increase and diffusion of knowledge." It took much time and debate to figure out what exactly this new Smithsonian Institution would be, and it wasn't until 1858 that it was designated as the National Museum. In the early years of the Smithsonian, the Institution focused on scientific research, with prominent American scientist Joseph Henry serving as its first Secretary.

Henry became interested in aeronautics in the 1830s when he saw a balloon ascent for the first time. He quickly began considering how balloons could be used to advance scientific goals, especially in weather forecasting. Henry formed relationships with pioneering American balloonists John Wise and Lowe, the latter of whom he encouraged to explore how ballooning might support the U.S. government in reconnaissance efforts during the Civil War. While Lowe was in D.C. to propose a Union Army balloon corps, Henry arranged for his balloon to be inflated, leading to Lowe's flight above what is now the National Mall.

The Smithsonian's third Secretary, Samuel Pierpont Langley, also had a keen interest in aviation. Langley conducted aerodynamic

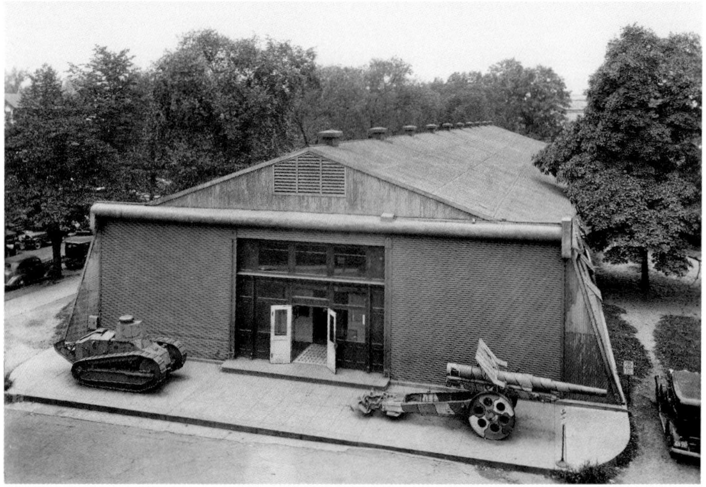

Built in 1918 (and pictured here in 1938), the Smithsonian's Aircraft Building housed most of the Institution's aviation collection for decades.

Smithsonian's National Air and Space Museum (NASM 2002-10653)

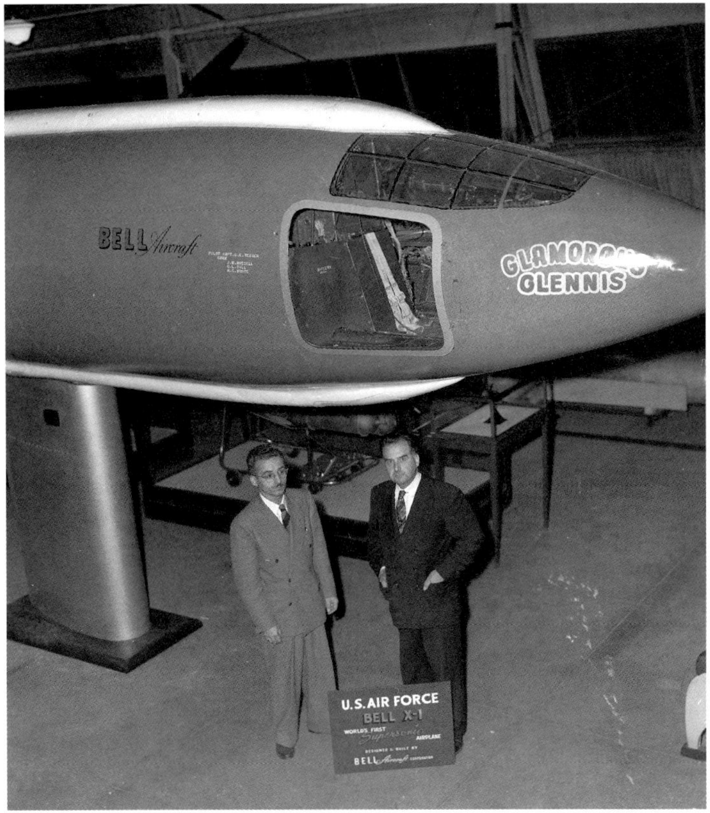

National Air Museum curator Paul Garber (right) was instrumental in the acquisition of the supersonic Bell X-1 in 1950.

Smithsonian's National Air and Space Museum (NASM 2003-25375)

research and built several small heavier-than-air machines that could fly without a human aboard, though he was unable to scale up his "aerodrome" for piloted flight. (Read about how Langley's attempts to build a flying machine eventually led to problems for the Smithsonian on page 114).

During these early years of the Smithsonian, the Institution collected its first aeronautical objects, starting with forty-three Chinese kites made of silk and bamboo from the 1876 Centennial Exposition in Philadelphia. After World War I, the Smithsonian began displaying airplanes and other wartime artifacts in the metal Aircraft Building behind the Smithsonian Castle, but its aviation collection really took off with the arrival of a twenty-year-old enthusiast named Paul Garber.

Garber began working at the Smithsonian in 1920, dedicating himself to the preservation of aviation history and sharing his passion for flight with Smithsonian visitors. In the 1920s, Garber, working as a junior curator in the Institution's U.S. National Museum, almost single-handedly amassed one of the finest collections of historic aircraft in the world, including Charles Lindbergh's *Spirit of St. Louis*.

As the story goes, in May 1927, while Lindbergh was flying *Spirit of St. Louis* across the Atlantic, Garber drafted a cablegram asking him to donate the aircraft to the Smithsonian. Garber was determined that Lindbergh's flight would be a turning point for aviation, so he asked Smithsonian Secretary Charles Abbot to send the note to Lindbergh. While Abbot was not immediately convinced, he did send the cablegram, and it arrived in Paris two days after Lindbergh, who eventually agreed to sell the *Spirit of St. Louis* to the Smithsonian for the nominal price of one dollar.

The acquisition of *Spirit of St. Louis* was a significant milestone for the Smithsonian, as the general public began associating the Institution with aviation and clamoring for more artifacts on the topic. Smithsonian leadership began paying more attention to the aeronautical collection, even reorganizing its management in 1931 to accommodate the increased focus. Garber and the Division of Engineering's new Section of Aeronautics continued to collect airplanes and other aviation artifacts, including Wiley Post's Lockheed Vega *Winnie Mae* (see page 90), the Wright EX biplane *Vin Fiz* (see page 328), and Lincoln Ellsworth's Northrop Gamma *Polar Star* (see page 344). In 1948, after the Smithsonian clearly stated that the Wright brothers invented the first piloted aircraft "capable of flight," not Langley, Garber was also able to acquire the 1903 Wright Flyer (read more about the Wright–Smithsonian feud that kept the Wright Flyer from the Institution for decades on page 114).

As the Smithsonian's aeronautical collection continued to grow, it became more and more clear that there was not enough room in the Aircraft Building and the nearby Arts and Industries Building to display its aeronautical treasures in a way that did justice to them. And so, Garber began to propose a museum dedicated to aviation alone. At the end of World War II, Army Air Forces commander Gen. Henry "Hap" Arnold spurred new discussions with his promise to donate the service's collection of surplus U.S. and Allied military aircraft and captured enemy planes.

On August 12, 1946, President Harry S. Truman signed Public Law 722, creating the National Air Museum as part of the Smithsonian Institution. The bill called for the Museum to memorialize the development of aviation; collect, preserve, and display aeronautical equipment; and provide educational material for the study of aviation. Although the bill established the Museum, it notably didn't set aside funds to create a museum building, a challenge that was compounded when, during the Korean War, the Air Force took back the buildings outside Chicago that stored the aircraft and missiles it had given to the Smithsonian. Garber cobbled together land and buildings to create a storage facility in Suitland, Maryland, that later was named the Paul E. Garber Preservation, Restoration, and Storage Facility. The Museum continued to display key artifacts for public view in the Aircraft and Arts and Industries buildings.

During the mid-1950s, Smithsonian Secretary Leonard Carmichael pushed to get a permanent location for a National Air Museum building. In September 1958, Congress designated the National Mall site where the building now stands, but Smithsonian efforts to get construction funds were still stalled. Eight years later, President Lyndon B. Johnson signed the National Air Museum Amendments Act on July 19, 1966. This legislation added "and Space" to the Museum's name and authorized the construction of a new building for the National Air and Space Museum. However, Congress did not want to appropriate funds for that purpose until Vietnam War expenditures declined.

In the wake of 1969's Apollo 11 Moon landing, Smithsonian leadership and Senator Barry Goldwater renewed the push to fund the building. Congress finally authorized its construction in 1971. Around the same time, Smithsonian Secretary S. Dillon Ripley selected Apollo 11 astronaut Michael Collins as the Museum's next director. In 1972, construction began, and in early 1975, the building was completed. Then it was time to fill the building with artifacts and exhibitions.

Collins hired the Museum's first professional historians to curate the exhibitions and tapped planetary scientist Farouk El-Baz to lead the Museum's new Center for Earth and Planetary Studies, which would conduct active research about the planets and moons in the solar system. Under Collins's leadership, and with the staff he needed to make it happen, the National Air and Space Museum opened on the National Mall "ahead of time and within its budget."

The National Air and Space Museum opened on July 1, 1976, just three days before the U.S. Bicentennial. The opening day ceremony was attended by a who's who of Washington, including President Gerald Ford, who praised the new museum as a monument to "the American spirit of adventure." After a ribbon cutting triggered by a spacecraft orbiting Mars, the doors opened and visitors began to stream in. With a seemingly endless number of aerospace treasures to feast their eyes on, visitors and the media alike were immediately taken with the National Air and Space Museum. In fact, on the official Bicentennial Day (July 4), a staggering sixty-five thousand people came to see the wonders it held. And the interest didn't slow down. The Museum welcomed its five millionth visitor just six months after opening.

The building itself, designed by architect Gyo Obata, was 685 feet long and covered in Tennessee pink marble and dark glass. Critics praised the building, calling it a "dignified, handsome work of architecture" and "an appropriate and harmonious finale to the grand architectural concert on the Mall." But despite containing 10 acres of exhibition space, it still wasn't large enough to display most of the Museum's collection.

Within just a few years of the opening of the Museum's dedicated building on the National Mall, officials had already begun scouting locations for a second public facility. Throughout the 1980s, various groups at the Museum and in the greater D.C. and Virginia community made efforts to advance the project, which was to be built on land leased from Washington Dulles International Airport. In 1993, President Bill Clinton signed Public Law 103-57, officially authorizing the Smithsonian to plan and design the annex.

In 1999, aviation entrepreneur Steven F. Udvar-Hazy donated $60 million for the construction of the facility, and the following year, the annex was named the Steven F. Udvar-Hazy Center in recognition of his generous gift. Construction of the newly named building began in 2001, and the Museum was once again up against the clock. Director Gen. John "Jack" Dailey committed the Museum to opening the Center in late 2003 as part of the national Centennial of Flight celebration, marking the one hundredth anniversary of the Wright brothers' first flight.

The Steven F. Udvar-Hazy Center officially opened to the public on December 15, 2003, two days before the Wright anniversary. Although the 1903 Wright Flyer was displayed at the Museum's building in D.C., a replica of the aircraft appeared in the official dedication ceremony on December 11, "flying" overhead and landing onstage, to trigger a curtain drop that was the official unveiling of the building. Despite frigid weather on December 15, the Center's opening day was very well attended, and over two hundred thousand people visited the Center in its first two weeks. The Udvar-Hazy Center is also home to state-of-the-art collections storage, conservation, preservation, and restoration facilities, most of which were completed in 2010.

In the fifty years since the National Air and Space Museum building opened in D.C., the nation's foremost aerospace museum has continued to acquire new artifacts, install new exhibitions, carry out educational programming, and hold special events. This has

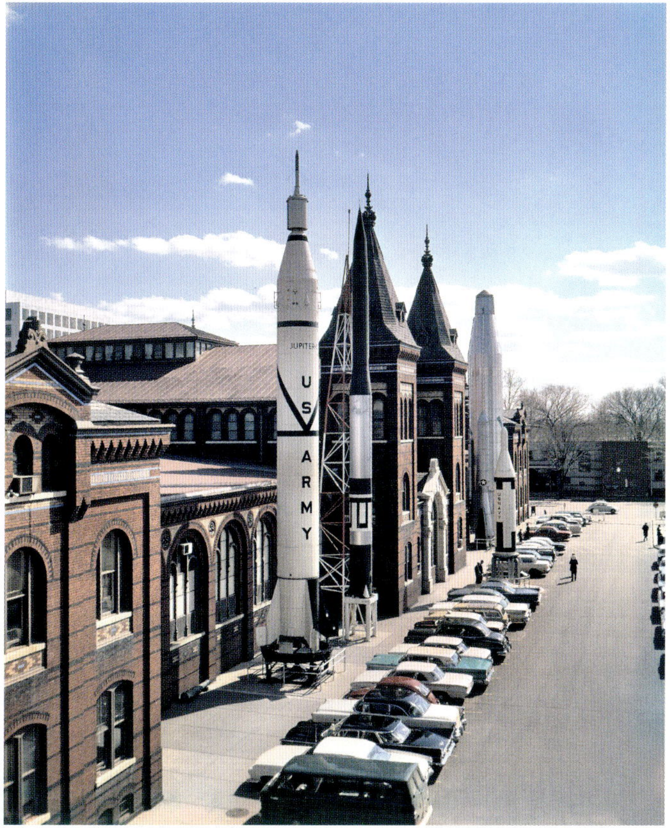

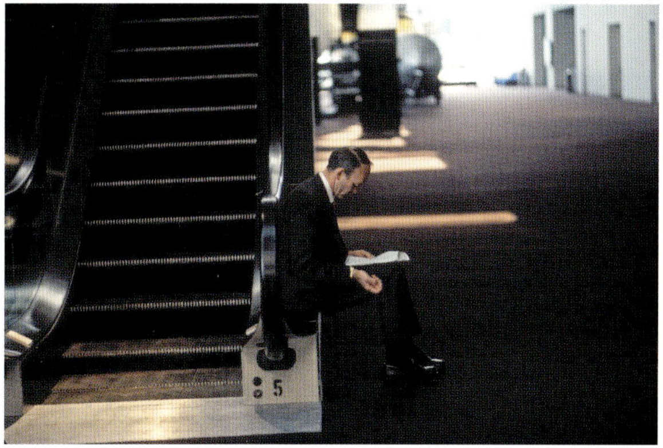

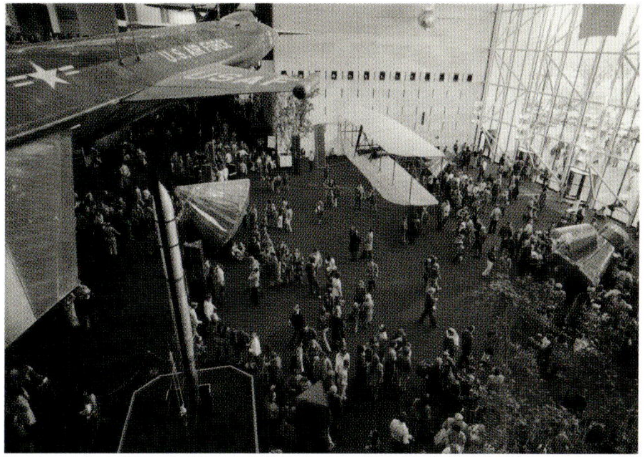

LEFT Before the National Air and Space Museum's flagship building opened, it displayed its collection around the National Mall, including its "Rocket Row" outside the Smithsonian's Arts and Industries Building.

Smithsonian's Institution Archives. Acc. 11-009 [73-7185]

RIGHT TOP Apollo 11 astronaut Michael Collins was the director of the National Air and Space Museum when its flagship building opened in 1976.

Smithsonian's National Air and Space Museum (NASM 2009-31387)

RIGHT BOTTOM *Milestones of Flight* was one of the most popular exhibitions at the National Air and Space Museum when it opened.

Photo by Richard B. Farrar, Smithsonian National Air and Space Museum (NASM 76-19265) included collecting artifacts as history is made, like SpaceShipOne (see page 288), a McDonnell Douglas F-15C Eagle, and Space Shuttle *Discovery* (see page 70); exhibitions about everything from Hawaiian air travel to Star Wars; and lectures by iconic aviation and space figures like Chuck Yeager and nearly all of the Apollo crews. The Museum has also been depicted in a number of Hollywood films. In *Night at the Museum: Battle of the Smithsonian*, the Museum comes to life; in *Captain America: The Winter Soldier*, the titular superhero visits an exhibition about his life; and in *Transformers: Revenge of the Fallen*, the SR-71 on display at the Udvar-Hazy Center transforms into the former Decepticon Jetfire.

One of the Museum's most showstopping events was its 2019 celebration of the fiftieth anniversary of the Apollo 11 Moon landing. As part of the weeklong celebration, the Museum hosted the *Apollo 50: Go for the Moon* projection show, which re-created the launch of Apollo 11 and told the story of the first Moon landing through full-motion projection mapping. For three nights, a Saturn V rocket was projected on the Washington Monument, and on July 19 and 20 the Museum showed a twenty-minute projection show, which played out on the face of the Monument and supporting screens. In total, over a half-million people came to see *Go for the Moon* during its five-day run.

When the National Air and Space Museum building in D.C. opened, a journalist at *The New York Times* declared that "the Smithsonian [had] finally moved into the 20th century." In the 2010s, it became clear to Museum officials that updates were needed in order to maintain the prestige of the Museum and keep up with current developments in both aerospace achievements and museum design—effectively moving it into the twenty-first century. The need to make upgrades to building systems presented the Museum with the opportunity to transform from the inside out, and in 2018, it began closing exhibitions as part of its renovation project.

In 2026, the Museum completed the renovation of the National Air and Space Museum in D.C., redoing all twenty of its galleries and transforming the visitor experience. The updated Museum features reimagined versions of some of its most popular exhibitions, like *Barron Hilton Pioneers of Flight* and *RTX Living in the Space Age* and brand-new exhibitions like *Futures in Space* and *Modern Military Aviation*. The Museum's most iconic artifacts, including the 1903 Wright Flyer, the Apollo 11 command module *Columbia*, and Lindbergh's *Spirit of St. Louis*, remain on display, joined by over 1,500 artifacts that are new to display at the Museum's D.C. location.

Never an institution to rest on its laurels, the Museum is now undertaking an expansion of the Steven F. Udvar-Hazy Center that will add nearly 45,000 square feet of display space to the Boeing Aviation Hangar, allowing it to showcase even more of the collection.

As aviation and space history forge ahead, the Museum will continue to collect and display new artifacts. Generations from now, when someone wants to know about the history of aviation and spaceflight, the Museum will have the artifacts and the exhibits that will tell that story all in one place. Its mission will continue to be "to commemorate, educate, and inspire" groundbreaking moments in air and space history for years to come.

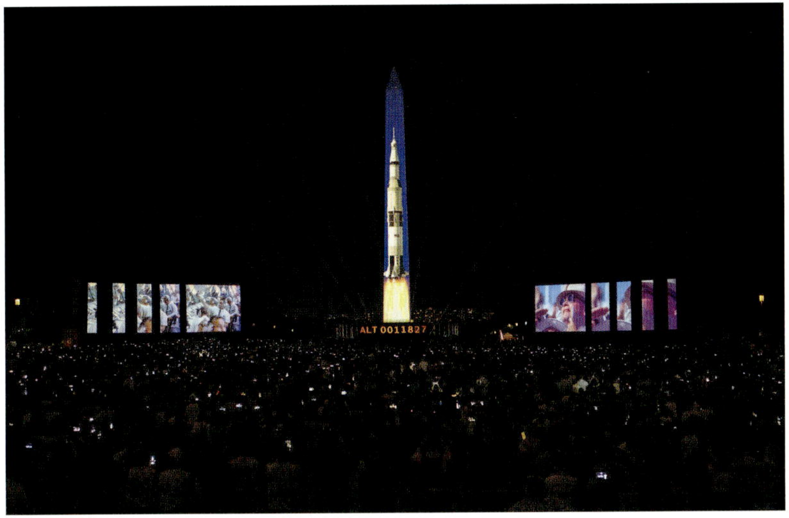

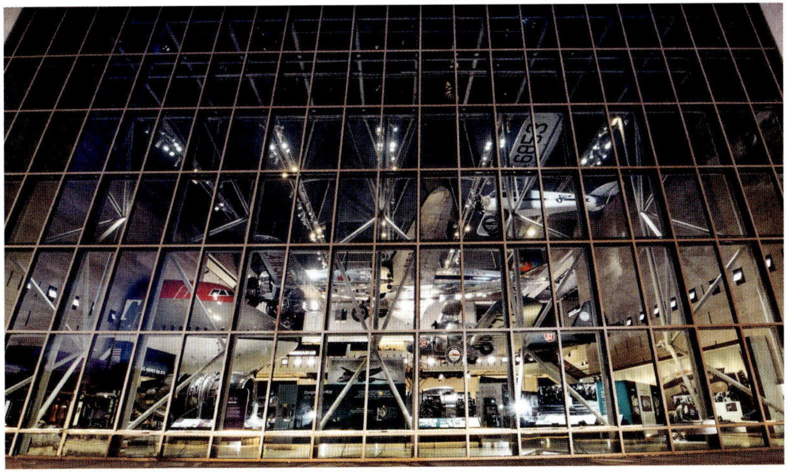

TOP To celebrate the 50th anniversary of the Apollo 11 Moon landing, the National Air and Space Museum projected a Saturn V rocket on the Washington Monument.

Smithsonian's National Air and Space Museum

BOTTOM In October 2022, the National Air and Space Museum began opening its renovated galleries, including the reimagined *America by Air* exhibition.

Smithsonian's National Air and Space Museum

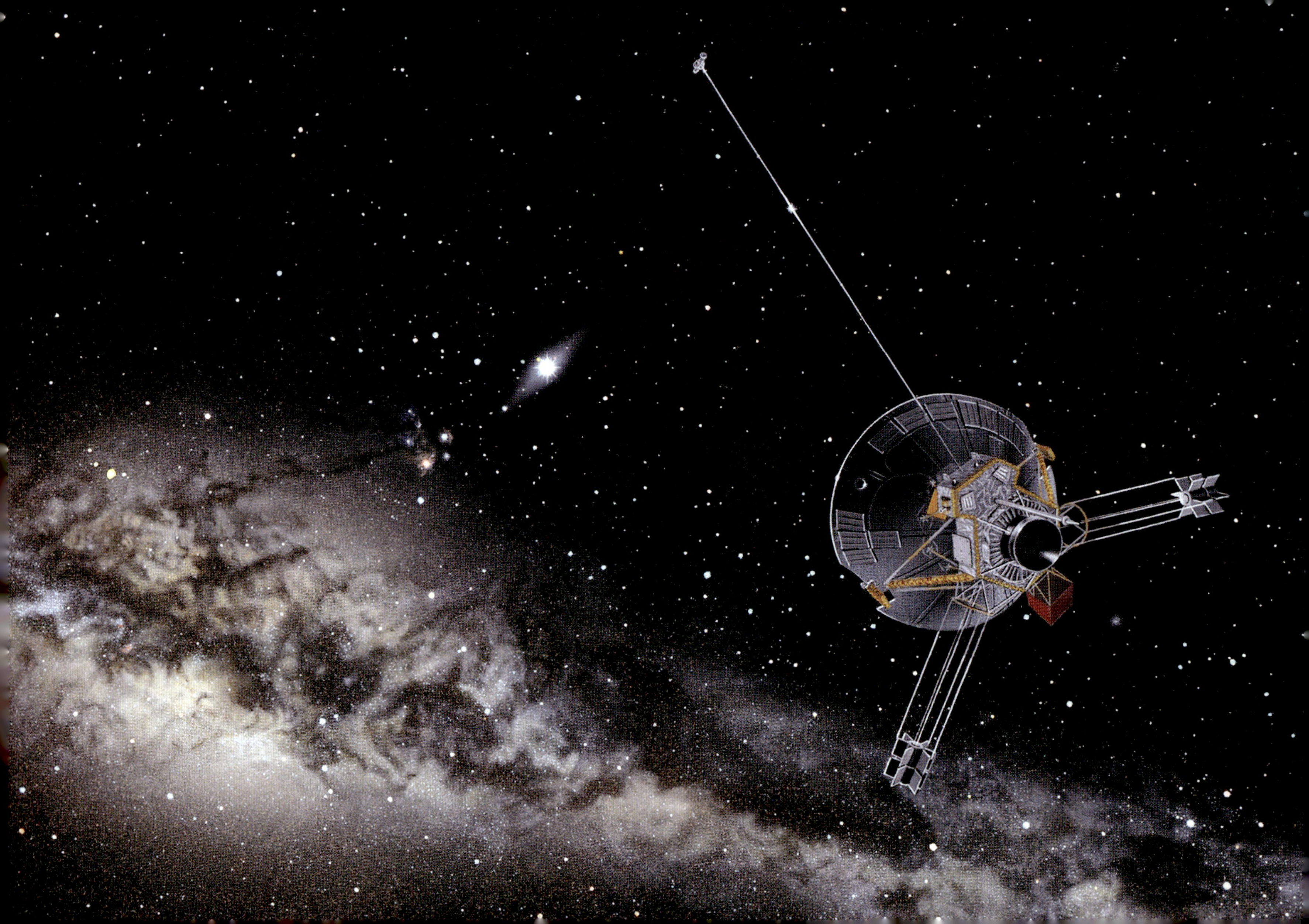

JANUARY

BETTY SKELTON BECOMES AN AEROBATIC CHAMPION

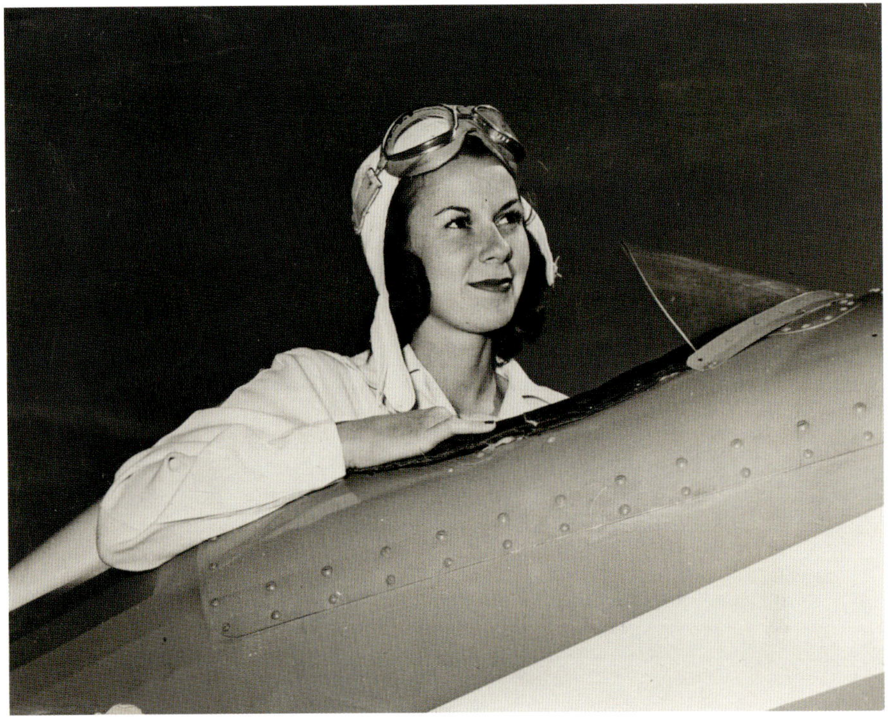

Betty Skelton began her aerobatic career flying a Great Lakes Model 2T-1A biplane.

Smithsonian's National Air and Space Museum (NASM 9A18937)

Betty Skelton won her first Feminine International Aerobatic Championship on January 1, 1948. This was just the beginning of Skelton's championship success, and she went on to three-peat, winning again in 1949 and 1950. She won her second and third championships in a Pitts Special S-1C nicknamed *Little Stinker*, which is part of the National Air and Space Museum's display at the Steven F. Udvar-Hazy Center.

As if setting records in the air wasn't enough, Skelton also became a record holder on land after retiring from aerobatics. Her career as a race car driver began when she met NASCAR founder Bill France in 1953. At his encouragement, she attended Speed Week at Daytona Beach the following year, driving the pace car and setting a stock car record. She was also the first woman to serve as a test driver for the auto industry and earned a total of four women's world land speed records.

STARDUST SPACECRAFT COLLECTS SAMPLES FROM COMET WILD 2

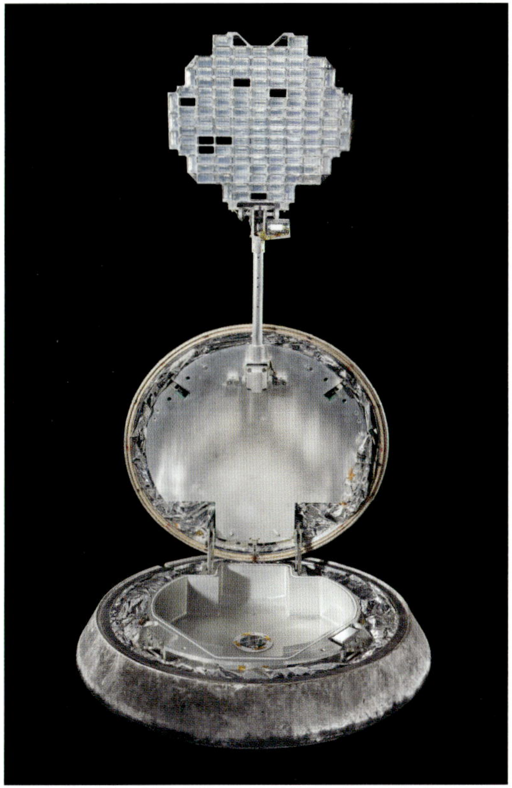

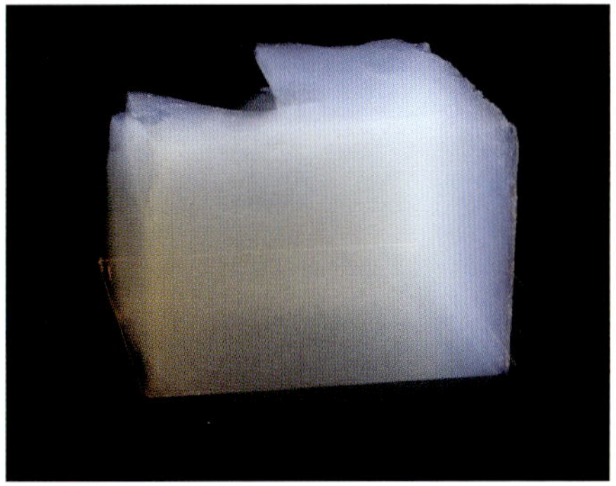

LEFT The only part of the Stardust spacecraft to land back on Earth was the return capsule, which is in the collection of the National Air and Space Museum.

Smithsonian's National Air and Space Museum

RIGHT Aerogel, the lightest solid ever made, was used to capture comet dust particles.

Smithsonian's National Air and Space Museum

On January 2, 2004, NASA's Stardust spacecraft flew through the tail of Comet Wild 2, collecting tiny particles. Flying at over 13,000 miles per hour, the Stardust capsule protected a grid of 132 filled tiles—small squares containing a porous, silicon-based material called aerogel to capture dust samples. With a spongelike structure that is 99 percent empty space, aerogel is the lightest solid ever made, only slightly more dense than air.

After collecting the samples, Stardust flew near Earth and released the return capsule, which parachuted down to the Utah desert. With the successful recovery of the samples, Stardust became the first U.S. spacecraft to bring back material from beyond the Moon. The material Stardust returned may date from the formation of the solar system, and scientific studies of the samples are altering our understanding of the universe.

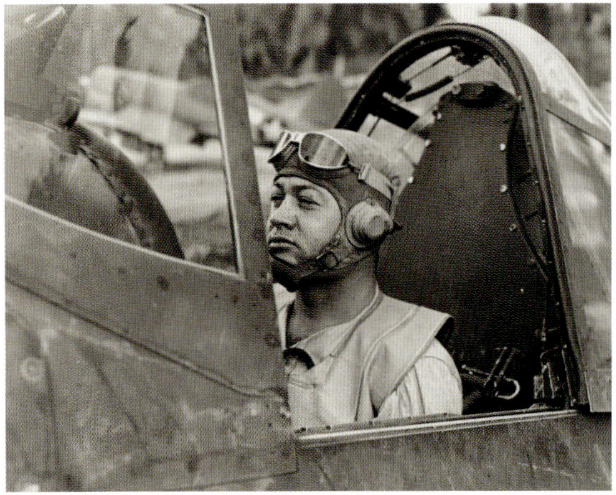

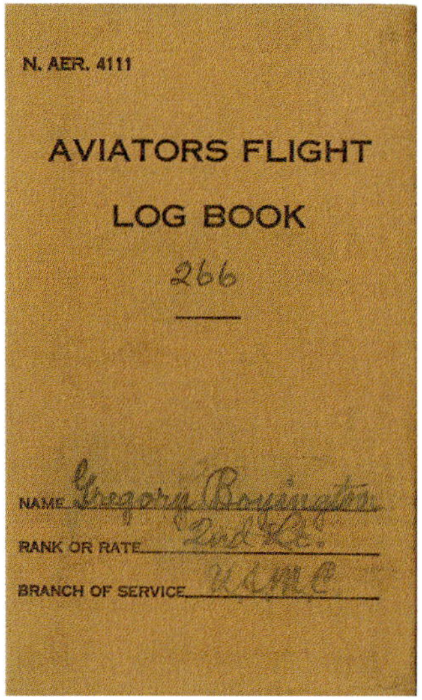
N. AER. 4111

AVIATORS FLIGHT

LOG BOOK

266

NAME Gregory Boyington

RANK OR RATE 2nd Lt.

BRANCH OF SERVICE U.S.M.C.

LEFT Pappy Boyington served in the South Pacific during World War II.

U.S. Navy/National Archives

RIGHT One of Boyington's logbooks, covering his flight training in the late 1930s, is in the collection of the National Air and Space Museum.

Smithsonian's National Air and Space Museum

Maj. Gregory "Pappy" Boyington was a U.S. Marine Corps aviator who served briefly with the First American Volunteer Group (AVG) of the Republic of China Air Force, which he joined before the United States entered World War II. While serving with the AVG, nicknamed the Flying Tigers, Boyington saw combat in Burma and downed six enemy planes, earning the title of flying ace.

Rejoining the Marine Corps in September 1942, Boyington served as commanding officer of Marine Fighting Squadron 214 (VMF-214), famed as the "Black Sheep Squadron." By the start of 1944, he had amassed an impressive record of twenty-four aerial victories. On January 3, the Marine ace attained two more kills during combat over Papua New Guinea, tying World War I ace Eddie Rickenbacker's record. Within minutes of these victories, however, Boyington was shot down and spent the remainder of the war in a Japanese prisoner of war camp. Following his release in August 1945, Boyington not only received the Congressional Medal of Honor and the Navy Cross but was also credited with another pair of aerial victories, bringing his total to twenty-eight kills.

F-14A TOMCATS DOWN TWO MIG-23S OFF THE COAST OF LIBYA

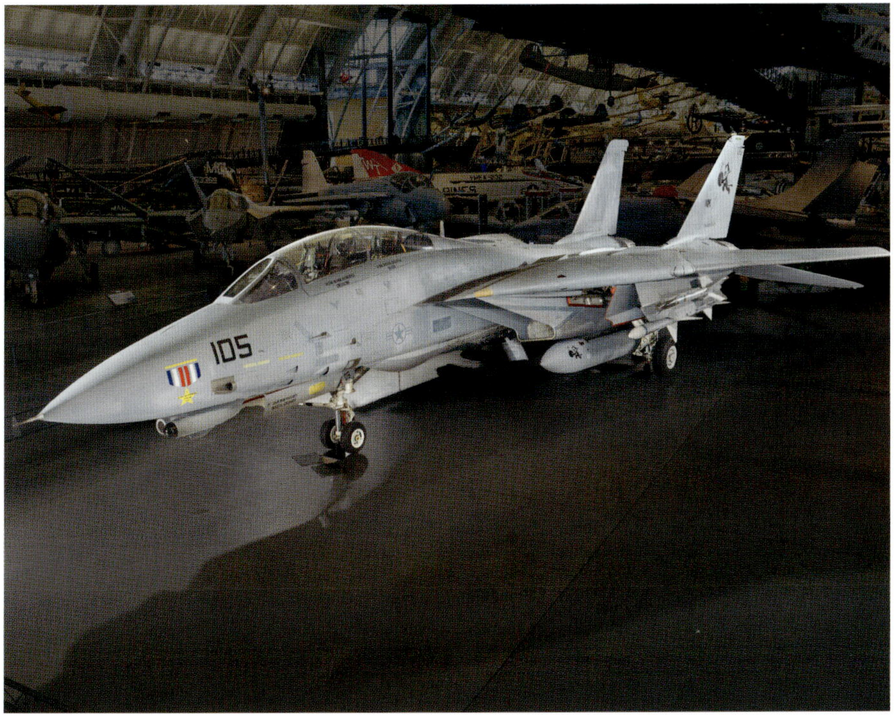

The Grumman F-14D(R) on display at the Steven F. Udvar-Hazy Center was involved in an air battle with two Libyan MiG-23s.

Smithsonian's National Air and Space Museum

On January 4, 1989, two Grumman F-14A Tomcats operating off the USS *John F. Kennedy* engaged with two Libyan Air Force MiG-23s near the coast of Libya. The F-14s locked the MiGs with their powerful AWG-9 radar. Normally such a radar lock resulted in the MiGs retreating to Libya, but not this time. During a tense six- to eight-minute air battle, the MiGs continued to threaten the Tomcats. After several attempts to evade the MiG radar threat, the Libyan aircraft were declared hostile, and the F-14 crews were cleared to engage.

One of the F-14As (AC207) fired an AIM-7 Sparrow missile, striking and destroying the first MiG-23. The second F-14A (AC202) then engaged the remaining MiG, firing an AIM-9 Sidewinder heat-seeking missile, which detonated in the Libyan aircraft's tailpipe. Both MiG pilots ejected safely from their destroyed aircraft. The F-14 that fired the first missile (AC207) was later modified as an F-14D(R) and is now in the collection of the National Air and Space Museum and on display at the Steven F. Udvar-Hazy Center.

SMITHSONIAN APPROVES RESEARCH GRANT FOR ROBERT GODDARD

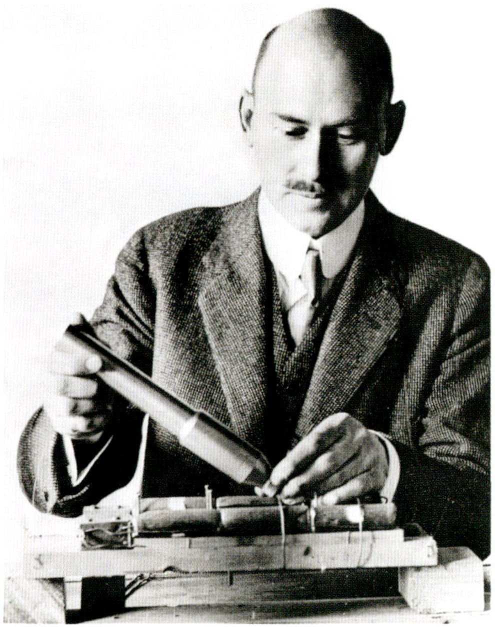

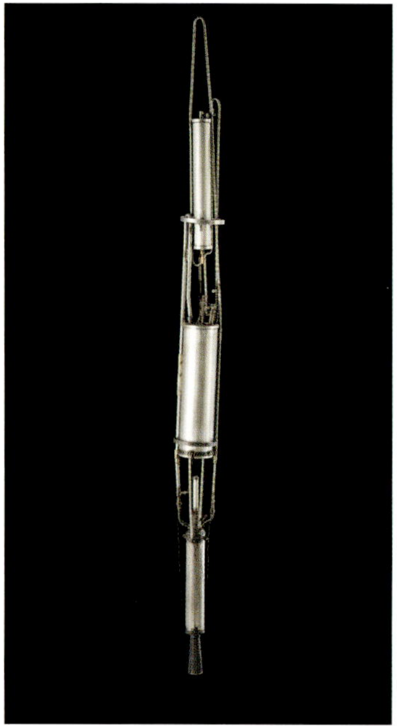

Rocket pioneer Robert Goddard wrote a letter to the Smithsonian Institution in September 1916 asking to discuss his rocketry experiments and requesting funding for his work. In a letter dated January 5, 1917, Smithsonian Secretary Charles Walcott informed Goddard that a $5,000 grant was approved from the Hodgkins Fund, which supported atmospheric research.

This was just the beginning of Goddard's relationship with the Smithsonian, which assisted his continued research for many years. In addition to financial support, the Smithsonian also published "A Method of Reaching Extreme Altitudes," Goddard's foundational paper in the field of rocketry.

"I feel that I cannot overestimate the value of your backing, at times when hardly anyone else in the world could see anything of importance in the undertaking."

—ROBERT GODDARD, IN A LETTER TO SMITHSONIAN ASSISTANT SECRETARY CHARLES ABBOT

LEFT Robert Goddard is considered the father of modern American rocketry.

Smithsonian's National Air and Space Museum (NASM 90-16506)

RIGHT Designed and built by Robert Goddard in 1926, the oldest surviving liquid-propellant rocket in the world is in the collection of the National Air and Space Museum.

Smithsonian's National Air and Space Museum

LUNAR PROSPECTOR MISSION LAUNCHES

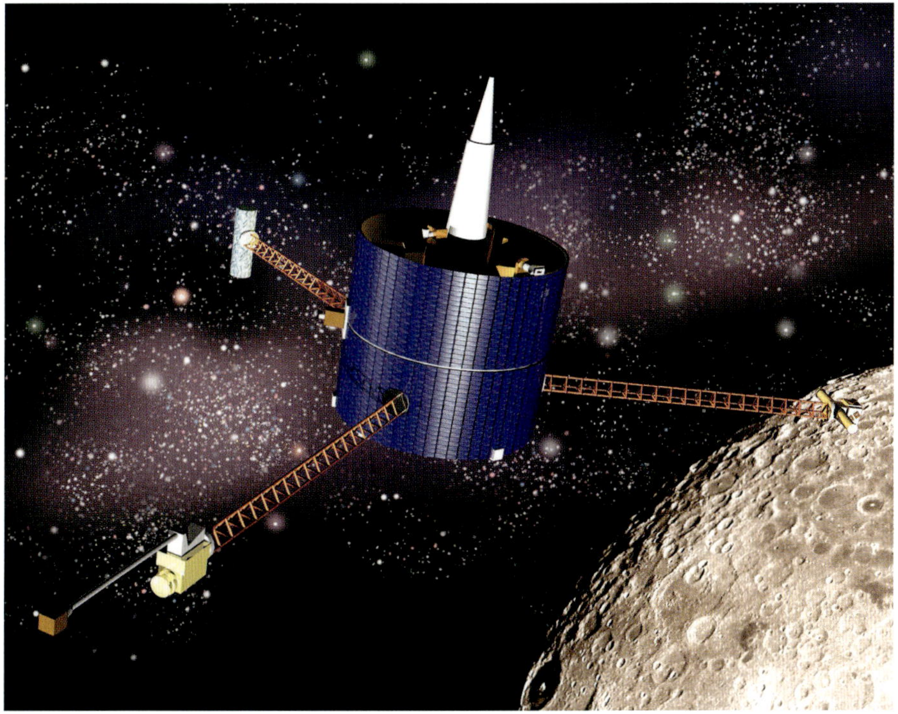

NASA's Lunar Prospector spacecraft, pictured here in an artist rendering, spent nineteen months orbiting the Moon.

NASA

NASA's Lunar Prospector began its mission to explore the Moon in low polar orbit on January 6, 1998. It launched on an Athena II rocket from Launch Complex 46 at Cape Canaveral Air Station in Florida. After a multiday voyage, the spacecraft entered lunar orbit and began studying Earth's only natural satellite. Lunar Prospector's primary mission, which lasted a little over a year, was to map the Moon's surface composition from a distance of sixty miles.

One of the mission's most significant discoveries was the presence of hydrogen at the poles, indicating that there is water ice on the Moon. After the completion of the primary mission, the spacecraft began an extended mission at a closer distance to the Moon—first eighteen miles above the surface, then six miles. Nineteen months after arriving at the Moon and with its mission complete, Lunar Prospector was intentionally crashed into a crater near the lunar south pole to remove it from the path of upcoming lunar exploration vehicles.

BUCK ROGERS IN THE 25TH CENTURY A.D. COMIC STRIP DEBUTS

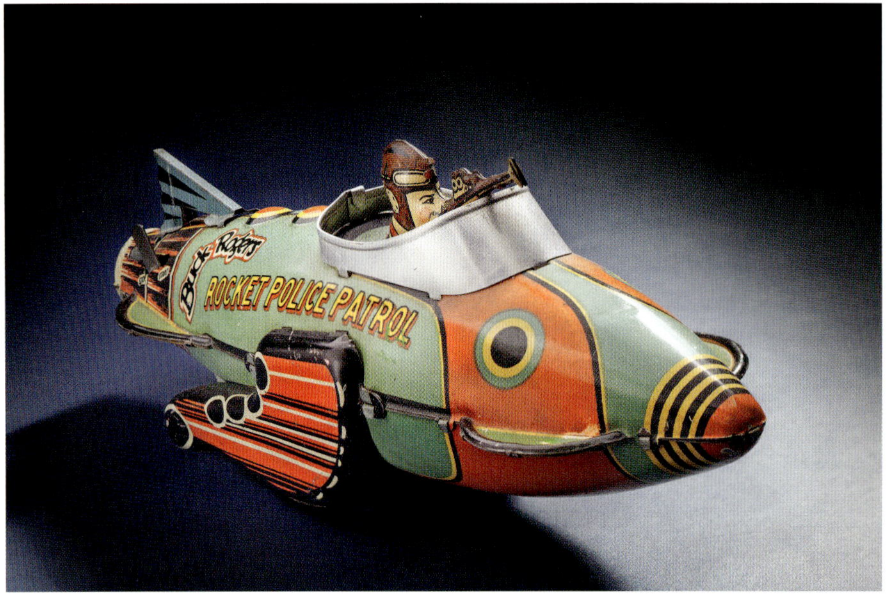

The National Air and Space Museum has a variety of *Buck Rogers* artifacts in its collection, including a Rocket Police Patrol Ship toy.

Smithsonian's National Air and Space Museum

The *Buck Rogers in the 25th Century A.D.* comic strip debuted on January 7, 1929, becoming the first syndicated science-fiction comic strip. The title character first appeared as Anthony Rogers in the Philip Francis Nowlan story "Armageddon—2419 A.D.," which was published in the pulp magazine *Amazing Stories* in August 1928. Soon after, the National Newspaper Service purchased the rights to the character for a comic strip, and he was renamed "Buck" to capitalize on the popularity of Westerns.

Buck Rogers, in its black-and-white printed form, was written by Nowlan and illustrated by Dick Calkins. They followed it up with a Sunday color comic strip in 1930, a radio program in 1932, and a film series in 1939. This led to extensive merchandise inspired by the franchise, including toy ray guns, games, uniforms, tin spaceships, and trading cards.

XP-80 *LULU-BELLE* FLIES FOR THE FIRST TIME

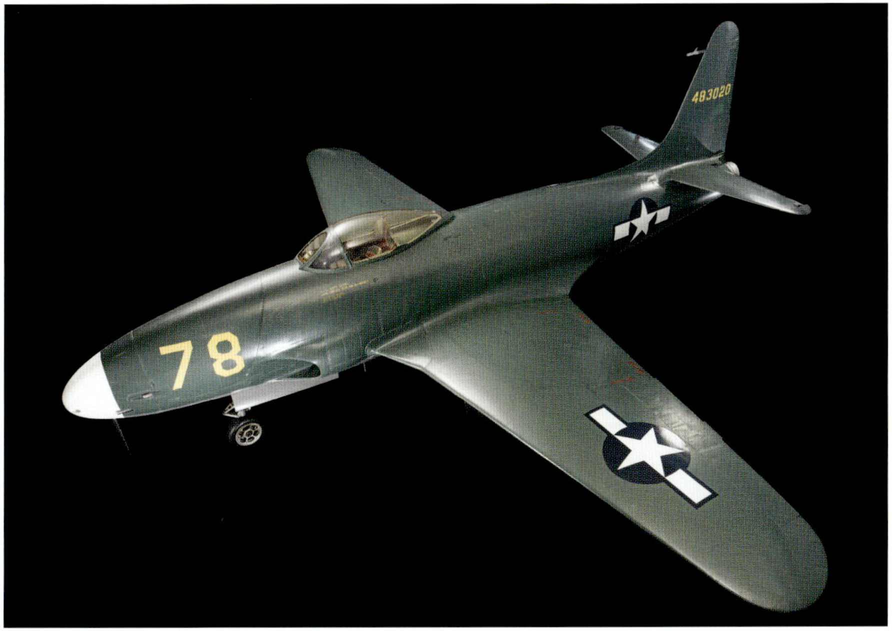

Lockheed XP-80 *Lulu-Belle* is in the collection of the National Air and Space Museum.

Smithsonian's National Air and Space Museum

In mid-1943, prolific aircraft designer Clarence "Kelly" Johnson and his team at Lockheed began developing a turbojet fighter for the Army Air Forces. To keep their work on the aircraft secret, Johnson walled off the production area with discarded engine crates and a circus tent. This was when Johnson's group got the nickname "Skunk Works," named for a mysterious remote factory in a *Li'l Abner* comic strip. On January 8, 1944, test pilot Milo Burcham took the prototype for the Lockheed P-80 Shooting Star—a turbojet-powered aircraft nicknamed the *Lulu-Belle*—into the sky for the first time.

During *Lulu-Belle*'s first flight, it reached an impressive speed of nearly 550 miles per hour while flying straight and level. Lockheed continued to refine the aircraft, and the first service-test models of the P-80 Shooting Star flew in September 1944. Although Lockheed did not produce enough P-80s to equip a frontline squadron before the end of World War II, the Shooting Star became a fine, reliable frontline fighter in the years after.

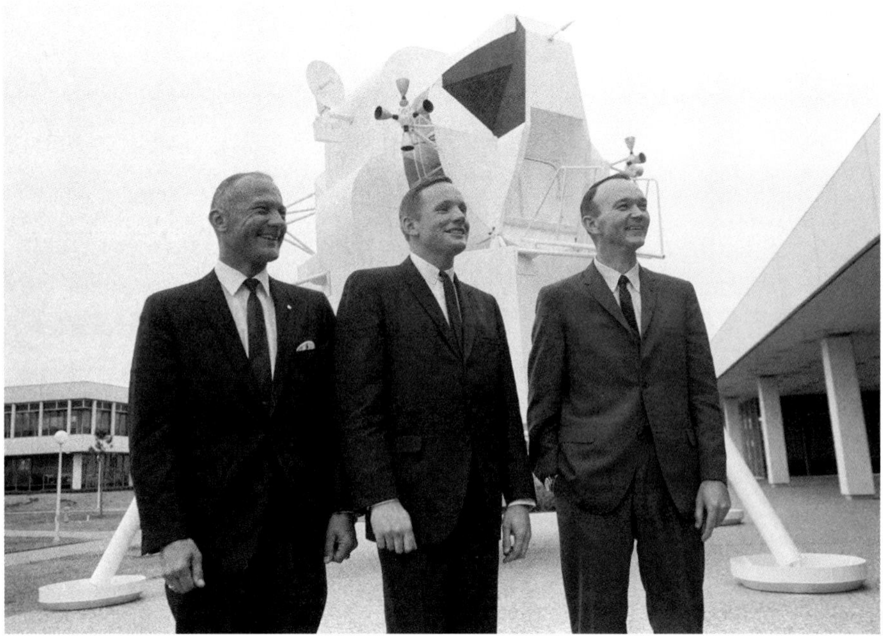

The Apollo 11 mission made Buzz Aldrin, Neil Armstrong, and Michael Collins, pictured here in front of a lunar module mockup at the Manned Spacecraft Center, household names.

NASA

On January 9, 1969, at long last, NASA announced to the public the three astronauts who would make history on the Apollo 11 mission: Neil Armstrong, Michael Collins, and Buzz Aldrin.

Mission commander Armstrong's first spaceflight was Gemini VIII in 1966 (see page 91). Before joining the astronaut corps, Armstrong served in the U.S. Navy and then as a NASA research pilot, flying the X-15 and other aircraft.

Command module pilot Collins's first spaceflight was the Gemini X mission. Before joining NASA, he was a test pilot in the U.S. Air Force, and after retiring from the agency, he continued his public service, including seven years as the director of the National Air and Space Museum (see page 200).

Lunar module pilot Aldrin was the first astronaut with a PhD, having written his thesis on orbital rendezvous (giving him the nickname "Dr. Rendezvous"). His first trip to space was on Gemini XII (see page 334). Before that, he graduated from West Point in 1951 and served in the U.S. Air Force.

JANUARY 10

PROJECT DIANA BOUNCES RADAR SIGNALS OFF THE MOON

NATIONAL SECURITY SPACE

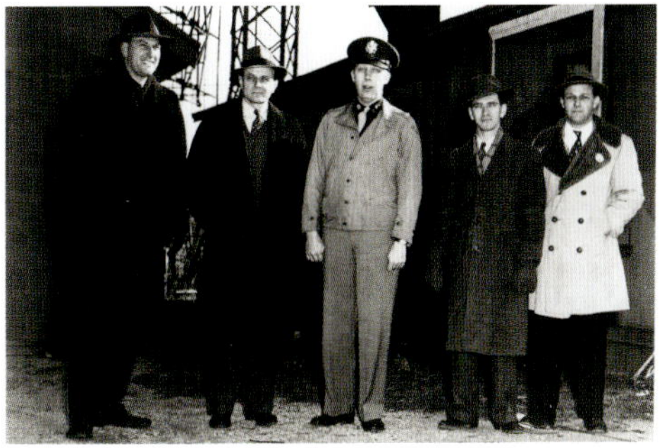

Lt. Col. John H. DeWitt Jr. was tasked with assembling the Project Diana team.

U.S. Army Communications Electronics Museum

The U.S. Army Signal Corps' "Project Diana" successfully bounced radar signals off the Moon for the first time on January 10, 1946. The project was based out of the Evans Signal Laboratory in New Jersey, which worked on radar technology during World War II. They used a modified SCR-271 radar antenna, aiming its signal at the Moon. The radio waves took about 2.5 seconds to travel to the Moon and back.

JANUARY 11

WILLIAM HERSCHEL DISCOVERS OBERON AND TITANIA

SPACE SCIENCE

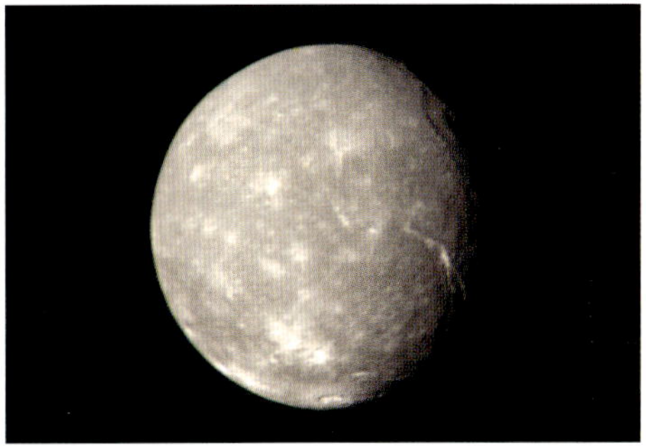

The Voyager 2 spacecraft flew by Uranus's moon Titania in 1986, taking photos that allowed a high-resolution color composite to be created.

NASA

On January 11, 1787, British astronomer William Herschel discovered the first two known moons of Uranus: Titania and Oberon. These discoveries came nearly six years after Herschel discovered the planet itself. The moons are named for the queen and king of the fairies in William Shakespeare's *A Midsummer Night's Dream*. In fact, most of Uranus's twenty-eight moons are named for Shakespeare characters, including Miranda from *The Tempest*, Juliet from *Romeo and Juliet*, and Ophelia from *Hamlet*.

JANUARY 12

BILL ODOM SETS LIGHT-PLANE DISTANCE RECORD FLYING FROM HAWAII TO MAINLAND U.S.

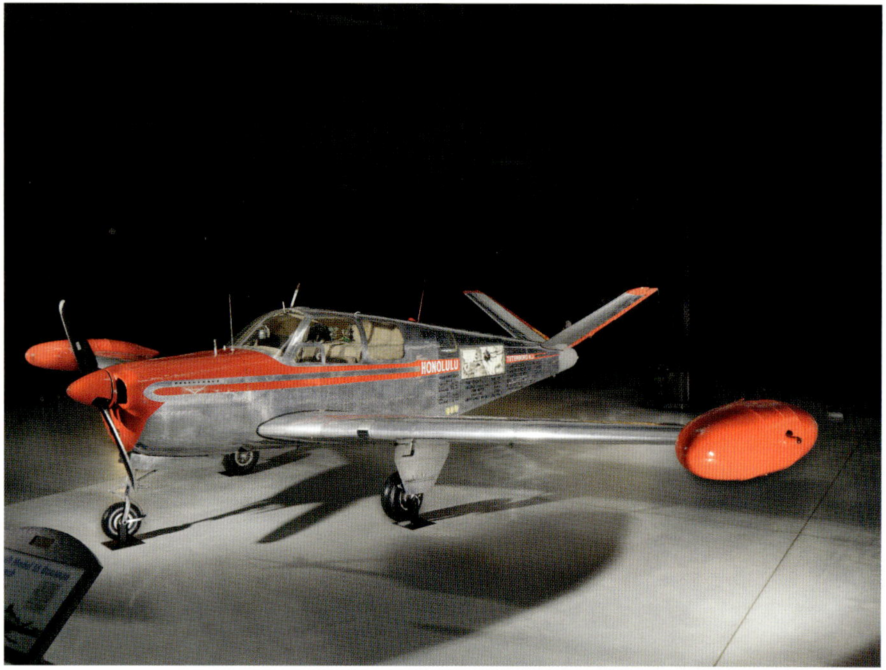

Bill Odom's Beechcraft 35 Bonanza *Waikiki Beech* is in the collection of the National Air and Space Museum.

Smithsonian's National Air and Space Museum

William "Bill" Odom flew a Beechcraft 35 Bonanza nicknamed *Waikiki Beech* over a distance of more than 2,400 miles from Honolulu, Hawaii, to Oakland, California, on January 12, 1949. Taking off with the intent of flying across the entire North American continent, Odom made it as far as Nevada before severe weather forced him to land in Oakland. By the time the Bonanza touched down, Odom had been in the air for twenty-two hours and six minutes and had covered some 2,900 miles.

Two months after that flight, Odom tried again, and this time succeeded in flying nearly 5,000 miles from Honolulu to Teterboro, New Jersey, a journey that lasted just over thirty-six hours. For both of these record flights, *Waikiki Beech* carried extra fuel tanks in the cabin and wing tips. Odom also made a point of flying in a business suit and landing cleanly shaven (making his Remington electric razor an important flight accessory). The Fédération Aéronautique Internationale (World Air Sports Federation) awarded Odom the 1949 Louis Blériot medal for these impressive long-distance flights.

JANUARY 13

SUSAN HELMS BECOMES THE FIRST ACTIVE-DUTY UNITED STATES MILITARY WOMAN IN SPACE

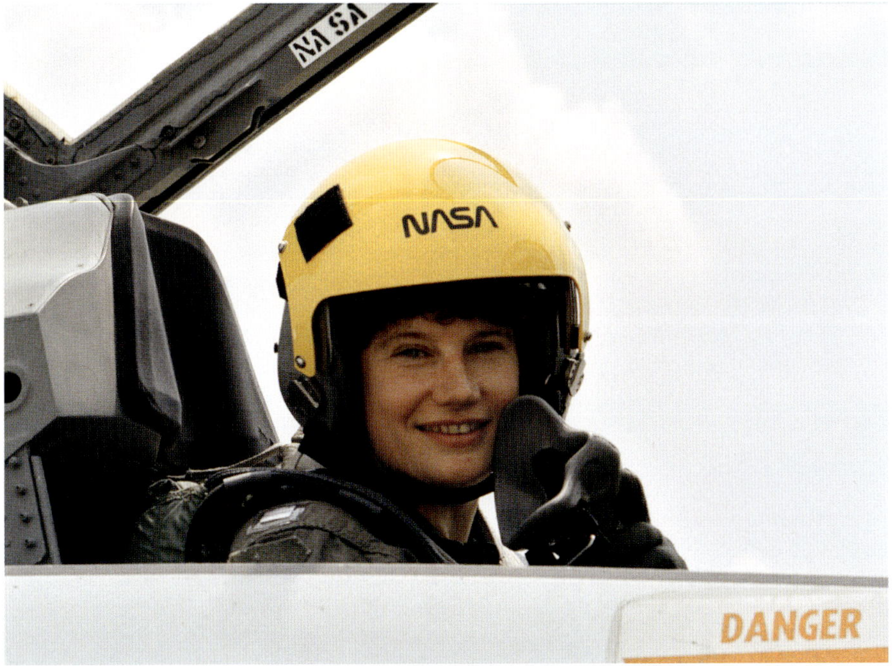

As an astronaut candidate, Susan Helms trained in a NASA T-38 jet (see page 92).

NASA

On January 13, 1993, U.S. Air Force Capt. Susan Helms became the first active-duty U.S. female military officer to fly to space. She was accepted in NASA's Astronaut Group 13 in 1990 alongside two other military women, U.S. Air Force Maj. Eileen Collins and U.S. Army Capt. Nancy Sherlock.

Helms was admitted to the U.S. Air Force Academy in the first year it accepted women cadets (1976) and was among the first women to graduate in 1980. She completed the flight test engineer course at the Air Force Test Pilot School in California and was named the outstanding flight test engineer of her 1988 class.

Helms's first spaceflight was January 1993's STS-54 mission aboard Space Shuttle *Endeavour*. In total, she flew on four space shuttle missions and an International Space Station (ISS) expedition, set a spacewalk duration record (eight hours and fifty-six minutes), and was the first woman to reside on the ISS for a long-duration mission.

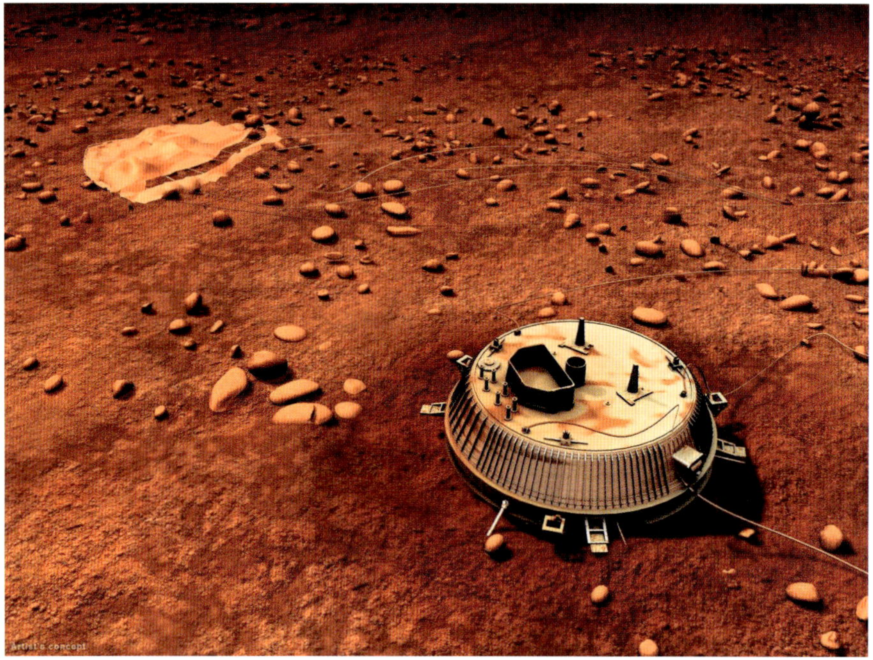

The Huygens probe traveled to the surface of Titan using a parachute to slow its descent.

ESA/C. Carreau

The European Space Agency's Huygens probe landed on the surface of Titan, Saturn's largest moon, on January 14, 2005. Titan is significant in the solar system because it is the only known moon with a substantial atmosphere. The Huygens probe traveled to Saturn's neighborhood aboard NASA's Cassini spacecraft, and the mission was officially called Cassini-Huygens (see page 275). After being released from the Cassini orbiter, Huygens coasted to Titan. When it entered the moon's atmosphere, the probe's real work began.

During Huygens's two-and-a-half-hour parachute-supported descent to the surface, it collected extensive data about Titan's atmosphere. After landing on the surface, Huygens continued transmitting data for an hour and ten minutes. With its successful landing, Huygens became the first spacecraft landing in the outer solar system and remains the farthest landing from Earth.

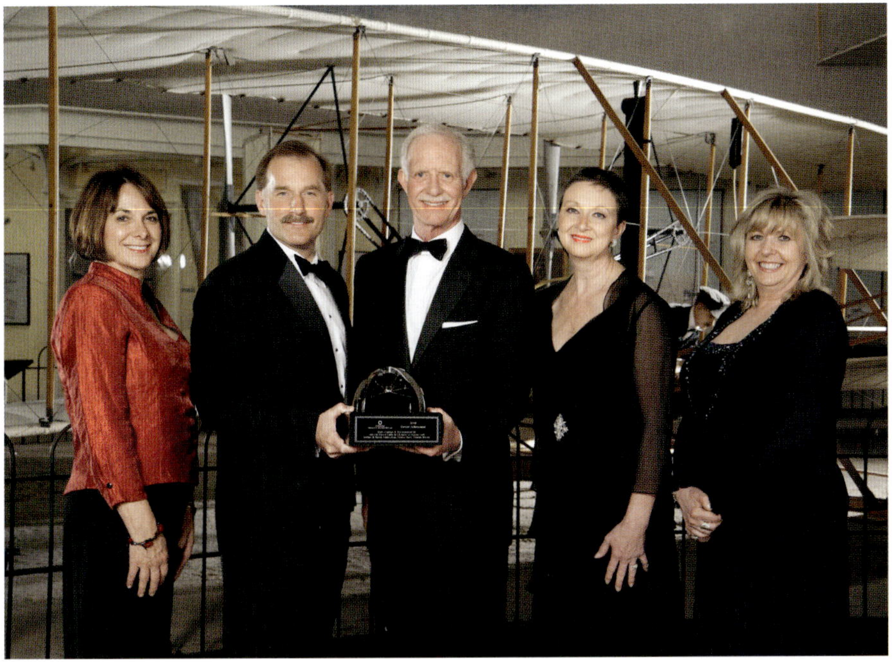

On January 15, 2009, US Airways Flight 1549 made an emergency landing after a flock of birds struck and disabled the engines of its Airbus 320 moments after takeoff from LaGuardia Airport in New York City. Gliding without power at 3,000 feet, Capt. Chesley "Sully" Sullenberger and First Officer Jeffrey Skiles reacted quickly, masterfully guiding the disabled airliner to a safe landing on the frigid Hudson River. Flight attendants Donna Dent, Doreen Welsh, and Sheila Dail quickly and safely evacuated all 150 passengers.

"I spent my life preparing for a challenge I never knew I would face," recalls Sullenberger. "I was always trying to be more knowledgeable, more skillful, and more experienced so I would have the judgment needed to handle the unexpected." Thanks to the actions of the flight crew, everyone on board survived and the event was dubbed the "Miracle on the Hudson."

The National Air and Space Museum awarded the crew of US Airways Flight 1549 its annual Trophy for Current Achievement in recognition of their lifesaving actions.

Smithsonian's National Air and Space Museum

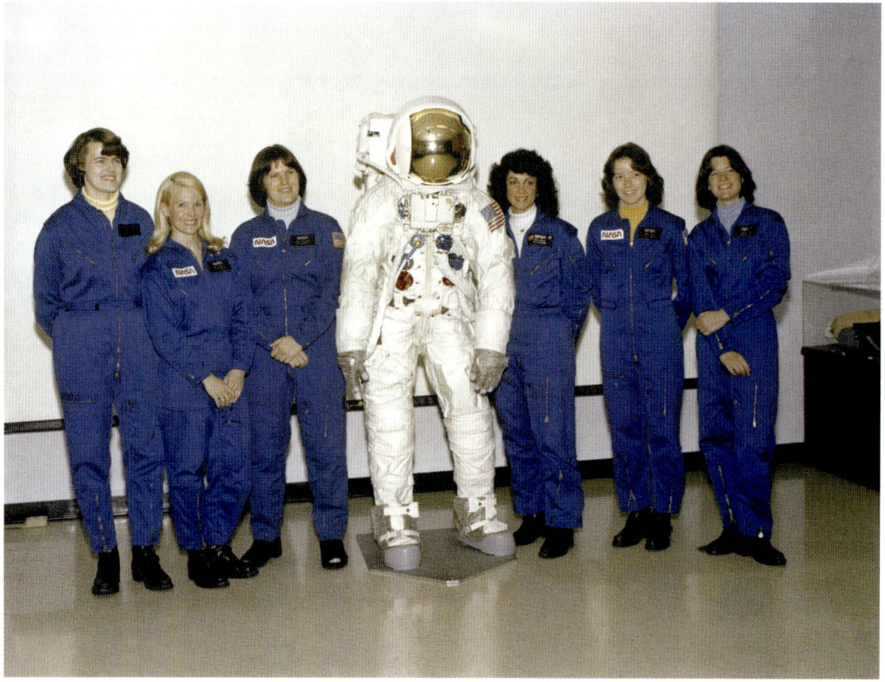

There were six women selected as astronauts in NASA's class of 1978.

NASA

After a campaign to finally include women and people of color in its astronaut corps, NASA announced its eighth group of astronauts on January 16, 1978. Known colloquially as the "Thirty-Five New Guys," these were the first astronauts selected specifically for the Space Shuttle program. They were expected to fill the roles of commanders and pilots, but also the new role of mission specialist. Those crewmembers would come from science and engineering backgrounds, training to operate the robotic arm, do spacewalks, and run experiments.

This class included NASA's first female astronaut candidates (pictured left to right: Shannon Lucid, Margaret Rhea Seddon, Kathryn Sullivan, Judith Resnik, Anna Fisher, and Sally Ride), NASA's first Black astronaut candidates (Ronald McNair, Guion Bluford, and Frederick Gregory), and NASA's first Asian American astronaut candidate (Ellison Onizuka).

AVIATION PIONEER GLENN L. MARTIN IS BORN

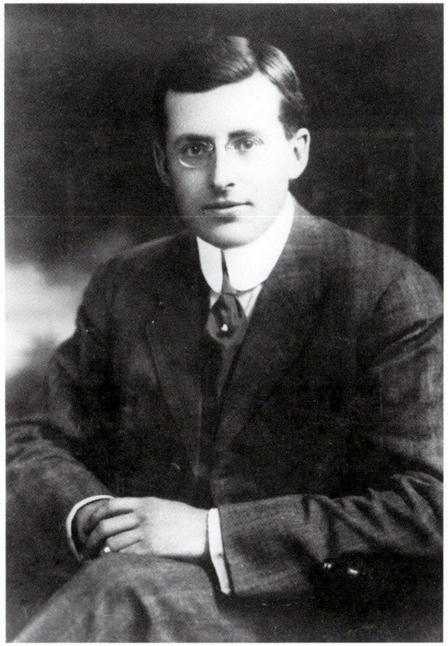

LEFT Glenn L. Martin taught himself to fly and earned his pilot's license in 1911, touring the country in flying exhibitions and becoming famous as a barnstormer.

Smithsonian's National Air and Space Museum (NASM A-54253)

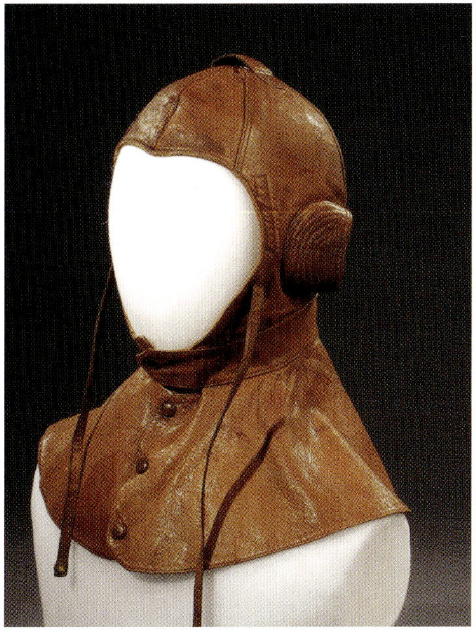

RIGHT Martin's leather flying helmet is held in the collection of the National Air and Space Museum.

Smithsonian's National Air and Space Museum

Pioneering aviator and aircraft manufacturer Glenn L. Martin was born in Macksburg, Iowa, on January 17, 1886. In August 1912, Martin and a group of investors incorporated the Glenn L. Martin Company "for the purpose of manufacturing and selling aeroplanes and hydroplanes." Later known simply as the Martin Company, this firm became one of the nation's premier builders of military aircraft, especially flying boats and bombers used in World War II.

Throughout his career, Martin received various awards and honors, including the Collier Trophy in 1932 for the company's development of the B-10 bomber, the Daniel Guggenheim Medal in 1940 for his contributions to the advancement of aeronautics, and the Officer of the French National Order of the Legion of Honor in 1949. Martin remained president of the company for over forty years and died in 1955. Following a series of corporate mergers in 1961 and 1995, the Martin Company was transformed into today's Lockheed Martin Corporation, which is one of the world's largest defense contractors.

PILOT MAKES FIRST SUCCESSFUL TAKEOFF AND LANDING FROM A NAVAL VESSEL

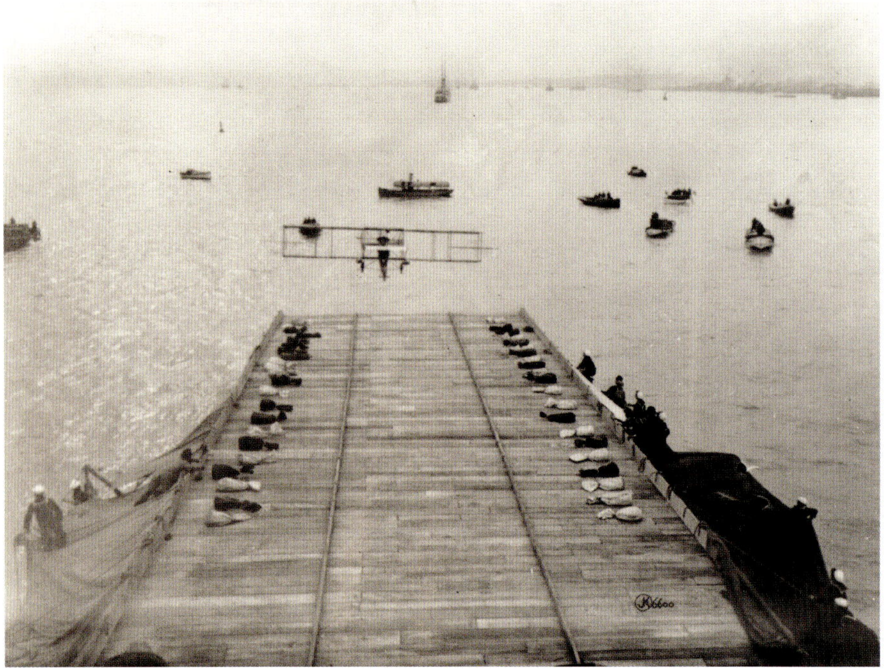

Eugene Burton Ely's historic flight landed and took off from the USS *Pennsylvania*.

Smithsonian's National Air and Space Museum (NASM 77-3592)

Pilot Eugene Burton Ely made the first successful takeoff and landing from a naval vessel on January 18, 1911, a dramatic demonstration of how the air and sea would soon come together for militaries around the world. Ely taught himself to fly in 1910, exhibiting natural skills as an aviator. Having quickly become a well-known pilot, Ely was tapped by the Navy to prove that an airplane could operate at sea. To accomplish this feat, a 120-foot platform was set up on the deck of the armored cruiser USS *Pennsylvania*. This wooden runway included ropes and sandbags stretched across its width to serve as a crude arresting system, as well as a canvas awning at the end to catch the airplane if it overshot.

As boats gathered in the San Francisco Bay harbor and crowds lined the shore to witness the daring flight, Ely's plane safely touched down on the ship platform and was brought to a complete stop by the makeshift arresting equipment. After lunch with the ship's captain, crewmembers cleared the platform and Ely took off, flying past the crowd before landing safely again onshore.

NEW HORIZONS SPACECRAFT LAUNCHES TO PLUTO

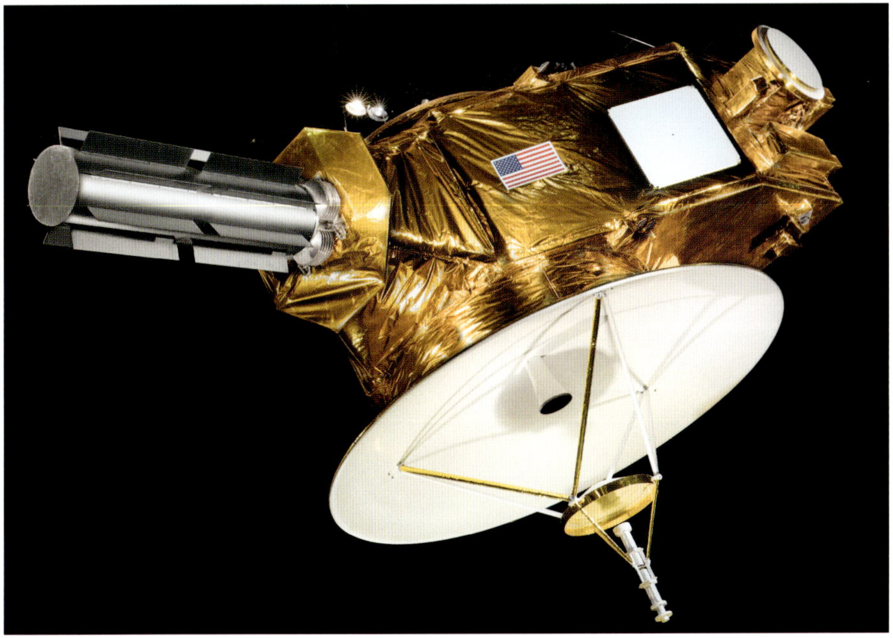

A full-scale model of the New Horizons spacecraft is in the collection of the National Air and Space Museum.

Smithsonian's National Air and Space Museum

On January 19, 2006, the New Horizons spacecraft launched aboard an Atlas V rocket from Cape Canaveral Air Force Base in Florida. New Horizons was the first and so far only mission to Pluto. Thirteen months after launch it flew near Jupiter, using the flyby as a gravity assist to gain acceleration for its journey to the outer solar system.

The spacecraft arrived at Pluto in July 2015, taking photos and providing the first up-close look at the dwarf planet. The spacecraft carried scientific instruments to map the composition and surface geology of Pluto and investigate its atmosphere. After it passed Pluto, New Horizons' mission continued, and it flew past the small icy world Arrokoth. Located in the Kuiper Belt beyond Neptune's orbit, Arrokoth is the farthest object from Earth ever explored up close. New Horizons is still traveling to the farthest reaches of the solar system today.

DID YOU KNOW? When New Horizons launched, Pluto was still considered a planet, but by the time the spacecraft arrived at its destination, Pluto had been reclassified as a dwarf planet (see page 251).

JANUARY 20

APOLLO COMMAND MODULE #002 LAUNCHES ON TEST FLIGHT

HUMAN SPACEFLIGHT

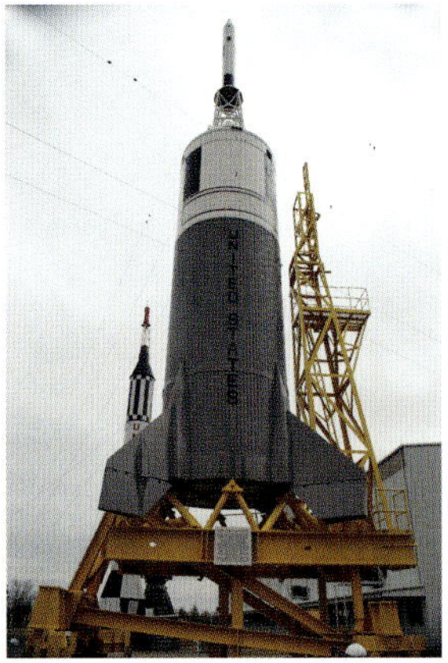

The prototype Apollo crew capsule launched on a Little Joe II rocket. The capsule is now in the collection of the National Air and Space Museum.

Smithsonian's National Air and Space Museum

While developing the Apollo spacecraft, NASA and its contractors conducted many tests to ensure the hardware and software performed correctly. On January 20, 1966, Apollo command module #002 launched aboard a Little Joe II rocket on a flight test from White Sands Missile Range in New Mexico. Designated mission A-004, the purpose of the flight test was to demonstrate the performance of the Launch Escape System (LES). At 61,000 feet, the abort signal was sent, and all components of the LES performed as planned.

JANUARY 21

PIONEERING EXPLORER AND AVIATOR UMBERTO NOBILE IS BORN

PIONEERS OF FLIGHT

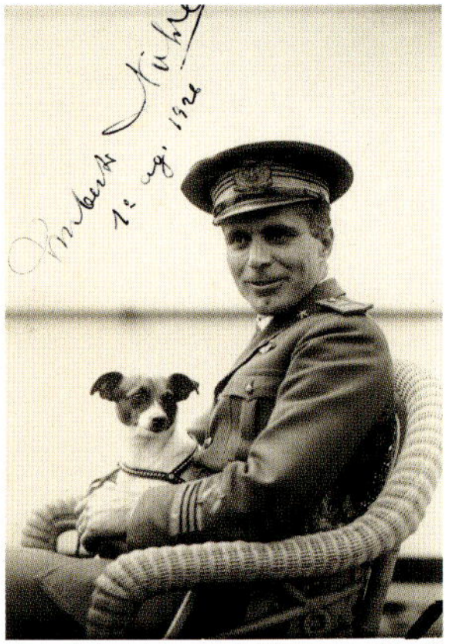

Umberto Nobile took his dog Titina on a polar voyage in 1926.

Smithsonian's National Air and Space Museum (NASM 2007-12775)

Born in Lauro, Italy, on January 21, 1885, Umberto Nobile was a pioneering figure in Italian aviation. Nobile not only invented the first Italian parachute and promoted construction of the first all-metal Italian airplane, but was also a well-known designer of airships. On May 12, 1926, Nobile piloted the airship *Norge* as it flew Norwegian explorer Roald Amundsen and fourteen others over the North Pole in history's first verified transpolar flight.

NASA RECEIVES LAST SIGNAL FROM PIONEER 10

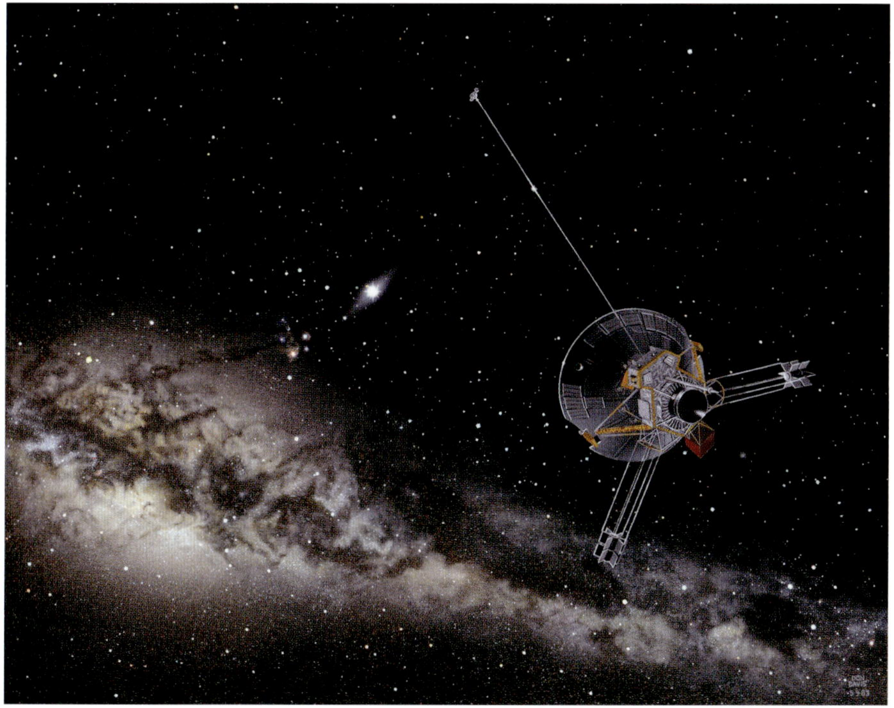

An artist rendering depicts the Pioneer spacecraft on its way to interstellar space.

NASA

NASA's Pioneer 10 spacecraft "phoned home" for the last time on January 22, 2003. The probe was about 7.6 billion miles from Earth, which at the time was farther into space than any other object sent from Earth—NASA's two Voyager spacecraft would later surpass it. After the final signal, NASA engineers reported that Pioneer 10's radioisotope power source had degraded and was not likely to allow future transmissions. It was a final farewell from a spacecraft that sent photographs and scientific information back to Earth for over thirty years.

Pioneer 10 launched in 1972 on a mission to fly by Jupiter. It reached speeds of 32,400 miles per hour on its way there, making it one of the fastest human-made objects. After completing its planetary investigation, Pioneer 10 continued to the outer regions of the solar system, studying solar wind and cosmic rays.

BLÉRIOT XI FLIES FOR THE FIRST TIME

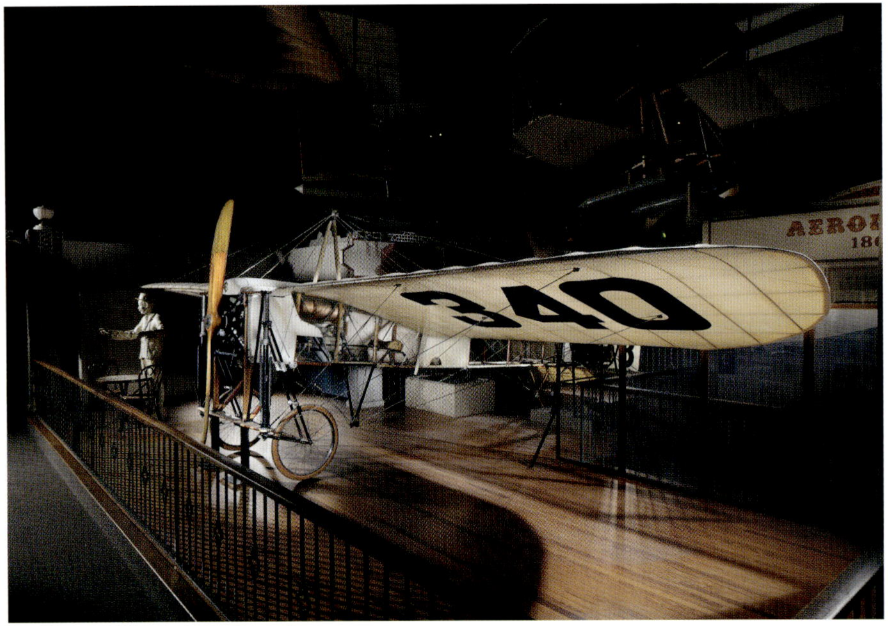

The National Air and Space Museum has a Blériot XI in its collection.

Smithsonian's National Air and Space Museum

The Blériot XI was the most famous and successful of several classic airplanes that emerged in Europe during the summer of 1909. On January 23, 1909, the Type XI, designed by French engineer and aviation pioneer Louis Blériot, flew for the first time at Issy-les-Moulineaux, a military parade ground turned flying field that was a hub of aviation activity in France.

Later that year Blériot made history when he completed the first air crossing of the English Channel in a Type XI, covering the twenty-five miles between Calais and Dover in thirty-six minutes and thirty seconds. Though it was not the longest or farthest flight to date, the symbolic impact of Blériot conquering the Channel made this the most widely lauded air journey before Charles Lindbergh's transatlantic crossing (see page 155). In addition to international acclaim, Blériot received $2,500 from the London *Daily Mail*, which had put up a prize for any successful cross-Channel airplane flight.

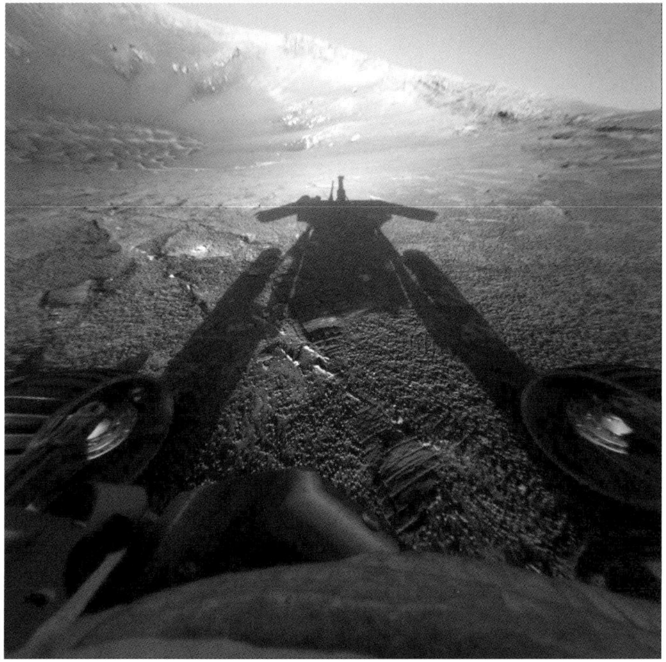

In 2004, Mars rover *Opportunity* took a self-portrait as it traveled farther into Endurance Crater.

NASA-Caltech

The Mars rover *Opportunity* landed on the Red Planet on January 24, 2004, joining its sister rover *Spirit,* which landed a few weeks before. Both made harrowing six-minute descents through the thin atmosphere to the Martian surface. One of the Mars Exploration Rover mission's main scientific goals was to search for and study a wide range of rocks and soils that may hold clues to past water activity on Mars. To do this, the rovers landed on opposite sides of the Red Planet in locations that appeared to have been affected by liquid water in the distant past.

The goal of the rovers was to travel up to two-thirds of a mile during a primary mission of ninety Martian days. Both rovers far exceeded these expectations before accumulating dust on their solar panels spelled the ends of their missions. *Spirit* traveled 4.8 miles over more than six years. *Opportunity* remained active on Mars for nearly fifteen years, traveling over twenty-eight miles.

CLEMENTINE SPACECRAFT LAUNCHES

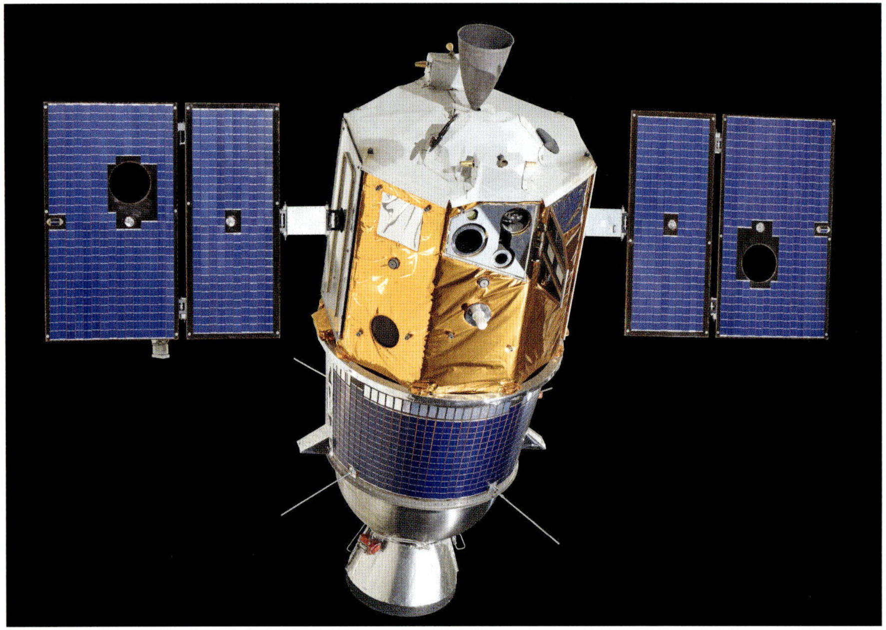

The Clementine spacecraft in the National Air and Space Museum collection is an engineering model acquired from the Naval Research Laboratory.

Smithsonian's National Air and Space Museum

In 1994, NASA and the Ballistic Missile Defense Organization launched the Clementine spacecraft on a mission that returned a U.S. spacecraft to the Moon for the first time since Apollo 17 more than two decades prior. Remarkably, Clementine went from the drawing board and into space in less than two years with a cost of under one hundred million dollars, a bargain for space probes. With a "cheaper, better, faster" philosophy, the mission's primary purpose was to evaluate the performance of commercial sensors and components under space conditions. Its secondary purpose was science—its advanced cameras captured 1.5 million images of the Moon's surface, enabling scientists to create a more detailed topographical map of the lunar surface than possible before.

The mission, launched on January 25, 1994, produced a surprise: the detection of ice embedded deep in a crater of the Moon's south pole, which astounded the public and sparked intense debate among scientists. NASA followed up on this discovery with the Lunar Prospector mission (see page 21).

JANUARY 26 MCDONNELL FH-1 PHANTOM PROTOTYPE FLIES FOR THE FIRST TIME

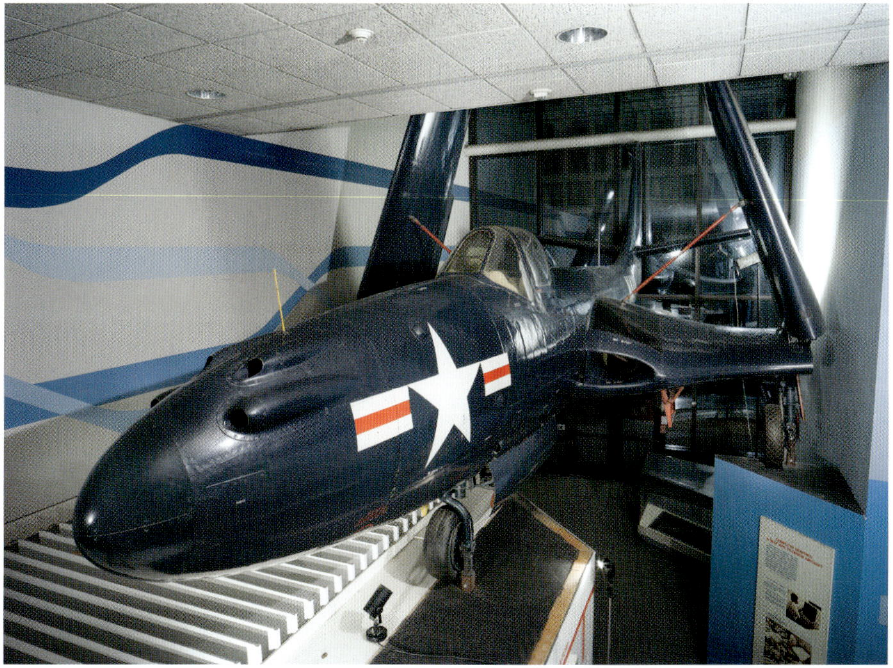

A McDonnell FH-1 Phantom is in the collection of the National Air and Space Museum.

Smithsonian's National Air and Space Museum

In 1943, the U.S. Navy asked the McDonnell Corporation to develop a jet-powered, carrier-based fighter aircraft. On January 26, 1945, the prototype XFD-1 Phantom flew for the first time. The project presented unique design challenges. Not only did the new aircraft have to take off from the relatively short length of a flight deck (less than 1,000 feet), but its engines also had to both decelerate and accelerate quickly enough to accommodate carrier landings and wave-offs.

McDonnell's engineers solved for these problems, and in July 1946, the Phantom became the first U.S. jet aircraft to take off from and land on an aircraft carrier. Following this achievement, the Navy ordered production versions of the FH-1 Phantom, which quickly proved the soundness of carrier-based jet aircraft. A new age in naval aviation had begun.

JANUARY 27

THREE ASTRONAUTS DIE IN APOLLO 1 FIRE

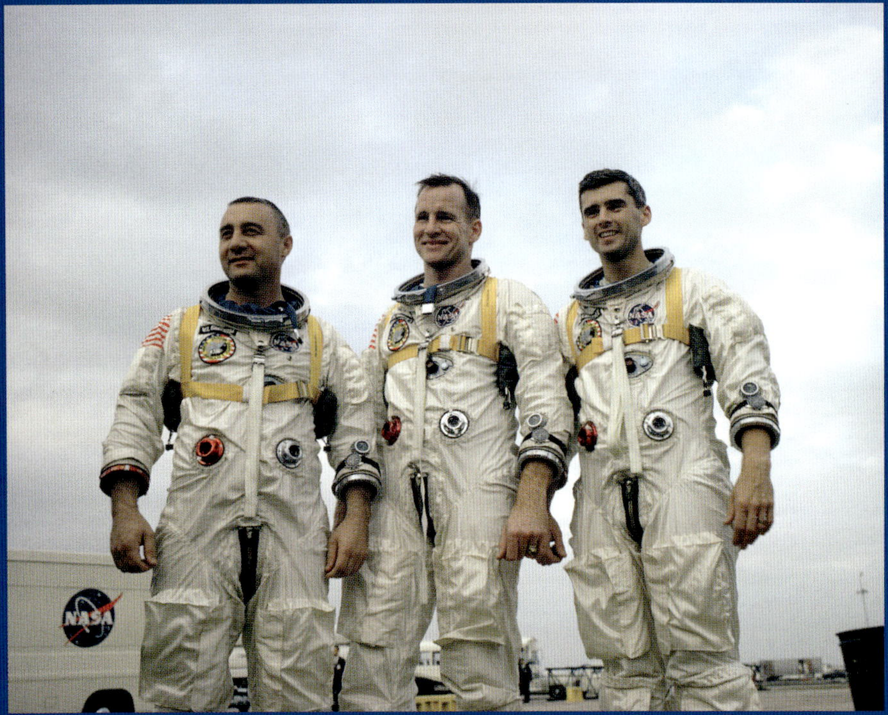

The three astronauts who were to fly on the first crewed Apollo mission were killed in the Apollo 1 fire.

NASA

On January 26, 1967, a fire broke out inside an Apollo command module during a countdown rehearsal for the first crewed Apollo mission. Unable to open the overly complicated spacecraft hatch, the astronauts were trapped inside. The three men died from carbon monoxide poisoning and a lack of oxygen. After the tragedy, the mission previously referred to as Apollo-Saturn 204 (AS-204) was officially designated Apollo 1. NASA responded to the event by fireproofing nearly all elements of the spacecraft, including a simplified hatch, the cabin's atmosphere, and all materials used by astronauts during missions.

REMEMBERING THE CREW OF APOLLO 1

(FROM LEFT TO RIGHT)

VIRGIL I. "GUS" GRISSOM, COMMANDER

EDWARD H. WHITE II, SENIOR PILOT

ROGER B. CHAFFEE, PILOT

JANUARY 28 SPACE SHUTTLE *CHALLENGER* AND CREW ARE LOST DURING LAUNCH

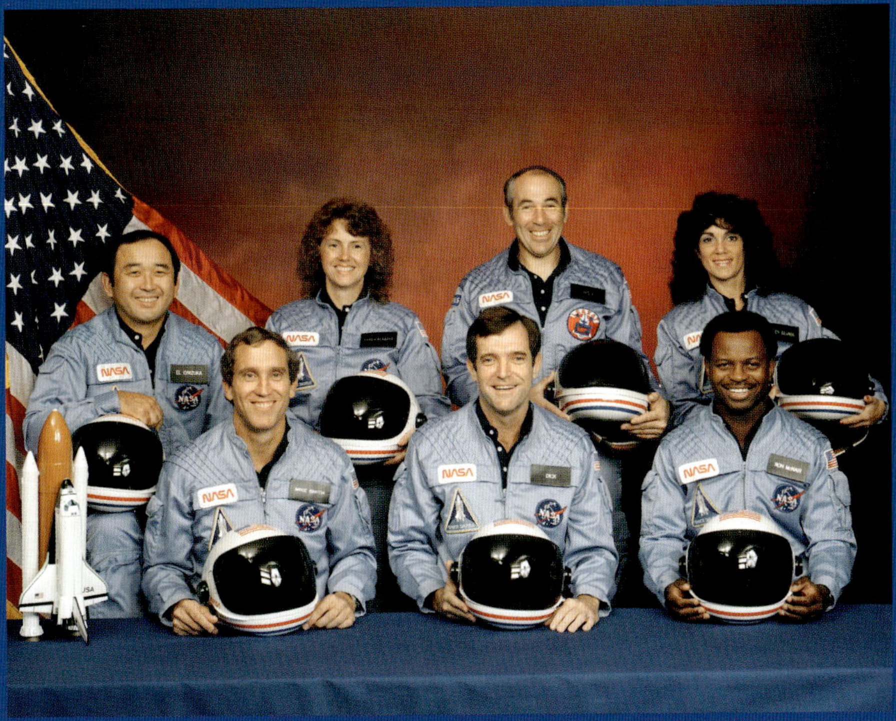

Seventy-three seconds after liftoff of Space Shuttle *Challenger* on STS-51L, the mission's crew was lost.

NASA

Space Shuttle *Challenger* broke apart just after liftoff of STS-51L on the morning of January 28, 1986. All seven crewmembers perished. Investigators traced the cause to a failed rubber O-ring between segments of a solid rocket booster. The O-rings, which were meant to prevent gases from escaping the booster's joints, became brittle due to the cold weather. The failed gasket allowed gas to escape as pressure increased during launch. This started a chain reaction that broke the vehicle apart. The presidential commission on the disaster also cited a flawed launch decision-making process that ignored long-standing engineering concerns and safety protocols.

REMEMBERING THE CREW OF STS-51L

(FROM LEFT TO RIGHT)

ELLISON S. ONIZUKA, MISSION SPECIALIST

CHRISTA McAULIFFE, PAYLOAD SPECIALIST

GREGORY B. JARVIS, PAYLOAD SPECIALIST

JUDITH A. RESNIK, MISSION SPECIALIST

MICHAEL J. SMITH, PILOT

FRANCIS R. SCOBEE, COMMANDER

RONALD E. McNAIR, MISSION SPECIALIST

FRONTIER AIRLINES HIRES EMILY HOWELL WARNER

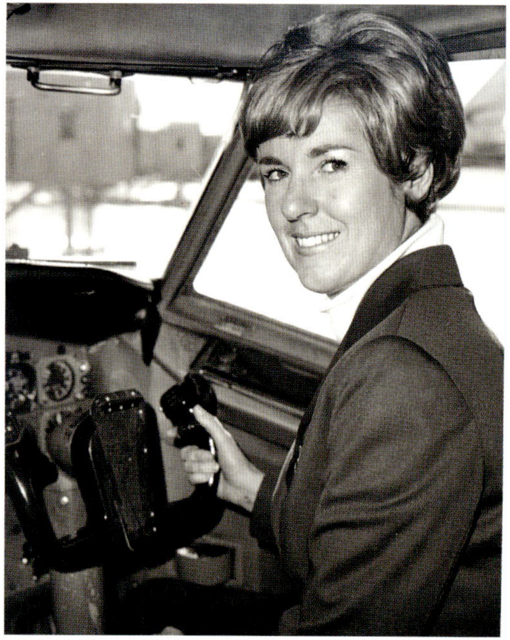

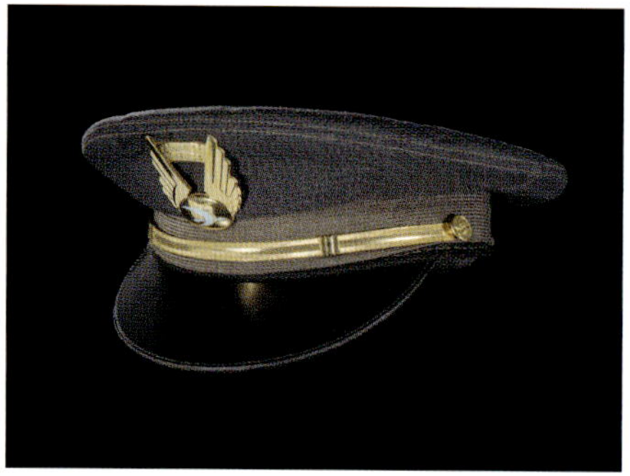

LEFT Emily Howell Warner was the first American woman to be hired as part of the permanent flight crew by a U.S. airline.

Smithsonian's National Air and Space Museum (NASM 92-16871)

RIGHT Warner's Frontier Airlines pilot cap is in the collection of the National Air and Space Museum.

Smithsonian's National Air and Space Museum

On January 29, 1973, Emily Howell Warner was hired as a second officer by Frontier Airlines, becoming the first American woman to fly routinely for a scheduled U.S. airline. In 1958, Warner took her first-ever airplane trip at age seventeen to decide if she wanted to be a flight attendant. By the time she finished her return flight, Warner had decided that she wanted to be a pilot instead.

Over the next few years, Warner earned her private pilot's license and several other ratings. She also secured work as a certified flight instructor and trained many men who went on to have their own airline careers. Warner began applying for airline pilot positions herself in 1968, but after five years of rejection, her hope was dwindling. By the time Frontier finally hired her in 1973, Warner had more than seven thousand hours in her logbook, over four times the minimum hours required to apply as an airline pilot. She soon advanced to first officer (co-pilot) and then to captain.

ARMY AWARDS CONTRACT TO DEVELOP A NIGHT FIGHTER

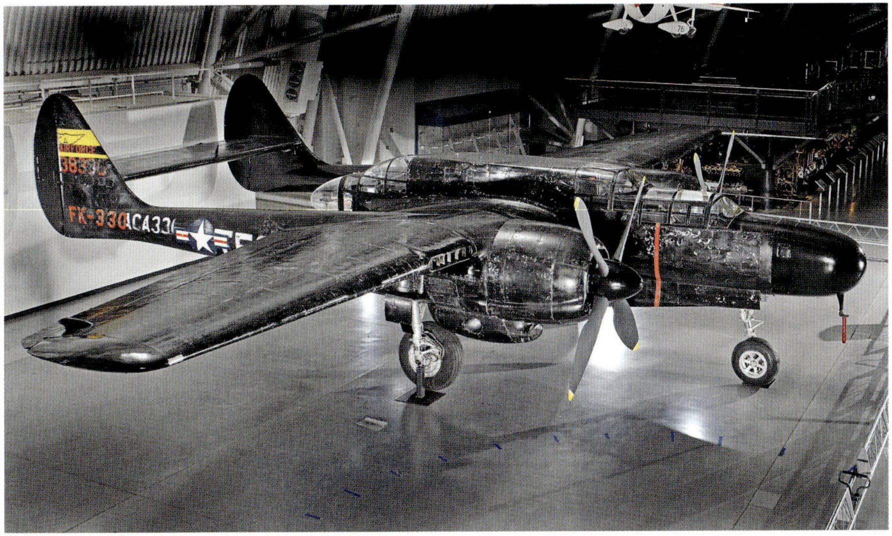

A P-61C Black Widow is on display at the National Air and Space Museum's Steven F. Udvar-Hazy Center.

Smithsonian's National Air and Space Museum

After the German Luftwaffe shifted to night bombing during the Battle of Britain and the London Blitz in 1940, it became clear to American military leadership that a night fighter would be essential if the U.S. entered World War II. On January 30, 1941, the U.S. Army awarded a contract to the Northrop Corporation to develop such a fighter. The resulting aircraft was the Northrop P-61 Black Widow.

The P-61 was the first U.S. aircraft designed to locate and destroy enemy aircraft at night and in bad weather, a feat made possible by the use of an onboard radar. P-61 combat operations began just after D-Day (June 6, 1944—see page 175) when Black Widows flew deep into German airspace, bombing and strafing trains and road traffic. By the end of the war, Black Widows had seen combat in every theater and were credited with destroying 127 enemy aircraft and eighteen German V-1 buzz bombs (see page 181).

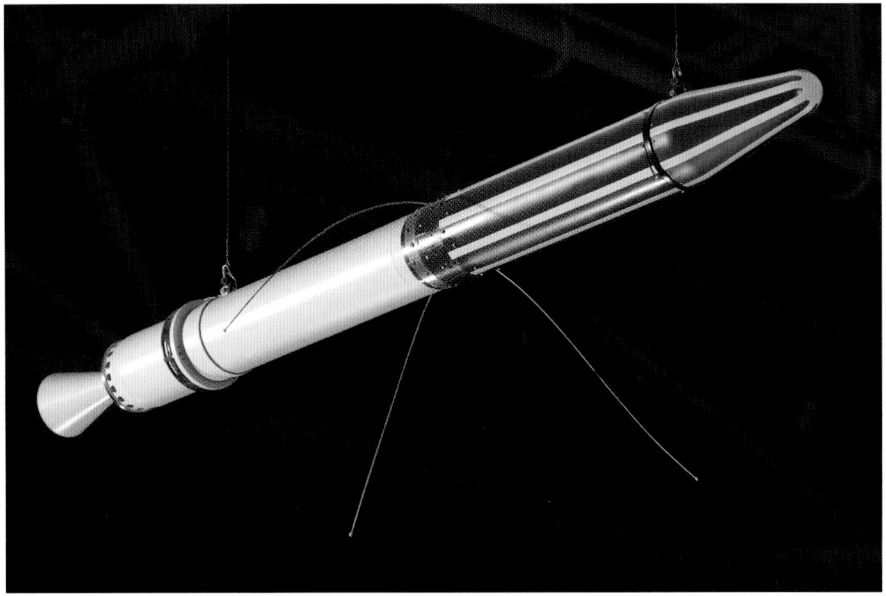

ABOVE A flight spare of Explorer 1 is in the collection of the National Air and Space Museum.

Smithsonian's National Air and Space Museum

OPPOSITE PAGE Explorer 1's successful launch followed the failed launch of TV-3 a few months prior.

NASA

On January 31, 1958, Explorer 1 was launched by a Jupiter-C missile from Cape Canaveral Missile Annex in Florida as part of the U.S. contribution to the International Geophysical Year. The stakes were impossibly high, and so were tensions: The Soviet Union had already achieved two successful launches—the first artificial Earth satellite, Sputnik, and a second Sputnik mission that took the dog Laika to space (see pages 294 and 326). Meanwhile, the U.S. Navy failed with its launch of the Vanguard satellite just two months prior (see page 356).

After Explorer 1's launch, scientists listened to telemetry data from the satellite until it dipped below the horizon—there were not yet global tracking stations capable of communicating the satellite's progress. When it was time to regain a signal from tracking stations in California, the signal didn't come. What followed were twelve minutes of pure, silent, palpable hell. But jubilation followed soon after when Explorer 1 finally reported home. The mission was a success, and the United States had put its first satellite into Earth orbit.

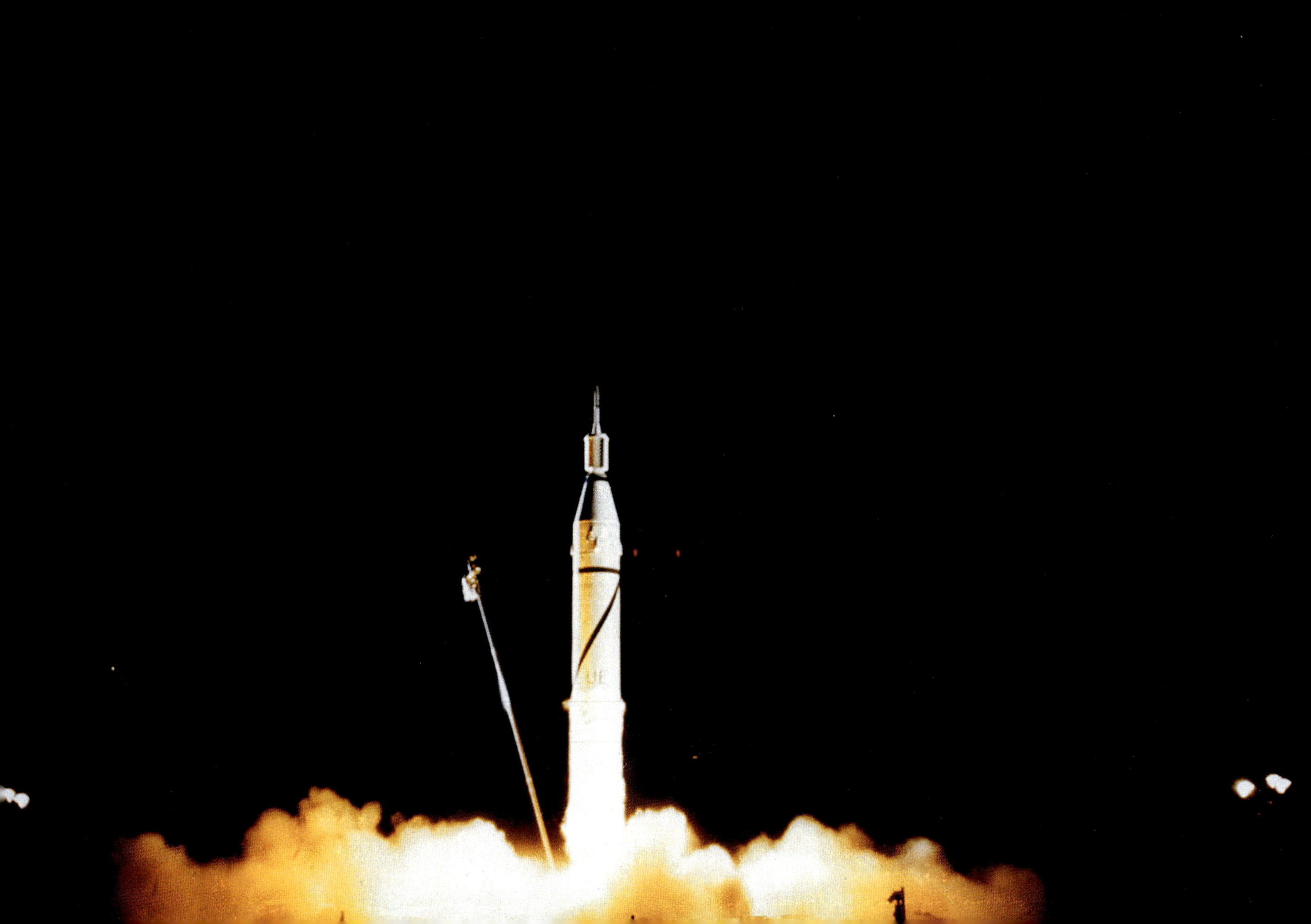

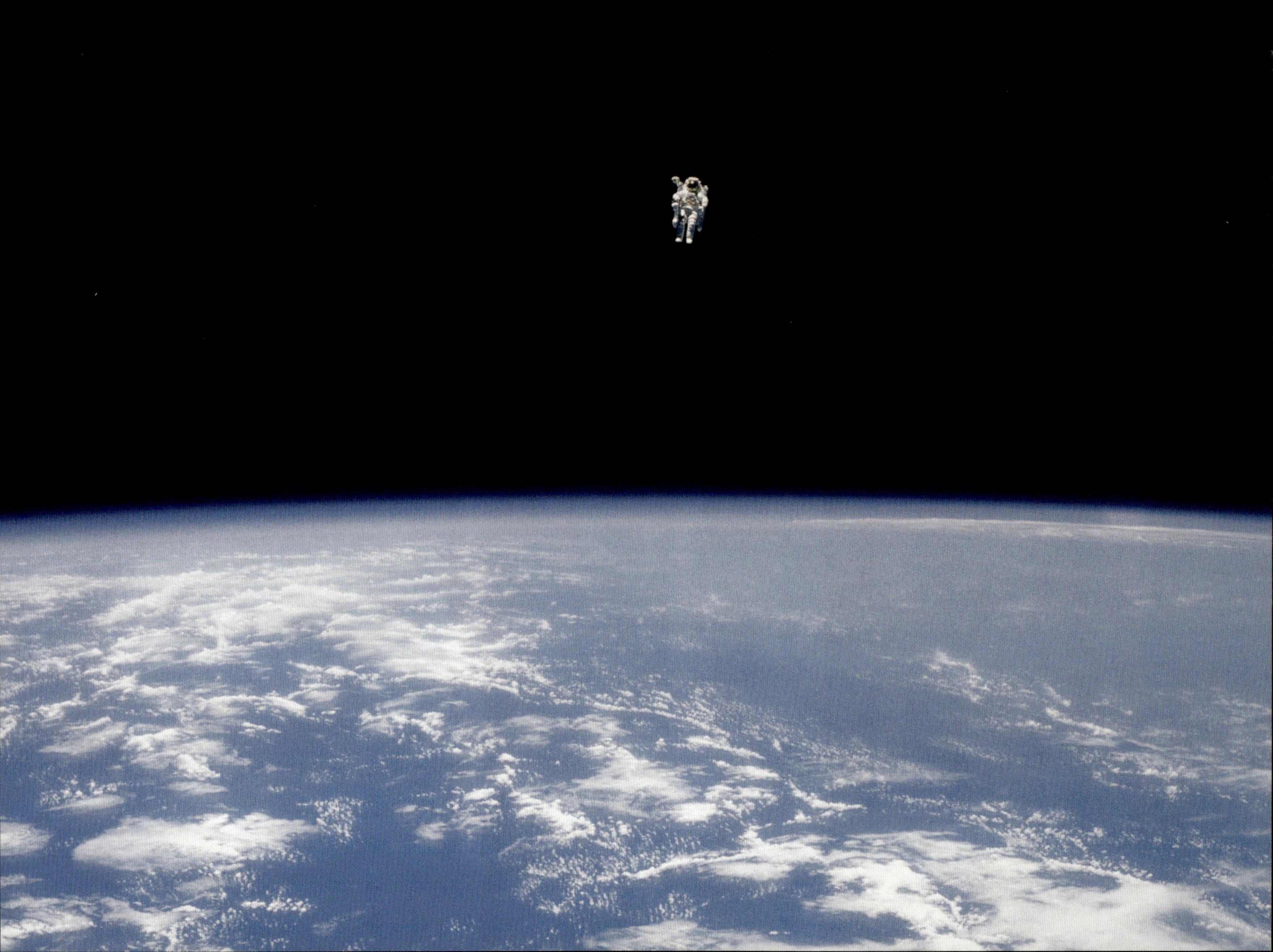

FEBRUARY

FEBRUARY 1

SPACE SHUTTLE *COLUMBIA* AND CREW ARE LOST DURING REENTRY

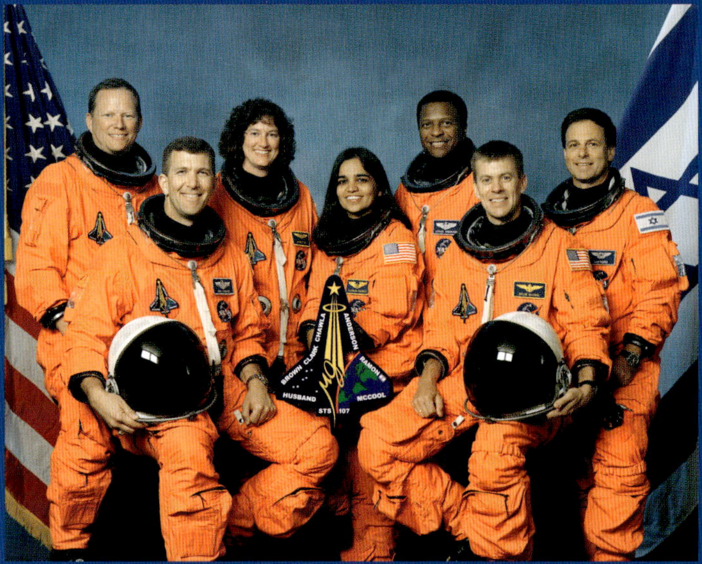

When Space Shuttle *Columbia* broke apart during reentry, the crew of STS-107 was lost.

NASA

Space Shuttle *Columbia* broke apart over Texas as it returned from space during the STS-107 mission on February 1, 2003. All seven crewmembers died. A piece of foam insulation fell from *Columbia*'s external tank during liftoff two weeks earlier, creating a hole in the orbiter's port side wing leading edge, crippling the thermal protection system. During reentry, hot gases entered the hole, melting the aluminum frame and causing the vehicle to come apart.

The *Columbia* Accident Investigation Board determined NASA had "a broken safety culture" that allowed management to ignore tank insulation loss and damage for decades. In the days after the tragedy, visitors from around the world used the National Air and Space Museum as an impromptu place of mourning, signing a condolence book and leaving small mementos to honor the crew.

REMEMBERING THE CREW OF STS-107

(FROM LEFT TO RIGHT)

DAVID M. BROWN, MISSION SPECIALIST

RICK D. HUSBAND, COMMANDER

LAUREL B. CLARK, MISSION SPECIALIST

KALPANA CHAWLA, MISSION SPECIALIST

MICHAEL P. ANDERSON, MISSION SPECIALIST

WILLIAM M. MCCOOL, PILOT

ILAN RAMON, PAYLOAD SPECIALIST

LILIENTHAL GLIDER IS PRESENTED TO THE SMITHSONIAN

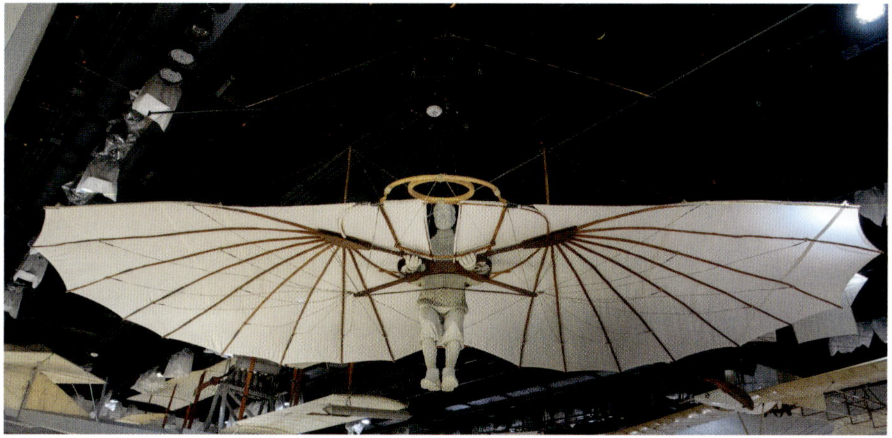

A Lilienthal glider is on display at the National Air and Space Museum in D.C.

Smithsonian's National Air and Space Museum

German glider pioneer Otto Lilienthal was the most accomplished aeronautical experimenter before the Wright brothers. During the 1890s, he built and flew a series of highly successful full-size gliders, making close to two thousand brief flights in sixteen different designs based on aerodynamic research he conducted in the decades prior. Lilienthal's research inspired other aeronautical innovators, most notably Orville and Wilbur Wright, who used his aerodynamic data as a starting point in their own research.

Only five Lilienthal gliders remain in the world. One of the surviving gliders was purchased by newspaper magnate William Randolph Hearst, who sponsored test flights of the aircraft on Long Island in April and May 1896 to create publicity and boost the circulation of the *New York Journal*. Hearst then gave the glider to *Cosmopolitan* magazine editor John Brisben Walker, who donated it to the Smithsonian Institution on February 2, 1906.

EILEEN COLLINS BECOMES THE FIRST WOMAN TO PILOT A SPACE SHUTTLE

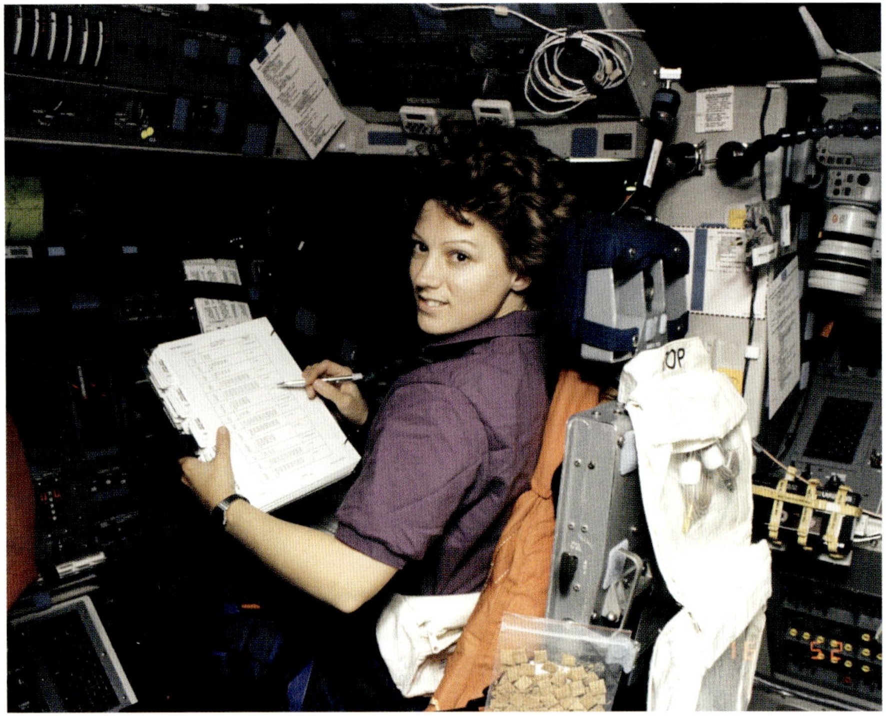

Eileen Collins piloted Space Shuttle *Discovery* on her history-making mission.

NASA

Growing up in Elmira, New York, Eileen Collins dreamed of going to space, but she thought her family and friends would tell her girls don't get to go to space. Collins kept that dream to herself until 1989, when she asked her boss at the Air Force Academy to write a letter of recommendation for her astronaut application. After over a decade as a pilot in the Air Force, including graduating from Air Force Test Pilot School, Collins's outstanding record earned her a place in the 1990 class of astronauts as a pilot.

On February 3, 1995, Collins flew to space for the first time on *Discovery*'s STS-63 mission, becoming the first woman to pilot a space shuttle orbiter. Four years later, she made history again as the first woman to command a space shuttle mission on STS-93, which deployed the Chandra X-Ray Observatory (see page 220). When Collins was asked about being the first and only woman to command the Space Shuttle, she replied, "Hopefully not for long!" That hope became reality in 2007, when Pamela Melroy commanded STS-120.

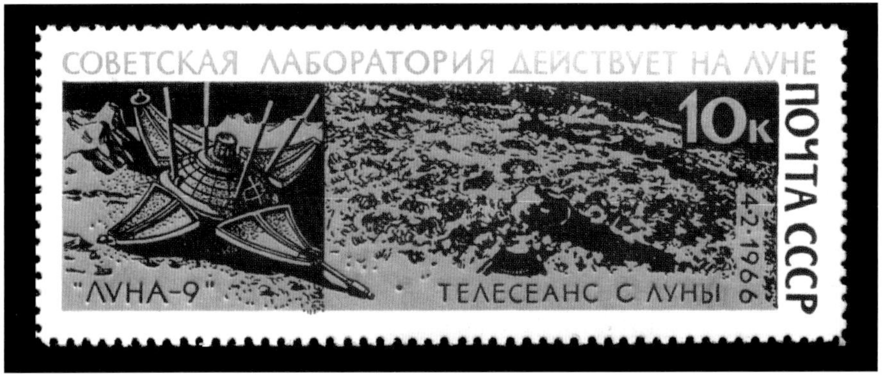

Like many of the Soviet Union's achievements in space, Luna 9's landing on the lunar surface was commemorated with a stamp.

USSR Post

With the Space Race well underway in the mid-1960s, the United States and Soviet Union were racing to see who could land a robotic spacecraft on the Moon first. The Soviet Union's Luna 9 thumped down on the vast lava plain known as *Oceanus Procellarum* (Ocean of Storms) in February 1966 after several failed attempts by previous Soviet spacecraft, achieving the first "soft landing" on another world.

Following Luna 9's landing, which used airbags to cushion its fall, the spacecraft took photos of the Moon using its turret camera. But the Soviets weren't the first to release the first images from the lunar surface. Radio signals containing the image data were intercepted by England's Jodrell Bank Observatory on February 4, 1966. Astronomers there worked with London's *Daily Express* to read the signals and print out the photos using a fax machine. The photos appeared in the *Daily Express* the following day, scooping the Soviet press.

MARINER 10 TAKES FIRST CLOSE-UP IMAGE OF VENUS

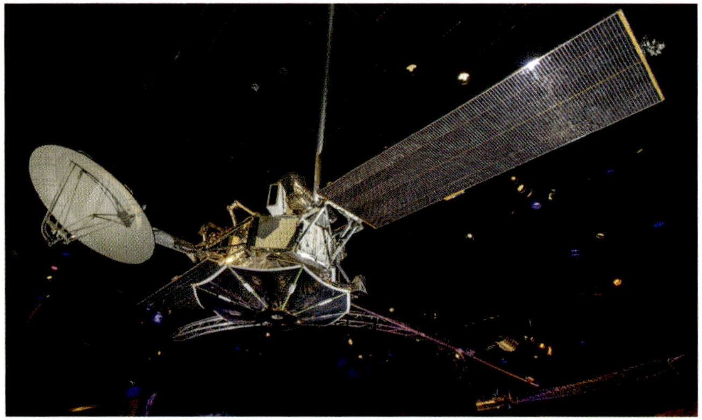

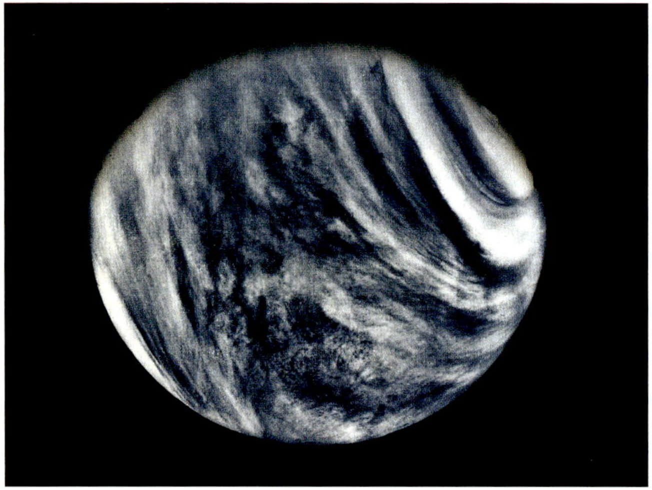

Mariner 10 was the first spacecraft to visit Mercury. Although its primary goal was to study the atmosphere, surface, and physical characteristics of Mercury, it also made some history during a flyby of Venus. It was the first spacecraft to use the gravitational pull of one planet (Venus) to reach another (Mercury). This maneuver, called a gravity assist, involved Mariner 10 speeding toward Venus to then slingshot itself around the planet to pick up speed and save fuel on the path to Mercury.

While Mariner was flying by on February 5, 1974, it took photos of Venus, giving scientists on Earth their first close-up look at the hellish planet. Measurements taken by the spacecraft also showed that Venus had a weak magnetic field and the ionosphere interacted with solar wind to form a bow shock. As for Mercury, Mariner confirmed that the planet had no atmosphere and a cratered, dormant moonlike surface.

TOP A Mariner 10 flight spare is on display at the National Air and Space Museum.

Smithsonian's National Air and Space Museum

BOTTOM The first close-up photo of Venus highlights its cloudy atmosphere.

NASA

ALAN SHEPARD PLAYS GOLF ON THE MOON

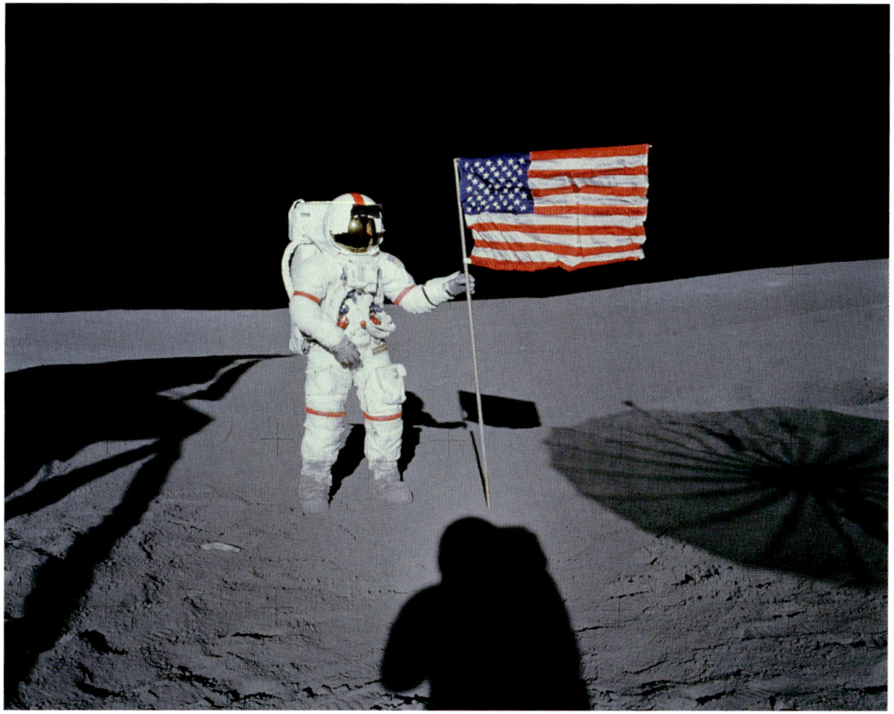

Alan Shepard was the only Project Mercury astronaut to walk on the Moon.

NASA

When Apollo 14 touched down on the Moon in the Fra Mauro highlands in February 1971, it was a big moment for mission commander Alan Shepard. After becoming the first American in space in 1961 (see page 143), Shepard was grounded from future spaceflight due to a diagnosis of Ménière's disease, an inner-ear disorder that causes dizziness and nausea. Years later, after an operation to relieve the symptoms of Ménière's, Shepard was cleared to fly again, and he returned to space on Apollo 14 to walk on the Moon.

An avid golfer, Shepard brought with him a few golf balls and a modified Wilson six iron club head he affixed to the handle of a sample return tool. Et voilà, he had a golf club. On February 6, 1971, Shepard played two shots on the most exclusive golf course in the solar system: the surface of the Moon.

BRUCE MCCANDLESS II MAKES FIRST UNTETHERED SPACEWALK

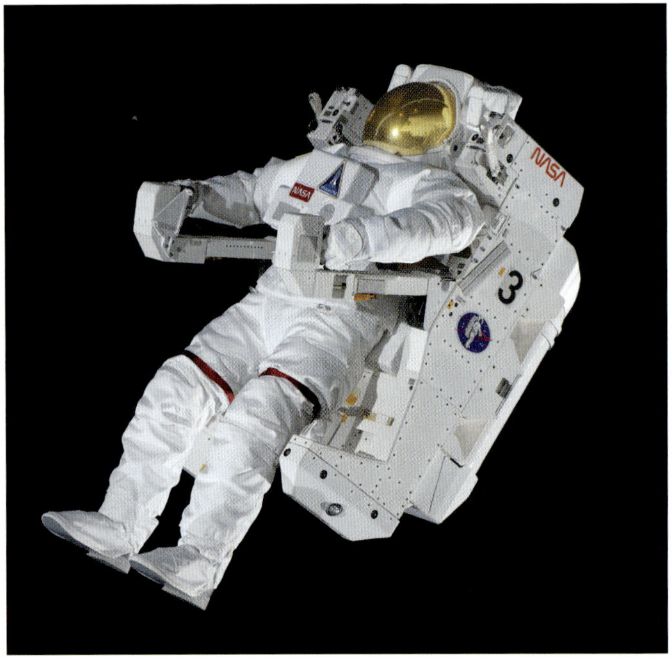

ABOVE The Manned Maneuvering Unit is on display at the National Air and Space Museum's Steven F. Udvar-Hazy Center.

Smithsonian's National Air and Space Museum

OPPOSITE PAGE The iconic photo of McCandless on an untethered spacewalk was taken during one of his 1984 test flights of the MMU.

NASA

Astronauts who need to complete tasks outside the spacecraft—extravehicular activity (EVA) or, more colloquially, spacewalking—require a tether to connect them to a spacecraft. Edward White II used an umbilical and small handheld maneuvering device for the first U.S. spacewalk in 1965 (see page 172), but the dream was always to move around a spacecraft with a jetpack. This became a reality, though only briefly, in 1984 with the introduction of the Manned Maneuvering Unit (MMU). NASA's backpack propulsion device allowed an astronaut to spacewalk without an umbilical or tether.

It was used for the first time on February 7, 1984, by astronaut Bruce McCandless II during Space Shuttle *Challenger*'s STS-41B mission, on a free flight lasting an hour and twenty-two minutes. A few days later, one of the most iconic space photos ever taken was captured from inside *Challenger* by mission commander Hoot Gibson of McCandless on another test flight. The MMU was only used on three missions in 1984 before NASA discontinued its use.

"It may have been one small step for Neil, but it's a heck of a big leap for me."

—BRUCE MCCANDLESS II

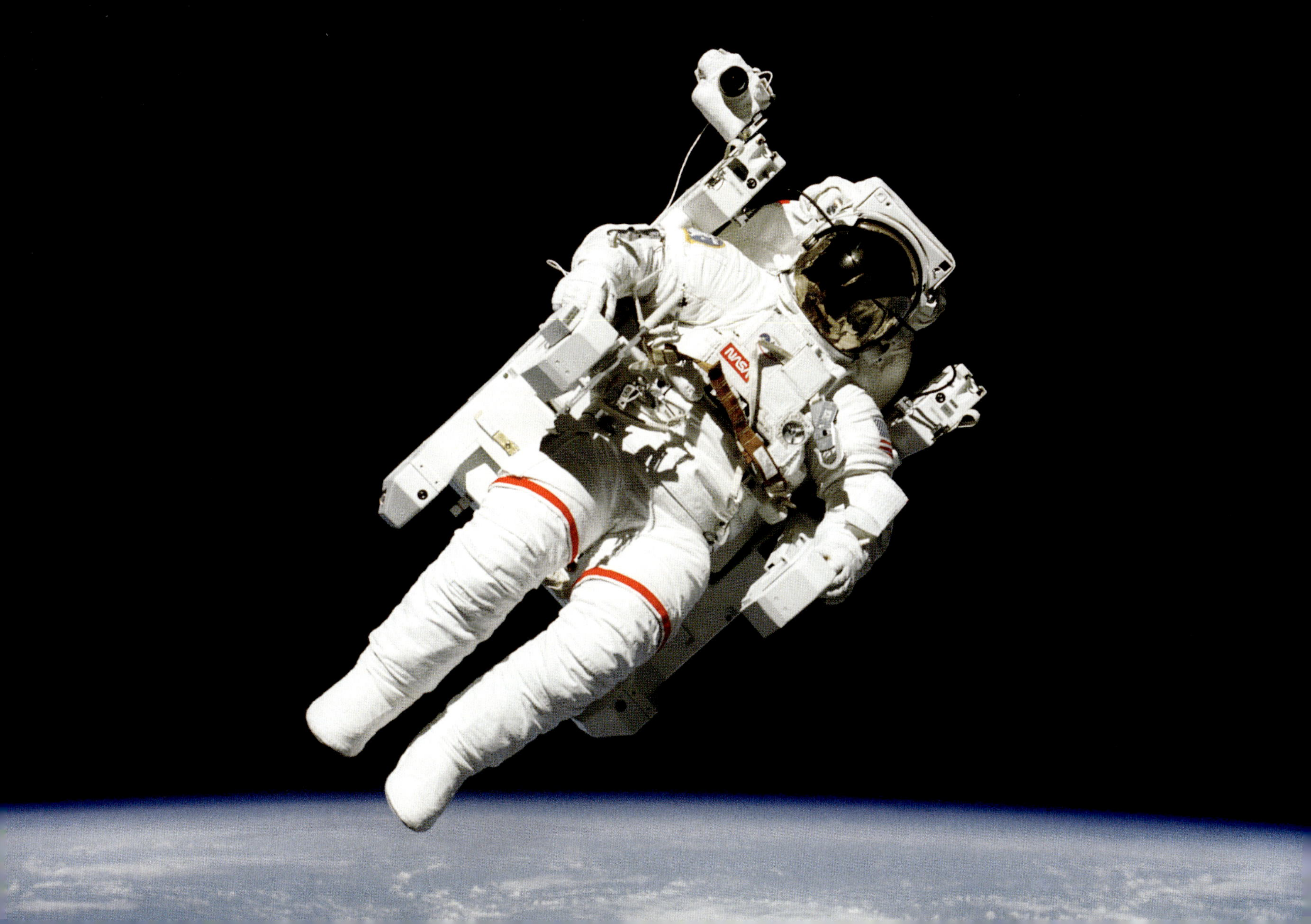
NASA

FEBRUARY 8

JULES VERNE IS BORN

SOCIAL AND CULTURAL SPACE

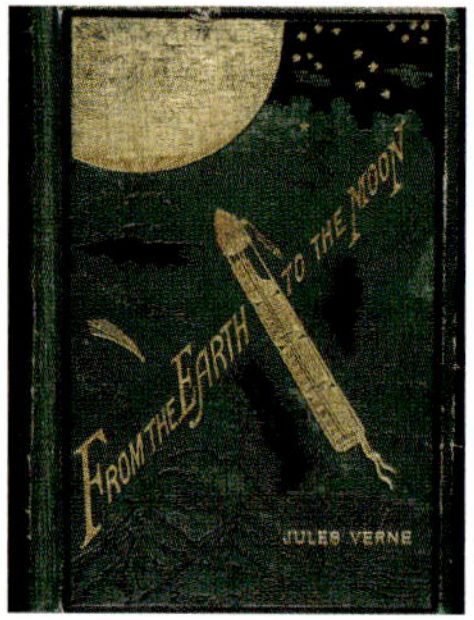

An 1874 copy of Jules Verne's book *From the Earth to the Moon* is held by Smithsonian Libraries.

Smithsonian Libraries

Aerospace innovators, from early rocket pioneers to engineers to today's astronauts, are often inspired by science fiction. Many early innovators drew inspiration from French author Jules Verne, who was born on February 8, 1828. Best-known for his novels *Journey to the Center of the Earth* and *Around the World in Eighty Days*, Verne also wrote space-inspired stories. *From the Earth to the Moon* featured a gigantic cannon based in Florida that fired a capsule around the Moon.

FEBRUARY 9

FIRST JUMBO JET TAKES FLIGHT

COMMERCIAL AVIATION

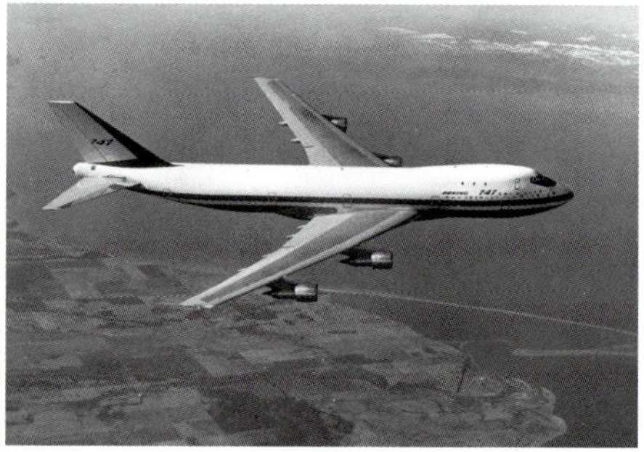

The Boeing 747 prototype was called the *City of Everett*, named for the site of the 747 factory.

Smithsonian's National Air and Space Museum/Boeing (NASM-7A07351)

Flying for the first time on February 9, 1969, the wide-body Boeing 747 revolutionized long-distance air travel when it officially entered service with Pan American Airways the following year. Powered by four efficient, high-bypass turbofan engines, the first 747s could seat up to four hundred passengers, and later versions carried even more. This allowed the 747 to have lower operating costs than other airliners at the time, making flying more affordable. The success of the "jumbo jet" spawned a new generation of wide-body airliners from Airbus, Lockheed, McDonnell Douglas, and later Boeing.

FEBRUARY 10

RESTORATION OF VOUGHT V-173 "FLYING PANCAKE" IS COMPLETED

WORLD WAR II MILITARY AVIATION

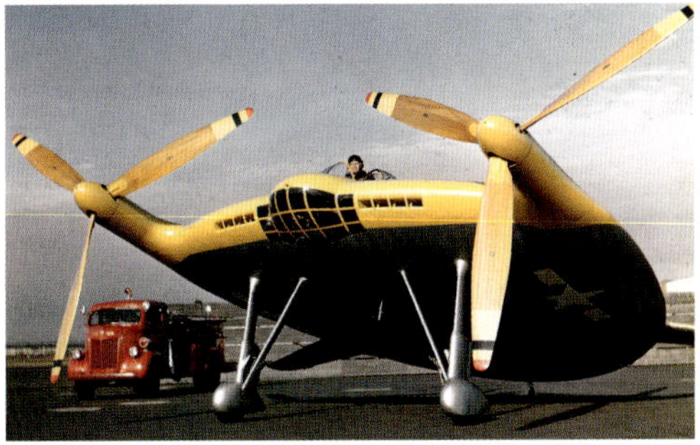

The Vought V-173 is in the collection of the National Air and Space Museum.

Rudy Arnold Photo Collection, Smithsonian's National Air and Space Museum (NASM 2009-1152)

First flown in November 1942, the Vought V-173 "Flying Pancake" featured an all-wing design with a disc-like body that served as the lifting surface. Its huge three-bladed propellers created gyroscopic forces that allowed the aircraft to behave similarly to a helicopter. After 131 hours of flight time, pilots gave the V-173 high marks, noting that it could almost hover. The Navy canceled the project when it decided to pursue turbojet engines and transferred the aircraft to the Smithsonian. Retired Vought employees finished restoring the "Flying Pancake" on February 10, 2012.

FEBRUARY 11

CHALLENGER BECOMES FIRST SPACE SHUTTLE TO LAND AT KENNEDY SPACE CENTER

HUMAN SPACEFLIGHT

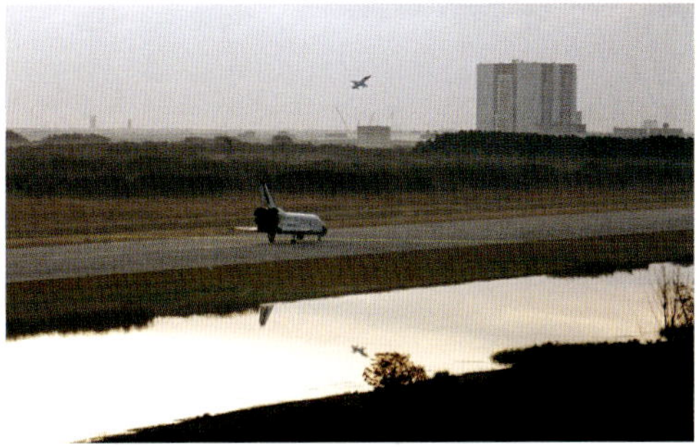

The famed Vehicle Assembly Building (VAB) can be seen in the background of this photo of *Challenger* making the first space shuttle landing at Kennedy Space Center.

NASA

Space Shuttle *Challenger* landed at Kennedy Space Center on February 11, 1984, becoming the first space shuttle orbiter to land at the Florida space facility. This was the first time that a spacecraft both launched and landed at the same location. The first nine missions of the Space Shuttle program landed at Edwards Air Force Base in California or White Sands Missile Range in New Mexico. With Kennedy's landing facility inaugurated, over half of the program's missions landed there until the program's end in 2011.

USS *MACON* CRASHES OFF COAST OF CALIFORNIA

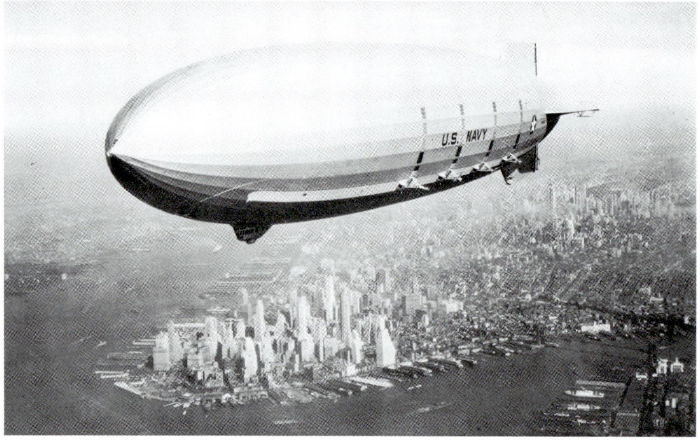

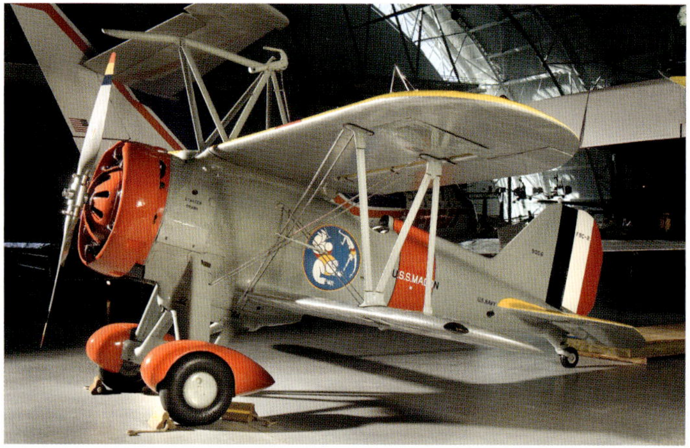

In the early 1930s, the U.S. Navy briefly operated airships as flying aircraft carriers. The USS *Akron* and USS *Macon* were helium-filled rigid airships built to serve as airborne coastal defense scouts. From their positions high in the sky, these airships had greater visual search capability than surface fleets alone and could keep watch for enemies approaching the United States.

Adapting the recently developed concept of the aircraft carrier, airplanes like the Curtiss F9C-2 Sparrowhawk could be operated from airships using an aerial trapeze hook for release and recovery. Using airships as carriers not only greatly increased the lighter-than-air vessels' search range but also improved their capability for attack and defense.

The Navy's experimental trials with airship-based fighter support were brief, officially ending when foul weather caused the *Macon* to crash off the California coast on February 12, 1935. This followed the loss of the *Akron* in a storm two years earlier.

TOP The USS *Macon* was one of two airships operated by the U.S. Navy as flying aircraft carriers.

U.S. Naval Historical Center

BOTTOM Several Sparrowhawks were lost in airship crashes in the 1930s. The only surviving Sparrowhawk is on display at the Steven F. Udvar-Hazy Center.

Smithsonian's National Air and Space Museum

FEBRUARY 13

CHUCK YEAGER IS BORN

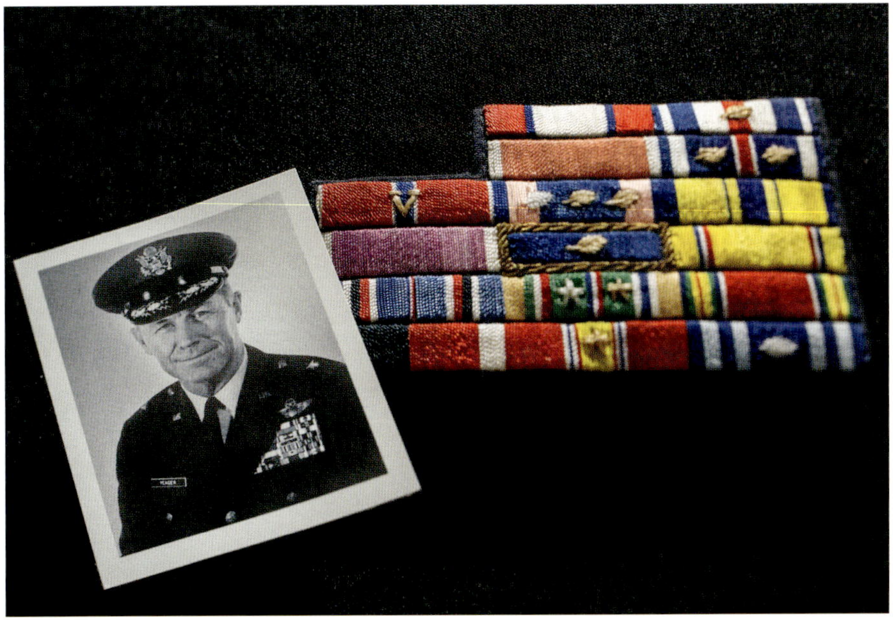

Gen. Chuck Yeager's ribbon bar highlights his many military accolades, including the American Defense Service Medal, Victory Medal, Silver Star, and Distinguished Flying Cross.

Smithsonian's National Air and Space Museum

Record-setting test pilot Gen. Charles "Chuck" Yeager was born in Myra, West Virginia, on February 13, 1923. Yeager grew up in nearby Hamlin, where he developed an interest in all things mechanical. His knowledge of machines made him an ideal test pilot, despite his lack of a formal college education. Piloting his North American P-51 Mustang during World War II, Yeager destroyed thirteen German aircraft in air-to-air combat, including five on a single mission.

After the war, Yeager flew experimental aircraft from Muroc Army Air Force Base (now called Edwards Air Force Base) in California. It was here that the famous test pilot cemented his legacy, becoming the first person ever to fly faster than the speed of sound in 1947 (see page 303). Yeager graduated from the Air War College in 1961 and became commandant of the Aerospace Research Pilot School in July 1962. He went on to hold various command roles in the U.S. Air Force and flew 127 missions in Vietnam.

Voyager 1 took the iconic "Pale Blue Dot" photo during its trip away from Earth on February 14, 1990. The spacecraft was 3.7 billion miles away when the photo of Earth in the distance was taken. The idea to take the photo originated with famed science communicator Carl Sagan, who was a member of the Voyager Imaging Team. Inspired by the photo, which pictured Earth as "a mote of dust suspended in a sunbeam," Sagan wrote his "Pale Blue Dot" excerpt: "Look again at that dot. That's here. That's home. That's us. On it everyone you love, everyone you know, everyone you ever heard of, every human being who ever was, lived out their lives."

On the same day, Voyager took additional photos as part of the "Family Portrait" series, which aimed to photograph all the planets in the solar system. It succeeded in taking photos of Venus, Earth, Jupiter, Saturn, Uranus, and Neptune, but was unable to photograph Mercury, Mars, and Pluto.

The "Pale Blue Dot" photo was taken by Voyager 1 in 1990.

NASA

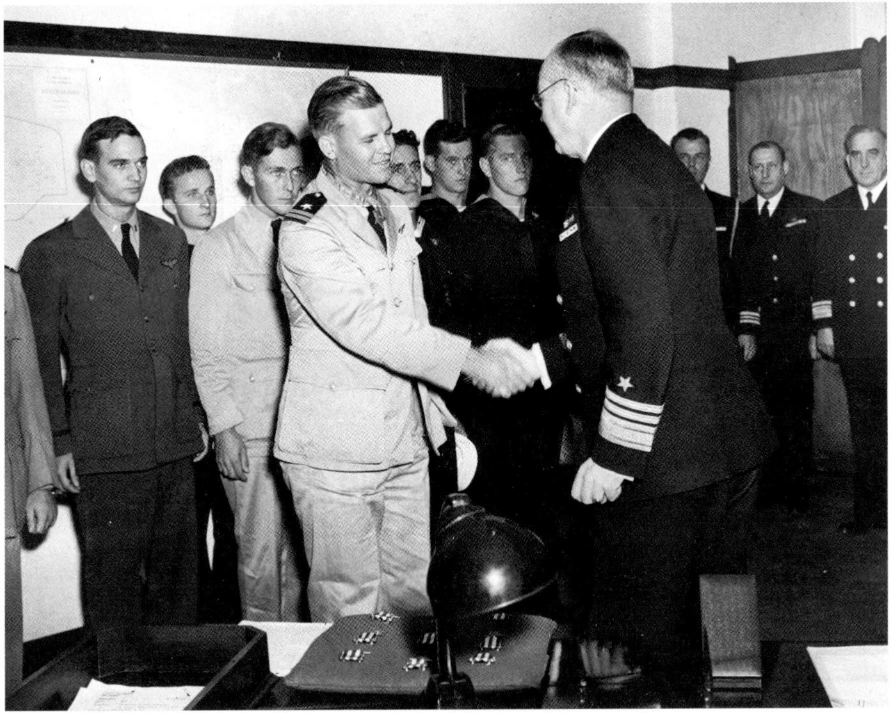

Vice Adm. Thomas Kinkaid presented Lt. Nathan G. Gordon the Medal of Honor for his heroic rescue of fifteen airmen.

Naval History and Heritage Command

On February 15, 1944, U.S. Navy Lt. (j.g.) Nathan G. Gordon was called to heroic action while flying his PBY Catalina *Arkansas Traveler* in support of a U.S. 5th Air Force attack on Kavieng, Papua New Guinea. Gordon's Patrol Squadron VP-34 was tasked with flying search-and-rescue missions that day. During the attack, several U.S. planes had been shot down by enemy antiaircraft fire, resulting in crewmembers ditching their aircraft in the waters near the target.

Gordon landed his PBY Catalina four times under intense enemy fire to pick up stranded aircrew. After his third landing, and with nine survivors on board, Gordon was flying back to base when he received reports of another stranded group. He turned back to land again under direct fire, picking up six more survivors and flying his very overloaded plane back to safety. Gordon was later awarded the Congressional Medal of Honor for his actions, which according to the award citation exhibited "exceptional daring, personal valor, and incomparable airmanship."

FEBRUARY 16

NEAR SHOEMAKER CAPTURES ROTATION VIDEO OF ASTEROID EROS

SPACE SCIENCE

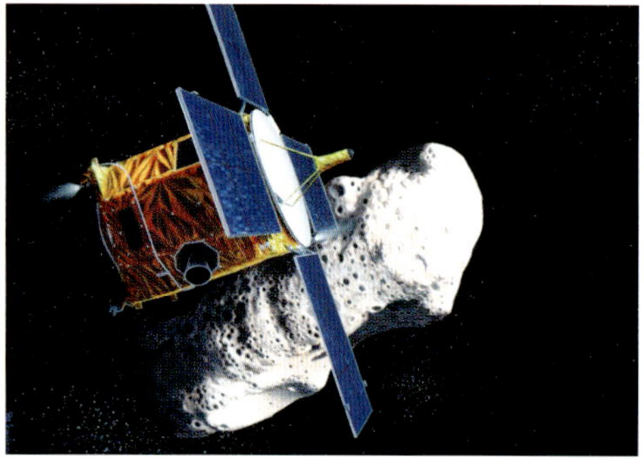

An artist rendering depicts NEAR Shoemaker at Eros.

NASA

NASA's Near Earth Asteroid Rendezvous (NEAR) Shoemaker spacecraft was the first spacecraft to orbit and land on an asteroid. Following its 1996 launch, it first flew by the asteroid Mathilde, then by Earth for a gravity assist, and arrived at the asteroid Eros. NEAR entered Eros's orbit in 2000, and on February 16, it captured a video from about 200 miles away in which the asteroid completed a full rotation. In 2001, it landed on the asteroid.

FEBRUARY 17

WISEMAN DELIVERS FIRST AIRMAIL FOR U.S. POST OFFICE DEPARTMENT

COMMERCIAL AVIATION

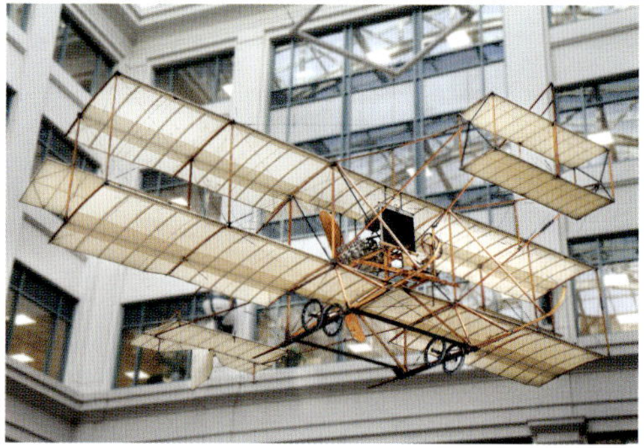

The Wiseman-Cooke aircraft is in the collection of the National Air and Space Museum and is on display at the Smithsonian's National Postal Museum.

Smithsonian's National Air and Space Museum

A sack of coffee, fifty newspapers, and three letters. That was the cargo on the first airmail flight sanctioned by the U.S. Post Office Department. On February 17, 1911, aviator Fred Wiseman took off in what is now known as the Wiseman–Cooke biplane to deliver letters from the mayor and postmaster of Petaluma, California, to their counterparts in Santa Rosa. The fourteen-mile delivery took two days due to mechanical difficulties. When Wiseman landed just outside Santa Rosa the following day, the town celebrated his historic flight.

CLYDE TOMBAUGH DISCOVERS PLUTO

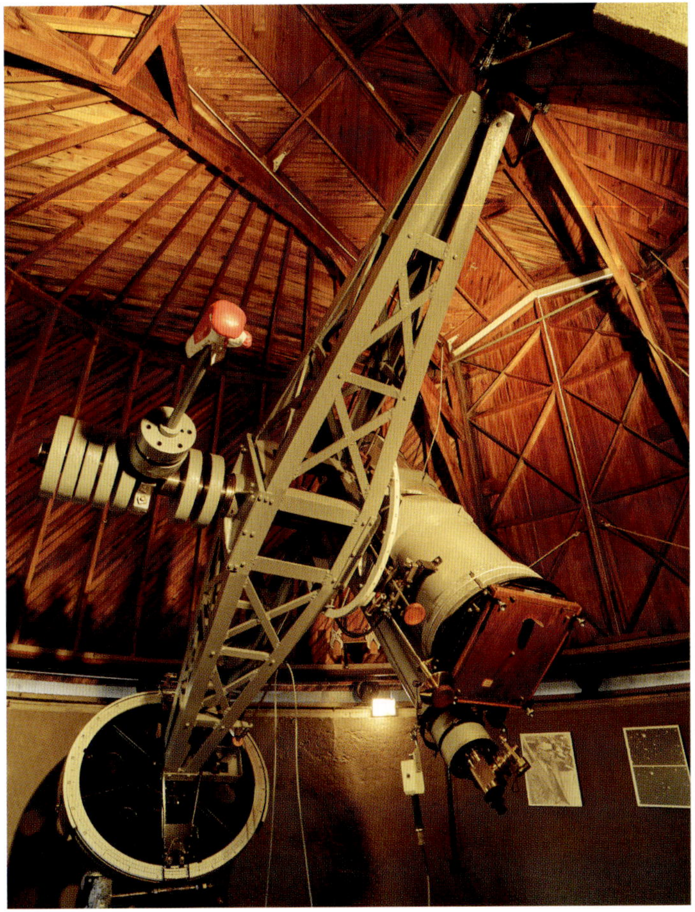

Astronomer Percival Lowell began to search for a planet beyond Neptune in the early 1900s. He thought (incorrectly) that a ninth planet would account for unexplained motions in the orbits of Uranus and Neptune. Clyde Tombaugh, a young astronomer at the Lowell Observatory in Arizona, later took up the search.

Tombaugh's work involved taking long-exposure photographic plates at night, covering areas of the sky where Lowell predicted something must be lurking. He then developed the glass plates and compared them, looking for something moving among the static stars exposed on the plates. He did this using an instrument called a "blink comparator," which allows users to rotate a small dial to flip a mirror back and forth between the beams from two microscopes, "blinking" between the two plates. Tombaugh discovered the object that he later named Pluto on February 18, 1930, when comparing a photographic plate from January 29 to one taken January 23.

DID YOU KNOW? To recognize Clyde Tombaugh's contributions to space science, his ashes were carried on the New Horizons spacecraft on its mission to Pluto (see page 33).

Clyde Tombaugh used a 13-inch telescope at Lowell Observatory to discover Pluto.

Library of Congress, Prints & Photographs Division, photograph by Carol M. Highsmith [LC-DIG-highsm-53341]

NEIL ARMSTONG SETS FIVE AVIATION RECORDS

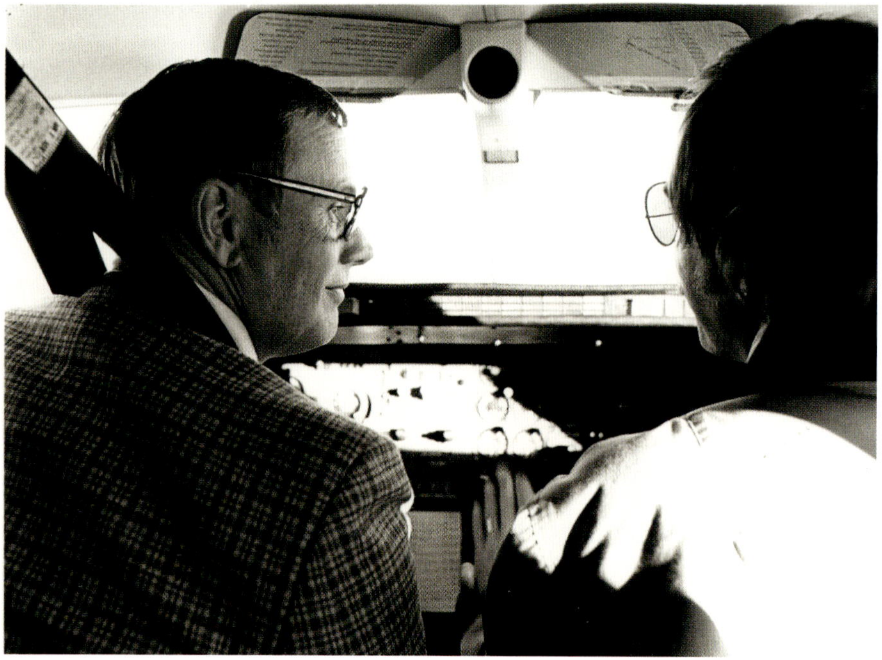

In addition to being an astronaut, Neil Armstrong was a skilled pilot, serving as a naval aviator and test pilot. He set five aviation records in a Learjet 28.

Neil A. Armstrong Archive, University of Cincinnati Libraries

It's well known that Neil Armstrong set records in space, but the renowned astronaut also set numerous terrestrial aviation records. On February 19 and 20, 1979, Armstrong set five world records for business jets in a Learjet 28. He set three records on the first day: altitude, altitude in horizontal flight (15,584.6 meters), and time to climb to a height of 15,000 meters (twelve minutes, twenty-seven seconds). The very next day, Armstrong broke both new altitude records, flying to 15,585 meters. The famous astronaut was joined on these record flights by Learjet 28/29 test pilot Peter Reynolds and National Aeronautic Association official observer Don Berliner.

DID YOU KNOW? Neil Armstrong's record-setting flights in the Learjet 28 took place in North Carolina near the location of the Wright brothers' first flight of the 1903 Wright Flyer.

JOHN GLENN BECOMES FIRST AMERICAN TO ORBIT EARTH

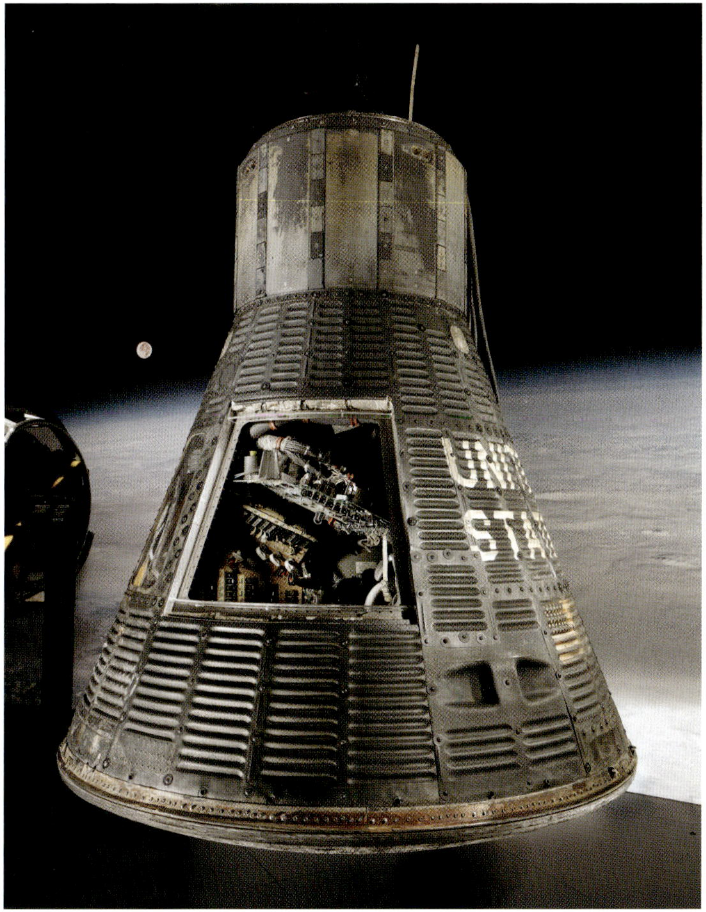

Mercury astronaut John H. Glenn Jr. became the first American to orbit the Earth on February 20, 1962. His three-orbit mission happened almost a year after cosmonaut Yuri Gagarin (see page 85) shocked the world by not just becoming the first person in space but also orbiting Earth. Glenn's spaceflight demonstrated that the United States could compete with the Soviet Union in the Space Race. His description of the experience? "Zero G, and I feel fine." This history-changing moment was the third human-crewed mission of Project Mercury, following two suborbital flights in 1961.

Glenn's Mercury capsule was nicknamed *Friendship 7*. He involved his children in naming his spacecraft, telling them: "There's only one ground rule. The world is going to be watching, so the name should represent our country and the way we feel about the rest of the world." Combining that idea with the fact that there were seven Project Mercury astronauts, the name *Friendship 7* came to be.

LEFT John H. Glenn Jr.'s *Friendship 7* capsule is on display at the National Air and Space Museum.

Smithsonian's National Air and Space Museum

NEXT PAGE "You don't get into it. You put it on," astronaut John Glenn said of the small Mercury capsule.

NASA

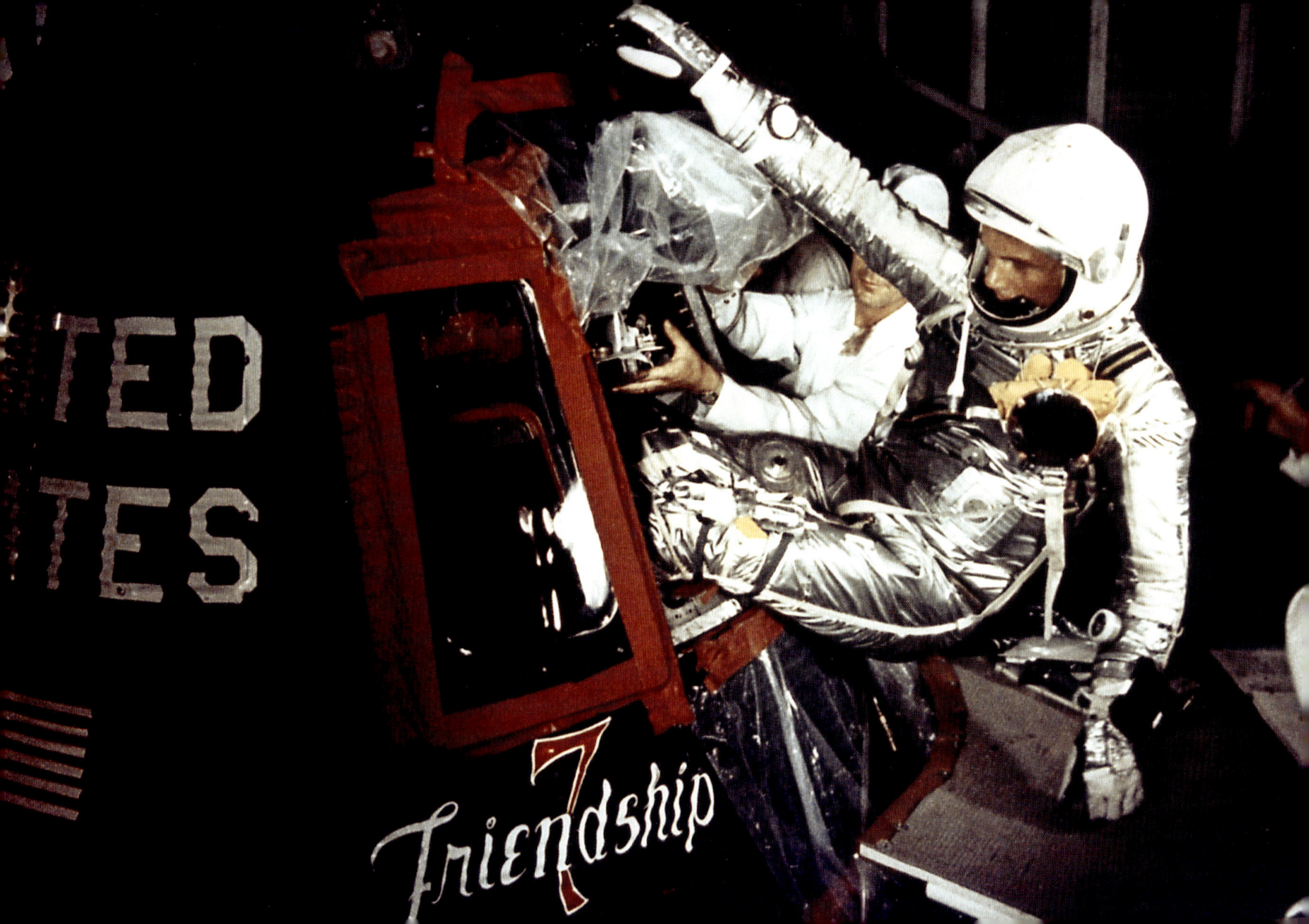

TED
TES
Friendship 7

STEVE FOSSETT SOLOS THE PACIFIC OCEAN IN A BALLOON

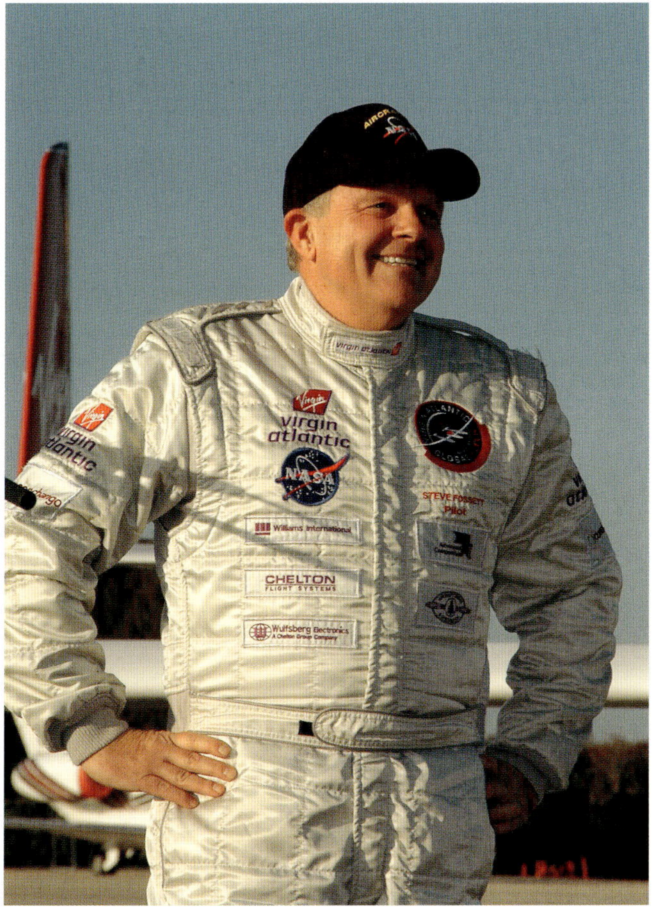

On February 21, 1995, aviator and adventurer Steve Fossett completed the first solo flight across the Pacific Ocean in a balloon. His nearly 5,500-mile transpacific flight began in Seoul, South Korea, and ended in Saskatchewan, Canada. While certainly an achievement, Fossett had his heart set on a more ambitious record, and the following year, he began his quest to fly all the way around the world in a balloon.

It wasn't until his sixth attempt in 2002 that Fossett achieved this lofty goal, becoming the first person to circumnavigate the globe by balloon solo in the Bud Light *Spirit of Freedom*. The 20,000-mile circumnavigation took fourteen days and nineteen hours to complete. In finally achieving his goal, Fossett demonstrated perseverance, determination, courage, and great skill in the air. He expressed the hope that his success would inspire others to "try and achieve something important to them."

Steve Fossett also set aviation records in airplanes, including a 2006 attempt to set a flight duration record in the Virgin Atlantic Global Flyer.

NASA

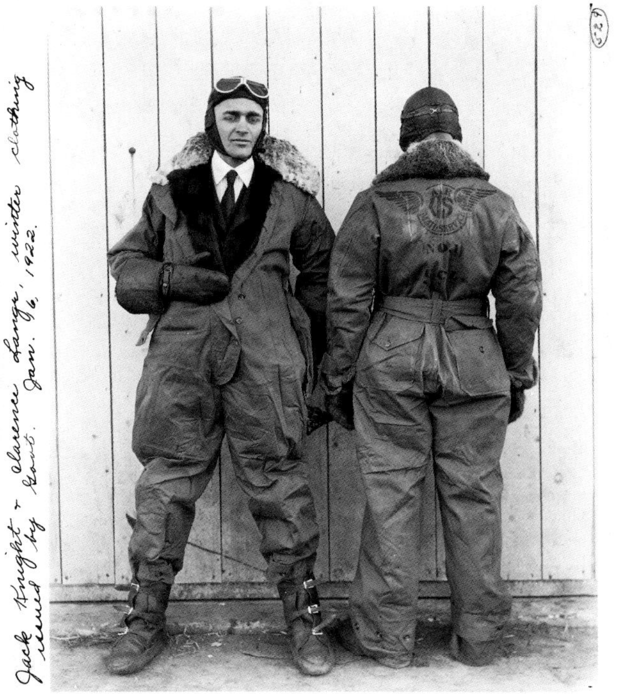

Jack Knight was the only pilot to succeed on a daring nighttime airmail flight in 1921.

Smithsonian's National Air and Space Museum (NASM 83-8165)

As the United States Post Office Department began to set up a burgeoning airmail business in the late 1910s, a problem emerged. Without flying at night, airmail was much slower and more expensive than mail delivered by railroad, but night flying was extremely dangerous. The first significant experiment to solve this problem began on February 22, 1921. Starting on opposite coasts, planes from New York and San Francisco flew the route between the cities assisted by scattered bonfires to aid night navigation.

Despite nearly running out of fuel due to a misunderstanding with the bonfire in Omaha, Nebraska, the plane piloted by Jack Knight completed the historic cross-country flight. Equipped with a railroad map and compass for navigation, Knight made the trip in thirty-three hours and twenty minutes, which was faster than the railroads. The experiment with bonfires was not repeated, but the post office later constructed chains of beacon lights along key routes.

PIONEER 11 CROSSES THE ORBIT OF NEPTUNE

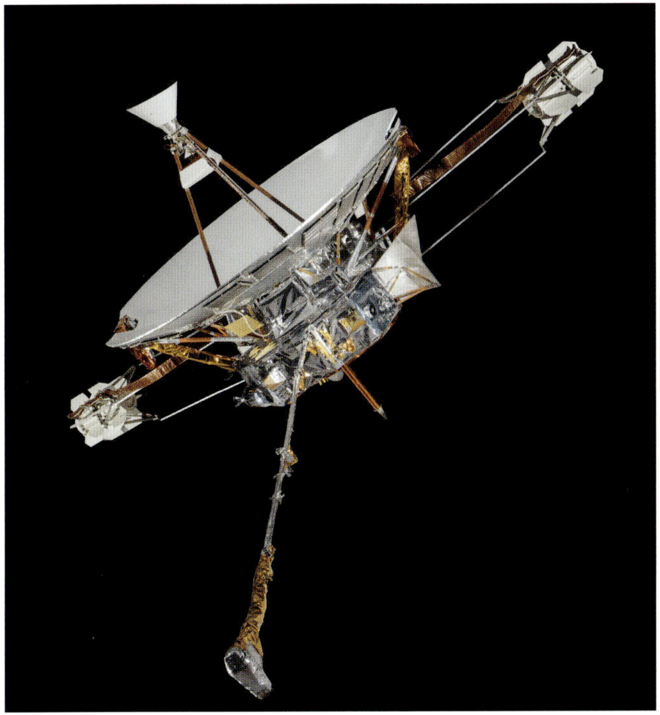

A prototype of Pioneer 10/11 was constructed for NASA by TRW, Inc. and is in the collection of the National Air and Space Museum.

Smithsonian's National Air and Space Museum

On February 23, 1990, Pioneer 11 crossed the orbit of Neptune, becoming the fourth spacecraft to travel beyond the outermost planets of our solar system. But in 1990, Pluto was still classified as a planet, so why did passing Neptune mean Pioneer had passed all planets in the solar system? It was thanks to Pluto's unusual orbit.

It takes 248 Earth years for Pluto to complete one orbit around the Sun, and its orbital path doesn't lie in the same plane as the eight planets. Rather, it is tilted at seventeen degrees. Pluto's orbital path is also more oval-shaped, or elliptical, than those of the planets and brings it closer to the Sun at certain times. That means sometimes, Pluto is nearer the Sun than Neptune. The last time this happened was from 1979 to 1999, and it won't happen again until 2227.

SPACE SHUTTLE *DISCOVERY* LAUNCHES ON FINAL MISSION

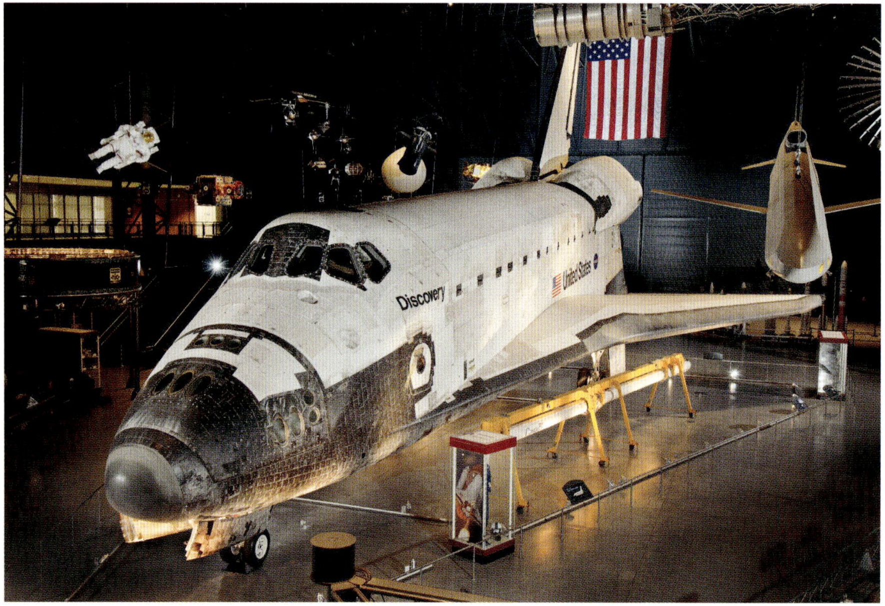

Space Shuttle *Discovery* is on display at the National Air and Space Museum's Steven F. Udvar-Hazy Center.

Smithsonian's National Air and Space Museum

Space Shutte *Discovery*, the third of NASA's Space Shuttle orbiter vehicles to fly in space, entered service in 1984 and retired from spaceflight as the oldest and most utilized orbiter. *Discovery* flew thirty-nine Earth-orbital missions, spending a total of 365 days in space, and traveling almost 150 million miles—more than any other orbiter. It shuttled 184 men and women into space and back, many of whom flew more than once, for a record-setting total crew count of 251.

Discovery was named after multiple renowned sailing ships of exploration. It was flown on many significant missions, including the mission to launch the Hubble Space Telescope, the "Return to Flight" missions after the losses of *Challenger* and *Columbia*, and the first mission to dock with the International Space Station (ISS). *Discovery* flew every kind of mission the Space Shuttle was meant to fly. *Discovery* began its final mission, STS-133, by launching from Florida on February 24, 2011. During the mission, *Discovery* and its crew delivered the robotic helper Robonaut and installed the Permanent Multipurpose Module on the ISS.

FEBRUARY 25

USSR SELECTS COSMONAUT TRAINING GROUP 1

INTERNATIONAL SPACE PROGRAMS

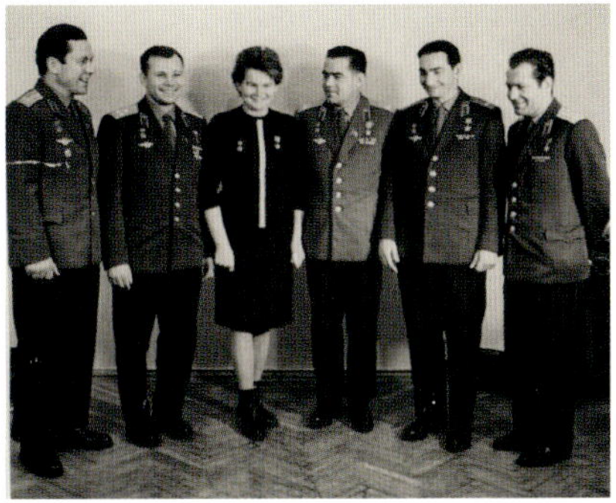

The first five Soviets to go to space were in Cosmonaut Training Group 1. The sixth, Valentina Tereshkova, was selected for training in 1962.

Smithsonian's National Air and Space Museum (NASM 2006-635)

The USSR selected its first group of cosmonauts almost a year after the announcement of the Mercury 7 (see page 115). Unlike NASA's first class of astronauts, which was announced with a big public relations campaign, the USSR kept its cosmonaut selection a secret. The names of cosmonauts, in fact, were not publicly shared until after their missions were successful. Information learned later shows that the group was finalized on February 25, 1960. There were twenty cosmonaut candidates in Group 1, which included Yuri Gagarin and Gherman Titov, and they began training a few weeks after their selection.

FEBRUARY 26

GEORGE SMITH SURVIVES SUPERSONIC EJECTION

MODERN MILITARY AVIATION

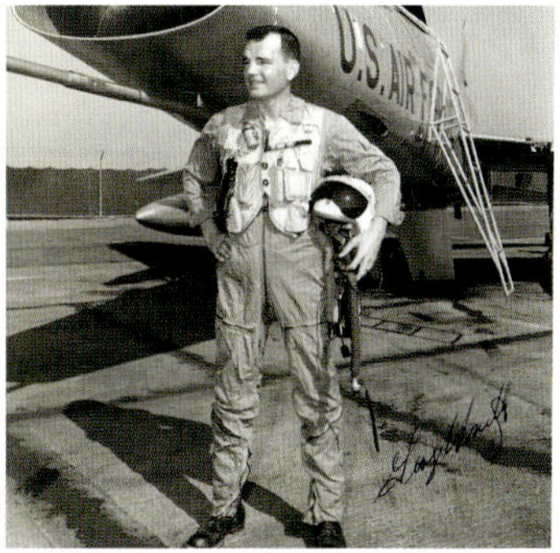

George Smith bailed out of a F-100 Super Sabre flying Mach 1.05.

Smithsonian's National Air and Space Museum (NASM 9A13995)

On February 26, 1955, George Smith became the first person to successfully eject from an aircraft flying at supersonic speeds. A test pilot for North American Aviation, Smith was flying an F-100 Super Sabre when a failure with the hydraulic system forced the aircraft into a dive. Unable to return to level flight, the F-100 increased in speed, reaching Mach 1.05. Smith was forced to eject from the aircraft, losing consciousness as he did so. Although critically injured, Smith survived the ejection and was eventually cleared to fly again.

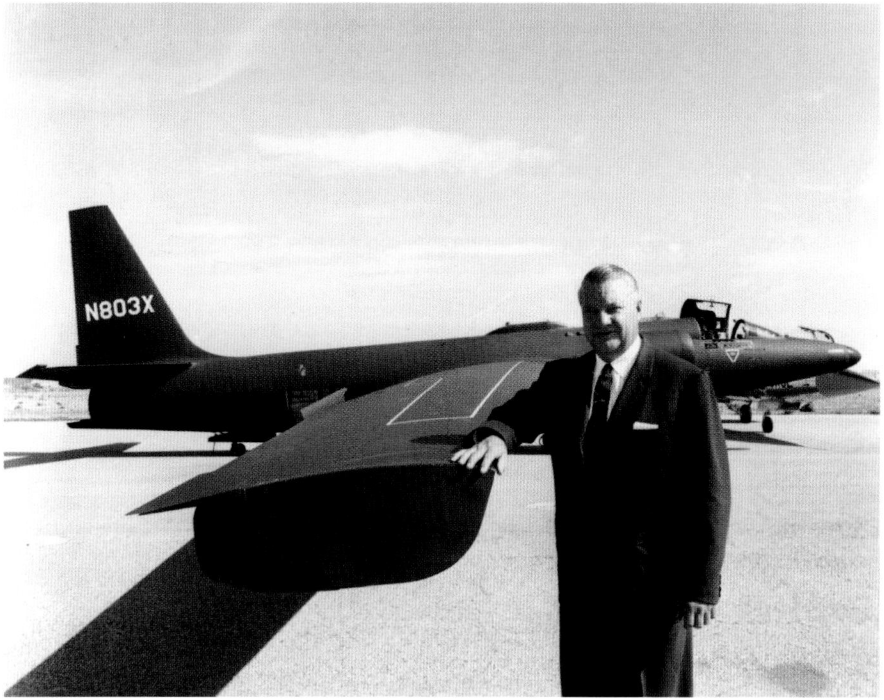

Aeronautical engineer Kelly Johnson designed the Lockheed U-2.

U.S. Air Force

"Be quick, be quiet, be on time." Aeronautical engineer Clarence L. "Kelly" Johnson lived by that motto. Born on February 27, 1910, in Michigan, Johnson developed an interest in aviation at a young age. He was later known as the "Architect of the Air" and contributed to the design of many of history's most iconic airplanes, including the SR-71, the P-38, and the U-2.

Lockheed hired Johnson as a tool designer in 1933, and by 1938 he had risen to become the company's chief research engineer. He is best known for leading Skunk Works, Lockheed's highly secretive engineering division. Johnson stayed at Lockheed his entire career, becoming chief engineer in 1953 and a vice president in 1956. Even after his retirement in 1975, Johnson remained involved as a senior advisor. Established in his honor by the Society of Flight Test Engineers, the Kelly Johnson Award recognizes outstanding achievement in the field of flight test engineering.

REPUBLIC XP-84 FLIES FOR THE FIRST TIME

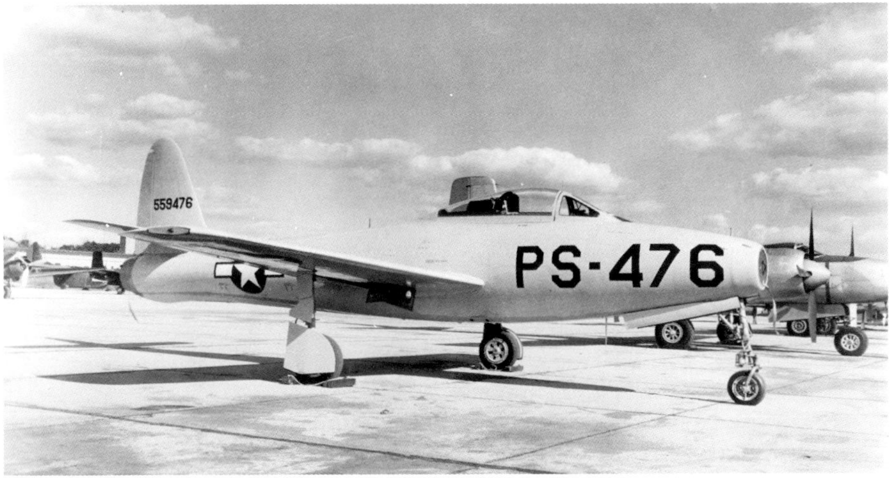

The jet-powered Republic F-84 was an important combat aircraft in the early Cold War. Piloted by Maj. William A. Lien, the first flight of the prototype XP-84 took place at Muroc Dry Lake in California on February 28, 1946, making it the first new American fighter to take its inaugural flight in the postwar years. The XP-84 was capable of achieving a maximum speed of 592 miles per hour at sea level, had a normal range of 1,300 miles, and could reach an altitude of 35,000 feet in thirteen minutes.

In mid-1948, the newly independent U.S. Air Force re-designated all pursuit (P) aircraft as fighters (F). Subsequently, the redesignated F-84 excelled at ground attack, air interdiction, and other close air support roles during the Korean War. With variants that included fighter-bombers and reconnaissance aircraft, the F-84 eventually equipped many Allied and NATO air forces until the advent of supersonic aircraft.

The nose section of the second XP-84 is in the collection of the National Air and Space Museum.

National Air and Space Museum

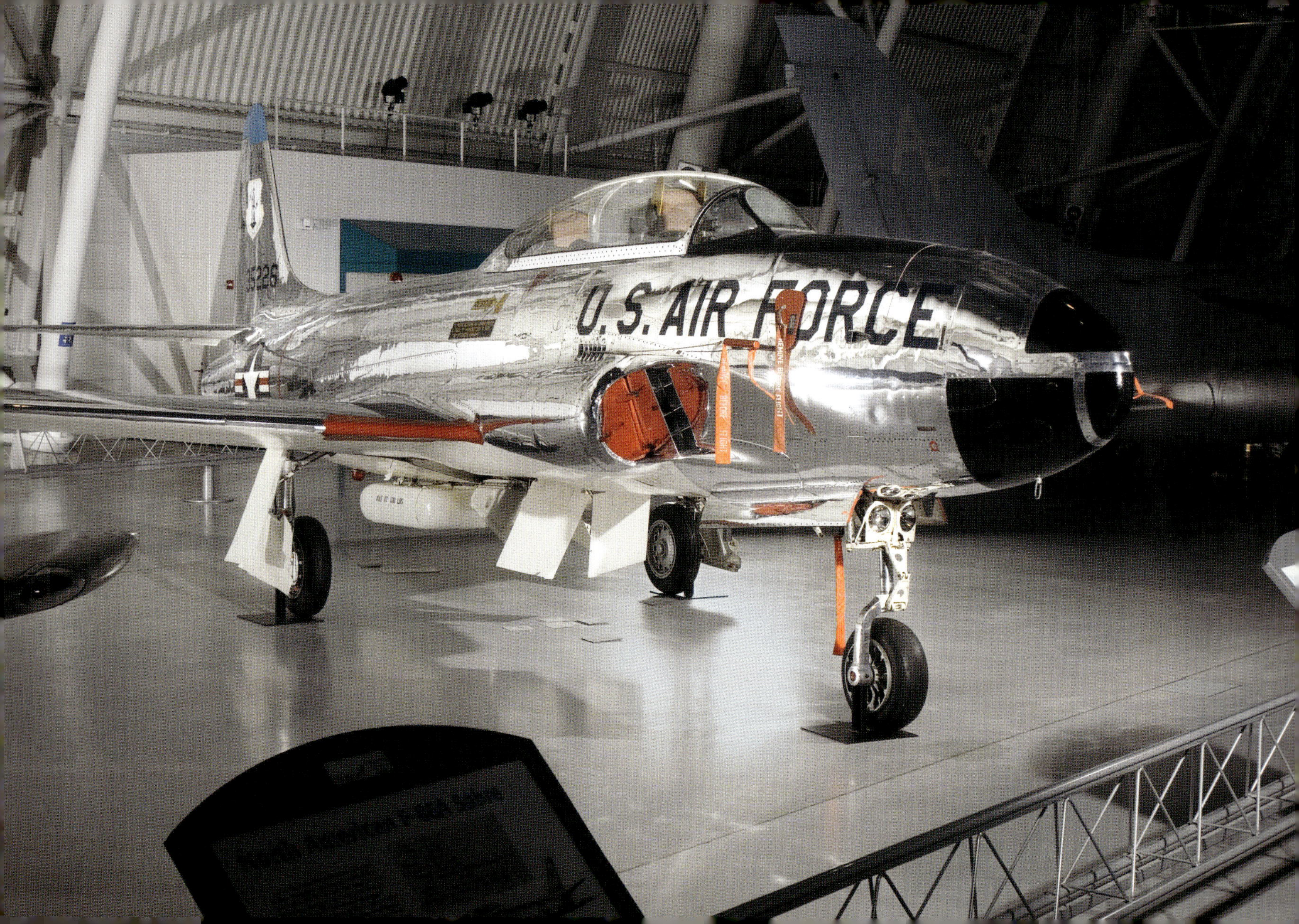
35226
U.S. AIR FORCE

MARCH

ALBERT BERRY MAKES PIONEERING PARACHUTE JUMP

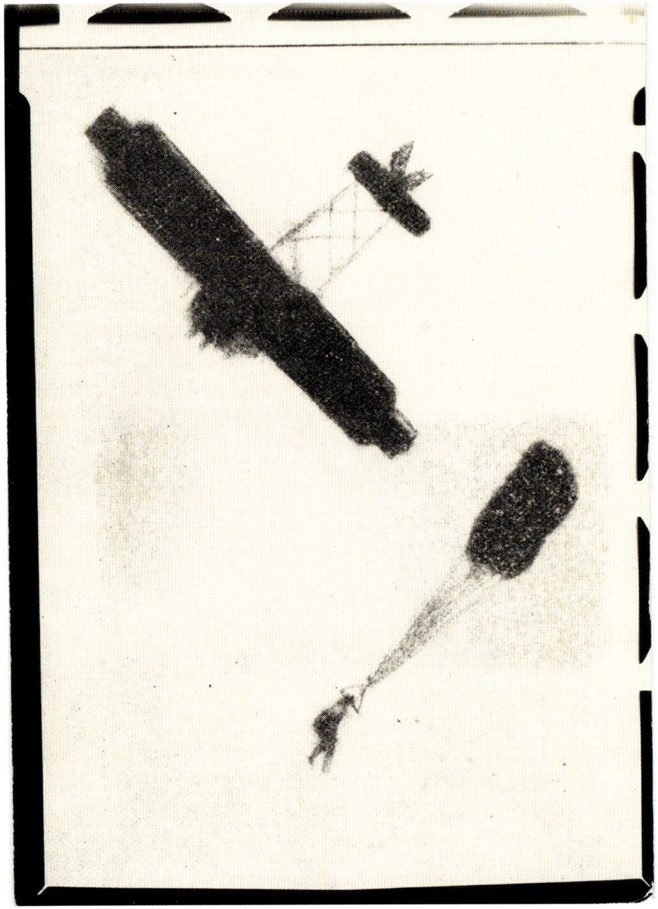

On March 1, 1912, Capt. Albert Berry made the first parachute jump from a powered airplane in the United States. His flight began at Kinloch Field (now home to the St. Louis Lambert International Airport). Flown aloft by pilot Tony Jannus in a Benoist pusher biplane, Berry climbed out of his seat as the aircraft approached Jefferson Barracks Army Base outside St. Louis, Missouri. After connecting himself to a trapeze bar at the front of the airplane and attaching the parachute to his harness, Berry released himself from the plane. He fell several hundred feet before the parachute opened and guided him safely to the ground.

DID YOU KNOW? Kinloch Field was also the site of an earlier aviation milestone: In October 1910, pilot Arch Hoxsey took Theodore Roosevelt for a short flight in a Wright Model B biplane, making Roosevelt the first U.S. president to fly in an airplane.

Albert Berry parachuted from a Benoist biplane in 1912.

Smithsonian's National Air and Space Museum (NASM A-33652)

SUPERSONIC CONCORDE MAKES FIRST FLIGHT

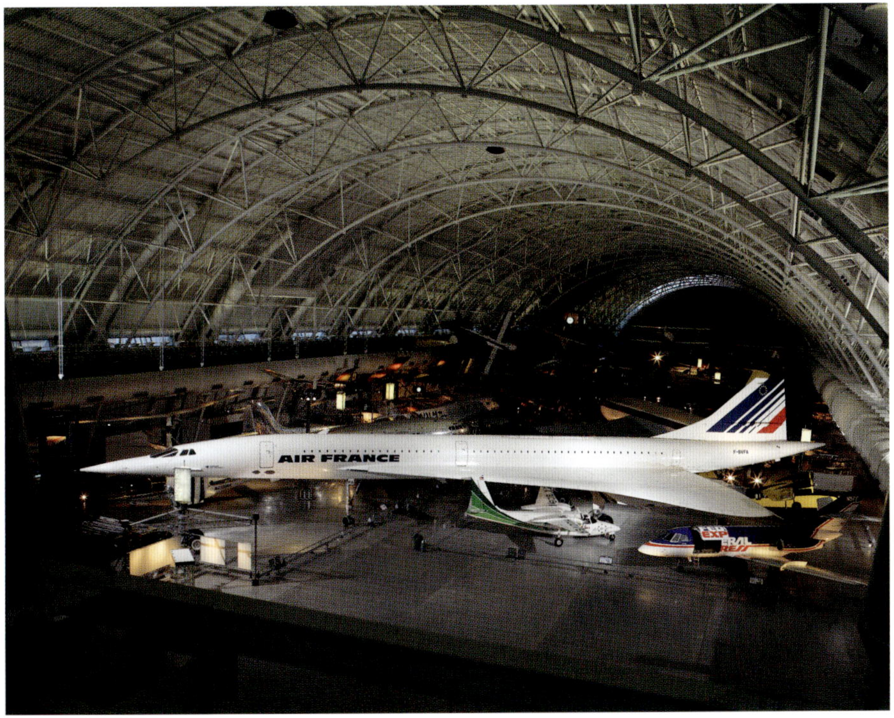

The Air France Concorde on display at the Steven F. Udvar-Hazy Center was flown nearly 18,000 hours.

Smithsonian's National Air and Space Museum

First conceived in the 1950s, the dream of supersonic passenger air travel came to fruition in the mid-1970s with the introduction of the graceful Anglo-French Concorde. For over twenty-five years, the Concorde flew thousands of passengers across the Atlantic at twice the speed of sound. Designed and built by the British Aircraft Corporation and France's Sud Aviation, the Concorde took off for the first time on March 2, 1969, and entered commercial service in 1976.

The Concorde was a technological masterpiece, flying so fast that its aluminum skin heated up and expanded during flight. The aircraft also cruised between 55,000 and 60,000 feet—high enough that passengers could see the curvature of the Earth. Despite its superior design and performance, the Concorde was very costly to operate. Concorde tickets were also prohibitively expensive, with an average round trip costing more than $12,000 per passenger. Unable to overcome these economic problems, Air France and British Airways retired the elegant supersonic aircraft in 2003.

APOLLO 9 LAUNCHES ON EARTH ORBITAL MISSION

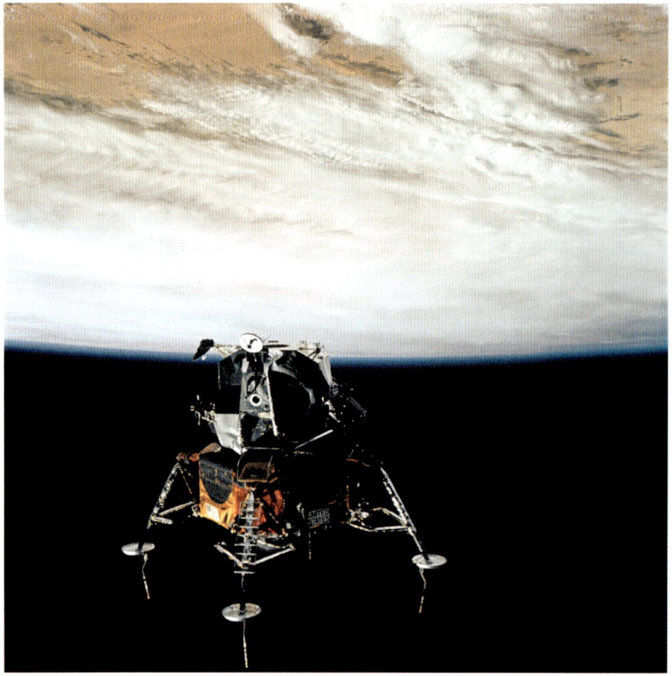

Lunar module *Spider* deployed its landing gear footpads as part of its tests during the Apollo 9 mission.

NASA

Before the Apollo lunar module flew in lunar orbit or landed on the Moon, it was tested in Earth orbit. Launched on March 3, 1969, Apollo 9 carried out a full test of the lunar module equipment and procedures while circling Earth, including the first crewed flight of the lunar module in space. Mission commander James McDivitt and lunar module pilot Russell "Rusty" Schweickart tested the lunar module by rendezvousing and docking with the command and service modules piloted by David Scott. Schweickart also tested the lunar spacesuit and life support backpack outside the spacecraft.

Apollo 9 was the first mission in the program that allowed call signs for its spacecraft. As a result, the Apollo 9 crew named their command module *Gumdrop* and their lunar module *Spider* after their overall shape and appearance. *Gumdrop* and *Spider* both functioned without problems, thus proving that the lunar module was ready for testing in lunar orbit.

LOCKHEED F-104 STARFIGHTER FLIES FOR THE FIRST TIME

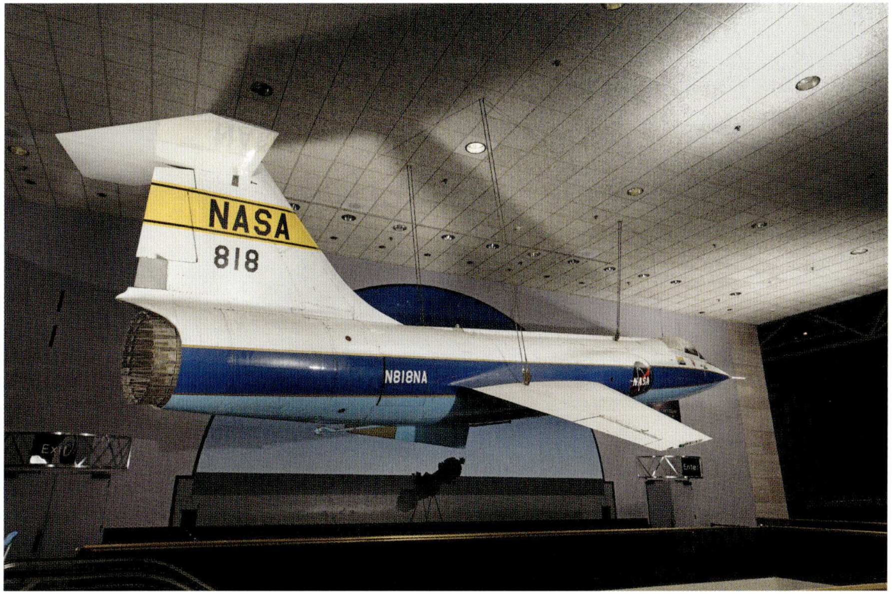

The Lockheed F-104A Starfighter in the National Air and Space Museum's collection flew for nearly twenty years as a NASA test bed and chase plane.

Smithsonian's National Air and Space Museum

Known as "the missile with a man in it," the stubby-winged Lockheed F-104 Starfighter was the first U.S. jet fighter in service to fly at Mach 2—twice the speed of sound. The high-performance day fighter took off for its first flight on March 4, 1954, exhibiting excellent acceleration and speed. The Starfighter's design was radical for its time, as its small, straight wings stood out against other contemporary aircraft with larger swept wings.

Four years after the aircraft's initial flight, the first production F-104As were delivered to the 83d Fighter-Interceptor Squadron at Hamilton Air Force Base in California. Almost immediately, squadron pilots began setting world speed and altitude records in the F-104. Though built for the U.S. Air Force, most Starfighters in service were flown by military pilots in other countries, particularly Canada, Italy, Germany, and Japan.

IGOR SIKORSKY FOUNDS SIKORSKY AIRCRAFT CORPORATION

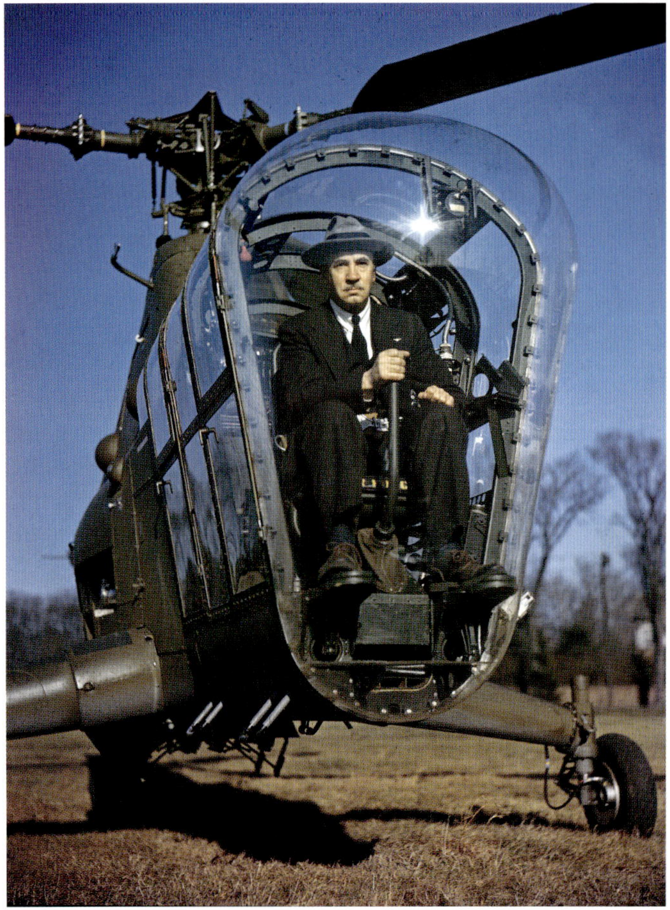

As a child, Igor Sikorsky developed an interest in science and aviation. While studying mechanical engineering, he resolved to build a helicopter and began building and testing his own aircraft designs. After fleeing the Russian Revolution and immigrating to the United States, Sikorsky founded the Sikorsky Aero Engineering Corporation on March 5, 1923. Sikorsky's first successful aircraft was a two-engine all-metal transport plane called the Sikorsky S-29-A that was released in 1924. The company also worked on flying boats and became part of United Aircraft and Transport Corporation in 1929.

By the late 1930s, Sikorsky had returned to his roots and began working on helicopter designs once again. Today, the Sikorsky Aircraft Corporation is known for its pathbreaking helicopter designs, including the R-4, the world's first mass-produced helicopter; the HH-52 Seaguard amphibious helicopter (see page 324); and the UH-60 Black Hawk utility helicopter. Sikorsky has been called the "father of the helicopter" and the Igor Sikorsky Kyiv Polytechnic Institute in Kyiv, Ukraine, where he was born, is named in his honor.

Igor Sikorsky is known as the father of the modern helicopter.

Smithsonian's National Air and Space Museum

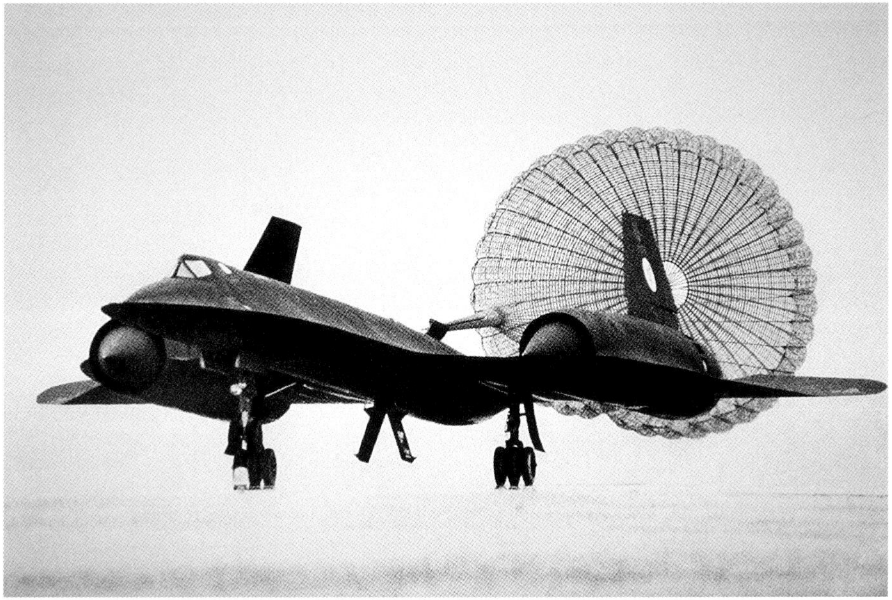

ABOVE The National Air and Space Museum's SR-71 Blackbird made its final flight while being delivered to join the Museum's collection.

Smithsonian Institution Archives. Acc. 11-009 [90-3299-10a]

NEXT PAGE The Lockheed SR-71 on display at the Steven F. Udvar-Hazy Center set several records on its final flight.

Smithsonian's National Air and Space Museum

On March 6, 1990, pilot Ed Yeilding and reconnaissance systems officer Joseph Vida flew an SR-71 Blackbird (serial number 61-7972) across the country to join the Smithsonian's collection. This was the last flight of a U.S. Air Force–operated Blackbird. The aircraft's service career ended on a high note—and a fast one: Yeilding and Vida set a speed record by flying from Los Angeles to Washington, D.C., in one hour, four minutes, twenty seconds, averaging 2,124 miles per hour.

But that wasn't the only record they set on the flight. They also flew from St. Louis to Cincinnati in eight minutes, thirty-two seconds; from Kansas City to D.C. in twenty-five minutes, fifty-nine seconds; and from the West Coast of the United States to the East Coast in one hour, seven minutes, fifty-four seconds. All four world speed records are still standing today. After landing at Dulles International Airport, the Air Force turned the record-breaking Blackbird over to the National Air and Space Museum, where it is now on display at the Museum's Steven F. Udvar-Hazy Center.

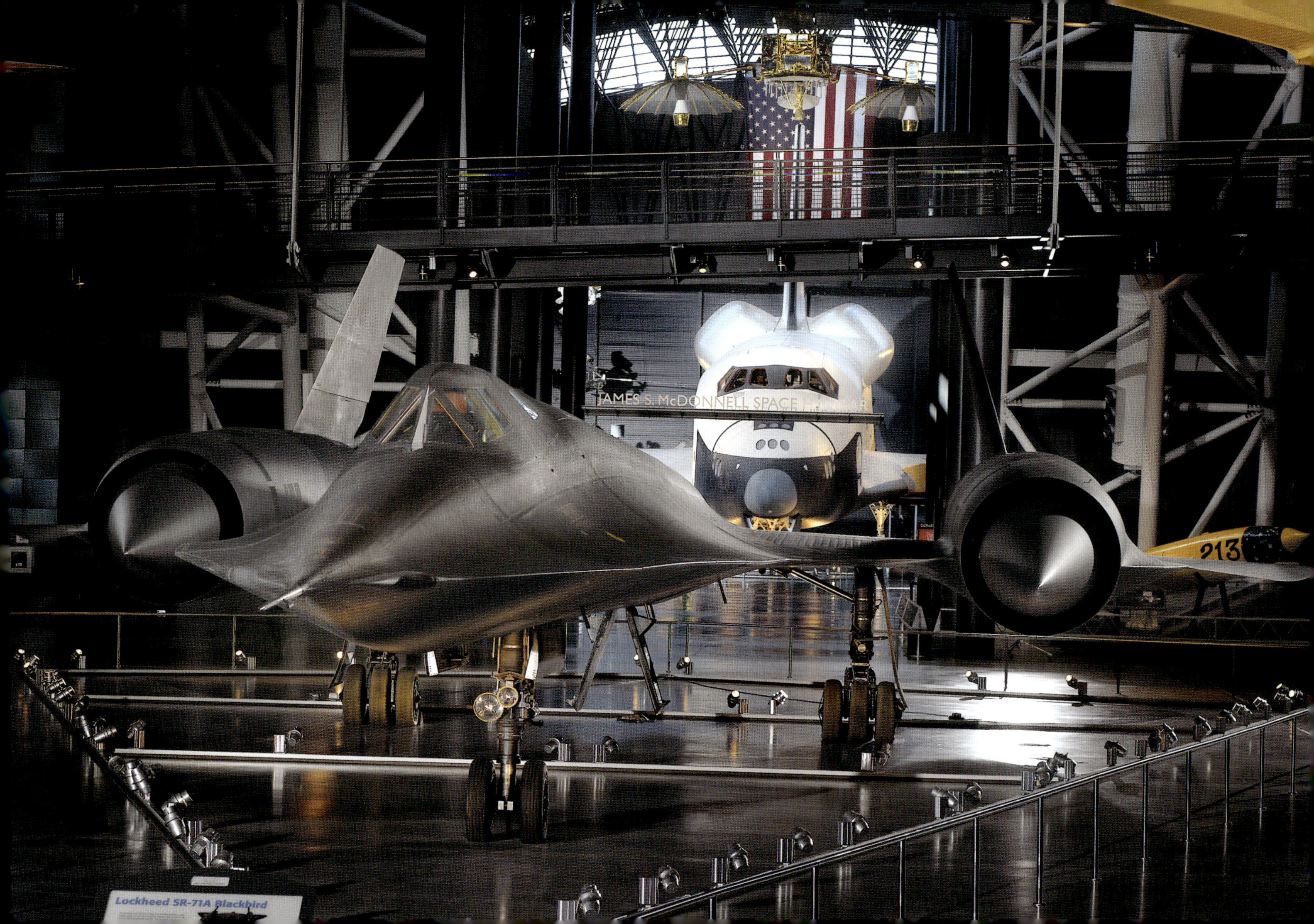
JAMES S. McDONNELL SPACE
213
Lockheed SR-71A Blackbird

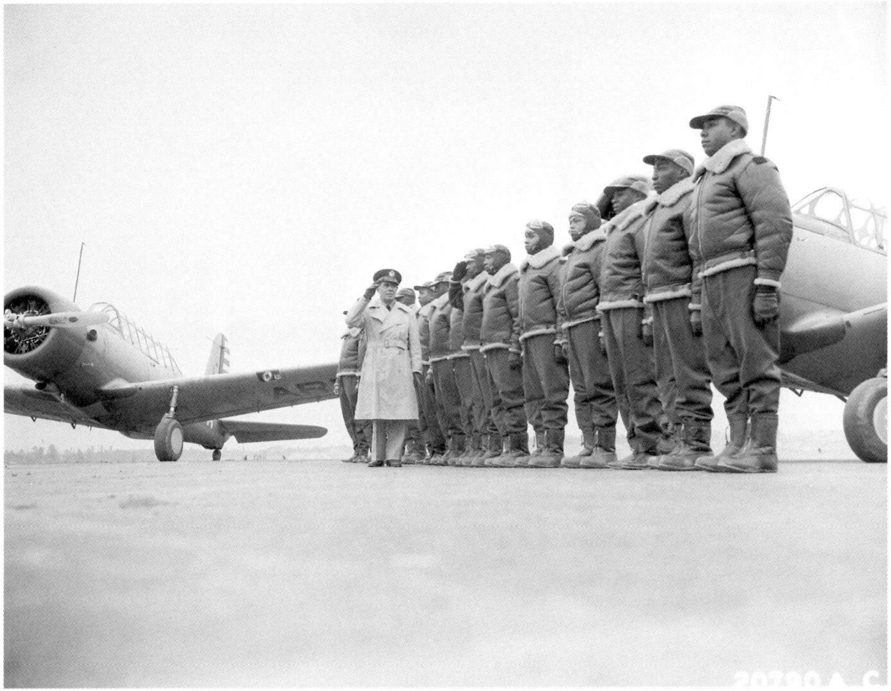

Mac Ross (saluting commandant Maj. James A. Ellison) was one of the first graduates of the Tuskegee Army Flying School.

U.S. Air Force

Prior to World War II, leaders of the U.S. Army Air Corps barred African Americans from serving in uniform as pilots or ground crew. Faced with public pressure from civil rights activists, however, the U.S. government ordered the removal of some restrictions against Black aviators and began accepting Black pilots into racially segregated units of the Army Air Corps in 1941. Military officials created a new air base at Tuskegee, Alabama, which became the center for training Black air personnel.

Lemuel R. Curtis, Charles DeBow, Mac Ross, George Spencer Roberts, and Benjamin O. Davis Jr. were the first Black pilots to graduate from the Tuskegee Advanced Flying School. The distinguished group earned their wings on March 7, 1942. Davis Jr. (see page 359) went on to become the leader of the Tuskegee Airmen. During World War II, the pilots who trained at Tuskegee contributed to the war effort in the 99th Fighter Squadron and later the 332nd Fighter Group. They served in the Mediterranean combat theater, flying from bases in North Africa and Italy while supporting operations against German forces.

BARONESS RAYMONDE DE LAROCHE EARNS HER PILOT'S LICENSE

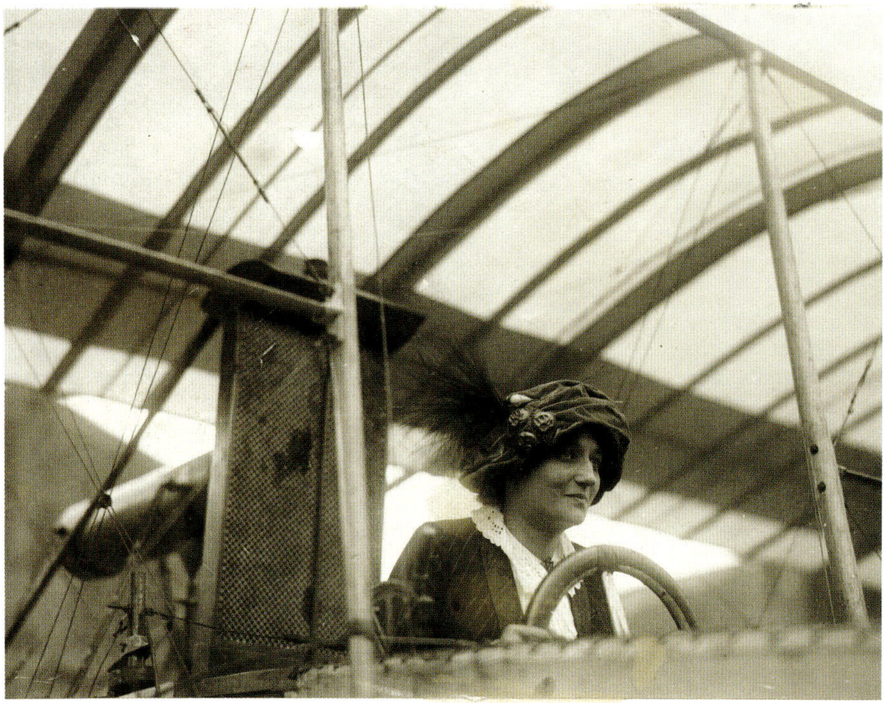

Raymonde de Laroche learned to fly in a Voisin biplane.

Smithsonian's National Air and Space Museum (NASM 81-3423)

In 1909, Baroness Raymonde de Laroche had dinner with French aircraft designer Charles Voisin and left with a new ambition to learn to fly. Taught by Voisin himself at the French flying grounds at Chalons, de Laroche received the first pilot's license awarded to a woman on March 8, 1910.

Shortly after this milestone, de Laroche entered the 1910 Reims meet as the only female participant and was seriously injured in a crash. Once she recovered, de Laroche went on to win the Femina Cup for a nonstop flight of four hours in 1913. Several years later, she also set a women's altitude record of 15,700 feet. In the summer of 1919, de Laroche reported to the airfield at Le Crotoy to copilot a new aircraft in hopes of becoming the first female test pilot. Unfortunately, the aircraft went into a dive on its landing approach and both de Laroche and the pilot were killed.

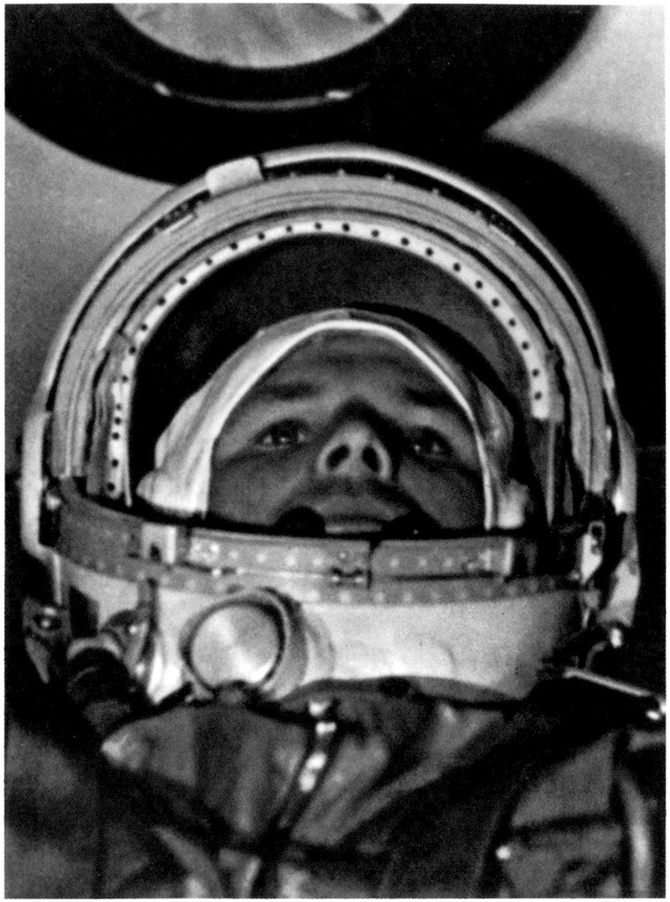

On March 9, 1934, Yuri Gagarin was born in a small village west of Moscow. He was a young Soviet Air Force pilot when a special commission interviewed him to find out if he might be qualified to fly a "new type of aircraft." He was selected with nineteen others for cosmonaut training in 1960 (see page 71).

Gagarin's historic single orbit around the Earth in April 1961 took only 108 minutes from ignition to landing. He launched on a modified R-7 intercontinental ballistic missile (ICBM) with an extra stage added atop the missile. Unlike NASA's Mercury missions that ended with the spacecraft splashing down in the ocean, Gagarin did not land inside his Vostok spacecraft. Instead, he ejected from the spacecraft as planned and parachuted back to Earth. After the Soviet press announced Gagarin's successful trip to space, he became an international celebrity and a national hero in the Soviet Union. He died in 1968 at age thirty-four when his MiG-15 crashed.

Yuri Gagarin made history as the first human to travel to space in April 1961.

Smithsonian's National Air and Space Museum (NASM 90-9056)

MARCH 10

ASTRONOMERS DISCOVER URANUS HAS RINGS

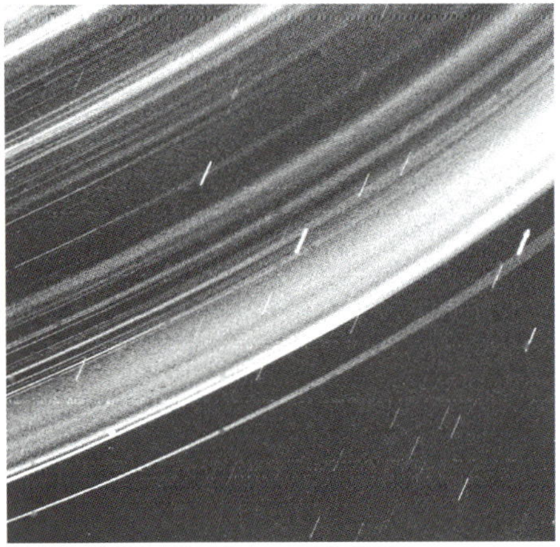

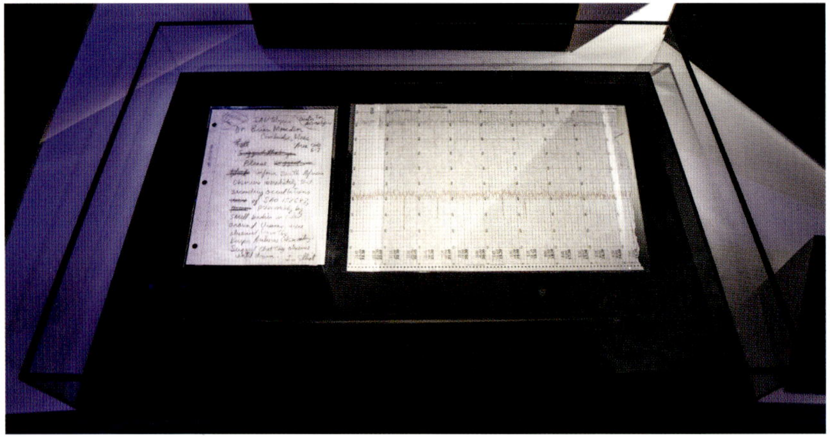

Although the planet Uranus was discovered in the 1700s, scientists didn't discover until much later that it had rings. Uranus's thirteen rings are made of particles and dust in orbit around the planet. They were discovered on March 10, 1977, by scientists onboard the Kuiper Airborne Observatory.

James Elliot, Edward Dunham, and Jessica Mink were using NASA's C-141 aircraft with an infrared telescope, the Kuiper Airborne Observatory, to study Uranus's atmosphere. Their observations involved the star SAO 158687, and they noticed that the light of the star was flickering. Looking at their data, the scientists deduced that the light intensity of the star was dipping when the rings of Uranus passed in front of it. Excited, they sent a telegram from the flying observatory to the Central Bureau for Astronomical Telegrams, the official center for reporting newly observed astronomical objects, to share their discovery.

LEFT The Uranian ring system was photographed by Voyager 2 in 1986.

NASA-Caltech

RIGHT The first draft of the telegram announcing the discovery of Uranus's rings is on display at the National Air and Space Museum.

Smithsonian's National Air and Space Museum

MARCH 11

PIONEER V LAUNCHES

SPACE SCIENCE

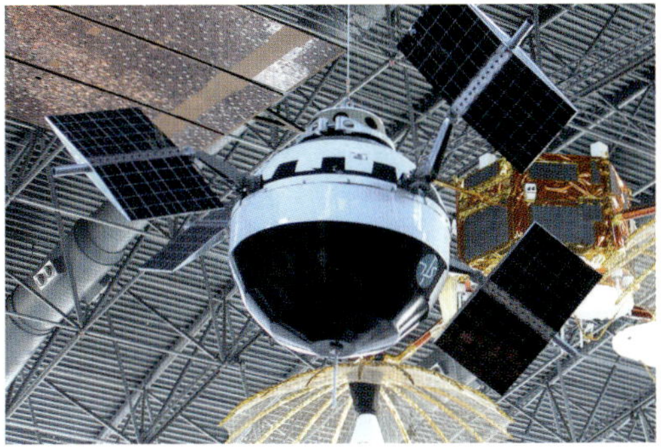

The Pioneer V replica on display at the Steven F. Udvar-Hazy Center is made from original parts that failed to meet flight specifications.

Smithsonian's National Air and Space Museum

On March 11, 1960, the Pioneer V satellite launched on a Thor-Abel IV booster and went into an orbital path around the Sun between the Earth and Venus. The spacecraft was designed to send back scientific data on interplanetary space while orbiting the Sun. Pioneer V provided a wealth of new data, including measurements of magnetic fields, cosmic radiation, electrical fields, and micrometeorites. It transmitted information for three and a half months until it was 22.5 million miles from home, too far for Earth to receive its weak signal.

MARCH 12

ARADO AR 234 V9 FLIES FOR THE FIRST TIME

WORLD WAR II MILITARY AVIATION

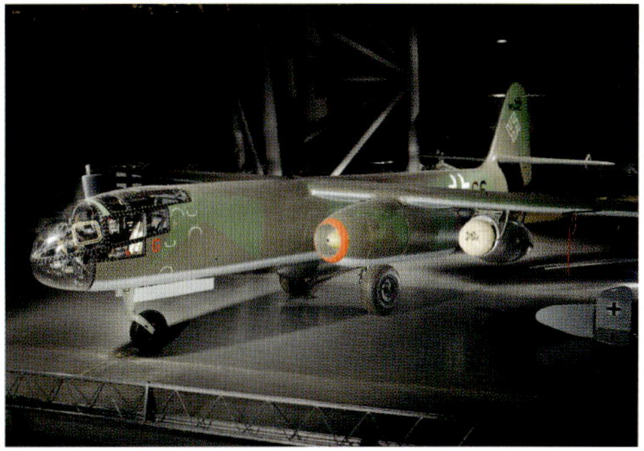

An Arado Ar 234 B-2 is on display at the Steven F. Udvar-Hazy Center.

Smithsonian's National Air and Space Museum

The German Arado Ar 234 B Blitz (Lightning) was the world's first operational jet bomber and reconnaissance aircraft. With a maximum speed of 459 miles per hour, the Blitz easily eluded Allied piston-engine fighters during the closing months of World War II in Europe. While less famous than the Messerschmitt Me 262 jet fighters, the Ar 234s that reached German Luftwaffe units provided excellent service, especially as reconnaissance aircraft. The prototype for the Blitz flew for the first time on March 12, 1944.

EILEEN VOLLICK BECOMES FIRST CANADIAN WOMAN TO EARN A PILOT'S LICENSE

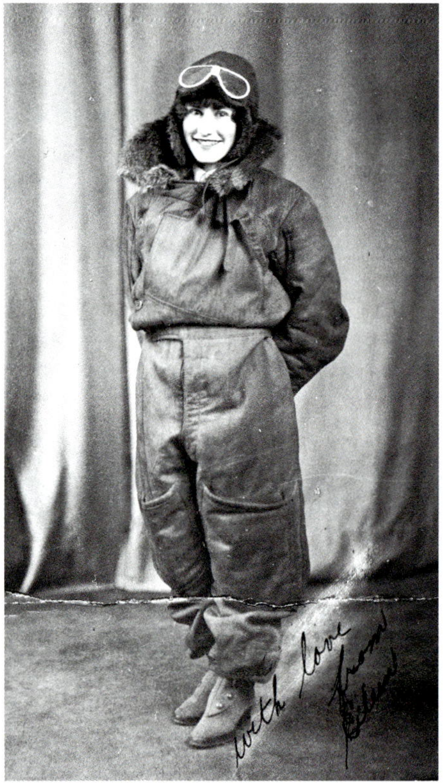

To earn her pilot's license, Eileen Vollick took flying lessons in the morning before work.

Ingenium; KM-08091

After a thrilling ride as a passenger in an airplane at age eighteen, Eileen Vollick knew she wanted to fly professionally, but no woman in Canada had yet earned a pilot's license. Determined to follow her dream, Vollick wrote a letter to the Canadian government requesting permission to train to become a commercial pilot. She received a reply informing her that once she turned nineteen and passed the required tests, she could earn a commercial license. With official permission in hand, Vollick began taking lessons at Elliot Air Service.

On March 13, 1928, Vollick and ten other students earned their pilots' licenses after demonstrating their flight skills and passing the Government Civil Aviation exam. Vollick's was the first pilot's license awarded to a Canadian woman and only the seventy-seventh pilot's license awarded in Canada.

"As I sat in the cockpit I felt quite at home, fear never entered my head and when I saw the earth recede as the winged monster roared and soared skyward . . . the pure joy of it, gave me a thrill which is known only to the air-man who wings his way among the fleecy clouds."

—EILEEN VOLLICK

WORLD WAR I ACE RAOUL LUFBERY IS BORN

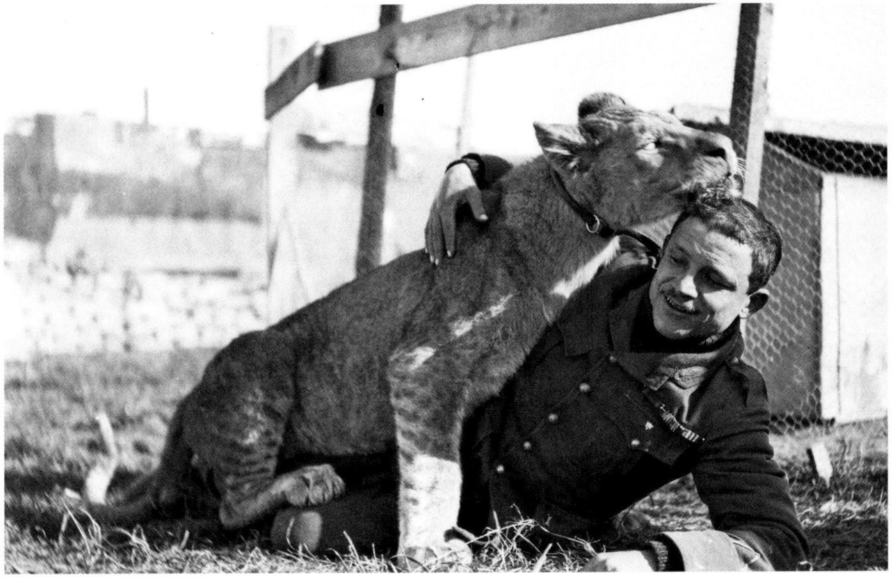

The Lafayette Escadrille had two lions, Whiskey (pictured here with Raoul Lufbery) and Soda, as mascots.

Smithsonian's National Air and Space Museum (NASM 2005-17461)

The expansion of military aviation in World War I gave rise to the first flying aces—pilots who shot down five or more enemy planes. Born March 14, 1885, Maj. Gervais Raoul Lufbery was America's first ace. Holding dual American-French citizenship, Lufbery joined the French Foreign Legion in 1914 and transferred to the French air service to begin aviation school.

In 1916, Lufbery joined the Escadrille de Chasse 124. Known more commonly as the Lafayette Escadrille, this squadron was composed of American volunteers who chose to fight for France. When the United States officially entered the Great War a year later, Lufbery transferred to the U.S. Army Air Service. Lufbery was killed in 1918 after being struck by enemy fire while flying a Nieuport 28. The distinguished pilot claimed sixteen confirmed aerial victories during his service in World War I.

"Everything I learned, I learned from Lufbery."

—FLYING ACE EDDIE RICKENBACKER

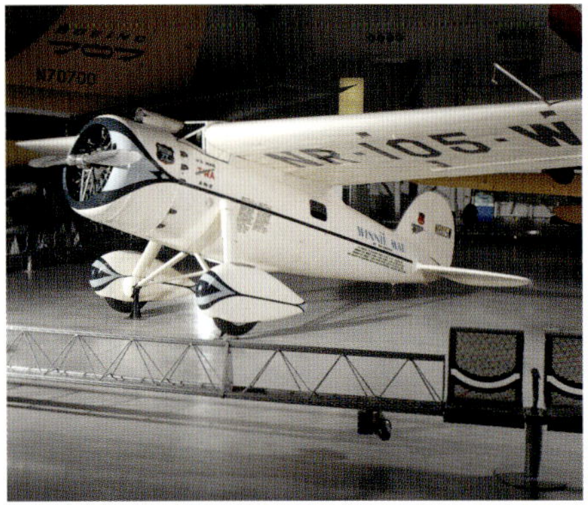

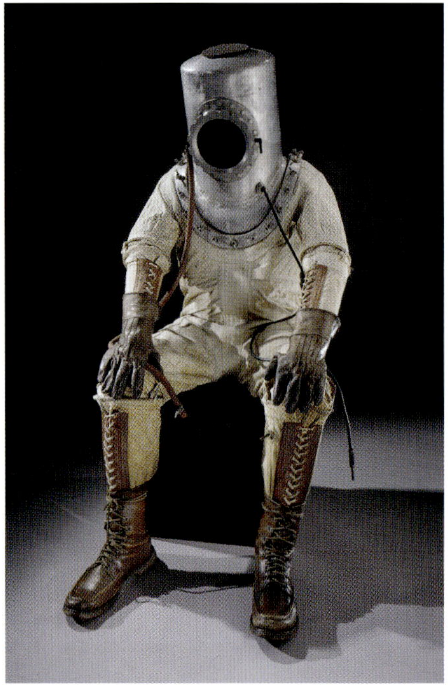

LEFT Wiley Post's *Winnie Mae* is in the collection of the National Air and Space Museum.

Smithsonian's National Air and Space Museum

RIGHT Post wore a specially made pressure suit while flying *Winnie Mae* through the stratosphere.

Smithsonian's National Air and Space Museum

Famed aviator Wiley Post set many records and pioneered several aviation technologies flying his specially modified Lockheed 5C Vega *Winnie Mae*. Post set his first record in the National Air Races in 1930, flying from Los Angeles to Chicago in nine hours, nine minutes, and four seconds. Post then flew *Winnie Mae* around the world twice: an eight-day flight in 1931 with navigator Harold Gatty and a seven-day flight in 1933 in which he became the first to fly around the world solo.

Having achieved his around-the-world goals, Post set his sights on the stratosphere and modified *Winnie Mae* for long-distance, high-altitude operation. Because the aircraft couldn't be equipped with a pressurized cabin, Post developed the first practical pressure suit to wear at high altitudes. On March 15, 1935, Post flew *Winnie Mae* from Burbank, California, to Cleveland, Ohio, at an altitude of more than 30,000 feet, making the 2,035-mile journey in seven hours and nineteen minutes. The flight showed that significant speed increases could be achieved by flying at high altitudes.

GEMINI VIII LAUNCHES ON A NEARLY DISASTROUS MISSION

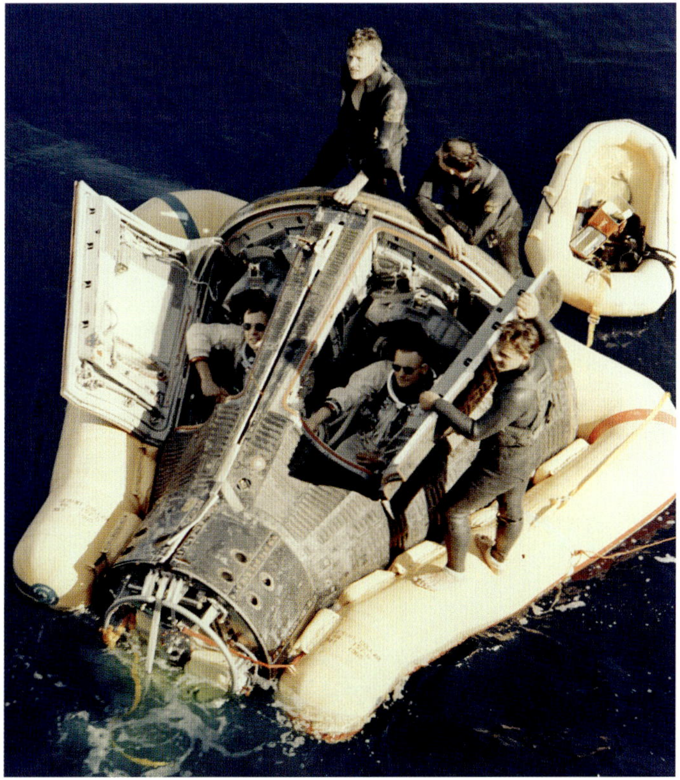

The Gemini VIII astronauts appeared cool, calm, and collected after splashdown.

NASA

On March 16, 1966, Neil Armstrong and David Scott launched on the Gemini VIII mission and rendezvoused with an uncrewed Agena vehicle. This accomplished the first docking of two spacecraft in history. That moment was quickly followed by the first life-threatening, in-flight emergency in the short history of the U.S. human spaceflight program. Gemini VIII, still joined to its Agena target vehicle, began spinning and vibrating.

When the astronauts undocked, Gemini VIII's rotation accelerated to the point where the crew nearly blacked out. The astronauts attempted to gain control of the spacecraft and stop its rolling, but to no avail. It became clear to Armstrong that the problem was a balky thruster in the Orbital Attitude and Maneuvering System (OAMS). Armstrong turned off the OAMS and activated the Reentry Control System (RCS), which slowed and eventually stopped the spin. This all happened while the spacecraft was out of contact with Mission Control. Armstrong and Scott's cool handling of the Gemini VIII crisis ensured their leading roles during the Apollo program.

T-38 TALON ENTERS SERVICE

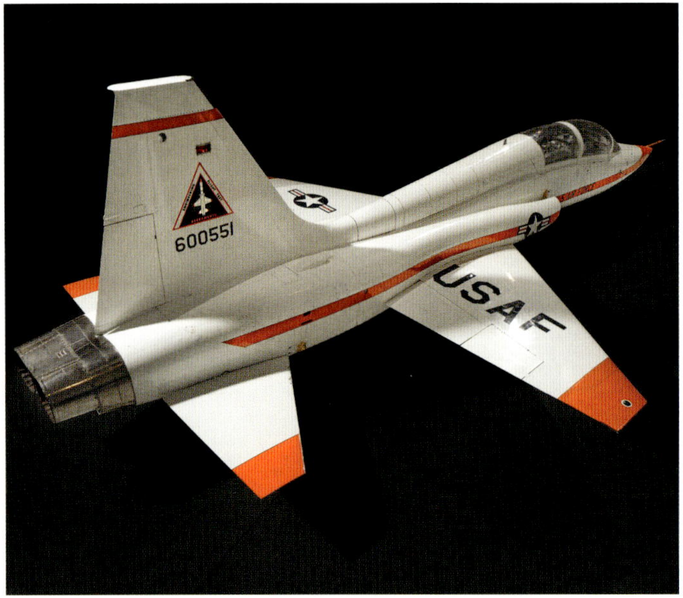

NASA astronaut Walter Schirra and pioneering aviator Jacqueline Cochran both flew the T-38 Talon on display at the National Air and Space Museum.

Smithsonian's National Air and Space Museum

Tens of thousands of pilots have honed their flying skills in the T-38 Talon, the world's first supersonic trainer. Thanks to its high performance, versatility, ease of maintenance, and affordability, the Talon is well-suited to train pilots for frontline fighter and bomber aircraft. The T-38 entered service on March 17, 1961, and remains operational today.

While the U.S. Air Force is the primary user of the T-38, the aircraft is also operated by the U.S. Navy and several NATO member nations. Additionally, NASA maintains a fleet of T-38s that are used as chase planes and flown by astronauts to maintain their flight proficiency. T-38s have also served as test beds for a variety of new technologies, equipment, and weapons systems. When pioneering aviator Jacqueline Cochran (see page 153) began her famous 1961 record campaign, she chose a T-38. Over the course of six weeks, Cochran and her Talon set eight world records for speed, altitude, and distance.

"During every touch-and-go landing in the T-37, I would see a T-38 flash by at nearly twice my speed. It looked like a comic book superhero."

—AIR FORCE PILOT LT. HOWARD MORLAND

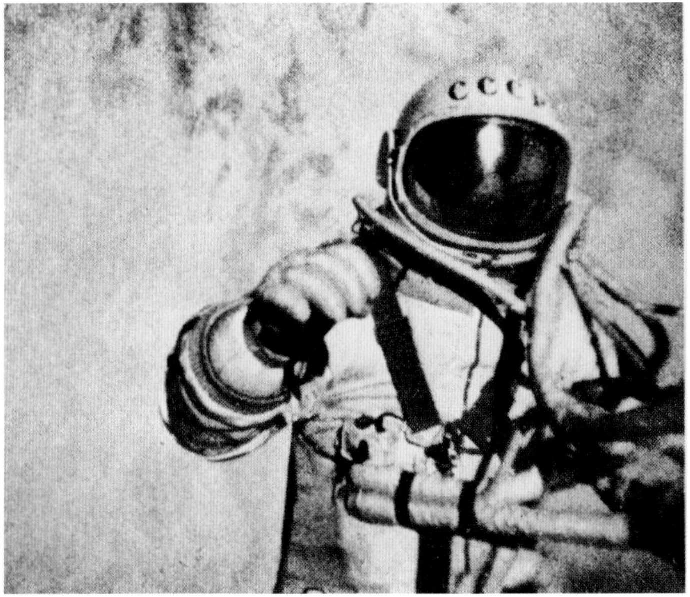

On March 18, 1965, cosmonaut Aleksei Leonov opened the airlock hatch of his Voskhod 2 spacecraft while in Earth orbit, becoming the first human to go outside a spacecraft into the vacuum of space. Nearing the end of his twelve-minute spacewalk, Leonov, ready to go back inside, discovered his spacesuit had unexpectedly swelled beyond its original size. When this and other challenges emerged, Soviet television and radio broadcasts of the event abruptly ended, leaving most people on Earth unaware of Leonov's plight.

Though it is now known that he vented air from his suit to squeeze back through the airlock—a bold and life-threatening move—the full extent of malfunctions that nearly claimed the lives of Leonov and mission commander Pavel Belyayev was not revealed until years later. After his 1965 mission, Leonov became a global ambassador for spaceflight, sharing the tale of his groundbreaking journey around the world.

Cosmonaut Aleksei Leonov gained international fame as the first person to spacewalk.

Smithsonian's National Air and Space Museum (NASM 00166589)

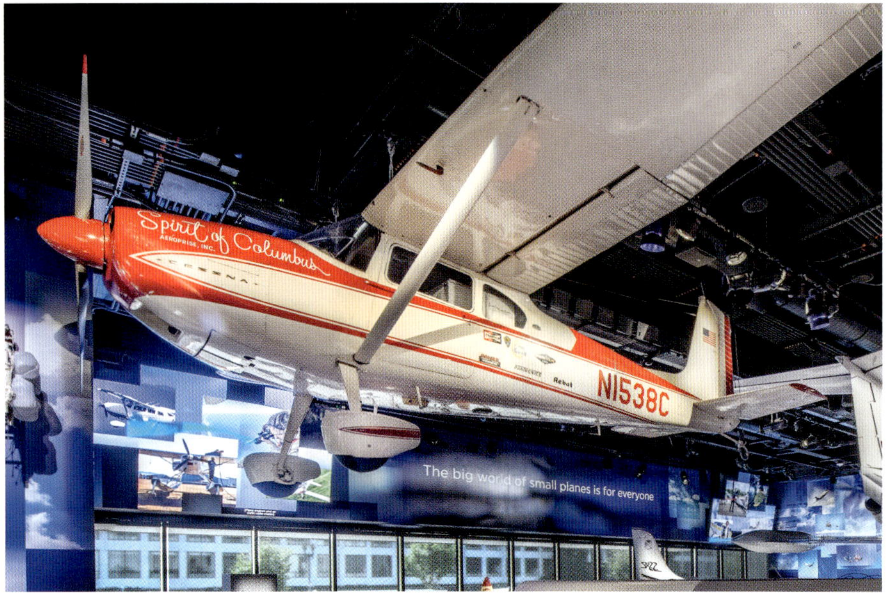

The Cessna 180 *Spirit of Columbus* that Geraldine Mock piloted around the world in 1964 is on display at the National Air and Space Museum.

Smithsonian's National Air and Space Museum

Geraldine "Jerrie" Mock's childhood dream was to see the world. She earned her pilot's license at age thirty-two and had accumulated 750 hours of flight time when her husband half-jokingly suggested she fly around the world. "Why not?" she replied enthusiastically. It was only after Mock contacted the Federal Aviation Administration to inquire about international flying rules that she learned no woman had made a solo round-the-world flight.

After earning her instrument flight rating, Mock prepared her route with help from friends in the Air Force, making sure she would exceed the required official distance for a round-the-world flight of 22,858.8 miles. On March 19, 1964, Mock embarked on her daring journey to become the first woman to complete a solo flight around the world. Twenty-nine days, eleven hours, and fifty-nine minutes later, Mock landed back in Columbus, Ohio. Her 23,103-mile journey cemented Mock's place in aviation history.

P-26 PROTOTYPE FLIES FOR THE FIRST TIME

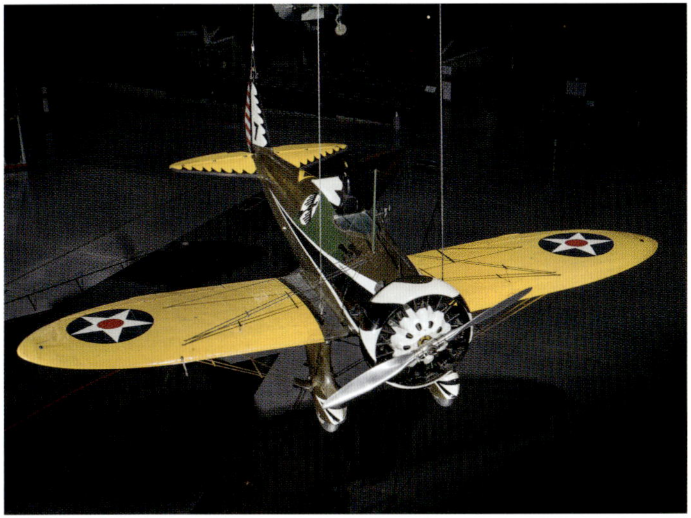

A Boeing P-26A Peashooter is on display at the Steven F. Udvar-Hazy Center.

Smithsonian's National Air and Space Museum

The Boeing P-26 was ahead of its time. Nicknamed the Peashooter, the aircraft introduced the concept of the high-performance, all-metal monoplane fighter design that became standard during World War II. When the prototype flew for the first time on March 20, 1932, observers were impressed with its success, and the U.S. Army contracted for over one hundred production aircraft. Hoping to further improve the P-26, Army officials next turned to the National Advisory Committee for Aeronautics (NACA) for help.

One of the first challenges tackled was the P-26's dangerously high landing speed and its tendency to flip upon touchdown. Working in the NACA's Full-Scale Wind Tunnel at the Langley Memorial Aeronautical Laboratory (see page 162), engineers sought a solution for the problem. The Full-Scale Wind Tunnel was so-named because it could hold full-size aircraft—a game-changer for testing and refining designs, as scale-model testing often returned inaccurate data. During two weeks of testing, engineers discovered that long split-flaps combined with shorter ailerons reduced the P-26's landing speed from 82.5 miles per hour to a much safer 73 miles per hour. Solution in hand, the Army retrofitted its existing Peashooters, and Boeing incorporated the updated design into all new aircraft.

MARCH 21

BREITLING ORBITER 3 COMPLETES FIRST NONSTOP BALLOON FLIGHT AROUND THE WORLD

LIGHTER-THAN-AIR FLIGHT

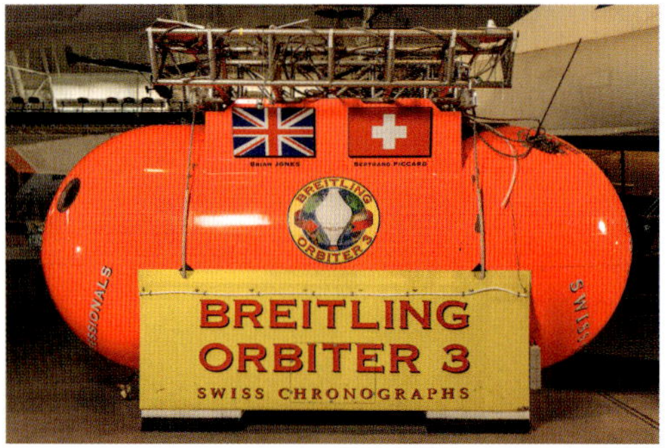

The Breitling Orbiter 3 gondola is on display at the Steven F. Udvar-Hazy Center.

Smithsonian's National Air and Space Museum

On March 21, 1999, Bertrand Piccard and Brian Jones completed the first nonstop flight around the world with a free balloon. The Breitling Orbiter 3 departed the Swiss Alpine village of Château-d'Oex on March 1, 1999, and landed in the Egyptian desert nineteen days, twenty-one hours, and fifty-five minutes later, having traveled over 29,000 miles. Piccard said of the flight: "Human beings always want to control nature, but . . . we must harmonize with nature, following the rhythm of the wind."

MARCH 22

LOCKHEED T-33 MAKES FIRST FLIGHT

MODERN MILITARY AVIATION

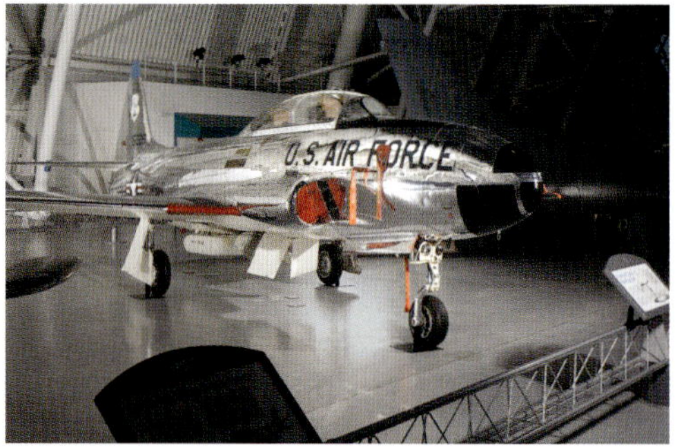

The T-33 on display at the Steven F. Udvar-Hazy Center was used by the D.C. National Guard.

Smithsonian's National Air and Space Museum

Known as the "T-Bird," the Lockheed T-33 Shooting Star served as an instrument trainer and utility aircraft as well as a test aircraft. In 1947, Lockheed initiated its design in response to an increasing number of accidents of the P-80 Shooting Star. The T-33 prototype first flew on March 22, 1948, piloted by acclaimed test pilot Tony LeVier. The aircraft was a success, with handling characteristics equal to those of the P-80C.

JOHN YOUNG SMUGGLES A CORNED BEEF SANDWICH INTO SPACE

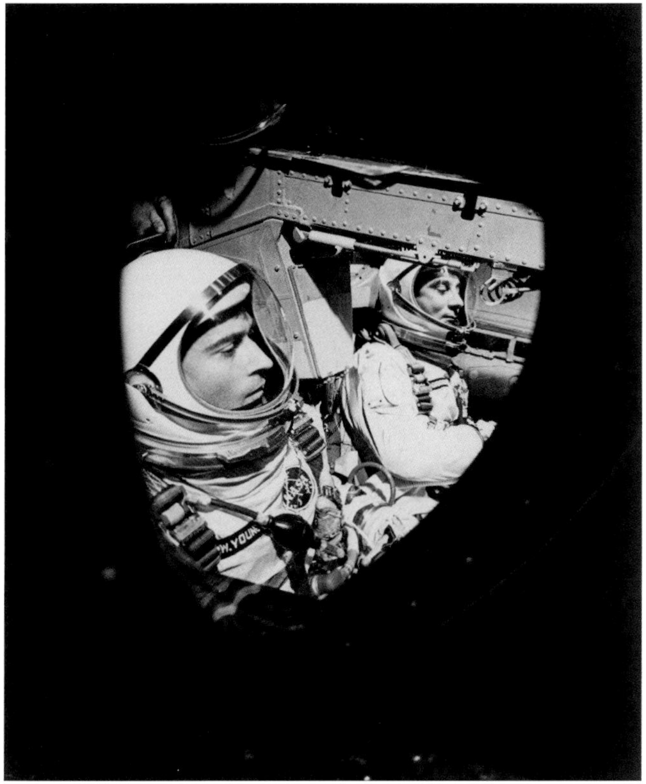

Gemini III was the first crewed mission of Project Gemini, which featured two-person crews.

NASA

One of astronaut John Young's assignments during the Gemini III mission on March 23, 1965, was to test space food. The food came in plastic bags and had to be rehydrated with a water dispenser. Not on the menu? A freshly made corned beef sandwich. But that didn't stop it from being brought on the mission. The contraband sandwich was smuggled on board in the pocket of Young's spacesuit.

According to Young, the idea came from fellow astronaut Walter "Wally" Schirra, who was a well-known practical joker. When the astronauts got hungry a few hours into the mission, Young pulled out the smuggled sandwich and mission commander Virgil "Gus" Grissom took a bite. Crumbs began floating around the spacecraft, which could have posed a threat if any got wedged in the equipment or instrument panel. Young's impromptu menu change didn't cause any harm during the spaceflight, but it became a larger issue back on Earth, resulting in a House of Representatives Appropriations Committee meeting to discuss it. The astronauts were sternly warned not to repeat the stunt.

RANGER 9 IMPACTS THE MOON INTENTIONALLY

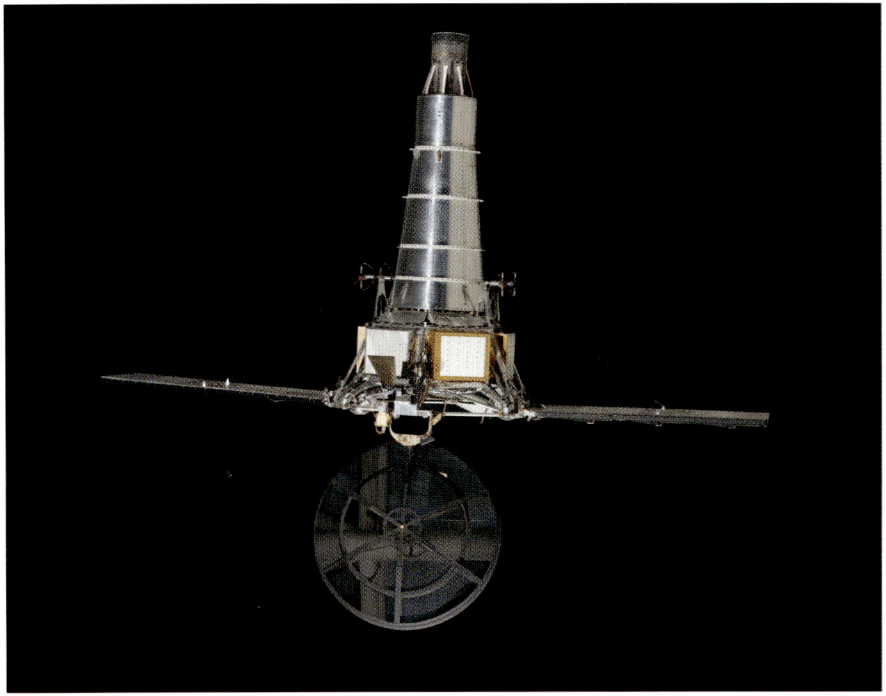

The Ranger spacecraft in the National Air and Space Museum collection is a replica made from parts of Ranger test vehicles.

Smithsonian's National Air and Space Museum

In the 1960s, the Ranger spacecraft gave scientists their first close look at the lunar surface. Nine Rangers were launched from 1961 through 1965. While the first six failed, Rangers 7, 8, and 9 successfully completed their 65-hour journeys to the Moon.

Each Ranger spacecraft had six cameras on board, and the three successful missions transmitted thousands of photos of the lunar surface, revealing details not visible through telescopes on Earth. The images provided better resolution than was available from Earth-based views by a factor of a thousand. These highly detailed images were used when selecting landing sites for the first crewed Moon landing.

At the end of each mission, NASA crashed the Ranger spacecraft into the Moon intentionally. During Ranger 9's impact on March 24, 1965, cameras were pointed in the direction of travel, allowing NASA to capture Ranger's impact on camera. Millions of viewers witnessed its descent to the Moon live on television.

MARCH 25

PROTOTYPE CHANCE VOUGHT CRUSADER TAKES FLIGHT

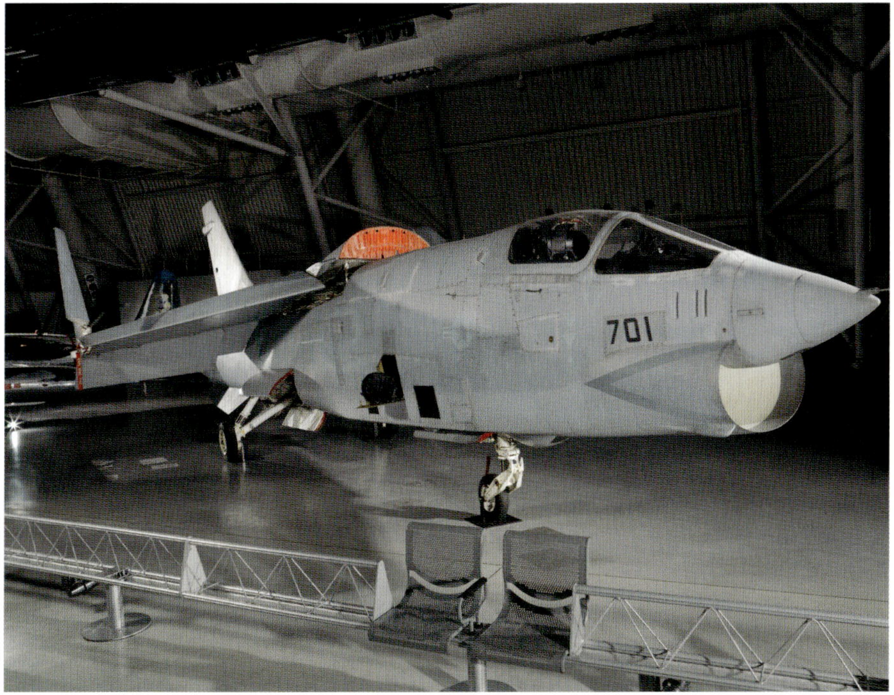

The Crusader on display at the Steven F. Udvar-Hazy Center is an RF-8G, the photo-reconnaissance model.

Smithsonian's National Air and Space Museum

On March 25, 1955, test pilot John Konrad piloted the prototype for the Vought F-8 (F8U) Crusader for the first time. The aircraft quickly reached supersonic speeds, making it the first fighter to do so on its first flight. The Crusader also featured an innovative variable-incidence wing that could rotate slightly, improving its flight characteristics at slow speeds and increasing pilot visibility for takeoff and landing.

During the F8U's first five years, it achieved an outstanding record as a carrier-based jet fighter. In 1956, the U.S. Navy and Chance Vought jointly accepted the Collier Trophy for the conception, design, and development of the first carrier-based aircraft to exceed 1,000 miles per hour. The Crusader was also the first aircraft to fly across the United States faster than the speed of sound—a record flight piloted by Marine aviator and future astronaut John Glenn (see page 65).

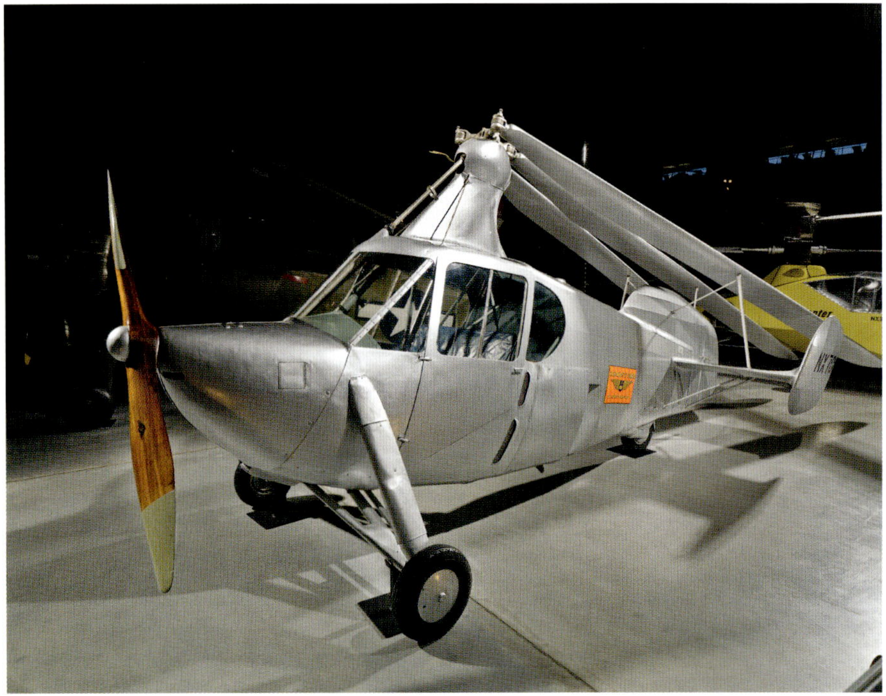

The AC-35 is on display at the Steven F. Udvar-Hazy Center.

Smithsonian's National Air and Space Museum

"An aircraft in every garage." That was the goal of the Autogiro Company of America's AC-35 roadable autogiro. Developed for a Department of Commerce competition to create an aerial "Model T," the AC-35 Autogiro could take off and land in less than 175 feet. After landing and folding back the aircraft's rotors, the pilot could switch engine power to the rear drive wheel and operate it like a car, reaching street speeds of twenty-five miles per hour.

The AC-35 flew for the first time on March 26, 1936, but initially suffered from stability problems. Further experimentation resulted in an aircraft that was safe and relatively easy to fly. The Autogiro Company of America proved the aircraft's viability when its chief pilot delivered the AC-35 to the Department of Commerce in style, landing in a small Washington, D.C., park and driving the vehicle to the Commerce Department building. While the AC-35 performed well, the $12,500 price tag was several times the average family income, so it did not meet the goal of an affordable aircraft for the suburbanite.

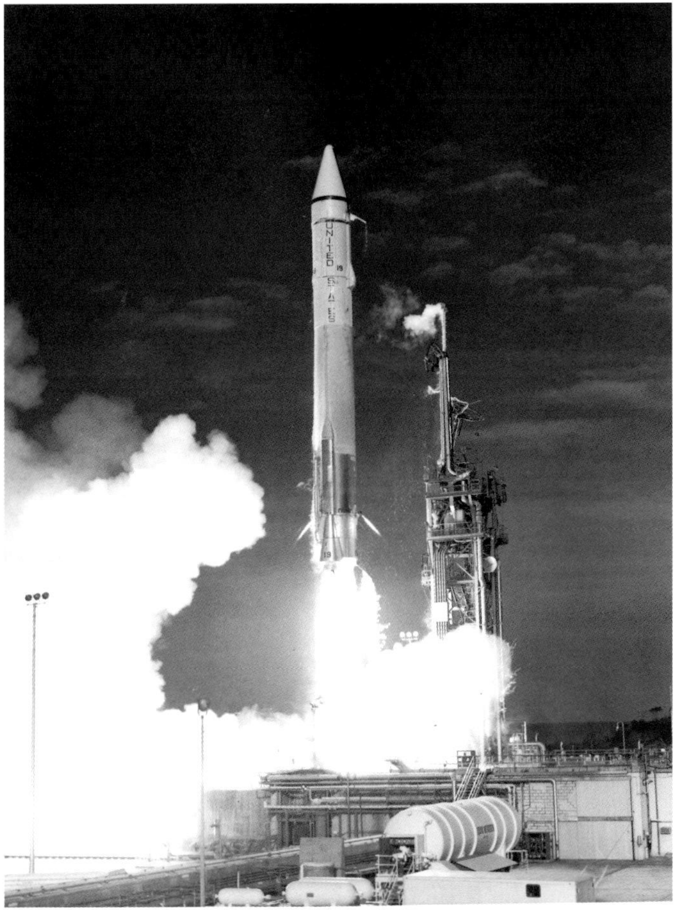

In March 1969, NASA launched twin spacecraft to fly by Mars—Mariner 6 and Mariner 7. Mariner 7 launched on March 27, 1969, a month after Mariner 6. The missions' objectives were to study the atmosphere and surface of the Red Planet and to test equipment to be used on future missions. Each spacecraft carried two vidicon television cameras, a wide-angle camera with medium resolution, and a narrow-angle camera with high resolution.

One benefit of the dual spacecraft mission was that scientists could determine Mariner 7's photo targets based on what they observed or learned from Mariner 6's flyby a few days earlier. During Mariner 7's flyby, scientists instructed the spacecraft to take additional photos of Mars's south pole after seeing intriguing things in Mariner 6's photos. As a result, the photos Mariner 7 sent back of Mars's south polar ice cap were higher quality than those sent by Mariner 6.

Mariner 7 launched on an Atlas-Centaur rocket.

NASA

CHESLEY BONESTELL'S *A LUNAR LANDSCAPE* MURAL IS UNVEILED

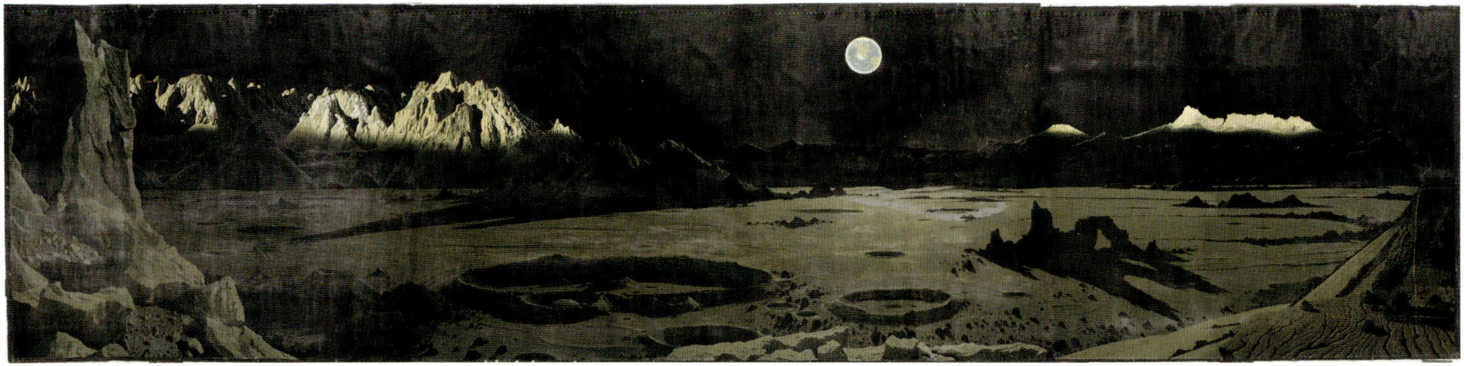

Before humans or spacecraft ever left Earth, artist Chesley Bonestell imagined the surface of the Moon with his masterpiece mural *A Lunar Landscape*. On March 28, 1957—six months before Sputnik kicked off the Space Race—the Museum of Science in Boston unveiled the work of art on the lobby wall of the Charles Hayden Planetarium.

Bonestell's matte paintings provided stunning backgrounds for Hollywood films of the 1930s and '40s, including *Citizen Kane,* but he remains best known for his profound influence on a generation of space enthusiasts, whose dreams were fueled by his images.

A Lunar Landscape, which stretched forty feet wide and ten feet tall, helped viewers imagine what it might be like to stand on another world. Given that there was little scientific information available about the Moon's surface, Bonestell took artistic license, presenting a dramatically lit moonscape with jagged peaks, deep canyons, and precipitous crater walls. After spacecraft and humans visited the lunar surface and revealed its true nature, Bonestell admitted that the Moon looked nothing like his masterpiece. "I tried to make it as dramatic as I could," he explained, noting that soft rolling hills "wouldn't have looked very interesting."

A Lunar Landscape is now on display at the National Air and Space Museum in Washington, D.C.

Smithsonian's National Air and Space Museum

MESSENGER PHOTOGRAPHS MERCURY FROM ORBIT

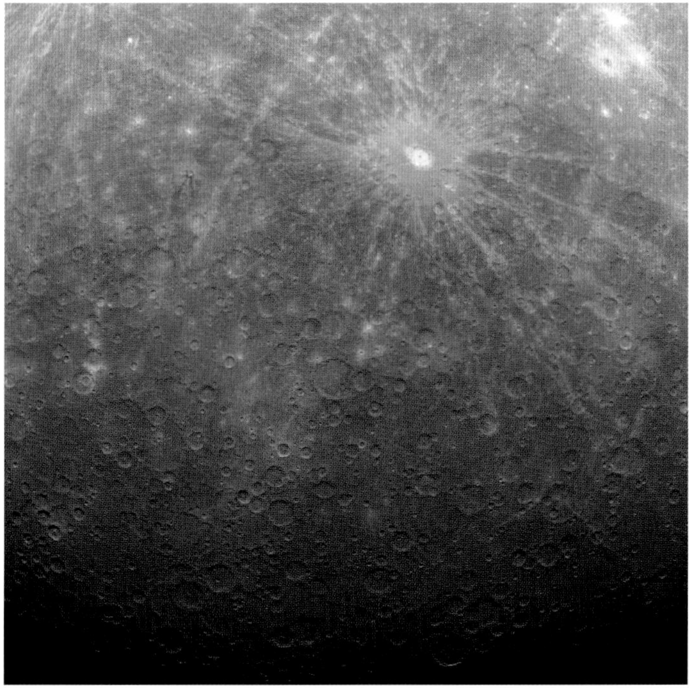

The first photo MESSENGER took of Mercury while in its orbit features the Debussy Crater.

NASA/Johns Hopkins University Applied Physics Laboratory/Carnegie Institution of Washington

In 1974, NASA's Mariner 10 mission was the first to visit Mercury (see page 52). Mariner 10 flew by the planet and took photos, but it was three decades before another spacecraft visited again. In March 2011, NASA's MESSENGER spacecraft became the first spacecraft to enter Mercury's orbit, and on March 29, it captured the first image of Mercury taken by a spacecraft in orbit around the planet.

In the years that followed, MESSENGER photographed 100 percent of Mercury's surface. The data it gathered allowed scientists to make many new discoveries about the solar system's innermost planet, from a well-preserved large impact basin with unique tectonic landforms, to evidence of water ice at the poles, to unusual ridges and troughs that resemble a "pie crust." The mission came to an end in 2015 after the spacecraft's propellants were depleted, and in April 2015, engineers commanded MESSENGER to crash intentionally into Mercury's surface at 8,750 miles per hour.

MARCH 30

BOEING DELIVERS FIRST MODERN AIRLINER TO UNITED AIR LINES

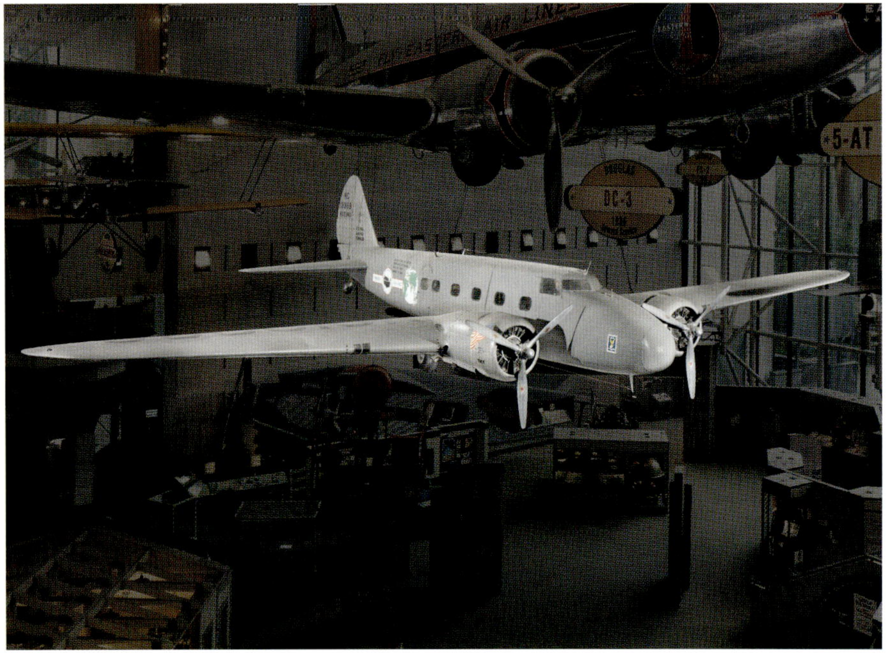

The Boeing 247-D on display at the National Air and Space Museum was flown in the 1934 England-to-Australia International Air Derby, better known as the MacRobertson Race.

Smithsonian's National Air and Space Museum

The Boeing 247 revolutionized air transportation when it entered service in 1933. The first commercial airframe was delivered to United Air Lines on March 30 of that year and entered service two months later. With its sleek, low-wing, all-metal construction; retractable landing gear; and supercharged, air-cooled engines, the Boeing 247 was 50 percent faster than its competitors. The 247 also established new standards in passenger comfort. Its ten passengers enjoyed excellent soundproofing, a low vibration level, plush seats, and, for the first time, cabin air-conditioning.

Considered the world's first modern airliner, the 247's innovative design launched a new generation of commercial airliners, most notably the Douglas DC series, which ultimately rendered the 247 obsolete. Though Boeing tried to respond to this competition with the improved 247-D, the new airplane did not have the necessary growth potential to compete and was soon relegated to shorter route segments and smaller airlines. Although the Boeing 247 did not stay on top for long, its impact on commercial aviation has earned it a place of honor in history books.

MARCH 31

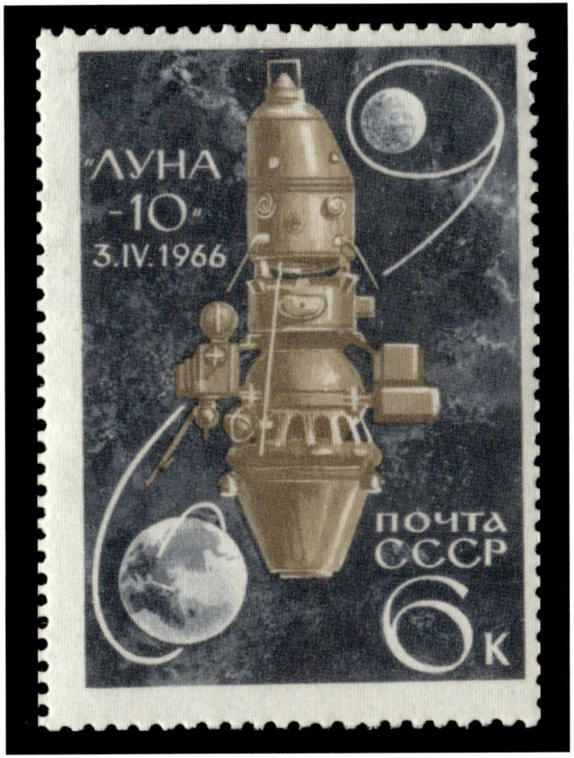

A Soviet stamp celebrated the Luna 10 mission.

Soviet Post

On March 31, 1966, the Soviet Union launched Luna 10 on a mission to become the first spacecraft to orbit the Moon—and in fact, to orbit any celestial body other than Earth. Luna 10's launch on the last day of the month was a follow-up to an unsuccessful launch with the same mission profile on March 1.

Because the Soviet Union only named missions after they were successful, that launch attempt was designated Kosmos 111 instead of a number in the Luna series. Kosmos is a name that is given to a variety of Soviet and Russian spacecraft, including prototypes, classified spacecraft, scientific spacecraft, and probes and satellites that failed; there are over 2,500 spacecraft designated with the Kosmos name.

But unlike Kosmos 111, Luna 10's launch was successful, and it entered lunar orbit a few days later. While operational in lunar orbit for over fifty days, Luna 10 gathered data about the Moon's magnetic field, atmosphere, gravity field, and more.

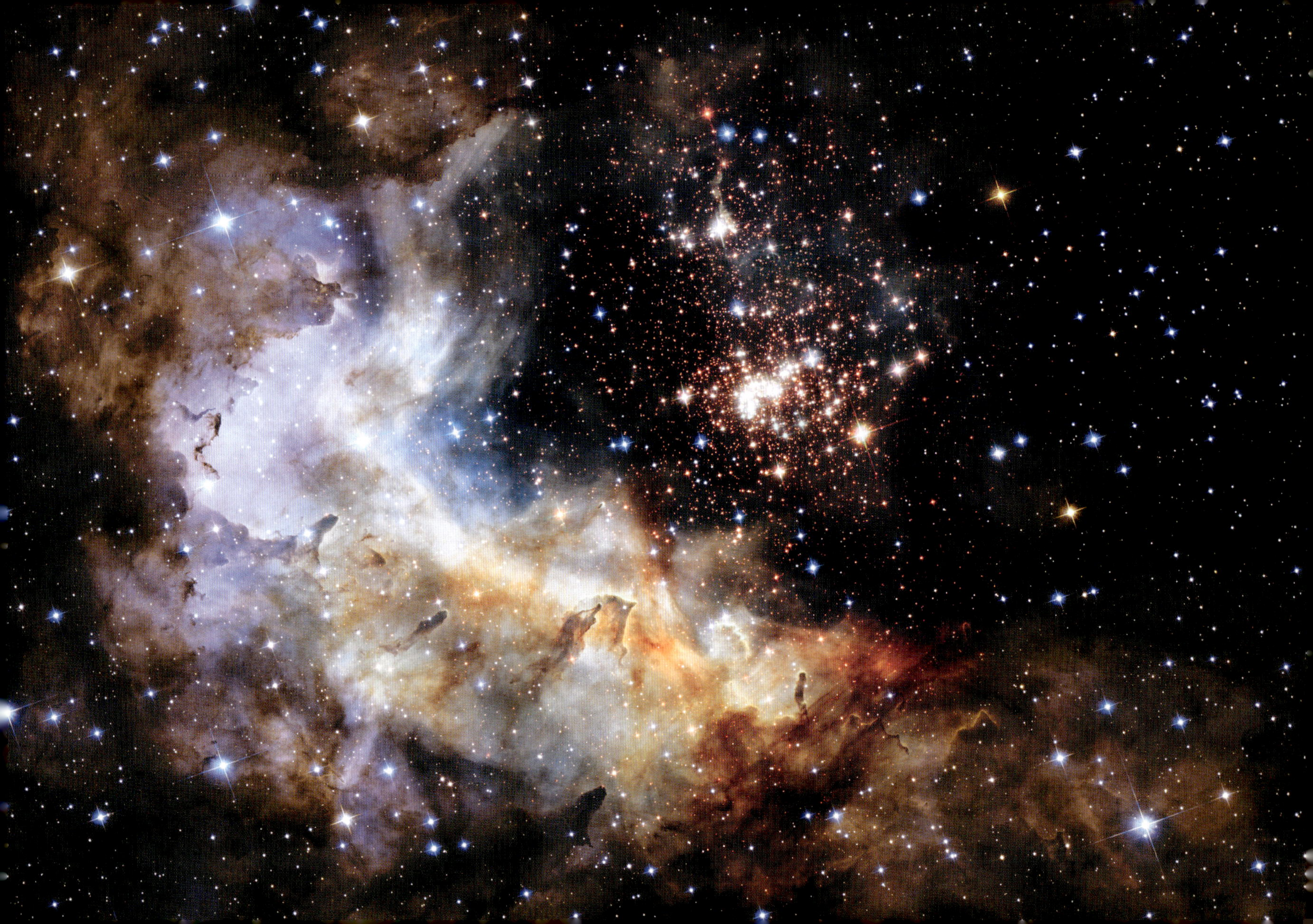

APRIL

TIROS-1 LAUNCHES

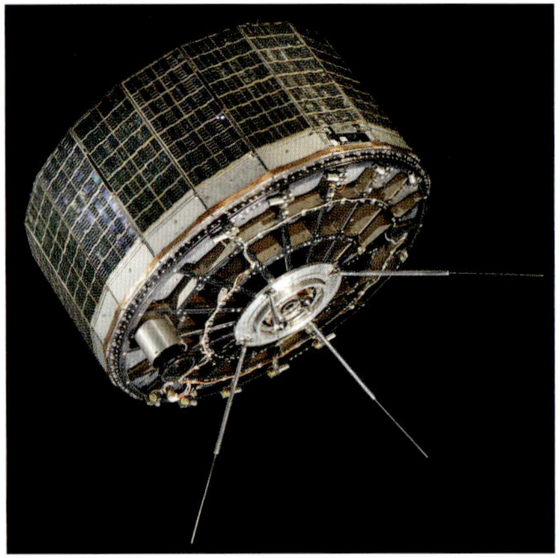

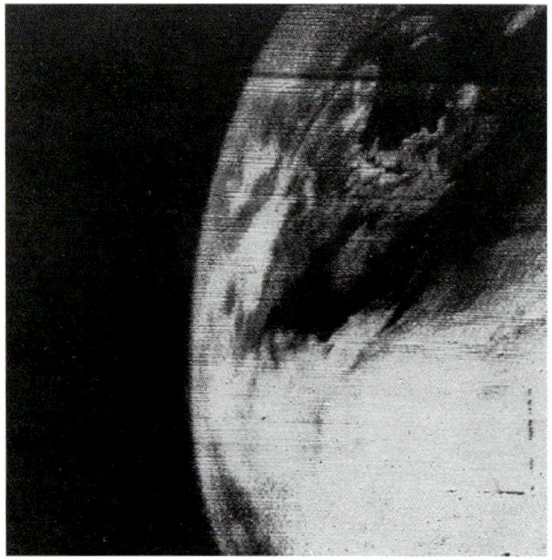

LEFT A TIROS backup is on display at the National Air and Space Museum.

Smithsonian's National Air and Space Museum

RIGHT TIROS-1 took the first television picture of Earth from space.

NASA

"The Earth doesn't look so big when you see that curvature." President Dwight D. Eisenhower uttered those words after seeing the first image sent back from space by TIROS-1 on April 1, 1960. This was the first photo of Earth taken from a weather satellite. TIROS imaged large swaths of Earth's surface, allowing forecasters and scientists to see, for the first time, large-scale features of our planet's weather systems.

The launch of TIROS-1 and the distribution of its first images made the front pages of newspapers across the country, each emphasizing the change brought by the space-based perspective. *The New York Times* wrote that the satellite and its successors held the promise "of illuminating vast areas of darkness in man's understanding of the weather." And the TIROS satellite series delivered on that promise. While TIROS-1 only operated for three months, its successor satellites still provide routine, daily weather observations today.

2001: A SPACE ODYSSEY PREMIERES

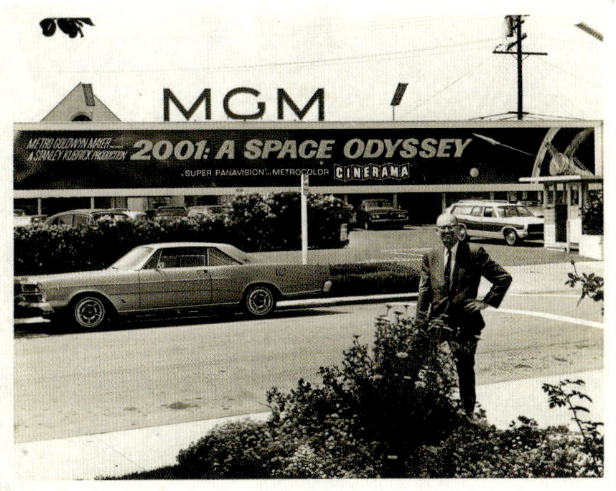

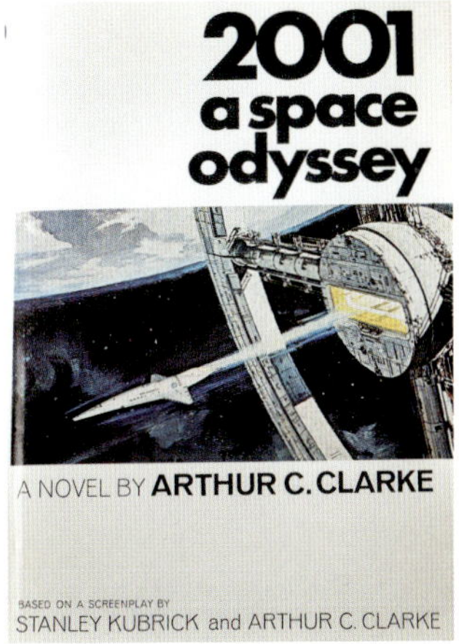

LEFT Arthur C. Clarke wrote the screenplay for *2001: A Space Odyssey* alongside director Stanley Kubrick.

Smithsonian's National Air and Space Museum (NASM 9A13527)

RIGHT Tom Jones took a copy of the *2001: A Space Odyssey* novel on the first spaceflight of the new millennium in 2001.

Smithsonian's National Air and Space Museum

Arthur C. Clarke was one of the twentieth century's preeminent authors of science fiction, a noted futurist, and a popularizer of science and technology. His collaboration with Stanley Kubrick on the classic film *2001: A Space Odyssey* was one signature moment in his impressive career. Kubrick based the film on Clarke's 1951 short story "The Sentinel," and they wrote the screenplay together.

The film premiered at the Uptown Theater in Washington, D.C., on April 2, 1968, and it was clear that the film's real magic was its special effects. The spacecraft moved realistically, and the film featured a fully realized vision of regular human spaceflights to Earth orbit and beyond, with an attention to detail that intrigued and delighted viewers. Months after *2001*'s release in theaters, Clarke published a novelization of the film. In 2001, astronaut Tom Jones, whose interest in space was sparked by repeat viewings of *2001: A Space Odyssey* as a young adult, carried a copy of the book with him on Space Shuttle *Atlantis*'s STS-98 mission to mark the first spaceflight of the new millennium.

GUS GRISSOM IS BORN

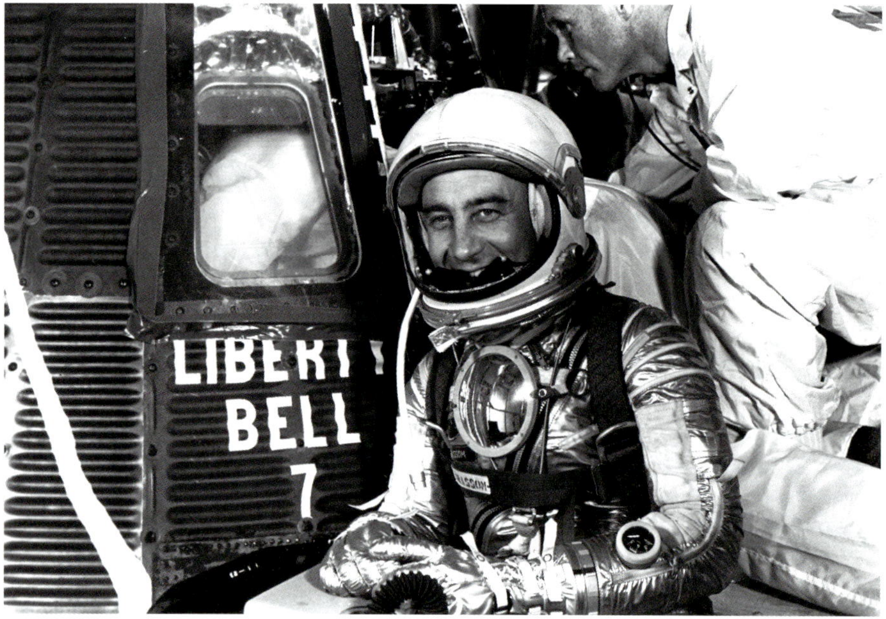

Gus Grissom's Mercury spacecraft was named *Liberty Bell 7.*

NASA

Virgil "Gus" Grissom was born on April 3, 1926. Grissom, the second American in space, was selected by NASA as one of its first astronauts in 1959 (see page 115). Before his selection, he served as a pilot in the U.S. Air Force, flying one hundred combat missions in Korea in F-86s and receiving both the Distinguished Flying Cross and the Air Medal with cluster for his service during the war. He graduated from Test Pilot School at Edwards Air Force Base and worked as a test pilot at Wright-Patterson Air Force Base.

In July 1961, Grissom took a suborbital ride inside the *Liberty Bell 7* spacecraft, launched atop a Redstone rocket. That trip almost ended in disaster when the capsule sank after a successful splashdown in the Atlantic Ocean. Grissom commanded the first crewed two-person Gemini flight in 1965 (see page 97) and was assigned to command the first Apollo mission. He and his Apollo 1 crewmates died on January 27, 1967, when a spark ignited a fire inside their sealed spacecraft during a preflight test (see page 40).

APRIL 4

TDRS-1 IS DEPLOYED

CIVILIAN APPLICATIONS SATELLITES

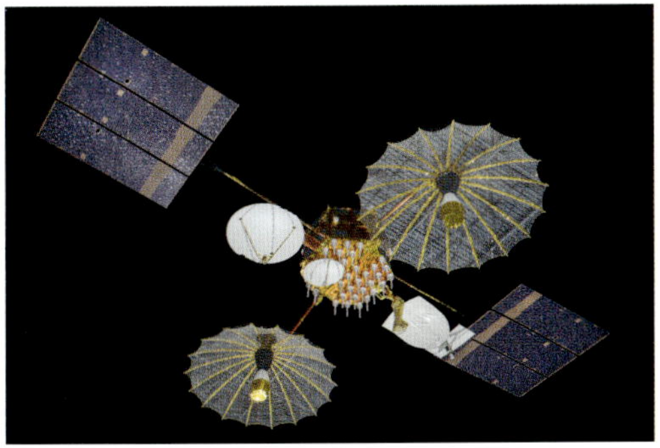

A high-fidelity model of the TDRS satellite is on display at the Steven F. Udvar-Hazy Center.

Smithsonian's National Air and Space Museum

How do astronauts in low Earth orbit communicate with mission control and their loved ones? Through a constellation of communications satellites called the Tracking and Data Relay Satellite (TDRS) system. These satellites, which transmit both voice and data communications with crewed and uncrewed spacecraft in low Earth orbit, are located in a high-altitude geosynchronous orbit 22,000 miles above Earth. TDRS-1 was released during STS-6 on April 4, 1983. It was the first satellite in the system, reaching its geosynchronous orbit months later, and was in use for over twenty-five years before NASA retired it in 2009.

APRIL 5

PEGASUS TAKES FLIGHT

ROCKETS AND MISSILES

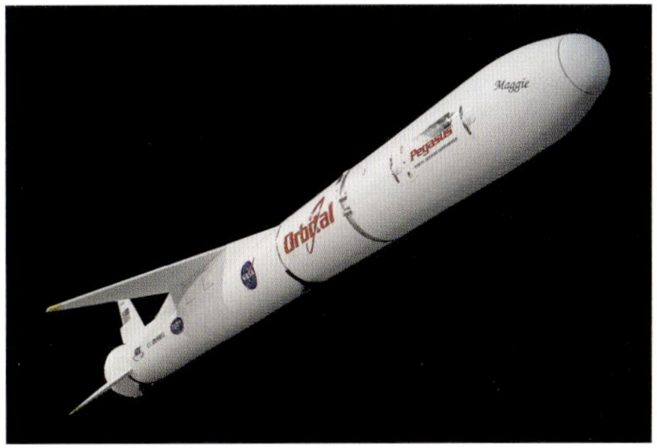

A Pegasus XL launch vehicle is on display at the Steven F. Udvar-Hazy Center.

Smithsonian's National Air and Space Museum

Orbital Sciences' Pegasus rocket was the first commercial air-launched vehicle capable of reaching orbit. On April 5, 1990, it was carried aloft by a NASA B-52 and released, free falling briefly before its rocket engine ignited and accelerated it to orbital velocity. Pegasus rockets were used to place small satellites, sensors, and other research tools into Earth orbit. Over the course of thirty years, Pegasus research craft completed forty-five missions, with a nearly 90 percent success rate.

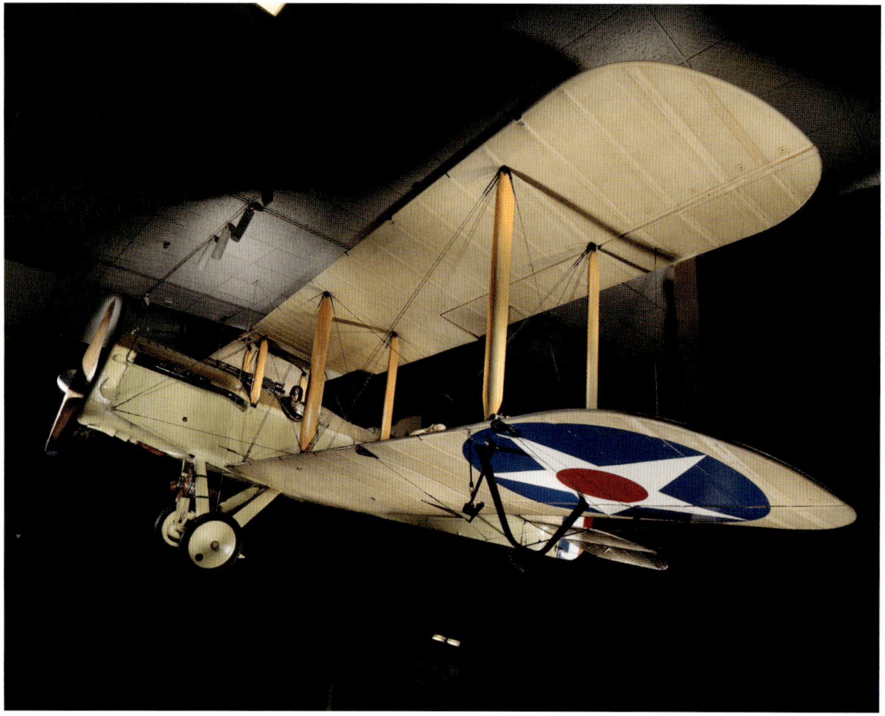

American pilots in World War I flew aircraft like the Dayton-Wright DH-4 to support the Allies. The prototype American-built DH-4 is on display at the National Air and Space Museum.

Smithsonian's National Air and Space Museum

Known variously as the Great War and "the war to end all wars," World War I was a turning point in human history. Between 1914 and 1918, countries around the globe mobilized over seventy million military personnel in a grand series of alliances that pitted Great Britain, France, and Russia (the Allies) against Germany, Austria-Hungary, and the Ottoman Empire (the Central Powers). Though it attempted to avoid involvement, the United States eventually entered the war on April 6, 1917, after Germany resumed unrestricted submarine warfare and proposed an alliance with Mexico against the U.S.

Contributing to the horrors of the trenches, World War I fostered unprecedented technological innovation. It was the first modern industrial war in which the combatants' material resources and manufacturing capability were as consequential as the skill of their troops. The conflict also made the recently invented airplane an essential element of both war and peace. Global warfare not only laid the foundation for military aviation but also helped establish the modern aviation industry and was a decisive test for aerial technology and tactics.

MUSGRAVE AND PETERSON MAKE FIRST SPACEWALK OF SPACE SHUTTLE PROGRAM

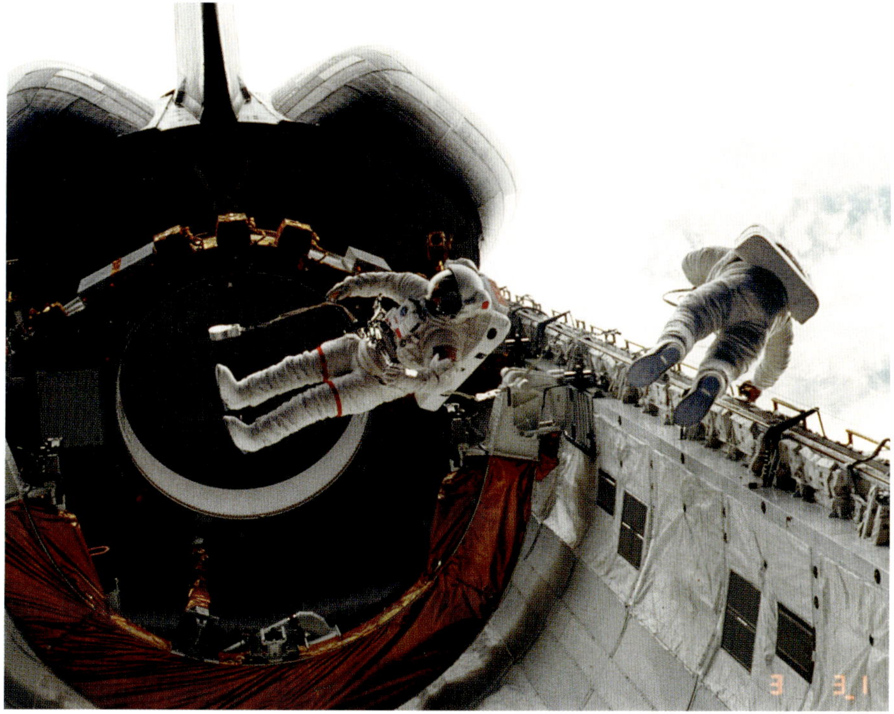

Story Musgrave and Donald Peterson were tethered during the first spacewalk of the Space Shuttle Program.

NASA

On April 7, 1983, during STS-6, Space Shuttle *Challenger*'s first mission, astronauts F. Story Musgrave and Donald Peterson conducted the first spacewalk of the Space Shuttle program. Musgrave and Peterson were STS-6's two mission specialists, and their job was to test new spacesuits designed for extravehicular activities (EVAs) outside the Space Shuttle orbiters.

Testing the new spacesuits required performing tasks expected to be regular features of any future EVA. Musgrave and Peterson worked on these demonstration tests inside *Challenger*'s payload bay. Their spacewalk lasted just over four hours, floating in the payload bay while attached to the orbiter by tethers.

DID YOU KNOW? In addition to flying on *Challenger*'s first mission, Story Musgrave is notably the only astronaut to fly on all five of NASA's Space Shuttle orbiters (*Atlantis, Challenger, Columbia, Discovery,* and *Endeavour*).

WRIGHT FLYER IS MOVED TO UNDERGROUND CHAMBER OUTSIDE LONDON

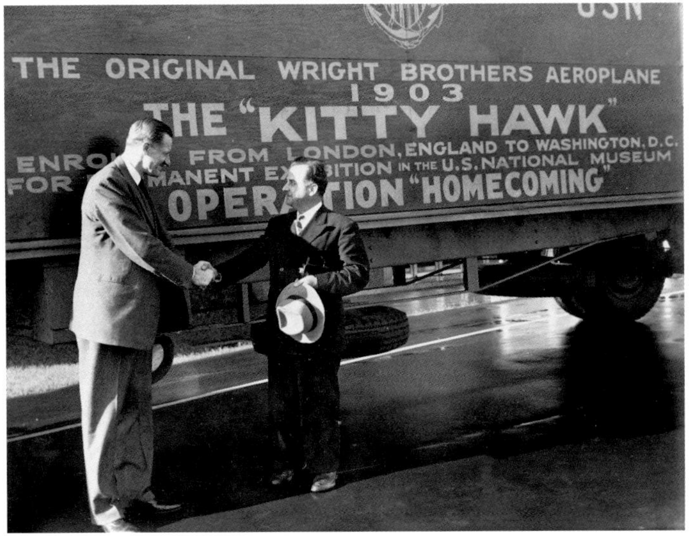

Operation Homecoming returned the 1903 Wright Flyer to the U.S. in 1948. Smithsonian curator Paul Garber (right) escorted the Flyer to D.C.

Smithsonian's National Air and Space Museum (NASM 2003-15995)

On April 8, 1942, the historic 1903 Wright Flyer was moved to an underground chamber outside of London. But why was the world's first successful powered airplane in the United Kingdom in the first place? The answer to this question involves a feud between the Smithsonian Institution and Orville Wright that began to grow in 1910. The dispute revolved around the Smithsonian's public display of an artifact label claiming that its former secretary Samuel P. Langley, had built the "first man-carrying aeroplane . . . capable of sustained free flight." This misleading assertion made the Institution reluctant to credit the Wright brothers as the true inventors of the airplane.

In the 1920s, Wright decided to use the Flyer as leverage to shame the Smithsonian into correcting its stance, loaning it to the Science Museum in London. The Flyer was still in London when World War II broke out, and it was moved to an underground chamber with other priceless artifacts for protection against German bombing raids.

In the aftermath of the war, the Smithsonian revised its false claims, and in 1948, the Wright Flyer returned to the U.S. It was displayed in the Smithsonian's Arts and Industries Building from 1948 to 1976, when it was moved to the new National Air and Space Museum building. The historic aircraft remains on display at the Museum today and is one of the crown jewels in the Smithsonian's collection.

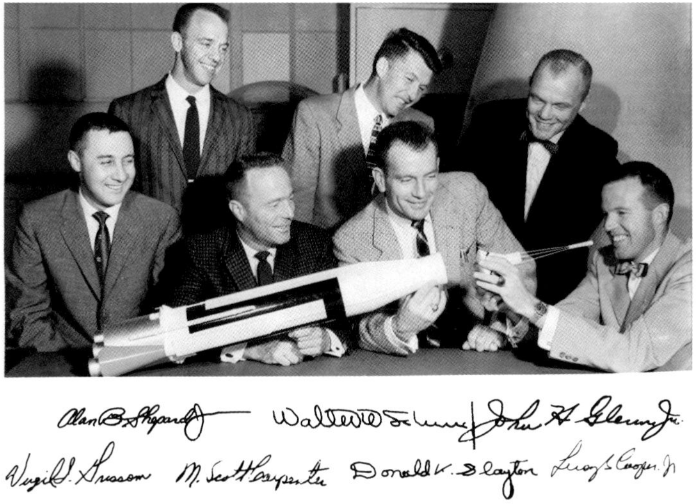

The lives of the Mercury 7 changed the day they were publicly announced as astronauts at a press conference in Washington, D.C.

NASA

NASA officially introduced its first class of astronauts on April 9, 1959: M. Scott Carpenter, L. Gordon "Gordo" Cooper Jr., John H. Glenn Jr., Virgil I. "Gus" Grissom, Walter M. "Wally" Schirra Jr., Alan B. Shepard Jr., and Donald K. "Deke" Slayton. At one point during the press conference, the Mercury 7, as they became known, were asked if they were confident that they would return from a space mission. All seven raised their hands, Glenn raising both. Six of the group flew on one-person Mercury missions between 1961 and 1963. Slayton was medically disqualified from his Mercury flight due to a previously undetected heart condition, but eventually flew to space on the Apollo-Soyuz Test Project in 1975 (see page 214).

Although the astronauts were announced in April, their selection process began months before. First, NASA had to determine how to find candidates who had the "right stuff." The community of United States military test pilots seemed a great place to start. One hundred ten pilots were tapped for a top-secret briefing and preliminary evaluations. NASA narrowed the pool to thirty-two, who underwent further psychological evaluation and health testing. The best candidates were selected as the Mercury 7.

FIRST IMAGE OF BLACK HOLE IS RELEASED

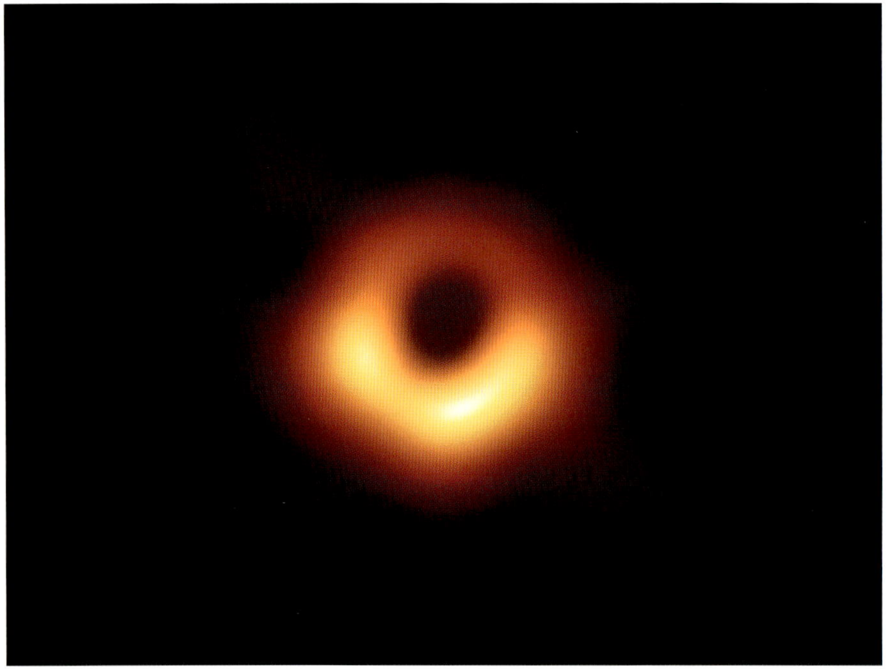

Using the Event Horizon Telescope, scientists obtained the first image of the black hole at the center of galaxy M87.

Event Horizon Telescope Collaboration

For a long time, taking an image of a black hole was thought to be impossible. After all, black holes by their very definition are invisible. They represent regions of space where the pull of gravity is so intense that nothing can escape it, not even light. To achieve the impossible, a team of international scientists created a network of telescopes known as the Event Horizon Telescope, synchronizing eight radio dishes around the globe.

Each of the telescopes recorded data from the black hole at their geographic locations, effectively forming a planet-size telescope array. The data was then combined and played back to create an image of a black hole. The first image of a black hole was released to the media on April 10, 2019. Sheperd Doeleman, founding director of the Event Horizon Telescope Collaboration, is an astrophysicist at the Center for Astrophysics, a collaboration between the Smithsonian Astrophysical Observatory and the Harvard College Observatory.

APRIL 11

PV-2 MAKES ITS FIRST FLIGHT

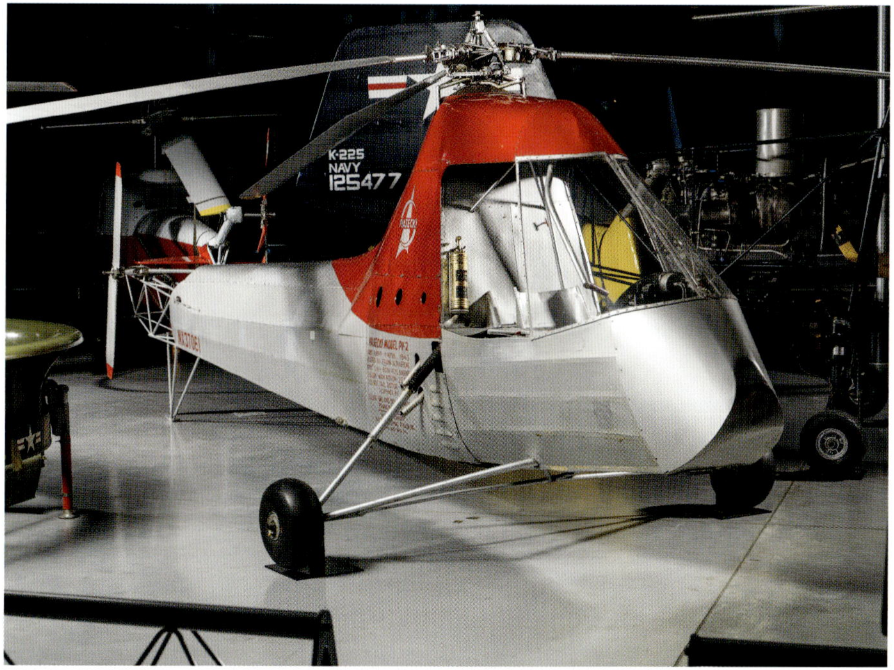

Frank Piasecki's PV-2 is on display at the Steven F. Udvar-Hazy Center in Virginia.

Smithsonian's National Air and Space Museum

In the early 1940s, helicopter designers were hard at work on an aerial version of the Model T. This group of innovators included Frank Piasecki. The American engineer's first design, the PV-1, did not advance beyond the drawing boards. After leaving his day job at Platt-LePage Aircraft Company to work on his designs full-time, however, Piasecki had more success. On April 11, 1943, Piasecki became the second American to successfully fly a helicopter of his own design, the Piasecki-Venzie PV-2.

The PV-2's first flight occurred by accident after a frayed clothesline that was intended to keep the aircraft tethered broke and the helicopter became airborne. The PV-2 flew with an unprecedented smoothness and stability. Ironically, Piasecki intended his first helicopter design to be the forerunner of a revolution in personal transportation, but instead his company evolved into one of the foremost manufacturers of large cargo helicopters sold to the military.

SPACE SHUTTLE LAUNCHES FOR THE FIRST TIME

Space Shuttle *Columbia* launched on the first orbital spaceflight of the program, STS-1, on April 12, 1981. This was the first full test of the Space Transportation System (STS), the completely assembled "stack" of two solid rocket boosters, an external tank, and an orbiter. Crews previously tested the orbiter's landing capabilities in the Approach and Landing Test program (see page 241), and the rockets and engines were tested separately from the full "stack," but STS-1 was the first time NASA ever included crew on the first launch of a fully assembled vehicle. The mission was commanded by Gemini and Apollo astronaut John Young and piloted by rookie astronaut Robert Crippen.

The Space Shuttle's first launch ushered in a new era of human spaceflight. It was the realization of NASA's decades-old dream of a reusable spaceplane that could perform a range of tasks: deploy large objects from a payload bay, serve as a scientific base for microgravity research, and create space for professionals and industries interested in the unique offerings of low Earth orbit. Science and technology research could even be done on space stations that the system could deliver in pieces for astronauts to assemble. Though the next three decades of Space Shuttle missions saw many successes, it wasn't without its share of failures, including the loss of *Challenger*, *Columbia*, and their crews (see pages 41 and 48).

DID YOU KNOW? Photos of the first two Space Shuttle launches look a bit different from all the rest: For STS-1 and STS-2, the orange external tank was painted white. By STS-3, they stopped painting the tank to save weight.

OPPOSITE PAGE NASA's Space Shuttle launched for the first time on the twentieth anniversary of Yuri Gagarin's first human spaceflight.

NASA

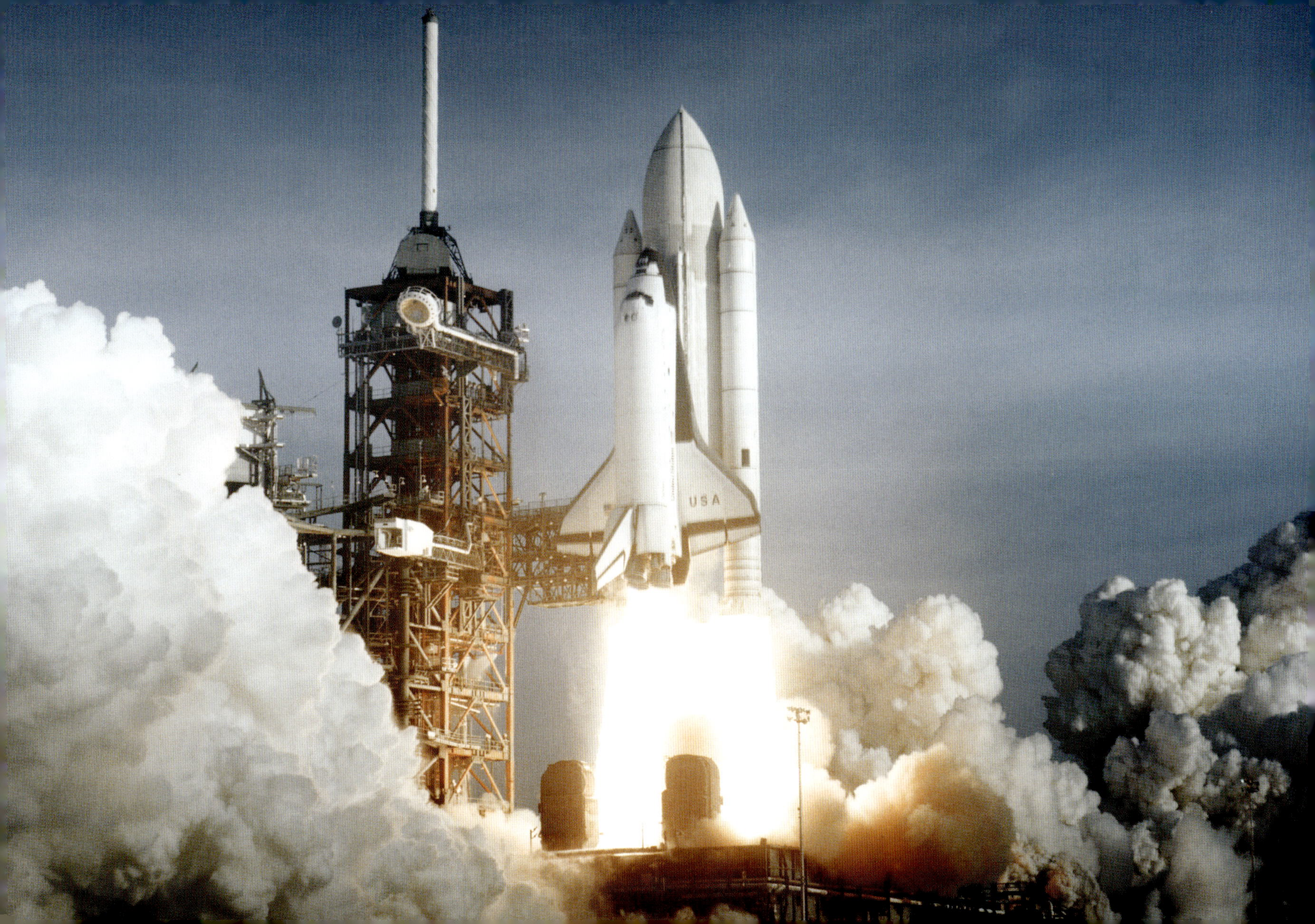
USA

DISASTER STRIKES THE APOLLO 13 MISSION

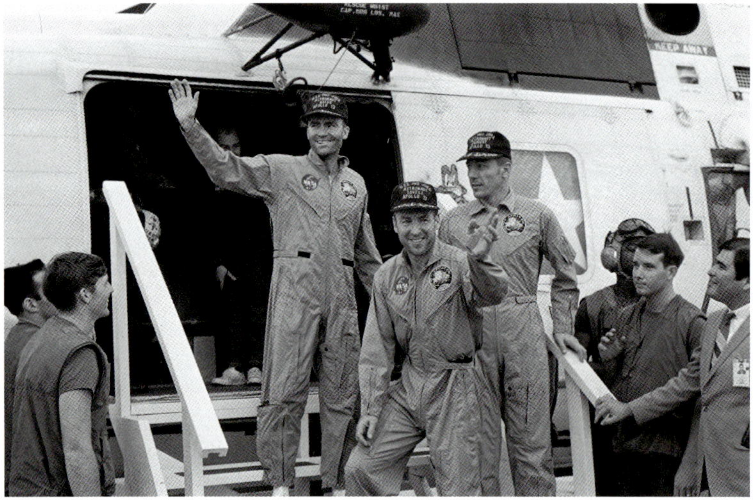

The Apollo 13 astronauts returned to Earth safely, despite a catastrophic explosion in the service module.

NASA

"Houston, we've had a problem."

—APOLLO 13 COMMANDER JIM LOVELL

"NASA's finest hour." "A successful failure." The Apollo 13 mission has been called many things and is one of the most famous Apollo missions despite never landing on the Moon. On April 13, 1970, the explosion of one of the service module's oxygen tanks seriously damaged the spacecraft. The crew was forced to fly around the Moon, using its gravity to send them back toward Earth without carrying out a lunar landing.

James "Jim" Lovell, John "Jack" Swigert, and Fred Haise piled into the lunar module, which had enough oxygen to support the astronauts, but had been designed for only two passengers. The carbon dioxide produced by all three astronauts exceeded the capacity of the lunar module's lithium hydroxide filters, and as Mission Control searched for a solution, they could only use materials the crew would have access to onboard the spacecraft. Using a plastic bag, cardstock, a spacesuit hose, and duct tape, engineers mocked up an altered lithium hydroxide filter converter, which the astronauts in turn re-created in space. A few days later, the crew climbed back into the command module for reentry and splashed down safely in the Pacific Ocean.

UNITED STATES DOWNS ITS FIRST ENEMY PLANES IN WORLD WAR I

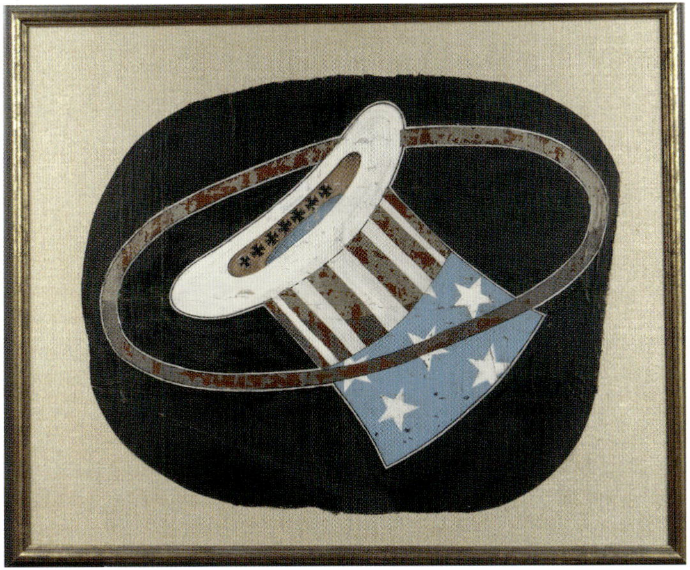

A "Hat in the Ring" insignia in the National Air and Space Museum collection was from a 94th Aero Squadron aircraft flown by ace H. Weir Cook.

Smithsonian's National Air and Space Museum.

The 94th Aero Squadron of the United States Army Air Service was one of the first American pursuit squadrons to see combat during World War I. As a result, the group was heavily publicized in American media, becoming popularly known as the "Hat in the Ring Squadron." The unit achieved great fame with its operations over the Western Front, in particular recording America's first official air combat victories of the war. Among the squadron's famous aces were Capt. Eddie Rickenbacker (see page 329) and Maj. Gervais Raoul Lufbery (see page 89).

On April 14, 1918, Lt. Douglas Campbell and Lt. Alan Winslow, flying French-built Nieuport 28s, downed two German aircraft. The pair were honored two days later with the French Croix de Guerre with Palm. The aircraft Campbell and Winslow flew that day were emblazoned with the squadron's official insignia, which depicted Uncle Sam's patriotic top hat upside down within a circle—signifying the United States throwing its hat in the ring of the war.

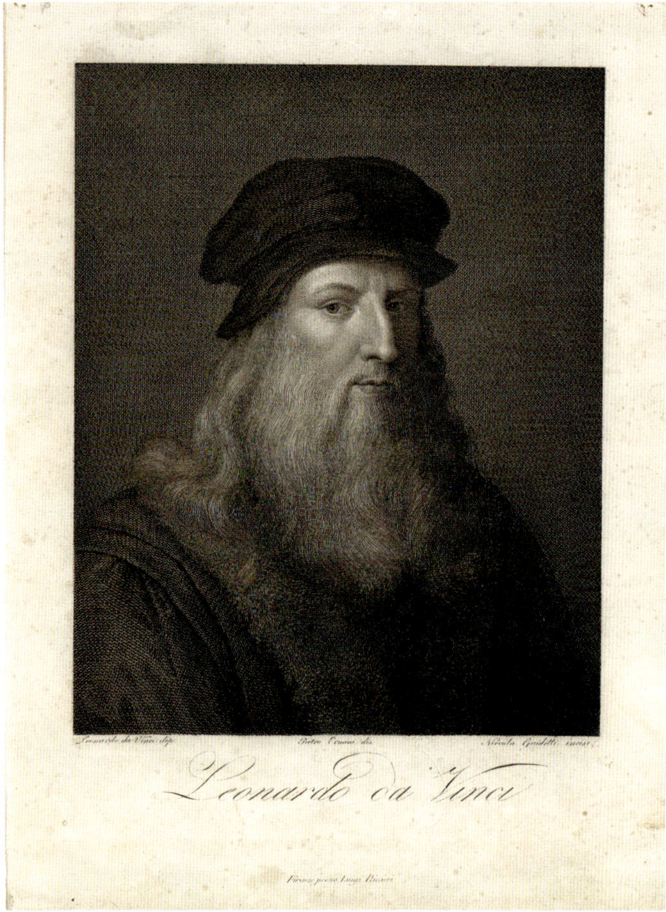

For centuries after his death, Leonardo da Vinci was known primarily as a painter. It was only in the nineteenth century that thousands of pages of Leonardo's writings and drawings began to resurface, revealing the full range of his intellectual and technical accomplishments. Leonardo was particularly fascinated with the possibility of human mechanical flight, producing more than thirty-five thousand words and five hundred sketches dealing with flying machines, the nature of air, and bird flight. Once he engaged with the notion of a flying machine, it became an obsession for the Renaissance inventor.

Most of Leonardo's aeronautical designs were ornithopters, machines that employed flapping wings to generate both lift and propulsion. Imaginative as these designs were, the limited muscle power and endurance of human beings makes ornithopters an impractical method of flight. Though Leonardo's designs weren't successful, the seeds of the ideas that would eventually lead humans to take flight were present in his research. In aeronautics, as with so many of the subjects he studied, Leonardo ventured where no one had before.

Leonardo da Vinci, painter, engineer, and all-around Renaissance man, was born on April 15, 1452.

Smithsonian's National Air and Space Museum

HARRIET QUIMBY FLIES SOLO ACROSS THE ENGLISH CHANNEL

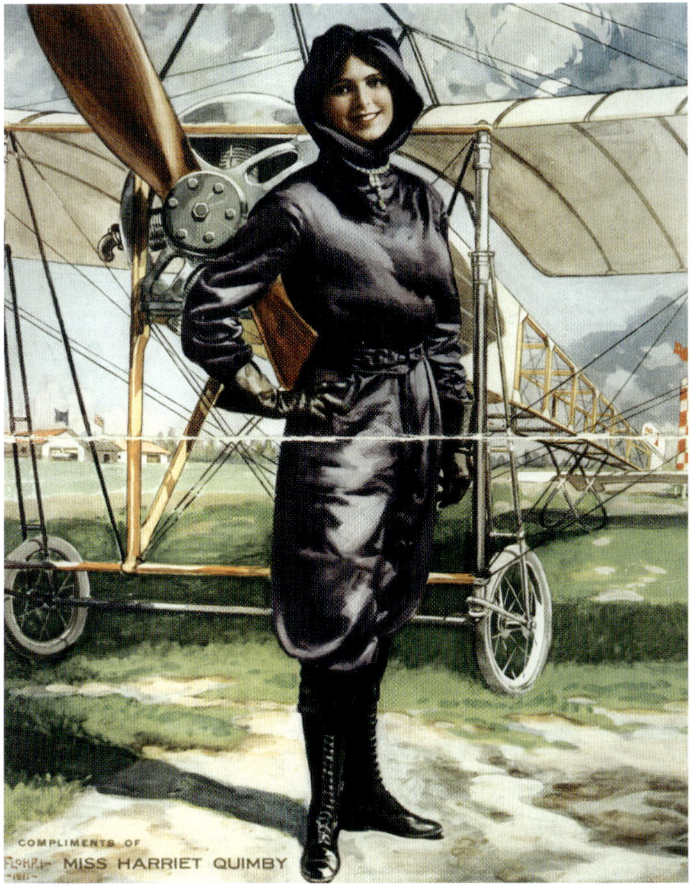

Soon after Harriet Quimby became the first American woman to earn a pilot's license (see page 230), she made history once more—this time in England. In March 1912, Quimby began preparing for a flight across the English Channel. Unsure of a woman's ability to make such a flight, advisor Gustav Hamel offered to disguise himself in Quimby's iconic purple flying suit and make the flight for her. By Quimby's own accounts, this suggestion only increased her determination to embark on the journey: "I was annoyed from the start by the attitude of doubt on the part of the spectators that I would never really make the flight," she reflected. "This attitude made me more determined than ever to succeed."

On April 16, 1912, Quimby flew through fog across the Channel from Dover, England, to Hardelot, France (about twenty-five miles south of Calais) in a little over an hour, landing on an isolated beach in France. Though she returned triumphantly to the U.S., her flight received limited fanfare and press coverage due to another world event that had occurred that week: the sinking of the *Titanic*.

Pioneering aviator Harriet Quimby was known for her stylish purple flying suit.

Smithsonian's National Air and Space Museum (NASM 2003-15995)

FLAK-BAIT FLIES ITS TWO HUNDREDTH MISSION

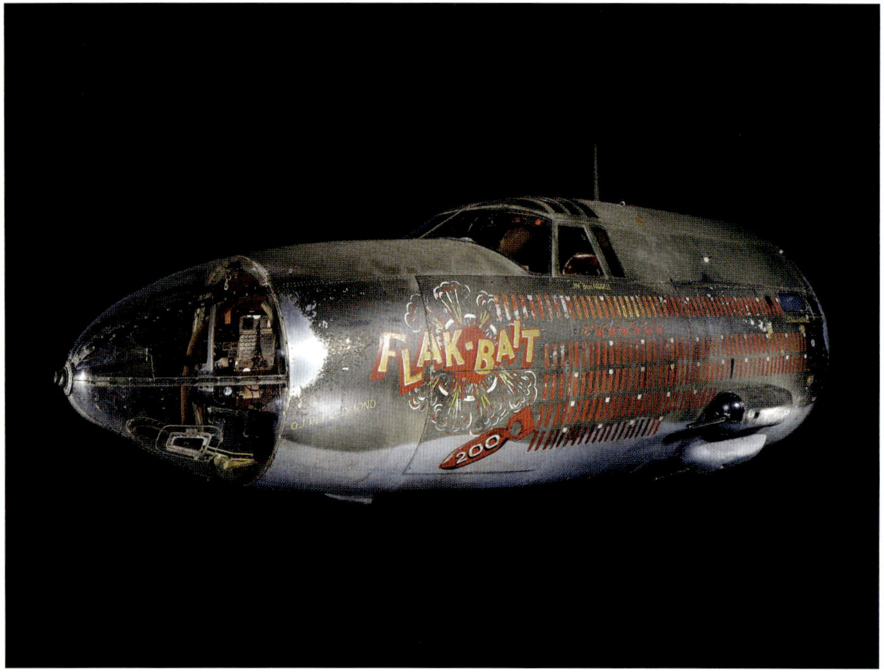

One only needs to look at the forward fuselage of *Flak-Bait*, in the collection of the National Air and Space Museum, to discover how many missions it flew. Painted on the side are two hundred bombs to represent bombing missions, six ducks for decoy missions, and a swastika for a mission with a confirmed kill of a German fighter.

Smithsonian's National Air and Space Museum

The Martin B-26 Marauder *Flak-Bait* survived more missions than any other American aircraft during World War II—207 to be exact. It operated in the skies over Europe for a year and nine months as the Allies prepared for the invasion of France and supported the armies on the ground as they pushed east toward Berlin.

During the aircraft's many missions, *Flak-Bait* and its crews attacked numerous targets, including cities; airfields; road, rail, and canal junctions; bridges; supply depots; fuel and ammunition dumps; gun emplacements; and even V-1 flying bomb launch sites. By spring 1945, *Flak-Bait*'s ground crew had repaired over a thousand holes in the aircraft caused by Nazi shrapnel, cannon shells, and machine gun bullets—hence the name *Flak-Bait*.

On April 17, 1945, an Army Air Forces crew flew *Flak-Bait*'s two hundredth mission. During the flight, the aircraft led the 322nd Bombardment Group of the Ninth Air Force against Magdeburg, Germany, a "defended area" on the Elbe River in Saxony. The next day, soldiers of the American Ninth Army occupied the city.

JIMMY DOOLITTLE LEADS DOOLITTLE RAID

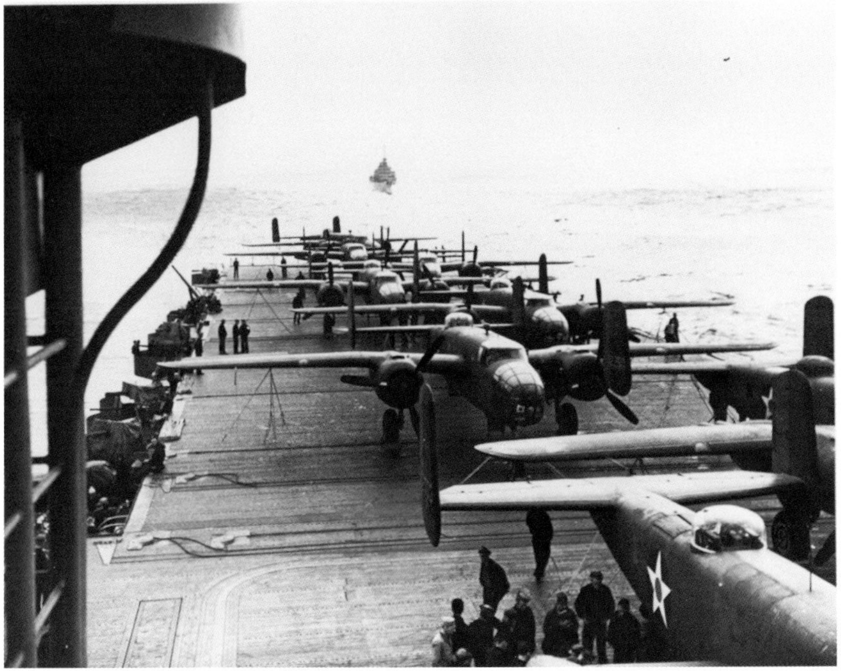

B-25B bombers were selected for the mission to bomb key targets in Japan.

U.S. Naval History and Heritage Command

After Japan's attack on Pearl Harbor in December 1941 (see page 357), American military and political leaders knew they needed to strike back quickly. In January 1942, military planners developed the "Joint Army-Navy Bombing Project," in which U.S. Army Air Forces bombers would launch from a Navy aircraft carrier within range of Japan. Lt. Col. James "Jimmy" Doolittle was chosen to command the Army Air Force elements, while B-25 bombers and the USS *Hornet* aircraft carrier were prepared for the mission.

On April 18, 1942, Doolittle led a force of sixteen B-25s to Japan, where they dropped ordnance on targets in Nagoya, Kobe, Tokyo, Yokohama, and Yokosuka. The attacks caught the Japanese by surprise and the B-25s faced little opposition. Although it did not cause much damage, the raid's psychological impact on the Japanese populace was significant. The attack also helped boost American home-front morale, a major goal of U.S. leaders after the dispiriting attacks the previous December. Doolittle received the Medal of Honor for his leadership of the mission, which has since become known as the Doolittle Raid.

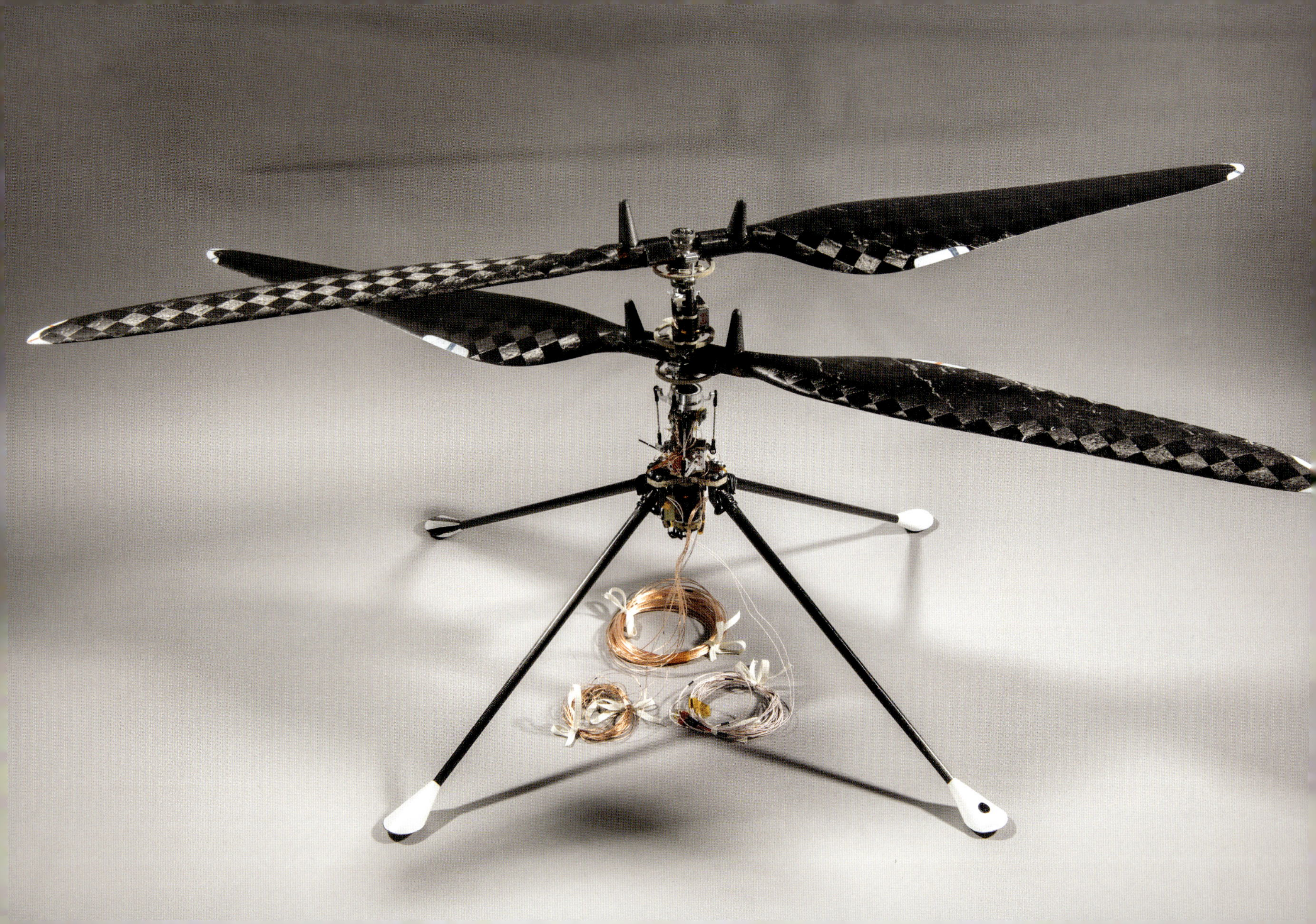

INGENUITY FLIES ON MARS FOR THE FIRST TIME

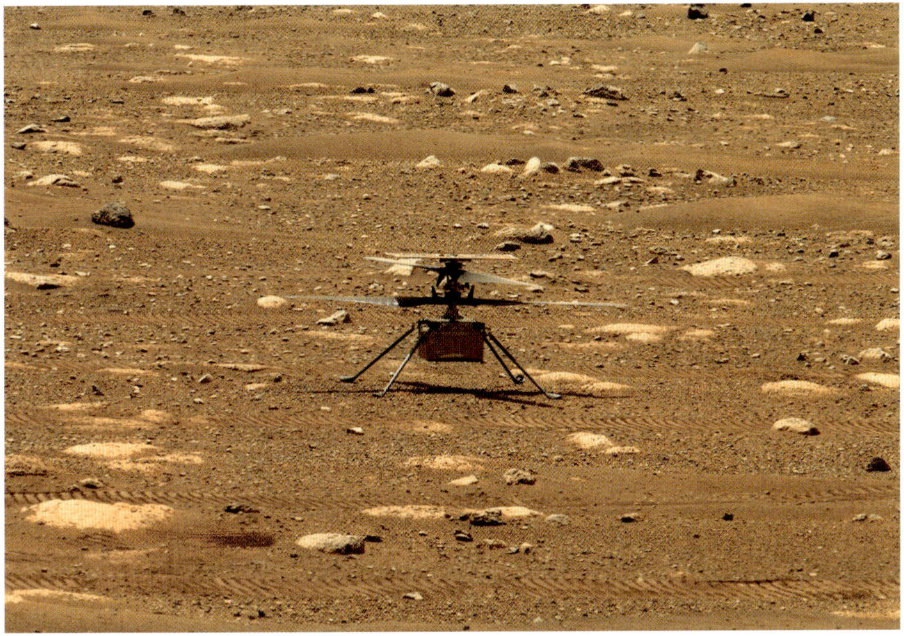

OPPOSITE PAGE An aerial prototype of *Ingenuity* was used in tests in a simulated Mars environment on Earth. It is in the collection of the National Air and Space Museum.

Smithsonian's National Air and Space Museum

ABOVE *Ingenuity* traveled to Mars on board Mars rover *Perseverance*.

NASA

On April 19, 2021, the *Ingenuity* Mars helicopter achieved the first powered, controlled flight of a human-made vehicle on another planet. The helicopter rose ten feet vertically and returned to its takeoff point. The craft hitched a ride to Mars with the *Perseverance* rover a few months prior, and its primary purpose was to show that robotic flight was feasible on Mars and test the technologies involved.

Even before it completed its five planned demonstration flights, NASA transitioned *Ingenuity*'s mission from a technology demonstration to an operational contribution to *Perseverance*'s mission. The helicopter flights were used to scout ahead for new sites to explore and map from the surrounding terrain. *Ingenuity* performed this role until it took its seventy-second and final flight in early 2024, which resulted in a crash. *Ingenuity* was so successful that plans for future Mars missions now include helicopters that will build on the achievements of the little Mars copter that could.

DID YOU KNOW? A piece of fabric from the 1903 Wright Flyer is attached to *Ingenuity*—connecting the first controlled, powered flight on Earth to the first controlled, powered flight on Mars.

BELL ROCKET BELT IS USED FOR THE FIRST TIME

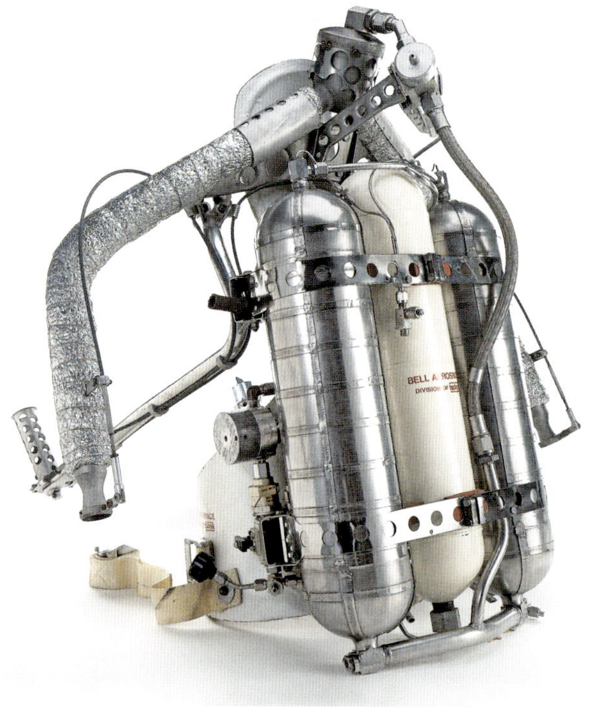

Bell Rocket Belt No. 2 is in the collection of the National Air and Space Museum.

Smithsonian's National Air and Space Museum

Imagine strapping on a backpack and flying to work or the grocery store. The idea is tempting enough that it's no surprise jetpacks appear time and time again in television shows and movies like *The Jetsons* and James Bond. In fact, jetpacks in fiction date back to the *Buck Rogers* comic strips in the 1920s (see page 22). But jetpacks aren't just sci-fi. Wendell Moore of Bell Aerosystems was the first to develop a real one, also known as a rocket belt, in the mid-1950s.

On April 20, 1961, Bell test pilot Harold Graham made the first free flight of the Bell Rocket Belt at the Pentagon, near Washington, D.C. This rocket belt was conceived as a small personal propulsion device that enabled a person to fly short distances using low rocket power produced by noncombustible gas. However, jetpacks weren't that practical and never really found a market. Today, they are mainly used for air shows, movie stunts, or half-time shows and other events.

APRIL 21

AEROBEE HI SOUNDING ROCKET MAKES ITS FIRST FLIGHT

ROCKETS AND MISSILES

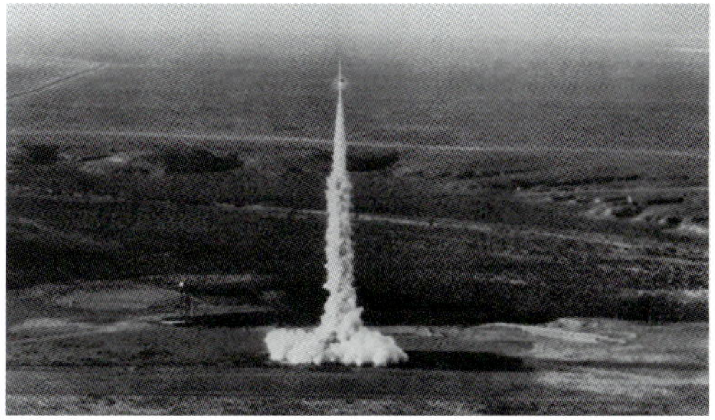

Aerobee rockets carried payloads of scientific instruments into the upper atmosphere.

Smithsonian's National Air and Space Museum (NASM 7B07689)

The Aerobee Hi was a sounding rocket initially built for research by Aerojet General for the U.S. Navy and Air Force. A two-stage rocket carrying scientific instruments, it first flew successfully and reached an altitude of about 168 miles on April 21, 1955. It launched from Holloman Air Force Base in New Mexico. Aerobee contributed to the scientific research of the International Geophysical Year (1957–58) with thirty-five Aerobee Hi rocket launches.

APRIL 22

THE FIRST EARTH DAY IS HELD

SOCIAL AND CULTURAL SPACE

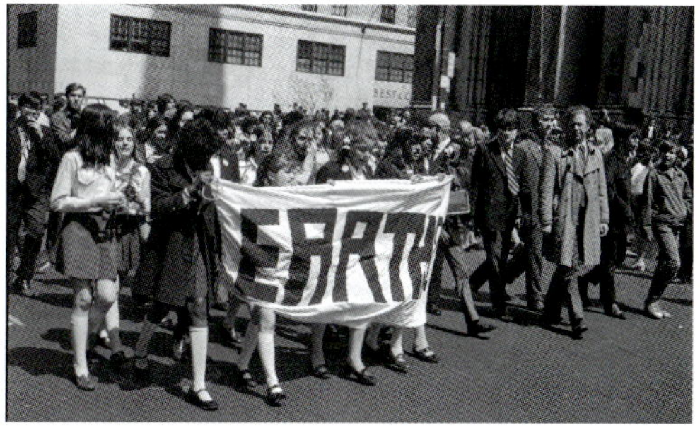

A parade was held in New York City on the first Earth Day.

Municipal Archives, City of New York

The first Earth Day was held on April 22, 1970, at community events in two hundred U.S. cities. In Manhattan, the city closed Fifth Avenue for throngs of marchers. Large outdoor crowds in Philadelphia heard speeches by poet Allen Ginsberg and activist Ralph Nader. Leaders of Earth Day also orchestrated national "teach-ins" to raise public awareness of environmental issues and to show how individuals could begin to improve the environment through their daily actions. More than two thousand colleges and ten thousand high schools organized teach-ins or other community events—all aimed at stimulating a grassroots movement for the environment. The movement started that day has continued since 1970, with Earth Day held every year on April 22.

RQ-4A GLOBAL HAWK FLIES NONSTOP ACROSS THE PACIFIC

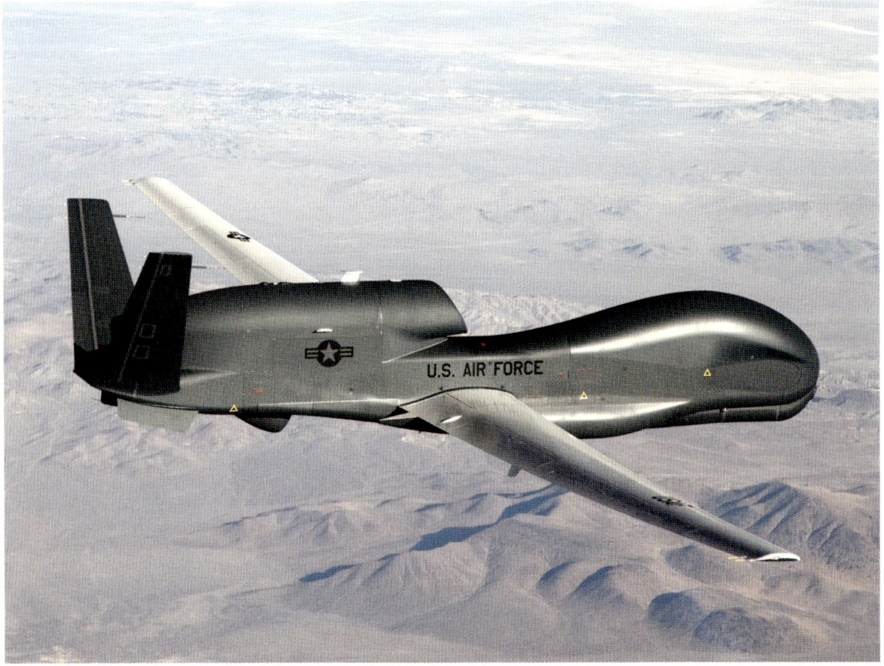

The RQ-4A Global Hawk is a surveillance drone operated by the U.S. Air Force.

U.S. Air Force

On April 23, 2001, an RQ-4A Global Hawk completed the first nonstop flight across the Pacific Ocean by an uncrewed powered aircraft. The Global Hawk is an Unmanned Aerial Vehicle (UAV), or drone, whose primary function is high-altitude, long-endurance intelligence, surveillance, and reconnaissance. Twenty-two hours after departing Edwards Air Force Base in California, the uncrewed aircraft arrived at the Royal Australian Air Force (RAAF) Base Edinburgh in southern Australia near Adelaide.

The record-setting drone was dubbed *Southern Cross II* for the flight, a name intended to honor the first-ever transpacific flight by four Australian aviators in 1928 (see page 178). During the UAV's journey, engineers were able to test its capabilities by having it detect and photograph vessels below as it flew. The more-than-8,000-mile flight had a purpose other than setting records: The drone was needed for joint exercises between the U.S. Navy, the RAAF, and the Royal Australian Navy. During its six weeks in Australia, *Southern Cross II* flew thirteen exercises with over two hundred hours of flight time.

HUBBLE SPACE TELESCOPE IS LAUNCHED

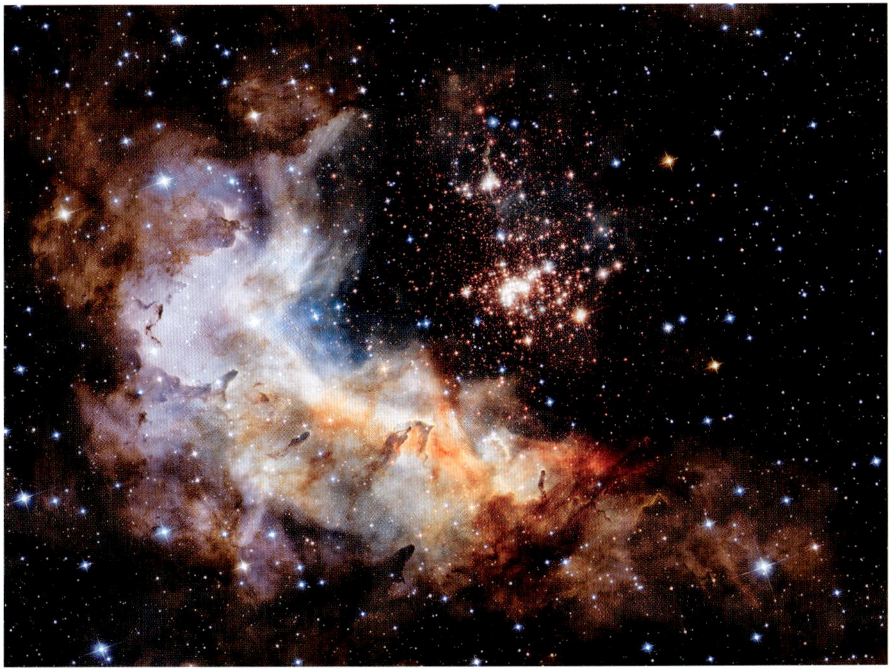

NASA released the "Celestial Fireworks" image of the Westerlund 2 star cluster for Hubble's twenty-fifth anniversary.

NASA, ESA, A. Nota (ESA/STScI), and the Westerlund 2 Science Team

The Hubble Space Telescope (HST) is one of the largest astronomical telescopes ever sent into space. It dramatically altered the way both scientists and the public alike understand the universe. From its vantage point high above Earth's obscuring atmosphere, the telescope provides astronomers with fascinating new views of the universe.

The Hubble Space Telescope was launched on Space Shuttle *Discovery* on April 24, 1990, and released into orbit the following day. As Hubble began sending data back, it became obvious there was a flaw with the primary mirror preventing it from focusing properly. This resulted in blurry photos. The optical flaw was corrected on the first Hubble servicing mission (see page 353), and a flood of spectacular images soon followed.

Both science and artistry are used to color, orient, and visualize the data technicians receive from the telescope. Hubble's images often reflect what the scientists want the public to understand about an object, rather than how the object would actually appear to human eyes. As a result, the images are popular with the public, who are constantly in awe of the vibrant and stunning images released by the HST team.

APRIL 25

KEN MATTINGLY PERFORMS A DEEP-SPACE EVA ON APOLLO 16

HUMAN SPACEFLIGHT

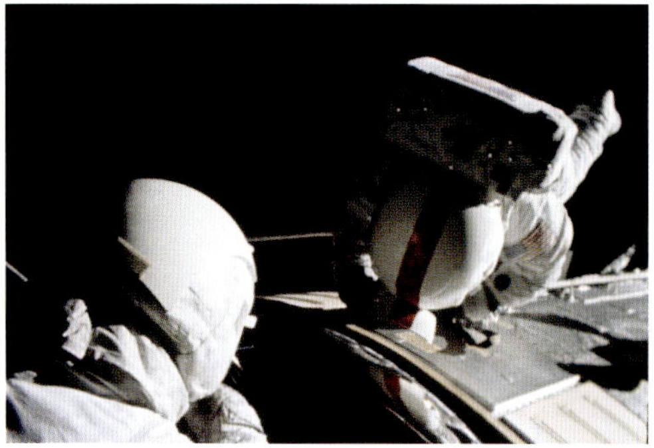

Apollo 16 lunar module pilot Charlie Duke assists Ken Mattingly as he performs a spacewalk in deep space.

NASA

On April 25, 1972, Apollo 16 command module pilot Thomas K. "Ken" Mattingly performed a deep-space extravehicular activity (EVA) as the Apollo 16 spacecraft journeyed back to Earth from the Moon. Mattingly ventured outside the command module to retrieve film cassettes from the scientific instrument module (SIM) bay in the service module. He collected film cassettes from two high-resolution cameras used to map the lunar surface accurately. Mattingly was the second person to perform a deep-space EVA after Alfred Worden did the same for the Apollo 15 mission the prior year.

APRIL 26

SECOND GERMAN SPACELAB MISSION LAUNCHES

INTERNATIONAL SPACE PROGRAMS

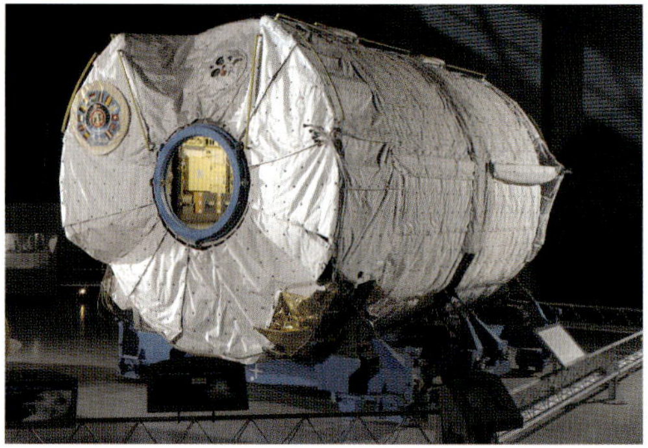

The flown Spacelab Module 1 is on display at the Steven F. Udvar-Hazy Center.

Smithsonian's National Air and Space Museum

Developed by the European Space Agency, Spacelab was a modular laboratory installed in the payload bay of a Space Shuttle orbiter. The pressurized module was outfitted with racks containing subsystems, computers, work-stations, stowage lockers, supplies, equipment, and experiments that changed from mission to mission. On April 26, 1993, STS-55 launched for the D-2 mission, the second German Spacelab spaceflight. During the mission, the crew divided into two teams and worked around the clock, conducting almost ninety experiments.

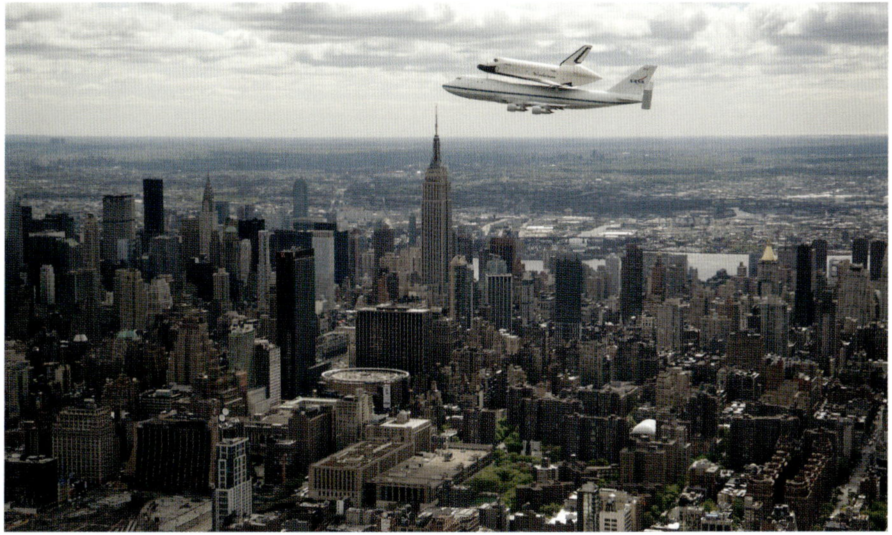

Space Shuttle *Enterprise*, atop the Shuttle Carrier Aircraft, flew over New York City on its journey to be displayed at the Intrepid Museum.

NASA

What does it take to move something as large as a Space Shuttle orbiter across the country when it's not flying under its own power? Enter the Shuttle Carrier Aircraft (SCA), two modified Boeing 747s NASA used to ferry orbiters back to Kennedy Space Center when they completed missions elsewhere. Space Shuttles were situated for transport using the Mate-Demate Device, a large gantry-like steel structure used to lift the shuttle. Transporting an orbiter was no small task!

In 2012, the SCAs had their work cut out for them as they contributed to the effort of distributing the now-retired orbiters to their final homes across the country. The Shuttle Carrier Aircraft flew Space Shuttle *Discovery* to Washington, D.C., for display at the Steven F. Udvar-Hazy Center; Space Shuttle *Enterprise* to New York City for display at the Intrepid Museum; and Space Shuttle *Endeavour* to Los Angeles for display at the California Science Center. *Enterprise*, an atmospheric test vehicle that never made it to space (see page 241), was previously on display at the Udvar-Hazy Center and departed for its new home on April 27, 2012.

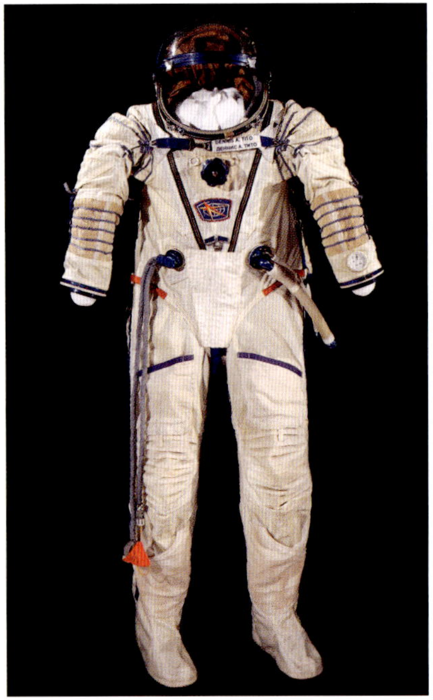

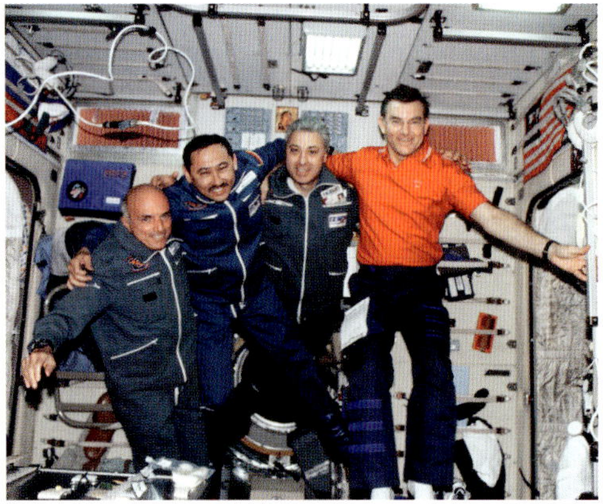

LEFT The Sokol pressure suit Dennis Tito wore during launch is in the collection of the National Air and Space Museum.

Smithsonian's National Air and Space Museum

RIGHT Tito (left) flew to the International Space Station with cosmonauts Talgat Musabayev and Yuri Baturin, and joined a crew already on station, including NASA astronaut Susan Helms.

NASA

While space tourism has become much more prominent and common recently, it all began in 2001 when California entrepreneur Dennis Tito paid a reported $20 million for a weeklong trip to the International Space Station (ISS). Tito spent months in Moscow and at the Cosmonaut Flight Training Center in Star City, Russia, training and preparing for the flight. On April 28, 2001, Tito launched aboard the Soyuz TM-32 from Baikonur, Kazakhstan, and spent six days at the ISS. In an interview with CNN after his spaceflight, Tito reflected: "To have six days where I had a constant high, no pun intended, was just the greatest experience of my life."

Between 2001 and 2009, six more space tourists traveled to the space station on board Soyuz spacecraft; subsequently, the ISS was temporarily closed to space tourism when the Space Shuttle was retired and Soyuz flights were reserved for professional astronauts only.

APRIL 29

CONVAIR XFY-1 POGO MAKES ITS FIRST TETHERED FLIGHT

VERTICAL FLIGHT

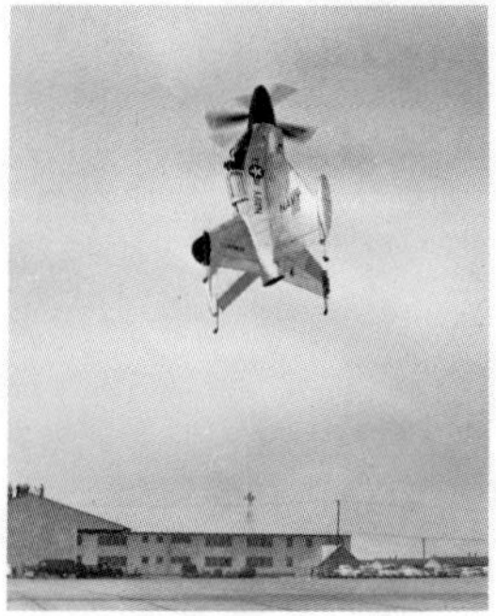

The XFY-1 could transition to horizontal flight and back.

Smithsonian's National Air and Space Museum

On April 29, 1954, James F. "Skeets" Coleman, a lieutenant colonel in the U.S. Marine Corps Reserve and Convair engineering test pilot, made the first tethered flight in the Convair XFY-1 Pogo. The XFY-1 was very much an experimental craft. No other propeller-driven aircraft of similar size, weight, and engine power had ever attempted to take off and land vertically. On early experimental flights, the Pogo required safety lines to protect the pilot and the aircraft. The tether on its nose streamed from a motorized reel that could be used to snatch the Pogo upright if Coleman lost control.

APRIL 30

TURI WIDERØE MAKES COMMERCIAL AVIATION HISTORY

COMMERCIAL AVIATION

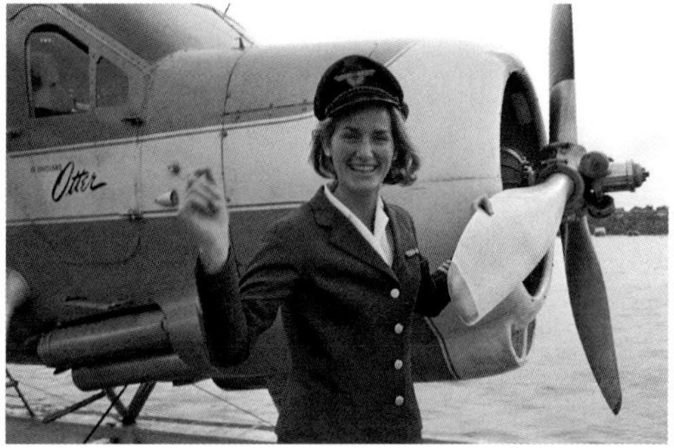

Turi Widerøe flew the de Havilland Otter seaplane early in her career.

NTB / Bridgeman Images

On April 30, 1969, Norwegian aviator Turi Widerøe became the first woman to work as a commercial airline pilot for a major airline in the Western world. Widerøe had earned her private pilot's license in 1962 and her commercial license in 1965. In 1968, she joined Scandinavian Airline Systems when she enrolled in the company's flight academy. After graduating, Widerøe was certified as a copilot on the Convair 440 Metropolitan, making history. In 1970, she received the Harmon Aviatrix Trophy, which is awarded annually for the most outstanding achievements by a woman in the arts or science of aeronautics.

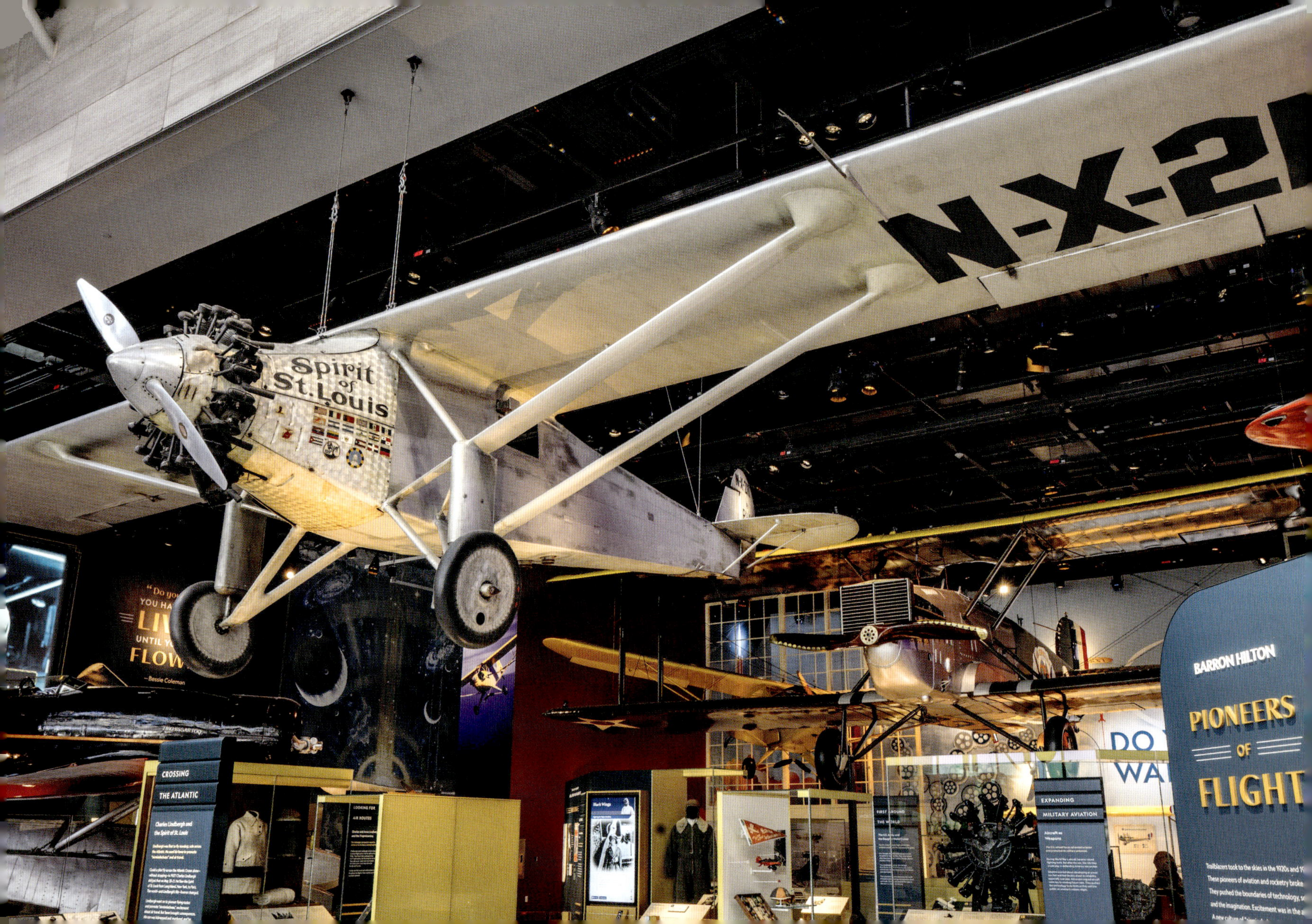

N-X-2
Spirit of St. Louis
BARRON HILTON
PIONEERS OF FLIGHT
CROSSING
THE ATLANTIC
EXPANDING
MILITARY AVIATION

MAY

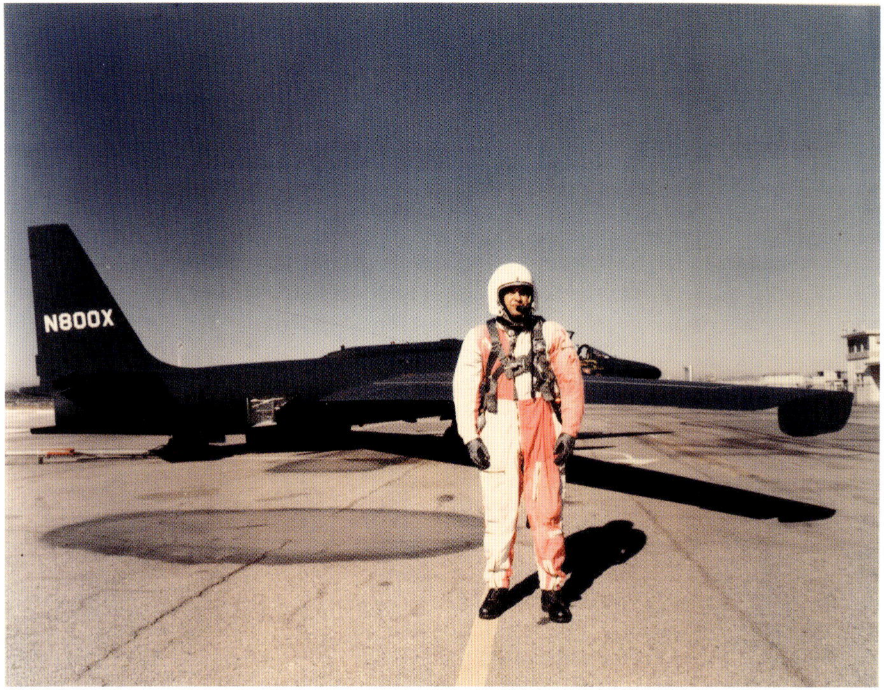

Francis Gary Powers was flying a Lockheed U-2 when he was shot down over the Soviet Union.

Smithsonian's National Air and Space Museum (NASM 93-16025)

Capt. Francis Gary Powers joined the U.S. Air Force in 1950 after graduating from college. In 1956, he resigned from the Air Force to become a "civilian employee" of Lockheed on loan to the National Advisory Committee for Aeronautics. In reality, Powers had been recruited as a covert employee of the CIA and began training to conduct highly secretive reconnaissance missions flying the Lockheed U-2.

On May 1, 1960, a surface-to-air missile struck Powers's plane while on a reconnaissance mission over the Soviet Union, and he was captured and imprisoned. The USSR publicly displayed pieces of the U-2 as proof of the United States' unauthorized overflights, triggering a diplomatic crisis. Two years after his capture, Powers was exchanged for convicted Soviet agent Rudolf Abel, and both men returned to their home countries. Back in the United States, Powers initially continued to work for the CIA but eventually left the agency to become a test pilot at Lockheed, fulfilling his initial cover story.

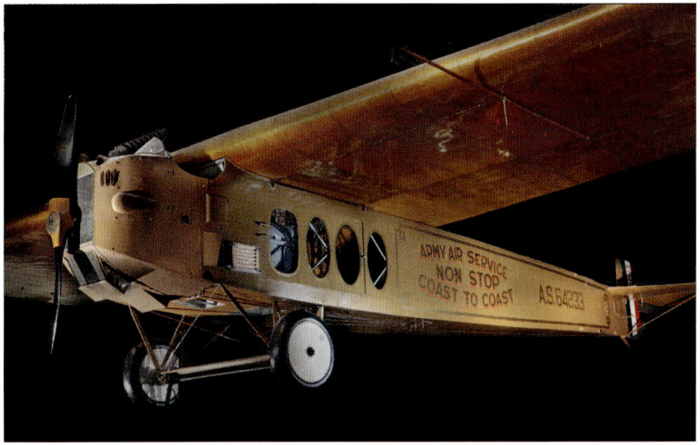

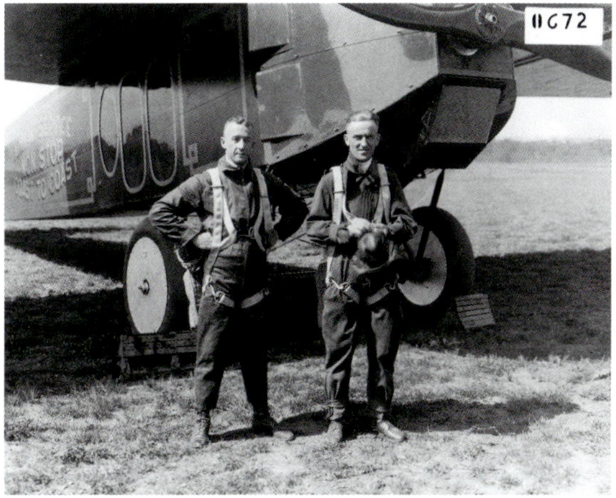

LEFT The Fokker T-2 flown on Macready and Kelly's historic flight is in the collection of the National Air and Space Museum.

Smithsonian's National Air and Space Museum

RIGHT Lieutenants Macready and Kelly were pilots in the U.S. Army Air Service.

Smithsonian's National Air and Space Museum (NASM 98-15780)

Third time's a charm: On May 2, 1923, U.S. Army Air Service pilots Lt. John Macready and Lt. Oakley G. Kelly began their third and final attempt to fly across the country nonstop. Unlike their first two attempts, which had been thwarted by weather and technical difficulties, this trip proved to be a success. Taking off from Roosevelt Field, Long Island, in a Fokker T-2, Macready and Kelly flew 2,470 miles west to Rockwell Field, San Diego.

Throughout the nearly twenty-seven-hour flight, the pair traded off who was at the controls, crawling through a tunnel to switch seats. Over half the journey took place at night and in storms. The Army Air Service approved the flight to test the capability and endurance of the new T-2 transport and its Liberty engine. The historic adventure also helped demonstrate the potential of military and commercial aircraft as practical long-distance technologies.

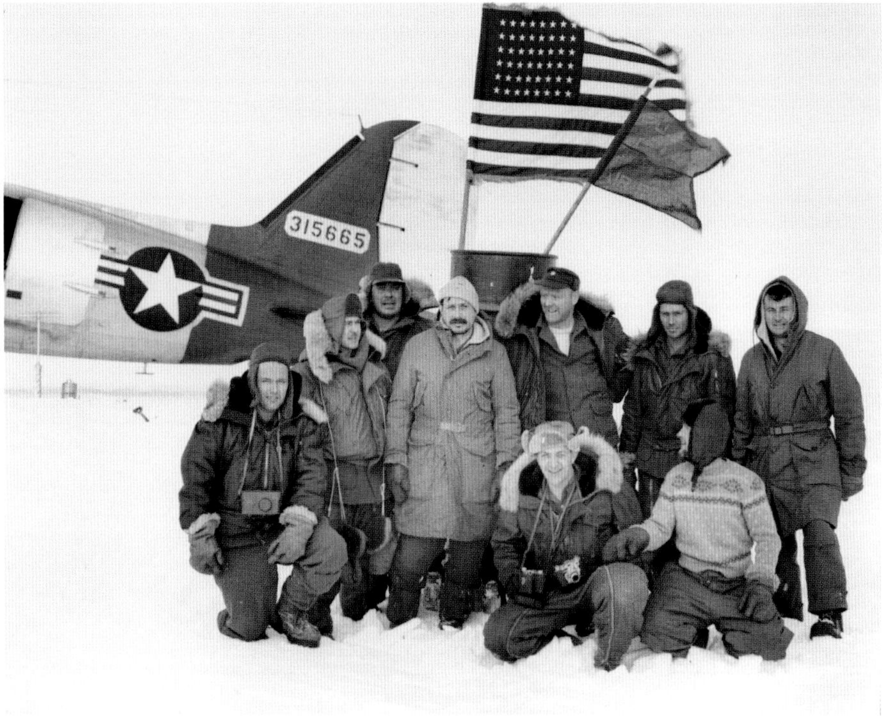

Both aviators and researchers were on board the flight that landed at the North Pole.

Smithsonian's National Air and Space Museum (NASM USAF-44277AC)

When Lt. Col. William Benedict and Lt. Col. Joseph Fletcher touched down in a Douglas C-47 at the North Pole on May 3, 1952, the pair became the first American aviators to land at the Earth's northernmost landmark. The aircraft they flew was equipped with skis and the flight was supported by navigator 1st Lt. Herbert Thompson, flight engineer Staff Sgt. Harold Turner, and radio operator Airman 1st Class Robert Wishard. After landing on the ice, Benedict radioed back to U.S. Air Force command: "Operational instructions carried out. No sweat."

The historic flight originated from T-3, a massive ice island 135 miles south of the pole on which the Air Force had built a weather observation station. Since the T-3 research station had been Fletcher's idea, the floating island eventually became known as Fletcher's Ice Island. Later that year, the C-47 that made the polar landing crashed on Fletcher's Ice Island and is now at the bottom of the Arctic Ocean.

DASSAULT FALCON FLIES FOR THE FIRST TIME

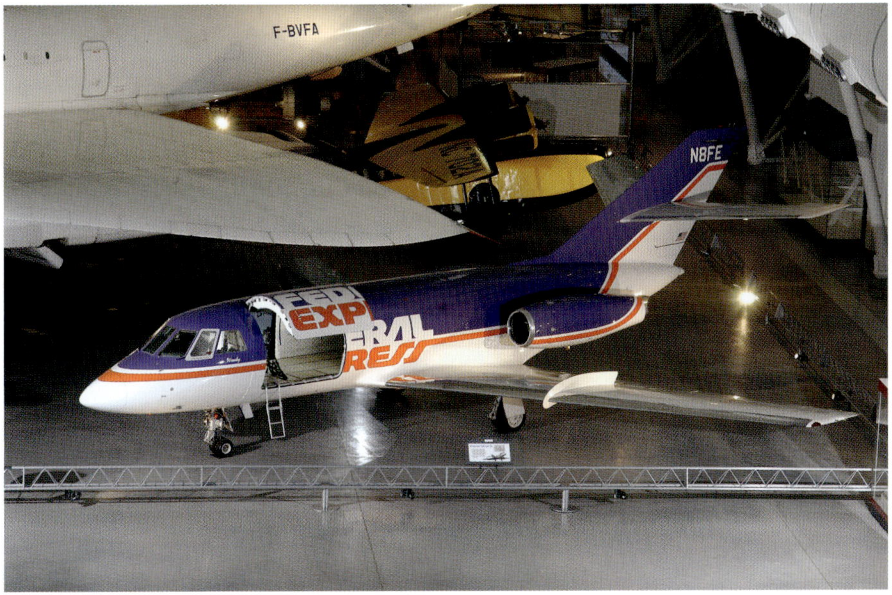

The Dassault Falcon on display at the Steven F. Udvar-Hazy Center carried the first Federal Express air express package.

Smithsonian's National Air and Space Museum

When Federal Express needed a small jet aircraft to carry packages for its new air express in the early 1970s, the company turned to the Dassault Falcon. Flying for the first time on May 4, 1963, the Falcon was the commercial version of the famous Mystere fighter aircraft and the first business jet developed by the French firm Dassault Aviation. Although marketed as an executive aircraft in competition with Learjet and other private business travel companies, the Falcon quickly became a prime candidate for the new package service.

The Falcon offered many advantages for Federal Express (which is today known simply as FedEx). With a top speed of 535 miles per hour, the aircraft was fast, allowing the company to offer overnight delivery. The Falcon could also be converted for the specialized needs of package delivery and was small enough to reduce the risk of carrying uneconomical loads during the company's first months of operation. Formally launched in April 1973, this package service was an immediate success. Within a year and a half, more than thirty Falcons were flying the spokes of the Federal Express delivery network.

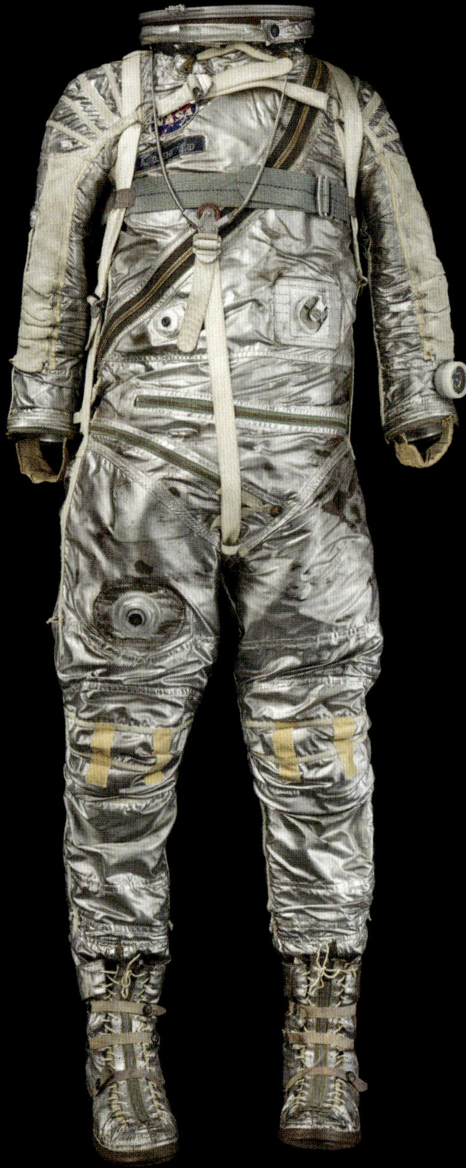

ALAN SHEPARD BECOMES FIRST AMERICAN IN SPACE

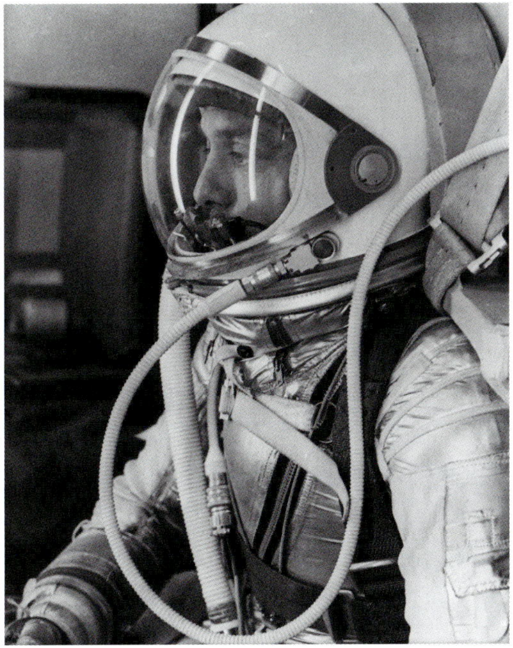

Navy test pilot and NASA astronaut Alan B. Shepard Jr. became the first American to travel to space on May 5, 1961. His historic mission in the *Freedom 7* capsule came a little over three weeks after the Soviet Union launched Yuri Gagarin aboard his Vostok spacecraft as the first person in space (see page 85). While Gagarin's spaceflight lasted 108 minutes and included a single orbit around Earth, Shepard's flight was a suborbital parabola and lasted fifteen minutes.

To launch Shepard, NASA turned to existing military ballistic missiles, modifying a U.S. Army Redstone rocket. NASA designed the Mercury capsule for a water landing, with a parachute that deployed at 24,500 feet to begin slowing the spacecraft.

Shepard's flight was a triumph, not least because it had been conducted live on national television and in front of the world press. In contrast, Gagarin's mission was only announced after it was completed safely. In the days after Shepard's successful spaceflight, he was honored with ticker-tape parades in D.C., New York, and Los Angeles, and received the NASA Distinguished Service Medal from President John F. Kennedy.

"I'm a hell of a lot cooler than you guys. Why don't you just fix your little problem and light this candle?"

—ALAN SHEPARD, IMPATIENTLY AWAITING THE LAUNCH OF HIS MERCURY MISSION

OPPOSITE PAGE Mercury astronauts wore a modified version of a U.S. Navy Mark IV flight suit. Alan Shepard's spacesuit is in the collection of the National Air and Space Museum.

Smithsonian's National Air and Space Museum

ABOVE Shepard became a national hero after his historic spaceflight.

NASA

MAY 6

HINDENBURG BURSTS INTO FLAMES

LIGHTER-THAN-AIR FLIGHT

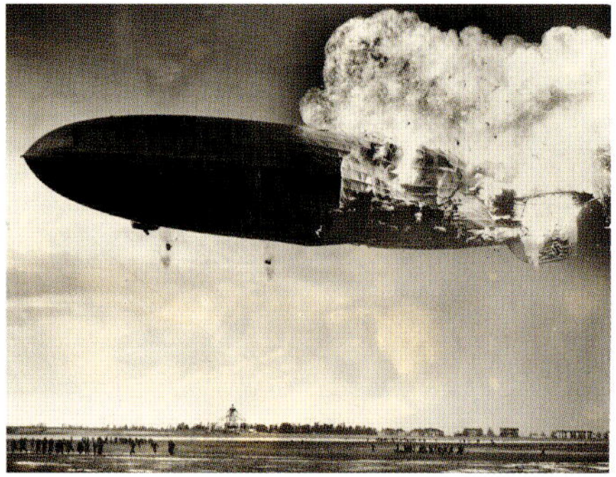

When the *Hindenburg* burst into flames, Navy sailors preparing to grab tether lines had to run for safety.

Smithsonian's National Air and Space Museum (NASM 73-8701)

At 7:25 P.M. on May 6, 1937, the German airship LZ 129 *Hindenburg* burst into flames. The fiery disaster began when the airship was attempting to moor at Naval Air Station Lakehurst in New Jersey. According to post-crash reports, hydrogen from a leaking gas cell mixed with outside oxygen and a spark, possibly from static electricity, set off the conflagration that consumed the airship. Of the ninety-seven people onboard, thirty-five died in the accident, as did one member of the ground crew. The *Hindenburg* fire marked the beginning of the end of the airship era and remains one of the most famous disasters in aviation history.

MAY 7

SPACE SHUTTLE *ENDEAVOUR* LAUNCHES FOR THE FIRST TIME

HUMAN SPACEFLIGHT

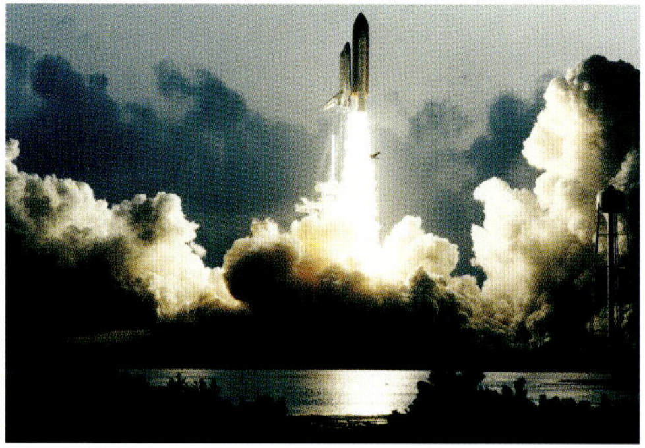

Space Shuttle *Endeavour* was the final Space Shuttle to make its debut.

NASA

On May 7, 1992, NASA's fifth and final operational Space Shuttle made its debut when the orbiter *Endeavour* launched from Kennedy Space Center in Florida. NASA built *Endeavour* as a replacement for *Challenger*, which had broken apart in a launch tragedy in January 1986. The orbiter was named for James Cook's HMS *Endeavour*, a name selected through a national competition that challenged students to propose a name based on a sea vessel. *Endeavour*'s first mission, STS-49, involved capturing, repairing, and redeploying the communications satellite INTELSAT VI.

NC-1, NC-3, AND NC-4 LEAVE ON FIRST TRANSATLANTIC FLIGHT

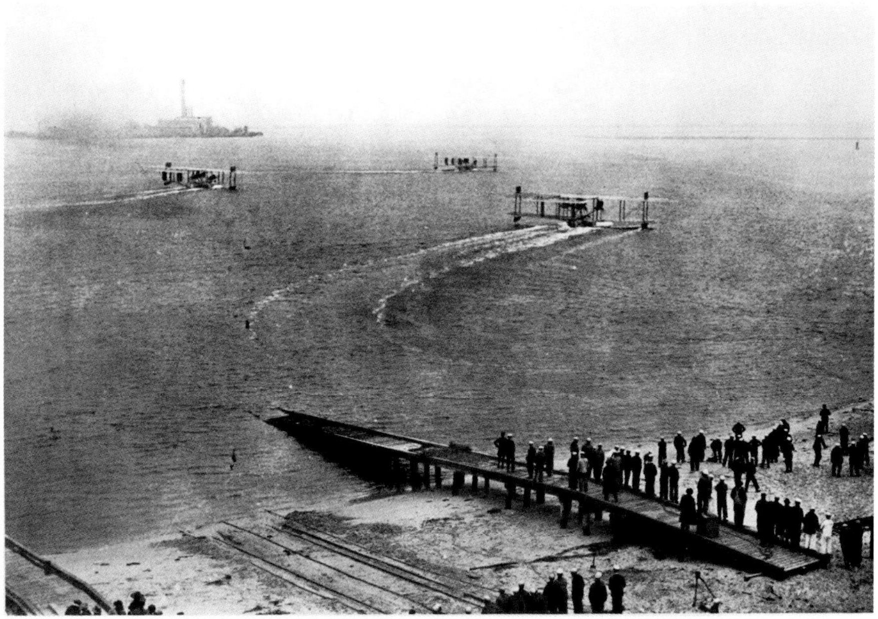

A sizable crowd gathered at Rockaway Beach to watch the NC flying boats leave for their transatlantic flight.

Smithsonian's National Air and Space Museum (NASM A-38529-A)

Though Charles Lindbergh achieved international fame as the first pilot to fly nonstop solo across the Atlantic Ocean in 1927 (see page 155), it was a U.S. Navy mission some eight years earlier that achieved the first transatlantic flight. Three Curtiss flying boats, each with a crew of six, were involved in the historic flight: NC-1, NC-3, and NC-4. The NC class of flying boats was intended to meet a U.S. Navy requirement for extended range aircraft for anti-submarine patrol. In authorizing the transatlantic flight, the Navy wanted to prove the capability of the airplane as a transoceanic weapon and technology.

The five-leg flight began on May 8, 1919, at the naval air station at Rockaway Beach, New York. After taking off, the aircraft followed a route that took them to Nova Scotia; Newfoundland; the Azores; Lisbon, Portugal; and Portsmouth, England. Only one airplane—the NC-4, commanded by Albert C. Read—completed the entire crossing, arriving at its destination twenty-four days after departing.

DRAGANFLYER X4-ES DRONE LOCATES INJURED ACCIDENT VICTIM

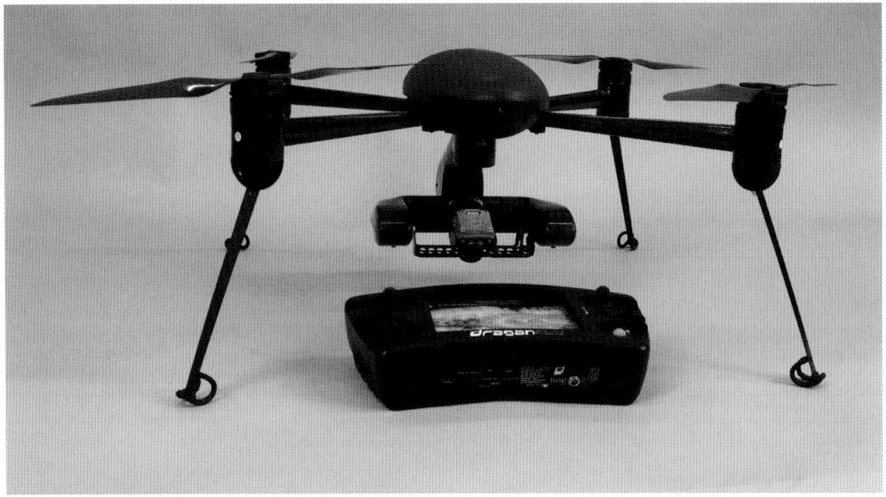

A drone that was used to locate an injured driver in Saskatchewan in 2013 is in the collection of the National Air and Space Museum.

Smithsonian's National Air and Space Museum

When officers from the Royal Canadian Mounted Police (RCMP) in Saskatchewan came upon a single car accident on the night of May 9, 2013, the vehicle's driver was nowhere to be seen. Though the crash victim had called emergency services, the officers could not identify the person's location. A search of the immediate vicinity proved unsuccessful, as did an aerial night vision search by an Air Ambulance helicopter. Knowing the person could be injured, the officers needed to locate them quickly.

That's when the RCMP officers turned to an unusual source for help. Using a Draganflyer X4-ES drone equipped with an infrared camera, the RCMP searched the area of the call's GPS coordinates and were able to pick up a heat signature for the driver, who was curled up near a snowbank and unresponsive. He was taken to the hospital, where he recovered from his injuries.

MAY 10

BRUCE PETERSON CRASHES THE M2-F2 LIFTING BODY

MODERN MILITARY AVIATION

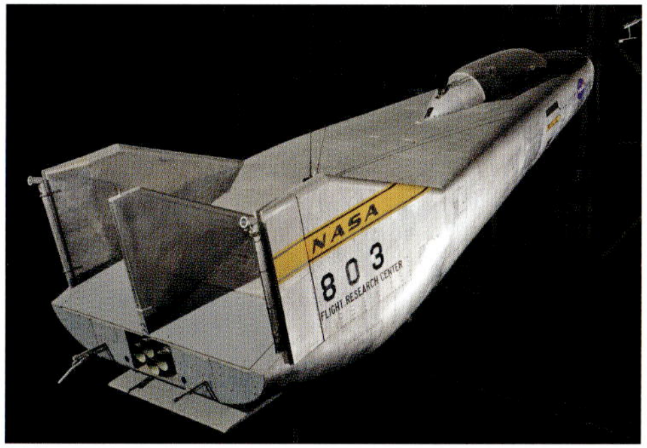

When the M2-F3 in the National Air and Space Museum's collection was rebuilt from the wrecked M2-F2, a third vertical stabilizer was added.

Smithsonian's National Air and Space Museum

On May 10, 1967, NASA test pilot Bruce Peterson lost control of the M2-F2 lifting body he was piloting and crashed on landing, rolling a half dozen times. Peterson was seriously injured and lost sight in one eye due to infection, but he did eventually recover. The accident inspired the television series *The Six Million Dollar Man*, which used footage of the crash landing in its opening credits. Though Peterson wasn't rebuilt with machine parts like the television show's title character Steve Austin, the aircraft he crashed was and received the new designation of M2-F3.

MAY 11

THEODORE VON KÁRMÁN IS BORN

SPACE SCIENCE

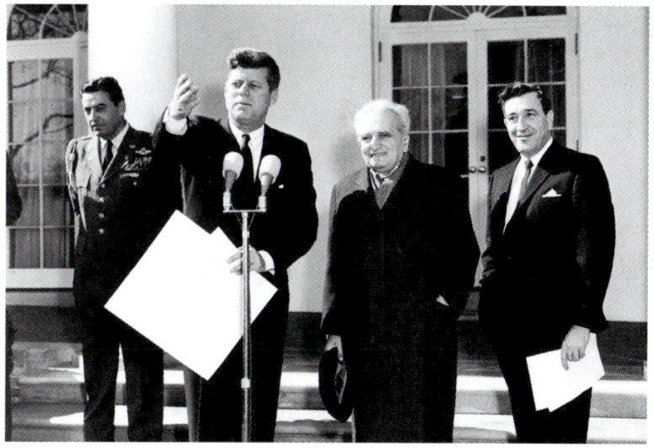

President John F. Kennedy awarded Theodore von Kármán the National Medal of Science in 1963.

Abbie Rowe. White House Photographs. John F. Kennedy Presidential Library and Museum, Boston

The Karman line is the boundary between Earth's atmosphere and space as recognized by the Fédération Aéronautique Internationale (World Air Sports Federation). The line is 100 kilometers (sixty-two miles) above sea level and is named for Hungarian scientist Theodore von Kármán. Von Kármán, born on May 11, 1881, was an accomplished physicist, aerospace engineer, applied mathematician, and science advisor. In 1930, he was appointed as director of the Daniel Guggenheim Aeronautical Laboratory at the California Institute of Technology and in 1944 helped found the Jet Propulsion Laboratory at Caltech, becoming its first director.

SOVIET UNION ENDS BLOCKADE OF WEST BERLIN

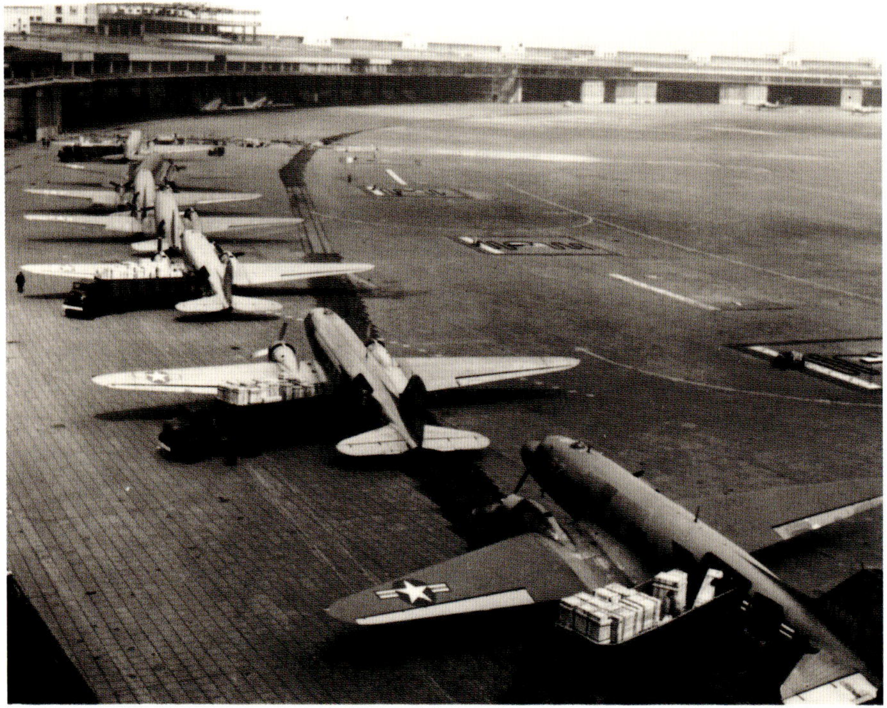

The first aircraft to deliver supplies to West Berlin as part of the Berlin Airlift were Douglas C-47 cargo planes. The C-47 was eventually replaced in that role by the larger Douglas C-54.

Smithsonian's National Air and Space Museum (NASM 86-12548)

In June 1948, the Soviet Union closed all surface routes into the western zone of Berlin, hoping to force the United States, Great Britain, and France to abandon the German city. Rather than retreat or start a military action, however, the Allies responded in a way that was only possible due to aviation—an airlift. Code-named "Operation Vittles," the airlift began landing transport planes in West Berlin within days of the Soviet blockade.

For eighteen months, American and British aircrews flew around the clock, bringing over 2.3 million tons of coal, food, medicine, and other necessities of life to the two million inhabitants of West Berlin. Despite nearly impossible odds, the Berlin Airlift succeeded in winning the first battle of the Cold War. On May 12, 1949, the Soviet Union called off its blockade of Berlin and reopened ground routes to the city. The airlift continued until September 1949 to ensure that Berlin would survive the winter if the Soviets resumed the blockade.

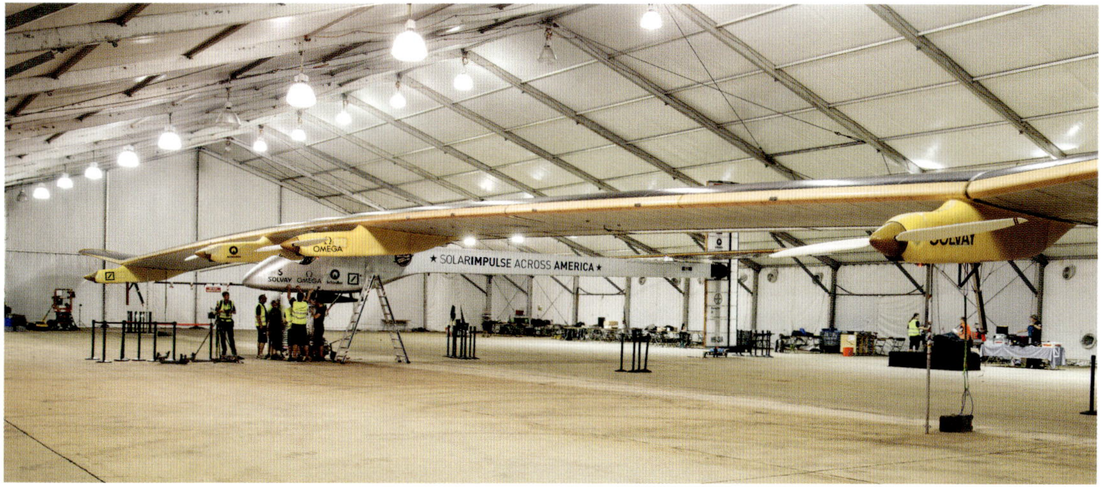

Solar Impulse 1 stopped at the Steven F. Udvar-Hazy Center during a transcontinental flight in 2013.

Smithsonian's National Air and Space Museum

In 2003, a team of Swiss entrepreneurs, engineers, pilots, and enthusiasts began designing a new electric aircraft. Their goal was to demonstrate that it was possible to fly an aircraft both day and night using only solar electricity. Known as Solar Impulse 1, the completed solar-powered aircraft had a wingspan of 200 feet—wider than a Boeing 777—and could fly at very slow speeds for up to thirty-six hours. Over eleven thousand individual solar cells powered the aircraft. Stored in onboard batteries, the electricity these cells generated turned propellers attached to four 10-horsepower electric motors when the Solar Impulse was in flight.

On May 13, 2011, engineer André Borschberg completed Solar Impulse 1's first international flight, traveling thirteen hours from Switzerland to Belgium. The team's ultimate goal was to eventually complete an around-the-world flight. While this wasn't achieved by Solar Impulse 1, its successor, Solar Impulse 2, did successfully circumnavigate the globe in 2015.

UNITED STATES' FIRST SPACE STATION LAUNCHES

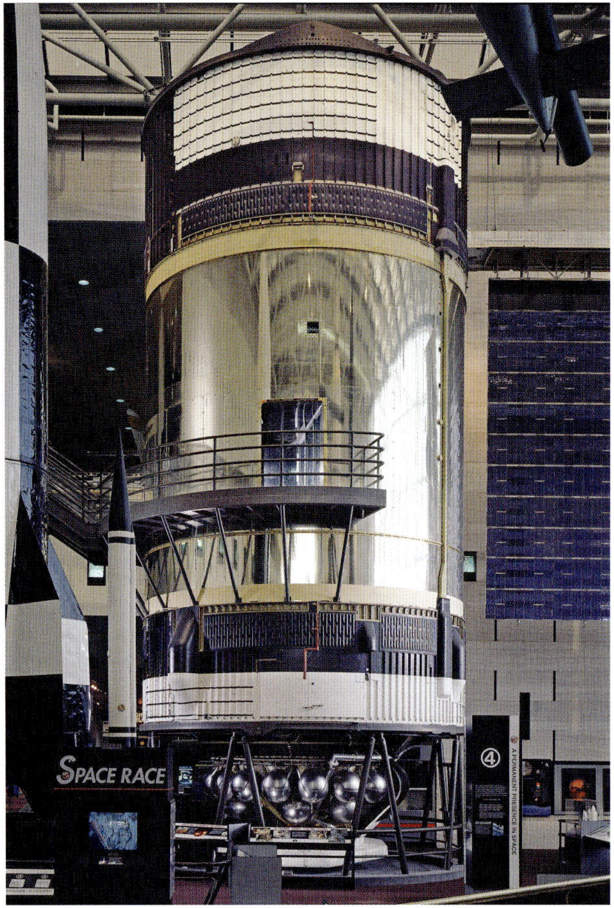

Before the International Space Station, the United States had a space station called Skylab. After the Apollo missions to the Moon, NASA used the last of its Apollo-era equipment to launch the first U.S. space station. On top of a Saturn IB, Skylab launched into orbit on May 14, 1973, and was intended as a temporary home in space. The space station was occupied on three missions in 1973 and 1974, each with a crew of three astronauts. The longest of these missions lasted over eighty days.

During the three Skylab missions, astronauts operated an attached solar observatory (the Apollo Telescope Mount), made Earth and astronomical observations, conducted microgravity and biomedical experiments, completed EVA maintenance and repair tasks, and proved how productively they could work in space. After the final Skylab mission, NASA powered the space station down, hoping to boost the orbit and reuse it once Space Shuttle orbiters came online in a few years. However, that program was delayed and Skylab drifted for five years. In 1979, it was deorbited in a controlled descent (see page 209).

Two complete Skylab space stations were manufactured and equipped for flight. The backup orbital workshop is on display at the National Air and Space Museum.

Smithsonian's National Air and Space Museum

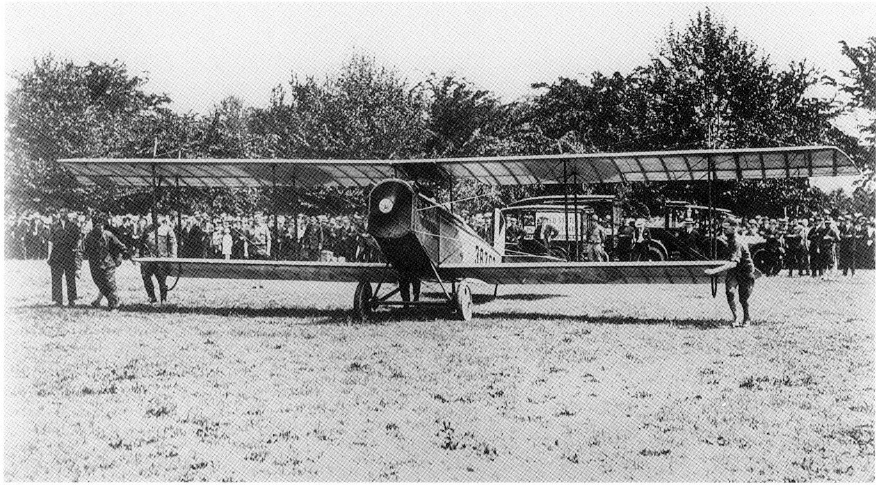

Army pilots flew Curtis JN-4H airplanes for the first U.S. airmail service.

National Postal Museum

When officials at the U.S. Post Office Department decided to use airplanes to carry mail in the late 1910s, they turned to U.S. Army Maj. Reuben Fleet for help. Using airplanes and crew provided by the Army, Fleet organized the first U.S. airmail service, which was officially inaugurated with a series of flights between New York and Washington, D.C., on May 15, 1918.

Despite Fleet's preparations, old-fashioned nepotism impeded the project. Lt. George Boyle used his connections as the son-in-law-to-be of the Interstate Commerce Commissioner to secure a spot as one of six pilots for the new airmail route. With only sixty flying hours in his logbook, Boyle's journey on the first flight out of Washington did not go as planned. The inexperienced pilot quickly got lost on the way to Philadelphia, ran out of fuel, and crashed less than twenty-five miles from Washington. Though Boyle survived the crash, his second airmail flight resulted in more wrong turns and another emergency landing, after which he was removed from the pilot list. Thankfully, the other airmail pilots who joined Boyle that first day fared much better on their flights, and the U.S. successfully began a service that would have important implications for aviation.

MAY 16

WINGS WINS BEST PICTURE AT FIRST ACADEMY AWARDS

WORLD WAR I AND INTERWAR MILITARY AVIATION

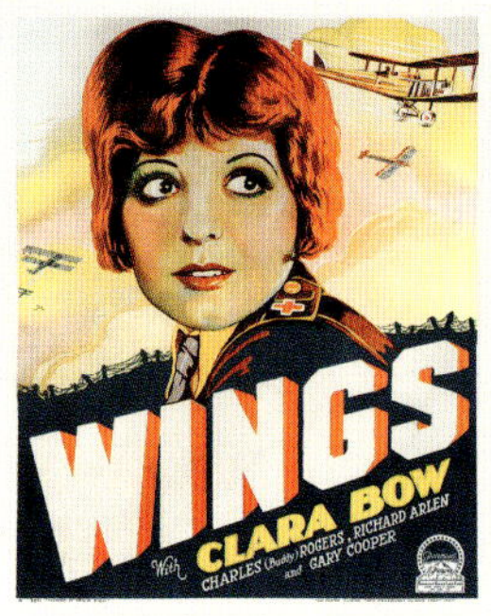

Wings set the standard for what an aviation film could and should be.

Paramount Famous Lasky Corporation

On May 16, 1929, the first Academy Award for Best Picture was awarded to the World War I aviation film *Wings*. Released just a few months after Charles Lindbergh's transatlantic flight (see page 155), the silent film capitalized on the public's feverish enthusiasm for flight. *Wings* received instant acclaim, and the cast was a who's who of early Hollywood legends, including Clara Bow, Buddy Rogers, Richard Arlen, and Gary Cooper. With its incredible aerial combat scenes, *Wings* also set the standard for other aviation films. Director William Wellman was an actual World War I fighter pilot, giving the film a skillful hand with the subject matter.

MAY 17

MOONEY M-18C MITE MAKES FIRST TEST FLIGHT

GENERAL AVIATION

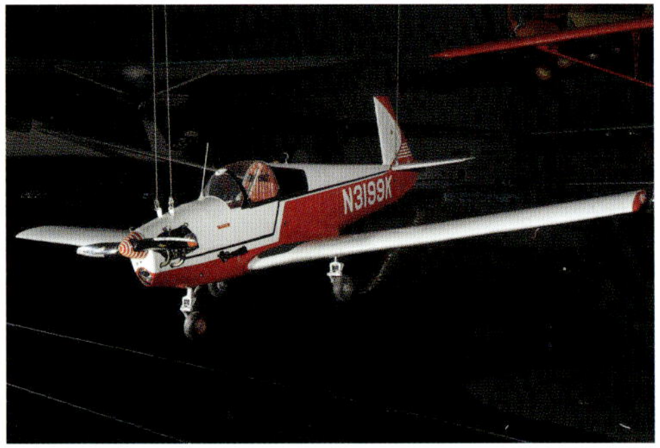

The Mooney Mite on display at the Steven F. Udvar-Hazy Center was the first aircraft of the series to be built.

Smithsonian's National Air and Space Museum

Produced between 1947 and 1955, the Mooney M-18 Mite was designed to be a fast and economical means of personal transportation for businessmen and private pilots. Produced by Mooney Aircraft, the Mite was the first in the company's successful line of private and corporate airplanes. Test pilot Bill Taylor flew the Mite on its inaugural flight on May 17, 1947. The compact, single-seat monoplane boasted retractable landing gear and wing flaps, new amenities for personal planes of that era. Pilots in search of a small but quick airplane appreciated the Mite's performance and maneuverability.

JACQUELINE COCHRAN FLIES FASTER THAN THE SPEED OF SOUND

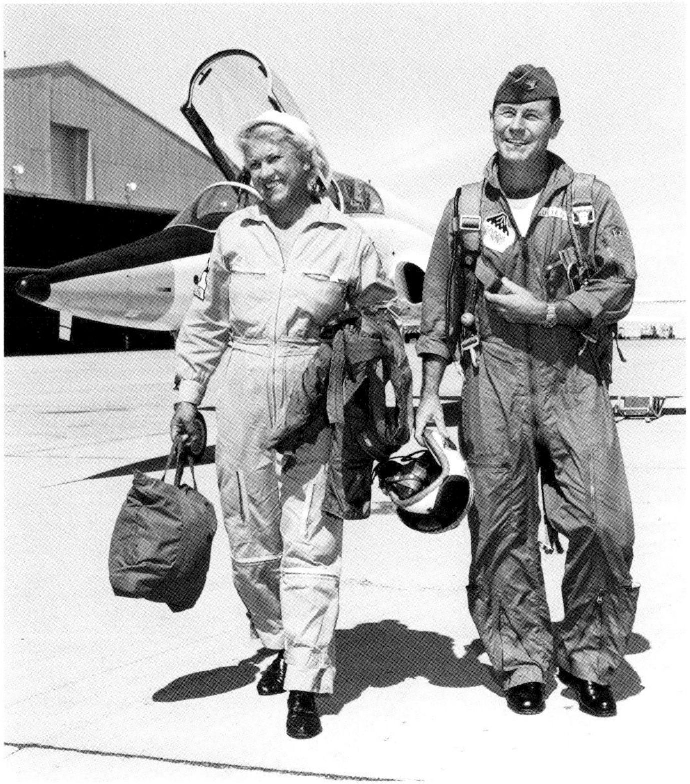

Aviation icon Chuck Yeager supported Jacqueline Cochran's many record-setting flights throughout her career.

U.S. Air Force

During her career as a pilot, Jacqueline "Jackie" Cochran broke records left and right. At the time of her death in 1980, the aviator held more speed, altitude, and distance records than any male or female pilot in history. Cochran was also the first woman to fly faster than the speed of sound and the first woman to fly twice the speed of sound.

To achieve the former record, Cochran first borrowed a Canadair F-86 Sabre jet, a military aircraft ordinarily not available to civilian, let alone female, pilots. Coached by Charles "Chuck" Yeager (see page 59), Cochran flew the F-86 on a closed circuit at Edwards Air Force Base on May 18, 1953, becoming the first woman to break the sound barrier. Nearly a decade later, she became the first woman to fly Mach 2 (twice the speed of sound) at the controls of a U.S. Air Force Lockheed F-104 Starfighter.

ED DWIGHT FINALLY MAKES IT TO SPACE

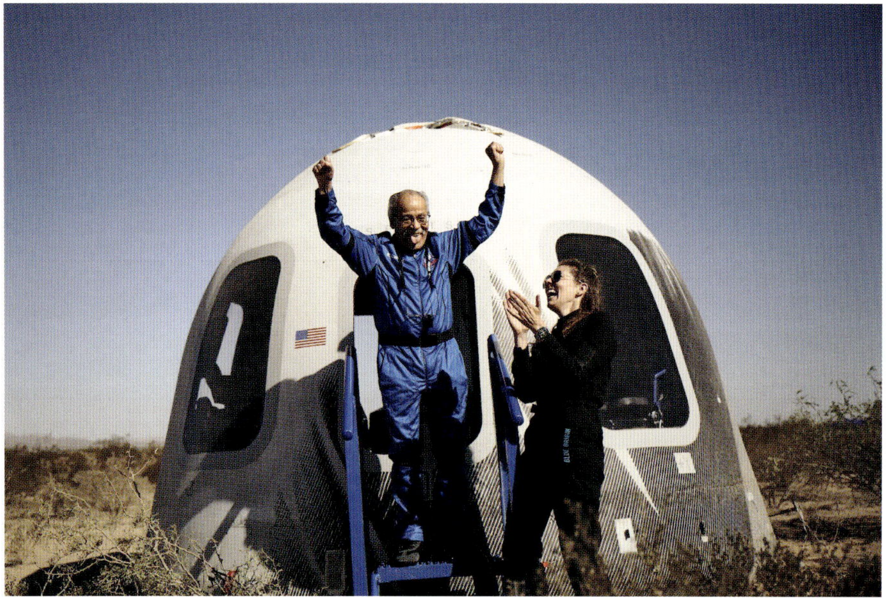

Edward Dwight flew to space on Blue Origin's RSS *First Step* crew capsule.

Blue Origin

The oldest person to travel to space so far, retired U.S. Air Force test pilot and prolific sculptor Edward "Ed" Dwight, launched at the age of ninety on May 19, 2024. Dwight's path to space was a long one. In 1963, at the request of the Kennedy Administration, Dwight joined the U.S. Air Force's Aerospace Research Pilot School, which was understood to be a pipeline to NASA's astronaut corps. Many expected him to become the country's first Black astronaut candidate. NASA even featured Dwight in public affairs campaigns. Dwight, however, left the Air Force in 1966—his dreams of space thwarted by a culture of exclusion.

In 2024, Dwight finally made it to space, riding on a suborbital mission on Blue Origin's New Shepard crew capsule RSS *First Step*. Dwight's spaceflight on the NS-25 mission was sponsored by Space for Humanity, a nonprofit organization dedicated to expanding humanity's access to space.

CHARLES LINDBERGH DEPARTS ON FIRST SOLO NONSTOP TRANSATLANTIC FLIGHT

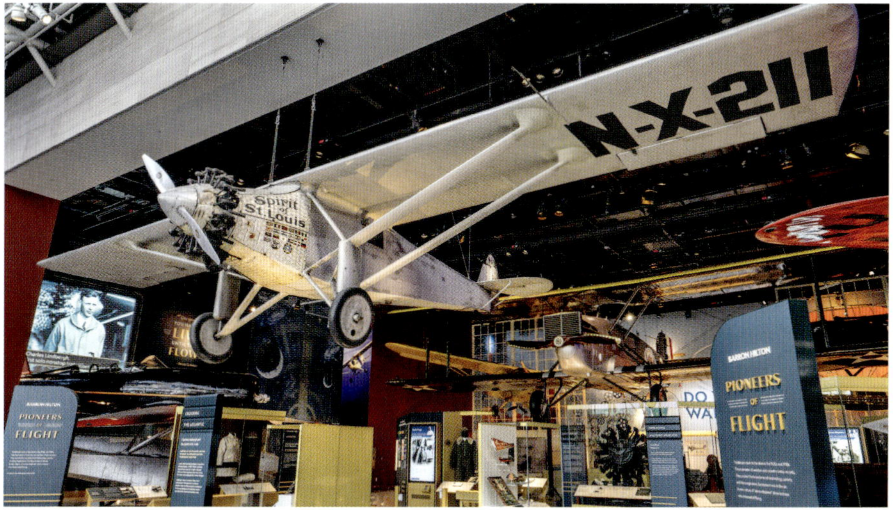

Charles Lindbergh's *Spirit of St. Louis* is on display at the National Air and Space Museum.

Smithsonian's National Air and Space Museum

On May 20, 1927, Charles Lindbergh departed Roosevelt Field on Long Island, New York, for a historic journey that changed his life. Thirty-three hours later, a crowd of 150,000 greeted the former airmail pilot and barnstormer as he landed his Ryan NYP *Spirit of St. Louis* at Le Bourget Field near Paris, France. Only twenty-five years old, Lindbergh was the first person to complete a solo, nonstop flight across the Atlantic Ocean.

Returning to the United States the following month, Lindbergh received a hero's welcome. The young pilot then took the *Spirit of St. Louis* on tour around the U. S. and Latin America (see page 313). The transatlantic flight and goodwill tour made Lindbergh a celebrity and established him as the face of aviation. The flights also began the "Lindbergh boom," causing interest in flying to skyrocket and aircraft industry stocks to explode in value.

DID YOU KNOW? Because the *Spirit of St. Louis* didn't have a front windshield, Lindbergh used a periscope or stuck his head out the window while banking the aircraft to see. These maneuvers also helped the young pilot stay awake during the long flight!

MAY 21

AMELIA EARHART BECOMES FIRST WOMAN TO FLY SOLO NONSTOP ACROSS THE ATLANTIC

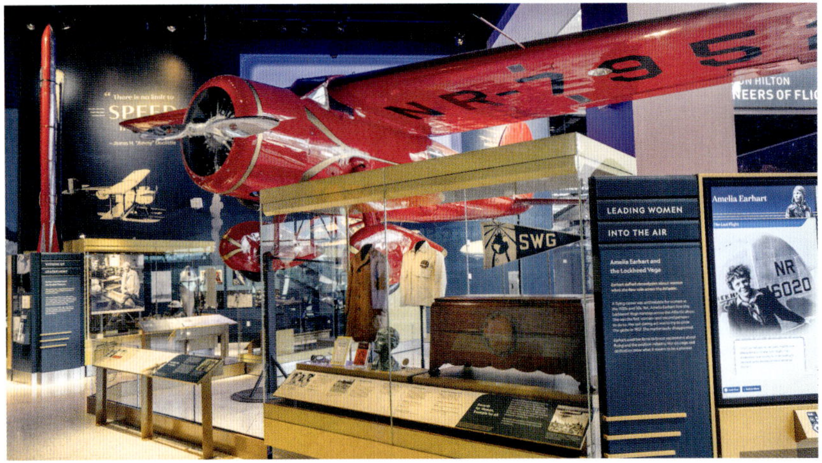

LEFT Amelia Earhart's Lockheed Vega is on display at the National Air and Space Museum alongside other artifacts from her life and career.

Smithsonian's National Air and Space Museum

OPPOSITE PAGE Earhart's record-setting flights in the 1930s made her one of the most famous pilots ever.

Smithsonian's National Air and Space Museum (NASM 80-11038)

In the year after Charles Lindbergh's historic transatlantic flight, another aviation celebrity began her journey to fame over the Atlantic Ocean. As a passenger onboard a flight from Newfoundland to Wales in 1928, Amelia Earhart became the first woman to cross the Atlantic by airplane. Using the international attention from this flight, Earhart launched her own aviation career in earnest and began traveling around the United States to speak, write, and fly.

Determined to prove herself and earn the respect of other pilots, Earhart decided to cross the Atlantic Ocean again, but this time she would fly the plane—solo. Taking off from Newfoundland, Earhart fought fatigue, a leaky fuel tank, and flames spewing out the side of her Lockheed Vega's engine cowling during the nearly fifteen-hour flight. At one point, ice formed on the airplane's wings and caused a dramatic descent to just above the waves. Realizing she was on a course far north of France, Earhart eventually landed in a farmer's field near Londonderry, Northern Ireland. When she touched down on May 21, 1932, Earhart became the first woman, and second person, to fly solo nonstop across the Atlantic.

DID YOU KNOW? Amelia Earhart's solo flight across the Atlantic was five years to the day after Charles Lindbergh's transatlantic flight (both left on May 20 and arrived at their destinations on May 21).

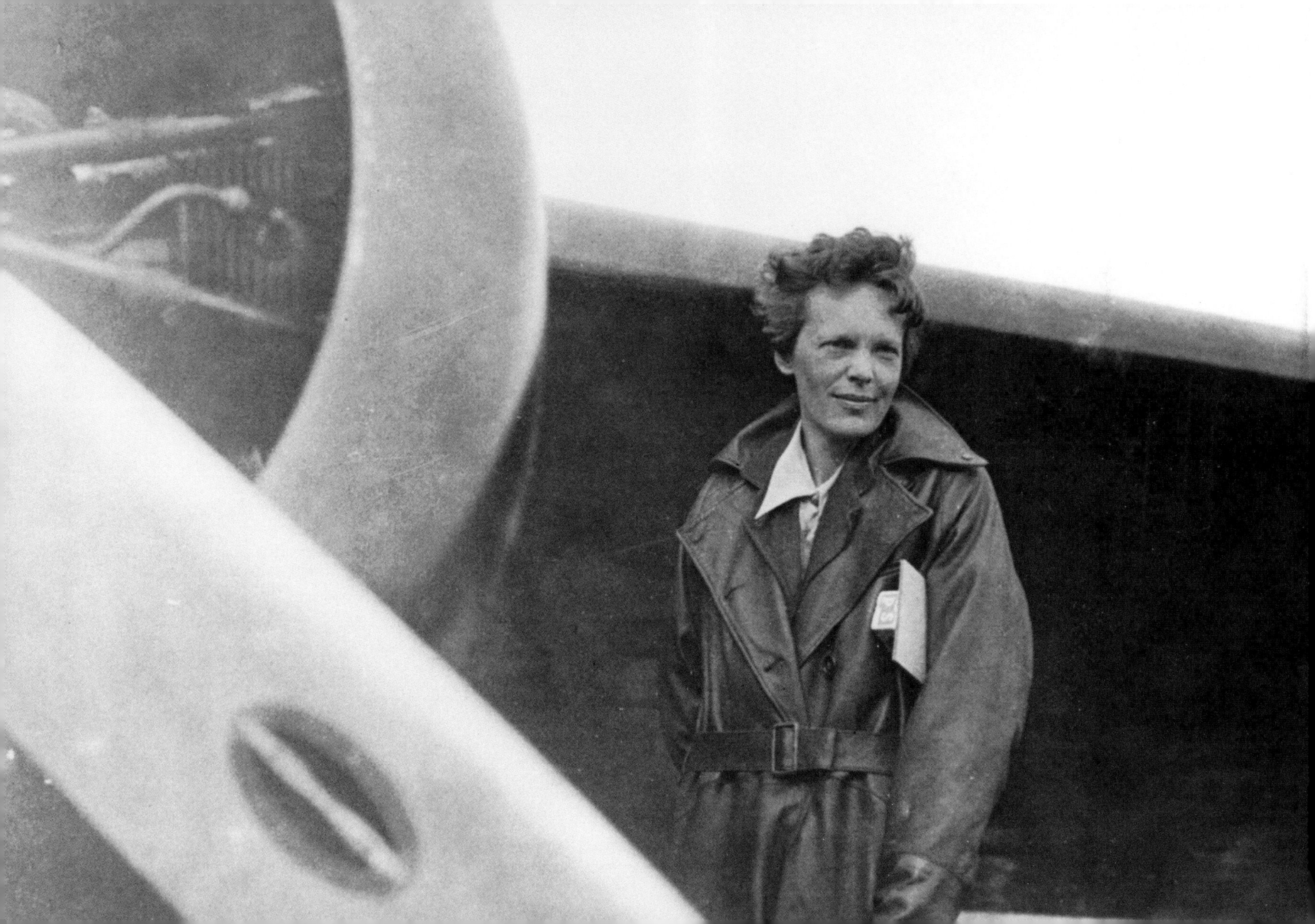

U.S. MARINE CORPS AVIATION BEGINS

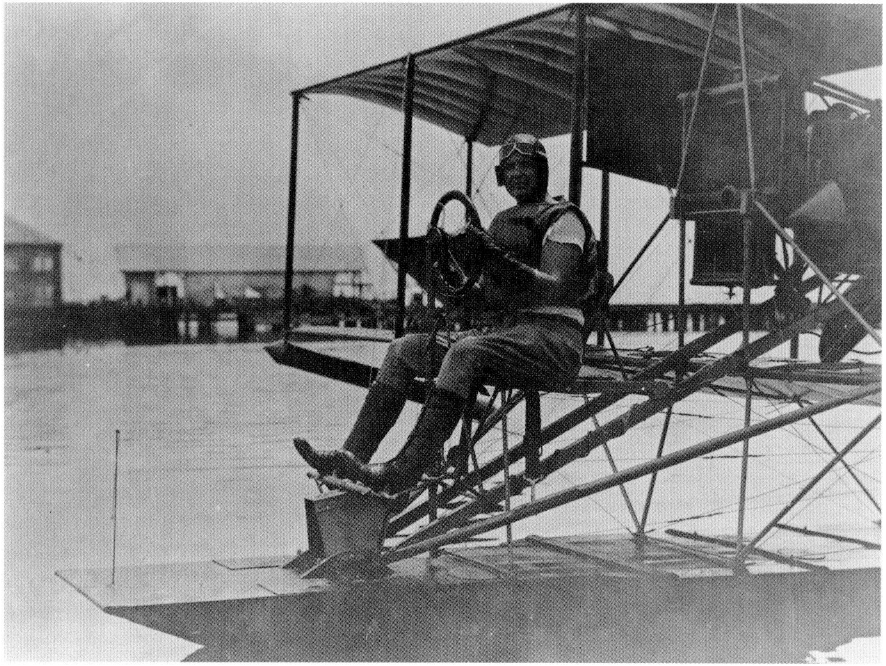

Alfred Cunningham, pictured in a Curtiss Hydroaeroplane in 1914, was the first Marine aviator.

Smithsonian's National Air and Space Museum (NASM 00156091)

Lt. Alfred A. Cunningham is widely considered to be the "Father of Marine Corps Aviation." Cunningham became interested in aviation soon after joining the Marines in 1909. Writing to the Marines' Advanced Base Force in 1912, he recommended that the school purchase airplanes. When military officials suggested that Marine Corps officers should be sent to train at the Navy's flying school, Cunningham reported to the aviation camp at the U.S. Naval Academy in Annapolis, Maryland, on May 22, 1912, and Marine Corps aviation was born.

Cunningham first took flight at the Burgess and Curtiss aircraft factory in Massachusetts a few months after reporting to Annapolis. During the year that followed, the Marine officer made four hundred sorties (military missions) in a Curtiss Model B-1, instructing others and working through tactics of air operations. From these modest beginnings, the Marine Corps built a formidable flying force that has engaged in combat throughout the world.

MAY 23

JAPAN LAUNCHES SEVENTH OPERATION KIKUSUI KAMIKAZE ATTACK

WORLD WAR II MILITARY AVIATION

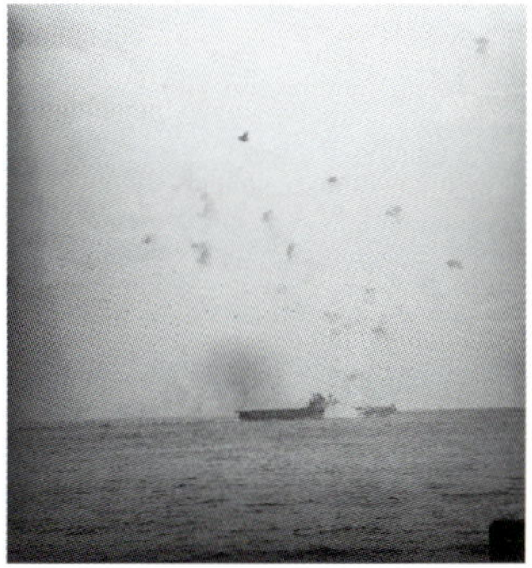

Kamikaze attacks damaged hundreds of Allied vessels during the Battle of Okinawa, including USS *Enterprise* (CV-6).

U.S. Navy Naval History and Heritage Command

During the United States' invasion of Okinawa from April to June 1945, vicious battles raged on the land, in the air, and at sea. Japanese forces struck back against the American ships surrounding the island with kamikaze planes. In these suicide air attacks, Japanese pilots flew directly into warships to damage and destroy them. Japanese forces launched a total of ten coordinated kamikaze assaults, known collectively as Operation Kikusui, during the Battle of Okinawa. Operation Kikusui VII began on May 23, 1945, and succeeded in sinking one American transport and damaging an escort carrier.

MAY 24

SCOTT CARPENTER LAUNCHES IN *AURORA 7*

HUMAN SPACEFLIGHT

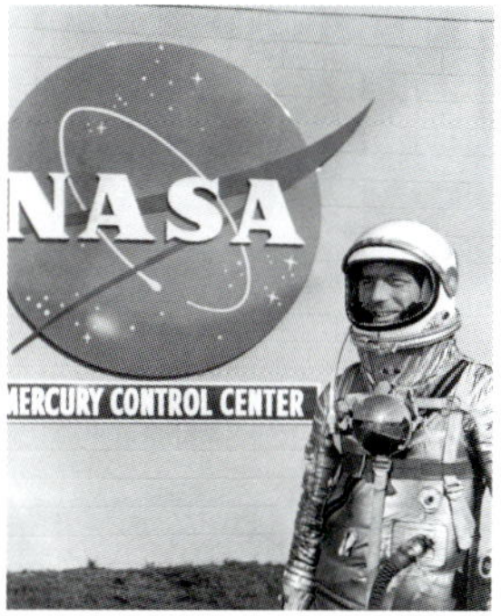

Scott Carpenter's trip aboard *Aurora 7* was his first and only spaceflight.

NASA

At the conclusion of NASA astronaut M. Scott Carpenter's May 24, 1962, spaceflight, he splashed down in the Atlantic Ocean near the U.S. Virgin Islands—and then had to wait for his ride. The fourth American in space and second to orbit, Carpenter's spaceflight on *Aurora 7* lasted nearly five hours. Due to a spacecraft alignment error when the retrorockets fired, Carpenter splashed down 250 miles off course. In the hour it took for the recovery ship to reach him, Carpenter climbed out of the capsule and waited in his life raft.

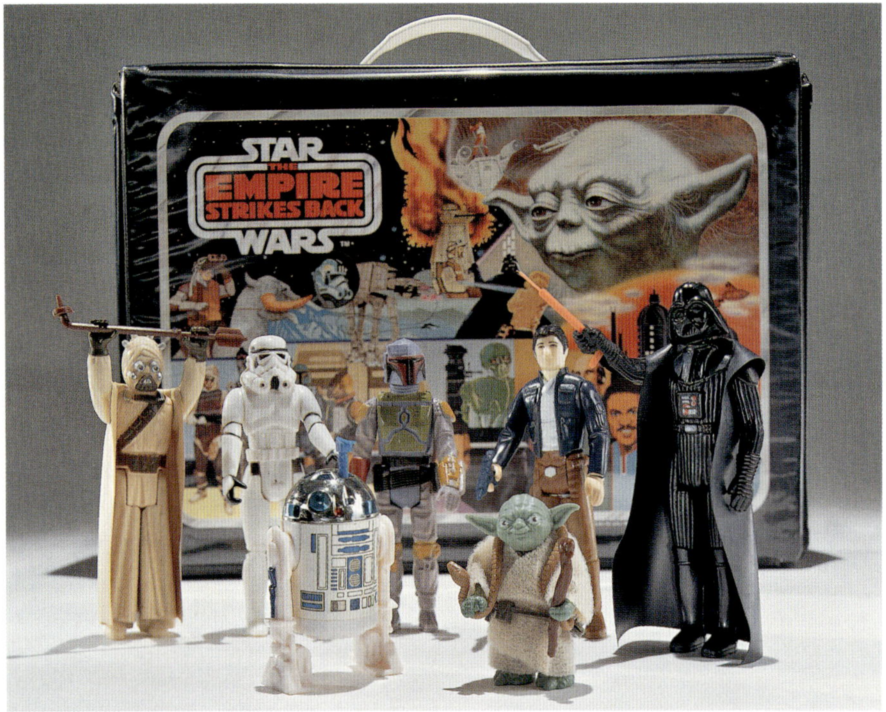

When the second *Star Wars* film was released in 1980, Lucasfilm and toy manufacturer Kenner were prepared for the merchandising boom, selling souvenirs like a set of toys now in the National Air and Space Museum collection.

Smithsonian's National Air and Space Museum

The first installment of George Lucas's famous *Star Wars* film franchise was released in theaters on May 25, 1977, becoming one of the biggest box office hits of all time. Though known today with the subtitle *A New Hope*, the first film in the series was just called *Star Wars* when it was released. Taking place in a galaxy far, far away, *Star Wars* revived the genre of space science fiction in the 1970s with a classic hero's journey told in the visual style popular in Westerns and war films of recent decades.

The original *Star Wars* trilogy revolutionized entertainment in other ways, giving rise to an innovative mass-marketing campaign for toys and other products that became an industry model. Through movie souvenirs, Lucas looked to strengthen the bond between filmgoers and the *Star Wars* universe beyond the theater, inspiring legions of children and adults to express interest in the film through the purchase of products. The hundreds of millions of dollars in revenue generated by *A New Hope* and its souvenirs resulted in a Hollywood first—a film's profits providing the financing for two sequels: *The Empire Strikes Back* (1980) and *Return of the Jedi* (1983).

APOLLO 10 COMMAND MODULE SPLASHES DOWN

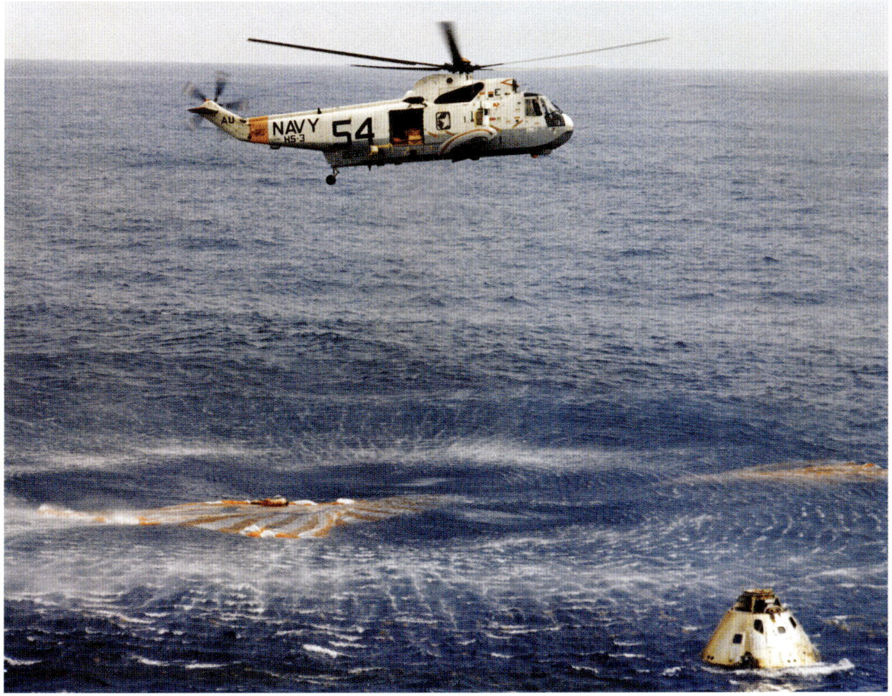

Thomas Stafford, John Young, and Eugene Cernan splashed down in the South Pacific at the conclusion of the successful Apollo 10 mission. The command module is now in the collection of the National Air and Space Museum.

NASA

The Apollo 10 mission in May 1969 served as a dress rehearsal for the first Moon landing a few months later. The mission plan staged all aspects of the Apollo 11 mission without actually landing on the Moon. Mission commander Thomas Stafford and lunar module pilot Eugene Cernan descended inside the lunar module to within eight miles of the lunar surface. Instead of landing, Apollo 10 performed a simulated abort that carried them away from the Moon.

This was the first flight of the lunar module in lunar orbit and the closest human approach to the Moon until Apollo 11 landed on the surface two months later. Nineteen color television transmissions (totaling five hours and fifty-two minutes) provided a global audience with the best exposure yet to spacecraft activities and spectacular views of the Earth and the Moon. The mission ended with splashdown on May 26, 1969, and with that, Apollo 11 was a go for the Moon.

DID YOU KNOW? Apollo 10's lunar module was nicknamed *Snoopy*, and the command module was *Charlie Brown.*

THE NACA TESTS FIRST AIRCRAFT IN FULL-SCALE WIND TUNNEL

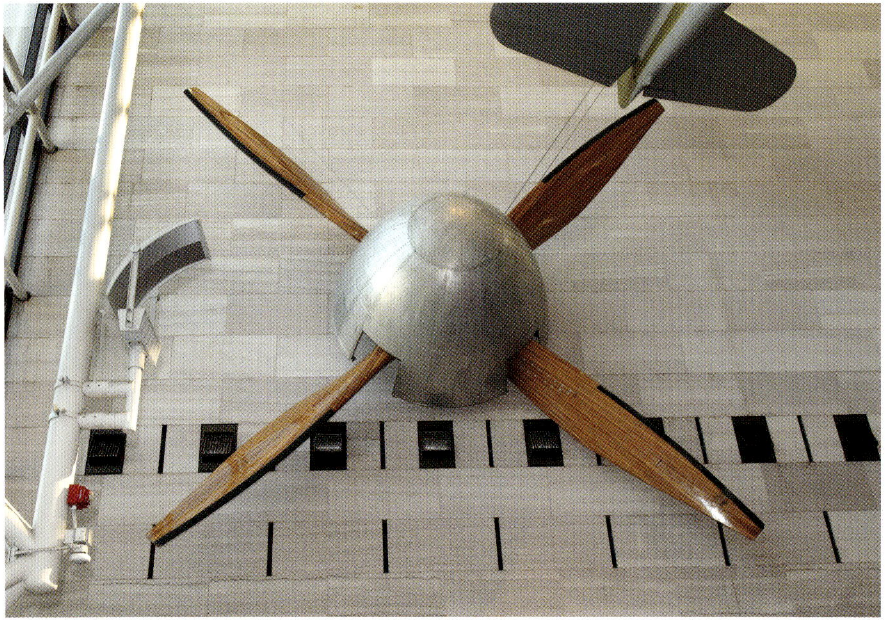

ABOVE The Full-Scale Wind Tunnel was demolished in 2011 and one of its fan assemblies is now on display at the National Air and Space Museum.

Smithsonian's National Air and Space Museum

OPPOSITE PAGE The first aircraft tested in the NACA Full-Scale Wind Tunnel was a Vought O3U-1 Corsair II.

NASA

On May 27, 1931, the National Advisory Committee for Aeronautics (NACA) placed a U.S. Navy Vought O3U-1 Corsair II in its Full-Scale Wind Tunnel at the Langley Memorial Aeronautical Laboratory in Hampton, Virginia. The first full-size aircraft tested in the tunnel, the Corsair II, was mounted on a test platform and began "flying" as its engines turned on. Though the airplane was stationary, wind produced by the tunnel's two 35.5-foot diameter blades blew over it at 120 miles per hour, allowing researchers to observe and measure sources of drag.

With a test section measuring thirty by sixty feet, the Langley Full-Scale Wind Tunnel held the record for the world's largest wind tunnel until 1944. The tunnel's size was so significant because it allowed engineers to conduct tests on actual airplanes, eliminating some of the uncertainty associated with testing scale models in smaller wind tunnels. From its opening in 1931 to its final run in 2011, the Full-Scale Wind Tunnel helped test and improve dozens of different American aircraft and spacecraft.

DID YOU KNOW? The NACA was the predecessor to NASA.

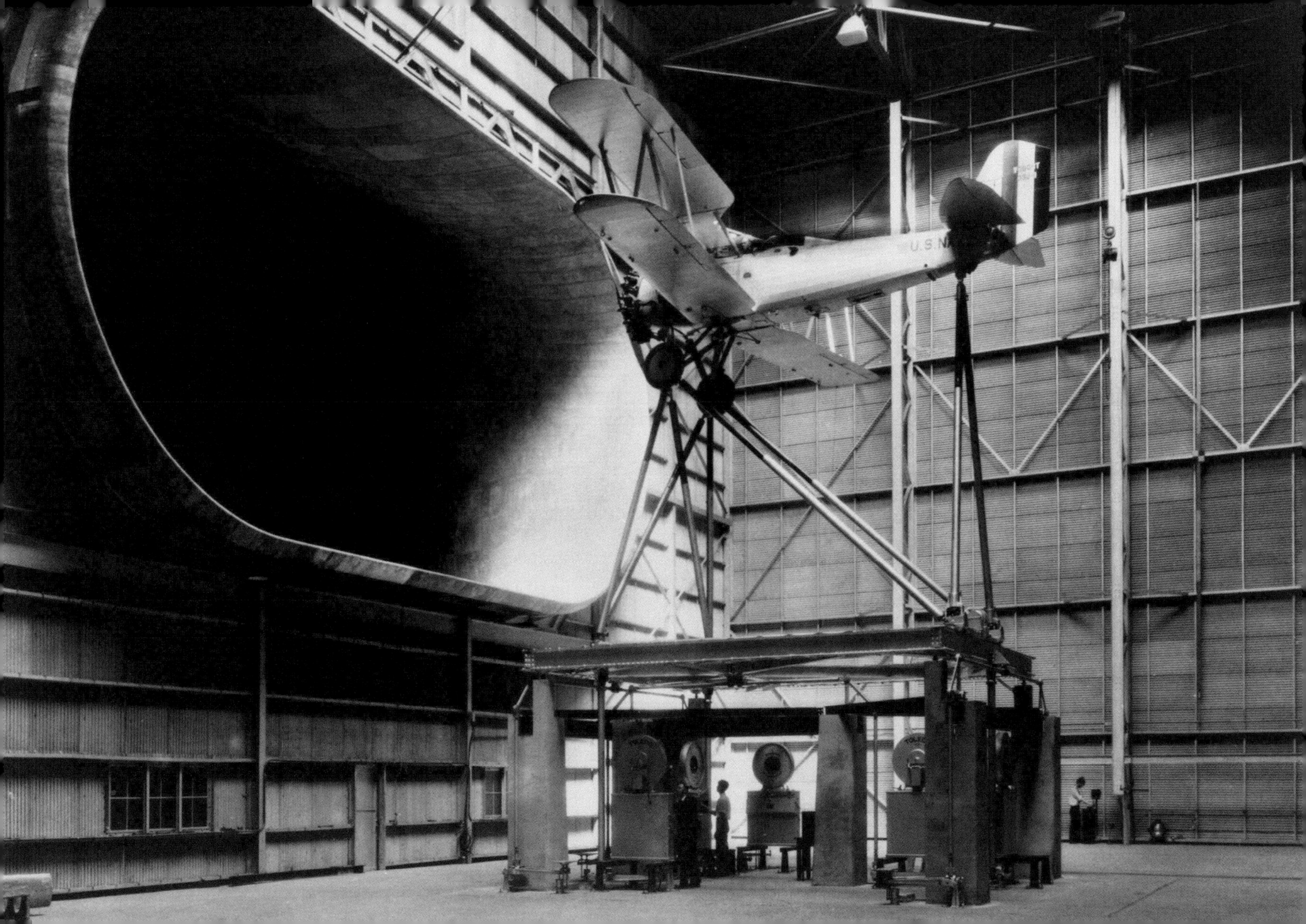
U.S.N

TWO MONKEYS LAUNCH INTO SPACE

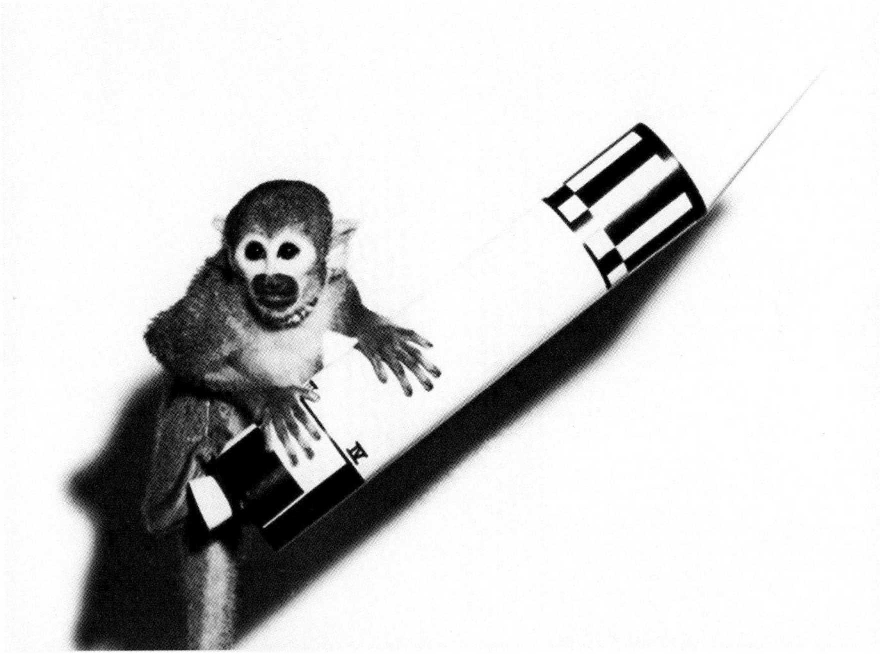

A squirrel monkey named Baker was one of two monkeys to fly to space.

Smithsonian's National Air and Space Museum (NASM 2003-4850)

On May 28, 1959, a rhesus monkey named Able and a squirrel monkey named Baker became the first American animals to travel to space and return safely. They were placed in separate space capsules in the nose cone of a Jupiter AM-18 rocket, secured by contour cradles made of fiberglass with sponge rubber lining specifically built for their bodies. The capsules had a life support system that included oxygen, moisture and carbon dioxide absorbers, and electrical heating and cooling systems.

Both primates survived the flight and were treated like celebrities upon their return, even appearing on the cover of *LIFE* magazine. Able died four days after the flight from anesthesia during a routine postflight operation. Baker survived for many years, dying at age twenty-seven.

CHARLES BLAIR FLIES OVER THE NORTH POLE

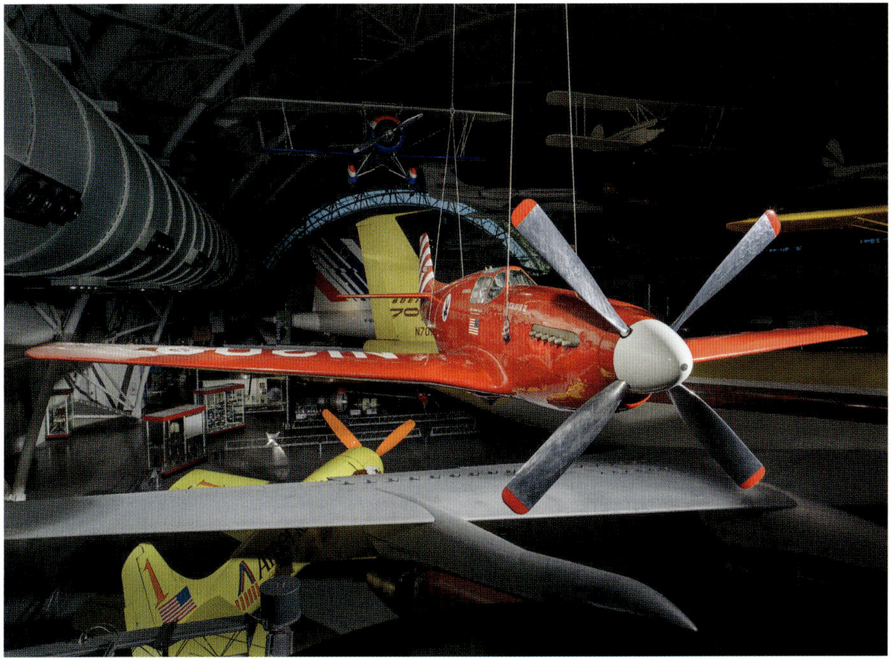

Charles Blair's *Excalibur III* is in the collection of the National Air and Space Museum and is on display at its Steven F. Udvar-Hazy Center in Virginia.

Smithsonian's National Air and Space Museum

It all began with a bar bet. At the beginning of the Cold War, aviator Charles Blair was discussing the fastest route to the Soviet Union while drinking with Air Force crewmembers. Magnetic compasses are unreliable in the polar regions, so flying over the North Pole to reach the USSR required at least three navigators and a thousand pounds of navigational equipment. A skilled navigator himself, Blair knew he could do better. By plotting sunlines at predetermined locations and times, he believed a more reliable form of navigation was possible. Putting his money where his mouth was, Blair bet the crewmembers that he could fly from Norway to Alaska with nothing more than a $12 surplus astrocompass.

On May 29, 1951, Blair set out in a converted P-51 Mustang nicknamed *Excalibur III* and made a 3,260-mile, record-setting flight over the North Pole. Blair's stunt was a major success and signified to U.S. military officials that there were some big changes to be made to their navigation systems.

SPACEX'S CREW DEMO-2 MISSION LAUNCHES

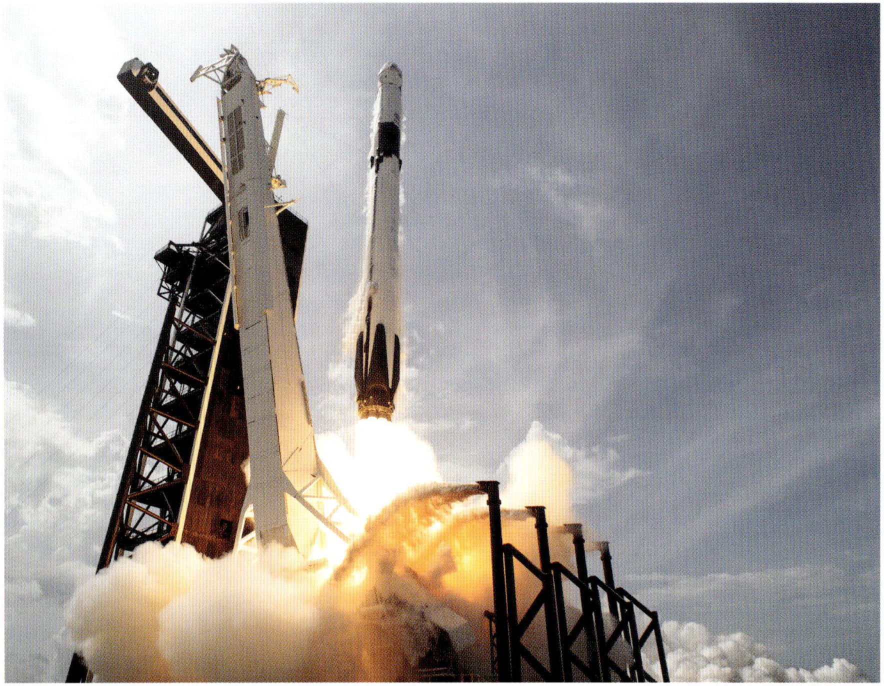

The Crew Demo-2 mission launched on a SpaceX Falcon 9 rocket.

NASA/Joel Kowsky

Even before the end of the Space Shuttle program in 2011, NASA knew changes were ahead. The U.S. civilian space agency would no longer have a launch vehicle or spacecraft to take American astronauts to space. For almost a decade, NASA relied on Russian Soyuz spacecraft to ferry its astronauts to the International Space Station. That changed in 2020, however, with the first crewed test flight of the Commercial Crew Development Program.

On May 30, 2020, NASA astronauts Robert Behnken and Douglas Hurley launched on the SpaceX Demo-2 mission aboard the company's Crew Dragon spacecraft. This marked a return of human spaceflight launches on American soil. It was also the first time NASA astronauts traveled on vehicles owned and operated by a private company. Following that successful test mission, SpaceX began operational flights for NASA, regularly launching astronauts to the ISS. SpaceX received the National Air and Space Museum's 2021 Michael Collins Trophy for Current Achievement.

DID YOU KNOW? Mission commander Douglas Hurley was the pilot of STS-135, the final Space Shuttle mission and the last crewed launch from the U.S. until Demo-2.

MAY 31

BUZZ LIGHTYEAR GOES TO SPACE

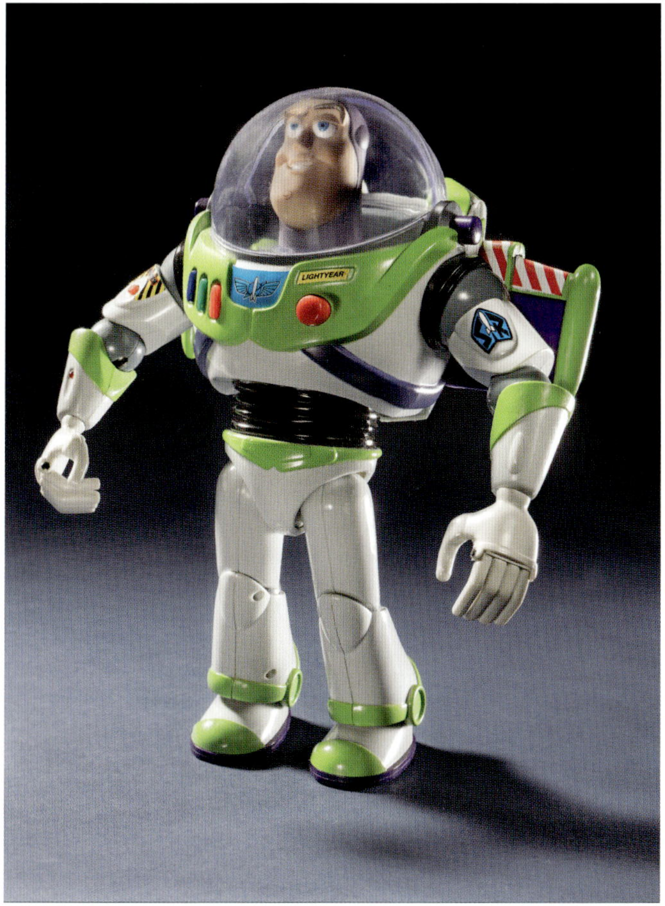

Pixar's *Toy Story* may have premiered in 1995, but it wasn't until 2008 that Space Ranger Buzz Lightyear made it to space for real. The action figure flew to the International Space Station (ISS) as part of NASA's "Toys in Space" project. The toy flew aboard Space Shuttle *Discovery* twice (to space on STS-124 and back home on STS-128), spending fifteen months aboard the ISS.

While on the station, the Buzz Lightyear toy was featured on videos for the project. NASA astronauts Gregory Chamitoff and Michael Fincke conducted science lessons from space with help from Buzz Lightyear, and the toy's presence provided much-needed levity for the busy crew. Back on Earth, the character was used in educational materials to promote STEM (science, technology, engineering, and math) learning.

The actual toy that flew to space was owned by the son of a Disney team member who coordinated the program with NASA. Unable to locate a Buzz Lightyear toy when he needed to ship one to NASA, Duncan Wardle sent a toy he found under his son's bed.

The Buzz Lightyear toy that spent fifteen months on the International Space Station is in the collection of the National Air and Space Museum.

Smithsonian's National Air and Space Museum

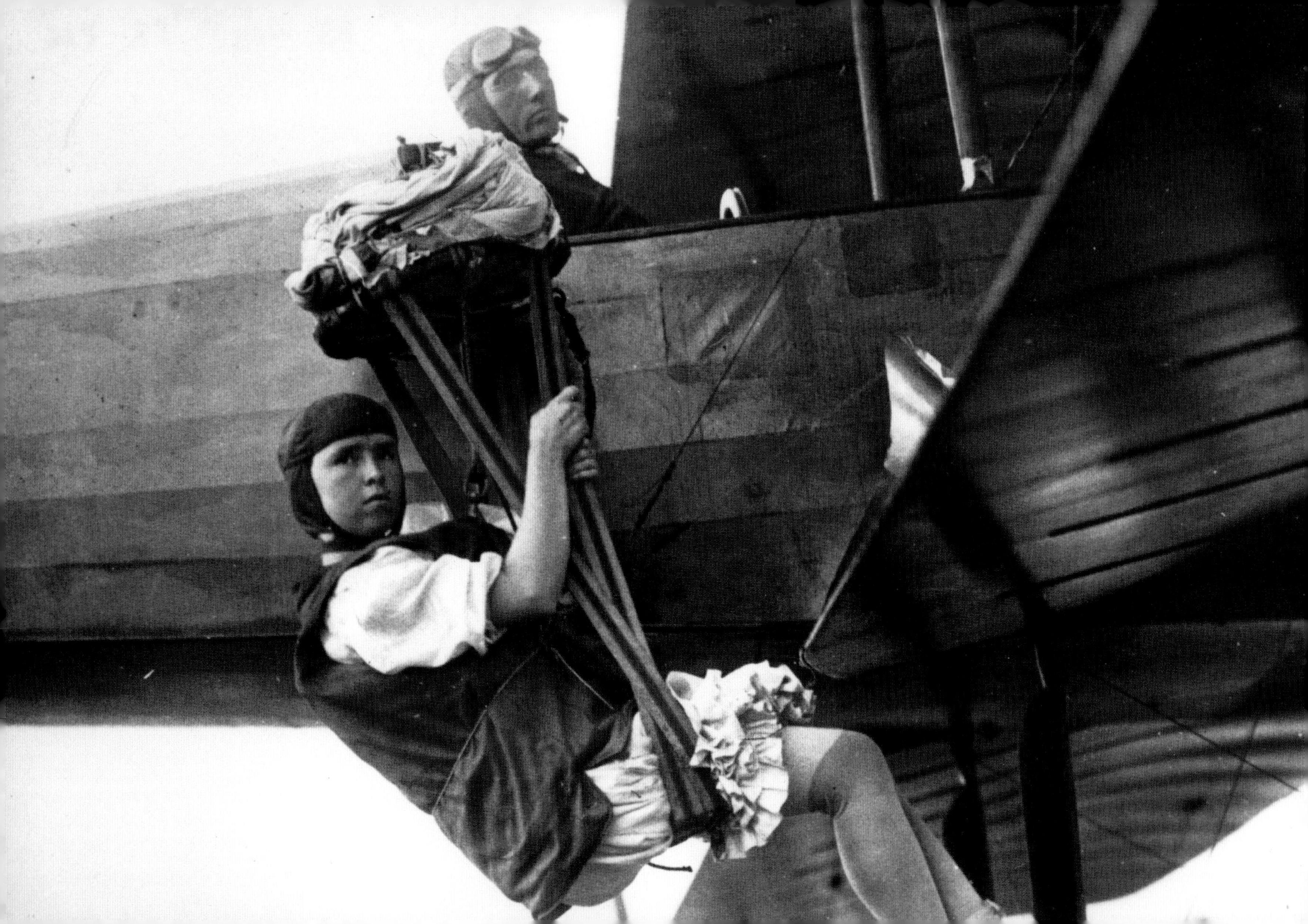

JUNE

U.S. AIR FORCE THUNDERBIRDS SQUADRON IS ACTIVATED

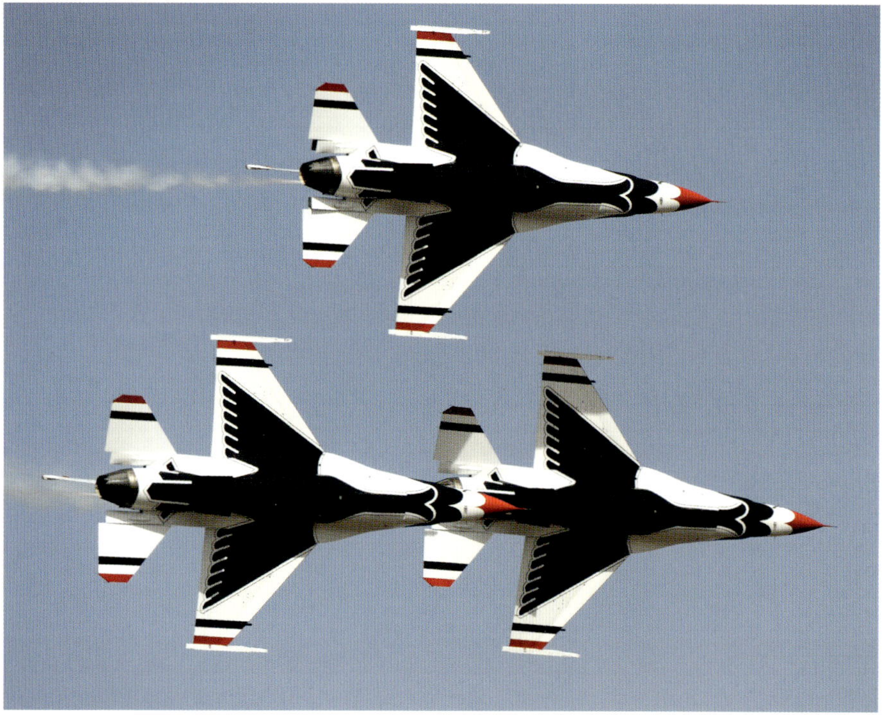

During air demonstrations, the U.S. Air Force Thunderbirds perform precision maneuvers, sometimes flying as close as 18 inches apart.

U.S. Air Force

On June 1, 1953, the United States Air Force Air Demonstration Squadron was activated at Luke Air Force Base. Originally called the 3600th Air Demonstration Team, the squadron is more popularly known today as the Thunderbirds, a supernatural bird found in Native American mythology. Along with the U.S. Navy Blue Angels, the Thunderbirds play an important role in connecting the American public with military aviation. These aerobatic flight teams perform at air shows and other events around the country and the world, demonstrating the capabilities and skill of the U.S. military's aircraft and pilots. Their popular shows include formation flying and solo routines that highlight precision flying.

During their first few years as a demonstration squadron, the Thunderbirds flew the F-84G Thunderjet and F-84F Thunderstreak. The Thunderbirds have since flown a variety of other aircraft over their seventy-year history, including the F-100 Super Sabre, the F-4E Phantom II, and the T-38 Talon. Thunderbird pilots today fly the F-16 Fighting Falcon.

SURVEYOR 1 LANDS ON THE MOON

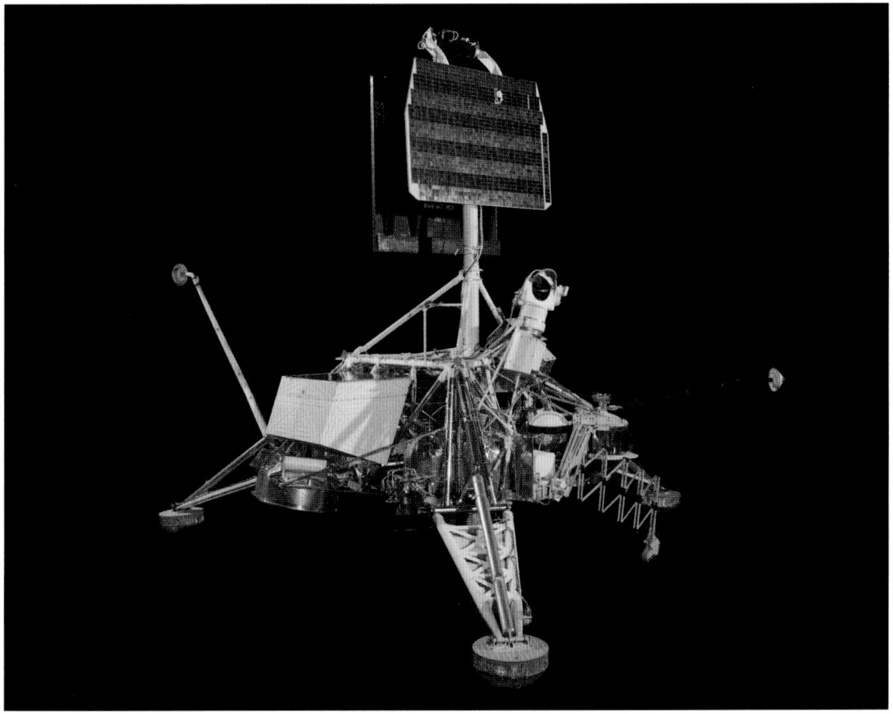

The Surveyor spacecraft on display at the National Air and Space Museum is an engineering model reconfigured to look like a flight model of Surveyor 3 or later.

Smithsonian's National Air and Space Museum

Before NASA sent the first humans to the surface of the Moon, it sent lunar landers to get up close with Earth's natural satellite. The Surveyor vehicles were designed to land on the Moon and send back data about its surface and possible atmosphere. NASA achieved a soft landing on the lunar surface on its first try—Surveyor 1 landed on the Moon in the Ocean of Storms on June 2, 1966. The tripod footpads on the spacecraft had shock absorbers and gauges that provided data about its landing to aid the development of the Apollo lunar lander.

After landing, Surveyor 1 sent back over eleven thousand detailed images of the surface taken by a television camera on board. NASA sent six more Surveyor spacecraft to the Moon over the next year and a half. Later Surveyors carried a soil scoop used to study the mechanical properties of lunar soil and some had tools that could perform simple chemical analyses on the soil. Over the course of the program, Surveyor spacecraft sent back nearly ninety thousand images, providing invaluable information about the Moon.

ED WHITE MAKES FIRST AMERICAN SPACEWALK

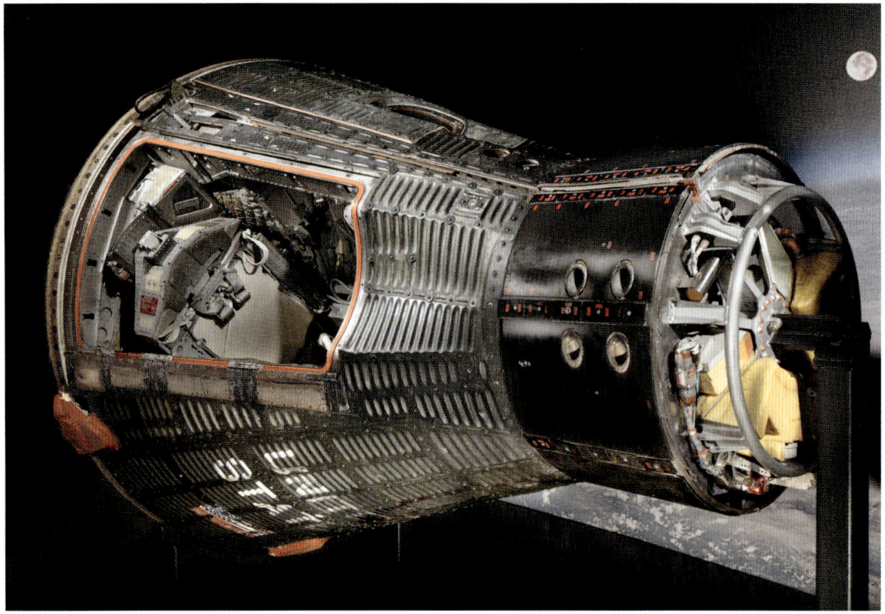

ABOVE The Gemini IV spacecraft from which Ed White II made the first American spacewalk is on display at the National Air and Space Museum.

Smithsonian's National Air and Space Museum

OPPOSITE PAGE White spent twenty-three minutes outside the spacecraft during the Gemini IV mission.

NASA

NASA astronaut Edward "Ed" White II became the first American to spacewalk on June 3, 1965. He ventured outside the spacecraft during the four-day Gemini IV mission. For twenty-three minutes, White floated in space, attached to the capsule by an umbilical tether and maneuvering with a handheld propulsion unit. NASA broadcast the audio from White's extravehicular activity (EVA) live and images released later of White floating in space with the backdrop of a beautiful blue-and-white Earth spread a sense of wonder around the world. This was the first time people saw, in color, an astronaut in space with Earth as the background.

While White's spacewalk was short, it was incredibly significant for America's future in space. Although the Soviets performed a successful spacewalk first (see page 93), NASA continuously achieved the necessary milestones for the U.S.'s goal to land a human on the Moon. Venturing outside the spacecraft was a critical step toward achieving that goal.

"I'm coming back in . . . and it's the saddest moment of my life."

—ED WHITE, AT THE END OF HIS SPACEWALK

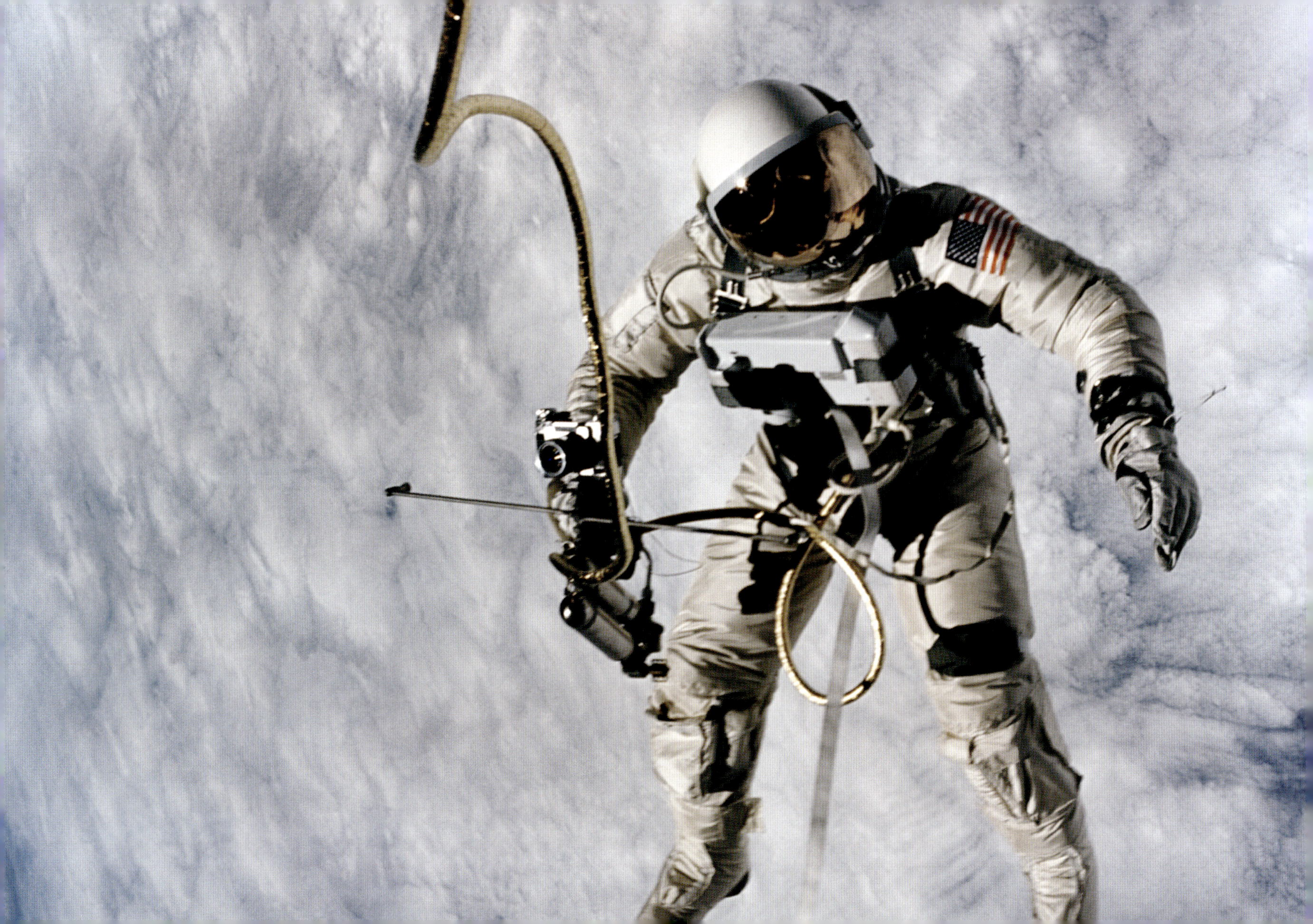

JUNE 4

BATTLE OF MIDWAY BEGINS

WORLD WAR II MILITARY AVIATION

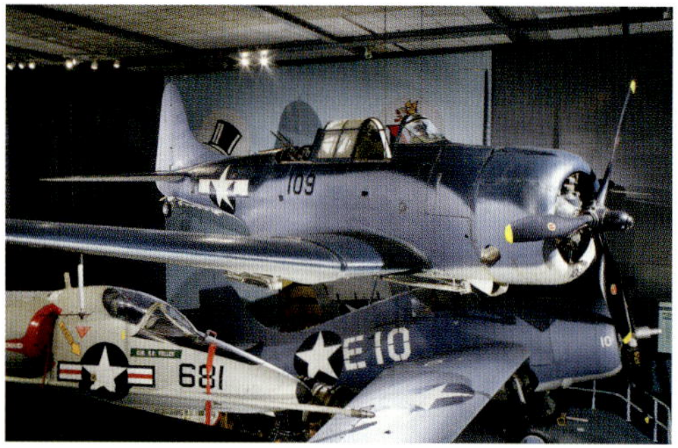

The Douglas SBD Dauntless played a major role in the United States' victory during the Battle of Midway.

Smithsonian's National Air and Space Museum

In May 1942, American codebreakers learned that Japan was planning an attack on the U.S. base at Midway Island northwest of Hawaii. Thanks to this intelligence, the U.S. Navy was ready when the Japanese began bombing Midway on June 4, 1942. Japanese ships found themselves unprepared for the waves of SBD Dauntless dive bombers and other aircraft deployed from American aircraft carriers nearby. By the time the Battle of Midway ended three days later, American planes had destroyed four Japanese aircraft carriers, giving the United States a decisive victory in the Pacific.

JUNE 5

ANTONOV AN-225 DEBUTS OUTSIDE USSR

GENERAL AVIATION

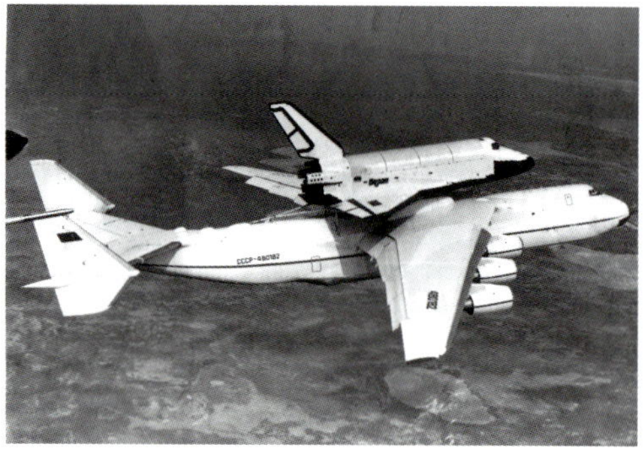

The An-225 was modified to carry the Soviet shuttle *Buran*.

Vasily Koba (CC BY-SA 4.0)

On June 5, 1989, the Antonov An-225 *Mriya* made its first public appearance outside the Soviet Union at the Paris Air Show. A strategic airlift cargo aircraft whose name comes from the Ukrainian word for dream, the massive *Mriya* showed off its capabilities by flying to France carrying the Soviet shuttle *Buran* (see page 337). In the years following its Parisian debut, the An-225 was a go-to for those with very large cargo, and it was frequently called up during crises around the globe. Once the world's largest plane, the only An-225 ever built was destroyed during Russia's 2022 invasion of Ukraine.

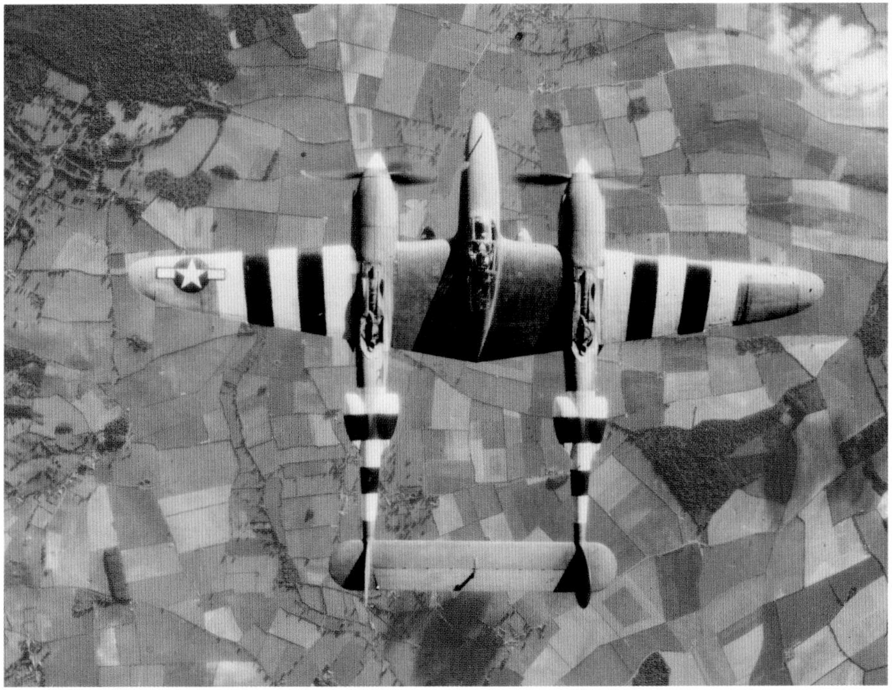

During Operation Overlord, Allied aircraft were painted with invasion stripes in order to avoid friendly fire.

Smithsonian's National Air and Space Museum (NASM 9A14039)

On June 6, 1944, thousands of Allied troops landed on the beaches of Normandy under the protective cover of American and British warships and aircraft. Codenamed "Operation Overlord," the D-Day invasion gave the Allies the foothold they needed to defeat Nazi Germany the following year.

The planners of Operation Overlord relied heavily on Allied aviation. Aerial photography produced by reconnaissance flights over the invasion area provided the Allies with the necessary information to organize the operation. Douglas C-47 military transports and other aircraft carried over twenty-three thousand paratroopers into battle, dropping them behind amphibious landing zones using parachutes and gliders. After the Allies secured bridgeheads on land, the skies over Normandy's liberated beaches were also protected by barrage balloons and fighter aircraft. Together with troops on the ground, aviators helped secure and reinforce the flanks for the entire Allied invasion, marking airpower as an essential element in the success of Operation Overlord.

JUNE 7 SOVIET UNION PERFORMS FIRST SUCCESSFUL DOCKING WITH A SPACE STATION

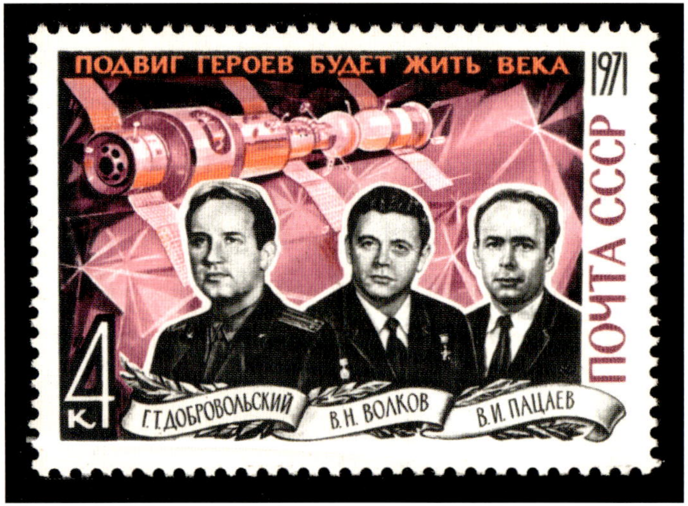

The crew of Soyuz 11 was memorialized with a Soviet stamp.

USSR Post

After the peak of the Space Race in the 1970s, the Soviet Union began pursuing the goal of establishing a permanent presence in space. They adapted existing hardware to launch a number of orbital space stations, using Soyuz spacecraft to ferry crews and supplies up for missions of increasing duration. In April 1971, the Soviet Union launched the world's first space station, Salyut. Two months later, on June 7, 1971, the Soyuz 11 spacecraft, with cosmonauts Georgi Dobrovolski, Vladislav Volkov, and Viktor Patsayev aboard, docked successfully with Salyut 1 and the crew transferred into the space station. This was the first successful docking with a space station.

Tragically, returning to Earth from a twenty-three-day stay on Salyut, the three cosmonauts died when an open valve on their Soyuz spacecraft caused it to depressurize before reentering Earth's atmosphere. Following this tragedy, the Soviet Union began requiring astronauts to wear pressure suits during both launch and landing, which is a mandate still in place today.

SCOTT CROSSFIELD MAKES FIRST UNPOWERED FLIGHT OF X-15

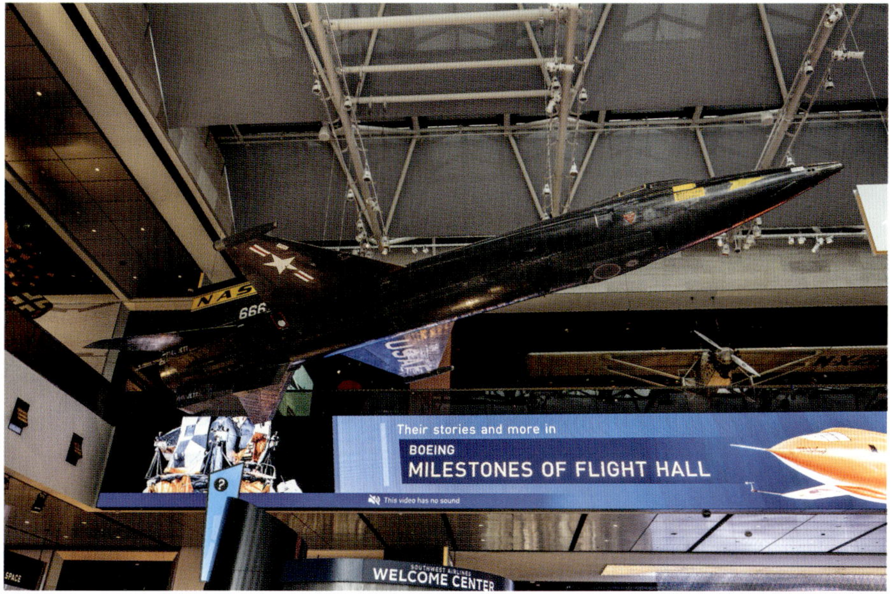

The North American X-15 on display at the National Air and Space Museum was once flown by Neil Armstrong.

Smithsonian's National Air and Space Museum

The North American X-15 bridged the gap between atmospheric flight and spaceflight. This rocket-powered research aircraft explored the hypersonic region—speeds above Mach 5 (five times the speed of sound)—and is the world's fastest crewed aircraft.

On June 8, 1959, test pilot A. Scott Crossfield made the air-launched X-15's first free flight after being carried to an altitude of 40,000 feet under the wing of a Boeing B-52 bomber and dropped. During the unpowered glide flight, Crossfield evaluated the aircraft, its systems, and its flying characteristics. Following these initial tests, the X-15 became the first aircraft to reach Mach 4, 5, and 6, and regularly operated above 100,000 feet. Over the course of 199 flights, a total of eight pilots flew the X-15 to an altitude higher than fifty miles. Having met the technical criteria for spaceflight, each of these pilots was eventually awarded astronaut wings for their flights in the X-15.

JUNE 9

FIRST TRANSPACIFIC FLIGHT TAKES PLACE

PIONEERS OF FLIGHT

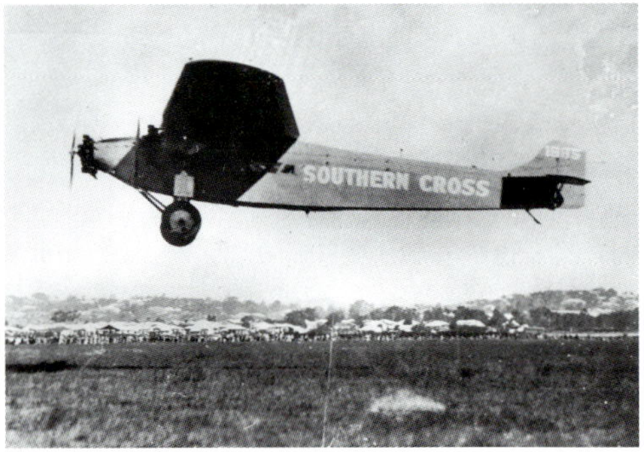

Southern Cross's transpacific flight ended at Eagle Farm Airport in Brisbane, Australia.

State Library of Queensland

Flying in a Fokker F.VIIB-3m named the *Southern Cross*, Australian aviator Sir Charles Kingsford Smith and crew were the first humans to complete a transpacific flight. The dangerous 7,500-mile flight required eighty-three total hours of flying time spread across three separate legs: California to Hawaii, Hawaii to Fiji, and Fiji to Australia. When *Southern Cross* landed in Brisbane, Australia, on June 9, 1928, thousands of people were at the airport to greet the flight crew. A celebration the next day in Sydney was attended by a crowd of three hundred thousand, a testament to the importance of the historic flight.

JUNE 10

RUTH LAW SETS ALTITUDE RECORD

PIONEERS OF FLIGHT

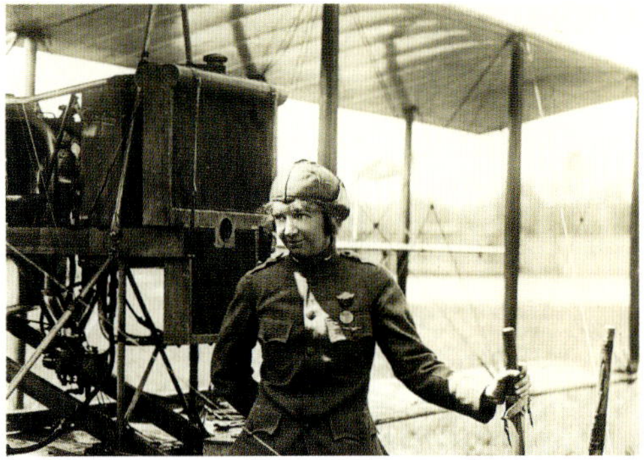

Ruth Law was permitted to wear a noncommissioned Army officer's uniform while flying recruiting trips during World War I.

Smithsonian's National Air and Space Museum (NASM A-5532)

Ruth Law enjoyed one of the longest and most colorful careers of any early aviator. The pioneering pilot was so successful that, in 1917, she earned as much as $9,000 a week for exhibition flights. Law set many records and achieved many firsts, including becoming the first known woman to fly at night, and carrying the first official airmail to the Philippine Islands. On June 10, 1919, Law set a new women's altitude record by flying to 14,700 feet. Law's record stood only a few days, however, before another famous woman aviator, Raymonde de Laroche (see page 84), flew to even greater heights.

FORD TRI-MOTOR FLIES FOR THE FIRST TIME

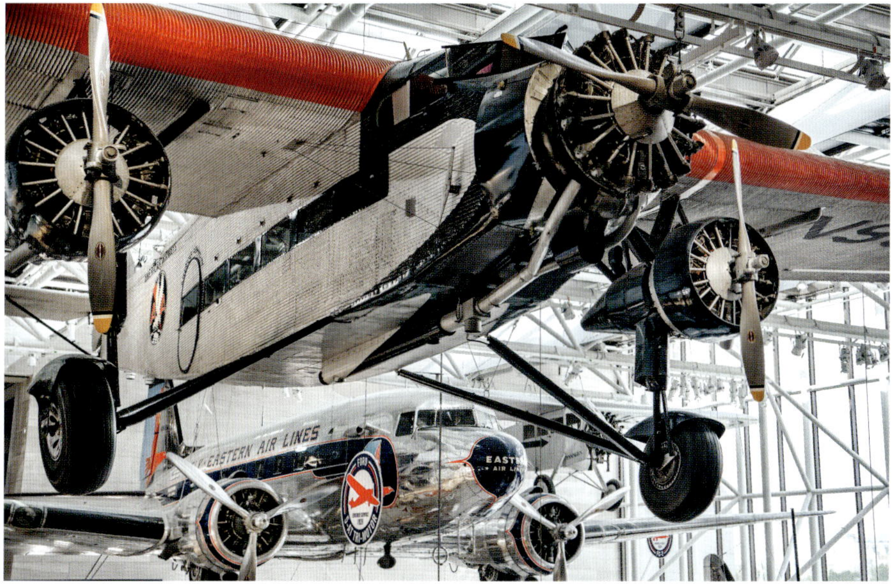

With more powerful engines, the 5-AT was the most numerous Ford Tri-Motor model built. An example of the aircraft is on display at the National Air and Space Museum.

Smithsonian's National Air and Space Museum

The Ford Motor Company first became involved in aviation building Liberty engines during World War I. It wasn't until the mid-1920s, however, that the automobile pioneer created an airplane of its own. In 1925, founder Henry Ford grandly remarked that aviation needed to be made "fool-proof" at a press conference announcing the acquisition of the Stout Metal Airplane Company. "What the Ford Motor Company means to do," Ford continued, "is prove whether commercial flying can be done safely and profitably."

The famous Ford Tri-Motor achieved exactly that. Affectionately known as the "Tin Goose," the 4-AT Tri-Motor was the largest civil aircraft in America when it first flew on June 11, 1926. Combined with the prestigious and reliable Ford name, the plane's all-metal, corrugated aluminum construction made it immediately popular with passengers and airline operators. Between 1926 and 1933, Ford produced a total of 199 Tri-Motors, and more than one hundred airlines flew the sturdy aircraft across the globe.

HUMAN-POWERED AIRCRAFT FLIES ACROSS ENGLISH CHANNEL

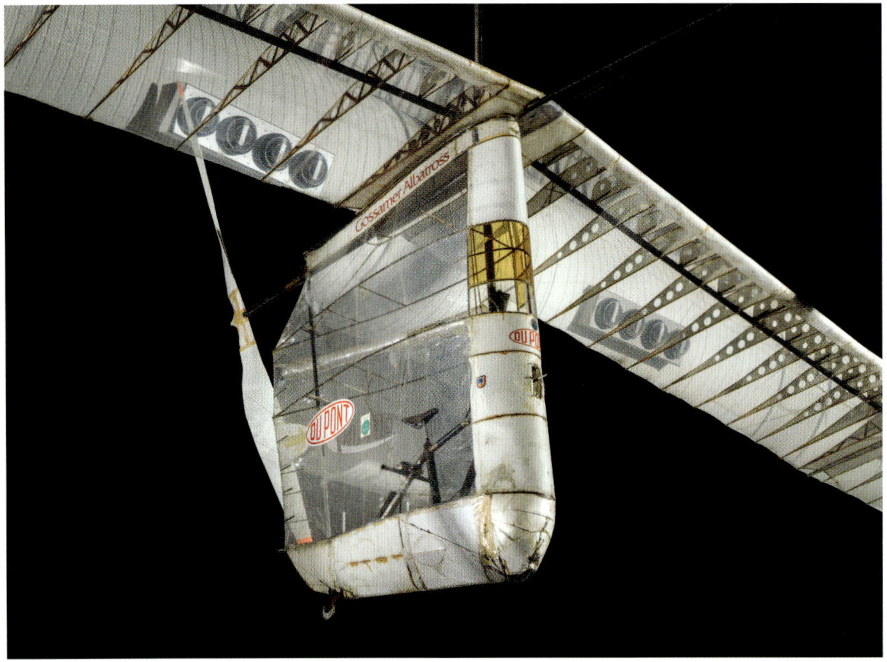

The first human-powered aircraft to fly across the English Channel is on display at the Steven F. Udvar-Hazy Center.

Smithsonian's National Air and Space Museum

In the early morning hours of June 12, 1979, pilot and long-distance cyclist Bryan Allen embarked on a flight that would make history. Pedaling at 75 rpm in the cockpit of an ultralight aircraft called the Gossamer Albatross, Allen successfully flew across the English Channel. The first human-powered aircraft to make the journey, the Gossamer Albatross took two hours and forty-nine minutes to cover the 22.5 miles between Folkestone, England, and Cap Gris Nez, France.

Designer Paul MacCready and his team of engineers from AeroVironment modeled the Albatross after the Gossamer Condor, which was the first successful human-powered aircraft. Built mostly from carbon fiber tubing and covered with clear Mylar, the Albatross was designed to be easily disassembled for shipping. In recognition of their accomplishment, MacCready and the Albatross engineers won their second Kremer Prize for human-powered aircraft.

GERMANY LAUNCHES FIRST OPERATIONAL CRUISE MISSILE

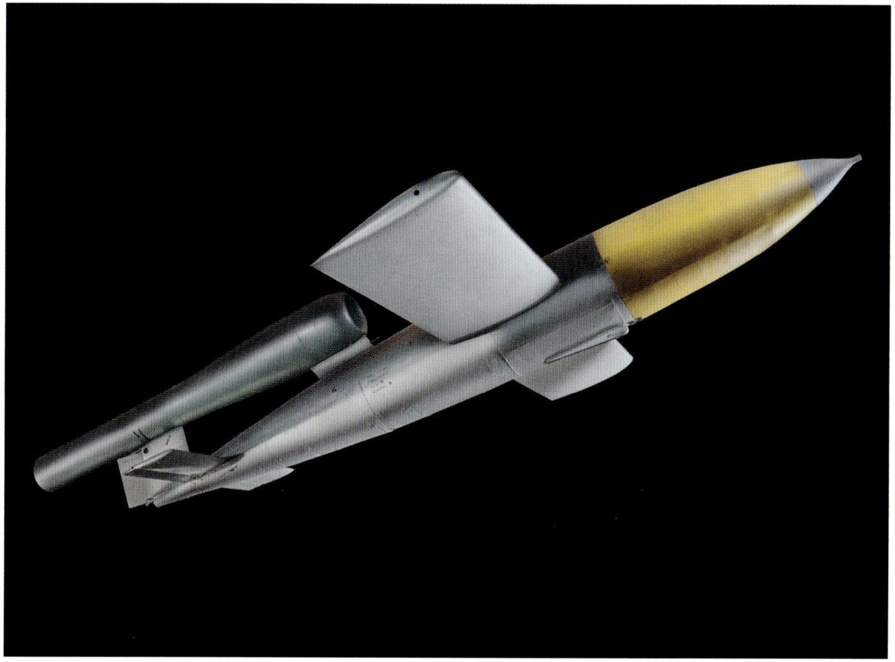

The V-1 on display in the National Air and Space Museum came into the possession of American military forces at the end of World War II and was given to the Smithsonian.

Smithsonian's National Air and Space Museum

The V-1 was the world's first operational cruise missile. The designation V-1 comes from "Vergeltungswaffe Eins" (Vengeance Weapon One), a name given to it by the Nazi Propaganda Ministry. It was powered by a simple but noisy pulsejet engine that earned it the Allied nicknames of "buzz bomb" and "doodlebug." In the early hours of June 13, 1944, the first V-1s were fired at England. Over the next year, Nazi Germany launched thousands of V-1s at British and continental targets, mostly London, England, and Antwerp, Belgium.

The V-1 was boosted into the air to function efficiently, normally launching from a firing tube mounted on a 150-foot-long inclined metal ramp about sixteen feet tall. After the missile reached 200 miles per hour, the pulsejet would be activated, and it would begin to travel toward its target. The V-1 carried a one-ton, high-explosive warhead. These cruise missiles caused over ten thousand deaths within their target areas.

ALCOCK AND BROWN MAKE FIRST NONSTOP FLIGHT ACROSS ATLANTIC

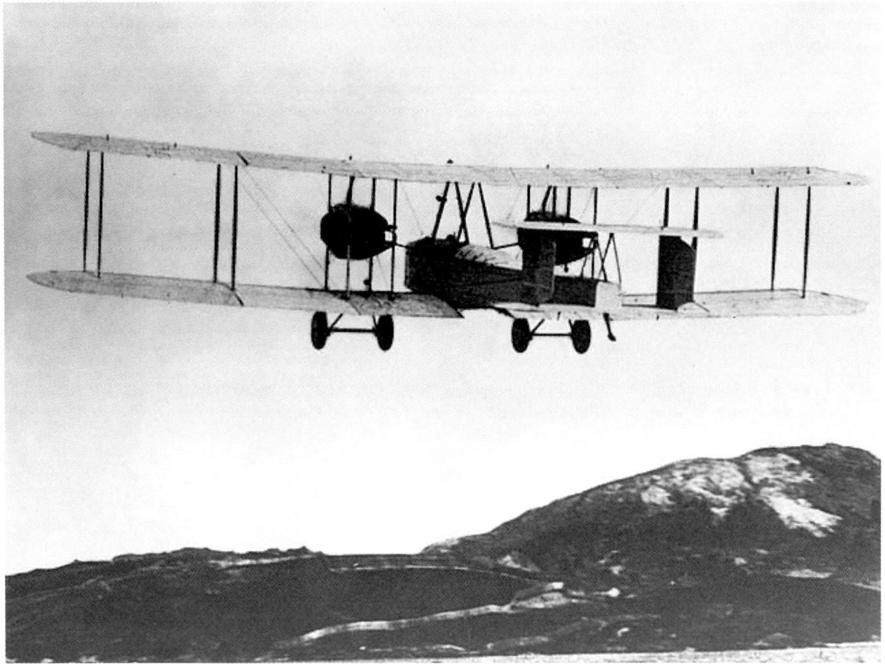

The first nonstop transatlantic flight took place in a Vickers Vimy biplane.

Canadian Forces

In 1913, Britain's *Daily Mail* newspaper offered a £10,000 prize for the first aviators to fly nonstop across the Atlantic Ocean. At the time, such a flight was nearly impossible, and no one took up the challenge. But five years later, wartime advancements in airplane technology made the journey seem more feasible, and the *Daily Mail* renewed the offer. Though multiple teams competed for the new prize, none were initially successful.

On June 14, 1919, British pilot John William Alcock and navigator Arthur Whitten Brown departed from St. John's, Newfoundland, on a treacherous and historic journey across the ocean. Soon after takeoff in their Vickers Vimy biplane, the aviators encountered thick fog and clouds that obscured the sky and sea, making navigation difficult. At one point during the flight, the aircraft emerged from a fogbank just one hundred feet above the water, but Brown was able to regain control and climb back to altitude. Sixteen hours after taking off, Alcock and Brown crash-landed in an Irish bog, making them the first aviators to complete a nonstop transatlantic flight.

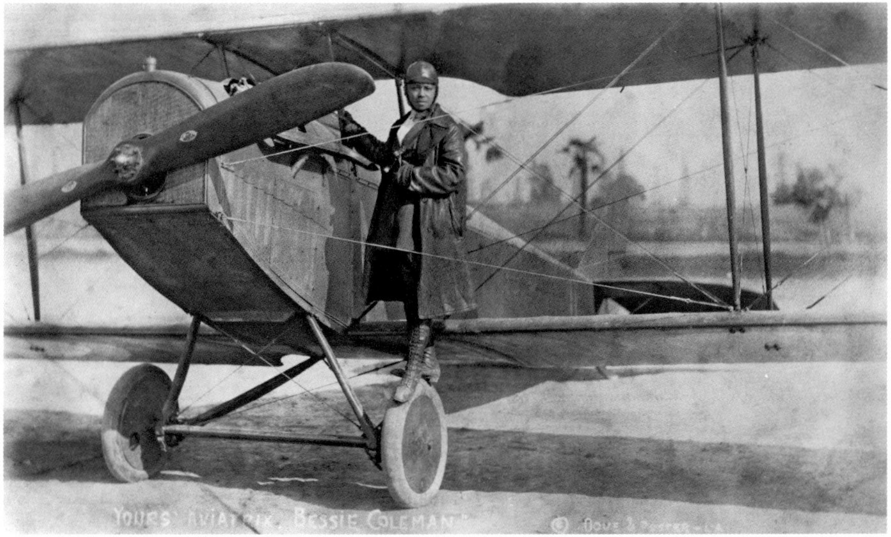

Bessie Coleman earned her pilot's license after seven months of training at the well-respected Caudron Brothers School of Aviation in France.

Smithsonian's National Air and Space Museum (NASM 92-13721)

In the early 1920s, pioneering aviator Bessie Coleman was flying loops through multiple glass ceilings. As a Black woman, getting a pilot's license in the United States proved impossible, so the twenty-four-year-old Coleman moved to France to learn to fly. On June 15, 1921, she earned her flying license from the Fédération Aéronautique Internationale—making Coleman the first African American woman to receive a pilot's certification.

Returning home to the U.S., Coleman got a job as a barnstorming pilot, performing stunts at aviation shows. In an era of intense racial prejudice and Jim Crow segregation, Coleman took a stand by only performing in exhibition shows if the crowds were integrated. Coleman's dream was to save enough money from her barnstorming work to open a flight school for African American students. Before she could achieve this goal, however, Coleman died in an airplane crash in 1926. In a fitting tribute to her dream, fellow Black pilot William Powell founded the Bessie Coleman Aero Club in 1929.

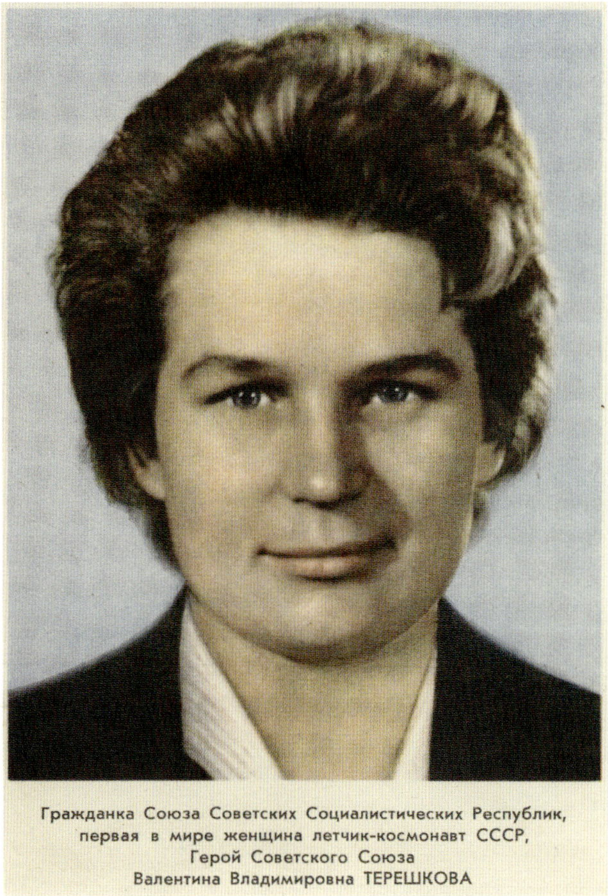

In the early 1960s, Soviet cosmonauts completed their spaceflights by parachuting out of their capsules and back down to Earth. Valentina Tereshkova, a skilled parachutist with nearly 150 jumps, was selected as a cosmonaut because of that experience. After a year and a half of general training, Tereshkova and another woman were selected to train for the Vostok 6 mission. Tereshkova was ultimately selected to carry out the mission.

On June 16, 1963, Tereshkova was launched into orbit aboard a Vostok spacecraft, becoming the first woman in space. During her nearly three-day spaceflight, she made forty-eight orbits of the Earth, operating her spacecraft with manual controls. At the end of the mission, Tereshkova reentered Earth's atmosphere in Vostok 6 and then parachuted from the spacecraft and landed in central Asia.

Although the Soviet Union broke the gender barrier of human spaceflight early, it would be almost two decades before Svetlana Savitskaya became the second Soviet woman in space in 1982, and yet another year until Sally Ride became the first American woman in space in 1983 (see page 186).

Valentina Tereshkova orbited Earth forty-eight times during her historic spaceflight.

Smithsonian's National Air and Space Museum (NASM 9A01693)

SPACE SHUTTLE *DISCOVERY* LAUNCHES ON STS-51G MISSION

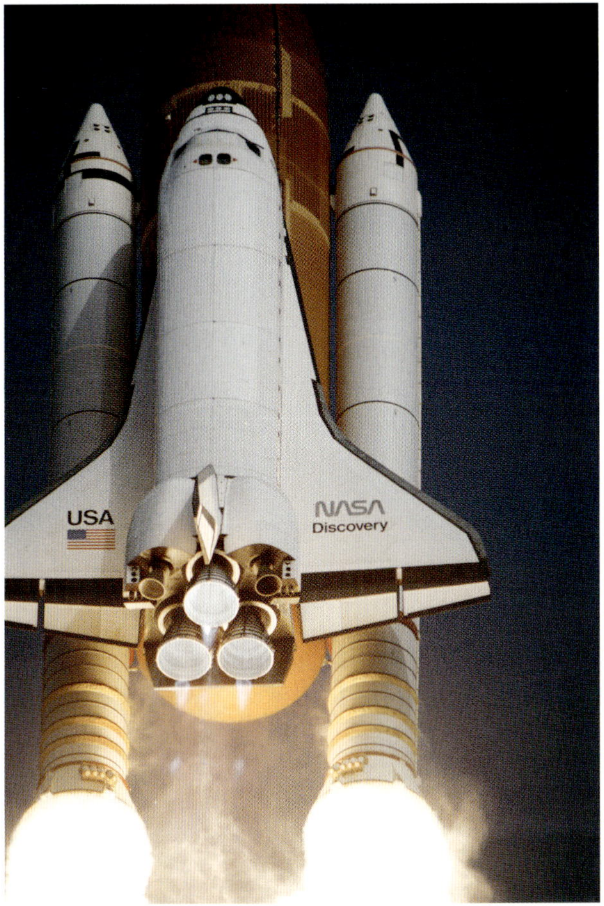

On June 17, 1985, Space Shuttle *Discovery* launched on the STS-51G mission. The orbiter had a full payload bay at launch, carrying three communications satellites and the SPARTAN-1 (Shuttle Pointed Autonomous Research Tool for Astronomy) spacecraft. The mission temporarily deployed the SPARTAN-1 spacecraft for forty-five hours to make X-ray observations of both the center of the Milky Way galaxy and the Perseus cluster of galaxies.

The crew also deployed and placed into orbit the Mexican communications satellite Morelos-A, which provided telecommunications access to remote areas of Mexico; the Arab Satellite Communications Organization's Arabsat-1, which provided telecommunications links between its member nations; and Telstar-3D, an AT&T satellite. After being ejected from the payload bay using spring mechanisms, the satellites were propelled into a transfer orbit by a Payload Assist Module, a small rocket attached to each satellite.

DID YOU KNOW? Saudi prince Sultan bin Salman Al Saud was a payload specialist on STS-51G, becoming the first member of a royal family to go to space.

STS-51G was Space Shuttle *Discovery*'s fifth trip to space.

NASA

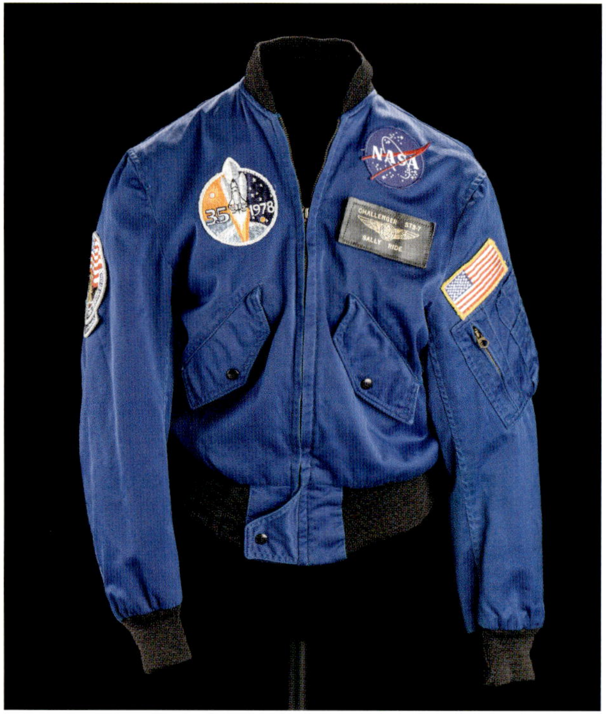

ABOVE The National Air and Space Museum has many artifacts related to Sally Ride, including her astronaut flight jacket.

Smithsonian's National Air and Space Museum

OPPOSITE PAGE Ride served as a mission specialist on Space Shuttle *Challenger*'s STS-7 mission.

NASA

Sally Ride became the first American woman to fly in space on June 18, 1983, as part of Space Shuttle *Challenger*'s STS-7 mission. Ride's journey to space began as a PhD student when she learned that NASA was recruiting scientist astronauts to serve as mission specialists in the Space Shuttle program. After passing NASA's preliminary interview process, she became one of 208 finalists and was ultimately selected as part of NASA's Astronaut Group 8 (see page 30).

After serving as backup orbiter capsule communicator (CAPCOM) for STS-2 and prime orbiter CAPCOM for STS-3, Ride was tapped for a mission and assigned to operate the robotic arm on STS-7. The following year, she flew to space a second time on STS-41G, the first spaceflight with two women on the crew. After leaving NASA, Ride became a physics professor and launched a variety of business ventures intended to inspire the next generation of astronauts and scientists.

In 2013, Ride was posthumously awarded the Presidential Medal of Freedom in acknowledgment of her role breaking the gender barrier in U.S. human spaceflight. Her partner, Tam O'Shaughnessy, accepted the medal on her behalf.

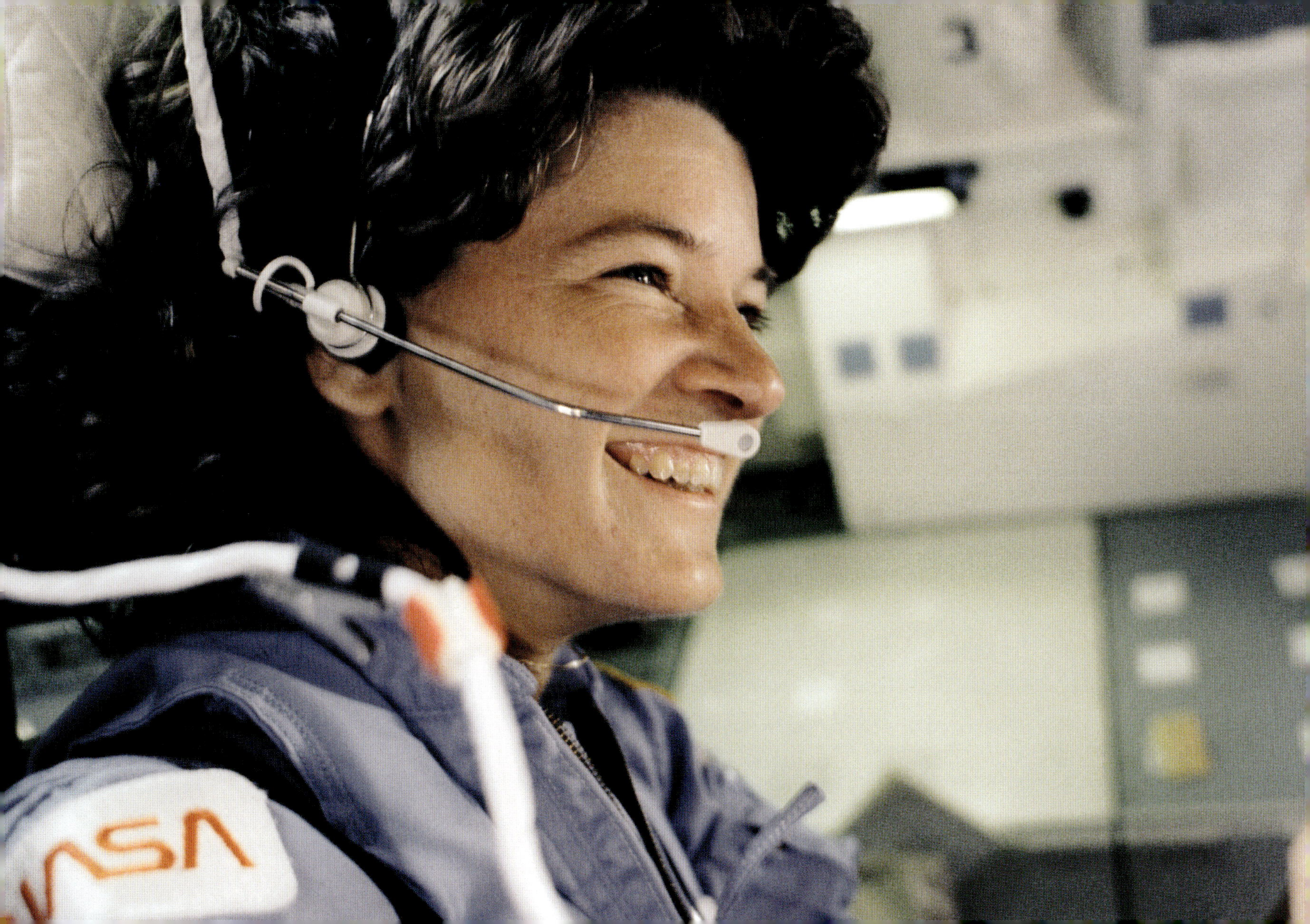
ASA

VIKING 1 SPACECRAFT ARRIVES AT MARS

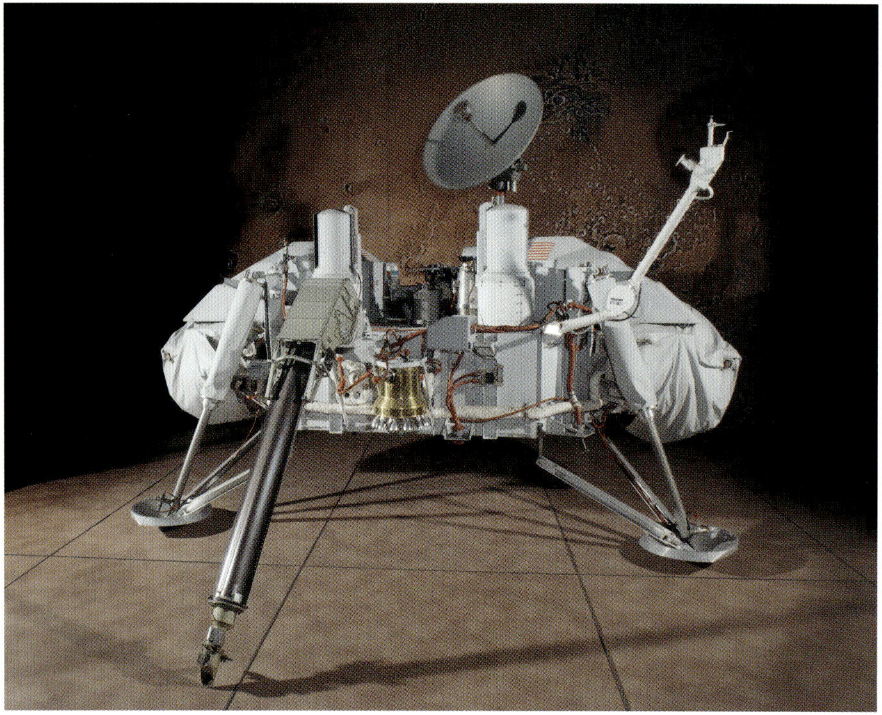

The Viking Lander on display at the National Air and Space Museum was used on Earth for testing and simulations before and during the Viking mission.

Smithsonian's National Air and Space Museum

Building on the Mariner missions to Mars in the 1960s and early 1970s, NASA's Viking program took humanity closer to Mars than ever before. Viking used two identical spacecraft, each consisting of a lander and an orbiter. Viking 1 and Viking 2 launched three weeks apart in summer 1975. On June 19, 1976, Viking 1 arrived at Mars, entering orbit around the planet. Soon after, it began transmitting photographs, including images of the Viking Lander's planned touchdown site. Because the area appeared rougher than expected, scientists used the new images to identify a better landing site in the same area.

A month after arriving at the Red Planet, the first Viking Lander touched down on the Martian surface. Viking was also NASA's first lander to carry instruments capable of doing chemical or physical analysis, and the spacecraft conducted experiments in search of signs of life. While Viking did not find organic molecules, NASA's *Curiosity* rover did decades later (see page 346).

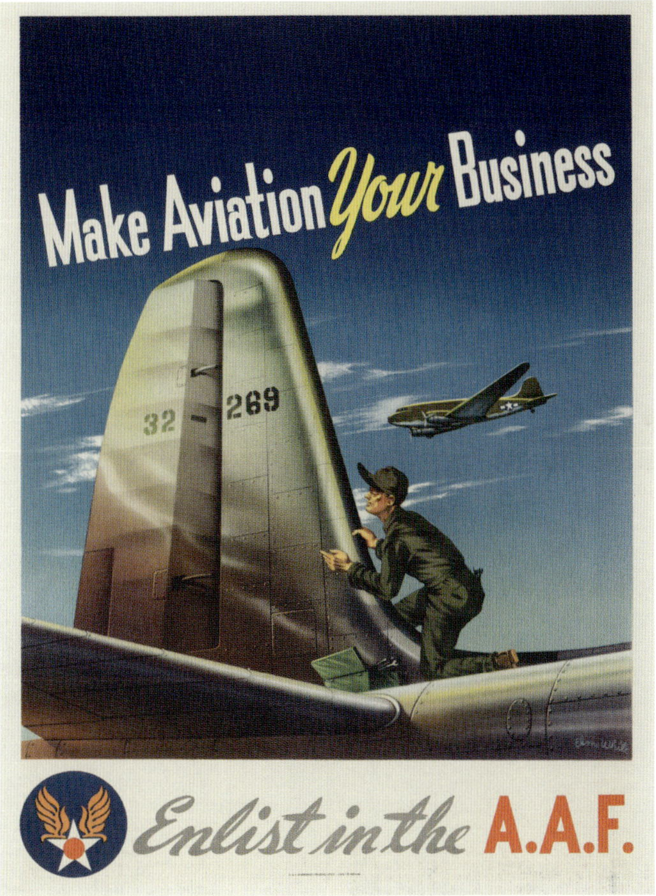

On June 20, 1941, U.S. Army Chief of Staff Gen. George C. Marshall established the United States Army Air Forces (USAAF) as a successor to the United States Army Air Corps. This change made the USAAF an autonomous arm of the Army, and by the following year it was on an equal footing with the other two U.S. Army Commands (Army Ground Forces and Services of Supply/Army Service Forces).

Gen. Henry "Hap" Arnold, a pilot and leader within the Air Corps, was selected as commander of the new Army Air Forces. Arnold led the USAAF throughout World War II, increasing the command's numbers from twenty-two thousand to 2.5 million airmen and 3,900 to seventy-five thousand aircraft. While in command, Arnold made a strong case for the need for an autonomous military force focused on aviation. In 1947, the USAAF became its own branch of the military, the United States Air Force.

The National Air and Space Museum has an extensive poster collection, including Army Air Forces recruitment posters.

Smithsonian's National Air and Space Museum

TINY BROADWICK BECOMES FIRST WOMAN TO PARACHUTE FROM AN AIRPLANE

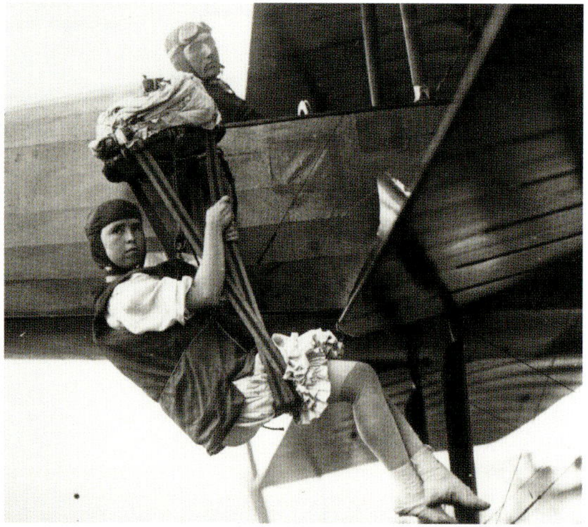

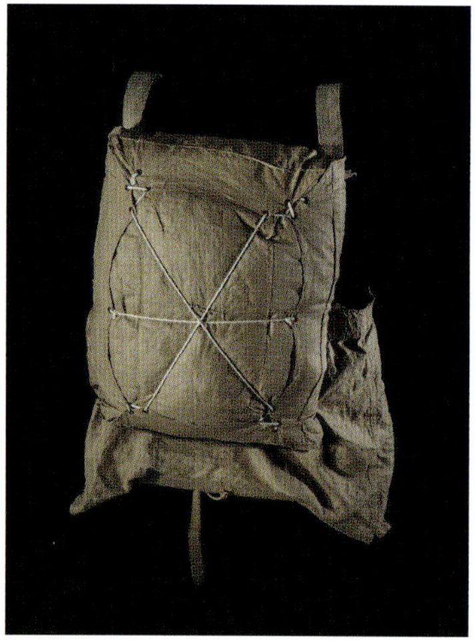

LEFT Tiny Broadwick's first parachute jump from an airplane was on a flight piloted by pioneering aviator Glenn L. Martin (see page 31).

Smithsonian's National Air and Space Museum (NASM 77-716)

RIGHT One of Broadwick's parachute backpacks is on display at the National Air and Space Museum.

National Air and Space Museum

When Georgia "Tiny" Thompson was fourteen, she saw an act called "The Broadwicks and Their Famous French Aeronauts" and became fascinated with parachuting. After joining the troupe and adopting the name of its founder, Tiny Broadwick made her first jump from a hot-air balloon at the 1908 North Carolina State Fair.

In the years following her first jump, the diminutive Broadwick became a darling of the aviation community. One day at a Los Angeles air meet, she met famed stunt flyer and aircraft manufacturer Glenn L. Martin and seized upon the idea of parachuting from an airplane. On June 21, 1913, Broadwick hung from a trapeze-like swing suspended beneath Martin's airplane as it flew over Griffith Park. When the plane reached 2,000 feet, she released a lever that made the seat drop out from under her. The parachute opened automatically, and she floated safely to earth, becoming the first woman to parachute from an airplane. Broadwick continued her parachuting career into the early 1920s and even worked with the Army to demonstrate jumping from a military airplane.

UNITED STATES LAUNCHES GRAB-1 SATELLITE

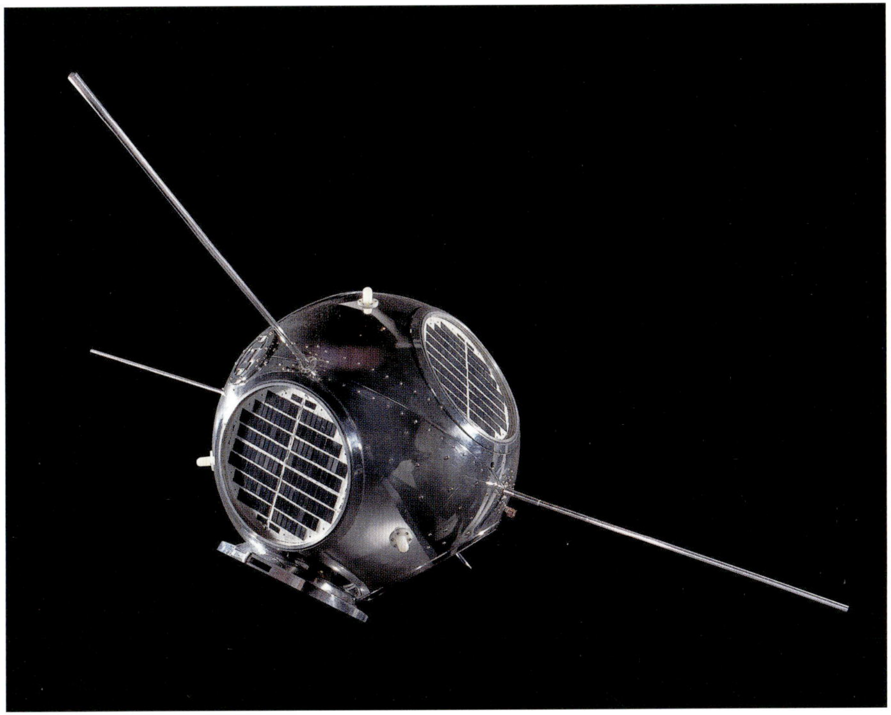

Four years after the GRAB program was declassified in 1998, the Naval Research Laboratory donated a GRAB-1 backup to the National Air and Space Museum.

Smithsonian's National Air and Space Museum

The Galactic Radiation and Background (GRAB-1) satellite was the world's first successful reconnaissance satellite. Built by the Naval Research Laboratory in Washington, D.C., the top-secret GRAB-1 was launched on June 22, 1960, as part of a highly classified program designed to obtain data on Soviet air defense radar installations. The U.S. Strategic Air Command used the information to develop electronic countermeasures and the most effective bomber routes. The satellite also carried instruments to measure solar radiation, part of an unclassified and publicly acknowledged project dubbed Solrad.

For eight months, GRAB-1 gathered information about the Soviet Union that was not possible to observe using military aircraft. In total, five GRAB satellites were launched from June 1960 to April 1962, but only the first and third reached orbit. Following the success of this first spy satellite, the United States secretly established the National Reconnaissance Office to oversee such projects. The GRAB program was kept secret until its declassification by the U.S. Navy in 1998.

JUNE 23

X-35B FLIGHT TEST PROGRAM BEGINS

MODERN MILITARY AVIATION

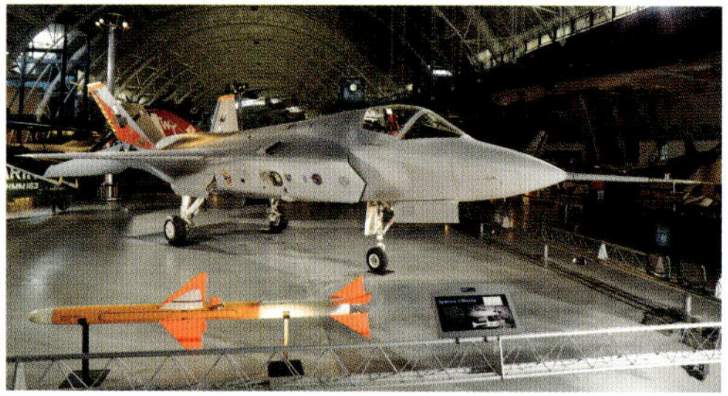

The Lockheed Martin X-35B on display at the Steven F. Udvar-Hazy Center is the first X-35 airframe ever built.

Smithsonian's National Air and Space Museum

The X-35B flight test program was one of the shortest and most efficient flight test programs in history. Beginning on June 23, 2001, and lasting until August 6, 2001, the program aimed to modify the X-35A, a technology demonstrator for the F-35 Joint Strike Fighter, into the short takeoff/vertical landing (STOVL) X-35B. Among its many test records, this aircraft was the first in history to achieve a short takeoff, level supersonic dash, and vertical landing in a single flight.

JUNE 24

TEENAGER BECOMES FIRST AMERICAN TO ASCEND IN A BALLOON

LIGHTER-THAN-AIR FLIGHT

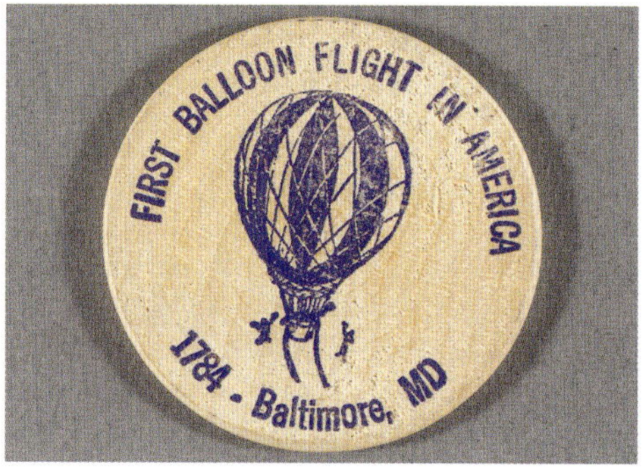

Though there are no known contemporary images of the 1784 Baltimore balloon flight, more recent memorabilia such as this wooden token commemorate the event.

Smithsonian's National Air and Space Museum

In 1783, a Maryland innkeeper named Peter Carnes read in wonder about the first balloon flights in France. Though he had never seen a balloon, Carnes was determined to build one of his own. Using details from the newspaper articles he found, he did just that, becoming the first American to build a full-scale hot-air balloon. On June 24, 1784, huge crowds gathered in Baltimore to watch Carnes ascend in his tethered balloon, but the would-be aviator quickly discovered he was too heavy. That's when a thirteen-year-old boy named Edward Warren volunteered to take his place, becoming the first American to ascend in a balloon.

KOREAN WAR BEGINS

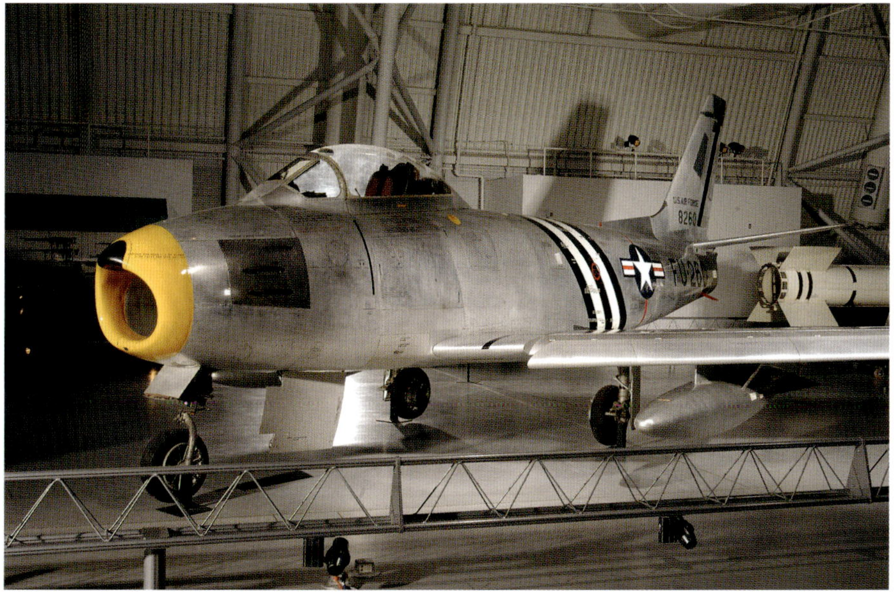

On June 25, 1950, the Korean War began when a massive force of North Korean ground troops and Soviet-manufactured aircraft invaded South Korea. The United States military led United Nations forces in a counterattack that turned back the initial invasion but eventually became bogged down in a protracted and costly conflict. One of the most brutal confrontations of the Cold War, the three-year-long struggle for Korea ended in a stalemate.

Aviation technology changed dramatically during the Korean War. Piston-driven aircraft fell out of favor as new jet-powered planes entered the conflict. The most famous American aircraft of the Korean War was the F-86 Sabre, a swept-wing air superiority fighter deployed to counter the Soviet MiG-15. At the end of 1950, an American pilot flying an F-86 shot down a MiG-15 in the first known aerial combat between swept-wing jet fighters.

The North American F-86 Sabre on display at the Steven F. Udvar-Hazy Center has the markings of the 4th Fighter Wing, the first F-86 unit in Korea.

Smithsonian's National Air and Space Museum

JUNE 26

HELLCAT PROTOTYPE TAKES FLIGHT FOR THE FIRST TIME

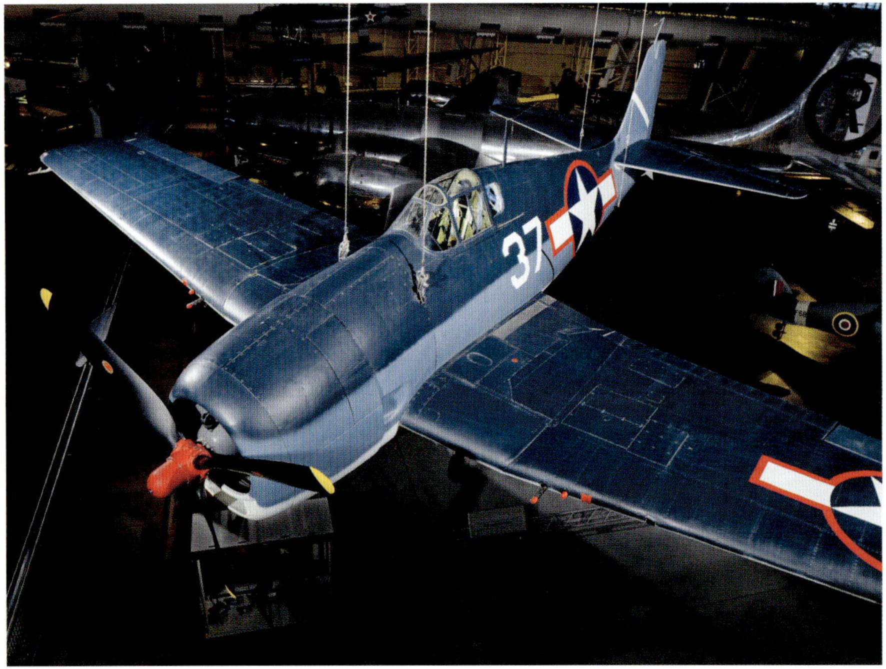

The Grumman F6F Hellcat on display at the Steven F. Udvar-Hazy Center was used during Operation Crossroads, the atomic bomb tests at Bikini Atoll.

Smithsonian's National Air and Space Museum

The Grumman F6F Hellcat was originally conceived as an advanced version of the U.S. Navy's then-current frontline fighter, the F4F Wildcat. Designed in the previous decade, by 1941 the performance of the Wildcat no longer matched that of other fighter aircraft, and the U.S. Navy asked Grumman to develop an improved version.

After adding a larger and more powerful engine, Grumman engineers soon made several additional changes to support the improved aircraft: a larger propeller, taller landing gear for increased ground clearance, more wing area, and an increase in the area of the vertical and horizontal tail surfaces. With all of these design modifications, Grumman had essentially created a new fighter, which became known as the F6F Hellcat. The XF6F-1 Hellcat prototype flew for the first time on June 26, 1942.

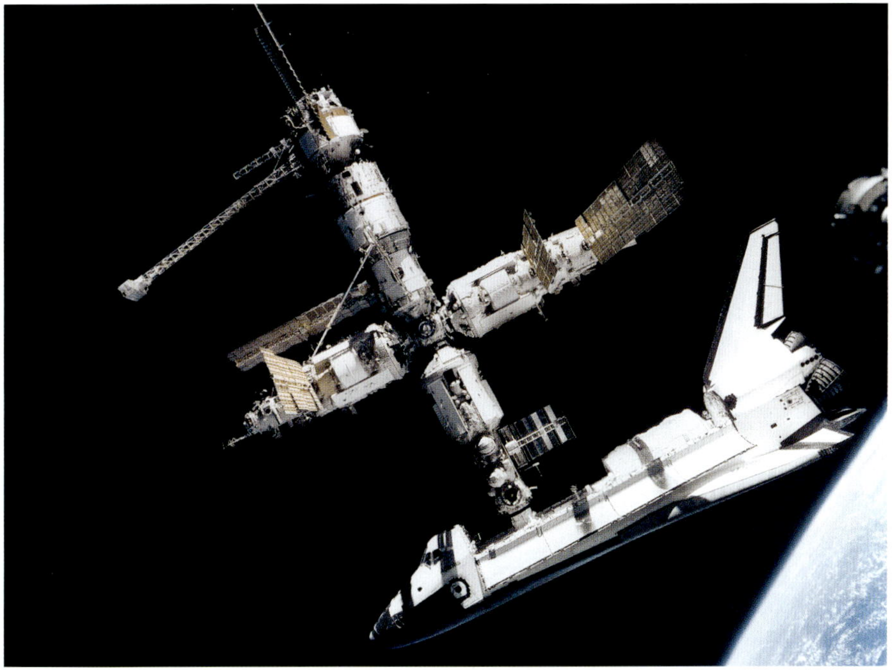

When *Atlantis* and Mir were docked, they weighed nearly half a million pounds, becoming the largest combined vehicle in orbit to date.

NASA

On June 27, 1995, Space Shuttle *Atlantis* launched on NASA's one hundredth human spaceflight. Two days later, it became the first Space Shuttle orbiter to dock with Russia's Mir space station. Prior to the orbiter's arrival, cosmonauts on Mir had to perform spacewalks to reconfigure the station to allow the vehicle to dock. Mission commander and five-time space veteran Robert "Hoot" Gibson piloted the Shuttle during the smooth docking with Mir.

After the pressure was equalized between the orbiter and the space station, Gibson and Mir commander Vladimir Dezhurov opened their hatches and shook hands at the threshold—recreating the famous handshake from the Apollo-Soyuz Test Project in 1975 (see page 214). The spacecraft remained docked for five days, during which the two crews collaborated on a variety of experiments in the orbiter's Spacelab module. The mission also involved a Mir crew exchange, with two cosmonauts launching on *Atlantis* and staying on board Mir, and three cosmonauts already on Mir returning to Earth on the orbiter.

BRITAIN'S WOMEN'S AUXILIARY AIR FORCE IS FORMED

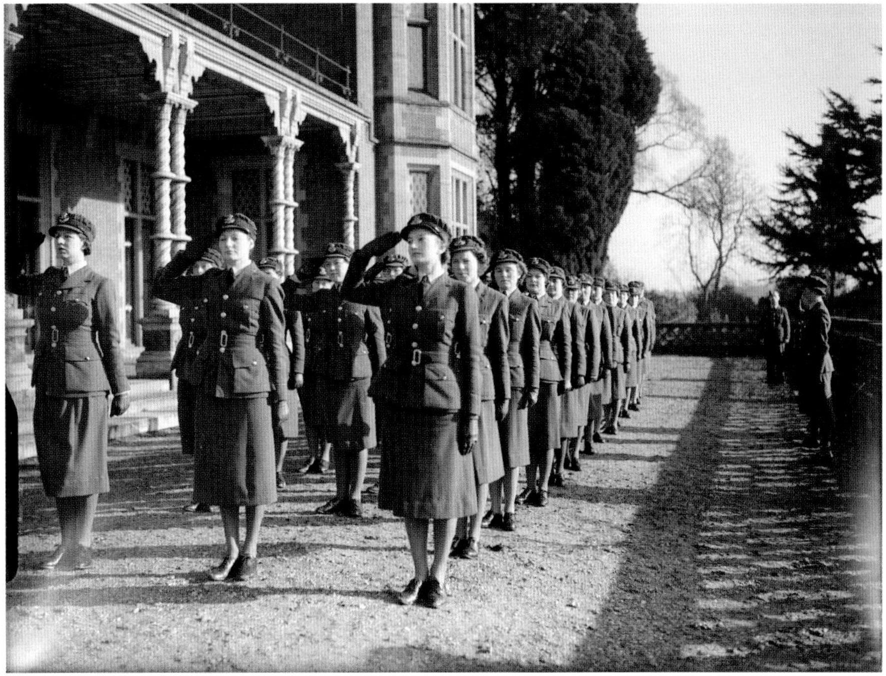

Women's Auxiliary Air Force officers were trained at the WAAF Officers School of Instruction in Gerrards Cross, Buckinghamshire.

Imperial War Museums

As World War II loomed, Great Britain's King George VI established the Women's Auxiliary Air Force (WAAF) on June 28, 1939. The women of the WAAF filled roles on the home front so that their male counterparts in the Royal Air Force could serve on the front lines. Unlike the United States' Women Airforce Service Pilots (WASP—see page 234), however, WAAF members were not pilots or aircrew. Instead, they filled a variety of roles, including completing standard administrative tasks, compiling weather reports, intercepting codes and ciphers, repairing aircraft, and even raising and lowering barrage balloons.

Tens of thousands of women volunteered for the WAAF within its first year. In December 1941, the British government passed the National Service Act, which extended conscription to women and designated the WAAF as one of the organizations they could join. As a result, WAAF membership grew to a quarter million by the time the war ended.

JUNE 29

DIXIE CLIPPER COMPLETES FIRST TRANSATLANTIC AIRLINE FLIGHT

COMMERCIAL AVIATION

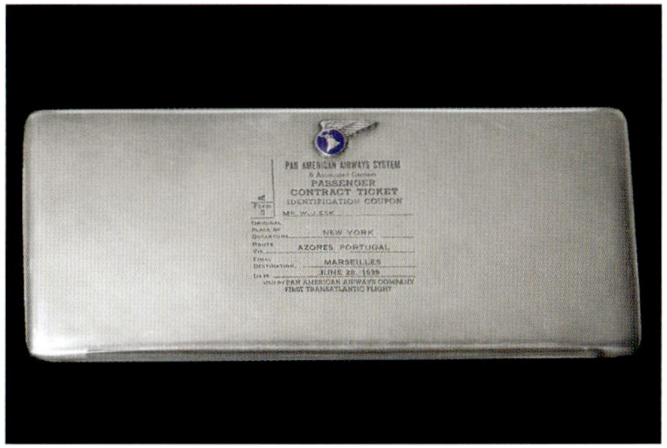

Pan Am presented a silver ticket holder to the first paying passenger to cross the Atlantic by aircraft. It is now part of the National Air and Space Museum collection.

Smithsonian's National Air and Space Museum

The first commercial airline flight across the Atlantic Ocean took place on June 29, 1939. A Boeing Model 314 named *Dixie Clipper* inaugurated Pan American Airways' transatlantic route by flying from New York to France. Among the eleven crewmembers and twenty-two passengers who made the journey were "Passenger Number One" William John Eck and Elizabeth Trippe, the wife of Pan Am president Juan Trippe. The entire flight took twenty-two hours, with stops in the Azores and in Lisbon, Portugal. Eck and the other passengers onboard were treated to fine dining with white table linens and all the comforts of home.

JUNE 30

RICHARD DU PONT SETS ALTITUDE RECORD FOR SAILPLANES

GENERAL AVIATION

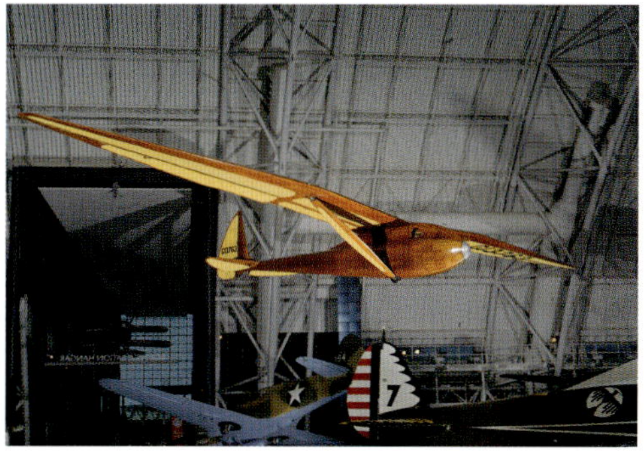

Made of a unique mahogany plywood skin, the Senior Albatross sailplane is on display at the Steven F. Udvar-Hazy Center.

Smithsonian's National Air and Space Museum

In 1933, American aviator Richard du Pont teamed up with engineer Hawley Bowlus to build gliders. The pair's most successful competition sailplane was the Senior Albatross, a unique aircraft that dominated American competitive soaring. Du Pont was also a talented pilot himself and soon began setting records with the glider, including two in 1934. On June 25, he established a world distance record of 158 miles, flying within two miles of New York City. Less than a week later, on June 30, 1934, du Pont set the U.S. altitude record for sailplanes by climbing to 6,223 feet.

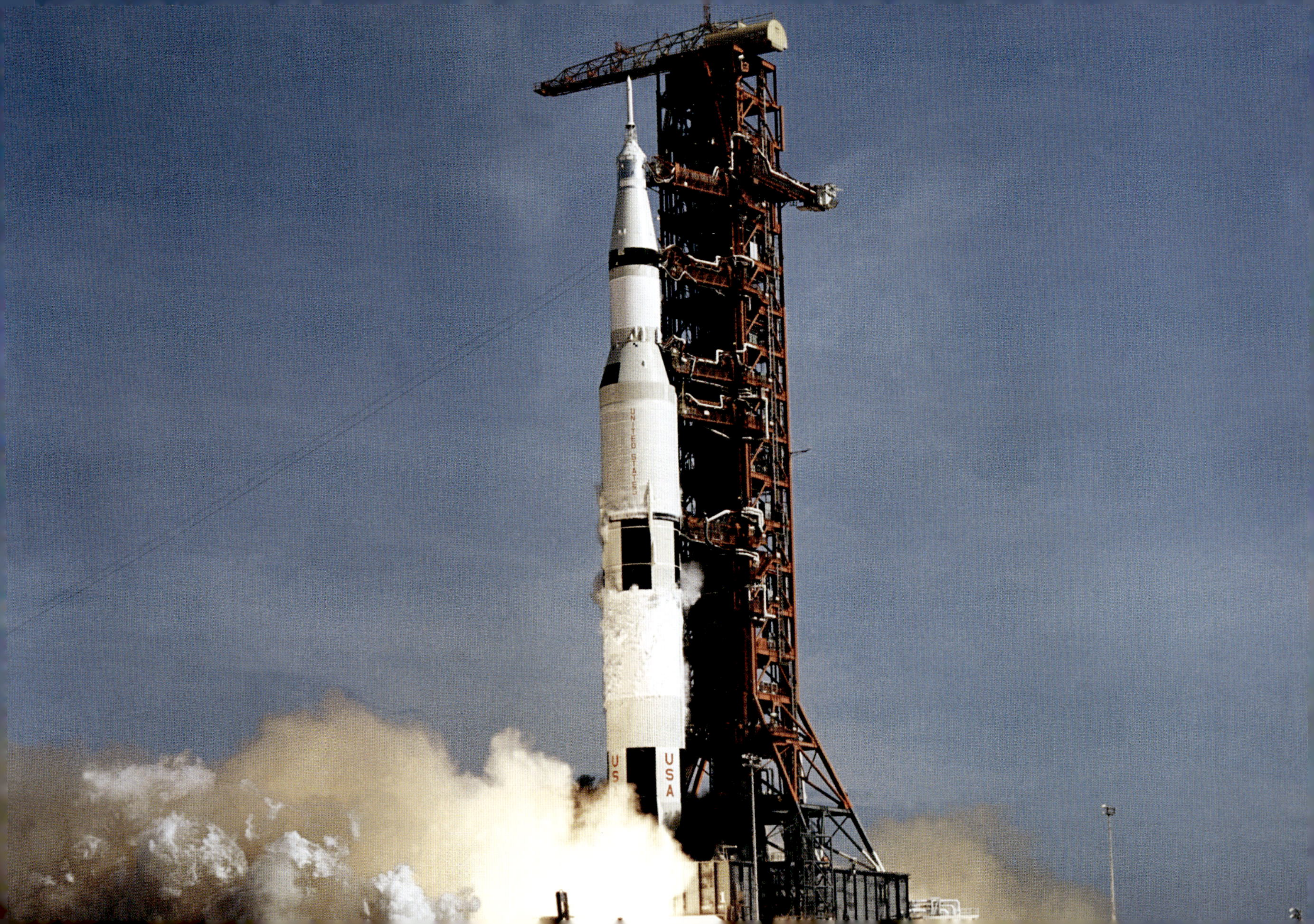
UNITED STATES
USA

JULY

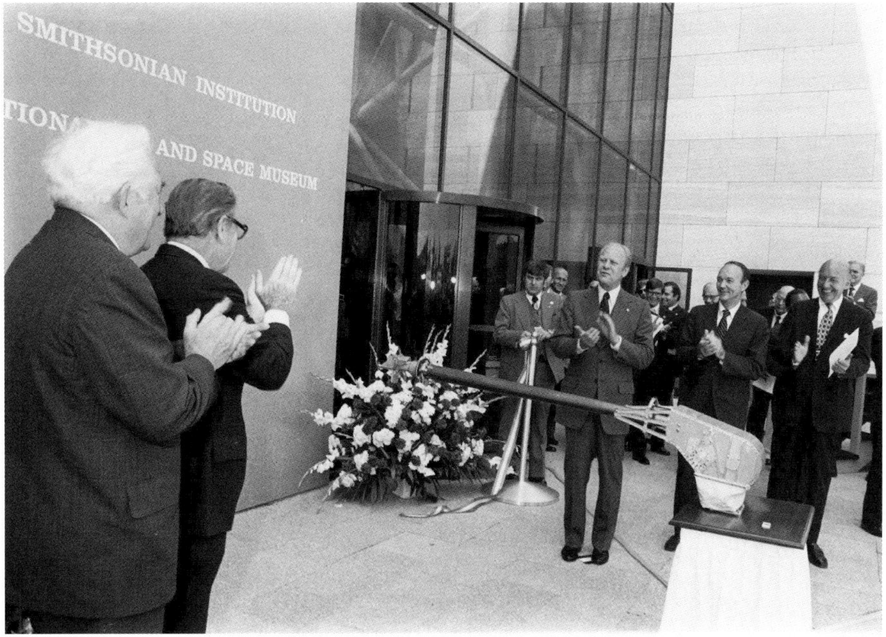

The ribbon cutting at the opening of the National Air and Space Museum in Washington, D.C., was triggered by a signal from the Viking 1 spacecraft in orbit around Mars.

Photo by Richard K. Hofmeister, Smithsonian's National Air and Space Museum (NASM 76-8434-16A)

On July 1, 1976, in the midst of the United States' bicentennial celebration, the Smithsonian Institution's National Air and Space Museum opened to the public to great fanfare. The official ribbon cutting began with a signal sent by the Viking 1 spacecraft in orbit around Mars. Relayed to NASA's Jet Propulsion Laboratory in California, the signal arrived at the Museum via ground lines. The signal activated a mechanical "arm" that cut the ribbon in two.

The Museum's opening was presided over by Museum director and Apollo 11 astronaut Michael Collins and other dignitaries, including President Gerald Ford, Vice President Nelson Rockefeller, Chief Justice Warren Burger, and Smithsonian Secretary S. Dillon Ripley. President Ford called the Museum "a perfect birthday present from the American people to themselves." Record crowds flocked to the Museum in the days and months after it opened. The five millionth visitor crossed the threshold only six months after opening day. In the fifty years since, over 350 million people have visited the National Air and Space Museum building on the National Mall in Washington, D.C.

LARRY WALTERS TAKES FLIGHT IN A LAWN CHAIR

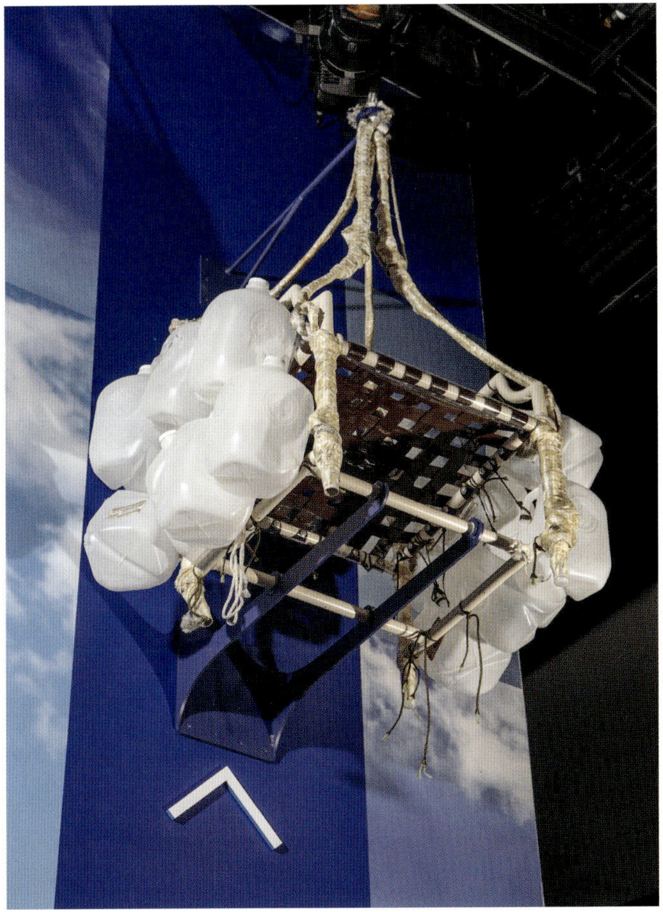

Before a man named Carl flew his house to South America using a bouquet of balloons in the animated film *Up*, there was a man named Larry, a lawn chair, and a cluster of weather balloons. On July 2, 1982, forty-two helium-filled weather balloons lifted Larry Walters and an aluminum lawn chair into the sky above San Pedro, California. As Walters reached 16,000 feet and drifted into the controlled airspace surrounding Los Angeles International Airport, commercial pilots reported sightings of the flying lawn chair to the control tower.

Walters faced freezing temperatures and lower oxygen levels during his amazing flight. To control his altitude, he popped balloons with a BB gun; to control his descent, he poured water from plastic jugs that acted as ballast. Upon landing, the Federal Aviation Administration (FAA) charged Walters with violating controlled airspace, flying without a balloon license, and operating a non-airworthy craft.

Larry Walters gave his aerial lawn chair to a child named Jerry Fleck in the neighborhood where he landed. Fleck later donated the chair to the National Air and Space Museum, where it is on display.

Smithsonian's National Air and Space Museum

NORTHROP N-1M FLYING WING MAKES FIRST FLIGHT

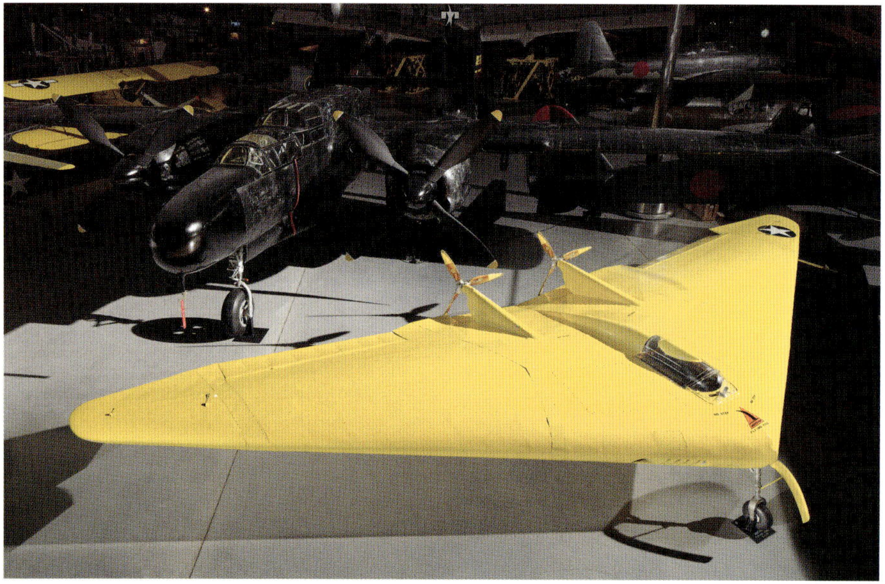

The bright yellow N-1M, on display at the Steven F. Udvar-Hazy Center, was built using plywood over a tubular steel airframe.

Smithsonian's National Air and Space Museum

John "Jack" Northrop's dream of an all-wing aircraft became a reality on July 3, 1940, when his Northrop Model 1 Mockup (N-1M) flew for the first time. As the designer of famous aircraft like the Lockheed Vega and Northrop Alpha, Northrop believed that conventional tailed aircraft were less efficient than all-wing aircraft since the latter would be unencumbered by non-lifting components like a fuselage and tail.

The N-1M was the first all-wing aircraft designed, built, and flown in the United States. Northrop planned to use the experimental prototype to determine how best to stabilize and control an all-wing aircraft. His ultimate goal was to build an all-wing heavy bomber, and he followed up the N-1M with a larger mockup called the N-9M. Though Northrop did eventually build a series of all-wing heavy bomber prototypes, none entered production before the Air Force ended the all-wing program in 1950.

PATHFINDER LANDS ON MARS WITH *SOJOURNER* ROVER

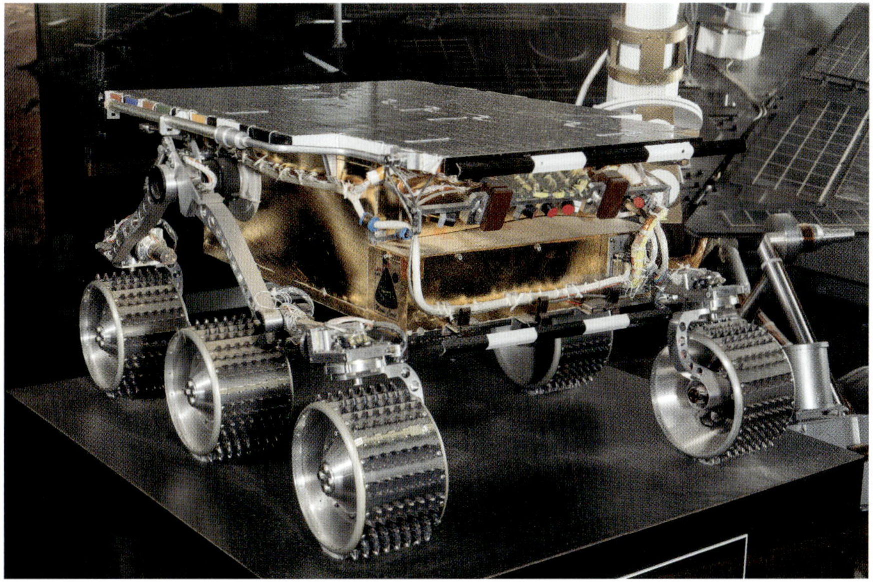

The *Sojourner* rover flight spare on display at the National Air and Space Museum is named *Marie Curie*, after the famed scientist.

Smithsonian's National Air and Space Museum

Over twenty years passed between Viking (see page 188) landing on Mars and the next spacecraft touching down on the Red Planet. On July 4, 1997, Mars Pathfinder entered the planet's thin atmosphere, was slowed by a parachute and rockets, and then landed on the surface encased inside inflated airbags that bounced to a stop. Pathfinder used a television camera and scientific instruments to gather data on the Martian weather and atmosphere, and its solar cells provided power for the spacecraft to operate and communicate.

Pathfinder is perhaps best remembered for delivering the first rover to the Martian surface. *Sojourner* was a technology demonstration, proving that it was possible to operate wheeled vehicles on Mars. After Pathfinder's protective shell unfolded to provide three flat platforms, *Sojourner* wheeled down a ramp from the spacecraft and onto the Martian surface. The rover, which was operational for eighty-five days, drove 330 total feet, took photos of the surface, and measured the composition of rocks near the lander. It was named for Sojourner Truth, the nineteenth-century abolitionist who also fought for women's rights.

JULY 5

CENTURY OF PROGRESS DEPARTS ON ROUND-THE-WORLD ATTEMPT

GENERAL AVIATION

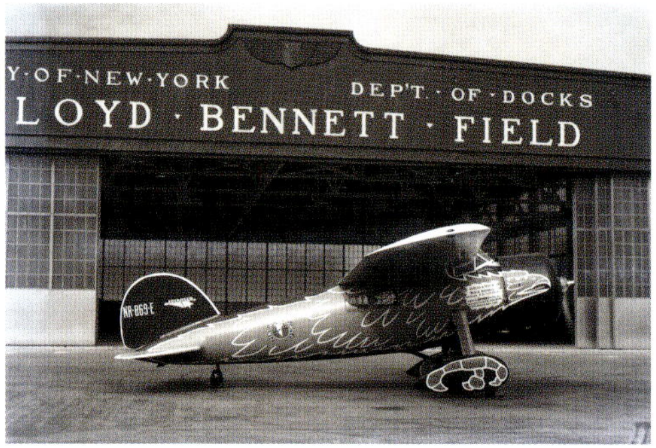

Mattern and Griffin named their Lockheed Vega *Century of Progress* in honor of the 1933–34 Chicago World's Fair.

Rudy Arnold Photo Collection, Smithsonian's National Air and Space Museum (NASM 91-17366)

On July 5, 1932, American pilots James "Jimmie" Mattern and Bennett Griffin took off from New York's Floyd Bennett Field in a Lockheed Vega named *Century of Progress*. Their goal was to fly around the world faster than famed aviator Wiley Post had done the year before. After departing New York, Mattern and Griffin flew to Newfoundland, Ireland, and Berlin before crashing in Belarus. Soviet officials briefly detained the pair on suspicion of espionage, but they were soon allowed to return to the U.S.

JULY 6

AIRSHIP R34 COMPLETES FIRST AIRSHIP CROSSING OF ATLANTIC

LIGHTER-THAN-AIR FLIGHT

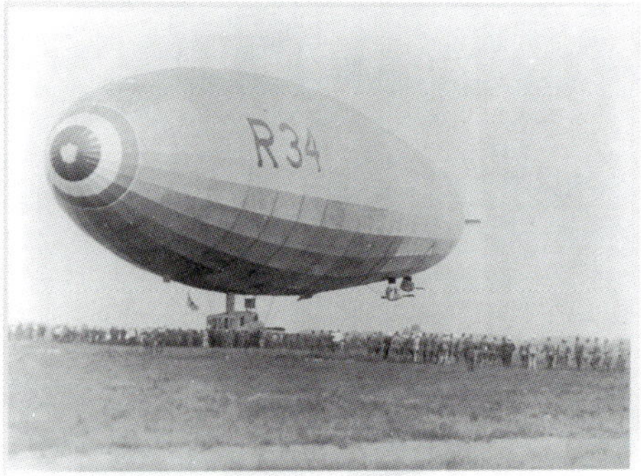

The 643-foot-long airship R34 was ironically known as *Tiny*.

Library of Congress

The British airship R34 was the first aircraft to fly nonstop across the Atlantic Ocean. Operated by the Royal Air Force (RAF), R34 completed its flight from East Lothian, Scotland, to Mineola, New York, on July 5, 1919. Upon the airship's arrival, RAF Maj. J. E. M. Pritchard became the first foreigner to reach United States soil by air. Since the landing crew in Mineola had no experience with large airships, Pritchard parachuted out to provide instructions to secure the R34.

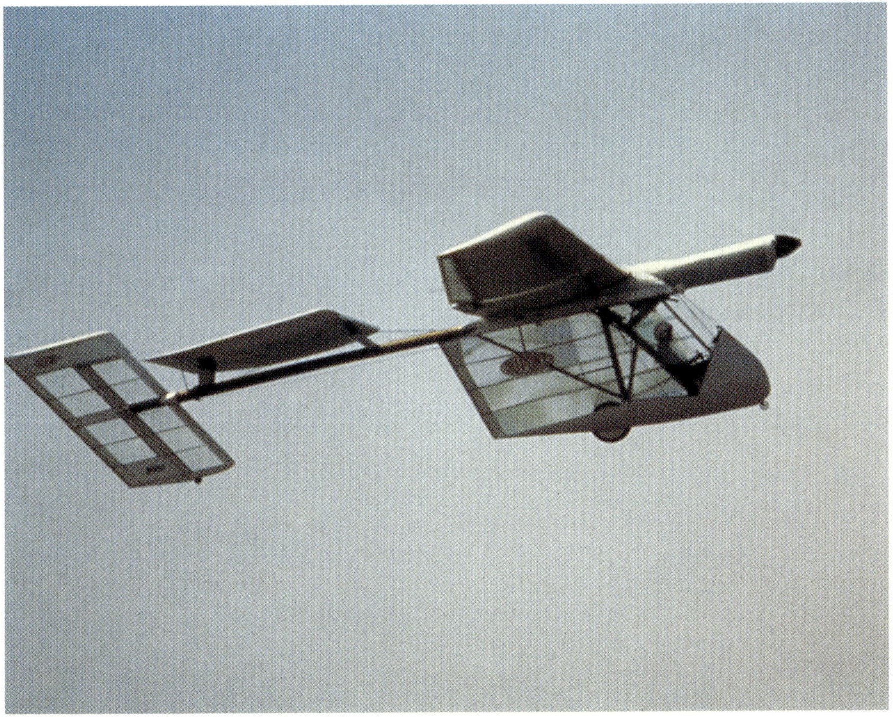

Solar Challenger was a solar-powered aircraft designed by Paul MacCready.

Smithsonian's National Air and Space Museum (NASM 2003-12991)

In the 1970s and 1980s, aeronautical engineer Paul MacCready's company AeroVironment built a variety of unusual aircraft that were powered using alternative energy sources. Some of the most notable aircraft designed by MacCready and his team were the Gossamer Condor, the first human-powered airplane; the Gossamer Albatross, the first human-powered airplane to fly across the English Channel (see page 180); and the Gossamer Penguin, a solar-powered version of the Albatross.

In November 1980, the team also launched the Solar Challenger, which soon became the first solar-powered aircraft to fly across the English Channel. Piloted by Stephen Ptacek, Solar Challenger's history-making flight took place on July 7, 1981. The 163-mile journey began at an airport north of Paris and ended at an air force base south of London some five and a half hours later. Sixteen thousand solar cells on Solar Challenger's 46.5-foot wingspan powered the aircraft on its flight.

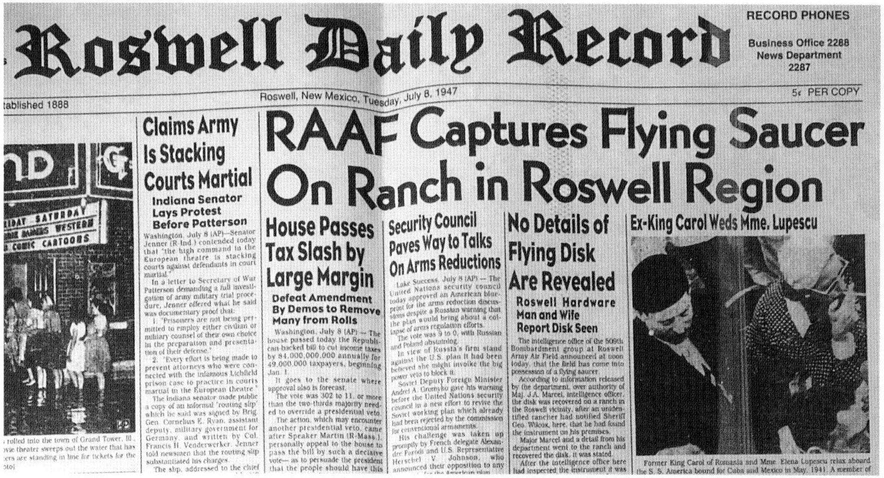

Roswell Daily Record

RECORD PHONES
Business Office 2288
News Department
2287

Established 1888 — Roswell, New Mexico, Tuesday, July 8, 1947 — 5¢ PER COPY

RAAF Captures Flying Saucer On Ranch in Roswell Region

Claims Army Is Stacking Courts Martial

Indiana Senator Lays Protest Before Patterson

Washington, July 8 (AP)—Senator Jenner (R-Ind.) contended today that "the high command in the European theatre is stacking courts against defendants in court martial."

In a letter to Secretary of War Patterson demanding a full investigation of army military trial procedure, Jenner offered what he said was documentary proof that:

1. "Prisoners are not being permitted to employ either civilian or military counsel of their own choice in the preparation and presentation of their defense."

2. "Every effort is being made to prevent attorneys who were connected with the infamous Lichfield prison case to practice in courts martial in the European theatre."

The Indiana senator made public a copy of an informal 'routing slip' which he said was signed by Brig. Gen. Cornelius E. Ryan, assistant deputy, military government for Germany, and written by Col. Francis H. Venderwerker. Jenner told newsmen that the routing slip substantiated his charges.

The slip, addressed to the chief

House Passes Tax Slash by Large Margin

Defeat Amendment By Demos to Remove Many from Rolls

Washington, July 8 (AP) — The house passed today the Republican-backed bill to cut income taxes by 84,000,000,000 annually for 49,000,000 taxpayers, beginning Jan. 1.

It goes to the senate where approval also is forecast.

The vote was 302 to 11, or more than the two-thirds majority needed to override a presidential veto.

The action, which may encounter another presidential veto, came after Speaker Martin (R-Mass.) personally appeal to the house to pass the bill by such a decisive vote— as to persuade the president that the people should have this

Security Council Paves Way to Talks On Arms Reductions

Lake Success, July 8 (AP) — The United Nations security council today approved an American blueprint for the arms reduction discussions despite a Russian warning that the plan would bring about a collapse of arms regulation efforts.

The vote was 9 to 0, with Russian and Poland abstaining.

In view of Russia's firm stand against the U.S. plan it had been believed she might invoke the big power veto to block it.

Soviet Deputy Foreign Minister Andrei A. Gromyko gave his warning before the United Nations security council in a new effort to revive the Soviet working plan which already had been rejected by the commission for conventional armaments.

His challenge was taken up promptly by French delegate Alexandre Parodi and U.S. Representative Herschel V. Johnson, who announced their opposition to any

No Details of Flying Disk Are Revealed

Roswell Hardware Man and Wife Report Disk Seen

The intelligence office of the 509th Bombardment group at Roswell Army Air Field announced at noon today, that the field has come into possession of a flying saucer.

According to information released by the department, over authority of Maj. J.A. Marcel, intelligence officer, the disk was recovered on a ranch in the Roswell vicinity, after an unidentified rancher had notified Sheriff Geo. Wilcox, here, that he had found the instrument on his premises.

Major Marcel and a detail from his department went to the ranch and recovered the disk, it was stated.

After the intelligence office here had inspected the instrument it was

Ex-King Carol Weds Mme. Lupescu

Former King Carol of Romania and Mme. Elena Lupescu relax aboard the S. S. America bound for Cuba and Mexico in May, 1941. A member of

A headline about a flying saucer in Roswell was just the beginning of the New Mexico town's alien legacy.

Roswell Daily Record

"RAAF Captures Flying Saucer on Ranch in Roswell Region." This lead headline in New Mexico's *Roswell Daily Record* on July 8, 1947, started an enduring legend. The crash debris found near Roswell kicked off a chain of events that led to many conspiracy theories and a tourism economy based on aliens.

A few days before the news broke, rancher Mac Brazel heard a loud explosion during a thunderstorm and found debris covering a three-quarter-mile area. When he reported it to military officials, they told him it was a weather balloon. But Brazel was suspicious. Because it was not like any weather balloon he'd seen, rumors about the official story began to circulate, and a cover-up seemed to be the only explanation.

In 1995, an explanation arrived when the Army released information about Project Mogul, a top-secret balloon built to detect Soviet nuclear testing in the atmosphere. Though the revelation seemed to dispel the myth of a flying saucer crash, by that point, it was too late—the story had taken on a life of its own, and Roswell remains associated with aliens to this day.

VOYAGER 2 MAKES CLOSEST APPROACH TO JUPITER

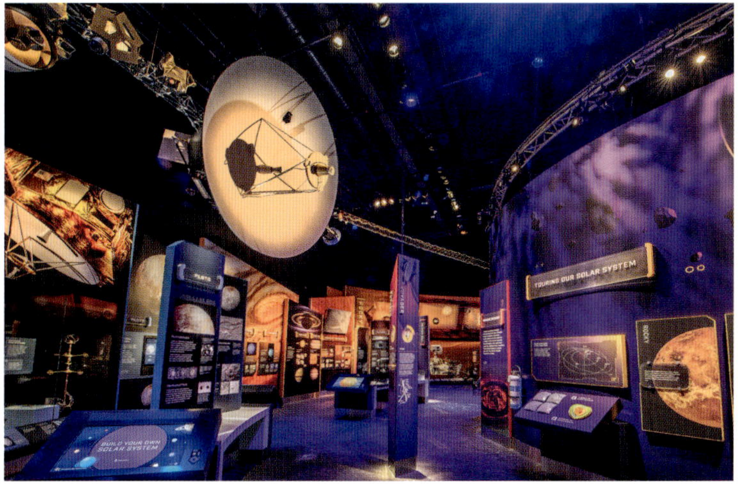

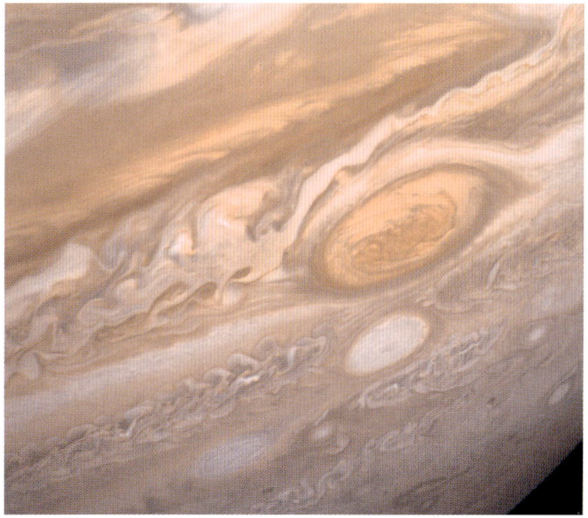

NASA began working seriously in the early 1970s on a new mission to explore the outer planets of our solar system. The mission involved launching two spacecraft to Jupiter and Saturn with the possibility of exploring more planets. The program's name, Voyager, was chosen through a 1977 naming competition. Voyager 1 explored Jupiter and Saturn, and its twin, Voyager 2, flew by Jupiter and Saturn and then shifted its path to visit Uranus and Neptune.

Voyager 2 arrived at Jupiter in April 1979. While in the Jovian system, it flew by the moons Callisto, Ganymede, Europa, Amalthea, and Io. The spacecraft made its closest approach to the gas giant on July 9, 1979, collecting data and transmitting photos. Among other discoveries, Voyager 2's exploration revealed that Jupiter's Great Red Spot was a complex storm moving in a counterclockwise direction.

LEFT A full-scale mock-up of the Voyager spacecraft is on display at the National Air and Space Museum.

Smithsonian's National Air and Space Museum

RIGHT While at Jupiter, Voyager 2 took photos of the gas giant's swirling clouds.

NASA-Caltech

TELSTAR 1 LAUNCHES

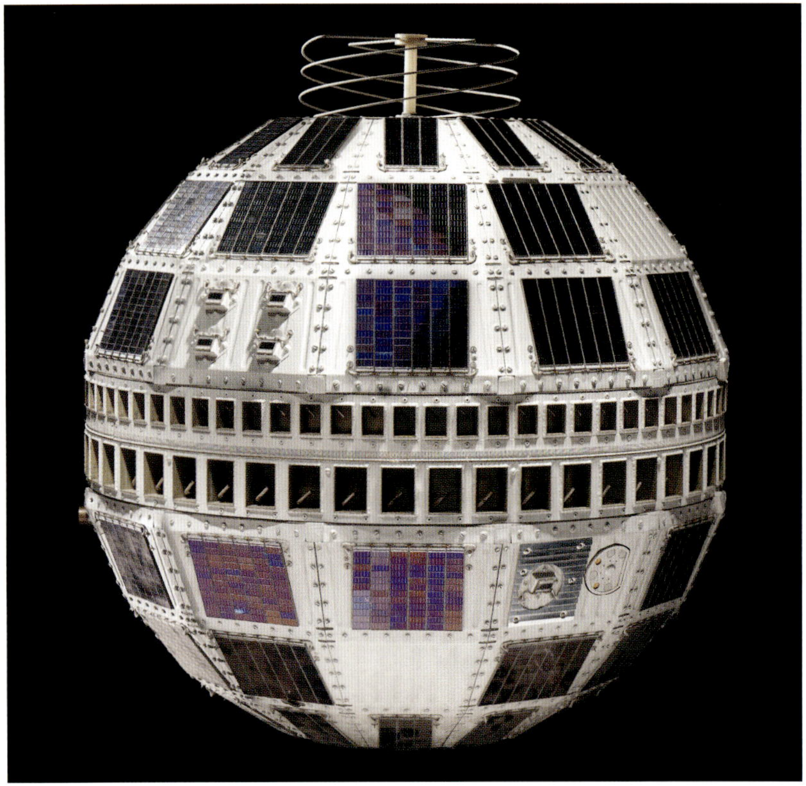

Telstar was covered with small solar cells to catch solar energy. A Telstar flight spare is on display at the National Air and Space Museum.

Smithsonian's National Air and Space Museum

Launched on July 10, 1962, Telstar 1 was the world's first active communications satellite. It was developed by AT&T, who used the satellite to test basic features of communications via space. Telstar began the era of live international television, enabling the first transatlantic television transmissions. Soon after launch, it relayed television images between the United States, France, and England. Images of a taped performance by French singer Yves Montand, a Philadelphia Phillies–Chicago Cubs baseball game, and a live news conference by President John F. Kennedy were the first audio-visual information exchanged in real time among the citizens of the "global village."

In November 1962, Telstar's electronics became compromised through exposure to Van Allen Belt radiation, resulting in the satellite's deactivation in February 1963. Although it operated for less than a year, Telstar was one of the most significant communications satellites of the early Space Age, raising the question of whether communications satellites should be operated and controlled by governments or by private corporations.

SKYLAB REENTERS EARTH'S ATMOSPHERE

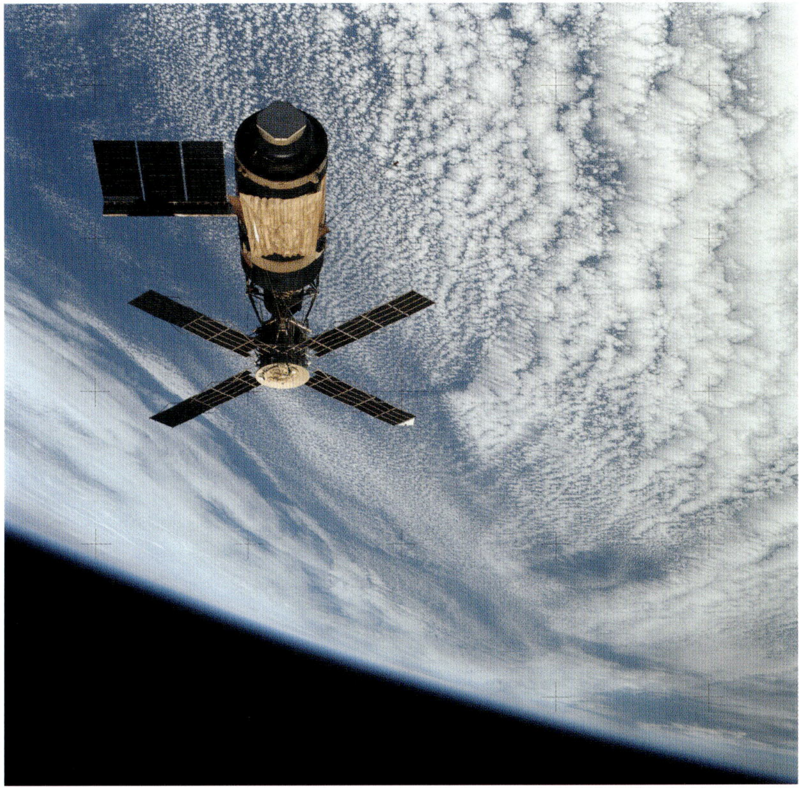

The Skylab space station was visited by three crews before it was deorbited.

NASA

On July 11, 1979, the first U.S. space station (see page 150) fell out of orbit. But it wasn't a surprise, error, or disaster. When NASA's third crewed Skylab mission left the space station in 1974, the space agency powered it down. Skylab drifted in a "parking orbit" for five years, but its orbit deteriorated more quickly than estimated because of a very active period of solar activity that affected the atmosphere and increased drag on the space station.

By 1978, it was clear that Skylab was losing altitude and would fall out of orbit without intervention. With the Space Shuttle program behind schedule and therefore unable to boost it higher, NASA began work on a controlled return for Skylab. When the orbital workshop reentered Earth's atmosphere, it was positioned by controllers to break up over the Indian Ocean, preventing debris from scattering in populated areas. While most debris fell in the ocean, some landed in western Australia. No one was hurt, and no significant property damage occurred.

JULY 12

EISENHOWER BECOMES THE FIRST U.S. PRESIDENT TO FLY IN A HELICOPTER

VERTICAL FLIGHT

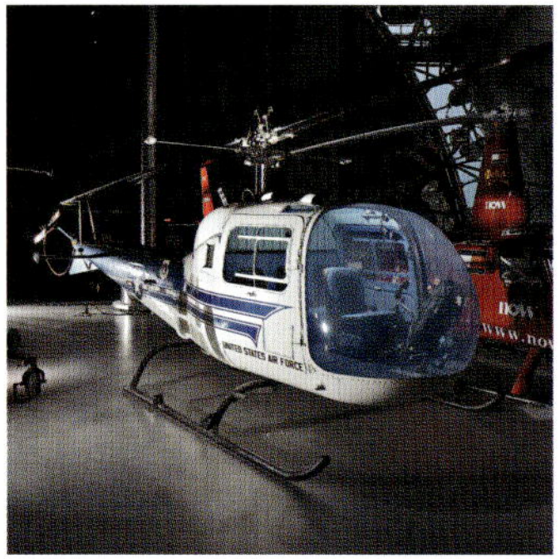

The Bell H-13J from the historic first presidential helicopter flight is on display at the Steven F. Udvar-Hazy Center.

Smithsonian's National Air and Space Museum

Dwight D. Eisenhower became the first American president to fly in a helicopter on July 12, 1957. The flight was part of a simulated nuclear alert staged to test how quickly the commander in chief and other government officials could reach a safe haven outside of Washington, D.C., in the event of an emergency. Eisenhower's personal helicopter pilot, U.S. Air Force Maj. Joseph E. Barrett, flew the rotorcraft and a Secret Service agent occupied the seat next to the president.

JULY 13

INTERNATIONAL SPACE PROGRAMS

LUNA 15 LAUNCHES

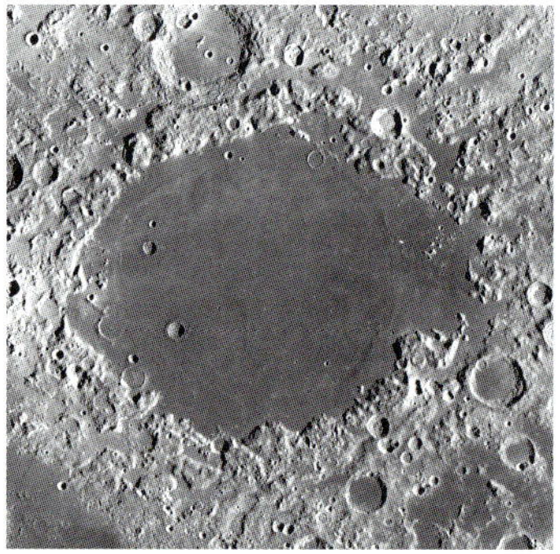

The Soviet Union's Luna 15 spacecraft crashed on the Moon in *Mare Crisium* (the Sea of Crises), nearly 350 miles from where Neil Armstrong and Buzz Aldrin landed on the Moon the day before.

NASA

Just three days before the Apollo 11 mission launched to the Moon, the Soviet Union launched its own lunar exploration mission on July 13, 1969—though not with a crew on board. The robotic Luna 15 spacecraft entered lunar orbit four days after launch and was programmed to land on the Moon the same day as the Apollo 11 astronauts. However, erratic readings from the spacecraft's altimeter delayed the landing. The Soviets instead made a landing attempt July 21, which ended with Luna 15 crashing into a lunar mountain.

JULY 14

MARINER 4 BECOMES FIRST SPACECRAFT TO FLY BY MARS

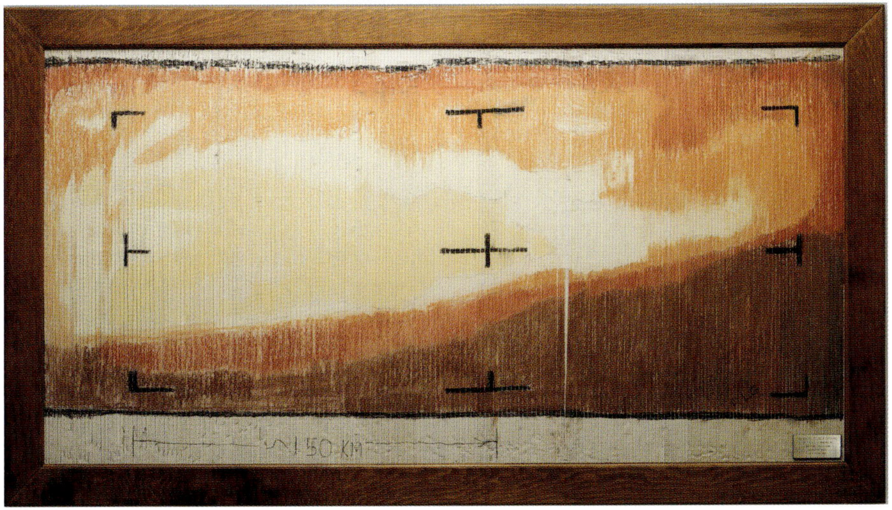

Employees at NASA's Jet Propulsion Laboratory created a hand-colored version of Mariner 4's image of Mars.

NASA/Dan Goods

Mariner 4 was the first spacecraft to fly by Mars and obtain and transmit close range images of the planet. It passed within 6,000 miles of Mars on July 14, 1965. With its state-of-the-art cameras, the spacecraft acquired surface images composed of two hundred lines of two hundred pixels each (with an average resolution of about 1.86 miles per pixel). Capturing data every forty-eight seconds, Mariner 4 completed its flyby with twenty-two television pictures of the Martian surface stored on its four-track tape recorder.

It took four more days to transmit the image information to Earth. Employees at NASA's Jet Propulsion Laboratory were understandably anxious to see Mariner 4's up-close photos of Mars. Once the data was received, they took a "paint by numbers" approach instead of waiting for the official processed image. Using a "real-time data translator machine" that converted the data into numbers on strips of paper, scientists assembled the strips and hand colored them based on the numbers.

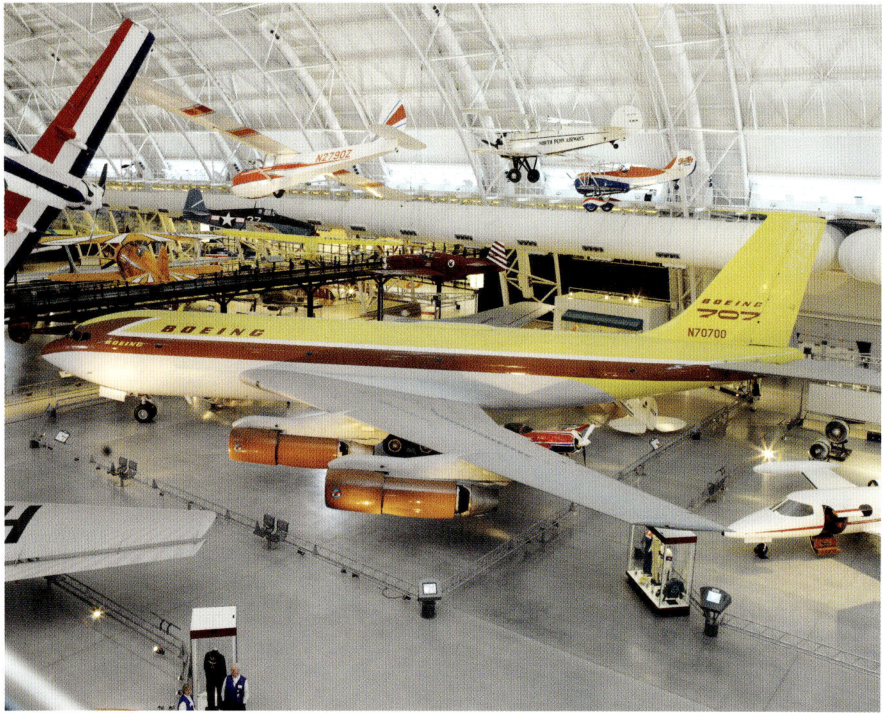

The Boeing 707 prototype is on display at the Steven F. Udvar-Hazy Center.

Smithsonian's National Air and Space Museum

On July 15, 1954, the Boeing 367-80 took flight for the first time in the skies over Seattle. The "Dash 80" revolutionized commercial air transportation when it entered service as the famous Boeing 707, America's first jet airliner. The first flight made clear that Boeing had a winner. Not only was the Dash 80 significantly larger than Britain's leading jet airliner, the de Havilland Comet, it could also fly a hundred miles per hour faster.

One of the Dash 80's most famous flights occurred in 1955 at Lake Washington in Seattle, where Boeing had assembled a group of airline representatives to witness a flyby of the new airliner. To the audience's intense delight—and Boeing's profound shock—test pilot Alvin "Tex" Johnston barrel-rolled the Dash 80 over the lake in full view of the astonished spectators. Johnston's stunt vividly displayed the superior strength and performance of Boeing's latest aircraft, readily convincing the airline industry to purchase the new model.

JULY 16

APOLLO 11 LAUNCHES

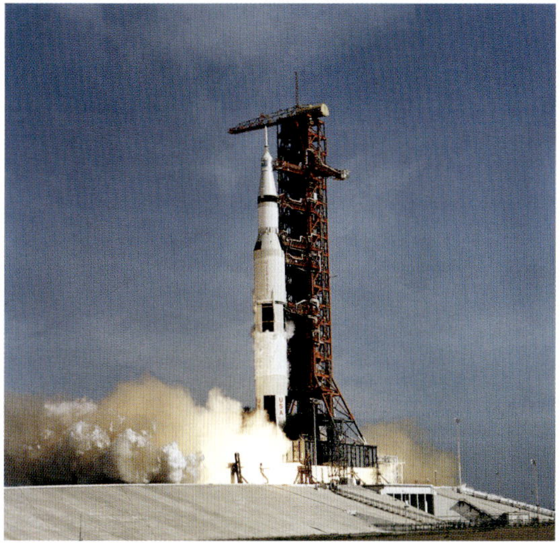

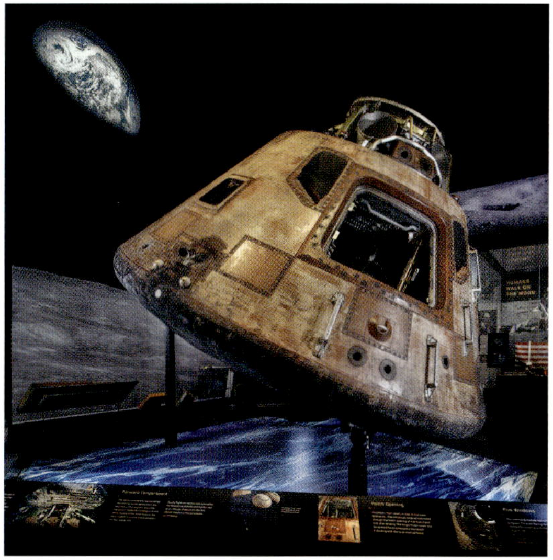

LEFT For five decades, the Saturn V rocket, which launched the Apollo 11 mission to space, was the largest and most powerful launch vehicle ever built.

NASA

RIGHT The command module that took Neil Armstrong, Michael Collins, and Buzz Aldrin to lunar orbit and back is on display at the National Air and Space Museum.

Smithsonian's National Air and Space Museum

"We have a liftoff, thirty-two minutes past the hour. Liftoff on Apollo 11!" Jack King, the "voice of Apollo launch control" uttered those words on July 16, 1969, as Apollo 11 launched on a Saturn V rocket from Kennedy Space Center. Over a million spectators, including Vice President Spiro Agnew and former president Lyndon B. Johnson, came to the launch. Hundreds of millions more around the world tuned in to watch as the crew of Apollo 11 (see page 24) began their journey to the Moon.

For most of the eight-day mission, the crew traveled in their command module named *Columbia*. Not much bigger than a large automobile, *Columbia* had just enough room for the astronauts to live and work and featured all of the essential elements for survival in outer space. The other part of the Apollo 11 spacecraft was the lunar module *Eagle*, which Neil Armstrong and Buzz Aldrin used to descend to the surface of the Moon halfway through the mission.

APOLLO-SOYUZ TEST PROJECT DOCKING TAKES PLACE

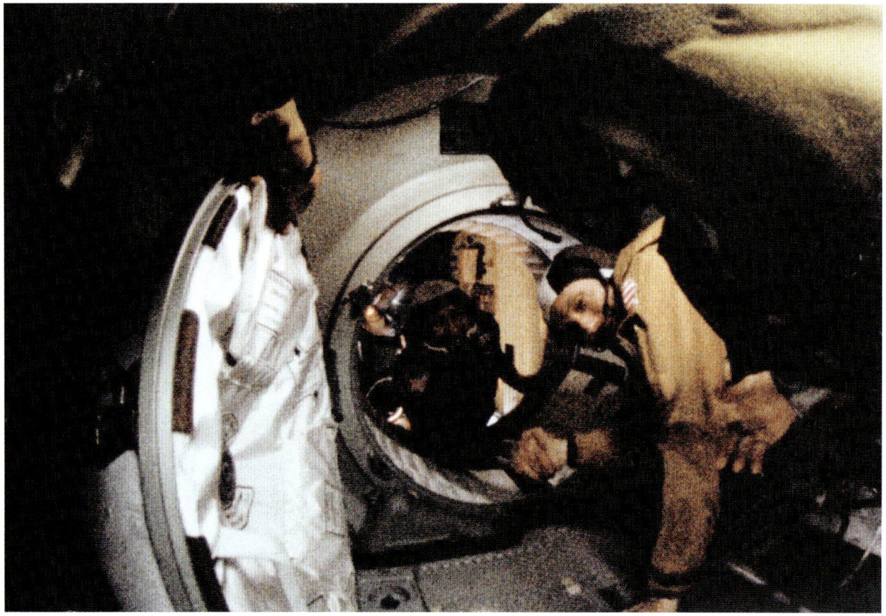

American astronaut Tom Stafford and Soviet cosmonaut Aleksei Leonov shook hands during the Apollo-Soyuz Test Project mission.

NASA

On July 17, 1975, American and Soviet spacecraft rendezvoused in the first international human spaceflight mission: the Apollo-Soyuz Test Project. This joint effort between the two major world superpowers and rivals in space was based on an agreement signed in 1972. That arrangement set a precedent for future joint efforts such as the Shuttle-Mir Program and the International Space Station.

The mission began when the United States launched an Apollo command and service module from Kennedy Space Center in Florida with astronauts Thomas Stafford, Donald "Deke" Slayton, and Vance Brand on board and the Soviet Union launched a Soyuz spacecraft from Baikonur Cosmodrome in Kazakhstan with cosmonauts Aleksei Leonov and Valery Kubasov on board. What came next were two different kinds of handshakes. First, the spacecraft rendezvoused and docked while in a circular Earth orbit. After hatches between the spacecraft opened, the crews greeted each other and the two commanders, Stafford and Leonov, shook hands. The spacecraft undocked two days later, and the U.S. command module splashed down on July 24.

JULY 18

MECHANIC AND PILOT EARNS THE NICKNAME "WRONG WAY CORRIGAN"

GENERAL AVIATION

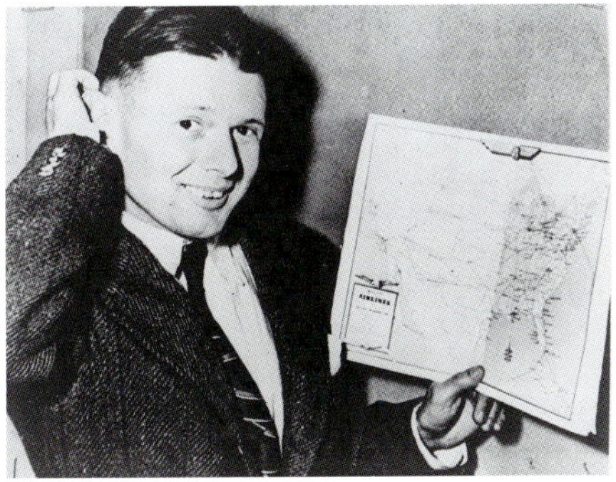

Douglas "Wrong Way" Corrigan never admitted to intentionally flying across the Atlantic instead of to California.

Library of Congress

Douglas Corrigan was an aircraft mechanic who worked on Charles Lindbergh's *Spirit of St. Louis*. On July 18, 1938, Corrigan made a transatlantic flight of his own that earned him the nickname "Wrong Way Corrigan." Although he had filed plans to fly his rebuilt 1929 Curtiss Robin across the Atlantic Ocean from New York to Dublin, the Bureau of Air Commerce deemed Corrigan's airplane unsafe for the journey. When he took off to fly west back to California, Corrigan instead flew east to Ireland, using the excuse that a navigational error and mistakes reading his compass resulted in him flying the wrong direction.

JULY 19

CURTISS-WRIGHT XP-55 ASCENDER MAKES FIRST FLIGHT

WORLD WAR II MILITARY AVIATION

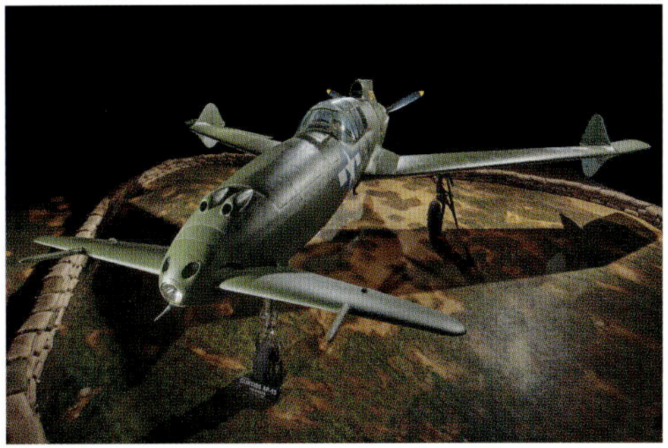

Only three XP-55s were built. The sole surviving Ascender is in the collection of the National Air and Space Museum.

Smithsonian's National Air and Space Museum

Curtiss-Wright defied convention with the XP-55 Ascender. Tasked with developing a pusher-type fighter aircraft—a configuration in which the propellers are behind the engines—engineers took a different approach. They placed the engine behind the pilot, mounted a canard near the nose, and placed two vertical tails at the end of swept wings. The XP-55 flew for the first time on July 19, 1943, but proved to be a failure despite multiple modifications. Besides its tendency to stall without warning, the unusual aircraft was slow compared to most other fighters already in production.

APOLLO 11 ASTRONAUTS TAKE HUMANITY'S FIRST STEPS ON THE MOON

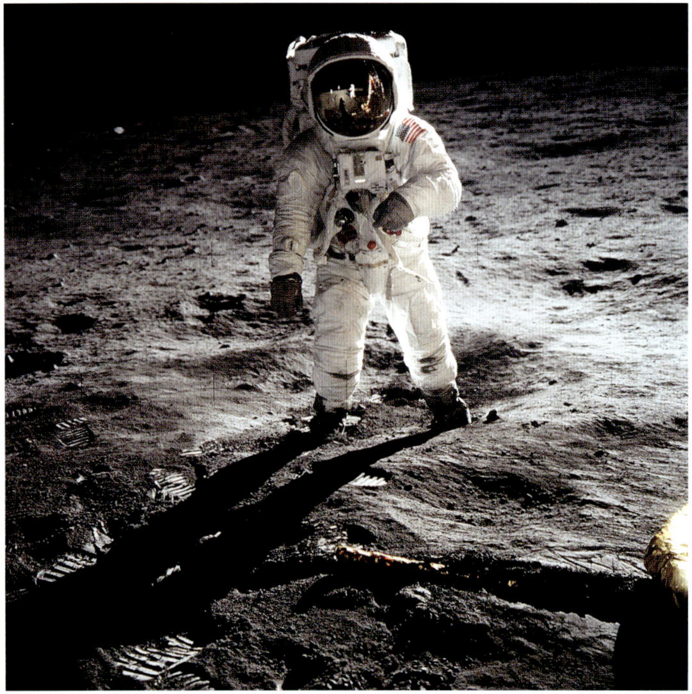

ABOVE The iconic photo of Buzz Aldrin on the Moon was taken by Neil Armstrong.

NASA

OPPOSITE PAGE Command module *Columbia* and Neil Armstrong's Apollo 11 spacesuit are on display at the National Air and Space Museum.

Smithsonian's National Air and Space Museum

The world was watching on July 20, 1969, when the Apollo 11 lunar module *Eagle* touched down on the Moon and mission commander Neil Armstrong and lunar module pilot Buzz Aldrin took their first steps on the lunar surface. At 1:44 P.M. Eastern time, *Eagle* separated from command module *Columbia* and began its descent to the surface of the Moon. Command module pilot Michael Collins stayed aboard *Columbia,* serving as a communications link and photographing the Moon.

At 4:17 P.M., the lunar module landed on the Moon. The landing wasn't without drama, however. *Eagle*'s computer became overloaded during the final minutes of the landing process, receiving more information than its memory could handle, and it blared out a 1202 alarm. The lunar module's fuel was getting perilously low, but Mission Control gave Apollo 11 a "go" for landing, and *Eagle* safely touched down.

At 10:39 P.M., Armstrong opened the hatch of the lunar module and began climbing down the ladder. And at 10:51 P.M., Armstrong stepped off the ladder and onto the lunar surface, becoming the first person to walk on the Moon. Some estimates state that 650 million people watched Armstrong take those steps live. Buzz Aldrin followed Armstrong soon after, and the two astronauts explored the Moon for over two hours before returning to the lunar module.

"That's one small step for man, one giant leap for mankind."

—NEIL ARMSTRONG

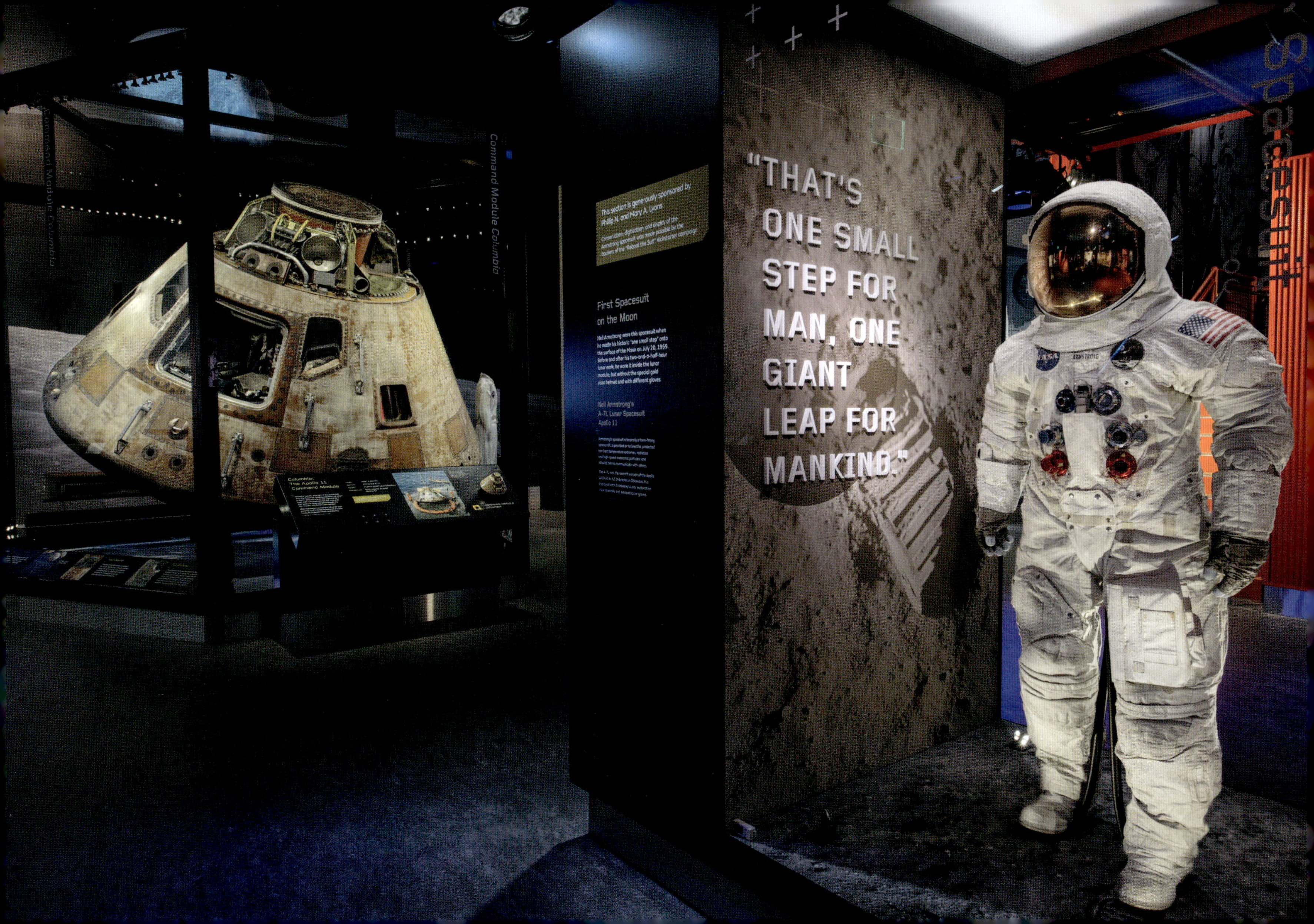
Command Module Columbia
This section is generously sponsored by
Phillip N. and Mary A. Lyons
First Spacesuit
on the Moon
Neil Armstrong wore this spacesuit when
he made his historic "one small step" onto
the surface of the Moon on July 20, 1969.
Before and after his two-and-a-half-hour
lunar walk, he wore it inside the lunar
module, but without the special gold
visor helmet and with different gloves.
Neil Armstrong's
A-7L Lunar Spacesuit
Apollo 11
"THAT'S ONE SMALL STEP FOR MAN, ONE GIANT LEAP FOR MANKIND."
ARMSTRONG
Spacesuit

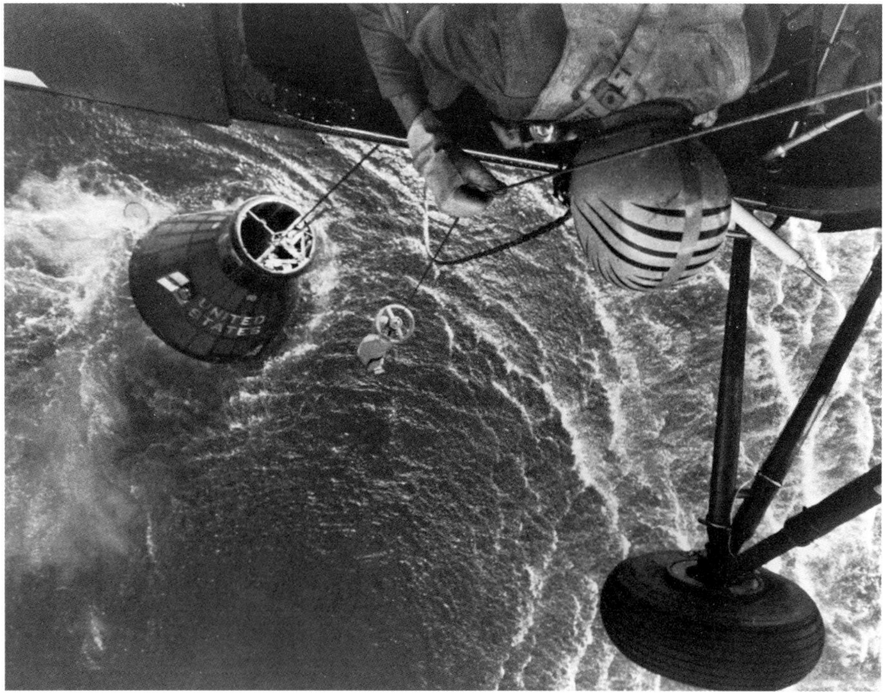

A Marine Corps helicopter was unsuccessful in retrieving the *Liberty Bell 7* spacecraft after it started to sink.

NASA

On July 21, 1961, Virgil "Gus" Grissom launched on the second Mercury mission, becoming the third human and second American in space. The fifteen-minute spaceflight itself, nearly identical to Alan Shepard's a few months before (see page 143), went off without a hitch. Soon after splashdown, though, the hatch of Grissom's *Liberty Bell 7* spacecraft suddenly blew off, and seawater poured in. Grissom got out and swam away from the sinking spacecraft.

When the awaiting Sikorsky UH-34D hooked onto *Liberty Bell 7* to lift it, the water inside made it too heavy for the helicopter. The helicopter pilot, intent on salvaging the spacecraft, even put all three wheels of his aircraft in the water as he gained leverage. Grissom, meanwhile, found himself slowly sinking as water leaked in through the oxygen hose inlet of his spacesuit. Blasted by the helicopter's rotor wash, Grissom waved frantically to the helicopter. After *Liberty Bell 7* sank, and fortunately before Grissom did, the helicopter crew gave up on the vehicle and lowered a rescue sling, taking the wet and exhausted astronaut back to the waiting aircraft carrier.

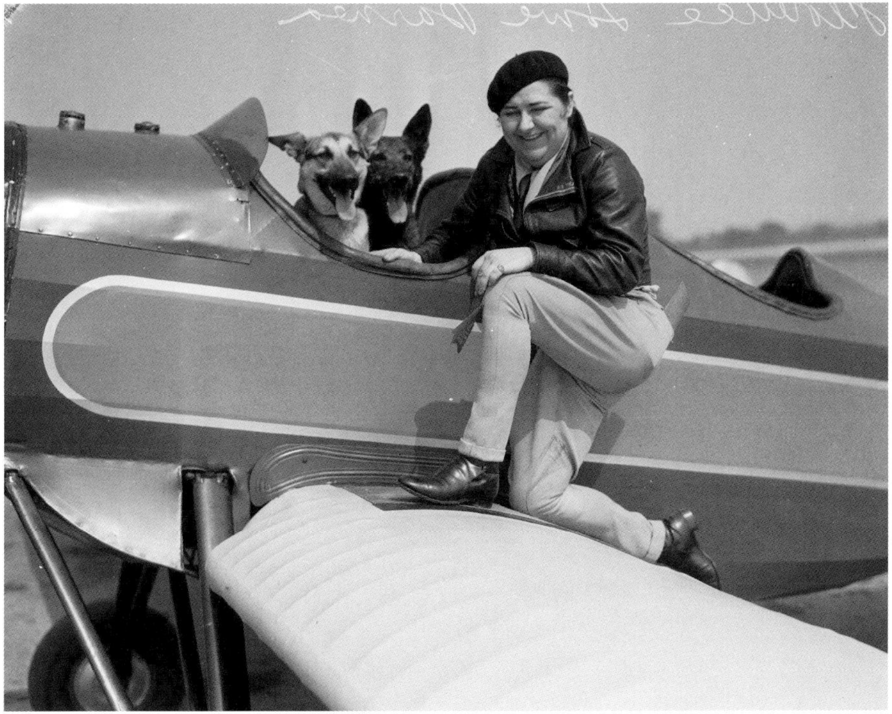

Pancho Barnes was an air racer, stunt flyer, test pilot, and entrepreneur who owned a ranch frequented by some of aviation's finest.

University of California, Los Angeles Library (CC BY 4.0)

Born into a life of privilege as Florence Lowe on July 22, 1901, pioneering pilot Pancho Barnes inherited a sense of aerial adventure from her grandfather, inventor and balloonist Thaddeus Lowe (see page 222). In her twenties, Barnes took flying lessons, bought several airplanes, and became hooked on aviation. Leveraging her connections in Hollywood, she started flying on film shoots and founded the Associated Motion Picture Pilots, the world's first union for stunt pilots. At the same time, Barnes was also flying in air races and working as a test pilot.

When the Great Depression hit, Barnes built a ranch and airstrip on a farm near Muroc Army Airfield in California (later Edwards Air Force Base). Known as the Happy Bottom Riding Club, the combination airport-inn-club-restaurant-ranch was frequented by military aviators and test pilots. One such visitor was Chuck Yeager, who famously broke two of his ribs riding a horse at Barnes's club days before breaking the sound barrier (see page 303).

CHANDRA X-RAY OBSERVATORY IS LAUNCHED

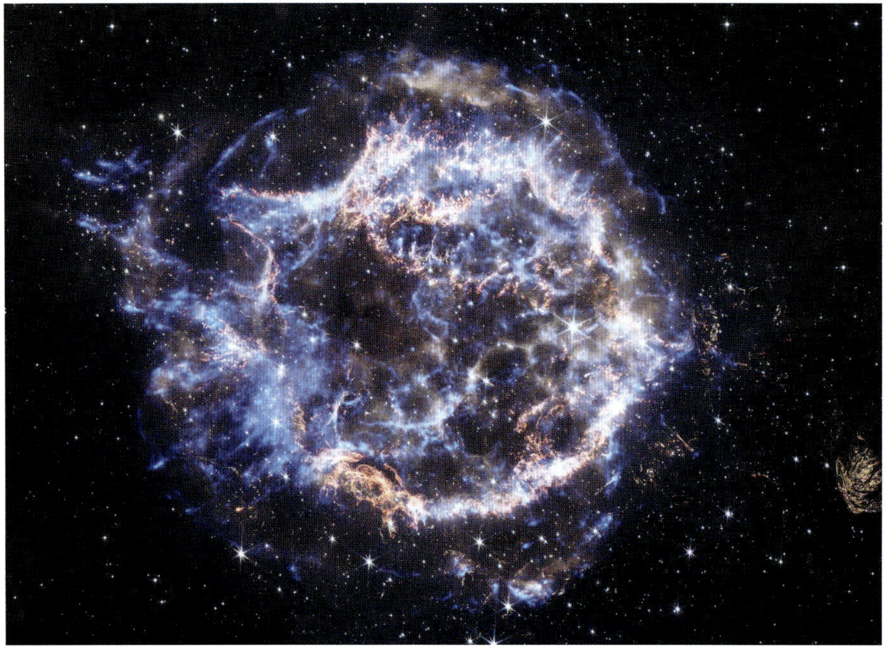

The Chandra X-ray Observatory has been imaging supernova remnant Cassiopeia A for over twenty-five years.

X-ray: NASA/CXC/SAO; Infrared: NASA/ESA/CSA/STScI/D. Milisavljevic (Purdue Univ.), I. De Looze (University of Ghent), T. Temim (Princeton Univ.); Image Processing: NASA/CXC/SAO/J. Schmidt, K. Arcand, and J. Major

NASA's Chandra X-ray Observatory was deployed from Space Shuttle *Columbia* during the STS-93 mission on July 23, 1999. The mission was commanded by Eileen Collins (see page 50), who became the first woman to lead a Space Shuttle mission. Soon after *Columbia* reached orbit, its payload door opened and the crew began preparations for Chandra's release. They placed the observatory in orbit, and over the course of nine days, a series of propulsion systems pushed Chandra to its final orbital position.

Three weeks later, Chandra's protective sunshade door flipped open and captured its first images. Scientists saw in stunning detail the debris field of a massive star, Cassiopeia A, which had exploded more than three centuries earlier. Designed to observe high-energy regions of the universe, Chandra's instruments can "see" high-energy electromagnetic radiation. These X-rays enable scientists to observe some of the most violent and energetic phenomena in the universe, like supernovae and black holes. The Chandra X-ray Observatory is operated by the Smithsonian Astrophysical Observatory in Cambridge, Massachusetts.

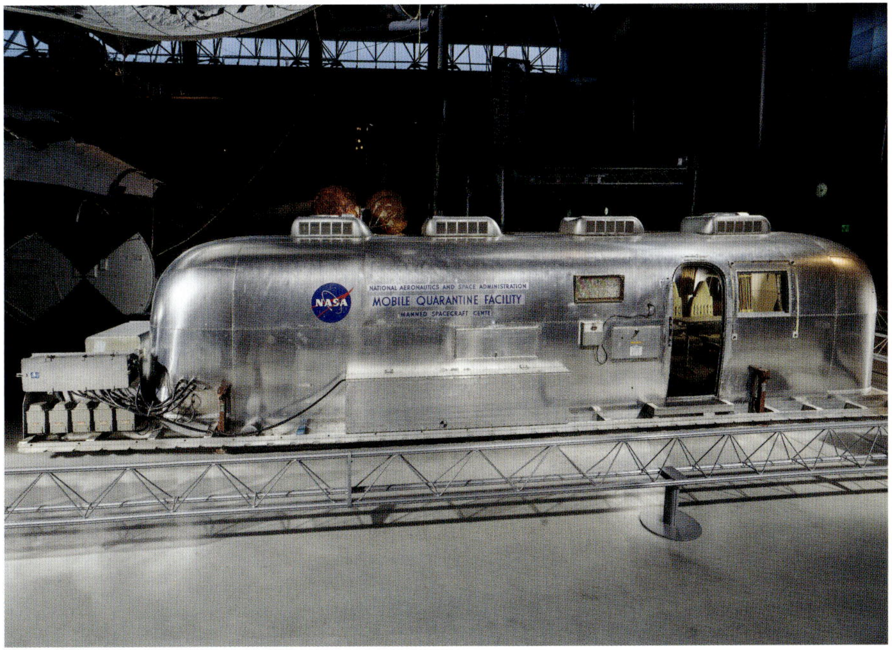

The Apollo 11 astronauts spent eighty-eight hours in the Mobile Quarantine Facility, which is now on display at the Steven F. Udvar-Hazy Center.

Smithsonian's National Air and Space Museum

The Apollo 11 command module *Columbia* splashed down in the Pacific Ocean on July 24, 1969, fulfilling the second half of President John F. Kennedy's Moonshot pledge: ". . . and returning him safely to Earth." After splashdown, Neil Armstrong, Michael Collins, and Buzz Aldrin donned protective isolation garments and were flown by helicopter to the USS *Hornet*, which was waiting nearby. After landing on the carrier, they were taken immediately to the Mobile Quarantine Facility (MQF), a converted Airstream trailer of a little over 300 square feet. The technique of immediate isolation after landing prevented the unlikely spread of "Moon germs."

The crew spent the first eighty-eight hours of their quarantine in the MQF, even greeting special guests—including their wives and President Richard Nixon—through a window at the back of the trailer. The astronauts remained in the Mobile Quarantine Facility as it was transported by ship to Hawaii and then flown on a cargo aircraft to Texas. Once it reached Johnson Space Center, the crew was transferred into more spacious quarantine facilities. They spent a total of twenty-one days in quarantine after the mission.

JULY 25

ABRAHAM LINCOLN WRITES LETTER ON BALLOON RECONNAISSANCE

LIGHTER-THAN-AIR FLIGHT

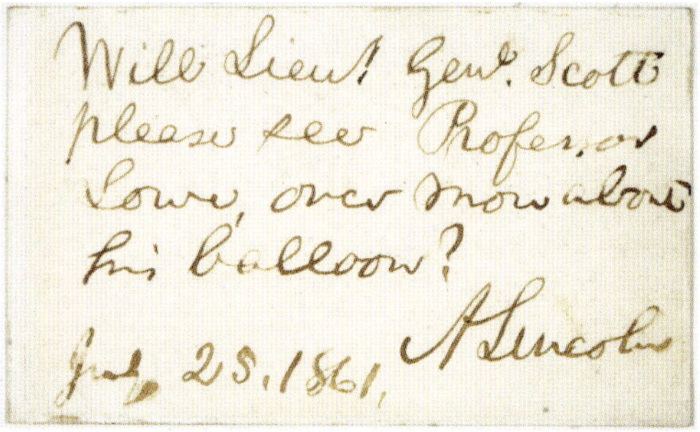
Will Lieut. Genl. Scott please see Professor Lowe, once more about his balloon?
July 25, 1861, A. Lincoln

Abraham Lincoln expressed interest in using balloons in the military during the Civil War.

Smithsonian's National Air and Space Museum (NASM 99-40777)

In June 1861, American inventor and balloonist Thaddeus Lowe had the attention of President Abraham Lincoln. From high above what is now the National Mall in Washington, D.C., Lowe demonstrated for the president how a tethered gas-filled balloon could be used to spy on Confederate forces. On July 25, 1861, Lincoln, clearly still thinking about Lowe's proposal, wrote a note that read "Will Lieut. Gen. Scott please see Professor Lowe once more about his balloon?" Later that year, the Union Army Balloon Corps was officially established, with Lowe as its "chief aeronaut."

JULY 26

DISCOVERY LAUNCHES ON RETURN TO FLIGHT MISSION

HUMAN SPACEFLIGHT

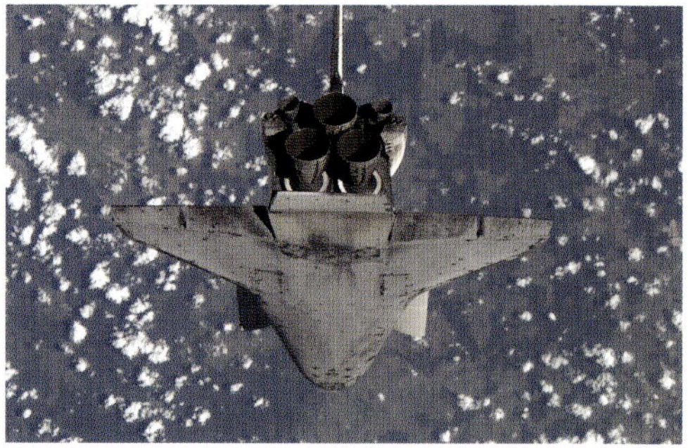

During STS-114, Space Shuttle *Discovery* did a "backflip" so that crew on the ISS could photograph its heat shield.

NASA

Following the loss of Space Shuttle *Columbia* in February 2003, NASA grounded the Space Shuttle fleet as it implemented improved safety measures. On July 26, 2005, Space Shuttle *Discovery* launched on NASA's second Return to Flight mission (it also carried out the first mission after the loss of *Challenger*). The STS-114 mission to the International Space Station (ISS) was led by experienced mission commander Eileen Collins. Once *Discovery* arrived at the ISS, Collins carried out the first rendezvous pitch maneuver—a "backflip" that allowed crew on station to take photos of the orbiter's heat shield to confirm critical thermal tiles were intact for a safe reentry.

JOSEPH KITTINGER IS BORN

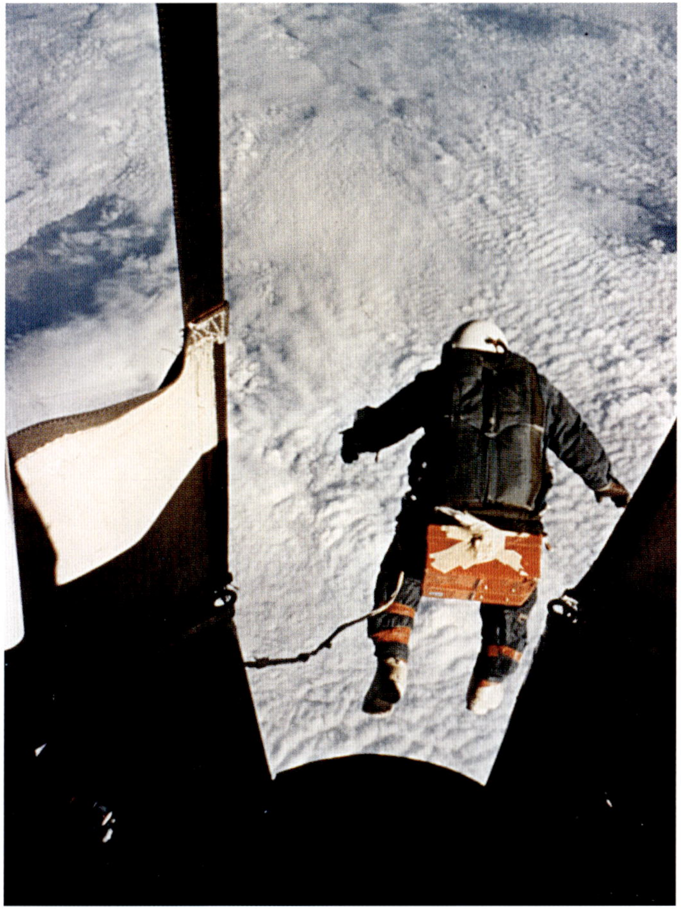

On July 27, 1928, record-setting aviator Joseph Kittinger was born in Tampa, Florida. Kittinger dreamed of becoming a fighter pilot after admiring the heroics of American aces in World War II. He enlisted in the Air Force at age twenty and earned his wings the following year. During the Korean War, Kittinger served with the 86th Fighter-Bomber Wing at Ramstein Air Base in West Germany and volunteered to test-fly F-86G Sabre jets in Copenhagen.

In 1960, Kittinger made a record-setting high-altitude parachute jump as part of the Air Force's Project Excelsior. After stepping from a balloon-supported gondola at an altitude of 102,800 feet, he free fell for four minutes and thirty-six seconds at speeds up to 614 miles per hour before opening his parachute at 17,500 feet. Kittinger's feat set world records for the highest parachute jump, the longest parachute free fall, and the fastest speed by a human being through the atmosphere. For a brief period, Kittinger was known worldwide. He was profiled in cover stories by *LIFE* and *National Geographic*, interviewed by Walter Cronkite, appeared on *The Ed Sullivan Show*, and met President Dwight D. Eisenhower.

Joseph Kittinger is best known for his record-setting parachute jump from the edge of space.

U.S. Air Force

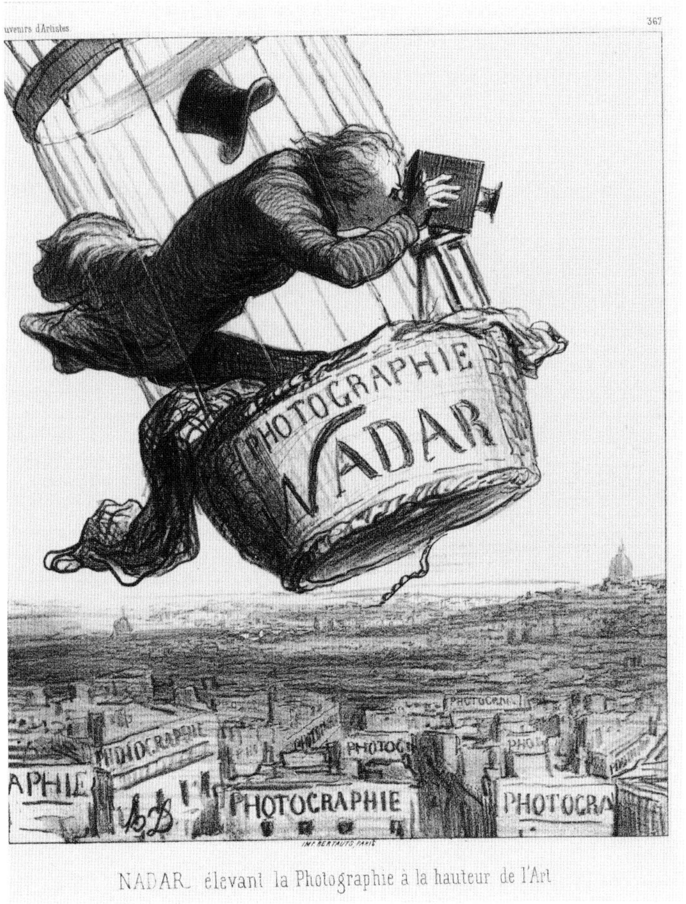

Snapping a photograph from the window seat of an airplane is now commonplace, but it is part of a much longer history of aerial photography. On July 28, 1858, French photographer Gaspar Félix Tournachon, better known as "Nadar," became the world's first aerial photographer when he captured views of the French village of Petit-Bicêtre (now Petit-Clamart) using a tethered hot-air balloon. The mid-nineteenth-century collodion process for fixing images was rather complicated, so Nadar carried a complete darkroom in his balloon's basket.

Though the images he took no longer exist, Nadar retains credit for the first aerial photographs. Two years later, photographer James Wallace Black captured the first aerial images in the United States. Black and his navigator, Samuel Archer King, made eight exposures from *The Queen of the Air,* a balloon tethered above Boston, Massachusetts, at 1,200 feet.

An 1862 lithograph by Honoré Daumier, titled *Nadar élevant la Photographie à la hauteur de l'Art*, depicts the beginning of aerial photography.

National Gallery of Art

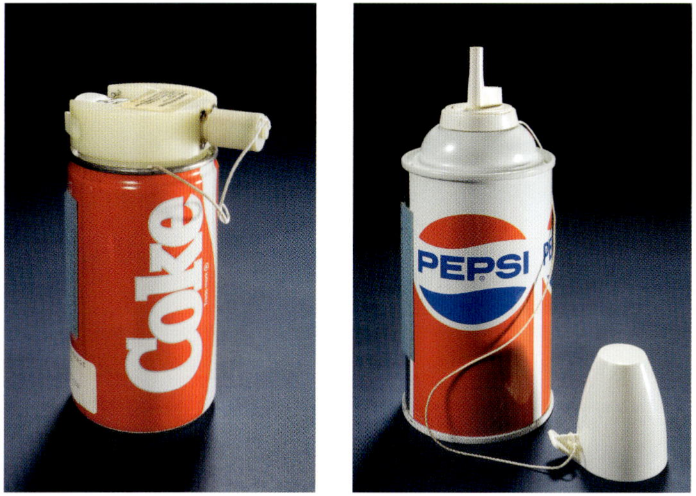

In 1985, specially adapted cans of Coke and Pepsi became the first soda consumed in space.

Smithsonian's National Air and Space Museum

Coke and Pepsi took their infamous "Cola Wars" to space in the 1980s. Researchers at Coca-Cola toyed with the idea of flying carbonated beverages in space starting in 1984 to give NASA astronauts more choices—and create a stellar advertising opportunity. They got to work developing a can that would work in weightlessness to keep the cola fizzy without spewing out of the can. When Pepsi found out about Coke's trip to space, it asked to participate as well.

The cans launched on NASA's STS-51F mission on July 29, 1985, as the "Carbonated Beverage Container Evaluation." These were the first carbonated beverages flown into space. The crew reported that although the taste was authentic, the carbonation proved an issue. In microgravity, the bubbles stay suspended in the soda, forcing astronauts to swallow all the bubbles. That gas goes straight into their stomachs, only to come up later as wet burps. Additionally, the cola from the Pepsi can, which resembled a shaving cream dispenser, came out very foamy. NASA did not add either company's product to the Space Shuttle's food pantry, but that did not stop Coke or Pepsi from running advertisements based on the mission.

MARS ROVER *PERSEVERANCE* LAUNCHES TO MARS

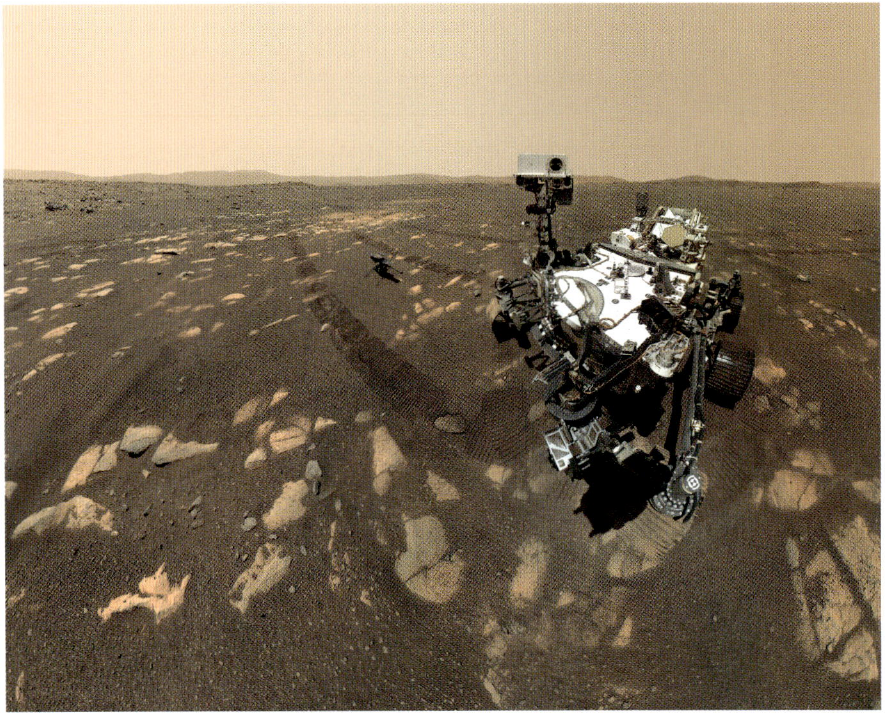

NASA's *Perseverance* rover took a "selfie" with the *Ingenuity* helicopter soon after it was deployed.

NASA-Caltech/MSSS

NASA's latest Mars rover, a car-size spacecraft named *Perseverance*, launched to the Red Planet on July 30, 2020. Officially called the Mars 2020 mission, the rover got the name *Perseverance* through a nationwide contest for K–12 students. In February 2021, the rover landed on Mars with the *Ingenuity* helicopter on board (see page 127). *Perseverance*'s mission is to search for signs of ancient microbial life. It is exploring the ancient lake at Jezero Crater to determine what it was like and whether there are any preserved biosignatures related to life on Mars.

Another of the primary objectives of the Mars 2020 mission is to acquire data and test technologies that will help human crews prepare for missions to Mars. Several new experiments onboard the rover directly address this objective, including one that attempts to turn Mars's carbon dioxide atmosphere into oxygen and one that uses radar to see below the surface and look for subsurface ice that could be used to produce fuel.

APOLLO 15 ASTRONAUTS USE LUNAR ROVING VEHICLE FOR THE FIRST TIME

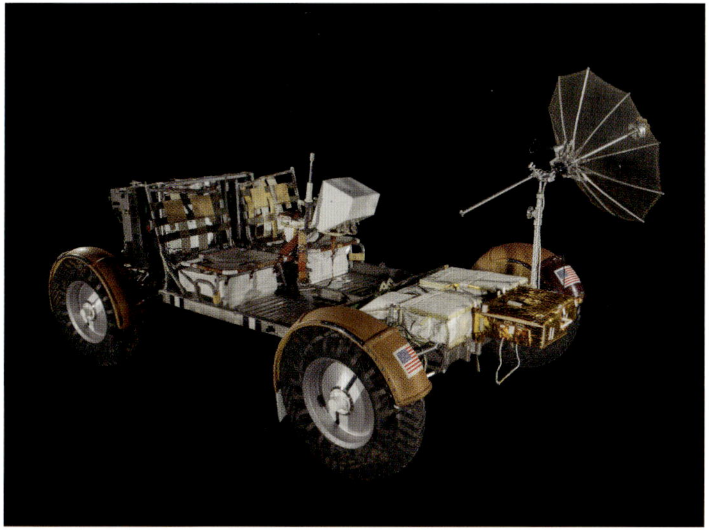

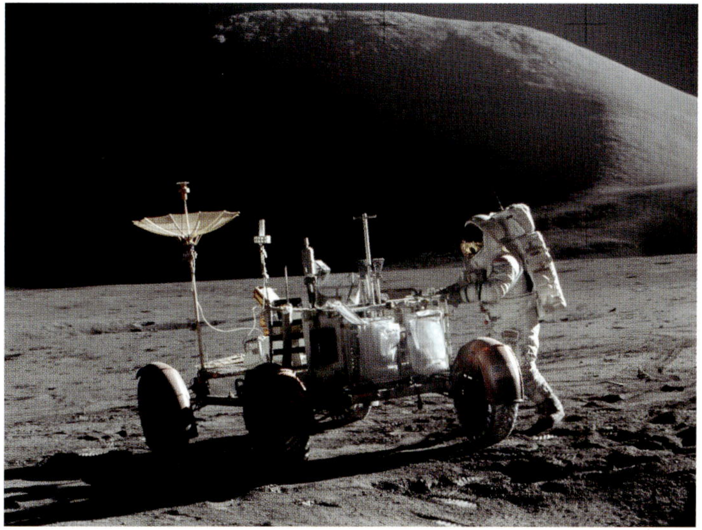

The Apollo moonwalkers had a limited time to explore the lunar surface and conduct experiments during just six missions. On the final three Apollo missions, the astronauts had a dune buggy–like vehicle that allowed them to travel farther and haul equipment and samples with ease. On July 31, 1971, David Scott and James Irwin used the Lunar Roving Vehicle (LRV) on the Moon for the first time during the Apollo 15 mission.

The LRV was stowed folded up inside the descent stage of the lunar module and deployed upon arrival at the lunar surface. It was powered by battery and was operated with a spacecraft "stick" rather than a steering wheel. The LRV could move forward and backward and reach speeds up to eight miles per hour. The Apollo 15 astronauts traveled over fifteen miles using the lunar vehicles during four moonwalks.

LEFT The three flown Lunar Roving Vehicles were left on the Moon, but a Qualification Test Unit is on display at the National Air and Space Museum.

Smithsonian's National Air and Space Museum

RIGHT The Apollo 15 astronauts used the Lunar Roving Vehicle to explore the Hadley-Apennine region of the Moon.

NASA

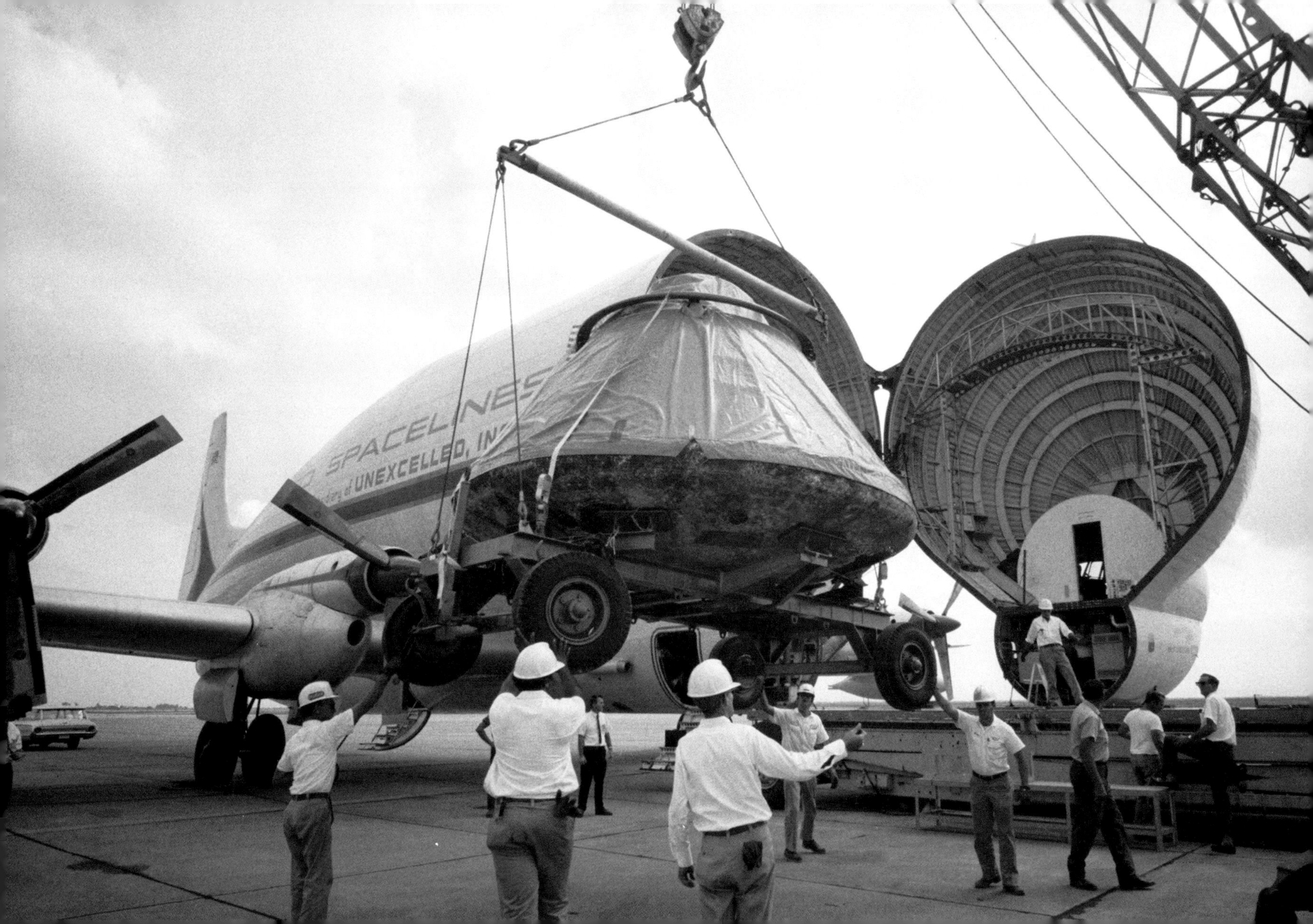
SPACELINES
UNEXCELLED, INC

AUGUST

HARRIET QUIMBY BECOMES FIRST AMERICAN WOMAN TO EARN A PILOT'S LICENSE

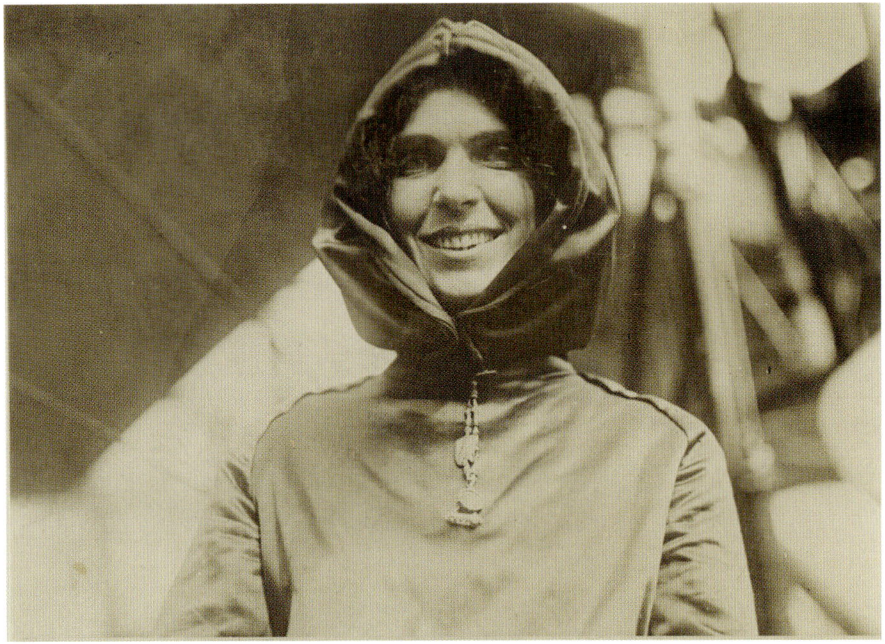

During her short aviation career, the press called Harriet Quimby "America's First Lady of the Air."

Smithsonian's National Air and Space Museum (NASM 9A18697-20B)

Despite a very short career, Harriet Quimby was one of the most popular early women aviators. Inspired by John Moisant's aerial performance at the 1910 Belmont Park Aviation Meet, Quimby began taking lessons from the American aviator soon after. She earned her pilot's license on August 1, 1911, and immediately joined the Moisant International Aviators exhibition team.

Quimby traveled with the Moisant group to Mexico, where she became the first woman to fly over Mexico City. The following year she also became the first woman to fly across the English Channel (see page 123). Having been a writer before becoming a pilot, Quimby wrote articles about her experiences in aviation for the magazine *Leslie's Illustrated Weekly.* Unfortunately, Quimby died in a flying accident less than a year after she earned her pilot's license.

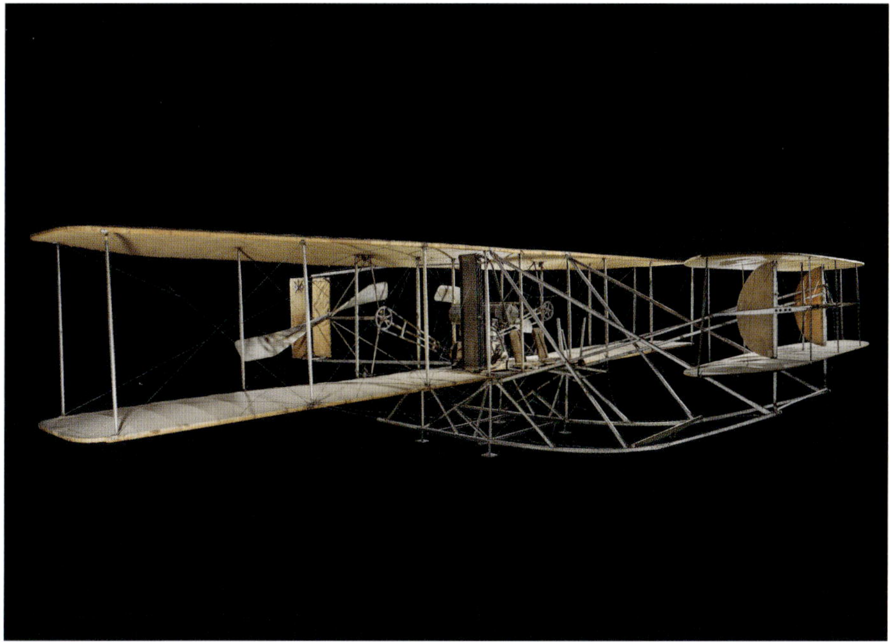

When the U.S. Army Signal Corps accepted the 1909 Wright Military Flyer on August 2, 1909, it was the first time an airplane was purchased and put into service by a government. Development of the aircraft began the year before when the Signal Corps sought competitive bids for a two-seat observation aircraft that could reach a speed of at least forty miles per hour, remain in the air for at least one hour, and land safely without needing a prepared spot or causing any damage that would prevent it from immediately flying again. The bid also required that the aircraft be able to carry two people and be easily assembled and disassembled so that an army wagon could transport it. The Wright Military Flyer achieved each of these requirements, and Wilbur and Orville Wright sold it to the government for $30,000.

Of the three Wright airplanes in the National Air and Space Museum collection, the 1909 Wright Military Flyer retains the largest percentage of its original material and components.

Smithsonian's National Air and Space Museum

FIRST SPACEWALK UNDER THE SHUTTLE IS CONDUCTED

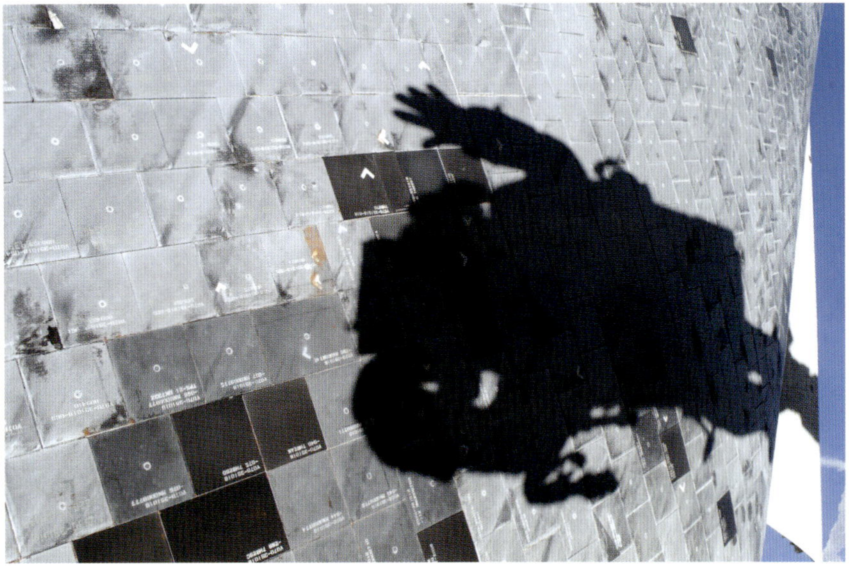

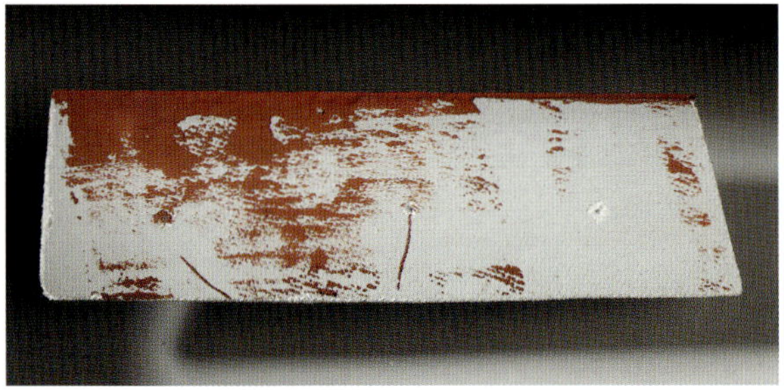

LEFT Stephen Robinson's shadow can be seen in a photo he took of the thermal protection tiles on *Discovery*'s underside.

NASA

ABOVE One of the tile gap fillers Robinson removed during the spacewalk is in the collection of the National Air and Space Museum.

NASA

On August 3, 2005, astronaut Stephen Robinson became the first person to do a spacewalk underneath a Space Shuttle orbiter. STS-114 mission managers sent Robinson to the underside of Space Shuttle *Discovery* to test possible thermal protection system repair techniques. The mission, the first following the loss of *Columbia* on STS-107, included several repair experiments. Imaging revealed a pair of protruding gap fillers that could have disrupted the aerodynamics of the orbiter during reentry.

Robinson traveled underneath *Discovery* mounted on the International Space Station's robotic arm controlled by astronauts Wendy Lawrence and James Kelly. As a result of being underneath the vehicle, Robinson was also out of sight of the crew. Once beneath *Discovery*, he was able to pull out the fillers by hand. Gap fillers were used to prevent tiles from scraping against one another and fill narrow gaps in its heat shield. There are thousands of gap fillers on each Space Shuttle.

SUPERMARINE SPITFIRE ENTERS SERVICE

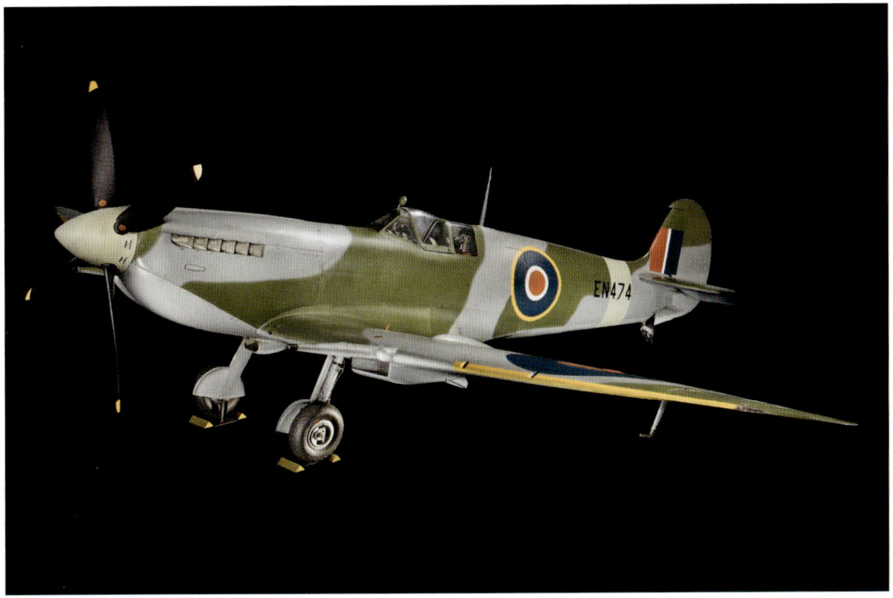

The National Air and Space Museum's Supermarine Spitfire is a high-altitude Mark VII version. Only 140 of this particular model were produced.

Smithsonian's National Air and Space Museum

The Supermarine Spitfire is a legend in British air history. The product of many years of design development at the Supermarine works in Woolston, England, the Spitfire first entered service with the Royal Air Force on August 4, 1938. Among the aircraft's many strengths were its outstanding maneuverability and easy handling. The combination of speed and firepower made the Spitfire an especially deadly machine.

Together with the Hawker Hurricane, the Spitfire successfully defended England against the German Luftwaffe during the Battle of Britain and saw service on every major front throughout World War II. Many variants of the Spitfire were developed as new needs arose. High-altitude versions like the Mark VII took on the Messerschmidt Bf 109, while low-altitude variants countered the Focke-Wulf Fw 190. Supermarine also produced photo reconnaissance versions to keep track of German movements on land and at sea. In total, over twenty thousand production Spitfires were built.

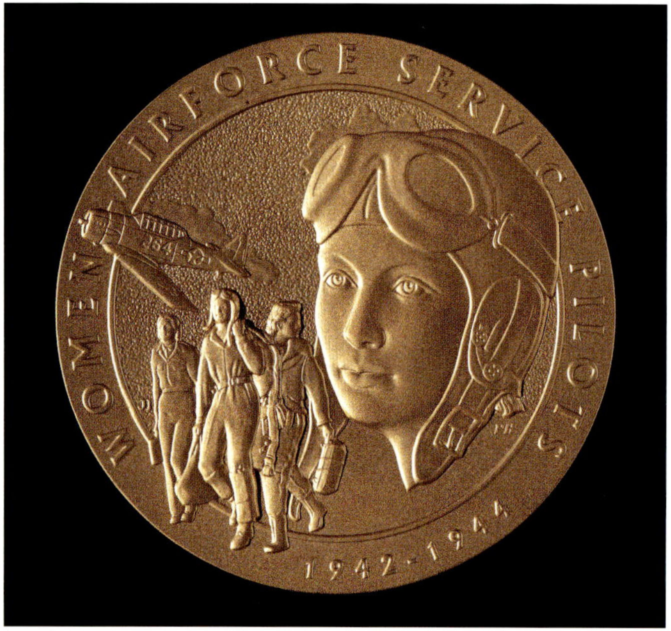

ABOVE The Women Airforce Service Pilots were awarded the Congressional Gold Medal in 2010. The medal is now on display at the Steven F. Udvar-Hazy Center.

Smithsonian's National Air and Space Museum

OPPOSITE PAGE WASP members Frances Green, Peg Kirchner, Ann Waldner, and Blanche Osborn trained in the B-17 *Pistol Packin' Mama*.

Smithsonian's National Air and Space Museum (NASM 97-17490)

The Women Airforce Service Pilots (WASP) was established on August 5, 1943, when the Women's Auxiliary Ferrying Squadron and the Women's Flying Training Detachment merged. As World War II raged, many women pilots were interested in serving their country and went through a rigorous selection and training process to join the WASP. Of the twenty-five thousand who applied, 1,820 were accepted and 1,074 graduated.

Though not trained for combat, WASP graduates flew a variety of missions, performing operational flights, towing aerial targets, transporting cargo, laying smoke, and testing aircraft. Skilled WASP pilots flew a total of sixty million miles in all types of military aircraft, including fighters and bombers. Although they had proven that women could capably fly any kind of military aircraft, WASP pilots were considered civilians and were not granted military benefits or burials. Their official recognition as part of military aviation only occurred decades later when they were granted retroactive military status in 1977.

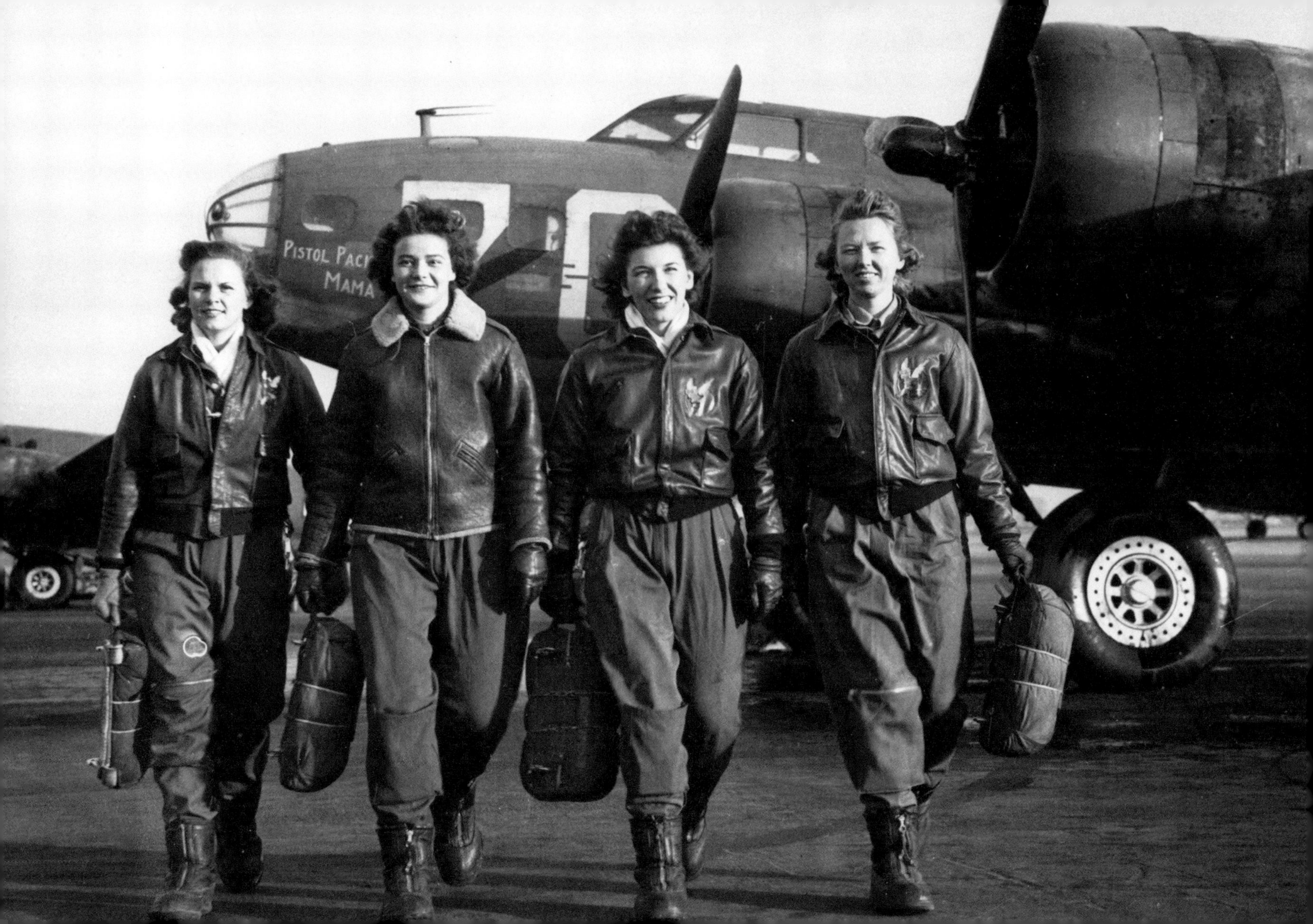
PISTOL PACK
MAMA

ENOLA GAY DROPS FIRST ATOMIC BOMB USED IN WARFARE

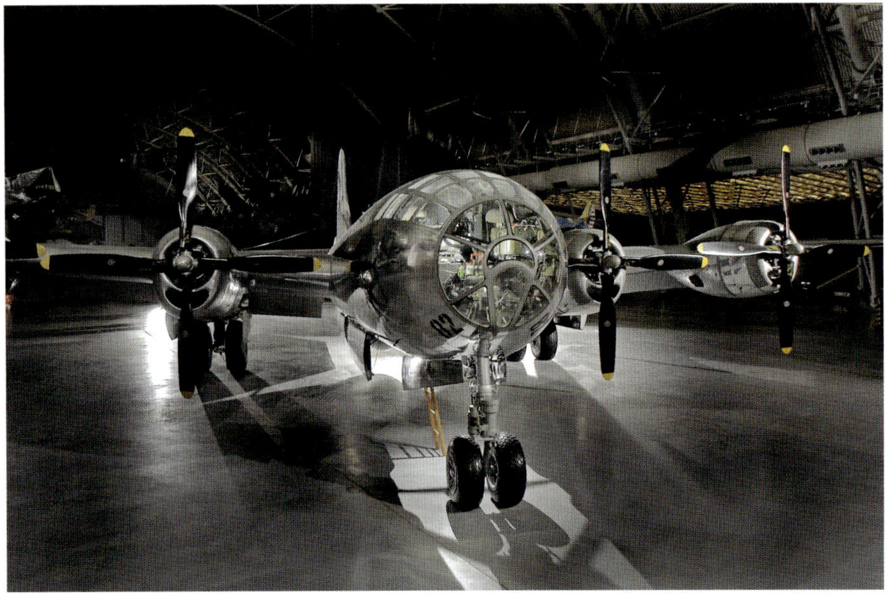

The Boeing B-29 Superfortress *Enola Gay* is on display at the Steven F. Udvar-Hazy Center.

Smithsonian's National Air and Space Museum

On August 6, 1945, the crew of a modified Boeing B-29 Superfortress named *Enola Gay* dropped the first atomic weapon used in warfare—a bomb called "Little Boy"—on the city of Hiroshima, Japan. The blast and resulting firestorm killed over 130,000 people. Another atomic attack on Nagasaki three days later helped force Emperor Hirohito's decision to surrender and forever changed how world powers considered and conducted war.

The delivery system for these atomic bombs, the B-29 Superfortress, represented the latest advances in American aeronautical engineering and bomber design. The aircraft's use in the skies over Japan also reflected the evolution of strategic bombing doctrine and the end of the war in the Pacific. As a new and deadly weapon, the atomic bomber *Enola Gay* facilitated a turning point in human history, ushering in the dawn of the Atomic Age and the threat of nuclear war.

APOLLO 15 SPLASHES DOWN WITH ONLY TWO PARACHUTES

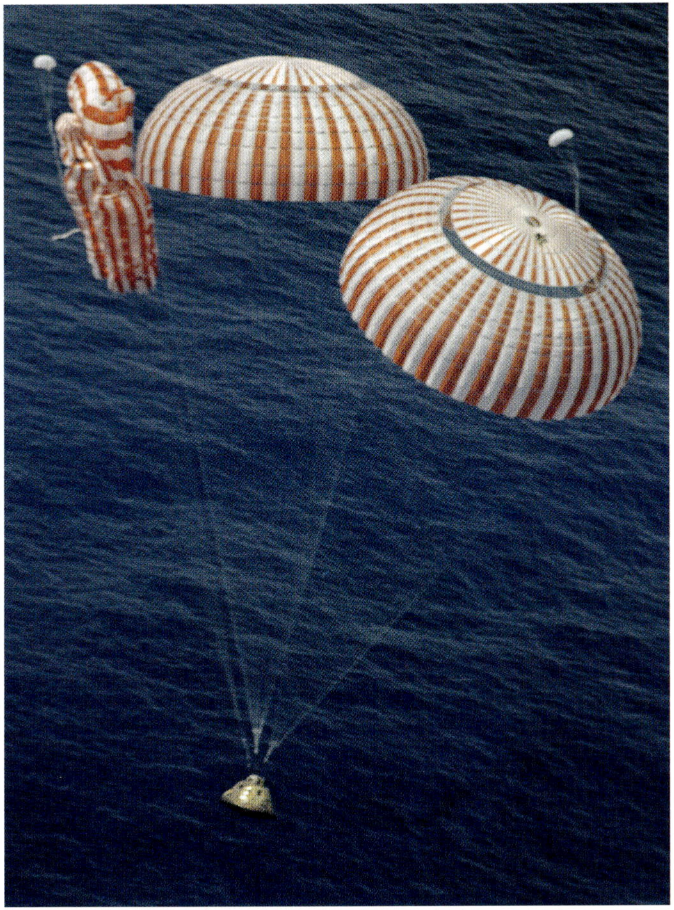

Like the Mercury and Gemini missions before, the Apollo missions ended with the spacecraft splashing down in the ocean. When the command module reentered the atmosphere, three main parachutes deployed to slow its descent. The parachutes were opened by the pilot at 10,000 feet, slowing the rate of descent from 175 miles per hour to 22 miles per hour. After splashdown, the risers connecting the main parachutes to the spacecraft were cut and the parachutes released.

On August 7, 1971, Apollo 15 command module *Endeavour* splashed down with only two parachutes. Thankfully, the parachutes were designed so that in the case of the failure of one parachute, the remaining two were able to decelerate the spacecraft to the needed twenty-five miles per hour. The parachutes held the command module at 27.5 degrees so the module's slanted corner would penetrate the water first, lessening the impact force.

During the descent of the Apollo 15 command module, one parachute malfunctioned.

NASA

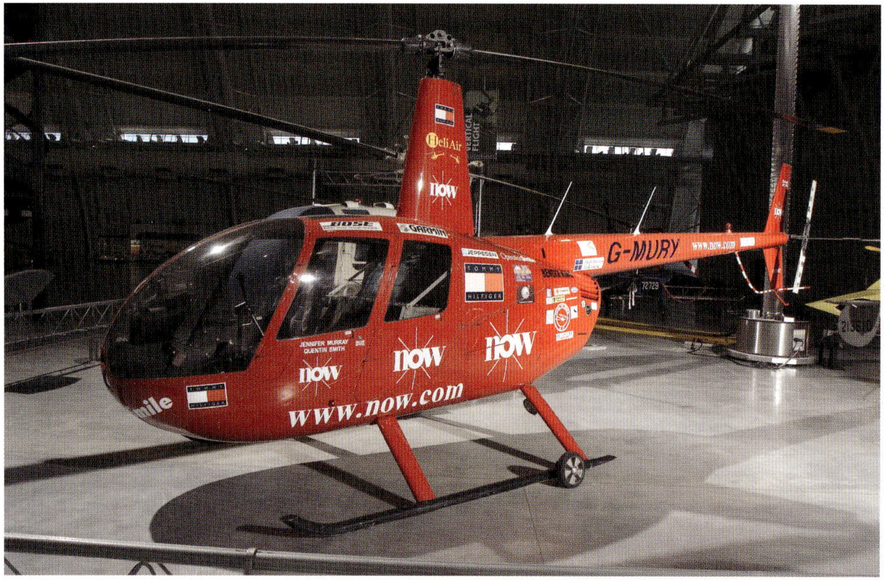

Jennifer Murray flew the R44 helicopter *G-MURY* around the world twice. It is on display at the Steven F. Udvar-Hazy Center.

Smithsonian's National Air and Space Museum

On August 8, 1997, British pilot Jennifer Murray became the first woman to fly around the world in a helicopter. She made the months-long flight in a Robinson R44 Astro piston-powered helicopter nicknamed *G-MURY* with her instructor, Quentin Smith, as copilot. Flying east from England, the flight took the pair through twenty-eight countries over the course of ninety-seven days—three days faster than Murray's goal.

A few years later, Murray again flew around the world in *G-MURY*, this time on her own, making her the first woman to circumnavigate the globe in a helicopter solo and the first person to do so without autopilot. "When I learnt that no woman had ever piloted a helicopter around the world and that only three men had ever done so—and they had all been flying larger, jet turbine helicopters with autopilot—the challenge was there," Murray later reflected.

AUGUST 9

CLIFFORD EVANS AND GEORGE TRUMAN BEGIN AROUND-THE-WORLD FLIGHT IN PIPER PA-12 SUPER CRUISERS

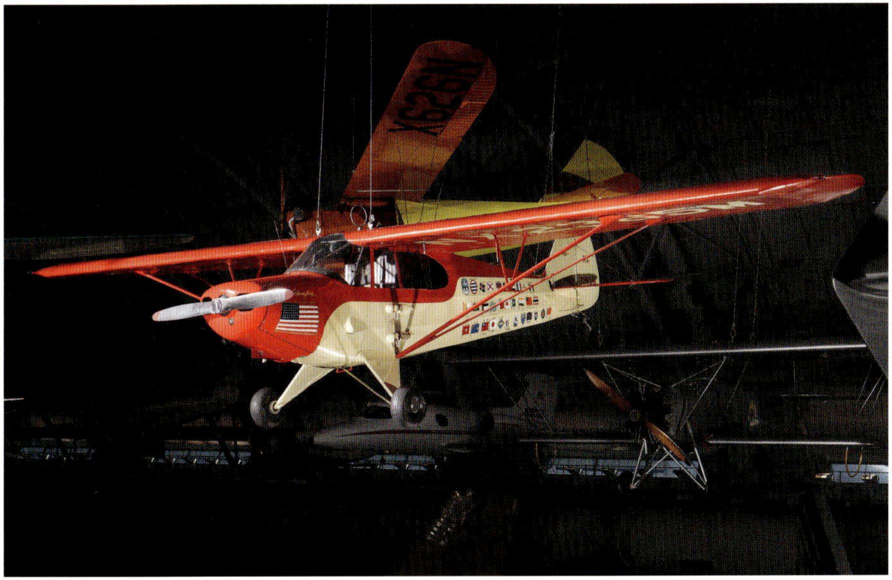

The Piper PA-12 Super Cruiser *City of Washington*, on display at the Steven F. Udvar-Hazy Center, is painted with the flags of the countries Evans and Truman visited on their flight.

Smithsonian's National Air and Space Museum

In 1947, Clifford Evans and George Truman circled the globe in a pair of Piper Super Cruisers, the first time light personal airplanes accomplished such a feat. On August 9, 1947, Evans and Truman left Teterboro, New Jersey, in aircraft named *City of Washington* and *City of the Angels*. The round-the-world flight took just over four months and covered 22,436 miles. Weather was the biggest challenge during the flight, confining them to the ground for many days and resulting in a number of slow-going legs of their journey.

When Evans and Truman arrived in Japan, they met a U.S. Air Force B-17 that escorted them across the north Pacific Ocean to the Alaska mainland, where they encountered the worst weather of the entire trip. Having overcome this poor weather, the "Modern Magellans," as they were billed, arrived back at Teterboro Airport on December 10, 1947. In Washington, D.C., they received heroes' welcomes and were greeted by President Harry S. Truman.

AUGUST 10

LUNAR ORBITER 1 LAUNCHES

SPACE SCIENCE

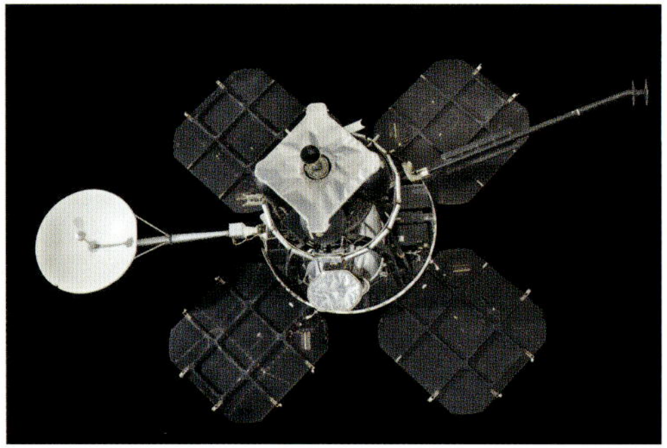

The Lunar Orbiter spacecraft on display at the National Air and Space Museum is an engineering mock-up built by Boeing.

Smithsonian's National Air and Space Museum

NASA's Lunar Orbiter project mapped the Moon in preparation for the Apollo landings. A total of five Lunar Orbiters were flown to the Moon, starting with Lunar Orbiter 1, which launched on August 10, 1966. The first three spacecraft in the series orbited around the Moon's equator and provided detailed photographic coverage of the primary Apollo landing sites. Because of the success of these earlier missions, the final two Lunar Orbiters were placed into a polar orbit to allow virtually the entire surface of the Moon to be mapped.

AUGUST 11

DOUBLE EAGLE II BEGINS FIRST BALLOON FLIGHT ACROSS THE ATLANTIC

LIGHTER-THAN-AIR FLIGHT

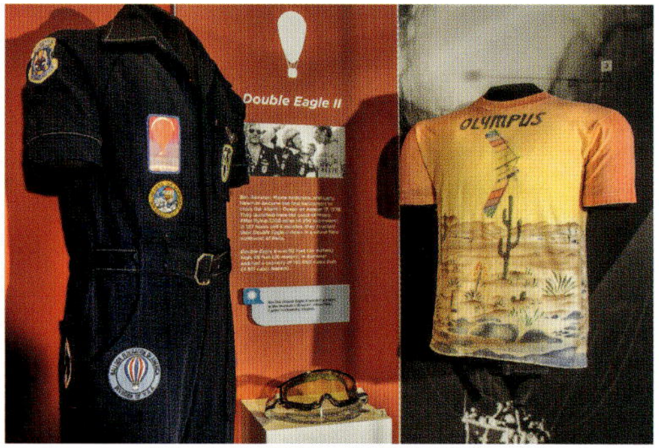

A variety of artifacts from *Double Eagle II*'s flight, including a flight suit, goggles, and T-shirt, are on display at the National Air and Space Museum.

Smithsonian's National Air and Space Museum

On August 11, 1978, Ben Abruzzo, Maxie Anderson, and Larry Newman departed Presque Isle, Maine, in the *Double Eagle II* balloon on the first successful balloon flight across the Atlantic. The 3,100-mile journey to Miserey, France, took 137 hours and six minutes to complete. Though the crew had hoped to finish at Le Bourget airfield, where Charles Lindbergh completed his solo transatlantic flight (see page 155), low ballast and fading daylight forced them down in the French province of Normandy. Despite this unscheduled landing, the balloon was immediately surrounded by crowds who had been following its path.

SPACE SHUTTLE *ENTERPRISE* FLOWN ON FIRST FREE FLIGHT

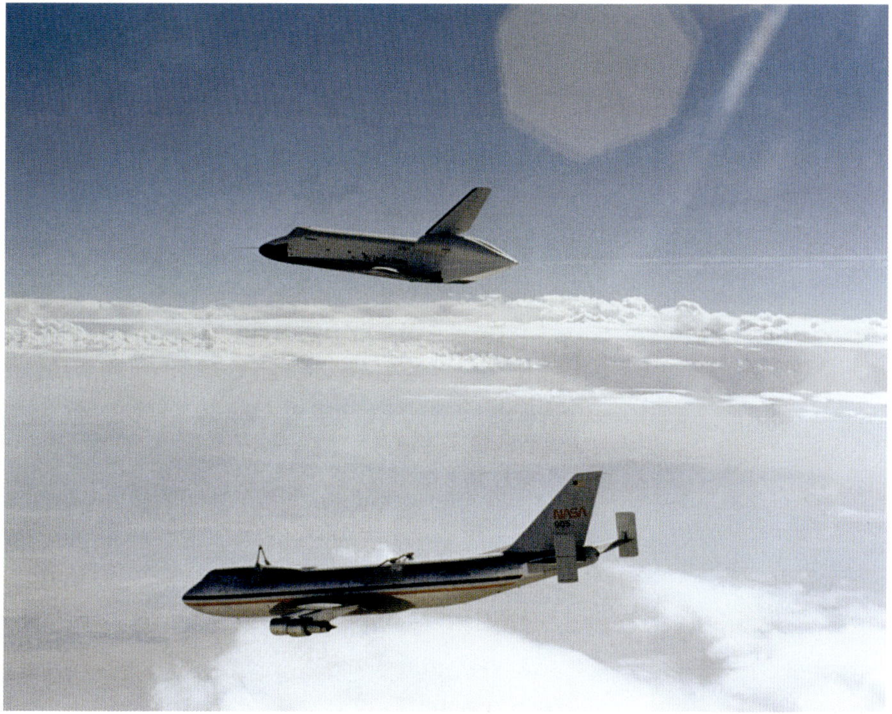

Space Shuttle *Enterprise*'s first free flight began on the back of a modified Boeing 747.

NASA

NASA built five Space Shuttles that launched to space—but one other never made it that far: *Enterprise.* A prototype orbiter, Space Shuttle *Enterprise* was used for testing in Earth's atmosphere. The Approach and Landing Tests (ALT) were conducted at NASA's Dryden Flight Research Center. During the first eight flights of the ALT program, *Enterprise* was mounted on a Boeing 747 Shuttle Carrier Aircraft (SCA) for lifting to certain altitudes.

After months of testing takeoff and ferrying flight dynamics, it was finally time for *Enterprise* to fly free. On August 12, 1977, Space Shuttle *Enterprise*, crewed by Fred Haise and Gordon Fullerton, made its first free flight. *Enterprise* was again carried into the skies by the SCA, and at 24,000 feet, it separated from the 747, and Haise and Fullerton took control of the vehicle. The astronauts glided *Enterprise* to a landing on a dry lakebed. Four more free flights followed, two crewed by Haise and Fullerton and two by Joe Engle and Richard Truly.

DID YOU KNOW? Space Shuttle *Enterprise* was originally going to be called *Constitution* but was renamed after a write-in campaign by *Star Trek* fans.

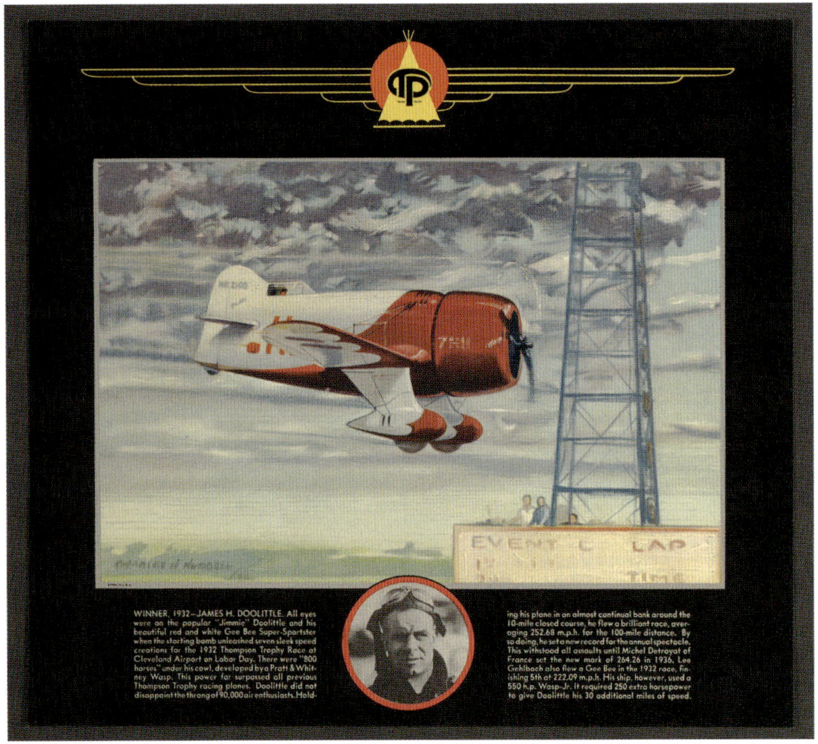

Jimmy Doolittle flew the Gee Bee R-1 in the 1932 Thompson Trophy Race.

Smithsonian's National Air and Space Museum

The Gee Bee Model R Super Sportster was an air racer manufactured by Granville Brothers Aircraft. The Model R was developed from the Granville Gee Bee Model Z, which won the 1931 Thompson Trophy Race with pilot Lowell Bayles at the controls. After the Z was destroyed in a crash in late 1931, Granville Brothers began working on its successors, the R-1 and R-2.

The R-1 flew for the first time on August 13, 1932. Less than a month later, famed World War I ace James "Jimmy" Doolittle piloted the aircraft in the 1932 Thompson Trophy Race, lapping most of his opponents. Doolittle later set an official Fédération Aéronautique International speed record in the R-1, averaging 294.4 miles per hour on a three-kilometer course.

PAUL GARBER IS MADE HONORARY NATIONAL AIR AND SPACE MUSEUM DIRECTOR FOR THE DAY

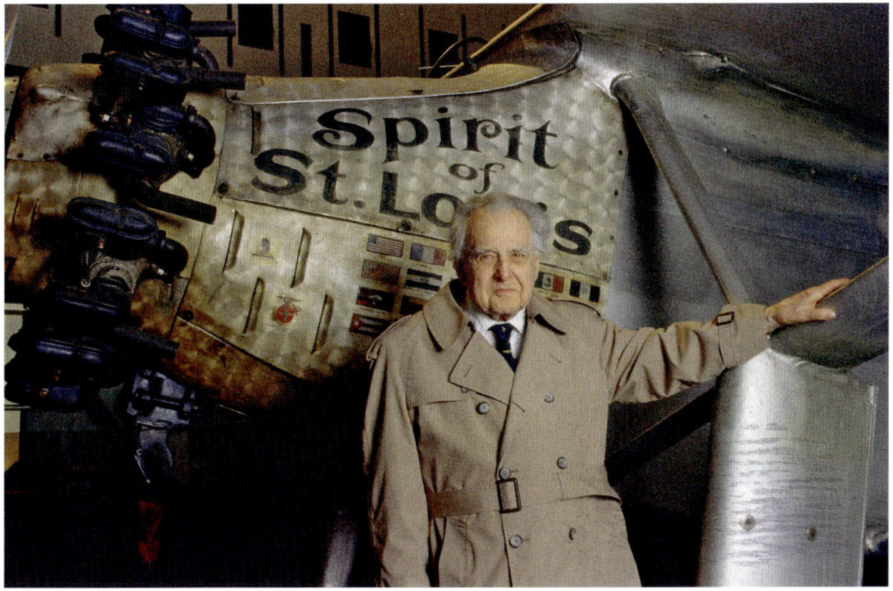

In May 1927, curator Paul Garber drafted a cablegram asking Charles Lindbergh to donate the *Spirit of St. Louis* while the pilot was still flying across the Atlantic. Smithsonian Secretary Charles Abbot sent the message two days after Lindbergh landed in Paris.

Photo by Mark Avino, Smithsonian's National Air and Space Museum (NASM 92-2946)

Paul Garber was a major figure in the history of the National Air and Space Museum. Born in Atlantic City, New Jersey, his interest in aviation began as a child when he saw Orville Wright fly the Wright Military Flyer in 1909. Garber took a job with the Smithsonian Institution in 1920, and for the next seventy-two years, dedicated himself to preserving the United States' aeronautical heritage.

Garber was the first curator of the National Air Museum and played a key role in its creation in 1946. He was also indispensable in the effort to construct the National Air and Space Museum building, which opened in Washington, D.C., in 1976 (see page 200). Most importantly, Garber helped amass the world's finest collection of historic aircraft, including one of the Museum's most prized possessions, Charles Lindbergh's *Spirit of St. Louis*. On August 14, 1987, Garber was made honorary director for the day in recognition of his contributions to the National Air and Space Museum.

AUGUST 15

EA-18G GROWLER MAKES ITS FIRST FLIGHT

MODERN MILITARY AVIATION

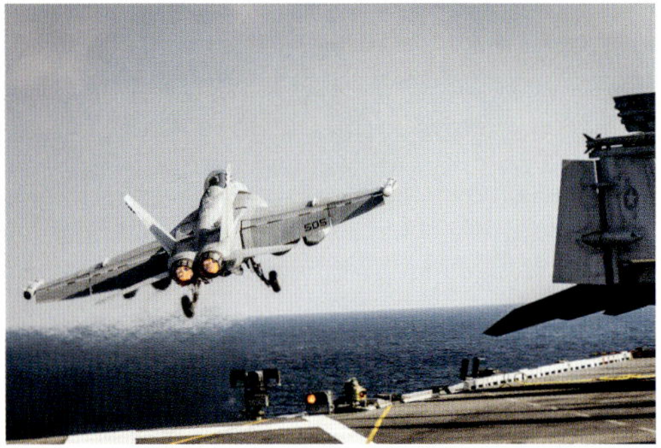

The U.S. Navy operates Boeing EA-18G Growlers off aircraft carriers like the Nimitz-class USS *George Washington*.

U.S. Navy

On August 15, 2006, the Boeing EA-18G Growler made its first flight. Designed to replace the Grumman EA-6B Prowler, the Growler is a carrier-based electronic warfare variant of the F/A-18F Super Hornet. The aircraft carries technology that allows it to jam enemy radar and communications while escorting other aircraft on strike and bombing missions. The U.S. Navy and the Royal Australian Air Force currently operate the EA-18G Growler.

AUGUST 16

DARRYL GREENAMYER SETS RECORD IN GRUMMAN F8F-2 BEARCAT *CONQUEST I*

GENERAL AVIATION

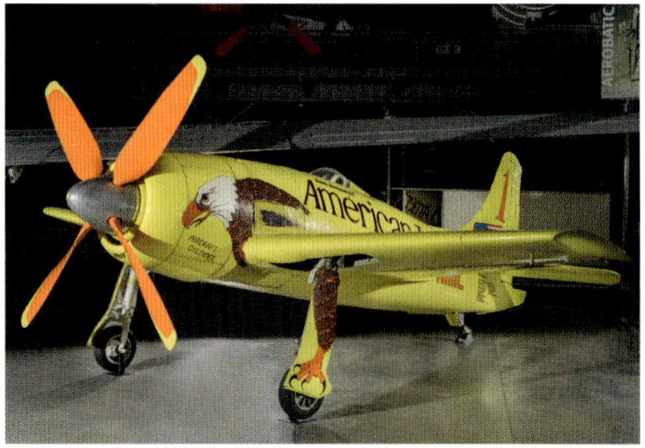

Darryl Greenamyer donated *Conquest I* to the National Air and Space Museum, where it is on display at the Steven F. Udvar-Hazy Center.

Smithsonian's National Air and Space Museum

For many years, test pilot Darryl G. Greenamyer competed in the Unlimited Class at the National Championship Air Races in a Grumman F8F-2 Bearcat nicknamed *Conquest I.* Greenamyer and a team of fellow Lockheed Skunk Works employees used their engineering talent to modify the U.S. Navy aircraft into a purpose-built air racer, winning the championship six times. Greenamyer also pursued records in the *Conquest I.* On August 16, 1969, Greenamyer flew just over 482 miles per hour in the *Conquest I,* breaking a thirty-year-old speed record for piston-engine aircraft previously held by German pilot Fritz Wendel.

MARGARET HAMILTON AND GENE KRANZ ARE BORN

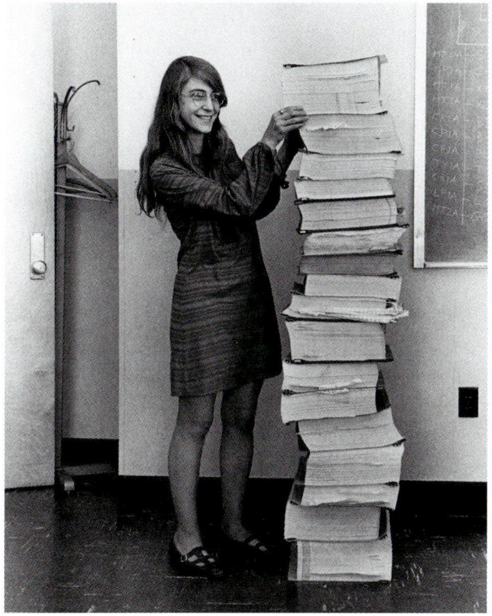

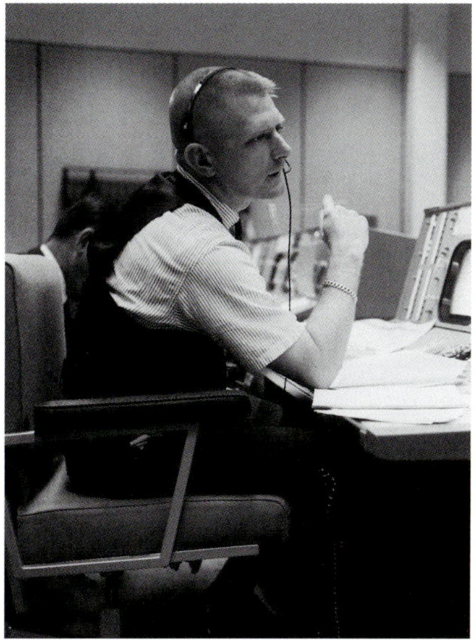

LEFT This now-iconic photo of Margaret Hamilton depicts her next to listings of the Apollo Guidance Computer source code.

NASA

RIGHT Flight director Gene Kranz was known for his vests. The white vest he wore during the Apollo 13 mission is in the collection of the National Air and Space Museum.

NASA

Two aerospace legends who made the Apollo missions possible were both born on August 17.

Computer scientist Margaret Hamilton was born on August 17, 1931. Her work leading the Software Engineering Division of the MIT Instrumentation Laboratory helped get the Apollo 11 astronauts to the Moon. Her team was responsible for developing the guidance and navigation system for the Apollo spacecraft and writing the code that brought astronauts into space and safely back home again.

Aerospace engineer, fighter pilot, and flight director Eugene "Gene" Kranz was born on August 17, 1933. Kranz was critical to many milestones in the U.S. space program, serving as flight director for seven Apollo missions. He played a key role in NASA's Mission Control for thirty-four years, from Project Mercury through the first Hubble servicing mission in 1993. Thanks to the 1995 film *Apollo 13*, Kranz is best known for his leadership during the Apollo 13 crisis.

DID YOU KNOW? Both Margaret Hamilton and Gene Kranz have been awarded the National Air and Space Museum's Michael Collins Trophy for Lifetime Achievement.

DISCOVERER XIV TAKES FIRST U.S. PHOTOGRAPH OF SOVIET MISSILE SITE FROM SPACE

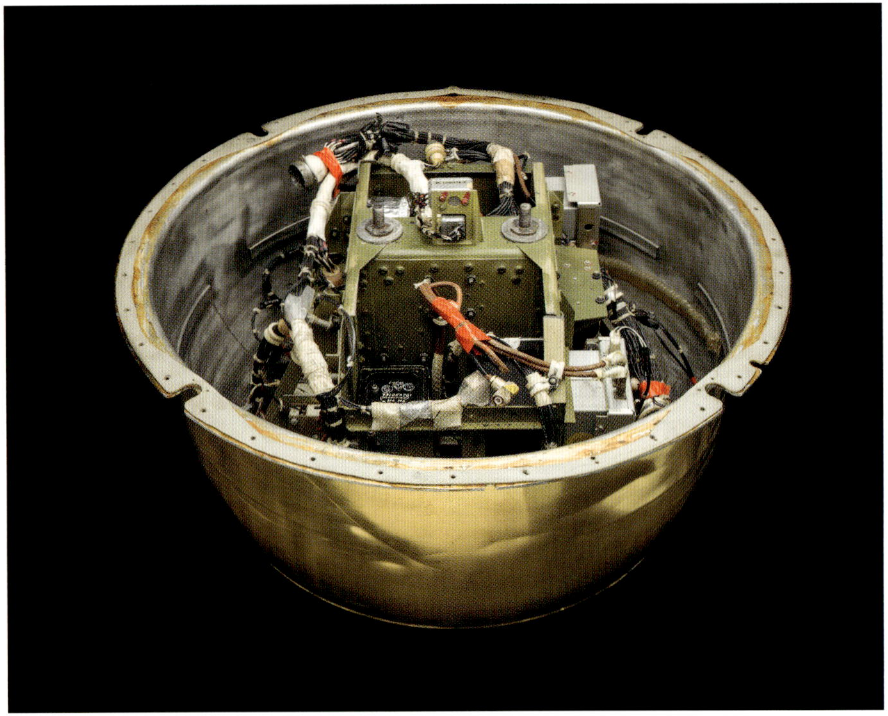

The Discoverer XIII reentry capsule on display at the National Air and Space Museum was launched one week before Discoverer XIV.

Smithsonian's National Air and Space Museum

The Discoverer satellite program began an age of spying from space in the 1960s that continues to this day. "Discoverer" was the cover name used in the early years of the highly classified Corona photoreconnaissance satellite program operated by the CIA and U.S. Air Force. In August 1960, Discoverer XIII became the first human-made object recovered from orbit. Although that satellite contained only self-diagnostic instruments, subsequent satellites in the Discoverer program carried cameras and film.

Discoverer XIV launched on August 18, 1960, and took the first U.S. photograph of a Soviet military site from space. The photograph showed a Siberian air base at Mys Shmidta near the Chukchi Sea. The following day, the capsule was ejected from the Agena spacecraft and reentered Earth's atmosphere. It floated back to earth with the aid of a parachute, and the Air Force retrieved it in midair by snagging the capsule's parachute lines with a hook trailing a small aircraft. By the end of the Corona program in 1972, over 120 Corona satellites had successfully flown and photographed the Soviet Union, China, and other nations.

ORVILLE WRIGHT IS BORN

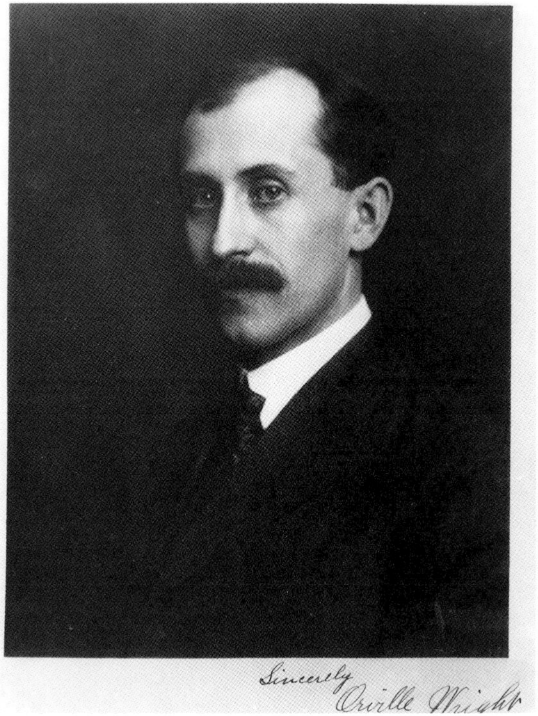

Orville Wright received eleven honorary degrees from universities in Europe and the United States, as well as dozens of medals and awards.

Smithsonian's National Air and Space Museum (NASM A-32497)

Aviation pioneer Orville Wright was born in Dayton, Ohio, on August 19, 1871. He fit the stereotype of the budding inventor, showing an interest in technology and science early in life and performing experiments and dismantling things to find out how they worked. Before achieving fame as the inventors of the airplane, Orville and his older brother Wilbur ran a local printing business in Dayton and owned a successful shop where they repaired, manufactured, rented, and sold bicycles.

The Wright brothers were fascinated with flight and used the money from their bicycle business to fund the design of a successful flying machine. Beginning with research on kites and gliders, the pair eventually achieved the first flight of a powered airplane in December 1903 with Orville at the controls (see page 368). Though Wilbur died of typhoid fever at the age of forty-five, Orville settled into the role of aviation elder statesman and national folk hero until the age of seventy-six. In 1939, President Franklin D. Roosevelt designated Orville's birthday, August 19, as National Aviation Day.

"Aviation has gone beyond my dreams."

—ORVILLE WRIGHT

U.S. AIR FORCE COMPLETES SECOND PROJECT MANHIGH FLIGHT

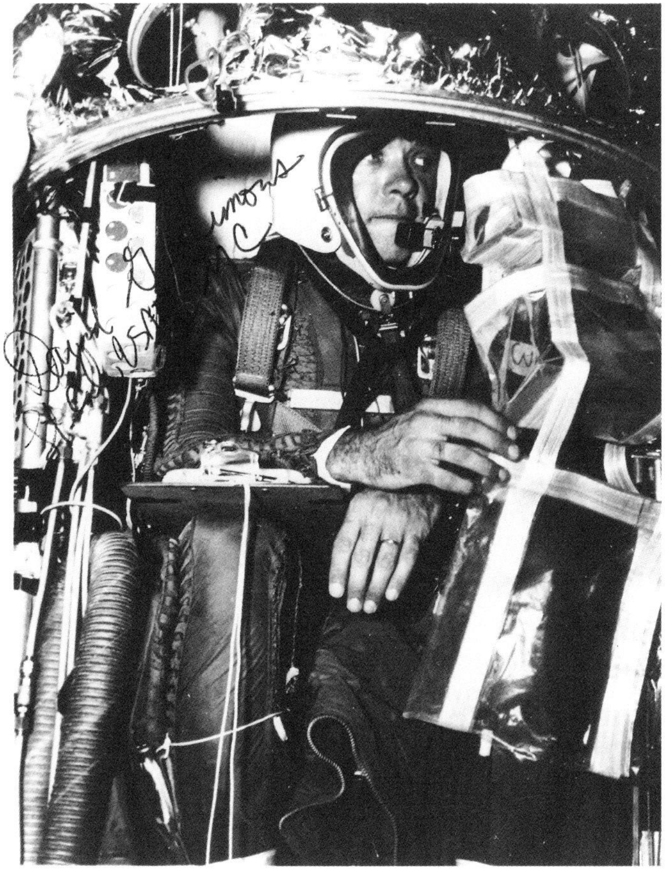

In the late 1950s, the United States Air Force conducted a series of three high-altitude balloon flights as part of Project Manhigh. Commanded by Col. John Paul Stapp, a flight surgeon with the Aerospace Medical Research Laboratory at Wright-Patterson Air Force Base, the research program flew military aeronauts to near space in pressurized gondolas suspended from balloons.

The first Manhigh flight took place in June 1957 and carried Capt. Joseph Kittinger (see page 223) to an altitude of about 95,500 feet. The second flight took place from August 19 to 20, 1957, and was the highest of the three, reaching a record altitude of 101,516 feet. During this thirty-two-hour flight, Maj. David Simons was taken aloft by a 200-foot-wide balloon filled with three million cubic feet of gas and conducted twenty-five aeromedical experiments. Simons also became the first person to see sunrise and sunset from above the Earth's atmosphere. The third and final Manhigh flight carried Lt. Clifton McClure to a height of 99,700 feet in October 1958.

Maj. David Simons flew on one of three Project Manhigh flights.

U.S. Air Force

DOUGLAS DC-8 GOES SUPERSONIC

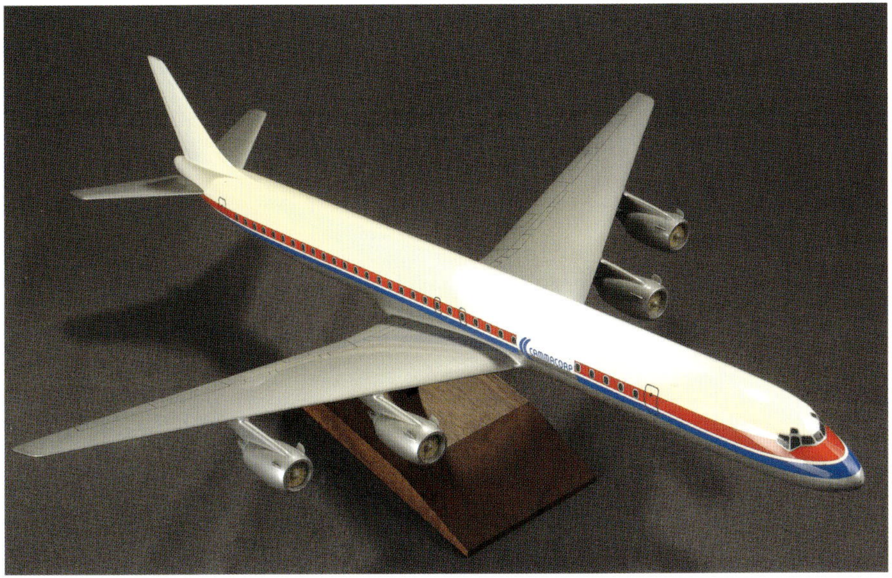

The Douglas DC-8 went into service in September 1959.

Smithsonian's National Air and Space Museum

The Douglas DC-8 was the first commercial airliner to break the sound barrier. Initially developed as a jet tanker, Douglas redesigned the DC-8 as a passenger jet after losing a military contract to Boeing. Early flight testing got the DC-8 to the edge of the sound barrier—Mach .95—but not any faster.

That changed on August 21, 1961, when test pilot Bill Magruder and copilot Paul Patten took off in a DC-8 from Edwards Air Force Base. After flying the aircraft to 52,000 feet—the highest a commercial airliner had ever flown—Magruder took the DC-8 into a dive and reached Mach 1.01 for just a few seconds before leveling off, though not without a bit of difficulty. The DC-8's speed record for a commercial airliner held for eight years, until it was broken by the Soviet supersonic airliner, the Tu-144.

DID YOU KNOW? The DC-8 was escorted on its test flight by an F-104 Starfighter piloted by Chuck Yeager.

AUGUST 22

WORLD'S FIRST MAJOR INTERNATIONAL FLYING MEET IS HELD IN FRANCE

EARLY FLIGHT

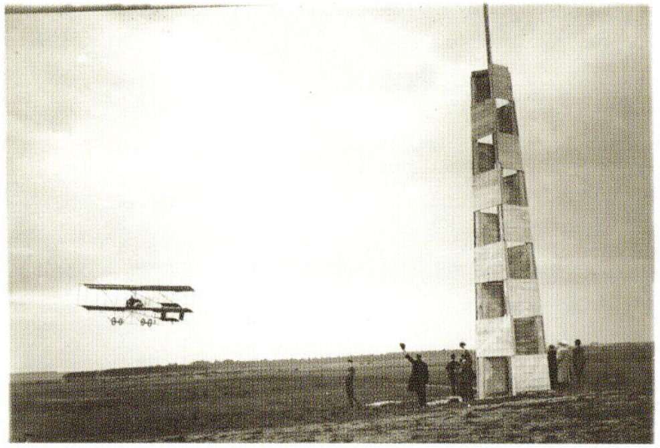

Twenty-three aircraft flew during the first international flying competition near Reims, France.

Library of Congress Technical Reports and Standards Unit, L'Aérophile Collection; Courtesy of Smithsonian's National Air and Space Museum (NASM 2001-11600)

The world's first major international flying competition began in France on August 22, 1909. Formally called La Grand Semaine de l'Aviation de la Champagne, thirty-eight airplanes entered various speed, distance, altitude, and passenger-carrying events. Though only twenty-three aircraft actually flew, and the Wright brothers did not attend, the event was a great success that turned many of the participating pilots into celebrities. Upward of a half-million spectators attended the competition, from the wealthy elite to the average aviation enthusiast.

AUGUST 23

LOCKHEED C-130 HERCULES FLIES FOR THE FIRST TIME

MODERN MILITARY AVIATION

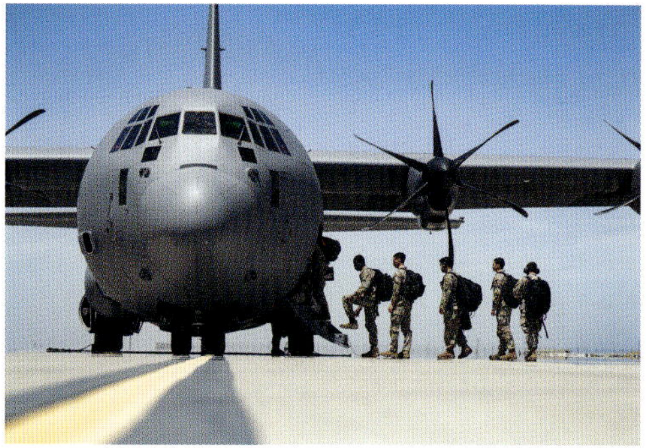

The Lockheed C-130 Hercules is used by militaries around the world, including the U.S. Air Force.

U.S. Air Force

On August 23, 1954, test pilots Stan Belz and Roy Wimmer were at the controls for the inaugural flight of Lockheed's prototype C-130 Hercules cargo aircraft. Though it certainly wasn't flashy, the rugged C-130 got the job done, flying a variety of missions including transporting cargo, airdropping supplies, retrieving satellites in midair, and supporting the U.S. Navy Blue Angels. This versatile aircraft now has over seventy variants for different purposes and locales.

PLUTO IS RECLASSIFIED AS A DWARF PLANET

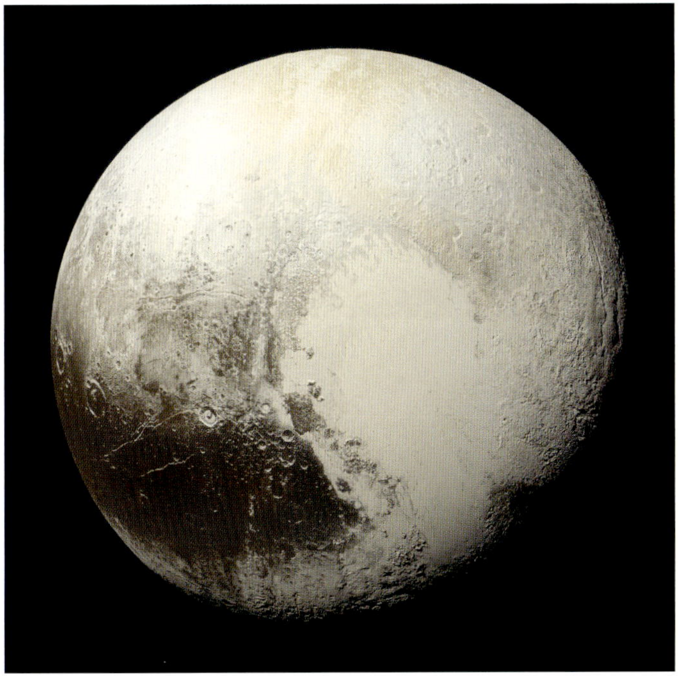

In 2015, the New Horizons mission returned the first high-resolution photos of the dwarf planet Pluto.

NASA

Pluto was reclassified as a "dwarf planet" on August 24, 2006, when the International Astronomical Union (IAU) passed a resolution redefining the criteria for planetary status. IAU criteria say that a planet is defined by three properties: It is a celestial body that orbits the Sun, it is massive enough that its own gravity causes it to form in a spherical shape, and it has cleared the neighborhood around its orbit. This means that its gravity caused other orbiting objects to crash into its surface or be ejected from the solar system.

It's that third element that's a strike against Pluto. Because Pluto resides in an area of the solar system still populated by numerous other objects, it could no longer be considered a planet. Pluto is now designated a dwarf planet—a celestial object that is not a satellite of another object and meets the first two criteria. Pluto's orbit just hasn't been cleared. Other dwarf planets are Ceres, which is the largest asteroid found in the Asteroid Belt between the orbits of Mars and Jupiter, and 2003 UB 313, which is an icy body that is larger and farther away than Pluto.

"You heard about Pluto? That's messed up, right?"

—BURTON "GUS" GUSTER, *PSYCH*

NASA LAUNCHES SPITZER SPACE TELESCOPE

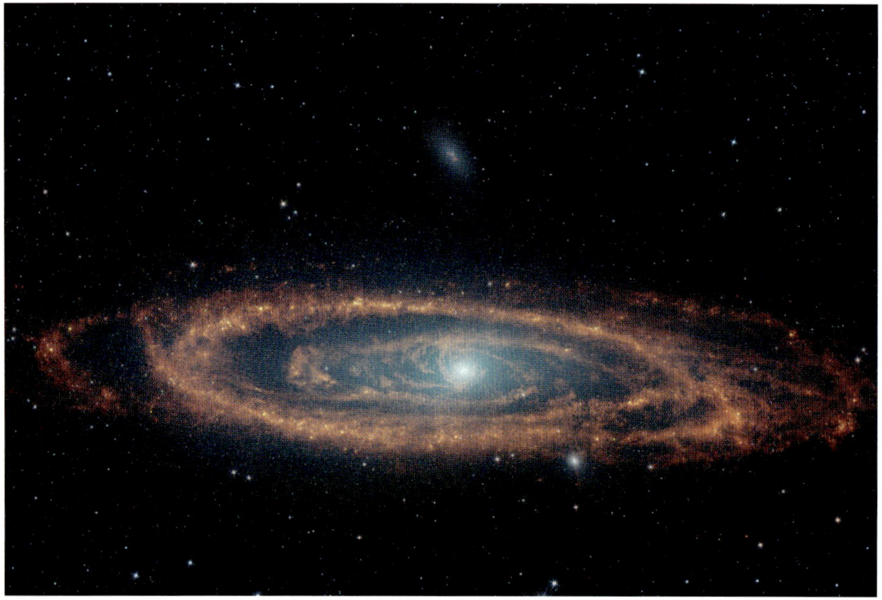

The Spitzer Space Telescope images celestial objects like the Andromeda Galaxy in infrared.

NASA/Caltech

The Spitzer Space Telescope launched atop a Delta 7920H rocket on August 25, 2003. At the time of its launch, it was called the Space Infrared Telescope Facility, but by December it had been renamed in honor of astrophysicist Lyman Spitzer Jr. The thirteen-foot-tall Spitzer Space Telescope had a 2.8-foot-wide mirror and was built by the Ball Aerospace Corporation and Lockheed Martin.

For seventeen years, Spitzer was the premier facility for infrared astronomy from space. Liquid helium on board the spacecraft cooled the telescope mirror and allowed instruments to function as needed. When its coolant was depleted in 2009, it completed its "cold mission" and entered "warm mode," which allowed some instruments to continue working, but not all.

Spitzer was the fourth in NASA's "Great Observatories," along with Hubble (see page 131), Chandra (see page 220), and the Compton Gamma Ray Observatory. The "Great Observatory Era" from 1989 to 2010 was a time of increased international collaboration in astronomy, but Spitzer was a completely U.S. project. It was, however, available to astronomers worldwide on a competitive peer-reviewed basis.

KATHERINE JOHNSON IS BORN

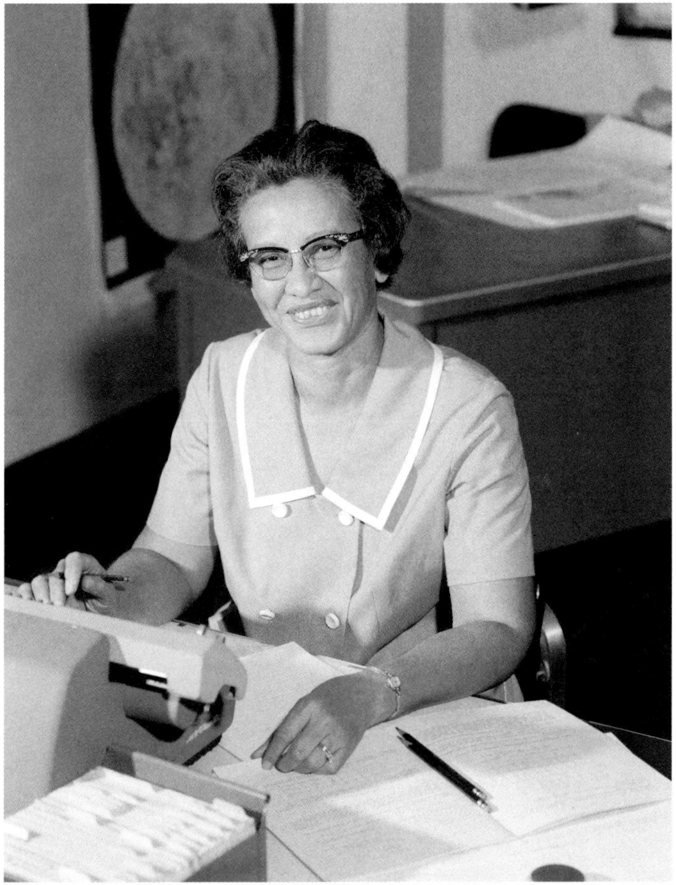

Pioneering aerospace mathematician Katherine Johnson was born on August 26, 1918, in White Sulphur Springs, West Virginia. Johnson was fascinated by numbers from a very young age, starting high school by the time she was ten, graduating at fourteen, and finishing college at just eighteen. After time as a teacher and stay-at-home mom, she went to work for the National Advisory Committee for Aeronautics, which later became NASA. In that role, she calculated results from tests at the famous wind tunnels at Langley Research Center (see page 162).

Johnson excelled as a "human computer" and the flights of the first Americans in space relied on her calculations. Even when NASA turned to electronic computers to tabulate trajectories, John Glenn famously asked that Johnson personally recheck the calculations on his flight before climbing aboard *Friendship 7*. Johnson's contributions to the early space program went unrecognized for decades, but the 2016 book and film *Hidden Figures* (see page 278) introduced a twenty-first-century audience to her story.

Katherine Johnson had a quiet, methodical approach to her work—even and especially when it was at odds with her expected role in society.

NASA

AUGUST 27

MARINER 2 LAUNCHES

SPACE SCIENCE

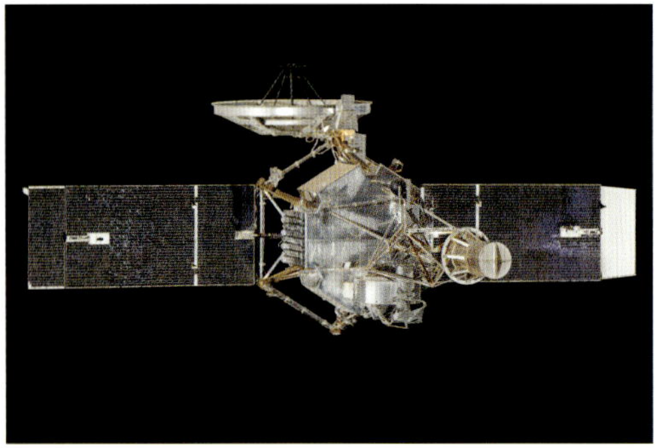

Unlike future Mariner spacecraft, Mariner 2 did not have cameras on board. The spacecraft in the collection of the National Air and Space Museum was constructed from test components.

NASA

Over the last six decades, many of NASA's signature achievements have been groundbreaking planetary science missions. It all began with Mariner 2, which launched on August 27, 1962. The world's first successful planetary science mission, Mariner 2 flew by Venus in December 1962, scanning the planet as it went. Using its six scientific instruments, the spacecraft gathered data on Venus's atmosphere and surface. Mariner 2 indicated that Venus is very hot and has no measurable magnetic fields or radiation belts.

AUGUST 28

TWO PILOTS SET ENDURANCE RECORD IN A DH-4B

WORLD WAR I AND INTERWAR AVIATION

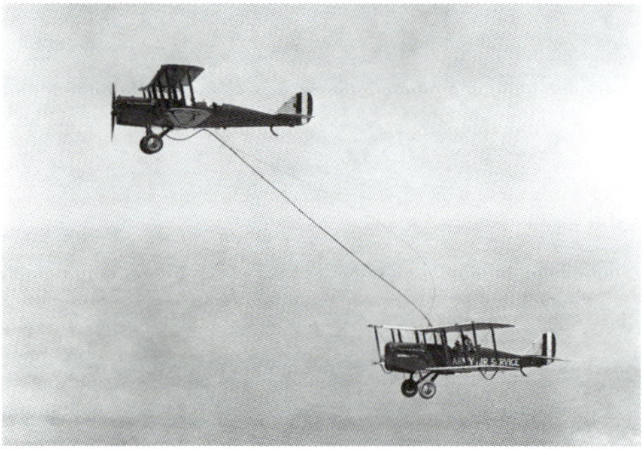

Lowell Smith and John Richter's endurance flight was only possible thanks to aerial refueling.

U.S. Air Force

On August 28, 1923, U.S Army Air Service lieutenants Lowell Smith and John Richter set an aerial endurance record piloting a DH-4B. During the more than thirty-seven-hour-long flight, the pair's DH-4 was refueled in midair sixteen times by another DH-4 using a hose to pass gasoline to their aircraft. The flight earned Smith and Richter sixteen world records for distance, speed, and duration. Smith continued to blaze new trails the following year when he and a team of U.S. Army Air Service pilots completed the first aerial circumnavigation of the world (see page 287).

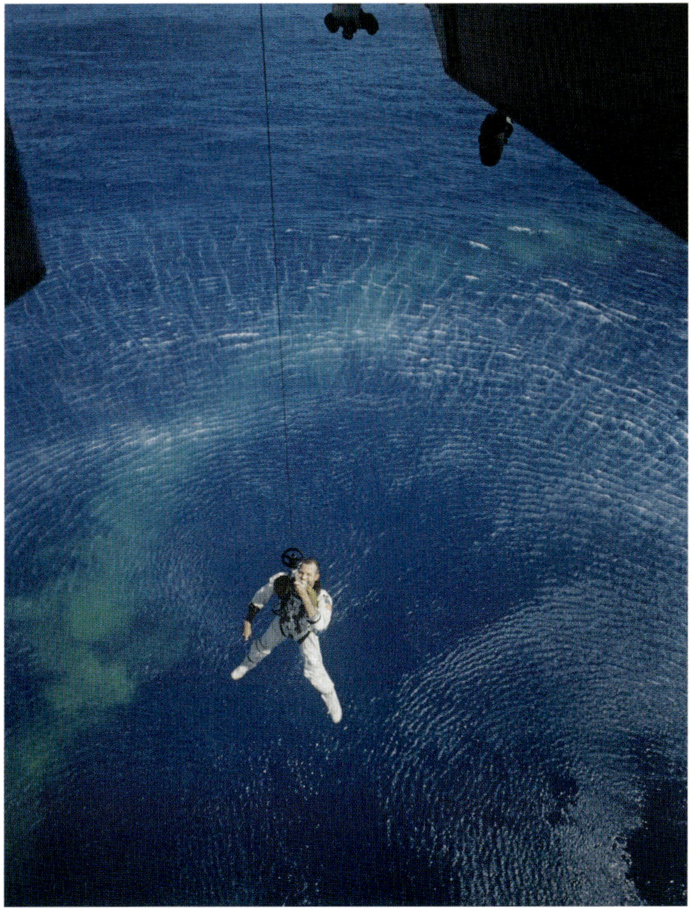

One of the goals of NASA's second human spaceflight program, Gemini, was to prove that humans could live in weightlessness for more than just a day or two. After all, with three days of travel time to get to the Moon and another three days back, Apollo missions would need to last at least a week. Gemini V, the program's third crewed spaceflight, was to fly in space for eight days. During the mission, astronauts L. Gordon Cooper and Charles "Pete" Conrad conducted medical experiments on their bodies to study the effects of long-term weightlessness.

On August 29, 1965, Gemini V splashed down in the Atlantic and the crew were recovered by helicopter and transferred to the USS *Lake Champlain*. The mission lasted seven days, twenty-two hours, and fifty-five minutes, just an hour shy of its eight-day goal. The mission set a new human spaceflight endurance record, exceeding the existing Soviet record of five days.

After splashdown, Gordon Cooper (pictured) and Pete Conrad were hoisted into a waiting helicopter.

NASA

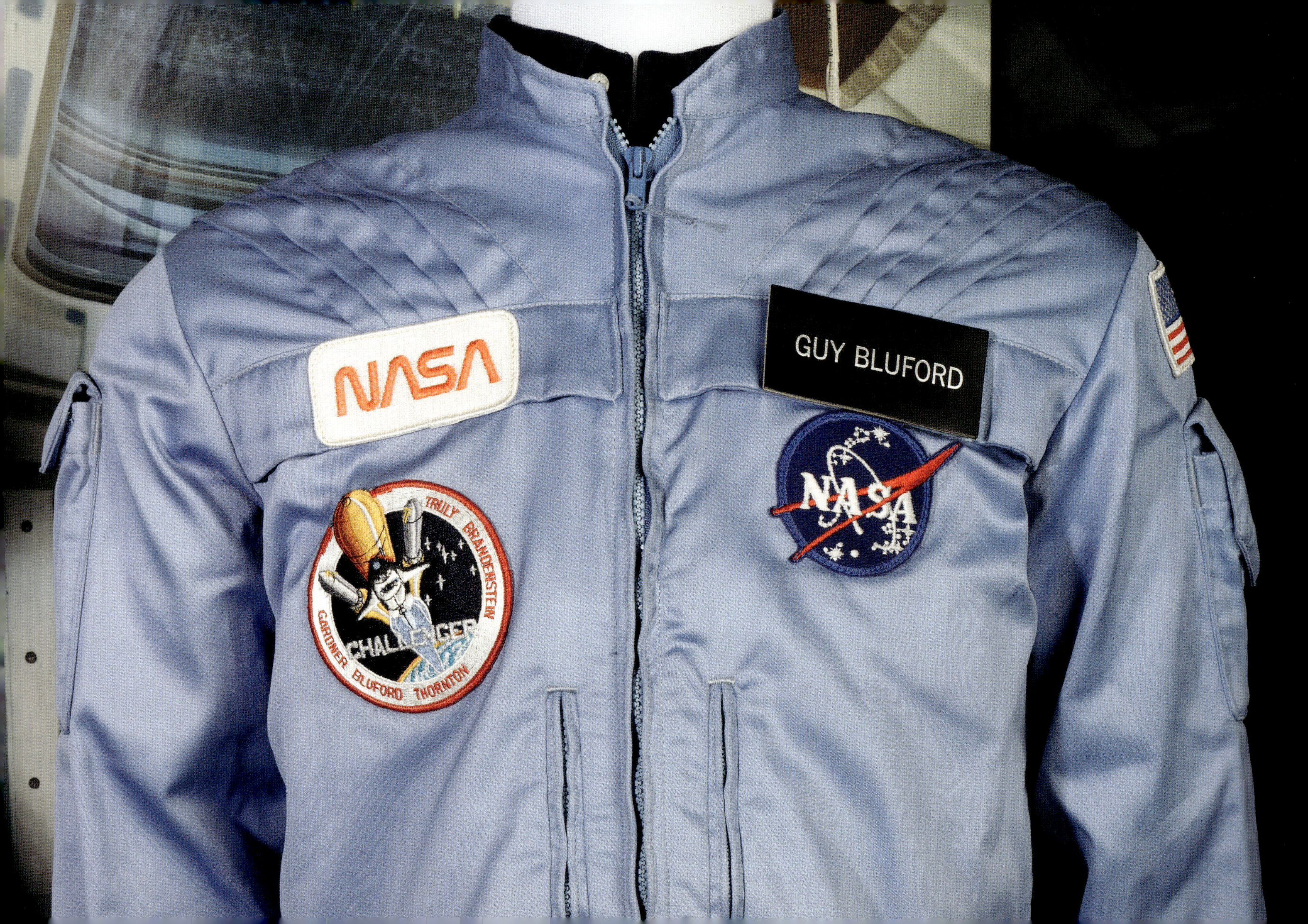
NASA
GUY BLUFORD
NASA
TRULY
BRANDENSTEIN
GARDNER
BLUFORD
THORNTON

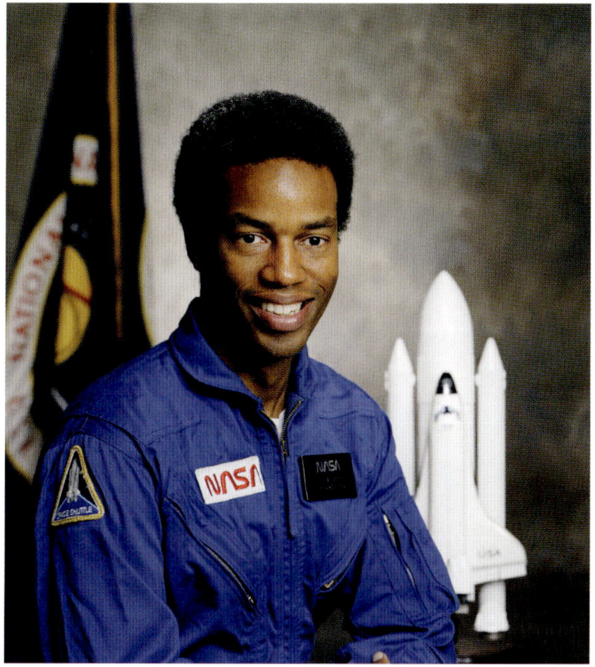

Guion "Guy" Bluford launched on Space Shuttle *Challenger*'s STS-8 mission on August 30, 1983, becoming the first African American astronaut to fly to space. As a mission specialist, Bluford's jobs were to deploy an Indian communications-weather satellite, perform biomedical experiments, and test the orbiter's fifty-foot robotic arm. Over the next decade, Bluford flew to space three more times on STS-61A, STS-39, and STS-53.

Bluford's path to space began in high school when he ignored the advice of his advisor to learn a trade or skill, instead enrolling at Penn State University to earn a degree in aerospace engineering. While there, he also participated in Air Force ROTC. Bluford flew F-4C fighters for the Air Force in Vietnam, completing 144 combat missions. After his deployment in Vietnam, he served as an instructor pilot. During this time, he went back to school, earning his master's and doctoral degrees in aerospace engineering from the Air Force Institute of Technology. In 1977, Bluford applied to be an astronaut, and the rest is history.

OPPOSITE PAGE Bluford's in-flight suit is on display at the National Air and Space Museum.

Smithsonian's National Air and Space Museum

ABOVE Guy Bluford spent twenty-eight days in space over the course of four Space Shuttle missions.

NASA

NASA'S SUPER GUPPY AIRCRAFT MAKES FIRST FLIGHT

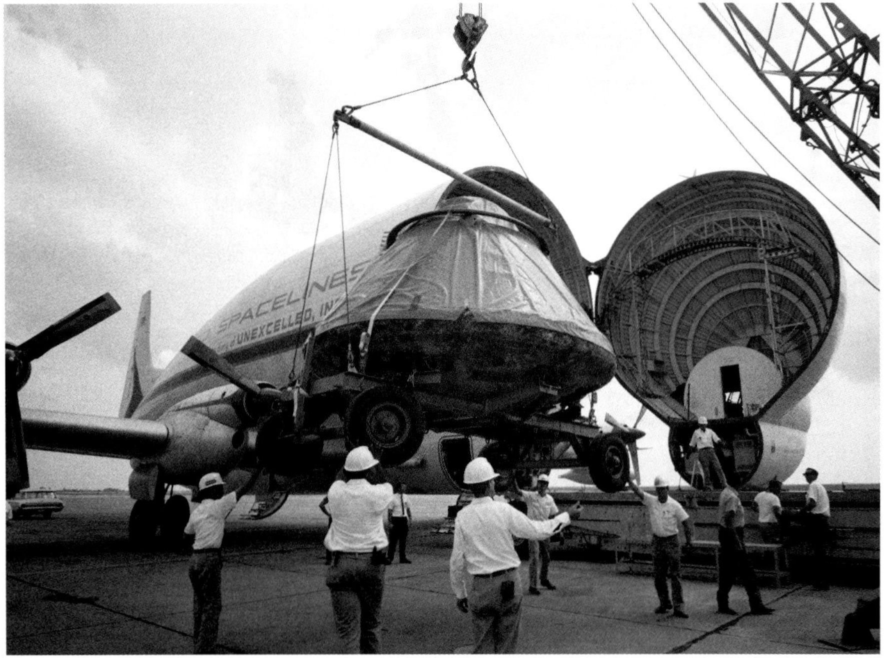

ABOVE The Super Guppy has a hinged nose that allows for loading large cargo into its cargo bay, including the Apollo 11 command module.

NASA

OPPOSITE PAGE NASA uses its Super Guppy aircraft to transport oversize cargo.

NASA/Kim Shiflett

As NASA began to stand up its human spaceflight program in the early 1960s, the agency recognized a need for a more practical way to transport large spacecraft components between its centers and contractors across the United States. Hoping to fill this need, ex-Air Force pilot John Conroy came up with the idea for the Guppy line of cargo aircraft. Built by Conroy's company, Aero Spaceline Industries (ASI), using a surplus Boeing 377 Stratocruiser, the first aircraft in the series was introduced in September 1962. Known as the Pregnant Guppy, the specialized aircraft had a cargo bay that was nineteen feet in diameter—large enough to carry the second stage of a Saturn I rocket.

But why stop there? ASI soon began work on a successor aircraft with a cargo bay that was twenty-five feet wide, twenty-five feet tall, and 111 feet long. Built from a retired Boeing YC-97J Stratofreighter and called the Super Guppy, it flew for the first time on August 31, 1965. One of the key innovations of the Super Guppy was its hinged nose, which allowed for easier loading of oversize cargo in the aircraft.

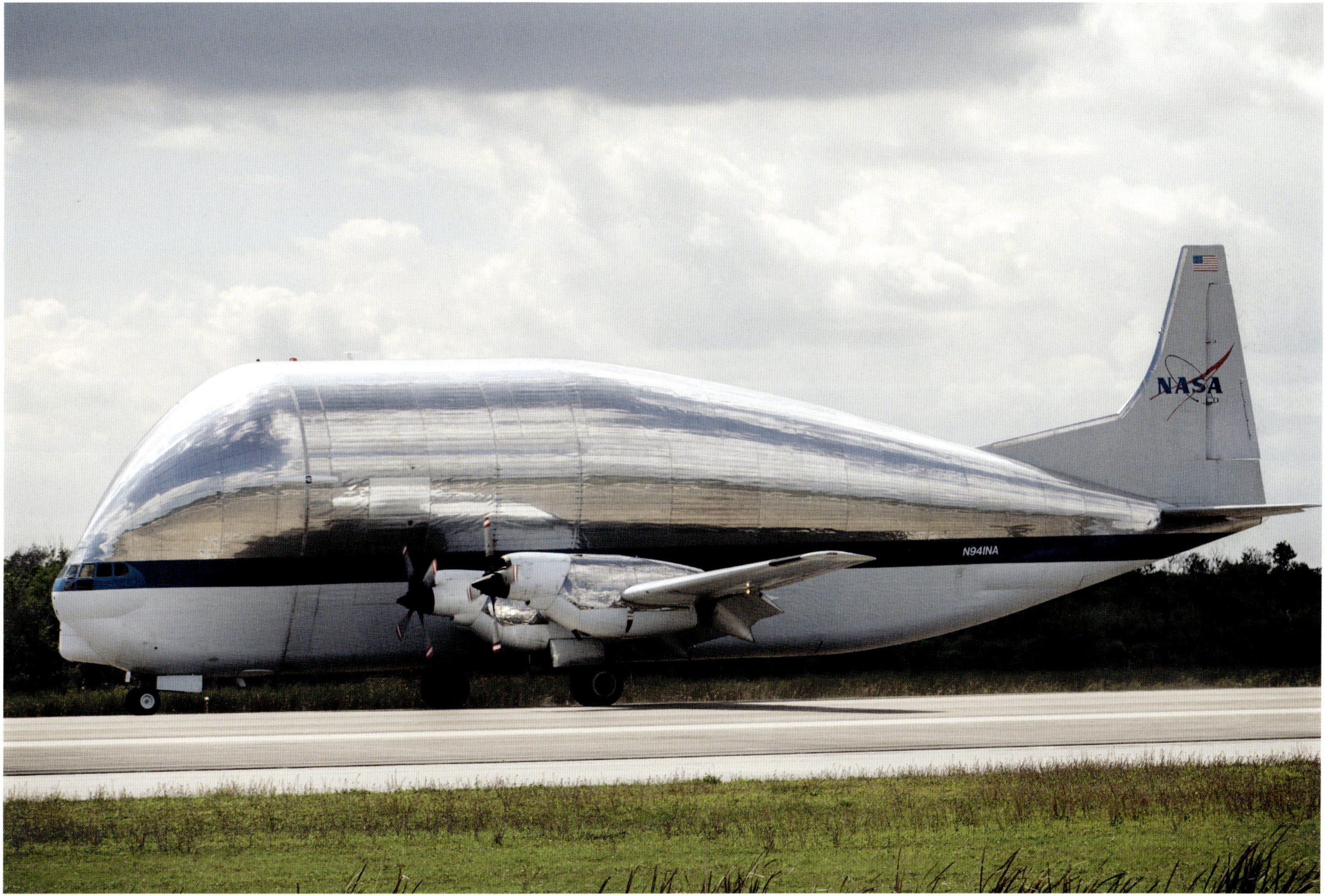
NASA
N941NA

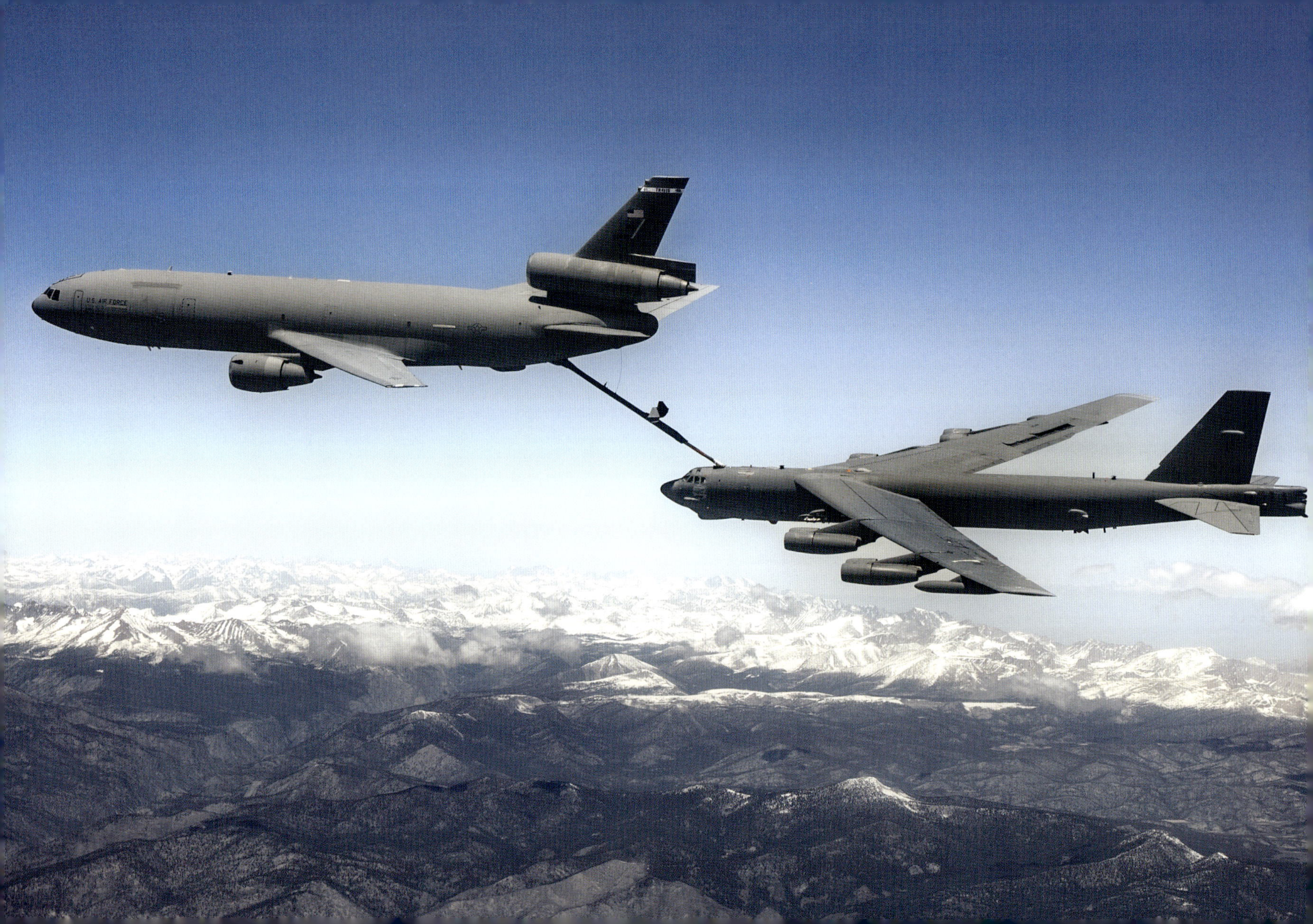
U.S. AIR FORCE

SEPTEMBER

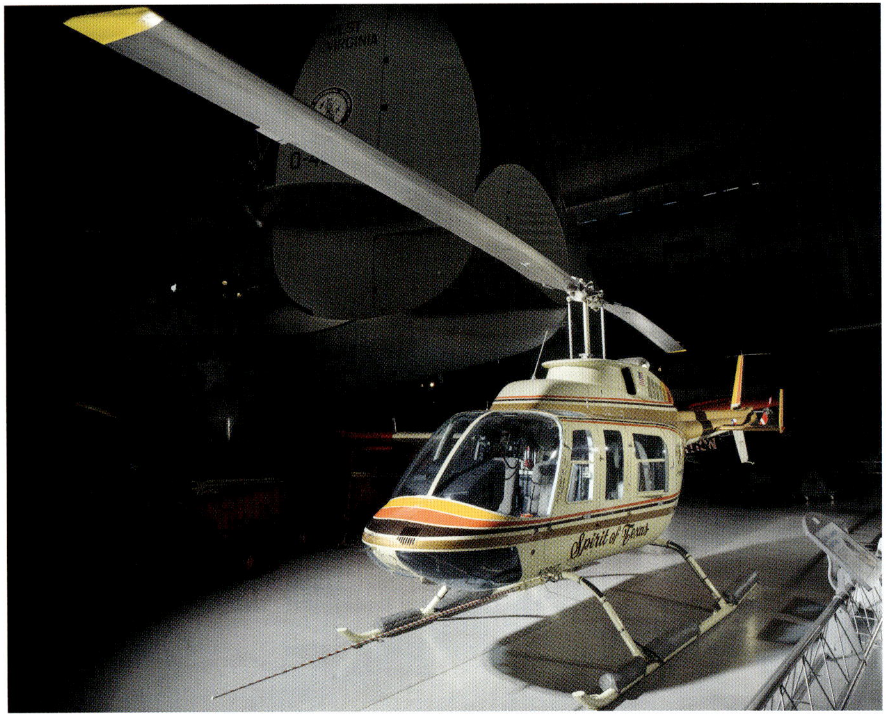

Spirit of Texas, now on display at the Steven F. Udvar-Hazy Center, was painted bright colors to enhance its visibility for its round-the-world flight.

Smithsonian's National Air and Space Museum

On September 1, 1982, H. Ross Perot Jr. and Jay Coburn departed Dallas, Texas, in a Bell 206L-1 LongRanger II named *Spirit of Texas* on the first round-the-world flight by helicopter. Flying an average of eight and a half hours per day, the pair traveled through twenty-six countries in twenty-nine days and refueled a total of fifty-six times. One especially harrowing refueling required Perot and Coburn to land on a container ship in the stormy waters of the northern Pacific Ocean.

The Bell LongRanger was a typical business and utility helicopter. To prepare the aircraft for their round-the-world trip, Perot and Coburn modified *Spirit of Texas*. This included removing nonessential items to make room for an extra fuel tank, which extended the helicopter's endurance by five hours. The pair also added additional navigation equipment, survival gear and emergency items, and pop-out floats to the rear seat of the helicopter.

MONTEREY PARK POLICE DEPARTMENT FLIES DOUBLE EAGLE ULTRALIGHT

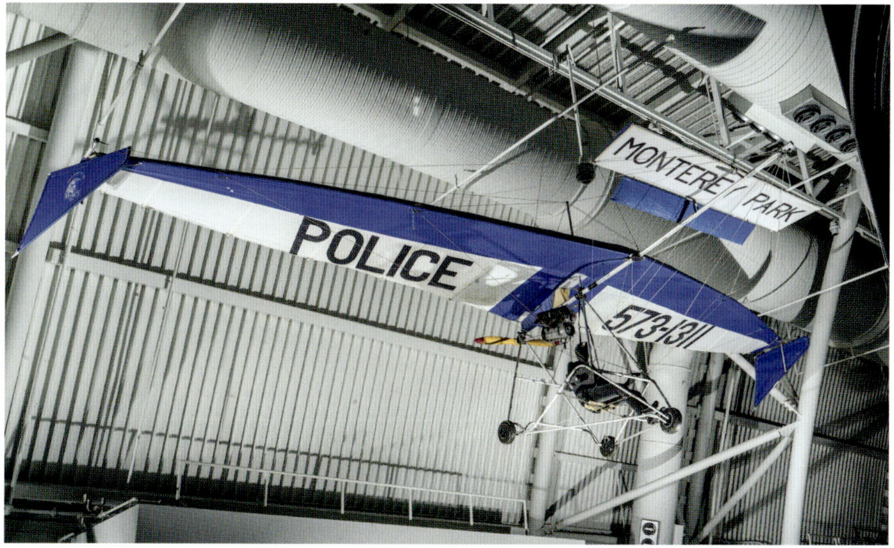

The Double Eagle ultralight is on display at the Steven F. Udvar-Hazy Center.

Smithsonian's National Air and Space Museum

"Our hilly terrain and lack of appropriate forced landing sites do not allow a viable program in this community, but the concept is good." This is how Lt. Joe Santoro of the Monterey Park Police Department in California described a novel but short-lived aviation experiment in the early 1980s. When Monterey Park police officers took flight in the American Aerolights Double Eagle on September 2, 1982, it was the first time that an ultralight aircraft was used to conduct police work. Though the Double Eagle was a valuable asset, the engine proved fragile, and Santoro grounded the aircraft after seven engine failures in six months.

The Double Eagle was designed by Larry Newman, a pilot and balloonist who had crossed the Atlantic in the *Double Eagle II* balloon in 1978 (see page 240). Newman's initial ultralight design, the Eagle, was a simple, low-powered beginner's machine with one seat. The ultralight flown by the Monterey Park Police was modified with a second seat, a stronger airframe, and more powerful engine, earning it the name Double Eagle.

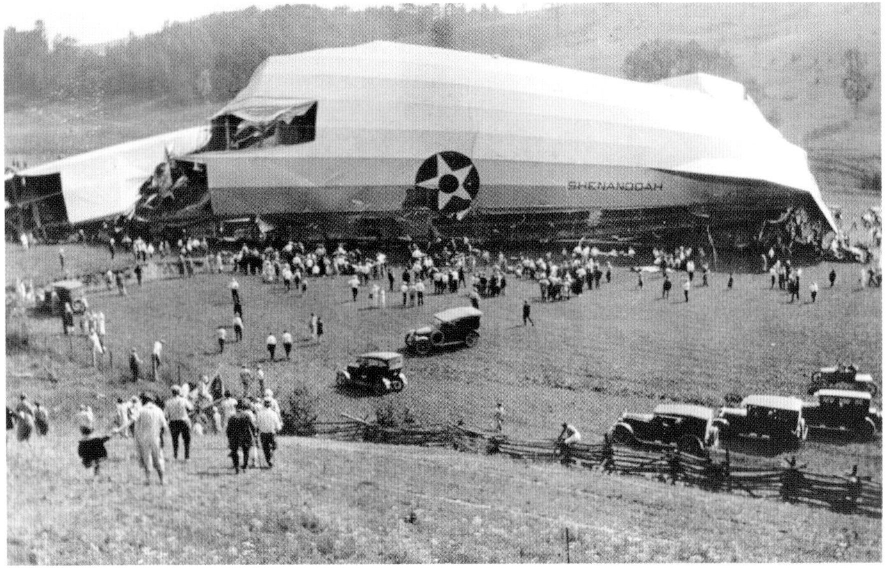

Thousands of people swarmed the USS *Shenandoah*'s crash site soon after the airship went down.

Smithsonian's National Air and Space Museum (NASM 2000-11498)

Launched in 1923, the USS *Shenandoah* was the U.S. Navy's first rigid airship. The aircraft's christening was seen by many as the beginning of a new era in which an entire fleet of American airships would sail the skies. Although this dream did not become reality, the USS *Shenandoah* did pave the way for future rigid airship pilots and crews and offered an invaluable platform for training.

Two years after it entered service, the USS *Shenandoah* crashed when it encountered stormy weather over Ohio on September 3, 1925. Initially, extreme air currents from the storm had caused the airship to rise rapidly. As the crew tried to level the creaking and groaning aircraft, a burst of cold air caused it to rapidly descend. These intense maneuvers were too much for the airframe to handle, and the USS *Shenandoah* broke up in midair. Tragically, fourteen members of the airship's forty-three-person crew died in the accident.

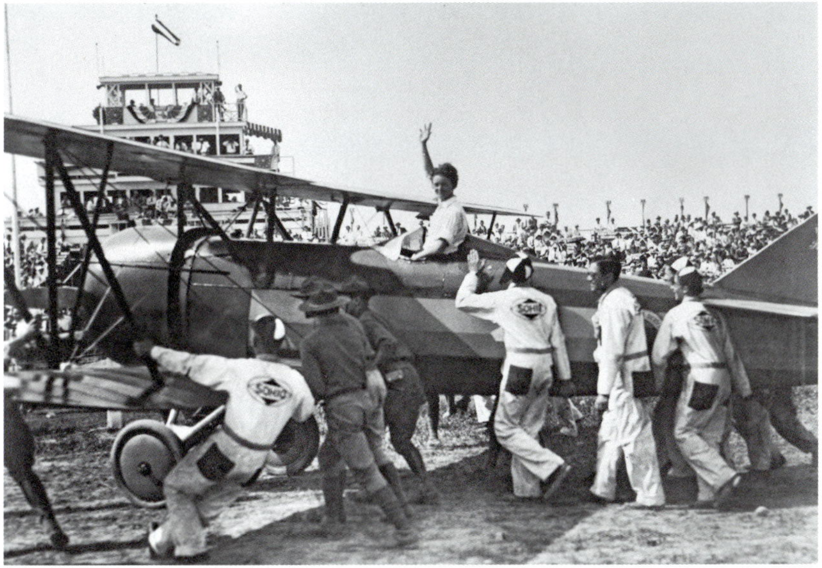

"If you have flown, perhaps you can understand the love a pilot develops for flight. It is much the same emotion a man feels for a woman, or a wife for her husband."

—LOUISE THADEN

Louise Thaden was the first woman to win the Bendix Trophy.

Smithsonian's National Air and Space Museum (NASM 89-22002)

Record-setting pilot Louise Thaden captured America's attention during the late 1920s and 1930s. In 1929, she gained recognition as a competitive flyer by becoming the first pilot to simultaneously hold the women's altitude, endurance, and speed records for light planes. That same year, Thaden also captured first place in the first annual Women's Air Derby, which was flown from Santa Monica, California, to Cleveland, Ohio.

Adding to these accomplishments, Thaden won the Bendix Trophy on September 4, 1936, the first year that women were allowed to compete against men in the transcontinental race. Later that year, she was awarded the Women's Harmon Trophy, an international prize given to the outstanding woman aviator of the year. Thaden did much to help popularize aviation and was a founding member of the Ninety-Nines (see page 325), a group formed by ninety-nine women pilots to mutually support other women in the aviation profession.

VOYAGER 1 LAUNCHES WITH THE GOLDEN RECORD

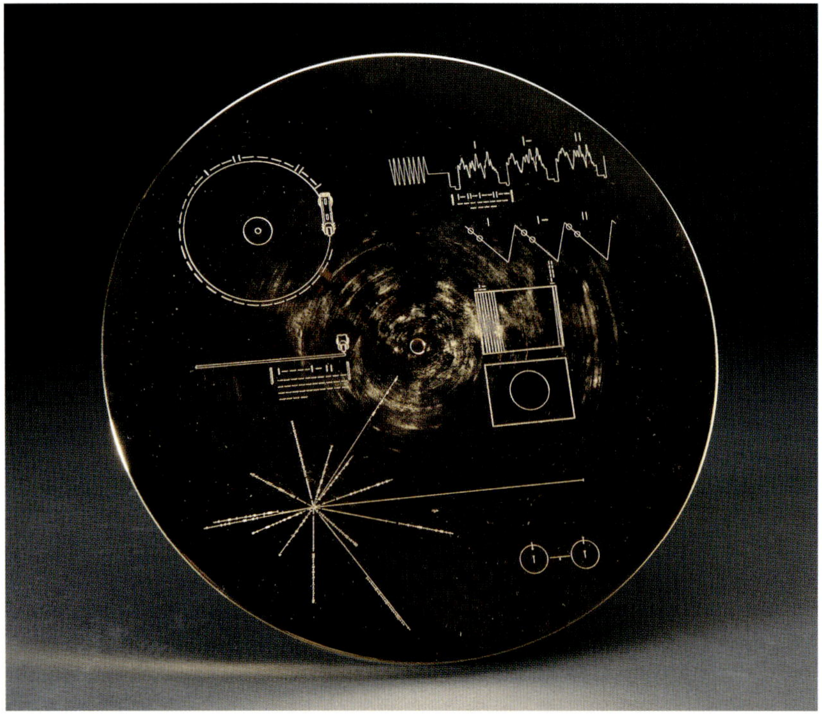

The cover of the Golden Record featured a pulsar map to Earth's solar system and instructions on how to play the record.

Smithsonian's National Air and Space Museum

NASA's Voyager 1 mission launched on September 5, 1977, with something special mounted on the outside of the spacecraft. The two Voyager spacecraft were expected to travel farther than any spacecraft had, so NASA decided to send along an analog disc record containing sounds and images selected to portray the diversity of life and culture on Earth. The disc, officially titled "Sounds of Earth" but better known as Voyager's Golden Record, was mounted in plain view on the exterior of both Voyager spacecraft, along with a stylus and pictographic instructions on how to play it.

NASA selected planetary scientist and science communicator Carl Sagan to chair a committee responsible for selecting what would go on the Golden Record. Ultimately, the record contained 122 images, a variety of natural sounds, spoken greetings in fifty-five languages, and ninety minutes of music, including Chuck Berry's "Johnny B. Goode" and Mozart's *The Magic Flute*.

SEPTEMBER 6

U.S. NAVY CONTRACTS WITH MCDONNELL AIRCRAFT TO BUILD GARGOYLE MISSILE

WORLD WAR II MILITARY AVIATION

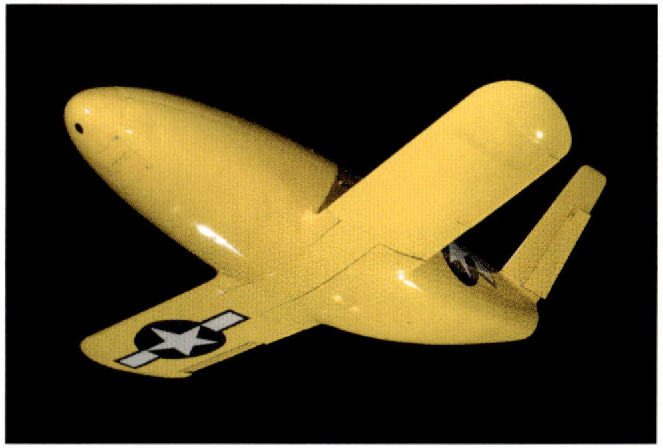

A Gargoyle is on display at the Steven F. Udvar-Hazy Center.

Smithsonian's National Air and Space Museum

On September 6, 1944, McDonnell Aircraft was awarded a contract by the U.S. Navy to develop a radio-controlled, rocket-propelled, air-to-surface missile. Called the Gargoyle, the missile was designed to be launched from carrier-based aircraft against ships. The Gargoyle carried a thousand-pound warhead and could travel at a speed of approximately 600 miles per hour for five to seven miles. Though developed too late for use in World War II, engineers continued testing the Gargoyle's autopilot and other components until the project's cancellation in 1974.

SEPTEMBER 7

BESSIE COLEMAN AERO CLUB HOLDS FIRST ALL-BLACK AIR SHOW IN THE U.S.

PIONEERS OF FLIGHT

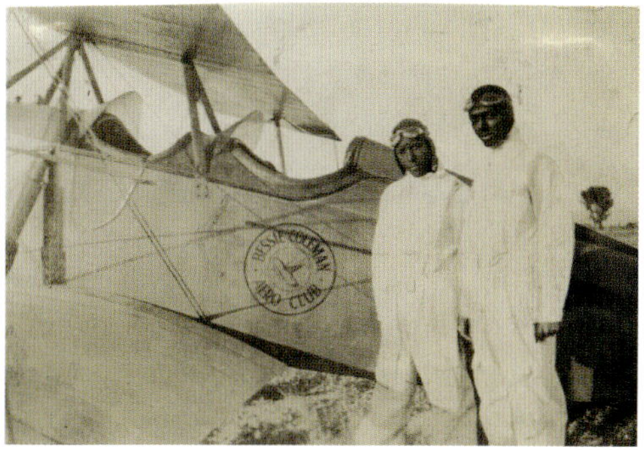

William J. Powell founded the Bessie Coleman Aero Club to support the Black aviation community.

Smithsonian's National Air and Space Museum (NASM 2009-9027)

In 1929, Black aviator William J. Powell founded the Bessie Coleman Aero Club in Los Angeles to raise aviation awareness in the Black community. Named for the first African American woman to earn a pilot's license (see page 183), the club was open to both men and women and trained pilots and mechanics. Powell was a talented visionary and avid promoter of Black involvement in aviation. On September 7, 1931, the Bessie Coleman Aero Club sponsored the first all-Black air show held in the United States. The event, which was held in Los Angeles, drew over fifteen thousand attendees.

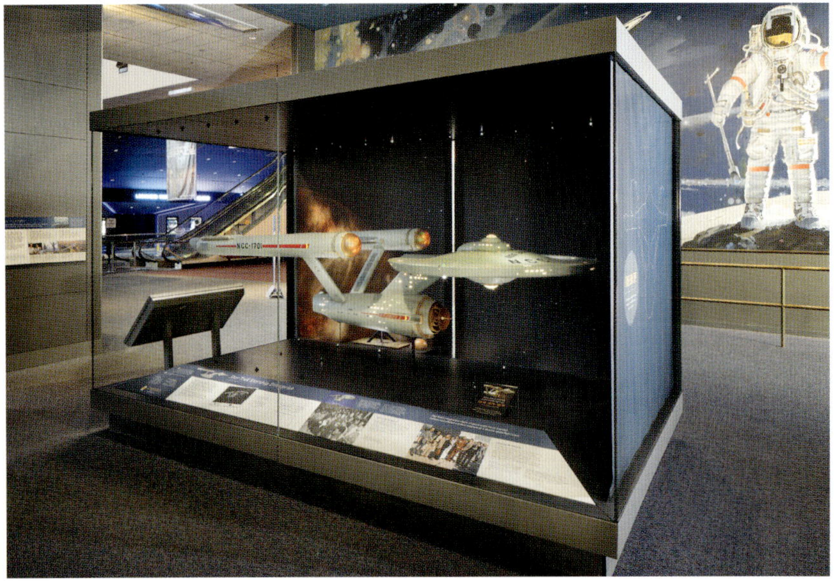

ABOVE The eleven-foot studio model of starship *Enterprise* used in the filming of *Star Trek* is on display at the National Air and Space Museum. The model appeared in all seventy-nine episodes of *Star Trek: The Original Series.*

Smithsonian's National Air and Space Museum

OPPOSITE PAGE The National Air and Space Museum has many *Star Trek* props including a model of a Klingon D7 Battle Cruiser, ear tips made for Leonard Nimoy to portray Mr. Spock, and a communicator badge prop from *Star Trek: Voyager* owned by Sally Ride.

Smithsonian's National Air and Space Museum

The first installment of the iconic science-fiction franchise *Star Trek* premiered on NBC on September 8, 1966. Despite its short initial run (only three seasons), *Star Trek* became one of the most influential shows in the history of television. The show depicted a racially integrated, multinational crew of men, women, and other creatures working together successfully. Its attention to contemporary social and political issues pushed the boundaries of network television and earned *Star Trek* a dedicated fan base that lobbied for the show's continuation.

Fans held the first *Star Trek* convention in New York City in 1972. In the decades since, multiple films and television series expanded the *Star Trek* canon. Passionate fans engage with, debate, and consume those programs as well as novels, reference books, comics, clothes, toys, and other branded items.

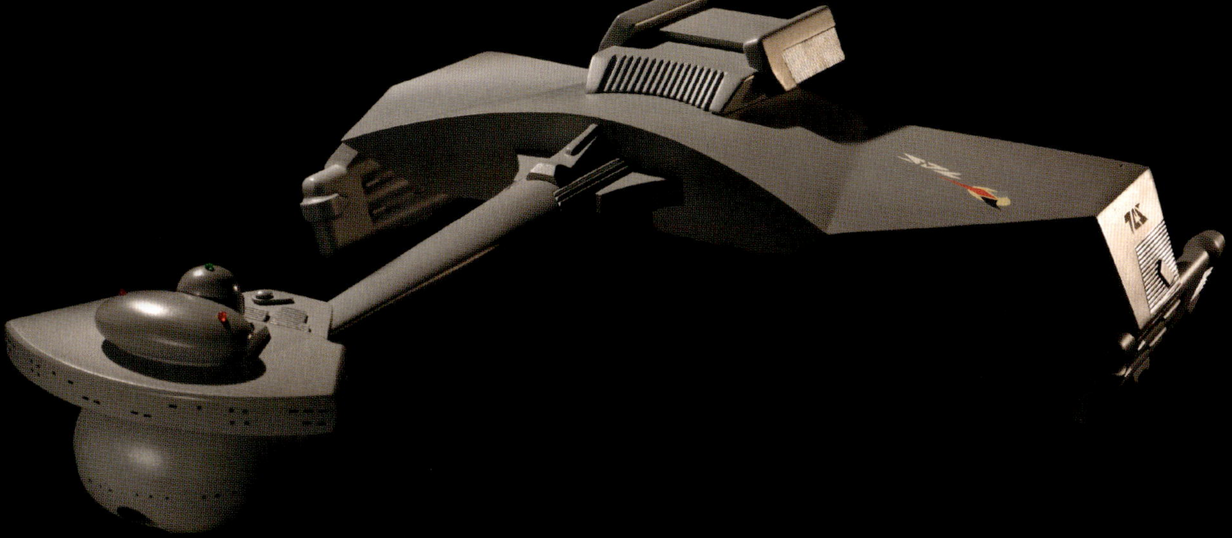

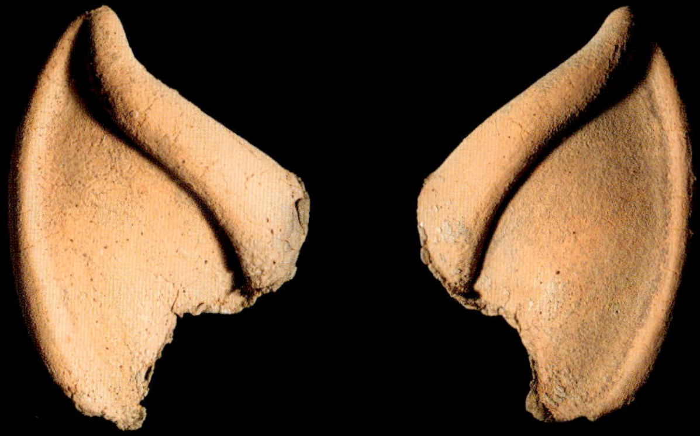

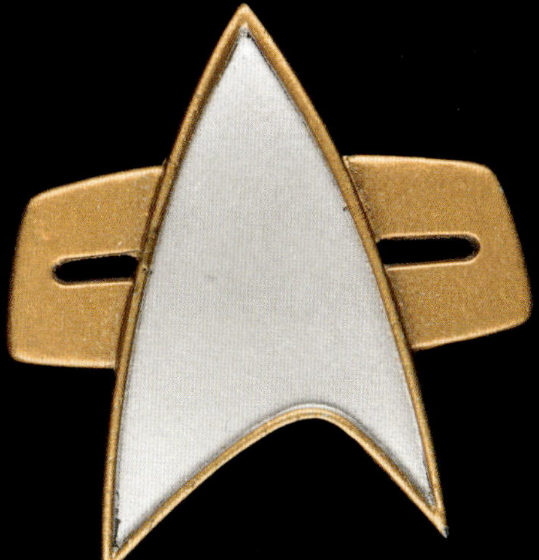

SEPTEMBER 9

NASA LAUNCHES UNCREWED MERCURY CAPSULE USING AN ATLAS BOOSTER

HUMAN SPACEFLIGHT

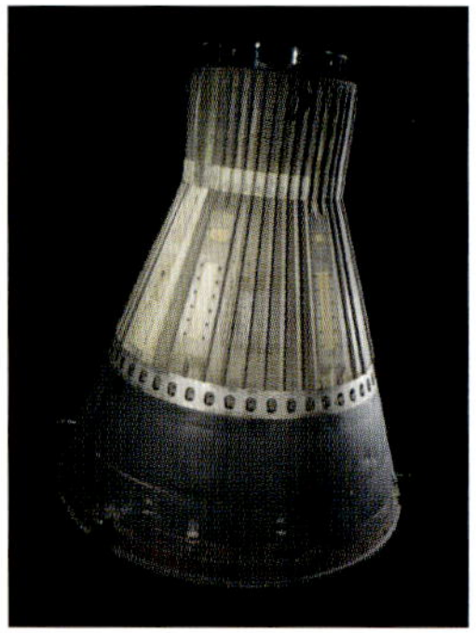

The *Big Joe* spacecraft is on display at the Steven F. Udvar-Hazy Center.

Smithsonian's National Air and Space Museum

NASA launched an uncrewed Mercury spacecraft called *Big Joe* from Cape Canaveral, Florida, on September 9, 1959. During the thirteen-minute suborbital spaceflight, the capsule reached an altitude of a hundred miles before successfully reentering the atmosphere. Its launch was the second in the Mercury program and the first using an Atlas booster. The heavily instrumented *Big Joe* was the most massive American spacecraft launched up to that time. The flight helped NASA evaluate the booster, the new ablative heat shield, the capsule's flight dynamics and aerodynamic shape, and spacecraft recovery systems and procedures.

SEPTEMBER 10

GRAIL MISSION LAUNCHES TO THE MOON

SPACE SCIENCE

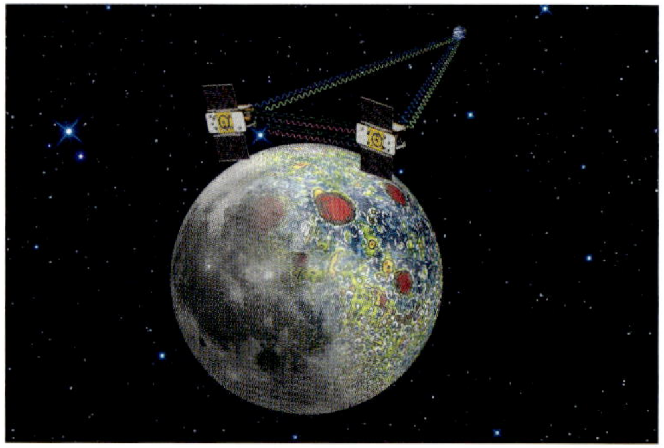

The twin spacecraft of NASA's GRAIL mission worked together to gather data about the Moon's gravitational field.

NASA-Caltech

On September 10, 2011, NASA launched its GRAIL mission to the Moon. Launched on a single rocket, the mission featured two identical spacecraft that arrived at the Moon a day apart after a three-and-a-half-month trip. The twin spacecraft were given the names *Ebb* and *Flow* by a national contest won by fourth graders in Montana. Once the spacecraft entered lunar orbit, they collected data on the Moon's gravitational field. Scientists used this data to determine the Moon's internal structure.

SEPTEMBER 11

AL-QAEDA TERRORISTS USE AIRLINERS TO ATTACK THE UNITED STATES

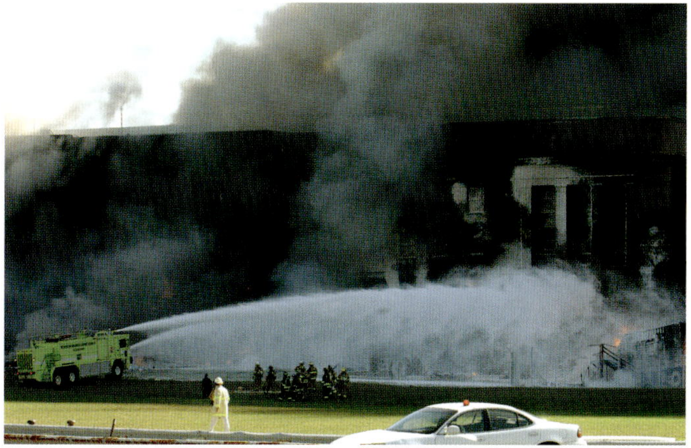

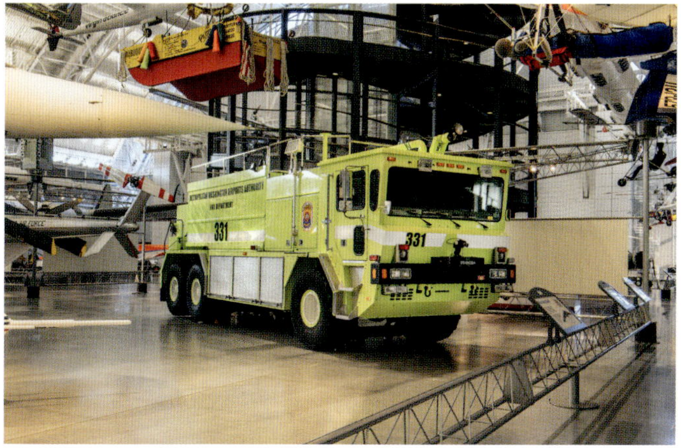

On September 11, 2001, nineteen terrorists hijacked four airliners in a coordinated attack on the United States. At 8:46 A.M., five of the hijackers flew American Airlines Flight 11 into the North Tower of the World Trade Center in New York City. A second airliner, United Airlines Flight 175, hit the South Tower at 9:03 A.M. Some thirty minutes later, at 9:37 A.M., the terrorists crashed American Airlines Flight 77 into the Pentagon in Washington, D.C. At 10:30 A.M., passengers and crew on board a fourth plane tried to regain control of the cockpit, preventing the terrorists from reaching their final target and crashing in a field in Pennsylvania.

Less than an hour after the first plane crashed into the Twin Towers, the Federal Aviation Administration closed all U.S. airspace. It was the first unplanned closure of airspace in United States history. In a matter of hours, all commercial air traffic was grounded. The National September 11 Memorial and Museum opened in 2011 to remember the nearly three thousand victims of these attacks and honor all those who risked their lives to save others.

TOP After the Pentagon was attacked on September 11, the Metropolitan Washington Airports Authority's rescue truck Foam 331 was the first foam-carrying rescue truck to arrive at the site.

National Archives and Records Administration

BOTTOM Rescue truck Foam 331 is on display at the Steven F. Udvar-Hazy Center.

Smithsonian's National Air and Space Museum

SEPTEMBER 12

JOHN F. KENNEDY DELIVERS "WE CHOOSE TO GO TO THE MOON" SPEECH

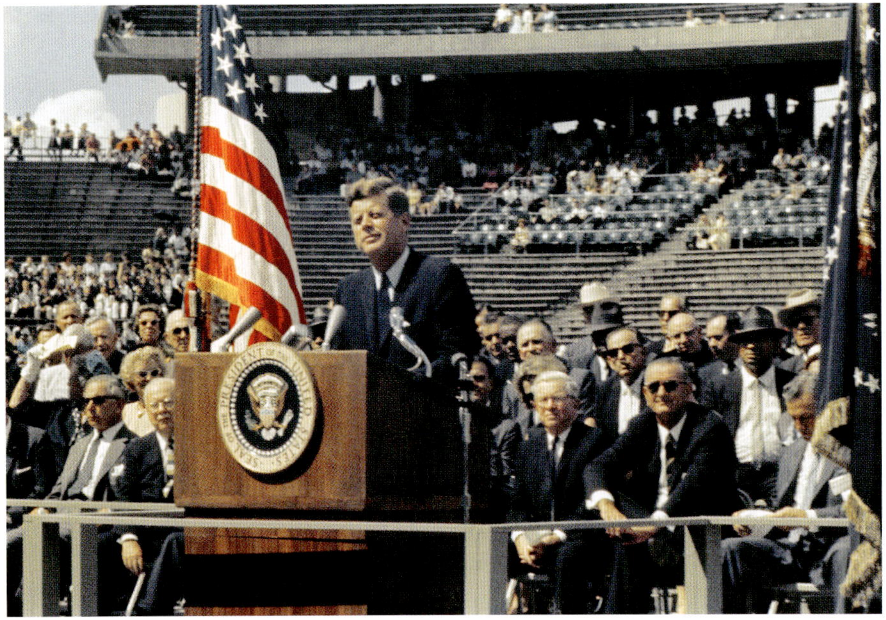

John F. Kennedy delivered his "We Choose to Go to the Moon" speech in Houston, Texas, home of NASA's Manned Spacecraft Center.

NASA

After President John F. Kennedy decided to enter the United States in a race to be the first to land on the Moon, he had to rally public support for the cause. After all, this was the most expensive civilian technology program in U.S. history. On September 12, 1962, Kennedy delivered his famous "We Choose to Go to the Moon" speech in front of a crowd of forty thousand people at Rice University in Texas.

Officially titled "Address at Rice on the Nation's Space Effort," the speech gets its more well-known name from a section in the middle of the speech: "We choose to go to the Moon in this decade and do the other things, not because they are easy, but because they are hard." Throughout the speech, Kennedy successfully laid out his argument that landing humans on the Moon was a worthy investment.

"But why, some say, the Moon? Why choose this as our goal? And they may well ask why climb the highest mountain? Why, thirty-five years ago, fly the Atlantic? Why does Rice play Texas?"

—PRESIDENT JOHN F. KENNEDY

HOWARD HUGHES SETS NEW WORLD SPEED RECORD IN H-1 RACER

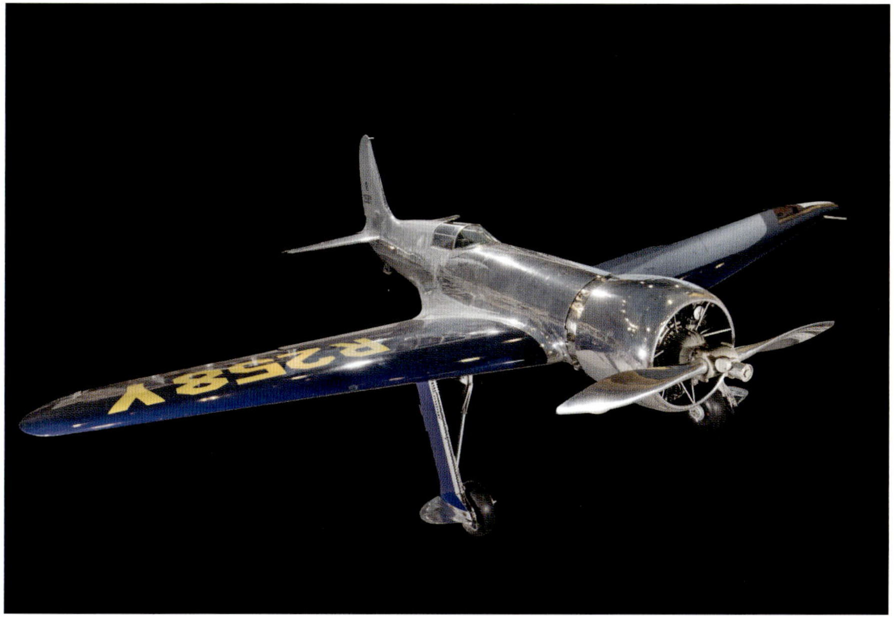

Businessman, filmmaker, and pilot Howard Hughes was passionate about flight. In the mid-1930s, Hughes and engineer Richard Palmer began work on developing the fastest landplane in the world. Built by Glenn Odekirk, the Hughes H-1 Racer achieved a new world speed record of 352.39 miles per hour on September 13, 1935. Hughes himself was at the controls of the H-1 during this record flight, which took place over a specially instrumented course near Santa Ana, California.

Interestingly, the H-1 had two sets of wings. The wings Hughes used to break the landplane speed record had a low aspect ratio and were shorter than those with which it is now fitted. Its second set of wings, spanning over thirty-one feet with a moderate aspect ratio, were used when Hughes broke the transcontinental speed record on another flight in 1937. The H-1 is displayed at the National Air and Space Museum with the thirty-one-foot wings.

Since Howard Hughes did not require a sponsor for the aircraft, the H-1 has no markings except the license number R258Y.

Smithsonian's National Air and Space Museum

SEPTEMBER 14 EUGENE BULLARD IS POSTHUMOUSLY HONORED BY U.S. AIR FORCE

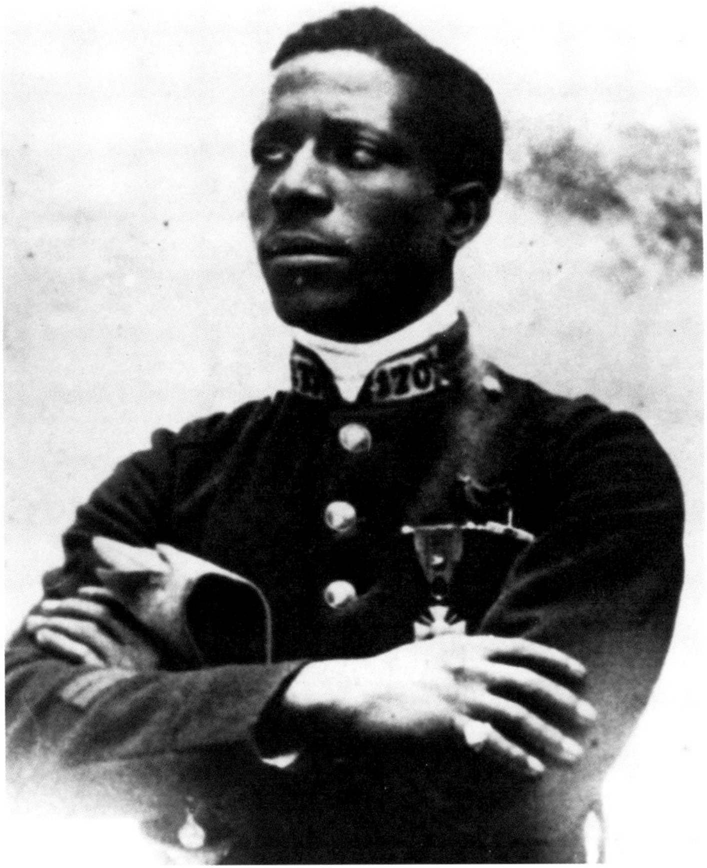

Though he never flew for the United States, Eugene Bullard was the only African American combat pilot and one of only a few Black combat pilots during World War I. Born in 1895 in Columbus, Georgia, Bullard fled the U.S. for France at age sixteen in an effort to escape racism. Bullard earned honors for fighting in the French trenches, and these accolades allowed him to volunteer for the French air service, Armée de l'Air.

After the United States entered World War I in 1917, Bullard attempted to join the U.S. Air Service. Despite his twenty-five combat missions and two unconfirmed aerial victories, the American military officials denied Bullard's request to fly. Bullard fought for France again during World War II and briefly found his way back to the U.S. during the Nazi occupation before returning once more to his adopted country. Though the people of France celebrated Bullard during his later years, he only became widely known in America after his death. The U.S. Air Force posthumously commissioned Bullard as a second lieutenant on September 14, 1994.

Eugene Bullard fought for France in two World Wars.

Smithsonian's National Air and Space Museum (NASM 91-6283)

CASSINI PLUNGES INTO SATURN IN "GRAND FINALE"

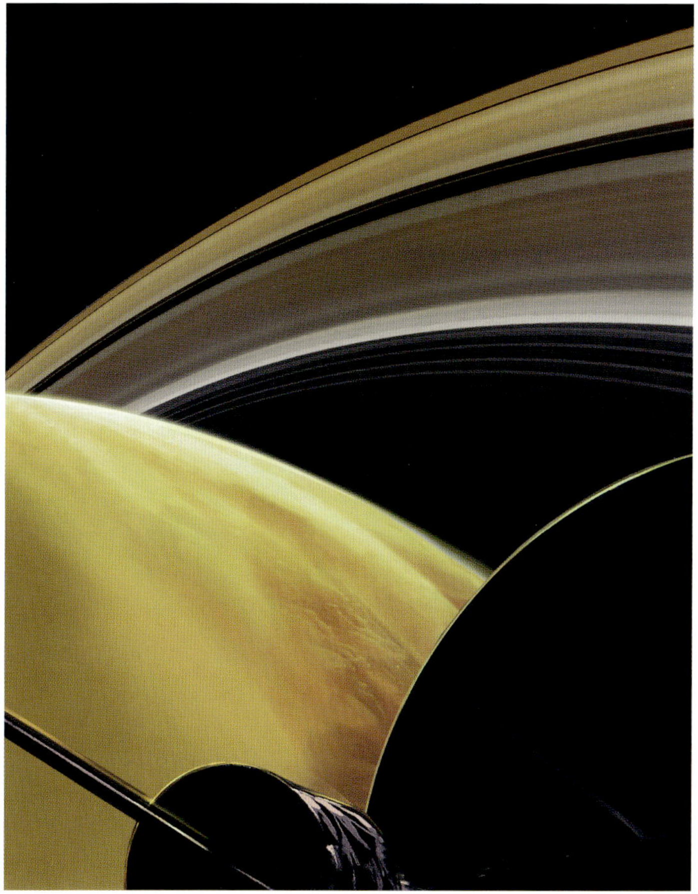

NASA's Cassini spacecraft plunged into Saturn on September 15, 2017, ending thirteen years of exploration of the giant ringed planet and its diverse moons. Cassini's journey began in 1997 when it launched as the Cassini–Huygens mission from Cape Canaveral Air Force Station in Florida. When it arrived in the Saturnian system in 2004, it went into orbit around the planet and began taking photos and collecting data. The Huygens lander separated and made its own trip to the surface of the moon Titan (see page 28). Scientists used data from Cassini to reveal seven previously unknown moons and discover new details about the planet's atmosphere and rings, the plumes of the moon Enceladus, and the hydrocarbon lakes of Titan.

The last stage of the Cassini mission was called the "Grand Finale." With fuel on board the spacecraft running out, NASA intentionally plunged Cassini into Saturn after a series of daring dives between the planet and its rings. Through these dives, Cassini collected data to refine measurements of Saturn's gravity, magnetic field, internal structure, and rotation rate. With these final measurements taken, Cassini plunged into Saturn's atmosphere, burning up and disintegrating.

During Cassini's "Grand Finale," the spacecraft made a series of daring dives between Saturn's rings, as depicted in this illustration.

NASA-Caltech

SEPTEMBER 16

BESSICA RAICHE MAKES FIRST ACCREDITED SOLO FLIGHT BY A WOMAN IN THE U.S.

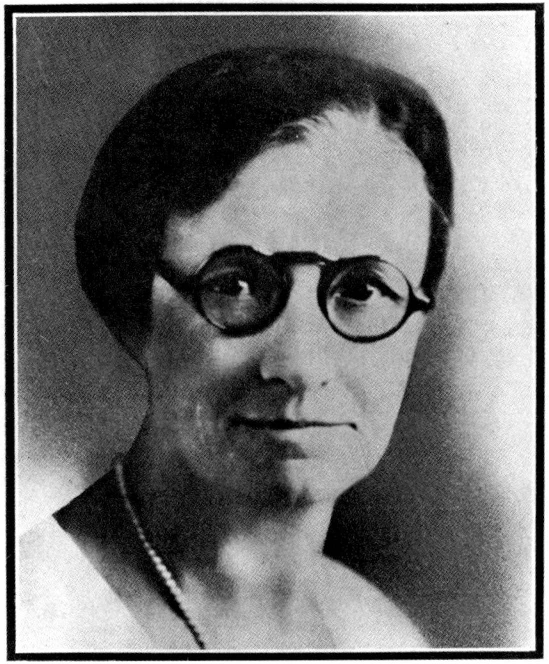

Bessica Raiche became a doctor after an early career in aviation.

Smithsonian's National Air and Space Museum (NASM 2007-5475)

While studying music in Paris, Bessica Raiche became intrigued by the flying of Baroness Raymonde de Laroche (see page 84). Raiche was considered a "new" woman of the twentieth century because she drove an automobile, wore bloomers, and participated in typically "masculine" activities like swimming and shooting. Adding to this list, Raiche and her husband, Francois, built their first airplane—a Wright type—in their living room in Mineola, New York.

On September 16, 1910, Raiche took off in a frail bamboo and silk aircraft on what has been recognized as the first accredited solo flight by a woman in the United States. Though Raiche never earned a pilot's license, the Aeronautical Society honored her with a dinner and a gold medal as America's first woman aviator.

Following Raiche's historic flight, the couple expanded their home-based silk, wire, and bamboo aircraft company into the French-American Aeroplane Company. Eventually, Raiche gave up flying for health reasons and embarked on another demanding career in medicine. She became one of America's first woman specialists in obstetrics and gynecology.

SPACE SHUTTLE *ENTERPRISE* ROLLS OUT

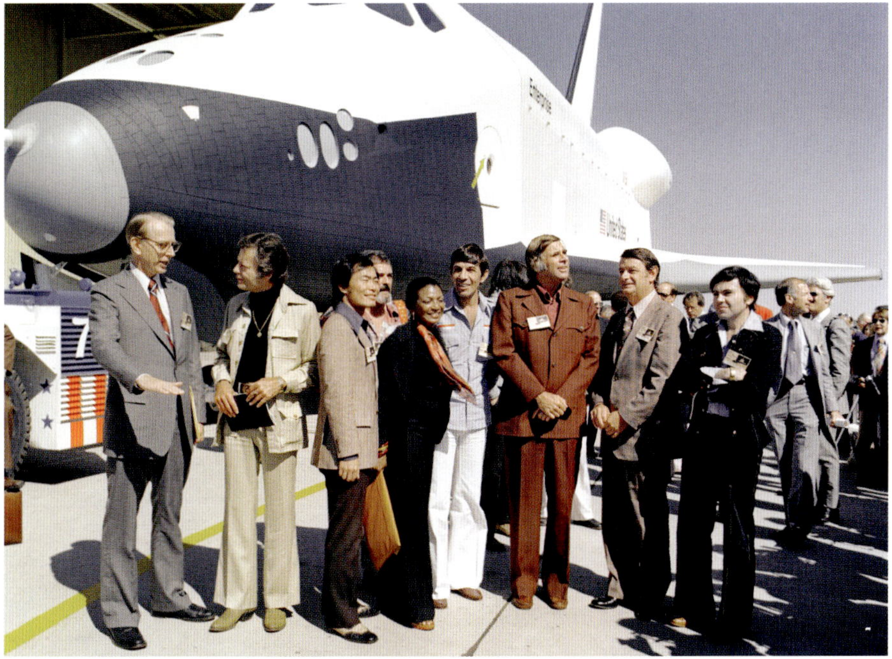

Cast and crew of *Star Trek* attended *Enterprise*'s roll-out ceremony, including George Takei, Nichelle Nichols, Leonard Nimoy, and Gene Roddenberry.

NASA

NASA's prototype orbiter, Space Shuttle *Enterprise*, rolled out of the Rockwell International manufacturing plant on September 17, 1976. The public debut of Orbital Vehicle-101 (OV-101) was planned for that day, Constitution Day, because OV-101 was initially going to be called *Constitution*. However, *Star Trek* fans conducted a write-in campaign to NASA and President Gerald Ford asking that the orbiter bear the name *Enterprise* instead, after the starship from the award-winning television show.

In early September, Ford instructed NASA to use the name *Enterprise* instead, noting that it was both a name from American naval history and one familiar to millions of fans: "To explore the frontiers of space, there is no better ship than the space shuttle, and no better name for that ship than the *Enterprise*." In honor of the vehicle's new name, members of the *Star Trek* cast attended the roll-out ceremony.

"*Star Trek* fans can be very persuasive."

—*STAR TREK* ACTOR LEONARD NIMOY

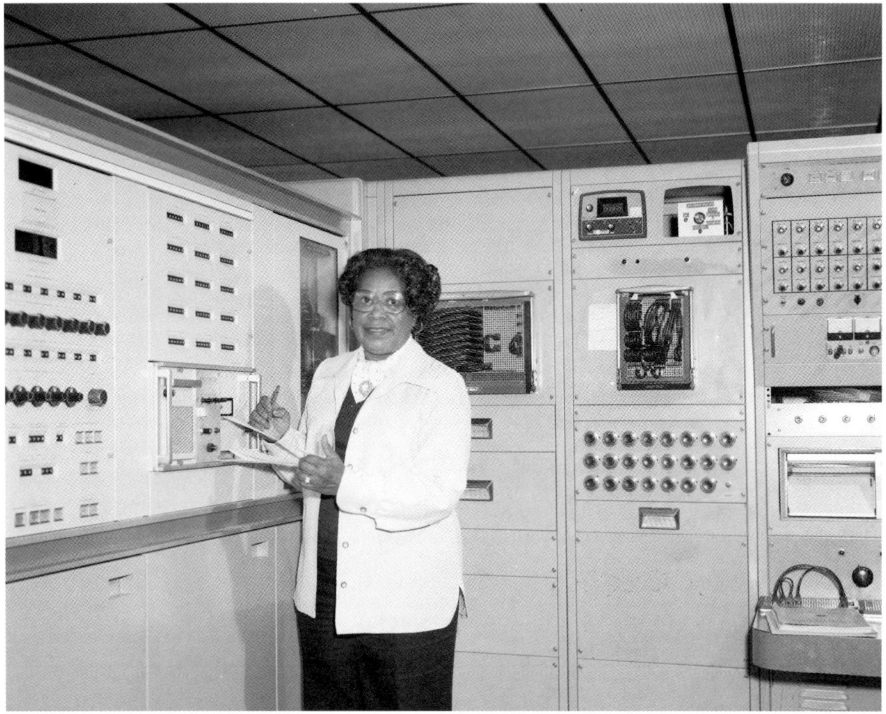

Mary Jackson, one of the women featured in *Hidden Figures*, was the first Black engineer at NASA.

NASA

In 2016, author Margot Lee Shetterly published *Hidden Figures: The American Dream and the Untold Story of the Black Women Who Helped Win the Space Race*, a book that finally shined a light on the contributions of the Black women who worked as mathematicians and engineers at NASA in the early days of the U.S. space program. The book and its subsequent film introduced millions of people to these women.

On September 18, 2024, these pioneering women, known collectively as NASA's "Hidden Figures," were honored with the Congressional Gold Medal at a ceremony held in Emancipation Hall at the U.S. Capitol Building in Washington, D.C. In addition to one medal awarded in "recognition of all the women who served as computers, mathematicians, and engineers at the National Advisory Committee for Aeronautics and NASA between the 1930s and the 1970s," individual Gold Medals were awarded specifically to aeronautical engineer Christine Darden, engineer Mary Jackson, mathematician Katherine Johnson (see page 253), and mathematician Dorothy Vaughan.

SEPTEMBER 19

THREE ANIMALS BECOME FIRST LIVING CREATURES TO FLY IN AN AIRCRAFT

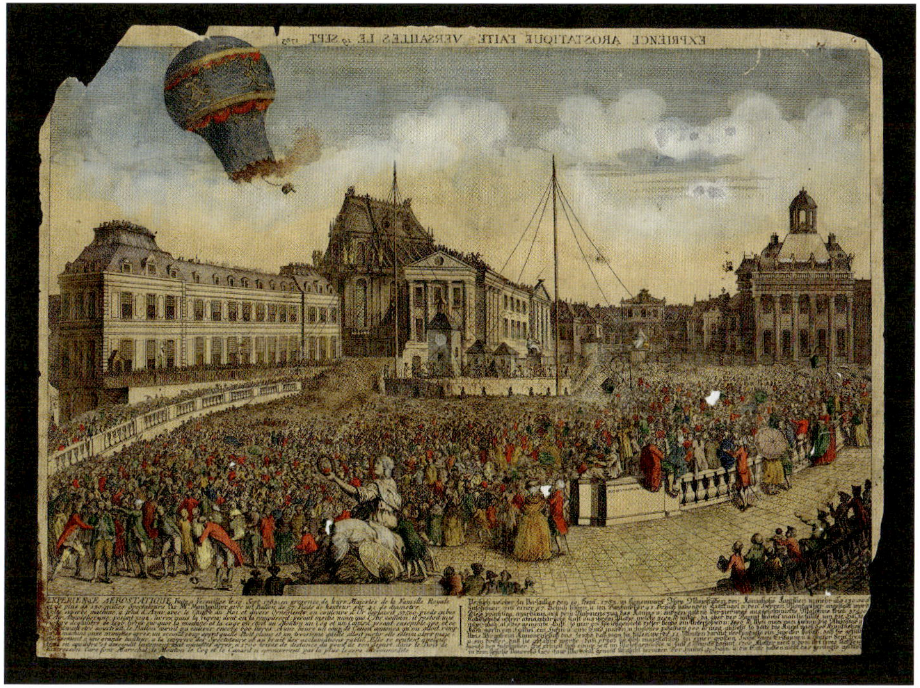

A color engraving in the National Air and Space Museum collection depicts the first balloon launch with living creatures on board.

Smithsonian's National Air and Space Museum

Before there were airplanes, there were hot-air and gas balloons. And before humans flew in these aircraft, animals went aloft first as test subjects. On September 19, 1783, lighter-than-air flight pioneers Jacques-Étienne and Joseph-Michel Montgolfier launched a duck, a rooster, and a sheep in a hot-air balloon they had built. Though the Montgolfier brothers had inflated and flown their balloons before, they had never put living creatures aboard. In fact, at the time it wasn't even known if humans could survive such a flight into the air.

The Montgolfiers were very deliberate in their selection of animals for the experimental flight. A sheep was chosen because they thought its physiology was most similar to humans; the duck because it could fly at high altitudes; and the rooster for comparison to the duck. The successful flight took place at the Palace of Versailles in full view of King Louis XVI and Marie Antoinette, with the balloon reaching 1,500 feet altitude and traveling some two miles before landing. Discovering that the animals had survived, the Montgolfiers scheduled the first human balloon flight a few months later (see page 342).

SEPTEMBER 20

U.S. LAUNCHES JUPITER-C ROCKET FOR THE FIRST TIME

ROCKETS AND MISSILES

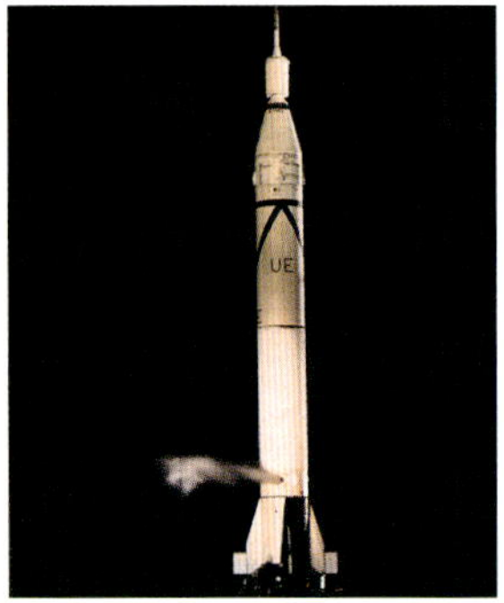

The Jupiter-C sounding rocket was launched for the first time from Cape Canaveral Launch Pad 5 on September 20, 1956. Jupiter-C was used to test components of the Jupiter intermediate-range ballistic missile (IRBM). The rocket used a U.S. Army Redstone ballistic missile as its first stage, with eleven solid rocket motors on its second stage, and three solid rocket motors on its third stage. When a modified Jupiter-C, redesignated Juno 1, was used to launch Explorer 1 the following year (see page 44), a fourth stage was added.

After the first successful Jupiter-C launches, a modified version of the rocket was used to launch the Explorer 1 satellite.

NASA

SEPTEMBER 21

CHINOOK HELICOPTER MAKES INAUGURAL FLIGHT

VERTICAL FLIGHT

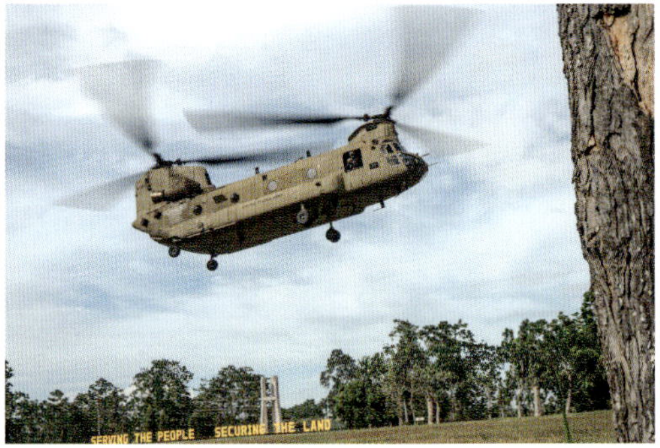

On September 21, 1961, the Boeing Vertol YHC-1B helicopter took flight for the first time. Built at the company's helicopter plant in Morton, Pennsylvania, and flown by test pilot Len LaVassar, the aircraft was the prototype for the tandem rotor Boeing CH-47 Chinook. The helicopter flown that day was Boeing Vertol's second prototype, the first having been damaged in ground testing. A highly capable aircraft, the Chinook has remained in production and frontline service with the U.S. Army continuously since 1962.

Over 1,200 CH-47 Chinook helicopters have been built since 1961.

U.S. Army

F-14 TOMCAT ENTERS SERVICE WITH THE U.S. NAVY

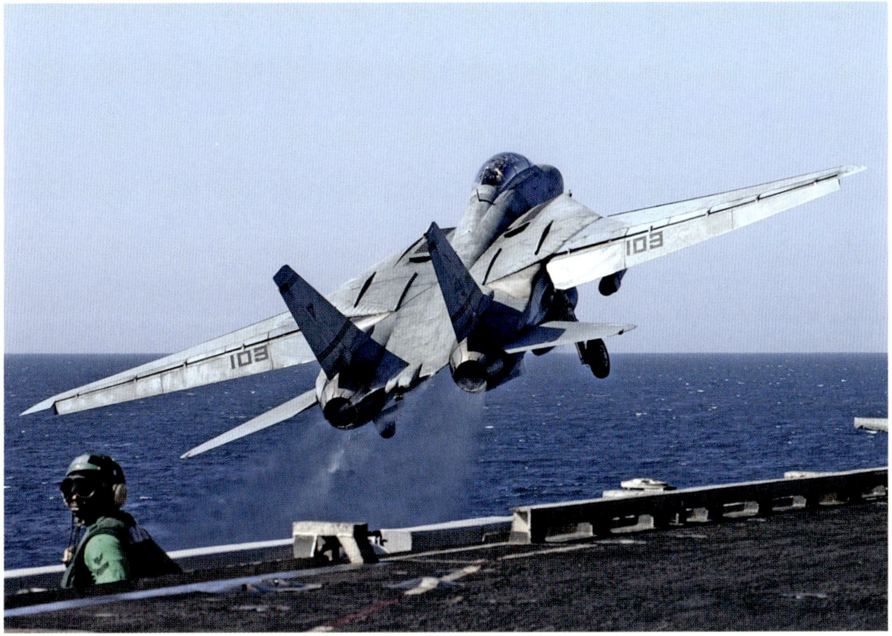

The F-14 Tomcat was a carrier-capable fighter aircraft.

U.S. Navy

Do you feel the need for speed? Although many people know the Grumman F-14 Tomcat as the aircraft Maverick and Goose flew in the 1986 film *Top Gun*, to aviation historians it was a powerful fighter used by the U.S. Navy from September 22, 1974, to September 22, 2006. The first two operational F-14A squadrons deployed in 1974, and almost all Navy fighter squadrons exchanged their F-4 Phantoms for F-14s between 1975 and 1983.

The versatile Tomcat had an official top speed of Mach 2.34 and was capable of carrying an assortment of both air-to-air missiles and air-to-ground ordnance. The Tomcat made its combat flying debut in air patrols during the 1975 evacuation of Saigon and was a vital asset in many subsequent military operations, including a notable incident in which a pair of F-14As shot down two armed Libyan MiG-23 fighters (see page 19).

SEPTEMBER 23

JORGE CHÁVEZ BECOMES FIRST PERSON TO CROSS THE ALPS BY AIRPLANE

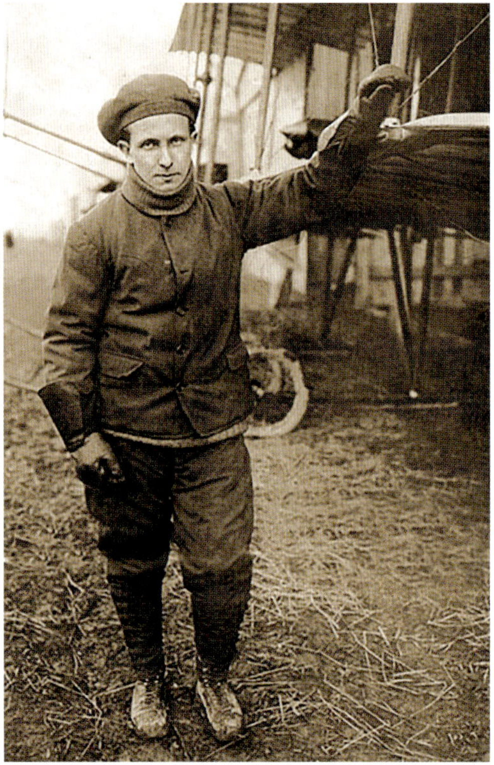

Jorge Chávez was just twenty-three years old when he flew over the Alps.

U.S. Air Force

Peruvian aviator Jorge Chávez was the first person to fly across the Alps. Having earned his pilot's license only months before, the twenty-three-year-old embarked on the flight in an attempt to secure a prize of 100,000 lira from the Aero Club of Italy.

On September 23, 1910, Chávez began his journey from the Swiss side of the Alps and flew through the Simplon Pass in a Blériot XI biplane. Though the fifty-one-minute flight was successful, Chávez crashed while landing in Domodossola, Italy, and died from his injuries four days later. According to an account by his friend Juan Bielovucic, Chávez's last words were "Higher. Always higher." In honor of his accomplishment, the international airport in Lima, Peru—Aeropuerto Internacional Jorge Chávez—is named for the aviator, who was born in France to Peruvian parents.

"Whatever happens, I shall be found on the other side of the Alps."

—JORGE CHÁVEZ

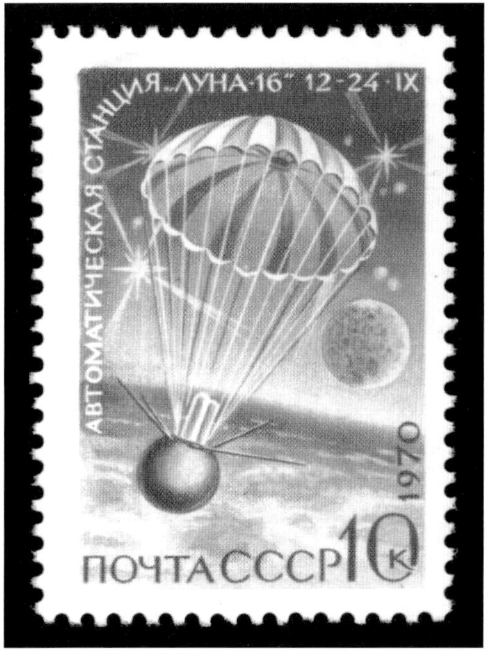

A Soviet stamp commemorates the return of Luna 16's lunar samples to Earth.

USSR Post

On September 24, 1970, a reentry capsule from the Soviet Union's Luna 16 mission returned to Earth with soil samples from the Moon onboard. Although Apollo astronauts returned lunar materials twice the year before, this was the first robotic return from the Moon's surface.

After Luna 16 landed in the Sea of Fertility, it drilled into the surface to collect its sample. On September 21, Luna 16's upper stage took off from the Moon's surface and began its flight back to Earth. The return capsule reentered the planet's atmosphere and parachuted into Kazakhstan, where it was recovered. The lunar soil was analyzed by scientists in the Soviet Union and the countries with whom the Soviets shared samples, including France, the German Democratic Republic, and Iraq.

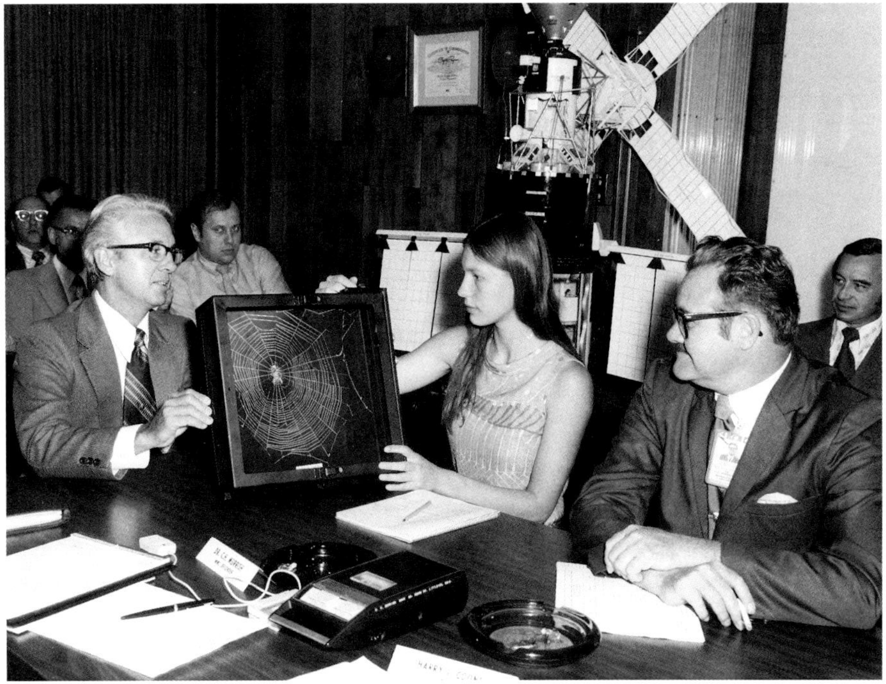

Skylab 3's spider experiment was proposed by a high school student from Massachusetts.

NASA

NASA's second crewed mission to the Skylab space station officially came to an end on September 25, 1973, when the Skylab 3 command module splashed down in the Pacific Ocean. The crew of Skylab 3—Alan Bean, Jack Lousma, and Owen Garriott—spent fifty-nine days on board the space station, completing 1,081 hours of experiments and three spacewalks totaling thirteen hours, forty-three minutes.

During the Skylab missions, scientists and students interested in the growth, development, behavior, and adaptation of organisms in weightlessness were able to propose a variety of biological experiments for flight in the orbital research laboratory. A web formation experiment suggested by a Massachusetts high school student named Judy Miles was carried out during Skylab 3. It involved two common cross spiders named Anita and Arabella. Both spiders were able to spin webs in microgravity that looked very similar to those spun on Earth, but the silk spun in space was thinner.

SEPTEMBER 26

KC-10 EXTENDER IS OFFICIALLY RETIRED BY THE U.S. MILITARY

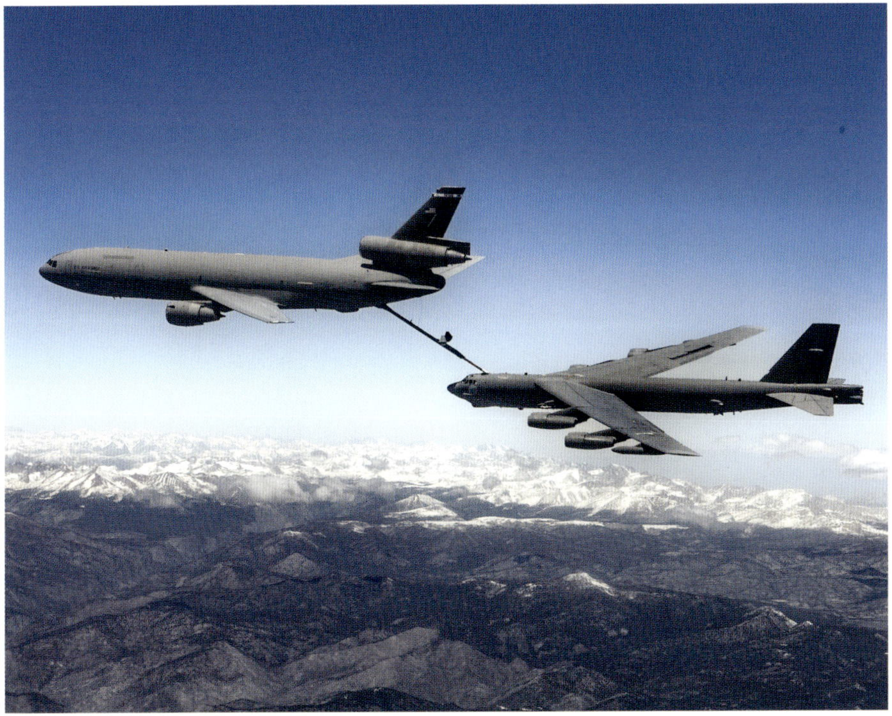

For four decades the U.S. Air Force used the McDonnell Douglas KC-10 to aerially refuel aircraft like the Boeing B-52.

U.S. Air Force

On September 26, 2024, the U.S. Air Force retired the final McDonnell Douglas KC-10 Extender—an aircraft nicknamed *Excalibur*—in a ceremony at Travis Air Force Base. Aerial refueling tankers like the KC-10 support U.S. military aircraft around the globe, allowing them to refuel without having to land. The KC-10 was a military variation of the DC-10 airliner. Instead of passenger seats, the tankers carried a system that allowed them to transfer up to 1,100 gallons of fuel per minute.

A distinguishing feature of the KC-10 was its ability to use both an aerial boom and a hose-and-drogue system depending on the type of aircraft it was refueling. The Extender could also double as a cargo transport and was capable of carrying 170,000 pounds of cargo. This incredible versatility made the KC-10 the U.S. military's go-to airborne refueling station for more than forty years. The mantle has now been taken up by the Boeing KC-46 Pegasus, whose technological advances make it a good fit for the modern battlefield.

VEREIN FÜR RAUMSCHIFFAHRT OPENS RAKETENFLUGPLATZ

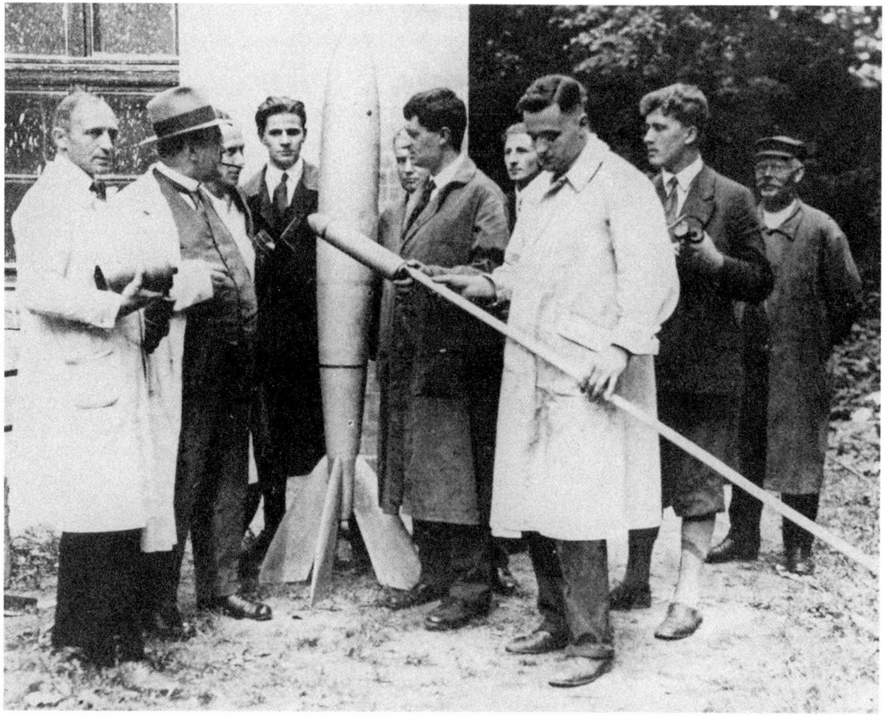

Notable members of Verein für Raumschiffahrt included Hermann Oberth and Wernher von Braun.

Smithsonian's National Air and Space Museum (NASM A-5347-H)

The Verein für Raumschiffahrt (VfR), or the Society for Space Travel, was a German rocket association founded by church administrator Johannes Winkler, rocket experimenter Max Valier, and science writer Willy Ley. Among its membership was Hermann Oberth, whose 1923 book *The Rocket into Interplanetary Space* aided in the rise in popularity of space travel and rocketry in Germany. In it, he predicted that liquid-fuel rockets could launch people into space.

Beginning in 1930, several VfR members conducted liquid-fuel rocket experiments. The society founded Raketenflugplatz (Rocketport) Berlin on September 27, 1930, a rocket launchpad where the society conducted many of its tests. However, Raketenflugplatz was put out of commission in 1934 as the military took over all research into rocketry in Nazi Germany. Several VfR members, notably Wernher von Braun, went on to be important in German Army rocket development, leading to the V-2 missile used during World War II (see page 293).

DOUGLAS WORLD CRUISERS COMPLETE FIRST ROUND-THE-WORLD FLIGHT

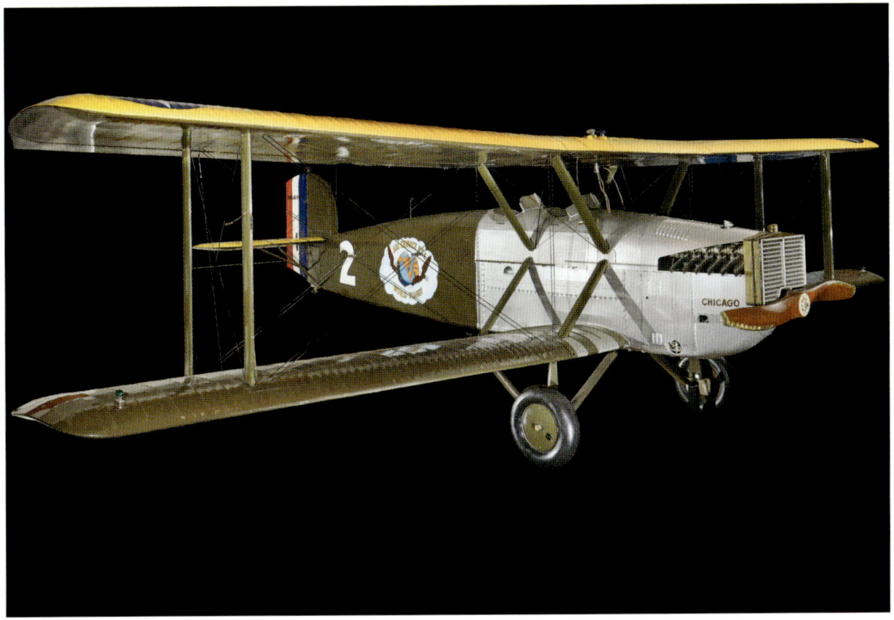

The Douglas World Cruiser *Chicago* is in the collection of the National Air and Space Museum.

Smithsonian's National Air and Space Museum

In the early 1920s, the U.S. Army Air Service commissioned the Douglas Aircraft Company to build four specially designed planes for the first flight around the world. Christened *Seattle*, *Chicago*, *Boston*, and *New Orleans,* the "World Cruisers" departed Seattle, Washington, in April 1924 carrying eight pilots and mechanics.

Over 175 days and 27,553 miles, these crews encountered climatic extremes from arctic to tropical as they flew over oceans and continents. Bad weather, repairs, forced landings, and other mishaps continually threatened the success of their journey. When *New Orleans, Chicago,* and a replacement aircraft called *Boston II* landed back in Seattle on September 28, 1924—both *Seattle* and the original *Boston* were unable to complete their journeys—it was the first time anyone had successfully circumnavigated the globe by air. A monumental accomplishment of airmanship and logistics, these historic flights marked an important step toward worldwide air transport.

SEPTEMBER 29

SPACESHIPONE MAKES FIRST OF TWO FLIGHTS TO WIN THE ANSARI X PRIZE

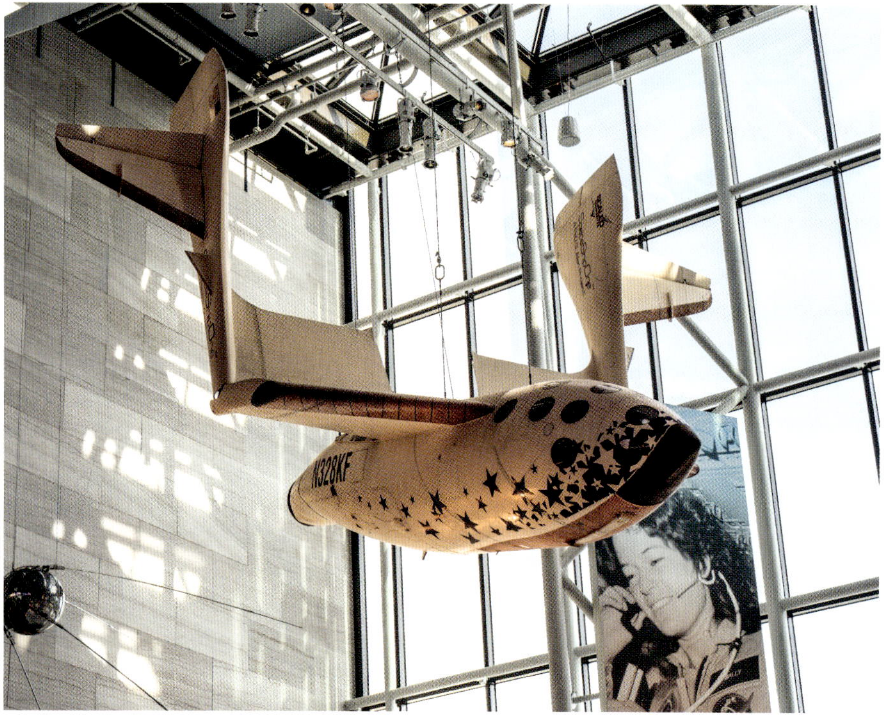

SpaceShipOne is displayed at the National Air and Space Museum nose down with its feather system at 65 degrees—just how it looked as it reentered Earth's atmosphere.

Smithsonian's National Air and Space Museum

In May 1996, the X Prize Foundation set up a prize for the first privately developed space vehicle capable of carrying three people into suborbital space and repeating the feat within two weeks. SpaceShipOne, funded by Microsoft cofounder Paul Allen and designed and built by Elbert "Burt" Rutan and his company Scaled Composites, won the $10 million prize.

On September 29, 2004, Michael Melvill, who piloted SpaceShipOne's first test flight in June, was assigned to fly the vehicle a second time and attempt at the first of the two flights of the challenge. Launched from its White Knight mothership, the rocket-powered SpaceShipOne and its pilot ascended just beyond the atmosphere, arced through space (but not into orbit), then glided safely back to Earth. Less than a week later, SpaceShipOne repeated the flight, with Brian Binnie at the controls, and the team officially won the X Prize. The success of SpaceShipOne inspired the creation of Virgin Galactic, a company founded to add private tourist flights to the existing world of commercial space.

HERBERT EKINS BEGINS FLIGHT AROUND THE WORLD ON REGULARLY SCHEDULED AIRLINES

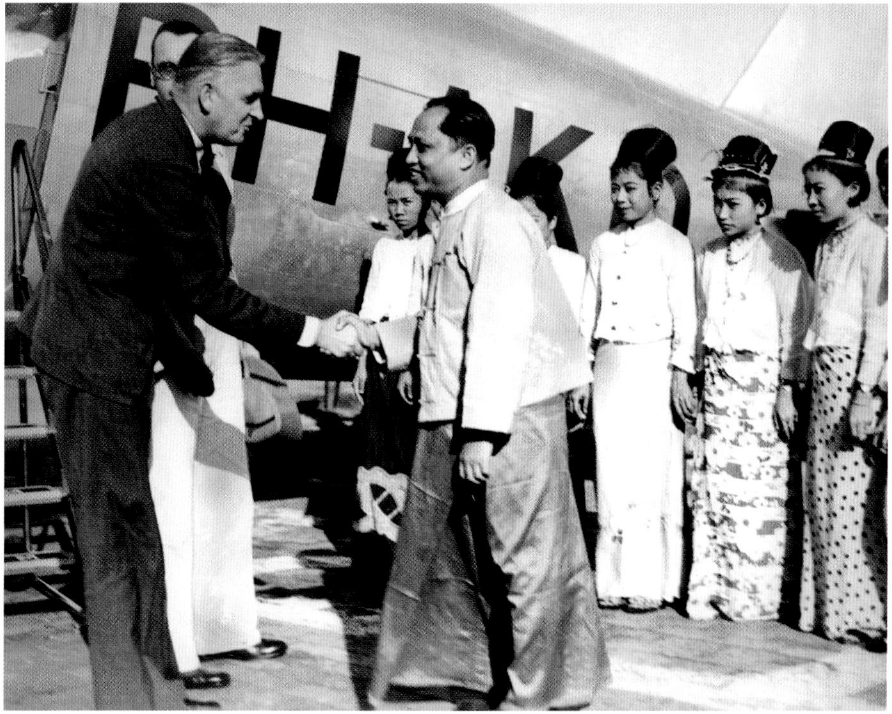

During his around-the-world flight, Herbert Ekins greeted officials in Rangoon, Burma.

Library of Congress

There are plenty of stories of round-the-world flights, but none quite like those of journalists Herbert Ekins, Leo Kieran, and Dorothy Kilgallen. As writers for three different newspapers—the *New York World-Telegram*, *The New York Times*, and *New York Evening Journal*—the trio was challenged to travel around the world using only "established means" of transportation open to the public. Officially timed by the National Aeronautic Association, the race opened on September 30, 1936, when the travelers left their New York offices.

The competitors began their journeys together, flying from New Jersey to Frankfurt, Germany, on the airship *Hindenburg*. Once in Europe, Ekins split off from Kieran and Kilgallen, determined to win the race alone by primarily sticking to air transportation. Though his rivals cried foul upon learning that Ekins had talked his way onboard a Pan Am trial flight as crew, the *World-Telegram* reporter completed the journey in eighteen days and was declared the winner. Kieran and Kilgallen each completed their travels in just over twenty-four days—respectable times to be sure, but who remembers second and third place?

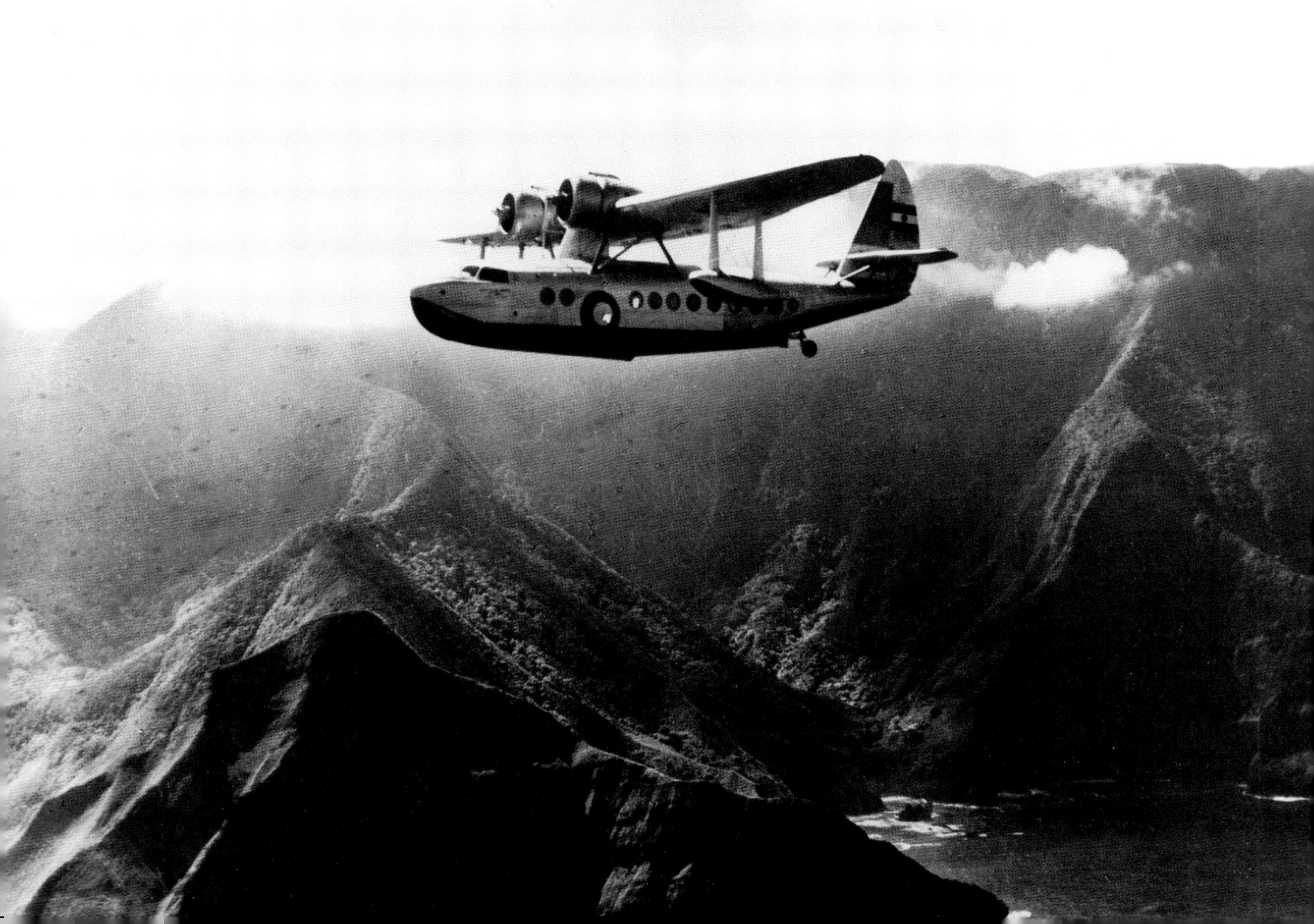

OCTOBER

BELL XP-59A AIRACOMET FLIES FOR THE FIRST TIME

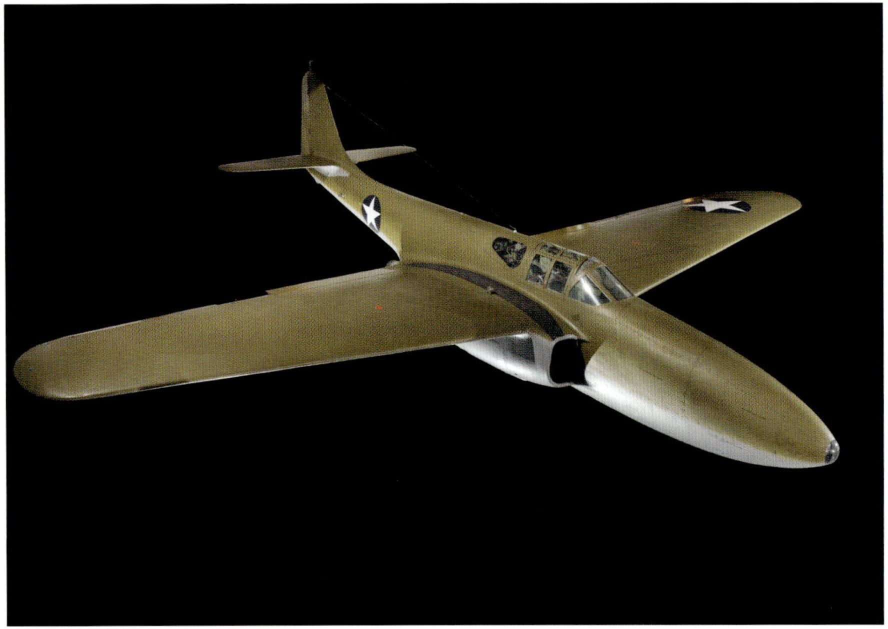

In 1944, an Army Air Forces engineer made the decision to save the prototype of the XP-59 for a museum. Today, America's first jet aircraft is on view at the National Air and Space Museum in Washington, D.C.

Smithsonian's National Air and Space Museum

The Bell XP-59A Airacomet was the first American jet aircraft. Development of the aircraft gave the U.S. military valuable experience with jet technology and helped pave the way for more advanced designs. Although the XP-59A flew for the first time on October 1, 1942, it did not see combat in World War II. The United States concentrated instead on mass-producing and fielding more conventional designs that could contribute quickly to the war effort.

To maintain secrecy during the Airacomet's first tests at Muroc Dry Lake in California, Bell mounted a dummy propeller on the jet aircraft's nose to disguise it as a conventional plane. Mechanics removed the propeller before flight and reinstalled it afterward. Although it was designed as a fighter, test flights revealed the Airacomet was underpowered and slower than conventional piston-engine fighters. After the conclusion of its test program, the XP-59A was used to train fighter pilots on how to fly a jet.

OCTOBER 2

CROWN PRINCE FRIEDRICH WILHELM OF GERMANY FLIES WITH ORVILLE WRIGHT

EARLY FLIGHT

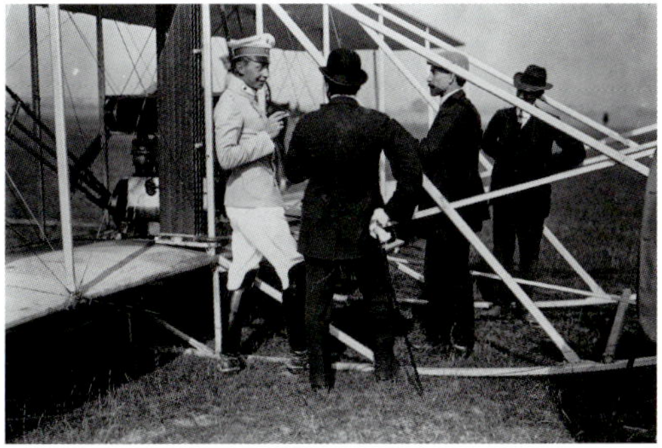

While in Europe, the Wrights were courted by the world's most influential people, including Crown Prince Friedrich Wilhelm (left).

Smithsonian's National Air and Space Museum

In 1908 and 1909, the Wright brothers traveled around France, Italy, and Germany to demonstrate their airplane. The pair made more than two hundred flights in Europe, dazzling crowds and turning critics and doubters into admirers. Practically overnight, the Wrights became world celebrities—wherever they appeared, aristocrats and heads of state came to see them fly. On October 2, 1909, Crown Prince Friedrich Wilhelm of Germany took a flight with Orville, becoming the first member of a royal family to fly in an aircraft.

OCTOBER 3

V-2 ROCKET LAUNCHES FOR THE FIRST TIME

ROCKETS AND MISSILES

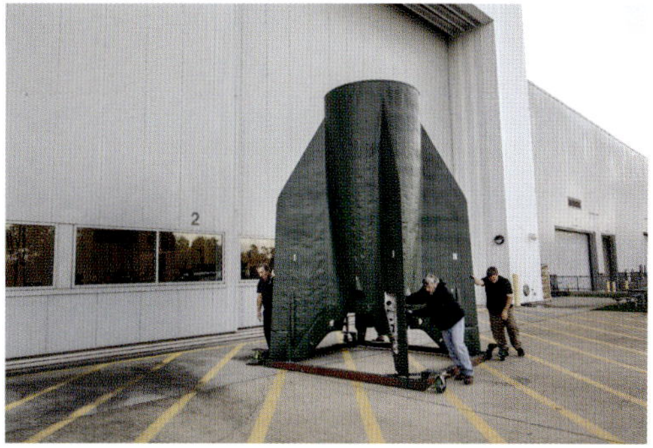

The National Air and Space Museum's V-2 was restored to its original color scheme before going back on display.

Smithsonian's National Air and Space Museum

The V-2 rocket, developed and used by Nazi Germany during World War II, was the world's first large-scale liquid-propellant rocket, the first long-range ballistic missile, and the predecessor of today's large rockets and launch vehicles. On October 3, 1942, a rocket engineering team led by Wernher von Braun successfully launched the V-2 for the first time from the Peenemünde testing grounds. The first operational launches of the V-2 took place two years later in September 1944. Nazi Germany launched over three thousand V-2s at Allied targets during the last year of the war.

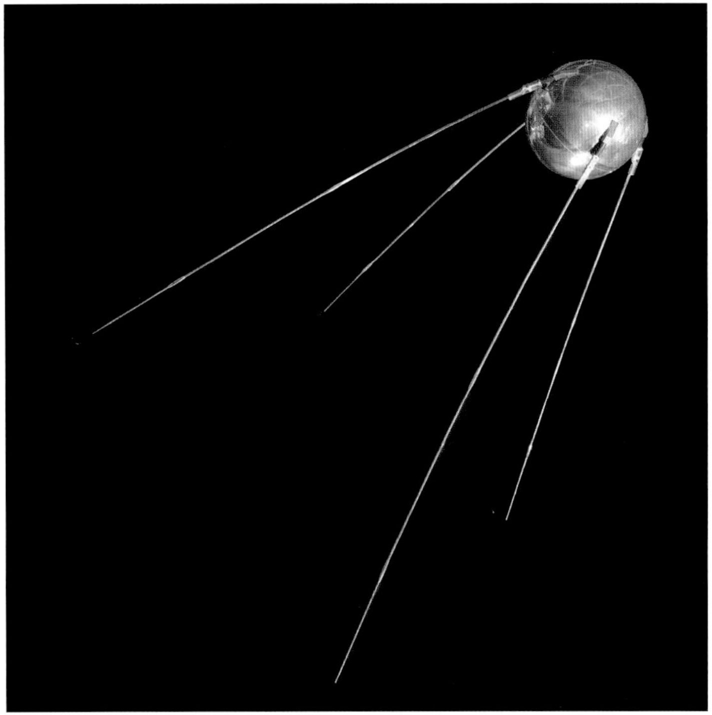

A replica of the Sputnik satellite is on display at the National Air and Space Museum.

Smithsonian's National Air and Space Museum

When the Soviet Union put Sputnik into Earth orbit on October 4, 1957, it became the world's first artificial satellite and kick-started the Space Race between the Soviet Union and the United States. In the West, the enduring memory of Sputnik is auditory: The "beep, beep, beep" signal its transmitters broadcast was a message to the world that the USSR was first in space. The beeping signals were broadcast at frequencies that amateur radio operators could hear around the globe.

Sputnik itself was not the satellite that the USSR intended to launch. Originally, it planned to launch a sophisticated scientific satellite as part of the country's contribution to international scientific cooperation for the International Geophysical Year. Those plans fell by the wayside when the USSR realized that they could not finish the advanced satellite in time to beat the Americans into space. Instead, they launched Sputnik, which carried only three batteries, two transmitters, a fan, and a barometric switch. All the satellite could do was proclaim its presence in orbit, but that was enough to claim its place in history.

NICOLE MANN BECOMES FIRST NATIVE AMERICAN WOMAN IN SPACE

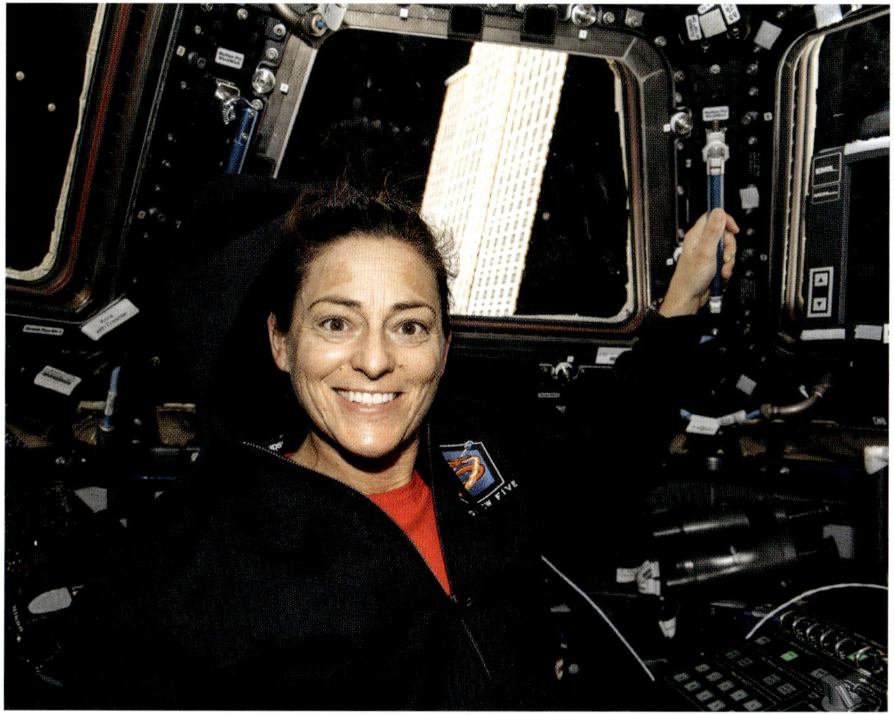

Nicole Mann spent five months on the International Space Station from 2022 to 2023.

NASA

NASA astronaut Nicole Aunapu Mann was the first Native American woman to travel to space. She was commander of the SpaceX Crew-5 mission, launching to the International Space Station (ISS) on October 5, 2022. While living on the ISS, she conducted scientific experiments and tested new technologies. Mann, a member of the Wailacki of the Round Valley Indian Tribes in Northern California, brought a dream catcher with her to space. This childhood gift from her mother was a reminder of her family and community. During the mission, she also became the first Native American woman to perform a spacewalk.

Before becoming an astronaut, Mann earned a bachelor's degree in mechanical engineering from the United States Naval Academy and was commissioned as a second lieutenant in the U.S. Marine Corps upon graduation. She earned a master's degree in mechanical engineering from Stanford University and then completed basic and flight training in Quantico, Virginia, and Pensacola, Florida, respectively. She later graduated from Naval Test Pilot School. As a fighter pilot and test pilot in the Marines, Mann flew the F/A-18 Hornet and Super Hornet aircraft.

ULYSSES SOLAR SPACECRAFT IS DEPLOYED DURING STS-41

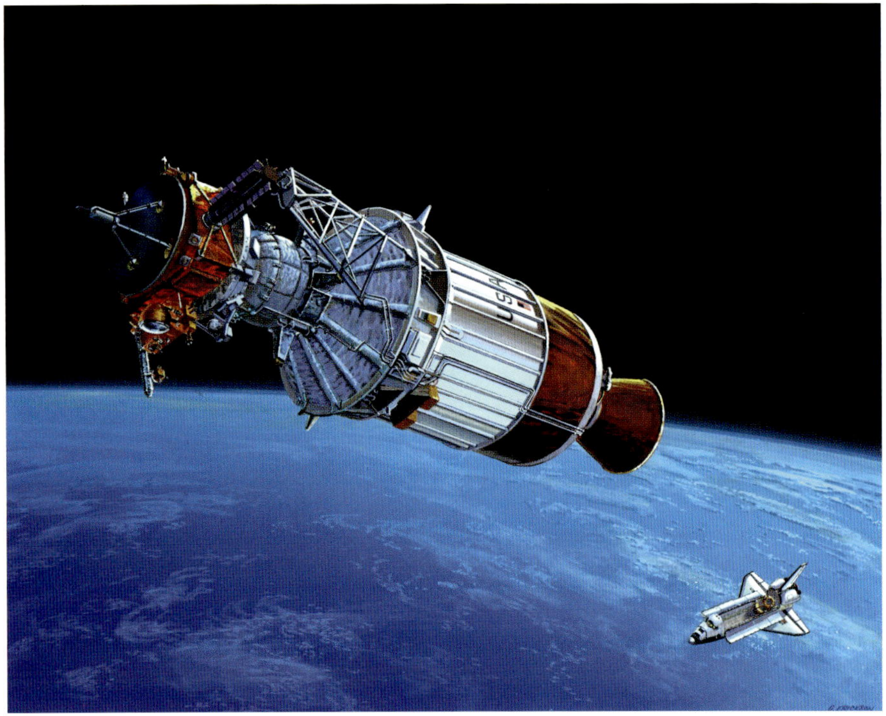

An artist rendering illustrates Ulysses soon after it was deployed by Space Shuttle *Discovery*.

NASA

The Ulysses spacecraft was deployed from Space Shuttle *Discovery* on October 6, 1990, as a joint mission between NASA and the European Space Agency. The solar spacecraft was initially called Odysseus, because its studies of the Sun required a lengthy and indirect journey echoing that of the hero in Homer's epic poem *The Odyssey*. Ultimately, it was renamed Ulysses, the Latin version of Odysseus, and a nod to the character from the *Inferno* section of Dante's narrative poem *The Divine Comedy*.

After the crew of STS-41 deployed Ulysses, the spacecraft used a gravity assist from Jupiter to achieve its ideal orbit around the Sun. The heliocentric orbits Ulysses achieved over the course of the mission allowed it to fly over both of the Sun's poles. Scientists analyzing data from the mission discovered that solar wind was weakening over time and that the magnetic fields at the solar poles were weaker than initially believed.

PETER MACK DEPARTS ON GOODWILL FLIGHT IN *FRIENDSHIP FLAME*

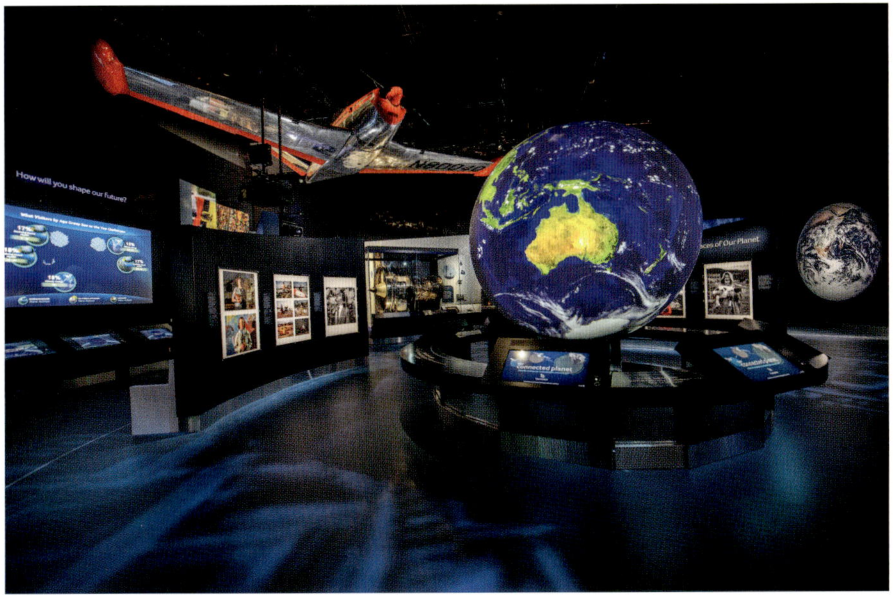

Peter Mack's *Friendship Flame* is on display at the National Air and Space Museum.

Smithsonian's National Air and Space Museum

On October 7, 1951, U.S. congressman and pilot Peter Mack Jr. departed on a solo goodwill flight in a Beechcraft 35 Bonanza. Refurbished and renamed *Friendship Flame*, the Bonanza that Mack flew was the same aircraft used by Bill Odom for his record-setting flights in 1949 (see page 26).

The idea for Mack's tour was born when a friend complained that world leaders only ever spoke with each other and not everyday people. During his self-directed and funded global dialogue and peace mission, Mack visited forty-five cities in thirty-one countries. He made a point of meeting with both dignitaries and ordinary citizens everywhere he visited. Mack flew over mountains, deserts, and water in all kinds of weather on his 113-day and 33,000-mile journey, becoming the first person to fly solo across the Pacific Ocean.

"Goodwill is everyone's job, and I am thoroughly convinced that it is the responsibility of every American citizen."

—PETER MACK JR.

OCTOBER 8

INTER-ISLAND AIRWAYS MAKES FIRST AIRMAIL FLIGHT IN HAWAII

COMMERCIAL AVIATION

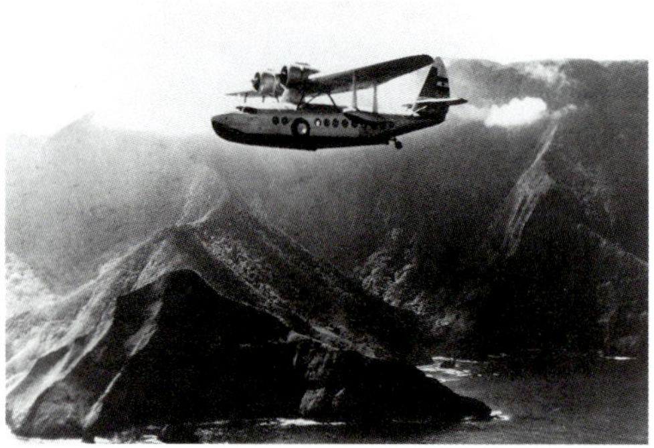

Inter-Island Airways, now known as Hawaiian Airlines, is one of the world's oldest air carriers.

Smithsonian's National Air and Space Museum (NASM 9A10176)

In the early days of flight, U.S. airlines helped carry the mail, a practice that provided them and commercial aviation with a strong economic foundation. This was the case for Inter-Island Airways, the first airline to offer travel among Hawaii's six largest islands. On October 8, 1934, Inter-Island conducted the first U.S. airmail flight in Hawaii. A few weeks prior, the airline had received a contract from the Post Office Department to transport mail between the islands of Oahu, Maui, Kauai, and Hawaii.

OCTOBER 9

HINDENBURG EMBARKS ON "MILLIONAIRES' FLIGHT"

COMMERCIAL AVIATION

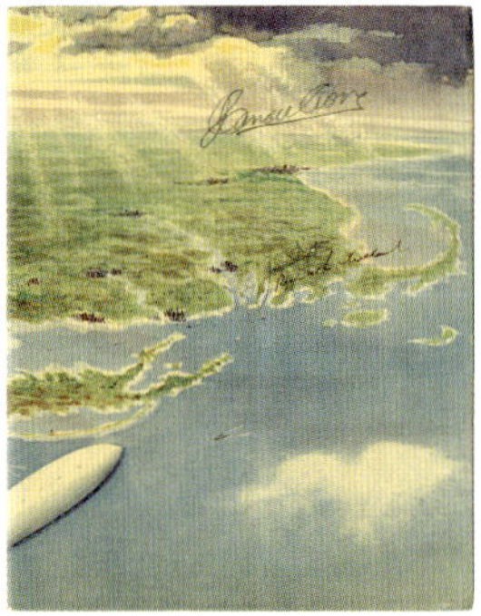

This souvenir program from the *Hindenburg*'s "Millionaires' Flight" belonged to flying ace Eddie Rickenbacker.

Smithsonian's National Air and Space Museum (NASM 9A19913)

On October 9, 1936, the German airship *Hindenburg* embarked on a voyage known as the "Millionaires' Flight." Airship builder Deutsche Zeppelin-Reederei and the Standard Oil Company invited a party of businessmen, politicians, and military officers aboard the *Hindenburg* for a 10-hour flight over the fall foliage of New England. Passengers included such notables as future vice president Nelson Rockefeller, Pan Am founder Juan Trippe, and World War I ace Eddie Rickenbacker. Also among the guests was U.S. Navy Cmdr. Garland Fulton, an advocate for lighter-than-air flight.

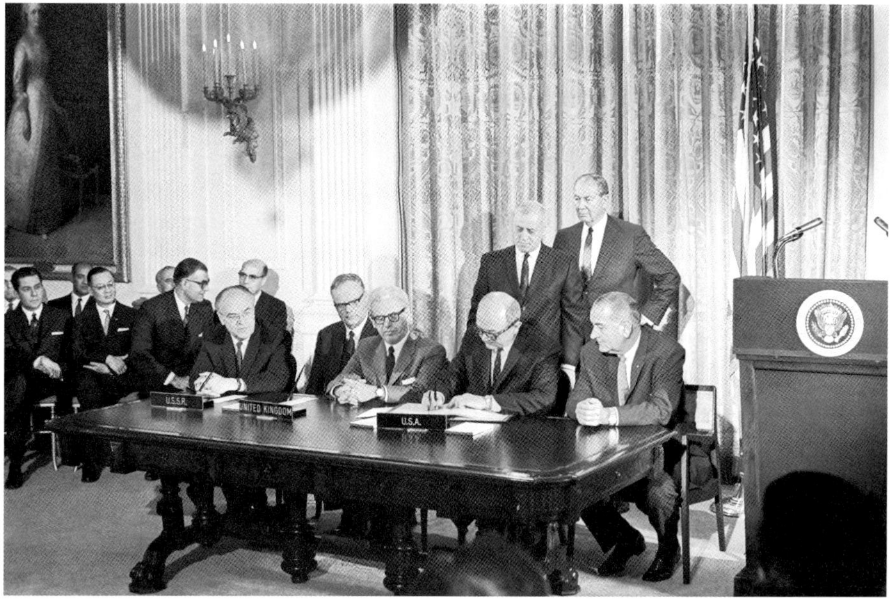

The Outer Space Treaty was signed at the White House by representatives from the United States, United Kingdom, and Soviet Union.

United Nations

In the late 1960s, space and rocket technology knowledge was constantly increasing, including the development of intercontinental ballistic missiles (ICBMs) that flew through space to reach targets far from their launch sites. It soon became clear that an international agreement on the use of space was needed. On October 10, 1967, the Outer Space Treaty officially went into effect. It opened for signature earlier that year and was initially signed by twenty-four countries. Today, nearly 140 countries have ratified or signed the treaty.

The succinctly named "Treaty on Principles Governing the Activities of States in the Exploration and Use of Outer Space, Including the Moon and Other Celestial Bodies" lays out the framework for international space law. Among its provisions are a prohibition on nuclear weapons in space and agreement that the Moon and other celestial bodies could only be used for peaceful purposes, that space is open to all countries, and that no country could own or claim sovereignty over a celestial body.

KATHRYN SULLIVAN BECOMES FIRST AMERICAN WOMAN TO SPACEWALK

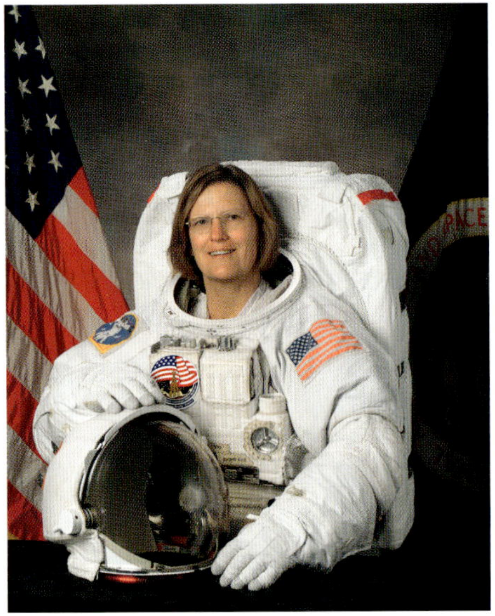

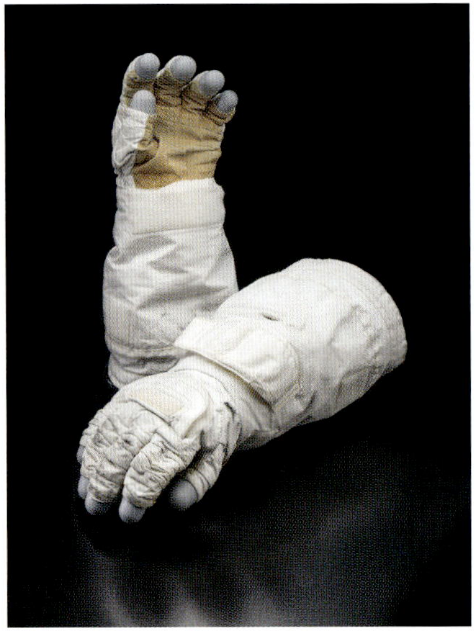

LEFT Kathy Sullivan flew on three Space Shuttle flights in the 1980s and 1990s.

NASA

RIGHT Sullivan wore these EVA gloves, now in the collection of the National Air and Space Museum, on her spacewalk in 1984.

Smithsonian's National Air and Space Museum

On October 11, 1984, Kathryn "Kathy" Sullivan stepped outside Space Shuttle *Challenger*, becoming the first American woman to conduct a spacewalk, or extravehicular activity (EVA). Sullivan and crewmate David Leestma ventured into the payload bay to conduct a trial fluid transfer to demonstrate that it was feasible to refuel satellites in orbit, a key task for satellite servicing. Sullivan was the first woman to wear the Space Shuttle-era spacesuit, the 225-pound Extravehicular Mobility Unit, to work in space. Designed by ILC Dover and Hamilton Sunstrand, the ready-to-wear suit was not custom made, but had interchangeable arms, legs, and torso units in different sizes.

After spending a total of 532 hours in space over three missions, Sullivan left NASA in 1993. An Earth scientist, geologist, and oceanographer by training and education, Sullivan became chief scientist and then administrator of the National Oceanic and Atmospheric Administration in 2014. In 2020, she became the first woman to dive to the bottom of Challenger Deep in the Mariana Trench, Earth's lowest point.

ILYUSHIN TSKB-57 PROTOTYPE TAKES FLIGHT FOR THE FIRST TIME

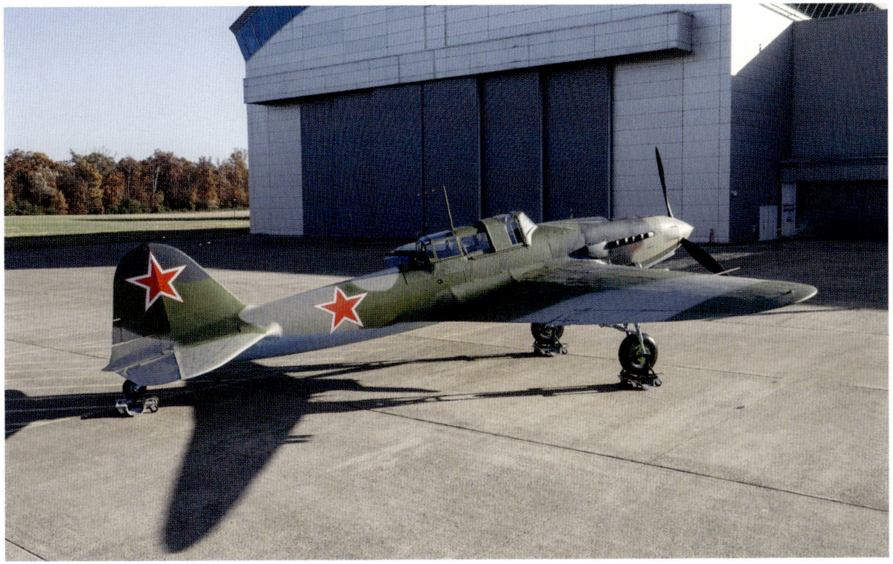

The Ilyushin Il-2 Shturmovik in the National Air and Space Museum collection was recovered from a lake in the 1990s and pieced together with parts from other Shturmoviks.

Smithsonian's National Air and Space Museum

During World War II, the Soviet Union manufactured between thirty-one thousand and thirty-six thousand Ilyushin Il-2 Shturmovik armored ground-attack airplanes, making it the second-most-produced aircraft ever. It was designed to meet the Soviet military's need for a low-flying, ground-attack airplane with armor-piercing guns and racks for bombs and rockets. The Il-2's adversaries had many nicknames for the rugged aircraft, including the "concrete plane," but designer Sergei Ilyushin referred to it as the "Flying Tank" when he approached Soviet leader Joseph Stalin with the concept in 1938.

Ilyushin's first Shturmovik design was for a two-seat aircraft, but it was redeveloped as a lighter single-seat plane dubbed the TsKB-57 when test flights revealed the engine could not support the original weight. This prototype Il-2 took flight for the first time on October 12, 1940, and deliveries to frontline units began the following year.

CHARLES MESSIER DISCOVERS WHIRLPOOL GALAXY

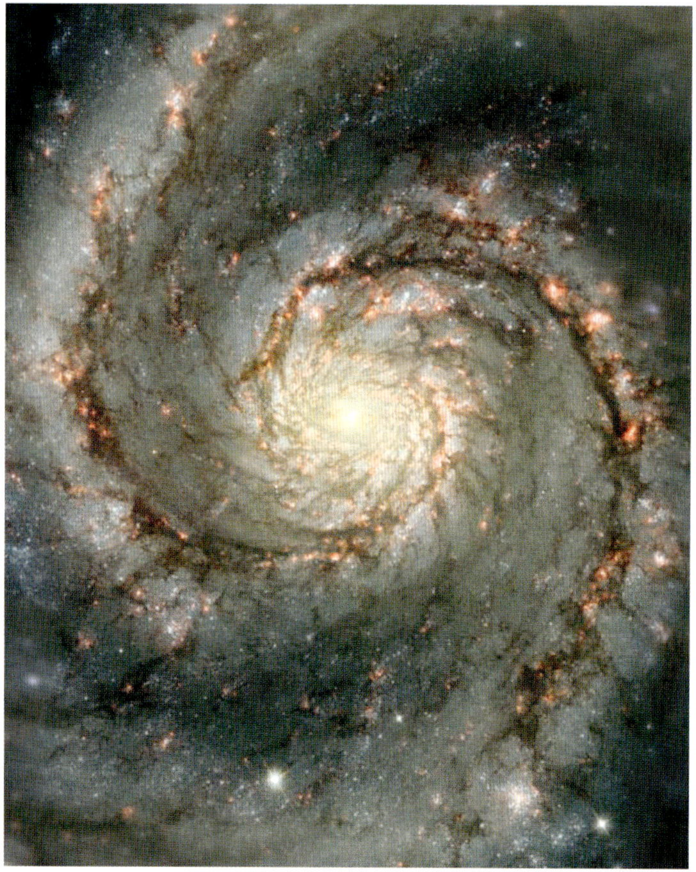

As a child in the late eighteenth century, astronomer Charles Messier was fascinated by the comets he observed at his rural French home. Eventually serving as chief astronomer of Paris's Marine Observatory, Messier spent his career searching for comets. He was so enthralled with them that King Louis XV even gave him the nickname "Comet Ferret."

Messier logged the non-cometary objects he discovered as "objects to avoid" for those on a comet hunt. Each of these "objects to avoid" that he discovered bore the name Messier and a number, so it tracks that the first was Messier 1 (M1)—known commonly as the Crab Nebula. On October 13, 1773, Messier discovered the Whirlpool Galaxy, which he logged as Messier 51 (M51), not realizing yet it was significantly larger than what Messier was looking for. Later, Edwin Hubble determined that M51 and objects like it were galaxies.

DID YOU KNOW? The Hubble Space Telescope has photographed at least 96 of the 110 objects in *Messier's Catalog of Nebulae and Star Clusters*.

The Hubble Space Telescope captured images of the Whirlpool Galaxy.

NASA, ESA, S. Beckwith (STScI), and the Hubble Heritage Team (STScI/AURA)

BELL X-1 *GLAMOROUS GLENNIS* BREAKS THE SOUND BARRIER

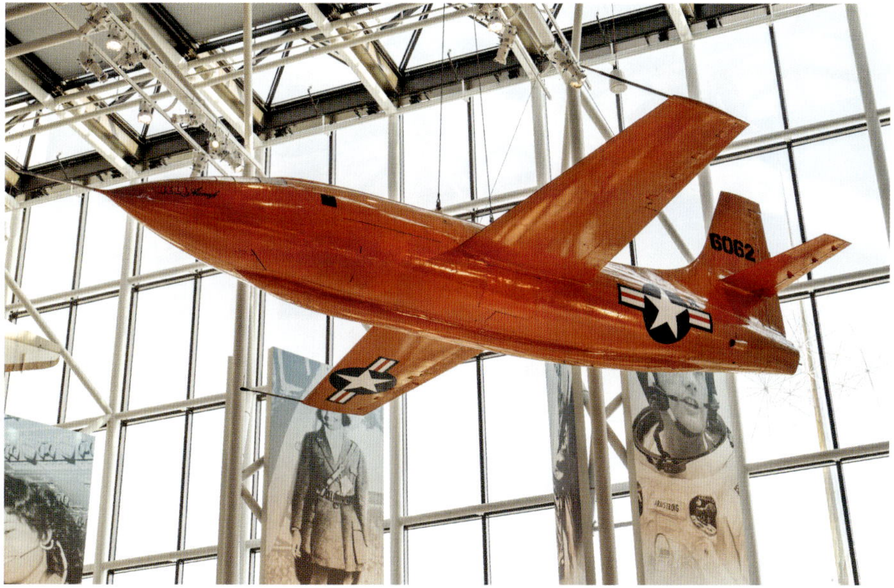

ABOVE The Bell X-1 *Glamorous Glennis* is on display at the National Air and Space Museum in Washington, D.C.

Smithsonian's National Air and Space Museum

NEXT PAGE Test flights of the Bell X-1 took place over the Mojave Desert near Muroc Dry Lake, California.

NASA

When the bullet-shaped Bell X-1 broke the sound barrier, it proved that an aircraft could travel faster than the speed of sound (Mach 1) and gathered transonic flight data that remains valuable today. Originally designated as the XS-1 for "experimental-supersonic," the X-1 was nicknamed *Glamorous Glennis* by test pilot Charles "Chuck" Yeager (see page 59) in tribute to his wife.

On October 14, 1947, the X-1 was air launched from a Boeing B-29, having been carried aloft in the bomb bay of the larger plane. When the aircraft reached altitude, Yeager climbed in the X-1 and famously closed the cockpit using a broom handle due to a pair of broken ribs he had suffered days before in a horseback riding accident. The bomber then released the X-1 and Yeager fired its engines once clear of the mothership. The unleashed X-1 accelerated rapidly, reaching 700 miles per hour (Mach 1.06) at an altitude of 43,000 feet over the Mojave Desert.

DID YOU KNOW? The X-1 was painted its iconic bright orange so that observers could better track the aircraft while it was in flight.

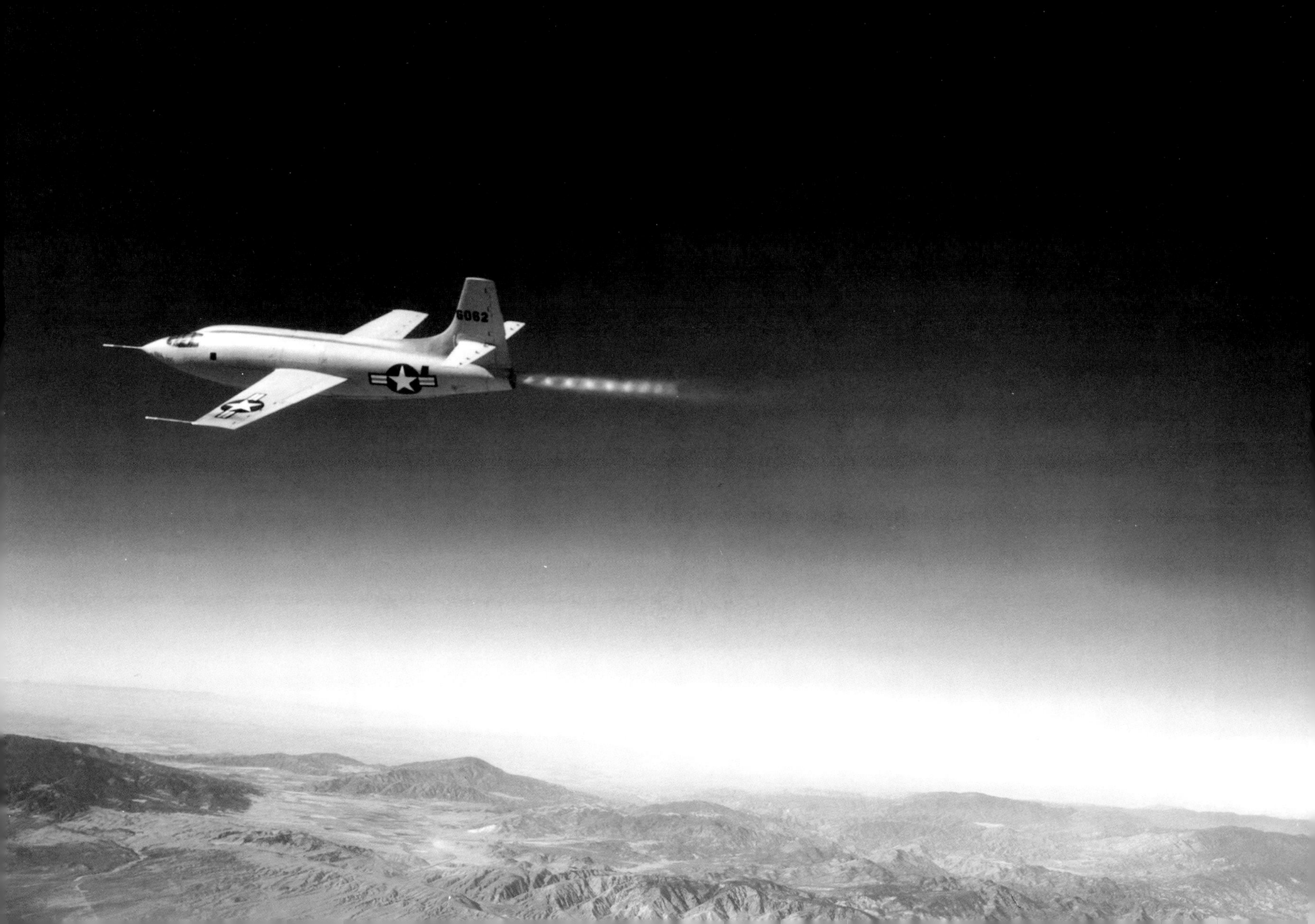
6062

KIDDO THE CAT STOWS AWAY ON AIRSHIP *AMERICA*

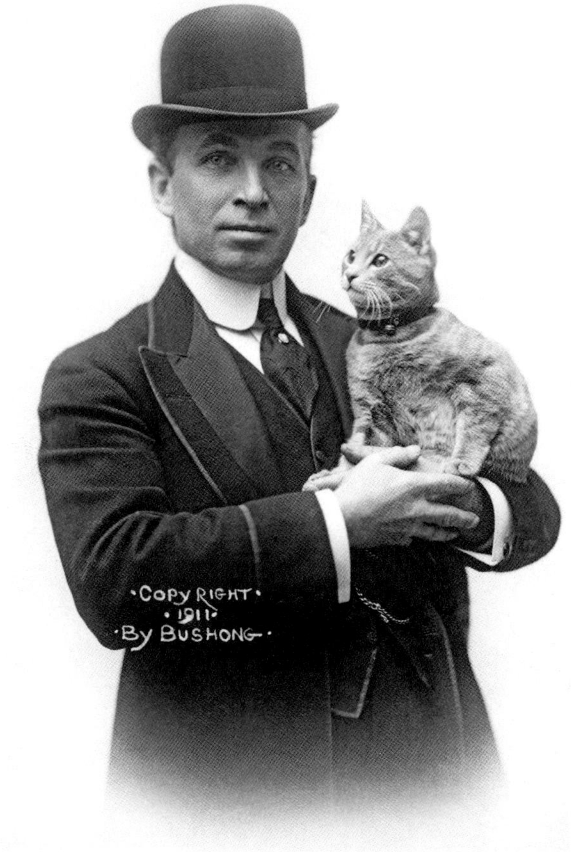

On October 15, 1910, a gray tabby named Kiddo became the first cat to attempt to cross the Atlantic Ocean by airship—and he wasn't very happy about it. Kiddo's journey began when he accidentally stowed away in the lifeboat of the airship *America*. After deciding he would rather not be on board, Kiddo began howling, which annoyed the airship's chief engineer, Melvin Vaniman. The feline soon earned the distinction of being the subject of the first wireless communication from an aircraft in flight when one of the crew radioed: "Roy, come and get this ***damn cat."

Kiddo and the airship crew only spent about seventy-one hours in flight before storms and engine failure required them to evacuate via the *America's* lifeboat to a Royal Mail steamship. The feline seemed to prefer the seafaring portion of the journey more than his time in the air and returned to dry land a hero. Kiddo even got to meet his adoring public during a brief residency in a gilded cage filled with pillows at a New York City department store.

Kiddo the cat, pictured here with engineer Melvin Vaniman, became famous upon returning from his unexpected airship journey.

Smithsonian's National Air and Space Museum (NASM 96-15130)

PRESIDENT KENNEDY IS BRIEFED ON AERIAL PHOTOS OF CUBA

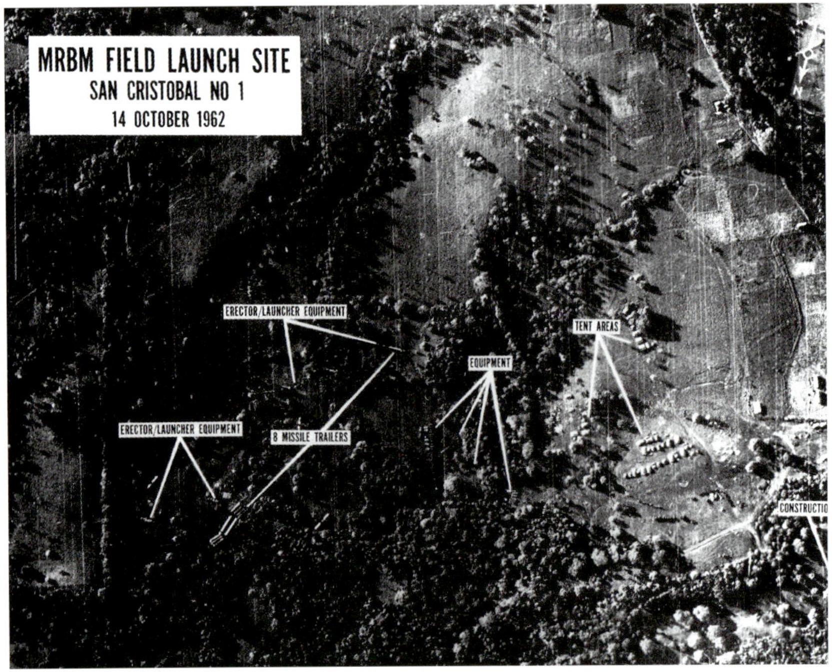

U-2 pilot Maj. Richard Heyser captured an image of medium-range ballistic missiles in Cuba in October 1962.

National Archives and Records Administration

In October 1962, a U.S. Air Force pilot flew over Cuba in a Lockheed U-2 and took 928 photographs of the island nation. The images revealed that the Soviet Union was building launch sites for nuclear missiles some one hundred miles off the coast of Florida and protecting those facilities with SA-2 surface-to-air missiles. This startling discovery kicked off the Cuban Missile Crisis when the military briefed President John F. Kennedy on October 16, 1962.

For the only time in U.S. history to date, the U.S. Air Force's Strategic Air Command was put at DEFCON 2—just one step below full-blown nuclear war. This status meant that at any given time there were fifty-six B-52 Stratofortress bombers in the air carrying nuclear weapons. The U.S. also implemented a naval blockade of Cuba, preventing Soviet ships from delivering any more weapons to the island. After thirteen tense days, negotiations ended the crisis, with the Soviet Union agreeing to remove its missiles from Cuba and the U.S agreeing to remove its own missiles from Turkey and never invade Cuba.

ASTRONAUT MAE JEMISON IS BORN

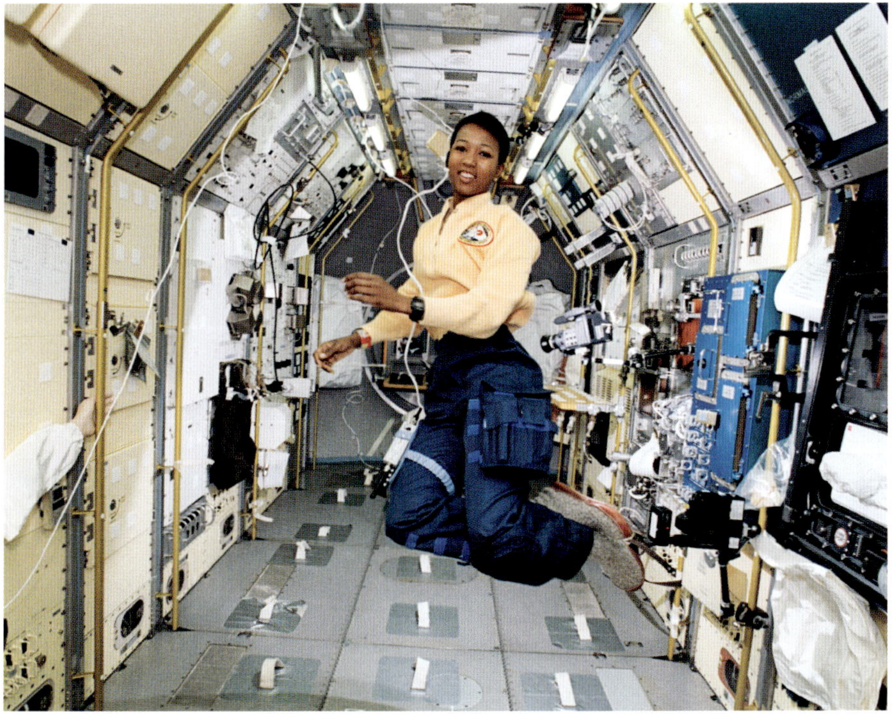

Mae Jemison became the first Black woman in space in 1992.

NASA

Dr. Mae Jemison was the first Black woman to go to space. She was born on October 17, 1956, in Decatur, Alabama, and grew up in Chicago, Illinois. After earning a bachelor's degree from Stanford University and a doctorate degree in medicine from Cornell University, Jemison began work as a physician. She later became a Peace Corps Medical Officer working in West Africa. She was selected as an astronaut candidate in June 1987 and began training for a mission.

In September 1992, Jemison launched on Space Shuttle *Endeavour*'s STS-47 mission, which carried a Spacelab module. On her eight-day spaceflight, Jemison served as a science mission specialist and carried out experiments on the effects of space motion sickness, frog fertilization in space, and bone loss during spaceflight. Jemison only went to space once, and after leaving NASA became a professor of environmental studies at Dartmouth College.

DID YOU KNOW? Mae Jemison was inspired to go to space by Lt. Uhura in *Star Trek* and later became the first real-life astronaut to appear on *Star Trek* (playing Lt. Palmer in a 1993 episode of *Star Trek: The Next Generation*).

OCTOBER 18

GALILEO SPACECRAFT IS DEPLOYED ON STS-34 MISSION

SPACE SCIENCE

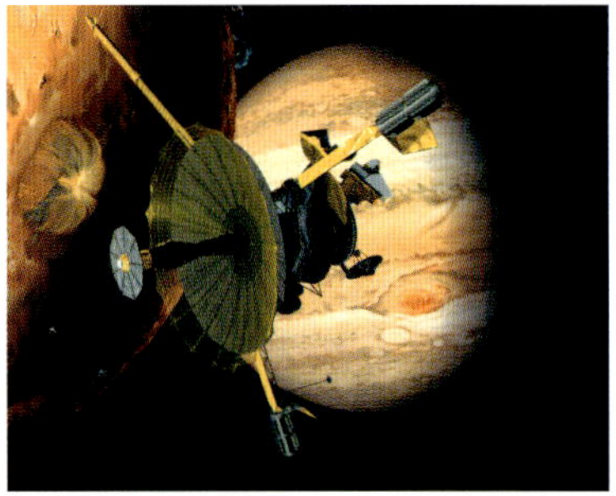

Galileo flew by Jupiter's moon Io during its mission, as depicted in an artist rendering.

NASA

Galileo Galilei made the first detailed observations of Jupiter in the early 1600s, so it's fitting that NASA's first mission to orbit Jupiter was named after the Italian astronomer and physicist. Space Shuttle *Atlantis* deployed the Galileo spacecraft on October 18, 1989. As the spacecraft approached the Jovian system in July 1995, Galileo released its descent probe, which collected data on Jupiter's atmosphere. It arrived at Jupiter that December and began studying the gas giant. It also made flybys of Jupiter's moons Ganymede, Callisto, Europa, and Io. The mission revealed that Ganymede is the only moon in the solar system with a magnetic field and provided evidence that Europa has a subsurface ocean.

OCTOBER 19

ALBERTO SANTOS-DUMONT FLIES AROUND THE EIFFEL TOWER IN A DIRIGIBLE

LIGHTER-THAN-AIR FLIGHT

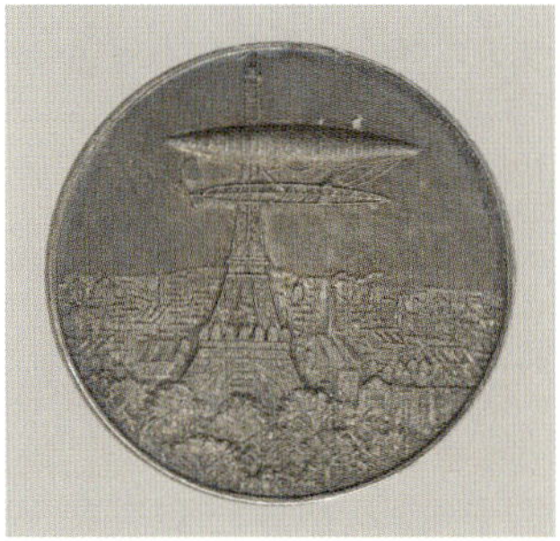

The National Air and Space Museum has a small silver commemorative medal of Santos-Dumont's Eiffel Tower flight in its collection.

Smithsonian's National Air and Space Museum

At the turn of the twentieth century, Brazilian aviation pioneer Alberto Santos-Dumont moved to France to study engineering. Fascinated by flight, he made headlines piloting a series of small, powered airships around Paris, becoming an early aviation celebrity. On October 19, 1901, Santos-Dumont won a prize of 100,000 francs for flying his airship No. 6 from a Paris suburb to the Eiffel Tower and back in roughly half an hour. Five years later, Santos-Dumont turned his attention to airplanes and made Europe's first public airplane flight in his famous 14-bis.

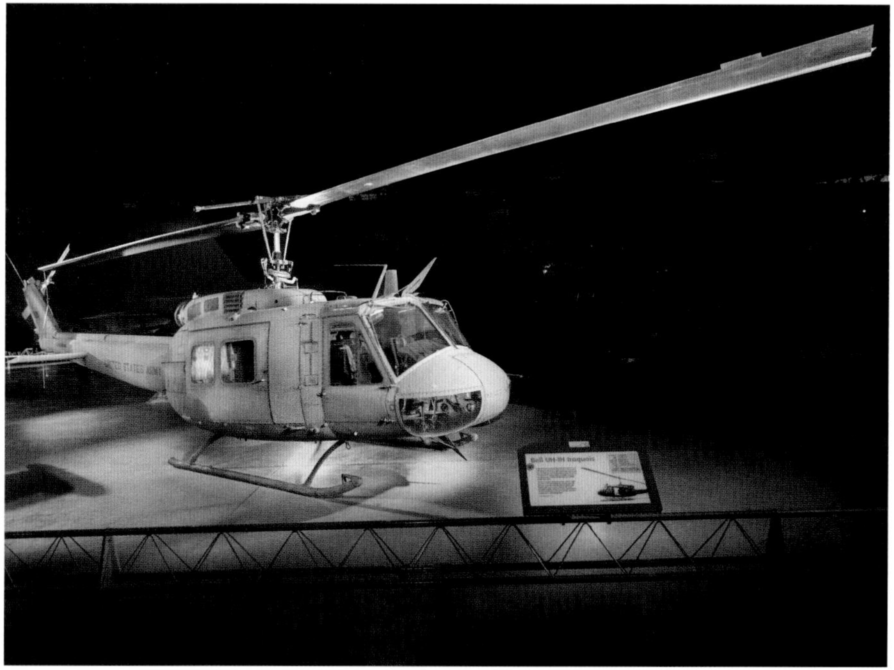

The Bell UH-1 Iroquois was designed as a replacement for the U.S. Army's H-13 medevac helicopter of Korean War fame. Commonly known as the "Huey," the UH-1 flew for the first time on October 20, 1956. By the end of the twentieth century, Bell had produced more Hueys than nearly any other American military aircraft. The versatile Huey was superbly suited for air mobility and medical evacuation missions but could also be modified for attack and other roles.

All branches of the U.S. military operated UH-1s during the Vietnam War, and the helicopter became an indelible symbol of that conflict. The distinctive "whomp-whomp" sound of the rotor blades is ingrained in the memory of most Vietnam veterans, nearly all of whom flew on a Huey at some point. For Americans watching the evening news back home, the Huey was a common sight in televised coverage of the battlefront.

The Huey in the National Air and Space Museum collection was given the name *Smokey III* by its crew because it operated as a "smoke ship," laying down smoke screens for air assault operations.

Smithsonian's National Air and Space Museum

EDDIE RICKENBACKER IS LOST AT SEA FOR TWENTY-FOUR DAYS

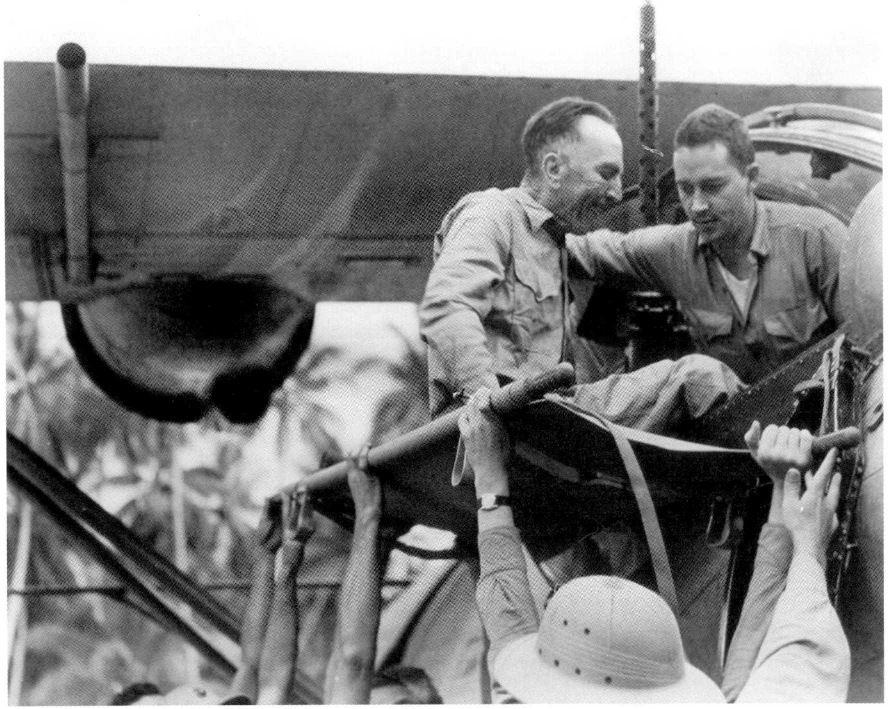

Eddie Rickenbacker and six other survivors of his crash were rescued by Navy pilots.

National Archives and Records Administration

On October 21, 1942, famed pilot Eddie Rickenbacker (see page 329) boarded a converted Boeing B-17 in Hawaii to deliver a secret message from President Franklin D. Roosevelt to General Douglas MacArthur in the South Pacific. Due to faulty navigation equipment, however, the transport plane became lost and was forced to crash-land in the waves below. After realizing that the water and food they gathered had not made it into the lifeboats, Rickenbacker and the other seven men on board spent more than three excruciating weeks at sea surviving on four oranges. Several times throughout the ordeal, the men saw aircraft flying miles away, but none spotted the survivors in the ocean.

On day twenty-four, an OS2U-3 Kingfisher seaplane finally found Rickenbacker and two of the survivors on their raft. The B-17 pilot, Capt. William Cherry, had split off from the group and been picked up the day before, allowing him to direct rescuers to Rickenbacker's raft. Three more survivors were eventually located on an uninhabited island nearby, and one member of the crew died at sea.

APOLLO 7 SPLASHES DOWN IN THE ATLANTIC OCEAN

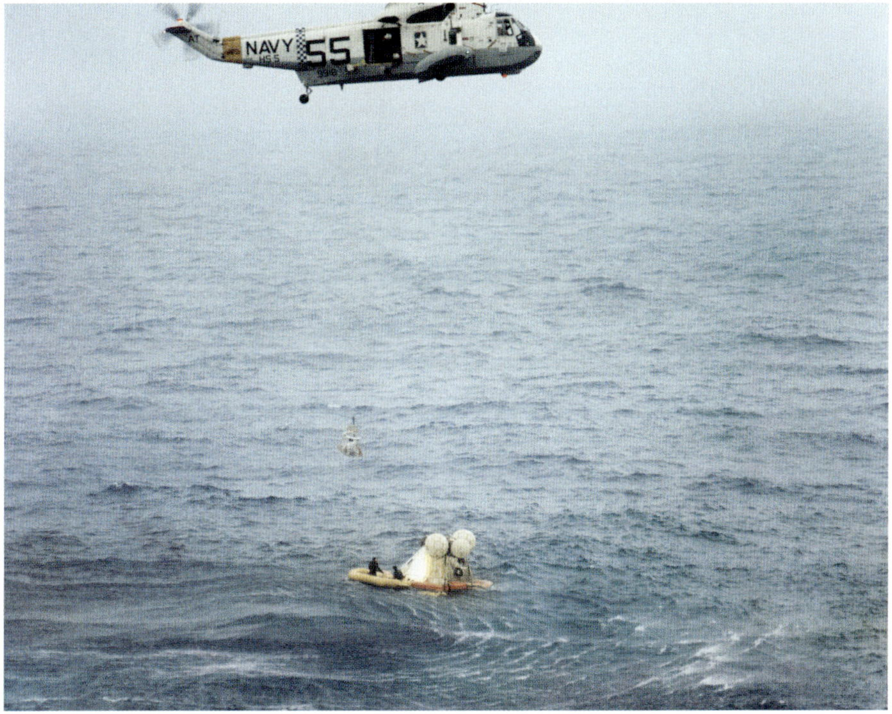

The Apollo 7 command module splashed down in the Atlantic Ocean on October 22, 1968, marking the successful completion of the first crewed Apollo mission. Apollo 7 launched earlier that month on a Saturn IB rocket, making it the only crewed Apollo mission to use the Saturn IB. The mission was the first test of the command and service module with a crew.

Astronauts Walter "Wally" Schirra, Donn Eisele, and Walter Cunningham orbited the Earth 163 times and spent ten days and twenty hours in space. The crew of Apollo 7 even won a special Emmy Award for being the first live television broadcast from space. They gave several video press conferences from Earth orbit using a small black-and-white camera that had three detachable lenses: a 10mm lens, a wide-angle lens, and an extra-wide-angle lens. This test of the Apollo spacecraft was a success. The only difficulty during the mission was that all three astronauts developed severe head colds.

After splashdown, the Apollo 7 crew were recovered by a helicopter from the USS *Essex*.

NASA

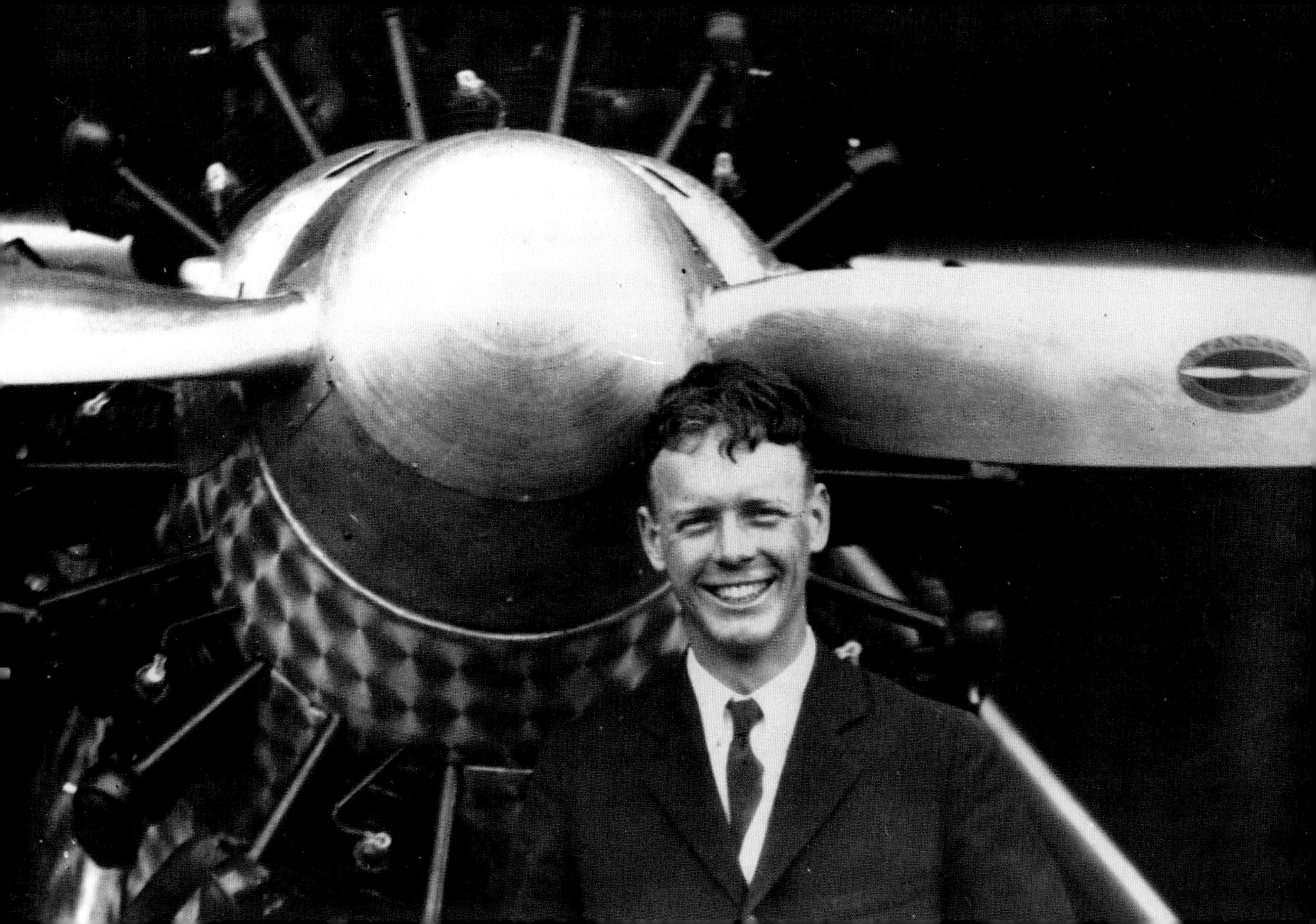

CHARLES LINDBERGH COMPLETES GOODWILL TOUR OF ALL FORTY-EIGHT STATES

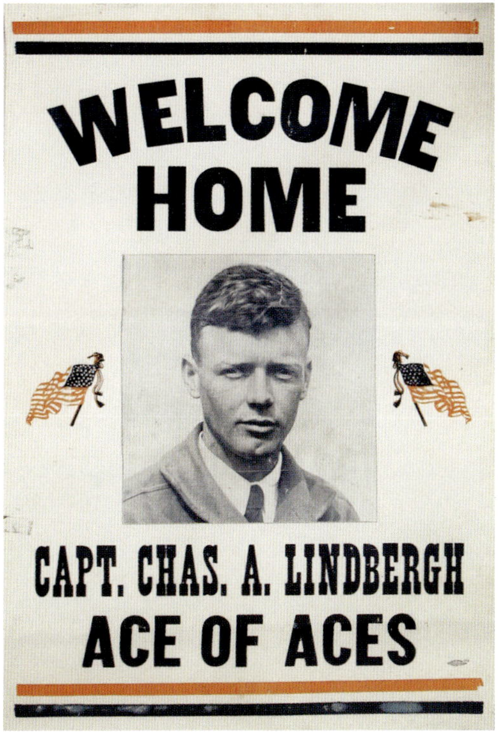

After Charles Lindbergh completed his historic transatlantic flight in 1927 (see page 155), he embarked on a ninety-five-day Goodwill Tour across the United States to connect with Americans and share information about aviation. Beginning at Mitchel Field, Long Island, Lindbergh flew the *Spirit of St. Louis* to eighty-two cities in all forty-eight states (Alaska and Hawaii were still territories). At each stop, the young pilot gave a short speech about aviation's potential as a commercial enterprise. About thirty million people came out to cheer Lindbergh and his famous plane.

Lindbergh completed his tour of the U.S. on October 23, 1927, in Philadelphia, Pennsylvania. A few months later, he embarked on a second leg of the tour, flying the *Spirit of St. Louis* to Mexico, Central America, Colombia, Venezuela, Puerto Rico, and Cuba. Beginning in Mexico City, the flags of the countries he visited were painted on both sides of the aircraft's cowling.

LEFT The National Air and Space Museum has a variety of Lindbergh memorabilia in its collection.

Smithsonian's National Air and Space Museum

OPPOSITE PAGE Charles Lindbergh became a worldwide celebrity after his transatlantic flight.

Smithsonian's National Air and Space Museum (NASM A-4819-A)

UNITED STATES AIR FORCE STARTS DYNA-SOAR PROGRAM

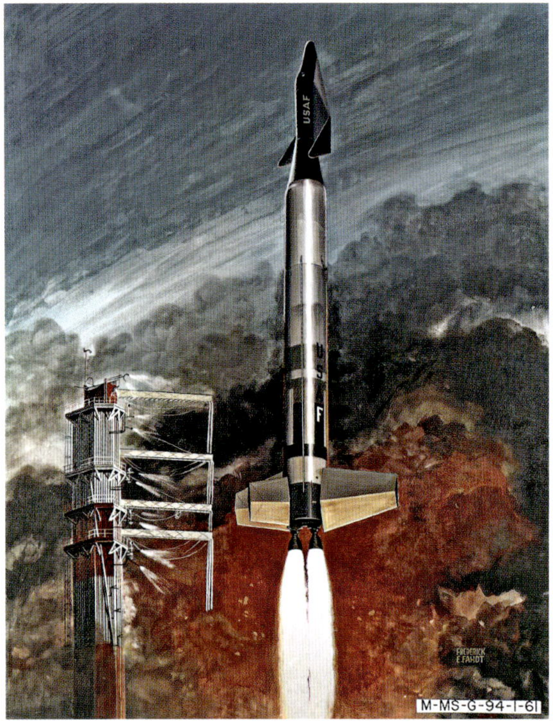

The U.S. Air Force planned to launch the X-20 using a Titan booster.

NASA

On October 24, 1957, the U.S. Air Force began the X-20 Dyna-Soar program. Short for "Dynamic Soaring," the Dyna-Soar was meant to be a research vehicle for exploring controlled atmospheric reentry, which could serve as a stepping stone to other military missions in space. Designed by Boeing, the single-pilot spaceplane was to be launched from atop a Titan IIIC booster, perform its mission in space, then glide back and land on Earth at an Air Force base.

The Dyna-Soar program was canceled in 1963 due to concerns with cost, capability, and a reluctance to weaponize space. Although it never got past the mock-up stage, the program influenced later vehicles like the Space Shuttle orbiters. After the X-20's cancellation, the U.S. military continued to explore opportunities in space, including developing the Manned Orbiting Laboratory project that never got off the ground. Although the military itself has never launched its own astronauts, its research has informed civilian human spaceflight endeavors.

OCTOBER 25

NATIONAL AIR AND SPACE MUSEUM BREAKS GROUND ON THE STEVEN F. UDVAR-HAZY CENTER

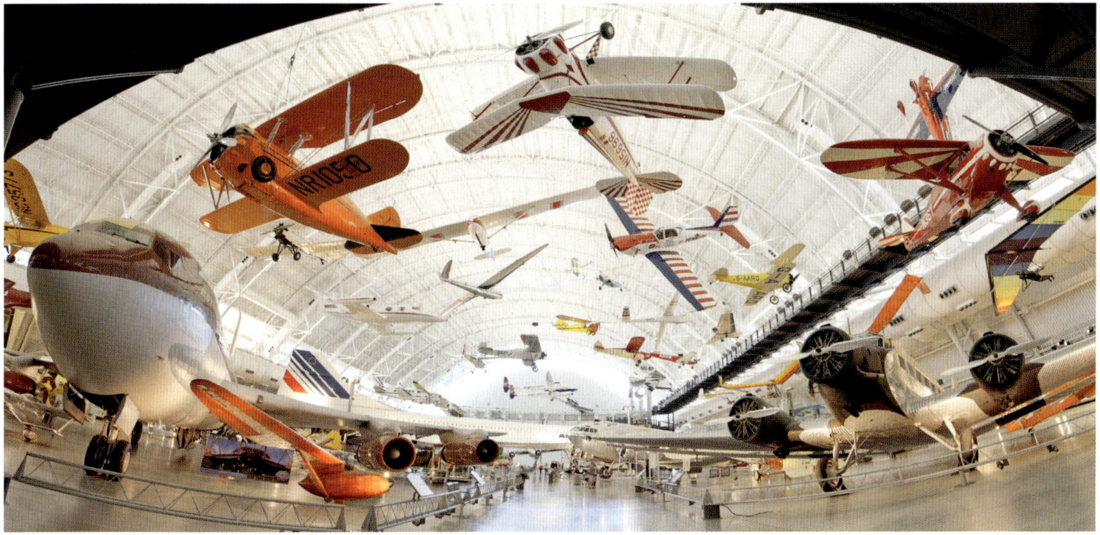

Artifacts at the Steven F. Udvar-Hazy Center are displayed in two connected hangars, the Boeing Aviation Hangar and the James S. McDonnell Space Hangar.

Smithsonian's National Air and Space Museum

Since the National Air and Space Museum opened in Washington, D.C., in 1976 (see page 200), size constraints allowed it to display only a fraction of its collection of large aircraft and space artifacts. The idea of constructing a second public building to supplement the one on the National Mall gained traction early on. Because modern aircraft are generally larger, heavier, and more difficult to move by road from one location to another, a museum located near an airport would make future acquisitions easier.

In 1993, President Bill Clinton signed legislation establishing an extension for the Museum near Washington Dulles International Airport in Virginia, and ground was broken at the site on October 26, 2000. The Steven F. Udvar-Hazy Center officially opened on December 15, 2003, just two days shy of the one hundredth anniversary of the first powered airplane flight. Today, over two thousand aviation and space artifacts are on display at the Center, including an SR-71 Blackbird, an Air France Concorde, and Space Shuttle *Discovery*.

JIMMY DOOLITTLE WINS SCHNEIDER TROPHY RACE IN CURTISS R3C-2 RACER

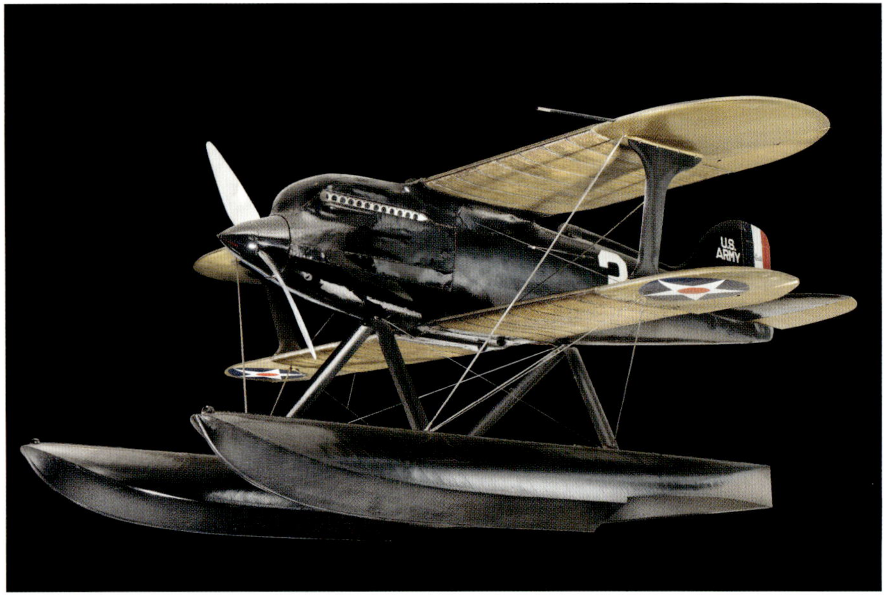

The Curtiss R3C-2 racer was in its floatplane configuration when Jimmy Doolittle flew it to win the Schneider Trophy.

Smithsonian's National Air and Space Museum

Racing planes became a worldwide phenomenon in the 1920s. The fierce contests thrilled crowds and boosted public support for flying, and racecourses served as "labs" to test and showcase aircraft technology and pilot skills. In 1925, 1st Lt. James "Jimmy" Doolittle flew a plane that was hard to beat: the Curtiss R3C Racer. A pilot for the U.S. Army Air Service, Doolittle also won fame and fortune flying as a private citizen.

With a molded-wood fuselage, thin airfoils, smooth engine covering, and minimal bracing, the sleek Curtiss R3C was built for speed. The racer's wheels could be replaced with floats, making it both a landplane and a seaplane. On October 26, 1925, Doolittle flew the Curtiss R3C-2 to victory in the Schneider Trophy Race, a seaplane race held at Bay Shore Park in Baltimore. His average speed in the race was 232.17 miles per hour. The next day he flew the R3C-2 over a straight course at a world-record speed of 245.75 miles per hour.

OCTOBER 27

SATURN I MAKES FIRST TEST FLIGHT

ROCKETS AND MISSILES

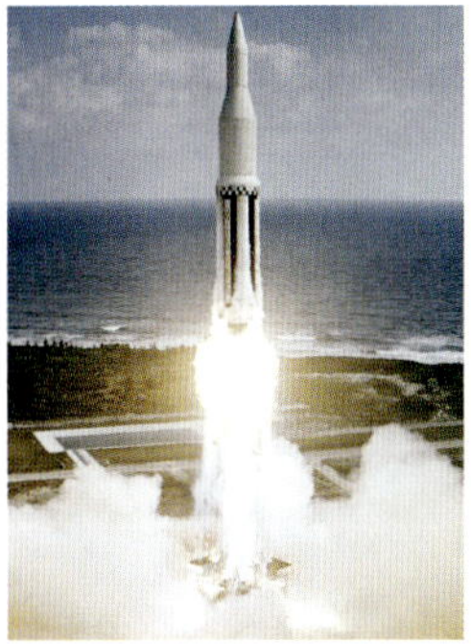

The Saturn I rocket was nearly two times as tall as the rocket that launched the first Americans to space.

NASA

Before there was the Saturn V (see page 331), there was the Saturn I. On October 27, 1961, the Saturn I rocket launched for the first time. The test flight was a success, and the launch vehicle flew an unprecedented 200-plus mile ballistic trajectory from the Kennedy Space Center in Florida. The 162-foot tall rocket was the basic test vehicle that led to the development of the Saturn V over the next few years, which carried humans to the Moon for Project Apollo.

OCTOBER 28

PAN AM MAKES FIRST SCHEDULED SERVICE BETWEEN KEY WEST AND CUBA

COMMERCIAL AVIATION

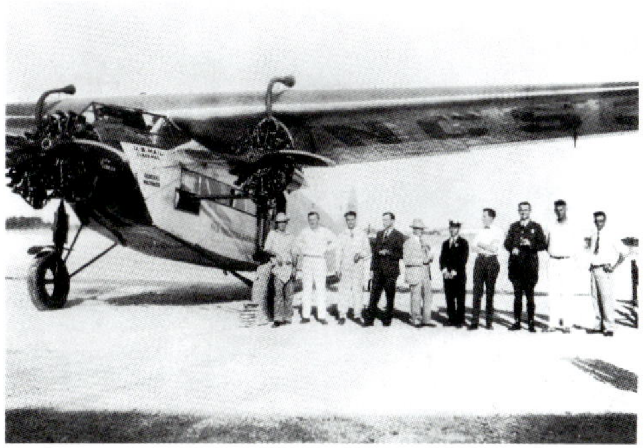

Pan American Airways' first scheduled flight carried airmail from Key West to Havana.

Pan Am Historical Foundation

Pan American Airways, led by Juan T. Trippe, became the dominant U.S. international airline in the early days of commercial aviation. Founded in 1927, Pan Am, as it was popularly known, opened regular commercial service throughout Latin America using both flying boats and land-planes. On October 28, 1927, a Pan Am Fokker F-VIIa/3m later christened *General Machado* departed on the new airline's first scheduled flight—an airmail delivery between Key West, Florida, and Havana, Cuba. With over 750 pounds of mail onboard, the flight took an hour and ten minutes to complete and was witnessed by hundreds.

JOHN GLENN RETURNS TO SPACE AT AGE SEVENTY-SEVEN

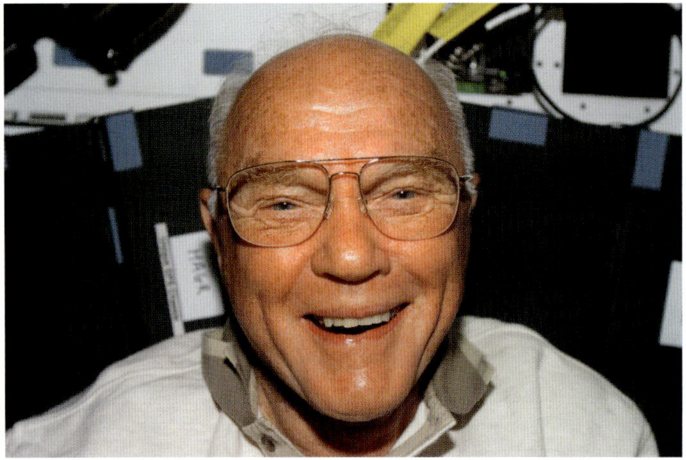

With one flight in 1962 and another in 1998, John H. Glenn Jr. uniquely bridged two eras in space history and left his mark in each.

NASA

In the 1960s, Mercury astronaut John H. Glenn Jr. flew to space just once, on his historic Earth-orbital mission (see page 65). It is believed that neither NASA nor President John F. Kennedy wanted to put Glenn at risk again after his first flight, as he had become extremely valuable to the nation as a hero and goodwill ambassador.

In 1998, Glenn finally got the opportunity to return to space. Serving on the Senate's Special Committee on Aging, Glenn proposed to NASA the benefit of flying an elderly person to space, because some of the bodily effects of spaceflight are similar to the bodily effects of aging, such as loss of bone density, compromised immune systems, and sleep disruption. On October 29, 1998, Glenn launched on board Space Shuttle *Discovery* as a payload specialist on the STS-95 mission. The SPACEHAB module in *Discovery*'s payload bay was loaded with life science and microgravity experiments.

There was a mixed reaction to Glenn's second space voyage. Some criticized the medical experiments as cover for a late-career victory lap, while others thought it was a fitting reward for Glenn's heroism and public service. Either way, there was a lot of interest in Glenn's return to space—especially because it earned him the title "oldest person in space." That record has since been broken (by Ed Dwight in 2024—see page 154), but Glenn remains the oldest person to orbit the Earth.

LUNAR LANDING RESEARCH VEHICLE FLIES FOR THE FIRST TIME

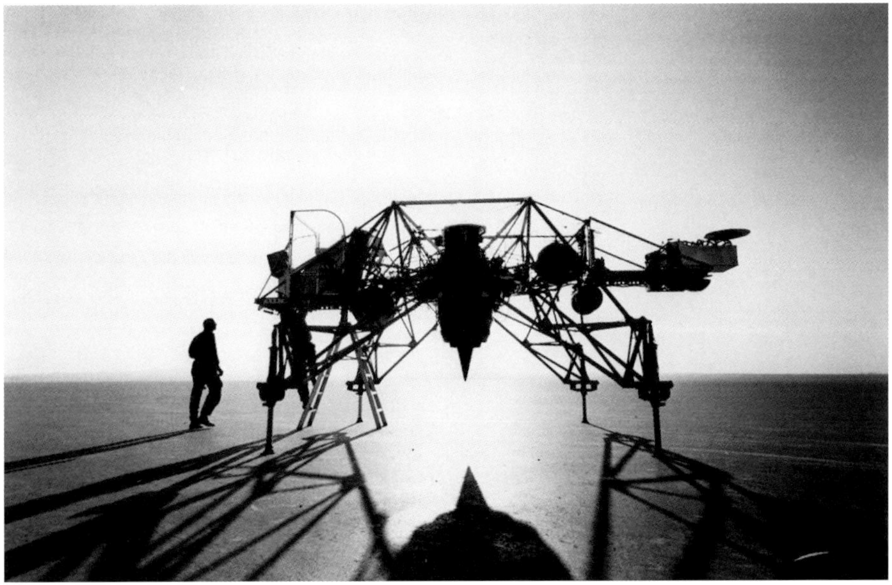

Like many experimental craft before and after it, NASA tested the Lunar Landing Research Vehicle on the dry lakebed at Edwards Air Force Base.

NASA

Before the Apollo lunar module (LM) could land on the Moon, NASA had to figure out how to fly in an environment with one-sixth of the gravity of Earth. Enter the Lunar Landing Research Vehicle (LLRV), a trainer/simulator that gave the astronauts a feel for what it would be like to pilot the LM to land on the lunar surface. A downward-pointing turbofan engine offset five-sixths of the LLRV's weight, effectively simulating the gravity on the Moon.

The Lunar Landing Research Vehicle was flown for the first time on October 30, 1964, with venerated test pilot Joseph "Joe" Walker at the controls. On this flight, Walker flew the LLRV for less than a minute to test its handling, only reaching ten feet off the ground before landing again. The astronauts and pilots who flew the LLRV affectionally called the oddly shaped vehicle the "flying bedstead" (it looked like an old metal bed frame), and Apollo 11 astronaut Neil Armstrong once said it was a "contrary machine, and a risky machine, but a very useful one."

EXPEDITION 1 LAUNCHES TO THE INTERNATIONAL SPACE STATION

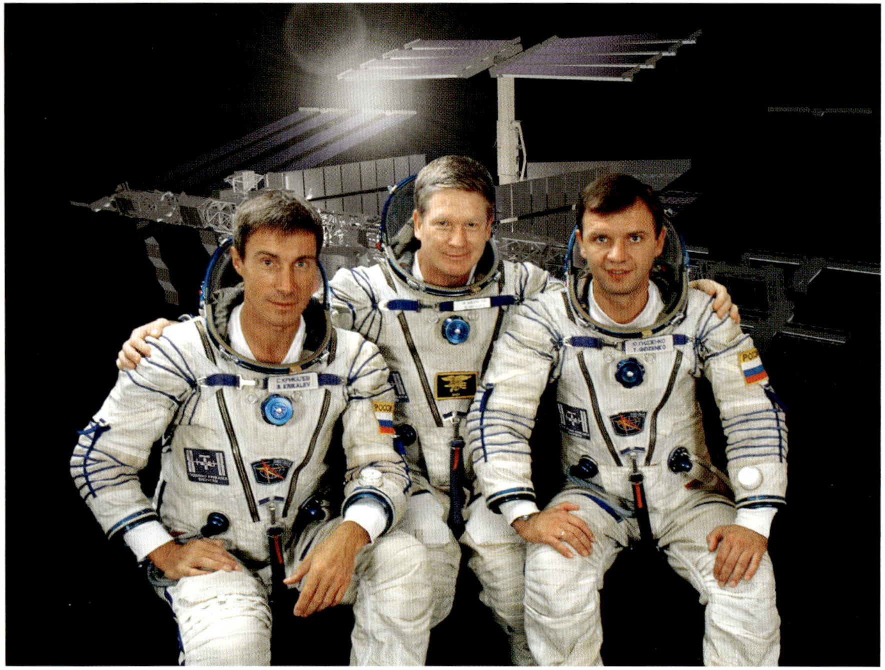

ABOVE The crew of International Space Station Expedition 1 launched on a Soyuz spacecraft wearing Sokol spacesuits.

NASA

OPPOSITE PAGE Major construction of the International Space Station finished in 2011. It is pictured here in 2021.

NASA

Expedition 1 launched to the International Space Station (ISS) on October 31, 2000. The crew of the first long-duration mission to the new space station consisted of NASA astronaut and mission commander William Shepherd and Roscosmos cosmonauts and flight engineers Yuri Gidzenko and Sergei Krikalev. They launched on a Roscosmos Soyuz rocket from Baikonur Cosmodrome and arrived at the ISS two days later. During their four-and-a-half-month mission on the station, the crew was visited three times by Space Shuttles carrying astronauts and equipment to continue constructing the station. The third of those, Space Shuttle *Discovery*'s STS-102 mission, delivered a new three-person crew (Expedition 2) to the station and took the Expedition 1 crew home.

Expedition 1 marked the beginning of over twenty-five years of continuous human presence in space that continues today. The ISS is a partnership between five space agencies representing fifteen countries. It features space for living, working, and sleeping, including bathrooms, a gym, and the iconic Cupola that provides stunning views of the Earth 250 miles below.

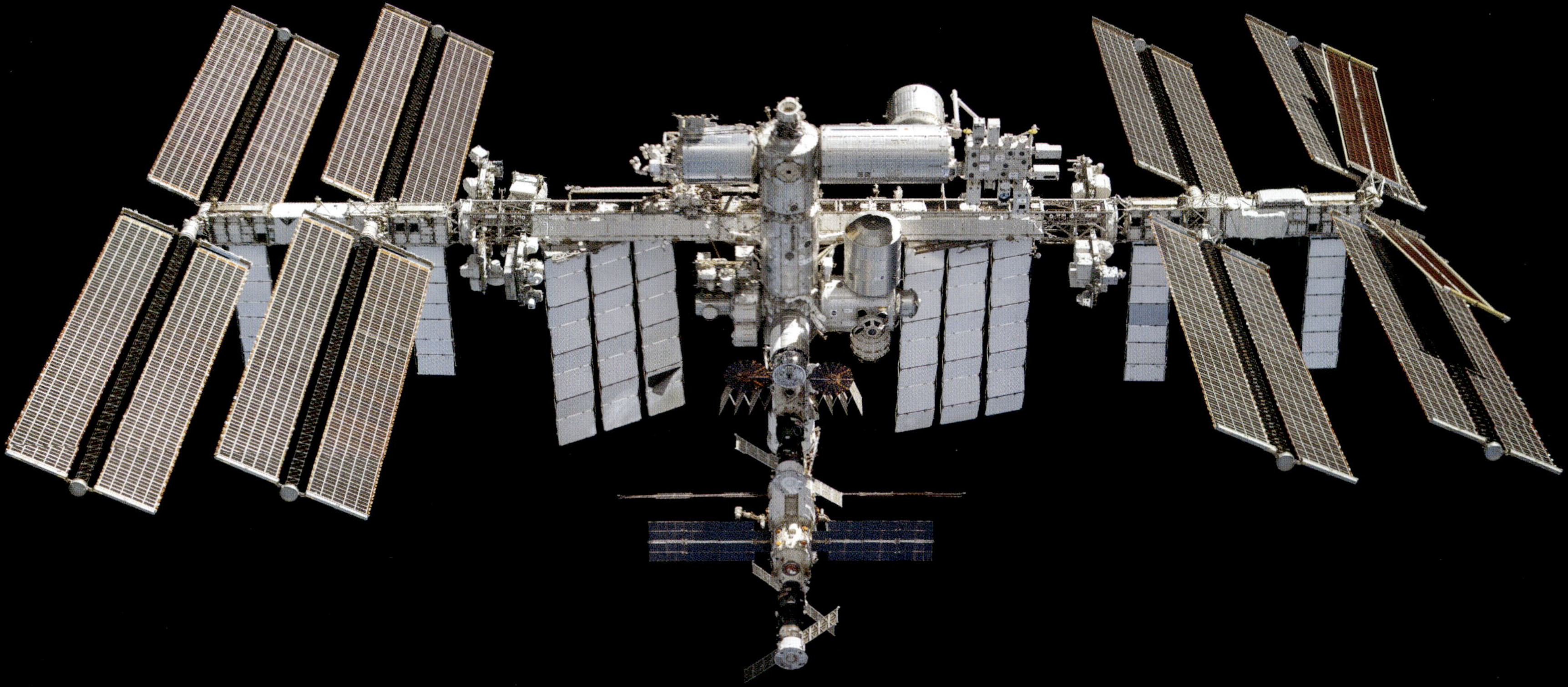

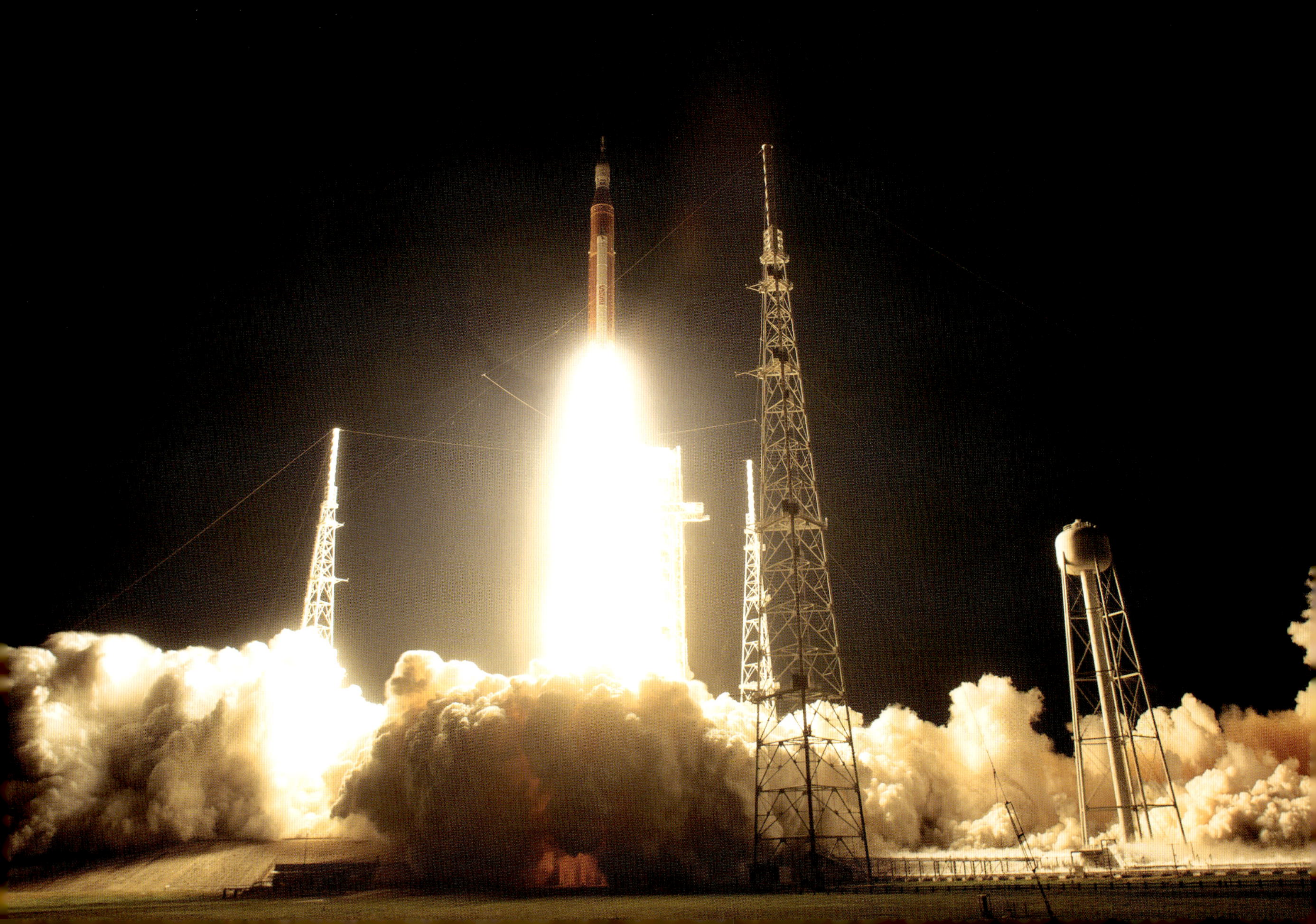

NOVEMBER

NOVEMBER 1

COAST GUARD CREW RESCUES TWENTY-TWO FROM A FIERY CRASH

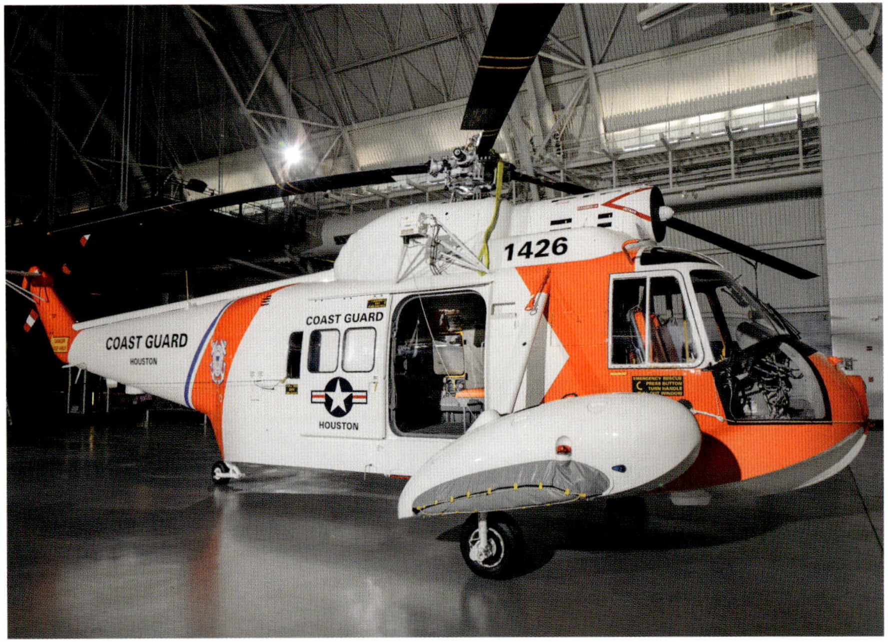

The HH-52A (#1426) on display at the Steven F. Udvar-Hazy Center made a daring rescue off the coast of Galveston in 1979.

Smithsonian's National Air and Space Museum

On November 1, 1979, the U.S. Coast Guard performed a daring rescue mission off the coast of Galveston, Texas. Flying a Sikorsky HH-52A Seaguard helicopter, Lt. (j.g.) Chris Kilgore, Lt. J. C. Cobb, and Petty Officer 2nd Class Thomas Wynn rescued twenty-two survivors from the oil tanker *Burmah Agate* and the freighter *Mimosa* after the vessels collided. The Seaguard helicopter evacuated twelve people from the inferno at one time—a record for the aircraft, which was designed to carry a maximum of ten crew members and passengers.

The HH-52 was the Coast Guard's first turbine-powered helicopter and the first that could land in the water without using awkward floats, making it the most effective air-sea rescue helicopter of its time. The aircraft was small enough to deploy aboard cutters, and its amphibious characteristics gave it a degree of safety in over-water operations that was missing in other helicopters. The Coast Guard operated ninety-nine HH-52s between 1962 and 1989, saving fifteen thousand lives.

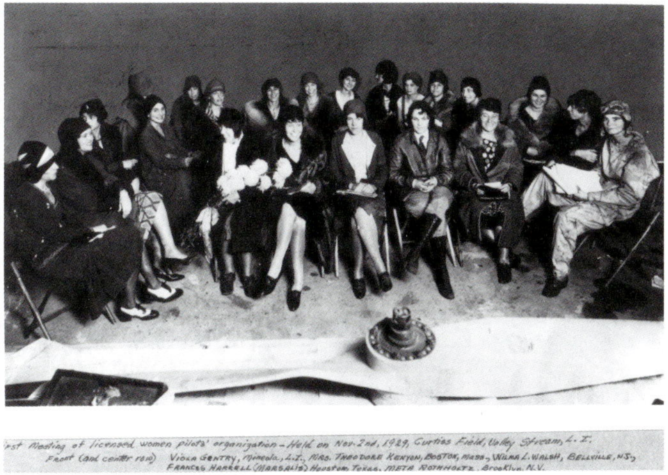

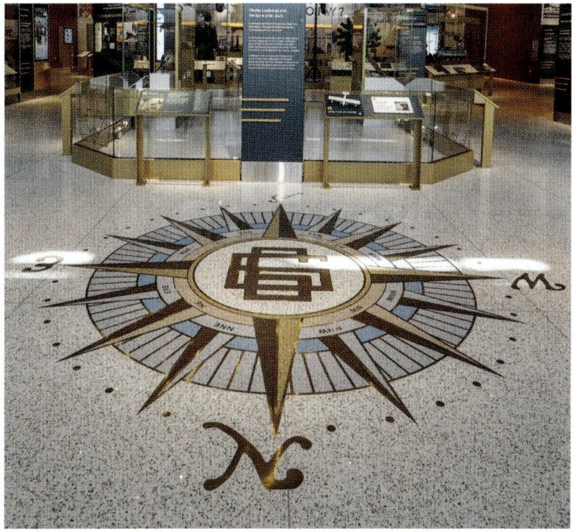

LEFT Ninety-nine women pilots formed an organization in 1929 to support the advancement of women in aviation.

Smithsonian's National Air and Space Museum (NASM 2005-7753)

RIGHT A compass rose with the Ninety-Nines logo in the middle is inlaid in the flooring of the *Barron Hilton Pioneers of Flight* gallery at the National Air and Space Museum.

Smithsonian's National Air and Space Museum

In August 1929, twenty women participated in the National Women's Air Derby, the first sanctioned race for women pilots. Fifteen of these women went on to complete the nine-day race from Santa Monica, California, to Cleveland, Ohio. Following the race, several of the competitors recognized there was a need for an organization of women pilots.

On November 2, 1929, this idea became a reality when twenty-six women pilots met at Curtiss Field near Valley Stream, Long Island, and chartered the new group. Living in a society that limited women's social and economic independence, the organization's mission was to mutually support each other in the aviation profession. Of the 285 licensed women pilots in the U.S. at the time, ninety-nine became charter members, inspiring the organization's name: the Ninety-Nines. Among the leaders of the early Ninety-Nines were president Amelia Earhart (see page 156) and secretary Louise Thaden (see page 265), who won the Women's Air Derby months before.

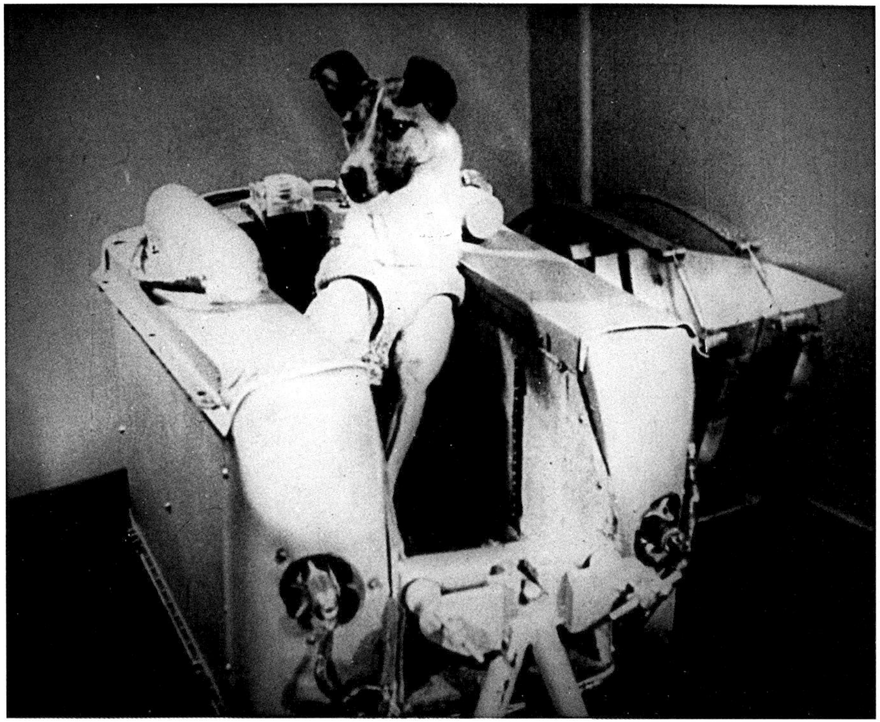

While Laika's breed is not known, she may have been part terrier and part husky or Samoyed.

Soviet Space Program

A dog named Laika became the first living creature to orbit the Earth on November 3, 1957. Launched on the Soviet Union's Sputnik II mission, Laika was a street dog in Moscow before she found fame in space. Of the stray dogs tested, Laika responded well when they recreated the unusual circumstances of a spaceflight, like changes in air pressure and sudden loud noises. Like the many other animals launched after her, Laika's purpose in space was to gather data on how aspects of spaceflight, including launch and microgravity, might impact human physiology.

While mission planners knew Laika would not survive the flight, she died sooner than expected. Sputnik II lost its heat shield soon after launch and the temperature in the capsule rose quickly. While the exact moment of her death is not known, it was likely within her first few orbits. For days after Laika's launch, the Soviet Union pretended she was still alive, going as far as to falsify documents. Nine days after launch, her tragic fate was finally announced.

HAWTHORNE GRAY FLIES TO 42,000 FEET IN A FREE BALLOON

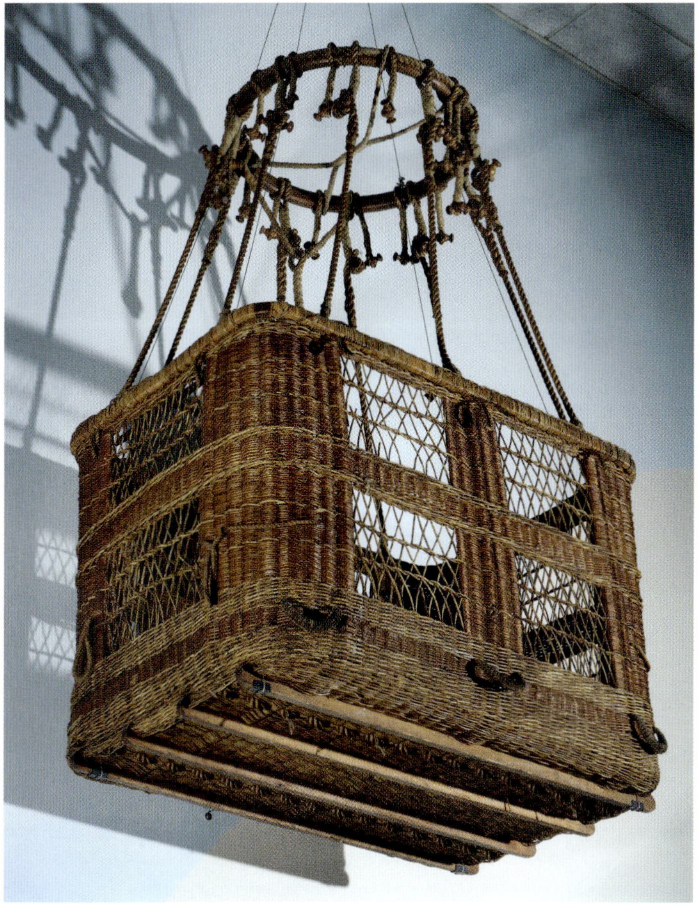

U.S. Army Air Corps balloonist Capt. Hawthorne Gray took off from Scott Field, Illinois, on November 4, 1927, on a mission to explore conditions and test equipment at altitudes over 40,000 feet. Unfortunately, Gray's trip aloft would be his last. Early the next morning, the balloon was found in a tree near Sparta, Tennessee, with Gray's lifeless body still in the basket. The balloonist had apparently become confused, throwing a full bottle of oxygen out of the basket in an effort to climb even higher. He died from lack of oxygen.

Gray had no illusions about the dangers involved in his quest—he knew that the reduced air pressure above 40,000 feet would have major impacts on his physiology. "His courage was greater than his supply of oxygen," the citation of his posthumous Distinguished Flying Cross suggested. Gray's flight took him higher than any other human being at that time, but he had not lived to tell the tale.

The balloon basket in which Hawthorne Gray made three high-altitude flights in 1927 is on display at the National Air and Space Museum.

Smithsonian's National Air and Space Museum

NOVEMBER 5

CAL RODGERS COMPLETES TRANSCONTINENTAL FLIGHT IN WRIGHT EX *VIN FIZ*

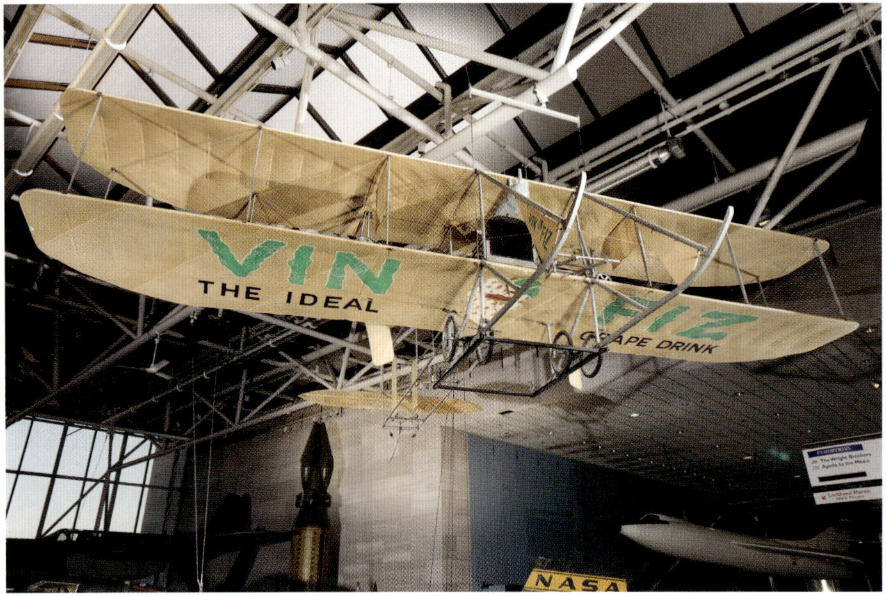

The Wright EX *Vin Fiz* is in the collection of the National Air and Space Museum.

Smithsonian's National Air and Space Museum

In 1910, publishing magnate William Randolph Hearst announced a $50,000 prize for the pilot who flew an airplane across the United States in thirty days or less. On November 5, 1911, Calbraith "Cal" Perry Rodgers completed the first transcontinental flight across the United States in the Wright EX biplane *Vin Fiz*—but not fast enough to claim the prize.

Rodgers's cross-country flight was punctuated by numerous stops, delays, and accidents. By the time Hearst's thirty-day time limit expired, Rodgers had only reached Kansas City, Missouri. Undaunted, the young pilot continued on, determined to make the first transcontinental airplane flight whether he received the money or not. Forty-nine days after setting out, Rodgers arrived to a hero's welcome in Pasadena, California. Although Pasadena marked the official end of his coast-to-coast journey, Rodgers flew on to Long Beach to complete the flight at the shore of the Pacific Ocean.

DID YOU KNOW? Calbraith Perry Rodgers's Wright EX biplane was named for his sponsor's Vin Fiz grape soda product. The drink's logo was emblazoned on a chaser train that served as a workshop to repair and maintain the aircraft during the journey.

EDDIE RICKENBACKER IS AWARDED THE MEDAL OF HONOR

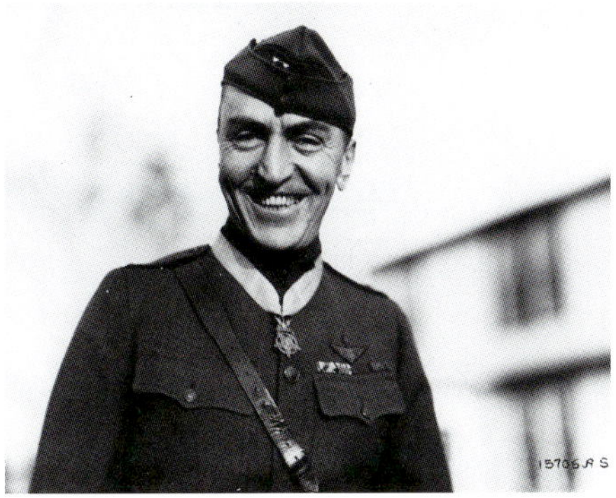

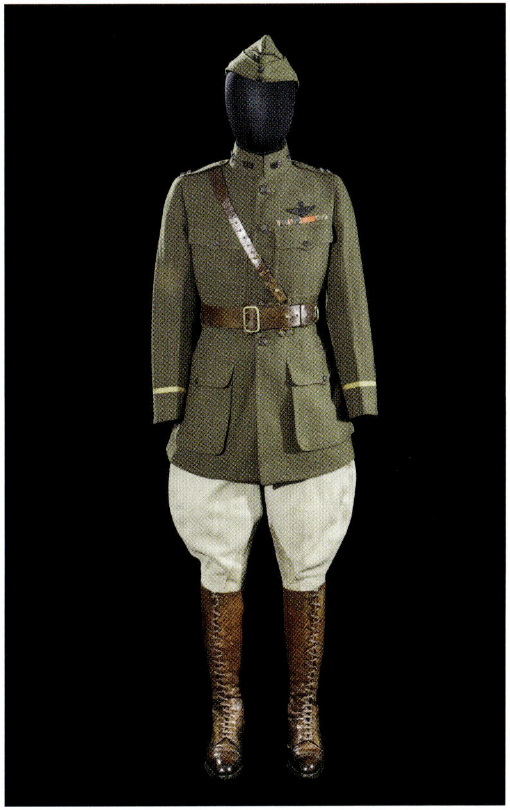

ABOVE A portrait of Eddie Rickenbacker was taken after he was presented with the Medal of Honor.

Smithsonian's National Air and Space Museum (NASM 73-7627)

RIGHT Rickenbacker's World War I uniform is on display at the National Air and Space Museum.

Smithsonian's National Air and Space Museum

Capt. Edward "Eddie" Rickenbacker was the United States' top-scoring ace of World War I. Before America entered the war, Rickenbacker was an accomplished race car driver. Because of his fame, he was offered the position of chauffeur to Gen. John J. Pershing, commander of U.S. forces in France. Soon after arriving in France in 1917, Rickenbacker was captivated by flying and requested a transfer to the fledgling U.S. Army Air Service. Following flight training at Tours, France, he was assigned to the famed 94th "Hat in the Ring Squadron" (see page 121).

Rickenbacker scored a total of twenty-six confirmed aerial victories (downed enemy planes) flying with the 94th. On November 6, 1930, President Herbert Hoover presented Rickenbacker with the nation's highest military decoration, the Medal of Honor, for boldly attacking seven enemy airplanes alone and shooting down two of them in September 1918.

NOVEMBER 7

BIPLANE RACES A CADILLAC

EARLY FLIGHT

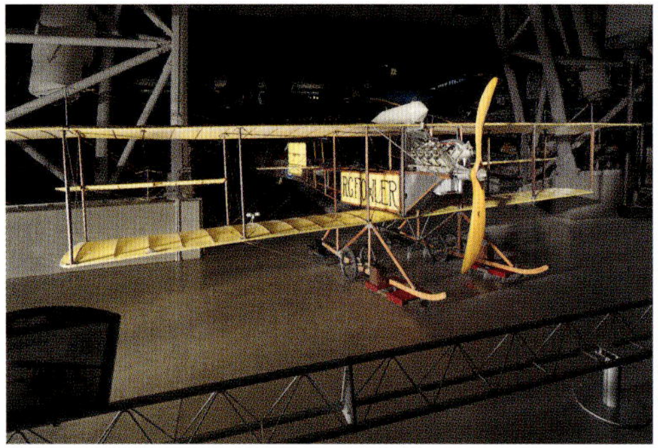

The Fowler-Gage biplane is on display at the Steven F. Udvar-Hazy Center.

Smithsonian's National Air and Space Museum

On November 7, 1912, pilot Robert G. Fowler departed Los Angeles in his Fowler-Gage biplane for a unique race against a Cadillac automobile. With Fowler in the skies and automobile racer Charles Soules on the road, the route to the finish line in San Francisco was selected so that neither racer had an advantage. Just northwest of Los Angeles at Saugus, Fowler crashed on takeoff and was forced to abandon the race to repair the aircraft before another flying engagement.

NOVEMBER 8

CHANDRAYAAN-1 ENTERS LUNAR ORBIT

INTERNATIONAL SPACE PROGRAMS

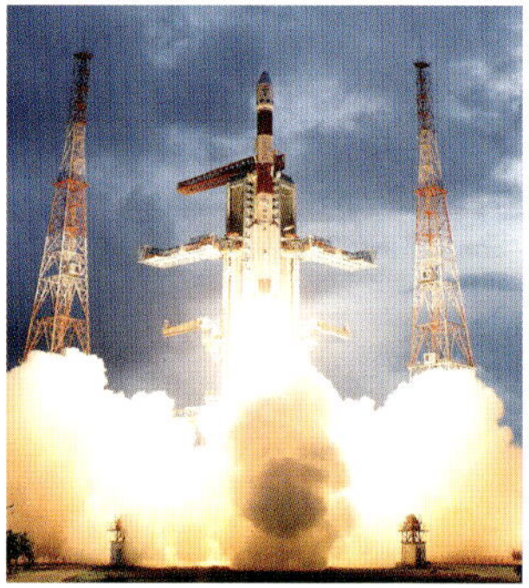

Chandrayaan-1 launched on India's Polar Satellite Launch Vehicle from Satish Dhawan Space Centre on an island off the coast of India.

ISRO

In October 2008, the Indian Space Research Organisation (ISRO) launched India's first mission to the Moon. The Chandrayaan-1 spacecraft entered lunar orbit on November 8, 2008, and eventually settled into a polar orbit sixty-two miles above the surface. Days after arriving at the Moon, Chandrayaan-1 released its Moon Impact Probe, which descended to the lunar surface in free fall, collecting data before its controlled impact at the lunar south pole. Chandrayaan-1 gathered important data that helped scientists discover evidence of water on the Moon.

SATURN V ROCKET LAUNCHES FOR THE FIRST TIME

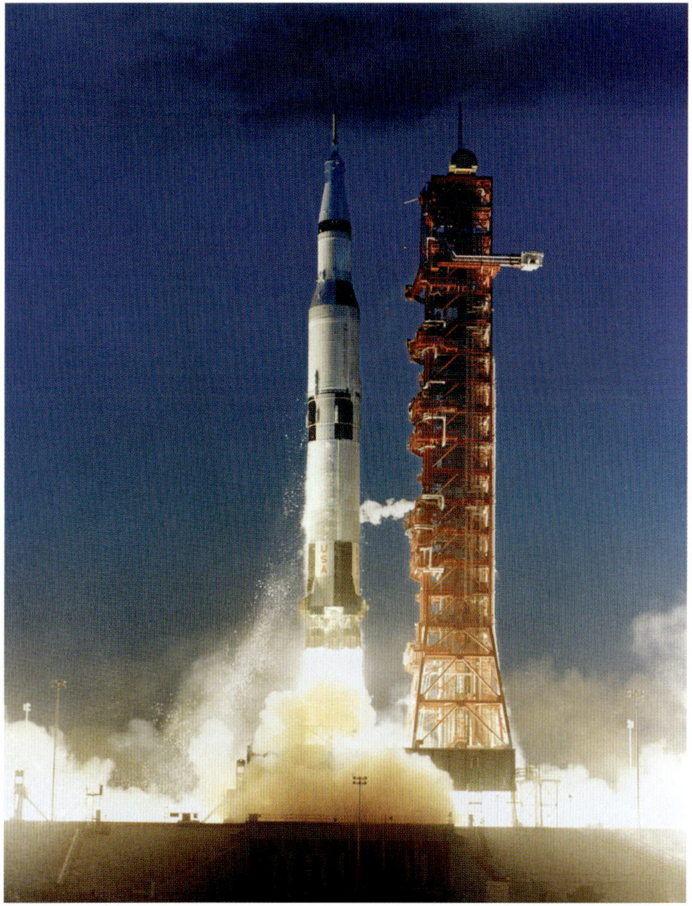

The Saturn V rocket launched for the first time on November 9, 1967, on the Apollo 4 mission. The uncrewed flight reached an altitude of 11,234 miles. The mission tested the United States' Moon rocket as well as the command and service modules. During the test, the spacecraft made two orbits, was placed on a trajectory that mimicked the approach an Apollo spacecraft would make returning from the Moon, and then was recovered in the Pacific Ocean.

For decades, the Saturn V was the largest and most powerful launch vehicle ever created. It had three stages: The first stage had five F-1 engines, producing nearly 7.7 million pounds of thrust. Those engines burned at liftoff and lasted about two and half minutes, taking the vehicle and payload to an altitude of thirty-eight miles. The second stage consisted of five J-2 engines and burned for approximately six minutes, taking the vehicle and payload to a 115-mile altitude. The third stage featured one J-2 engine that boosted the spacecraft to an orbital velocity of about 17,500 miles per hour.

LEFT The first launch of the Saturn V rocket was an important milestone on NASA's quest to land humans on the Moon.

NASA

NEXT PAGE The Saturn V rocket was powered by five F-1 engines. One and a quarter F-1 engines are on display at the National Air and Space Museum.

Smithsonian's National Air and Space Museum

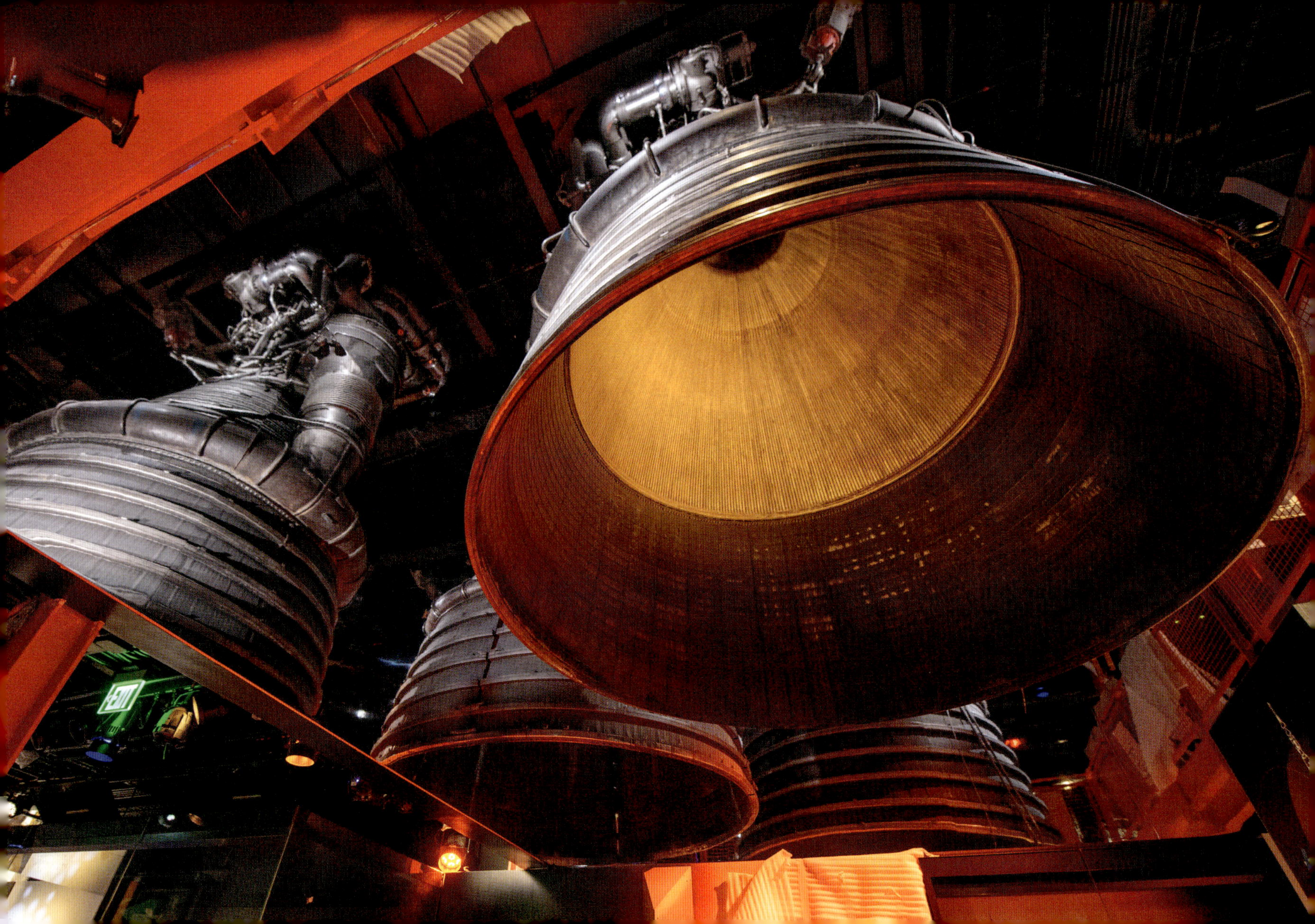

NOVEMBER 10

U.S. AIR FORCE PUBLICLY UNVEILS THE F-117 NIGHTHAWK

MODERN MILITARY AVIATION

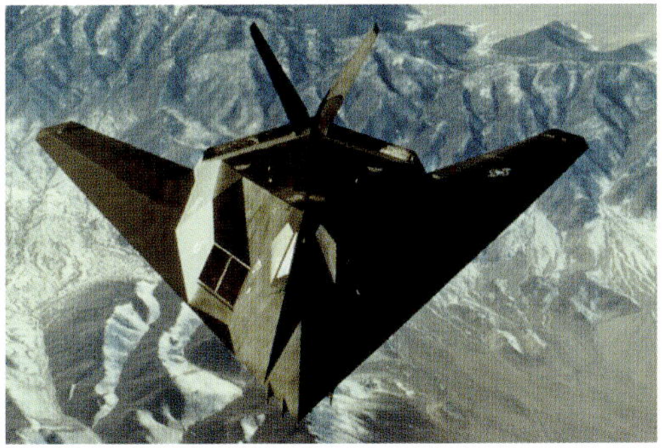

The F-117 was designed by Lockheed Martin's secretive Skunk Works division.

Department of Defense

On November 10, 1988, the United States military publicly unveiled the Lockheed F-117 Nighthawk in a press conference at the Pentagon. Fittingly for a stealth aircraft, the F-117 was a closely guarded secret during its first years of operation. In fact, the attack aircraft had entered service five years before it was even announced, having flown for the first time in 1981. The F-117 was the world's first operational stealth aircraft and was virtually invisible on radar screens thanks to its sharp angles, slanted tail, and radar-absorbent materials.

NOVEMBER 11

ARMISTICE FORCES GERMANY TO SURRENDER FOKKER D.VIIS

WORLD WAR I AND INTERWAR MILITARY AVIATION

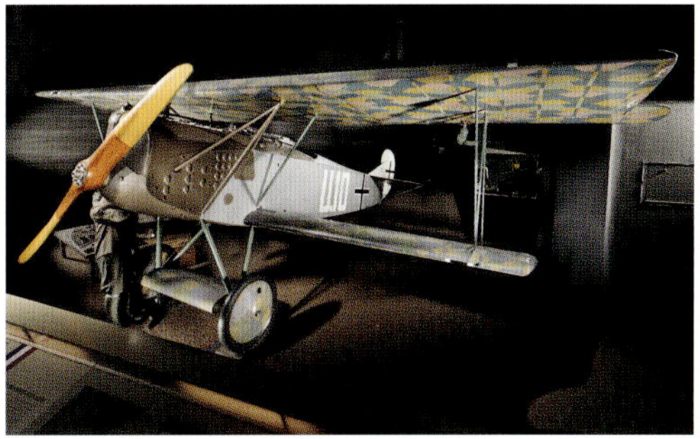

The National Air and Space Museum's Fokker D.VII was captured by American forces days before the armistice.

Smithsonian's National Air and Space Museum

At the eleventh hour of the eleventh day of the eleventh month in 1918, an armistice went into effect between the Allied forces and Germany, ending World War I. One of several such agreements signed with the Central Powers, the armistice of November 11 required the withdrawal of German troops from occupied territory and the release of Allied prisoners of war. The agreement also required that Germany surrender all of its Fokker D.VII aircraft. In August 1918 alone, D.VIIs shot down 565 Allied planes. The fighter aircraft's inclusion in the armistice was indicative of its fearsome reputation.

BUZZ ALDRIN TAKES A "SPACE SELFIE" DURING GEMINI XII EVA

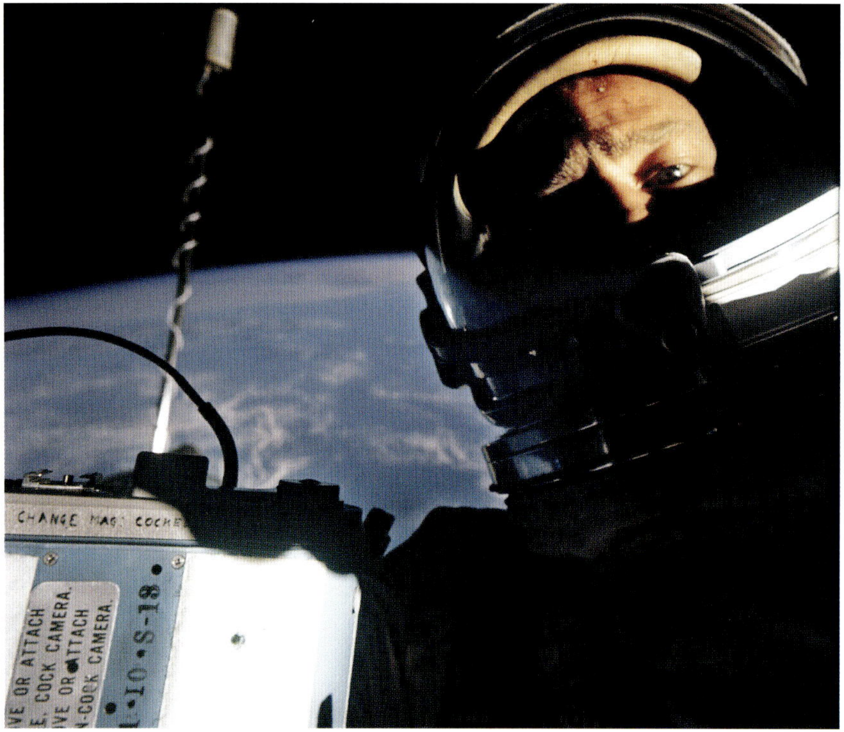

Buzz Aldrin describes his Gemini XII self-portrait as the "first space selfie."

NASA

Decades before the term "selfie" was coined, NASA astronaut Buzz Aldrin took a self-portrait during the final Gemini mission. During his first stand-up extravehicular activity (EVA) of the Gemini XII mission on November 12, 1966, Aldrin took pictures of landmarks on Earth, and while doing so, set his camera on the edge of the hatch, pointing it in his direction. Posing with Earth over his shoulder, Aldrin took the first known "selfie" from outside the spacecraft.

The purpose of Aldrin's EVA was to install a handrail between his hatch and the docking collar of the Agena target vehicle, which he would then use during his spacewalk the following day. To do this task, he opened his hatch (each astronaut had their own) but did not fully exit the spacecraft. As he photographed Earth, he transmitted a message to CAPCOM (capsule communicator) Charles "Pete" Conrad: "Okay, tell everybody down there to smile." Right before snapping his selfie, he remarked, "Now let me raise my visor and I'll smile."

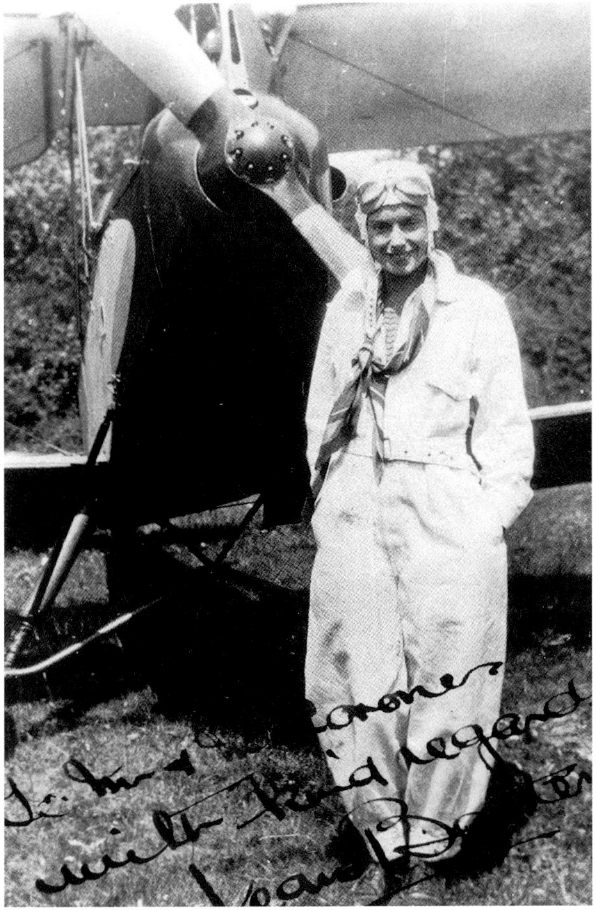

Growing up, New Zealand aviator Jean Batten developed a fascination with flight. In 1929, her love was solidified when she flew as a passenger in famed Australian pilot Charles Kingsford Smith's *Southern Cross* airplane (see page 178). Though her father did not approve of her aviation enthusiasm, Batten convinced her mother to move with her to England, where she could learn to fly. After earning her pilot's license, Batten began planning a flight from England to Australia. Her first two attempts failed, but she found success in 1934 and became an instant sensation in Australia, New Zealand, and England.

In 1935, Batten continued to prove her aviation skills with a record-setting flight from England to South America. Upon landing in Port Natal, Brazil, on November 13, 1935, Batten became the first woman to fly solo across the South Atlantic, and she was once again greeted with acclaim as she toured South America. Batten continued to make impressive flights throughout the 1930s, receiving the Harmon International Trophy for outstanding flights by a woman three times.

Jean Batten was nicknamed the "Greta Garbo of the Skies."

State Library of Queensland

NOVEMBER 14 ROSCOE TURNER SETS NEW EAST-WEST TRANSCONTINENTAL SPEED RECORD

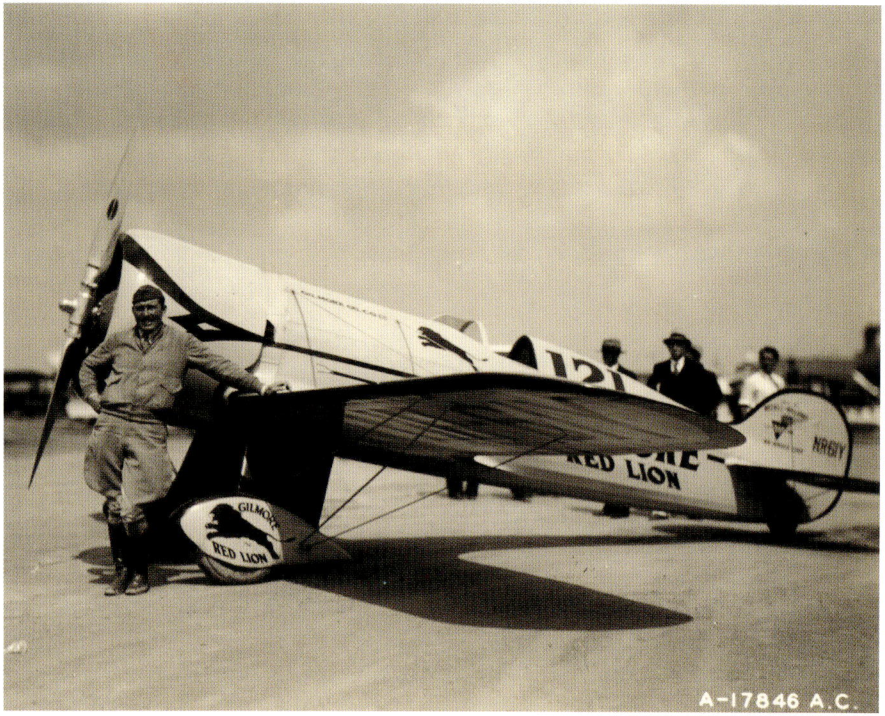

Roscoe Turner set a record and won his first Thompson Trophy in a Wedell-Williams air racer.

Smithsonian's National Air and Space Museum (NASM A-580-A)

American aviator Roscoe Turner was the most famous air racer of the 1930s. Flamboyant and charismatic, Turner's fame as a "speed king" transcended aviation into popular culture in the 1930s. On November 14, 1932, Turner set an east-west transcontinental speed record in his Wedell-Williams Model 44 air racer, flying from New York City to Burbank, California, in twelve hours and thirty-three minutes. Two years later, he won his first Thompson Trophy in the same plane.

Concerned that his Wedell-Williams was beginning to be outclassed by newer, faster racers, Turner began flying an RT-14 Meteor in the 1937 National Air Races. Though he finished third in the Thompson Trophy race that year, Turner returned victorious in 1938 and 1939, making him the only three-time winner of the award.

DID YOU KNOW? Roscoe Turner was sponsored by Gilmore Oil Company, which was well known for its Red Lion gasoline brand. To help promote the company, Turner adopted a lion cub he named Gilmore, whom he had as a passenger on dozens of flights.

SOVIET UNION LAUNCHES BURAN SPACE SHUTTLE

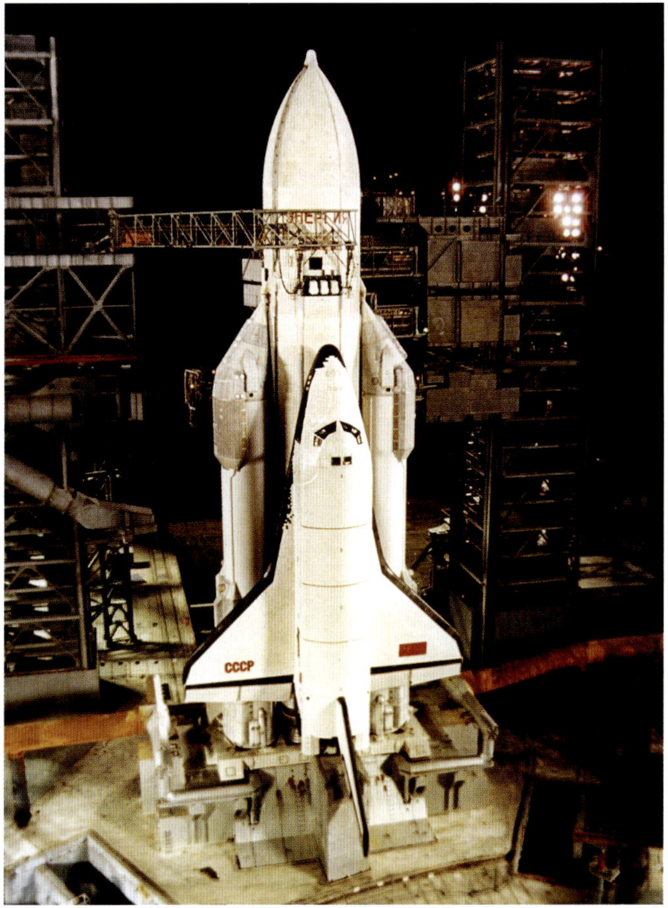

The United States was not the only country interested in developing a space shuttle. However, while NASA's shuttle orbiters launched on 135 missions (see page 118), the Soviet shuttle never made any crewed spaceflights. Named Buran (Russian for "snowstorm"), the Soviet Union's first full-scale reusable space shuttle resembled the American shuttle quite closely—not by coincidence. Through espionage, the Soviets obtained the design specifications of the U.S. orbiter. Experts have determined that the Soviets stole NASA's designs early in the space shuttle's development because Buran's tile pattern is reflective of NASA's original plan.

Buran was tested extensively in the atmosphere with trained pilots, but the first and only orbital flight, which took place on November 15, 1988, was made without a crew. It was launched on the Soviet launch vehicle Energia. The response to the Buran program from within the Soviet aerospace community was immediately and resoundingly negative, due to its cost and a legacy that linked it to the Soviet tradition of sacrificing the needs of civil society for ostentatious military build-up. Two Buran shuttles were manufactured, but after that single uncrewed test mission, the program was canceled.

The Soviet space shuttle Buran only launched once, on an uncrewed spaceflight.

Smithsonian's National Air and Space Museum (NASM 9A21214)

ARTEMIS I LAUNCHES ON UNCREWED LUNAR MISSION

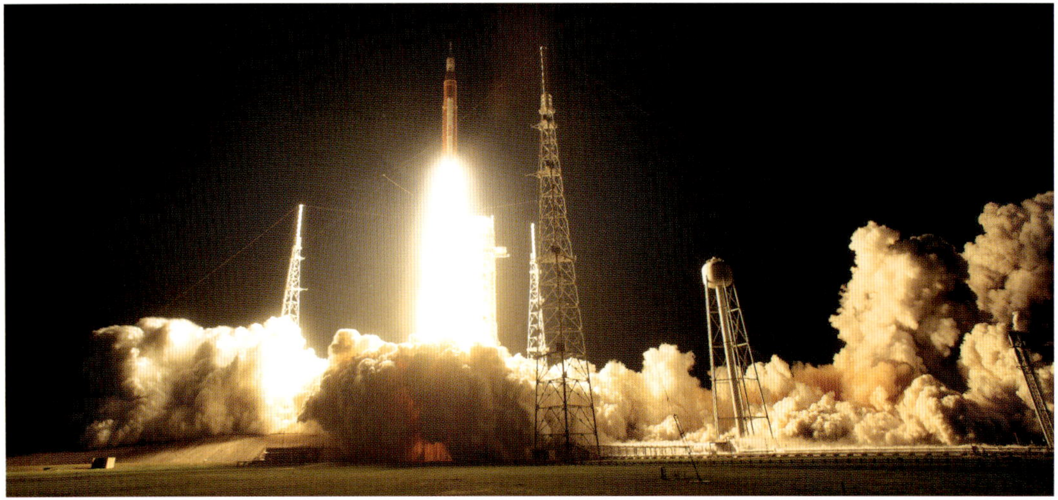

The SLS rocket, which launched Artemis I on its lunar mission, is the most powerful rocket ever used by NASA.

NASA/Joel Kowsky

The last person to set foot on the Moon did so in late 1972 (see page 365). Now, over fifty years after the end of the Apollo program, NASA's Artemis program aims to land American astronauts on the lunar surface once again. The first mission of the Artemis program to leave Earth orbit, an uncrewed mission called Artemis I, launched from Kennedy Space Center on November 16, 2022. It was a flight test of NASA's Deep Space Exploration Systems, which includes the SLS (Space Launch System) rocket and Orion spacecraft.

Artemis I was the first launch of NASA's SLS rocket, a super heavy-lift rocket designed to send crew and cargo to the Moon for the Artemis program. The mission tested the Orion spacecraft, which took a crew of four astronauts to the Moon for the Artemis II mission in 2026 (see page 382). On the Artemis I mission, however, the Orion spacecraft carried three mannequins with radiation sensors—and an astronaut Snoopy zero-G indicator. The mission concluded twenty-five days after launch when the Orion spacecraft splashed down in the Pacific Ocean.

DID YOU KNOW? The Artemis program is named for Artemis, the Greek goddess of the hunt, who is also the twin sister of Apollo, for whom NASA's first Moon landing program was named.

NOVEMBER 17

DULLES AIRPORT OPENS IN VIRGINIA

COMMERCIAL AVIATION

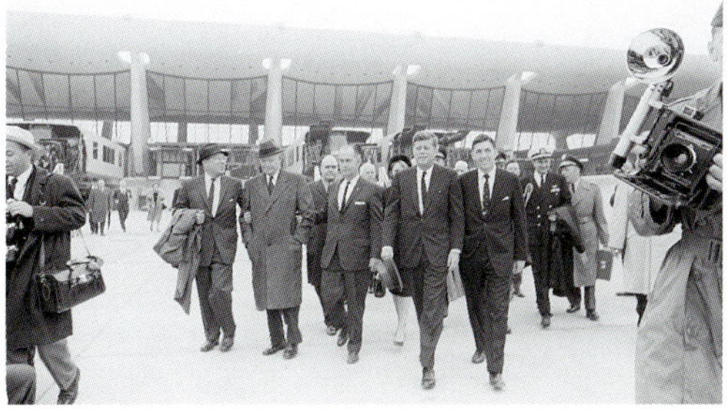

President John F. Kennedy attended the Dulles Airport dedication.

Robert Knudsen. White House Photographs. John F. Kennedy Presidential Library and Museum, Boston

On November 17, 1962, President John F. Kennedy spoke at the dedication ceremony for Washington Dulles International Airport, which began commercial flights two days later. Located twenty-six miles from downtown Washington in Chantilly, Virginia, Dulles was the second airport to serve the National Capital Region and the first in the United States specifically designed for jetliners. The airport was named for former Secretary of State John Foster Dulles, who had died several years earlier.

NOVEMBER 18

P-38 LIGHTNING PILOTS ATTACK JAPANESE FIGHTERS

WORLD WAR II MILITARY AVIATION

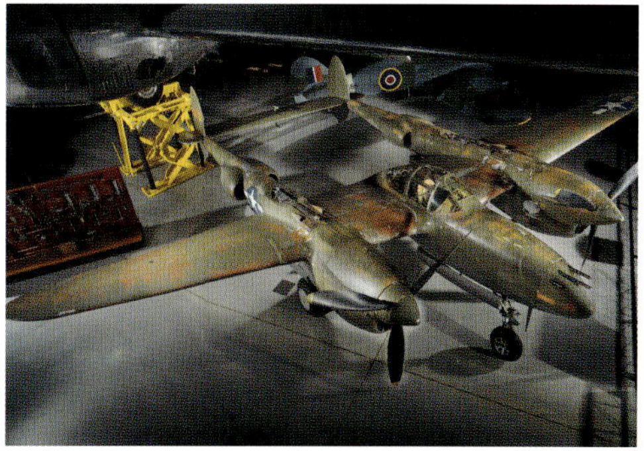

A P-38J Lightning is on display at the Steven F. Udvar-Hazy Center.

Smithsonian's National Air and Space Museum

The Lockheed P-38 Lightning was one of the most successful twin-engine fighters ever flown by any nation. From 1942 to 1945, U.S. Army Air Forces pilots flew P-38s over Europe, the Mediterranean, and the Pacific. Lightnings were among the first American fighter aircraft capable of consistently defeating Japanese fighters in aerial combat—by war's end, P-38 pilots in the Pacific Theater had downed more Japanese aircraft than their counterparts in any other Army Air Forces warplane. On November 18, 1942, pilots of the 339th Fighter Squadron became the first Lightning pilots to attack Japanese fighters, claiming three victories during a B-17 escort mission.

APOLLO 12 LANDS ON THE MOON

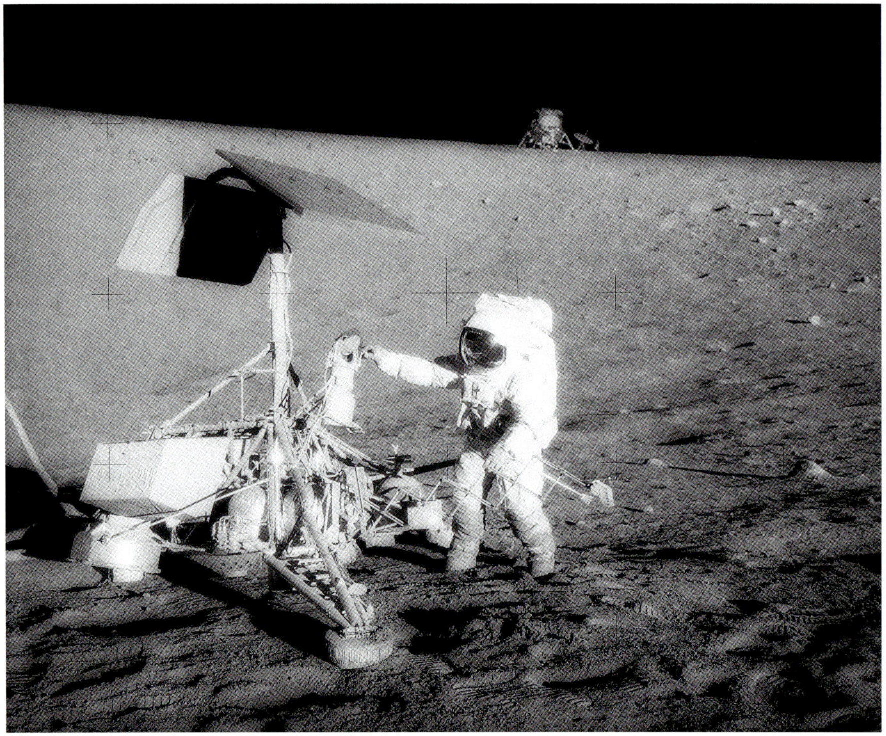

After landing on the Moon, the Apollo 12 moonwalkers (including Alan Bean, pictured here) walked to the Surveyor 3 lander nearby.

NASA

Just a few months after Apollo 11 made history as the first human landing on the Moon (see page 216), NASA repeated the feat with Apollo 12. On November 19, 1969, the Apollo 12 lunar module *Intrepid* touched down on the lunar surface. Mission commander Charles "Pete" Conrad and lunar module pilot Alan Bean carried out a precision landing to touch down on the Moon with almost pinpoint accuracy. Conrad exclaimed "Yippee!" upon setting foot on the surface—properly capturing the excitement many felt about a successful return to the Moon.

The lunar module landed within easy walking distance of the Surveyor 3 lander, which had arrived on the Moon two years prior. This allowed the astronauts to bring back instruments from the robotic spacecraft, including its camera, to examine the effects of long-term exposure to the lunar environment. While Conrad and Bean were on the lunar surface, command module pilot Richard Gordon remained in command module *Yankee Clipper.*

DID YOU KNOW? The Apollo 12 mission got a shocking start: Thirty-seven seconds after launch, the Saturn V launch vehicle was struck by lightning.

NOVEMBER 20

DOUGLAS D-558-2 FLIES FASTER THAN TWICE THE SPEED OF SOUND

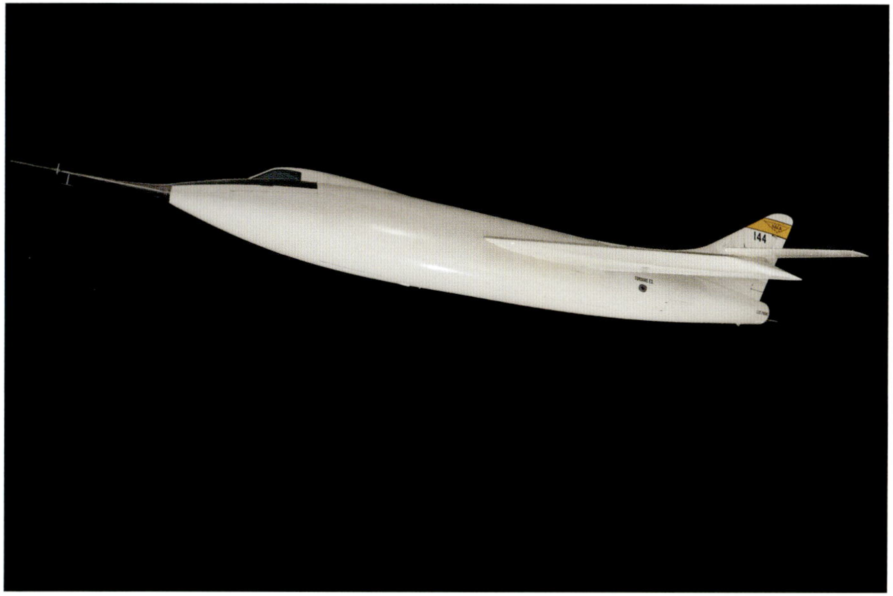

The first plane to fly twice the speed of sound is in the collection of the National Air and Space Museum.

Smithsonian's National Air and Space Museum

On the morning of November 20, 1953, American test pilot Scott Crossfield became the first pilot to fly at twice the speed of sound. Crossfield accomplished this feat in the experimental rocket-propelled Douglas D-558-2 Skyrocket. Air-launched from a Boeing B-29 Superfortress, the swept-wing, rocket-powered D-558-2 reached Mach 2.005 in a shallow dive at 62,000 feet. Seconds afterward, the plane's XLR-8 rocket engine exhausted its fuel supply and shut down. Crossfield glided to a smooth dead-stick landing on Muroc Dry Lake at Edwards Air Force Base, California.

The D-558 series of aircraft was developed by Douglas under the direction of Edward H. Heinemann for the U.S. Navy to explore transonic and supersonic flight. The D-558-1 and early D-558-2 aircraft were jet-powered, but the aircraft flown by Crossfield was modified to all-rocket propulsion, using the space formerly taken up by its turbojet engine for additional rocket fuel.

HUMANS MAKE FIRST FREE FLIGHT IN A BALLOON

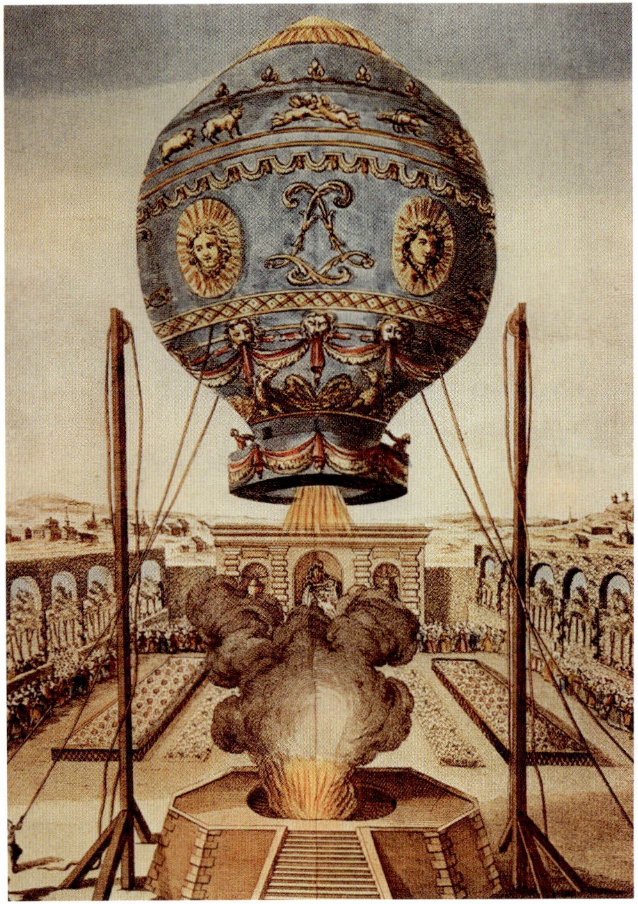

After brothers Joseph-Michel and Jacques-Étienne Montgolfier successfully sent three animals aloft in a hot-air balloon in September 1783 (see page 279), they were ready to attempt their first human free flight. Said to have been the first person to reach the balloon carrying the animals when it landed, Jean-François Pilâtre de Rozier launched a successful campaign for the honor of being the first human to make such a flight.

On November 21, 1783, the Montgolfier brothers launched de Rozier and the Marquis d'Arlandes on the first free balloon flight from the Chateau de la Muette in Paris. They flew to an altitude of approximately 3,000 feet and landed the hot-air balloon after about twenty-five minutes in flight. A week and a half later, Montgolfier competitor J. A. C. Charles and his flying companion M. N. Robert made the first free flight in a gas balloon from the Jardin des Tuileries in Paris.

A hand-colored engraving in the archival collection of the National Air and Space Museum depicts the flight of Jean-François Pilâtre de Rozier and the Marquis d'Arlandes.

Smithsonian's National Air and Space Museum (NASM 80-2357)

FREDERICK GREGORY BECOMES FIRST BLACK SHUTTLE COMMANDER

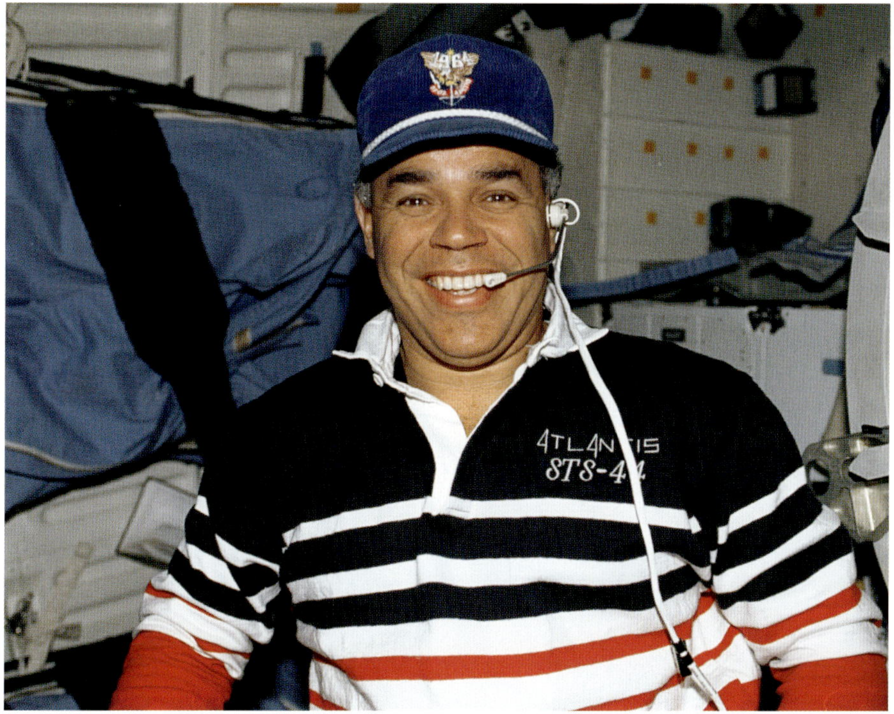

Frederick Gregory commanded two Space Shuttle missions.

NASA

When Frederick Gregory was selected as an astronaut, he was among the first Black astronaut candidates at NASA. Prior to his selection, Gregory gained extensive aerospace experience, serving as a helicopter rescue pilot in the U.S. Air Force (including 550 combat rescue missions in Vietnam) and attending U.S. Naval Test Pilot School. He was serving as a research test pilot at NASA's Langley Research Center when he joined the astronaut program in 1978.

Gregory went to space for the first time on STS-51B, becoming the first African American to pilot a Space Shuttle orbiter. On November 22, 1989, he became the first Black astronaut to command a spaceflight on Space Shuttle *Discovery*'s STS-33 mission, a role he repeated on the STS-44 mission in 1991. In total, Gregory spent 455 hours in space across three Space Shuttle missions. He went on to serve in leadership roles at NASA, retiring in 2005 after three years as deputy administrator of the agency.

NOVEMBER 23

ELLSWORTH AND HOLLICK-KENYON ATTEMPT TO CROSS ANTARCTICA BY AIR

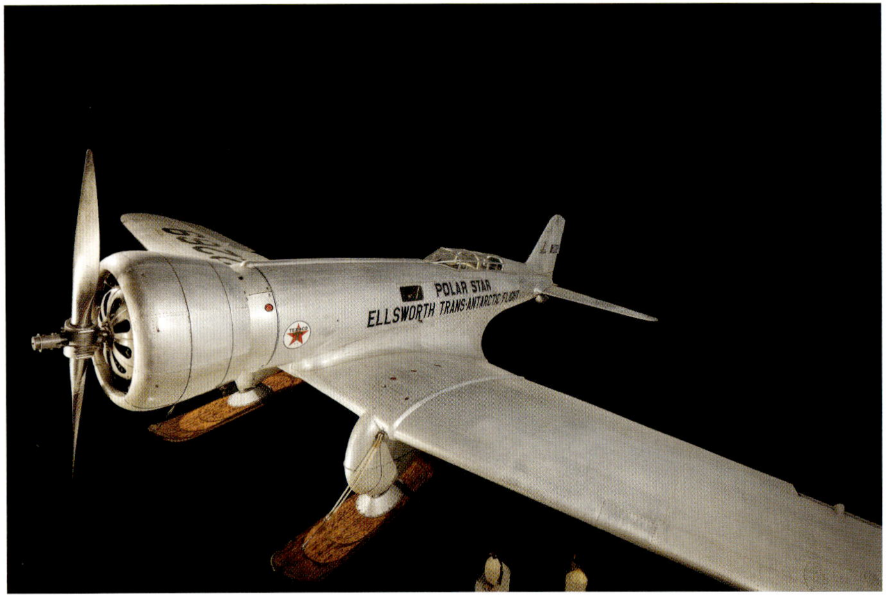

Lincoln Ellsworth donated the Northrop Gamma *Polar Star* to the Smithsonian in 1936.

Smithsonian's National Air and Space Museum

On November 23, 1935, American explorer Lincoln Ellsworth and Canadian pilot Herbert Hollick-Kenyon left on a flight across Antarctica. They took off from Dundee Island in the Weddell Sea and began flying across the continent in the Northrop Gamma *Polar Star*. Flying at an altitude of 13,400 feet, the pair crossed the 12,000-foot peaks of the Eternity Range, becoming the first humans to visit western Antarctica. Ellsworth named a portion of that area James W. Ellsworth Land in honor of his father.

Ellsworth and Hollick-Kenyon's destination was the Little America exploration base, but in early December, low fuel forced them down about twenty-five miles short of their goal. The pair walked six days to reach the base and then settled down in the camp abandoned by Richard E. Byrd (see page 348) several years earlier. A month later, the British Research Society ship *Discovery II* rescued the men.

NOVEMBER 24

D.B. COOPER HIJACKS A PLANE

COMMERCIAL AVIATION

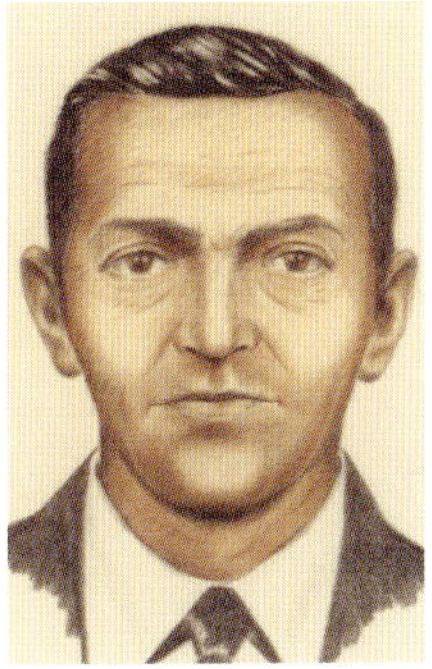

The FBI created an artist rendering of the hijacker referred to as D. B. Cooper.

Federal Bureau of Investigation

On November 24, 1971, a man calling himself Dan Cooper boarded a Northwest Orient Airlines Boeing 727 to Seattle. Soon after takeoff, he revealed that he had a bomb and demanded four parachutes and $200,000 in cash. Upon landing in Seattle, thirty-six passengers were exchanged for the money and parachutes and the airplane took off once more for Mexico City. Before the airliner arrived at its destination, "Cooper" jumped out of the plane, taking the money with him. Despite an extensive investigation, the crime was never solved, and the hijacker's identity remains a mystery.

NOVEMBER 25

FIRST NUCLEAR-POWERED AIRCRAFT CARRIER IS COMMISSIONED

MODERN MILITARY AVIATION

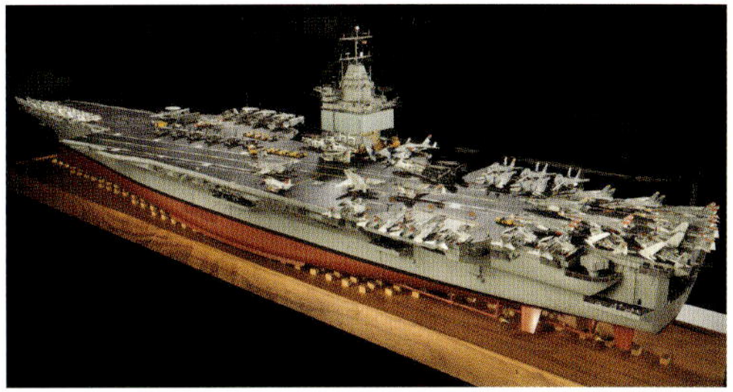

The 1:100 scale model of the USS *Enterprise* in the collection of the National Air and Space Museum took twelve thousand hours over the course of twelve years to complete.

Smithsonian's National Air and Space Museum

Launched on November 25, 1961, the USS *Enterprise* [CVA(N)-65, later CVN-65] was the United States' first nuclear-powered aircraft carrier. Measuring 1,123 feet, it is also the longest naval vessel ever built. *Enterprise* became an iconic symbol of the projection of U.S. naval air power during the Cold War following deployments to Vietnam and other hot spots during the 1960s, '70s, and '80s. In September 1974, *Enterprise* became the first carrier to deploy with the new F-14 Tomcat fighter aircraft (see page 281).

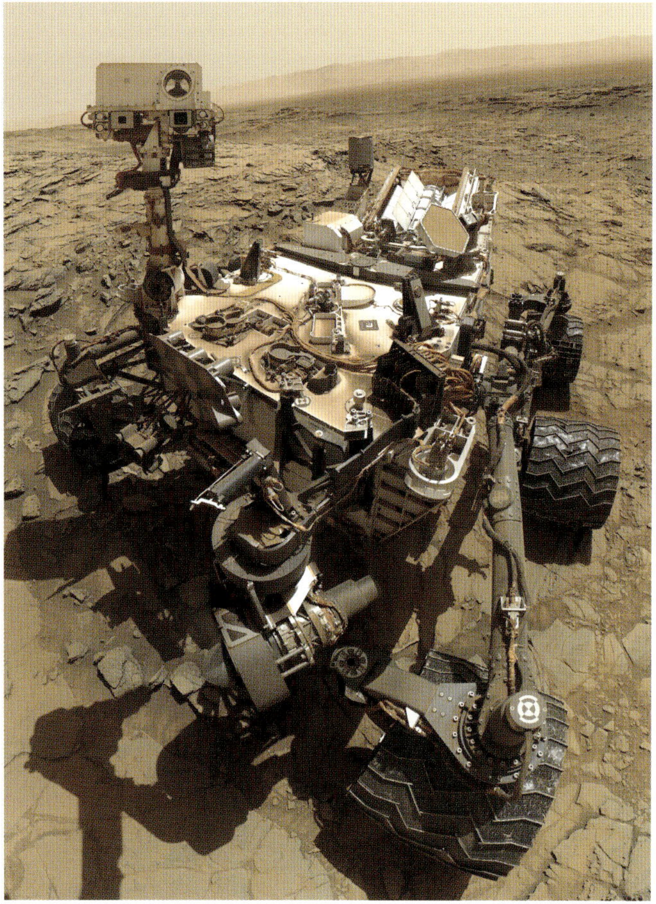

The Mars Science Laboratory *Curiosity* launched atop an Atlas V rocket on November 26, 2011. After an over eight-month journey to Mars, the *Curiosity* rover arrived on the Red Planet in August 2012. Weighing about a ton (1,000 kilograms), it landed by means of what engineers called a "sky crane" maneuver—lowered safely to the surface from a hovering platform. It then began a multi-year mission to explore the Gale Crater and climb the mountain in its center.

Curiosity was the first full-scale astrobiology mission to Mars since the Viking Landers of 1976 (see page 188). It brought a formidable life sciences laboratory to the Martian surface that may eventually help resolve beyond serious doubt whether or not life ever existed in space. Having followed the water and found evidence of it, *Curiosity* now seeks to answer if Mars could have supported—or might still support—life. *Curiosity* has ten different instruments designed to help find the answer to this question, like the Alpha Particle X-Ray Spectrometer that measures chemical elements in the Martian soil, the Rover Environmental Monitoring Station that provides Martian weather reports, and the Radiation Assessment Detector that measures high-energy radiation.

Curiosity took a self-portrait at the "Big Sky" site on Mars's Mount Sharp.

NASA

NOVEMBER 27

ATLAS-CENTAUR ROCKET MAKES FIRST SUCCESSFUL LAUNCH

ROCKETS AND MISSILES

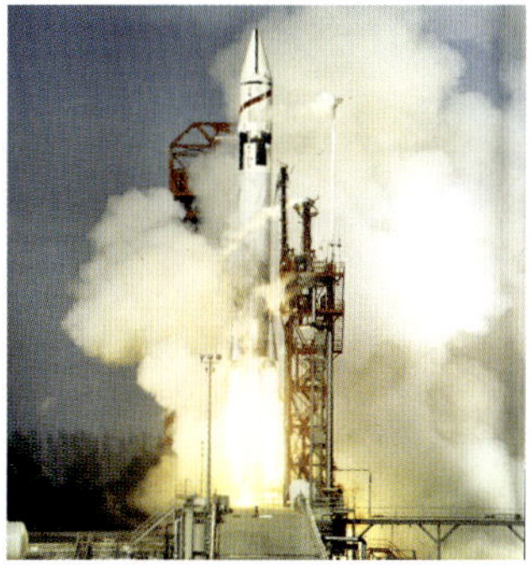

The first successful Centaur launch took place at Cape Canaveral's Launch Complex 36A.

NASA

On November 27, 1963, NASA successfully launched the first Atlas-Centaur rocket—an Atlas D with a powerful Centaur upper stage for putting satellites and probes into space. The space agency attempted its first Atlas-Centaur launch in May 1962, but the Centaur upper stage exploded after fifty-five seconds. NASA engineers got to work figuring out what went wrong and finally found success in November 1963. NASA proceeded to launch a number of spacecraft using Atlas-Centaurs, including missions in the Surveyor, Pioneer, and Voyager programs. Versions of the rocket are still used today.

NOVEMBER 28

RYAN X-13 VERTIJET MAKES FIRST TRANSITION FROM HORIZONTAL TO VERTICAL FLIGHT AND BACK AGAIN

VERTICAL FLIGHT

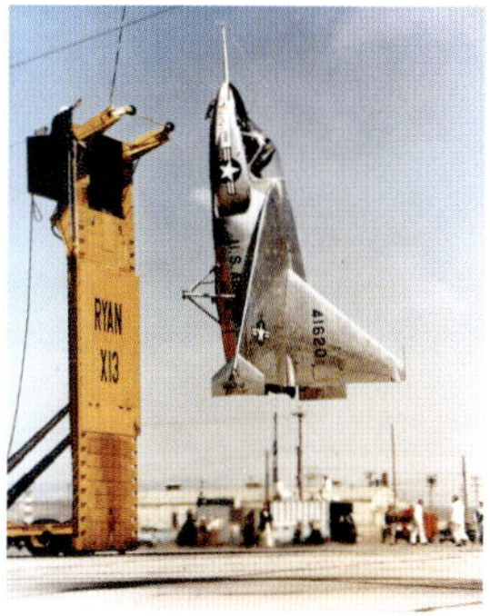

The Ryan X-13 Vertijet could take off vertically or horizontally.

U.S. Air Force

The Ryan X-13 Vertijet was an experimental vertical takeoff and landing (VTOL) aircraft. As its name implies, the Vertijet was designed to take off vertically and then transition into horizontal flight. Although vertical takeoff was its defining characteristic, the X-13 could also take off like a conventional airplane using a runway. On November 28, 1956, test pilot Pete Girard took off horizontally in the X-13, transitioned to a vertical hover, and then transitioned back to horizontal for landing.

RICHARD BYRD AND CREW COMPLETE FIRST FLIGHT OVER SOUTH POLE

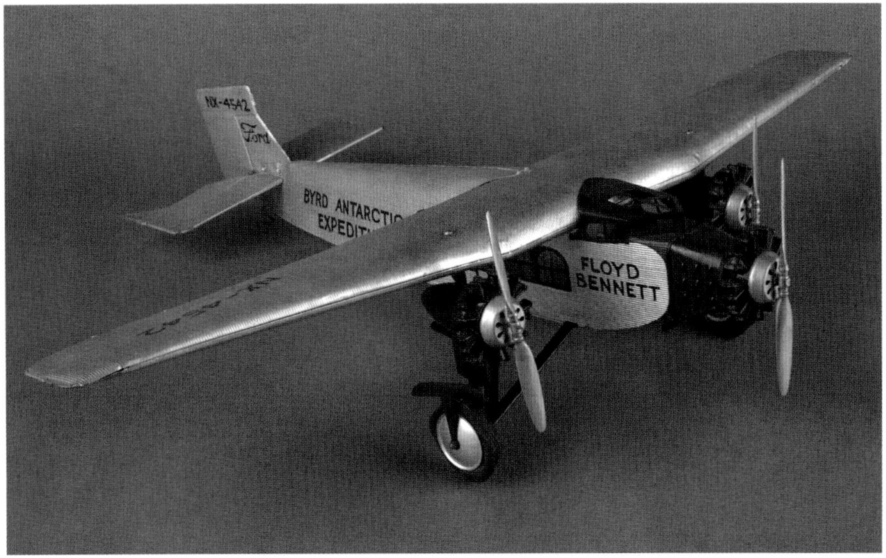

On November 29, 1929, pilot and explorer Richard E. Byrd became the first person to fly over the South Pole. Byrd's overflight of the pole took place during his first Antarctic expedition (1928–30), which was based at a camp called Little America on the Ross Ice Shelf.

After conducting various aerial mapping and reconnaissance missions in a modified Fairchild FC-2W2, Byrd, pilot Bernt Balchen, and two additional crew set out for their historic South Pole flight in a Ford 4-AT Tri-Motor nicknamed *Floyd Bennett*. Magnetic compasses do not work near the pole, so Byrd used a sun compass and his skill as a navigator to find it, and the crew flew extra miles on each side of the pole to account for any errors in navigation. Before heading back to base, Byrd dropped a small American flag onto the pole, securing his place in history.

Richard E. Byrd flew over the South Pole in the Ford 4-AT Tri-Motor *Floyd Bennett*. A 1/32 scale model replica of Byrd's aircraft is in the collection of the National Air and Space Museum.

Smithsonian's National Air and Space Museum

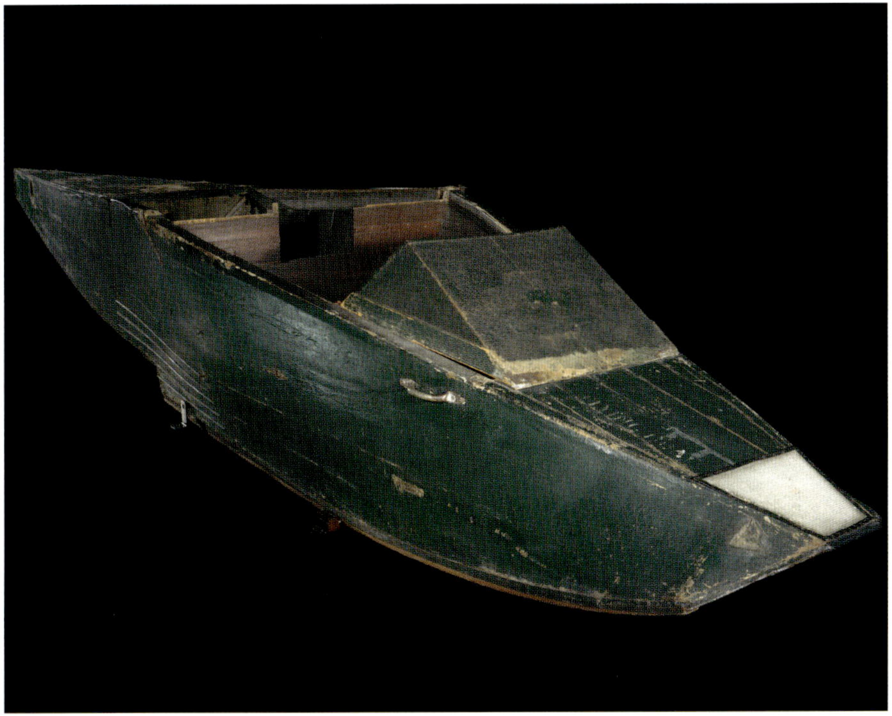

The hull of a Curtiss Model E flying boat is in the collection of the National Air and Space Museum.

Smithsonian's National Air and Space Museum

The first aircraft purchased by the U. S. Navy was a Curtiss Model E hydroaeroplane. Navy modifications to one of these Model Es made it a true flying boat—the entire fuselage being a hull as opposed to mounting the aircraft on a separate float—and it was redesignated as the C-1. On November 30, 1912, Lt. Theodore Ellyson began test flying the new C-1 at Hammondsport, New York.

Building on the C-1, the most successful version of the early Curtiss flying boats was the Model F (designated the C-2 by the Navy). Produced in far greater numbers than any other flying boat, the Model F replaced the flat-bottomed hull of the Model E with a more efficient V hull, which soon became a standard design feature of flying boats. The Model F was well received by U.S. military and civilian markets.

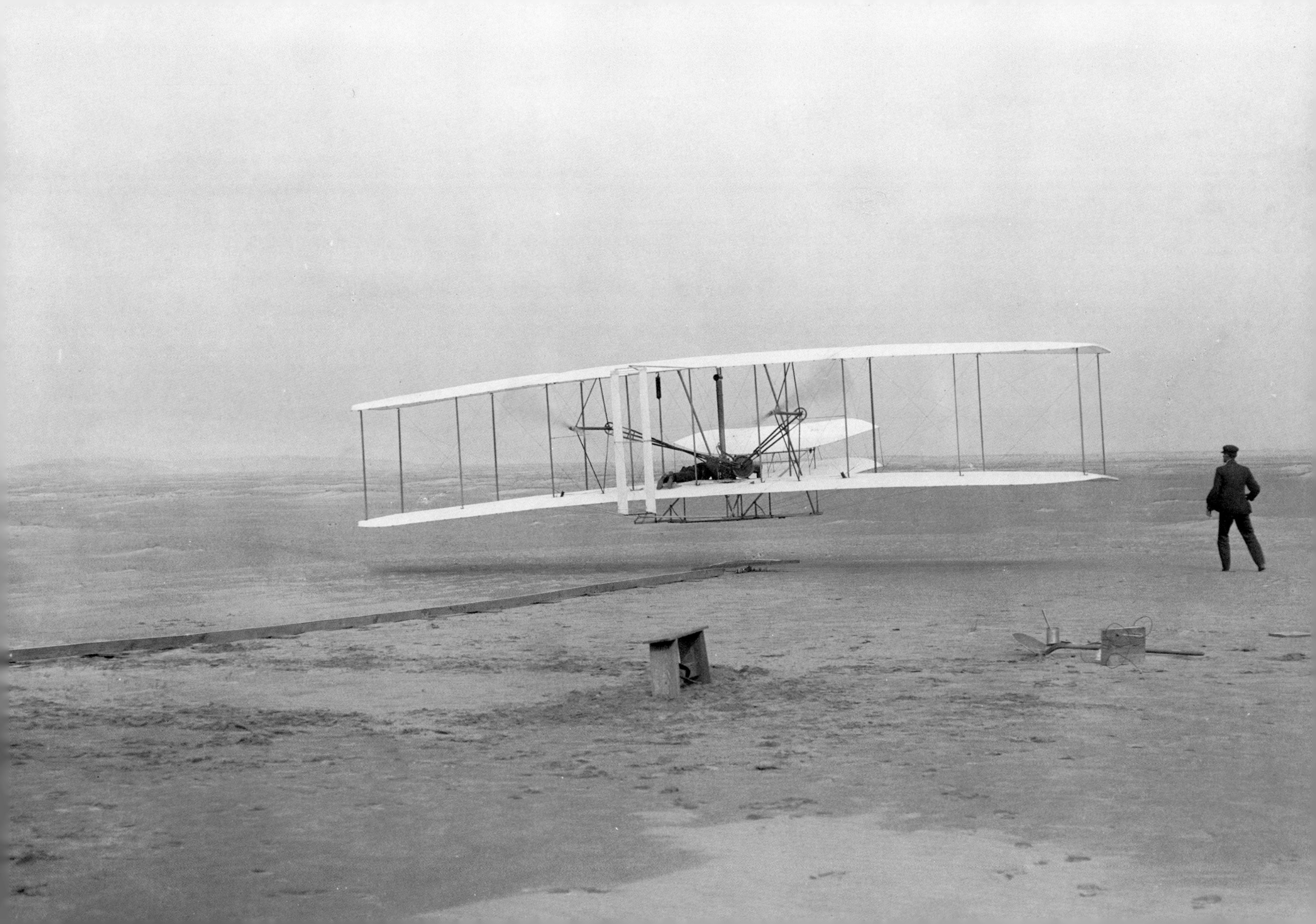

DECEMBER

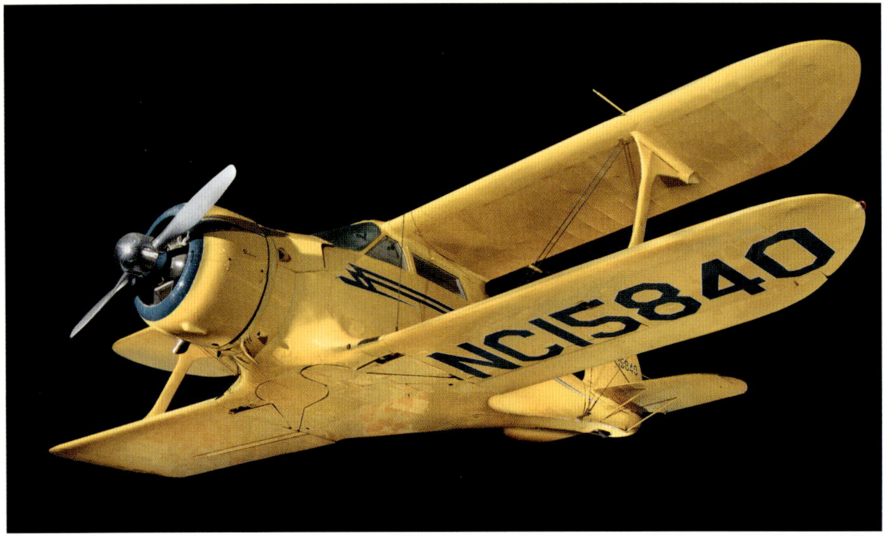

The Beechcraft C17L Staggerwing in the National Air and Space Museum collection was flown by Civil Air Patrol pilots on coastal patrols during World War II.

Smithsonian's National Air and Space Museum

The Civil Air Patrol (CAP) was established on December 1, 1941, to organize civilian aviators to help with air defense. The volunteer force was officially announced a week later after Japan's attack on Pearl Harbor (see page 357). Over the next several months, CAP pilots started picking up jobs including search and rescue, disaster recovery, medical flights, and border patrol. But CAP's biggest wartime job was coastal patrol.

CAP pilots conducted patrol flights along the East Coast of the United States looking for enemy U-boats and providing protective cover for merchant vessels carrying supplies. These CAP patrols freed up Army and Navy pilots to serve on the front lines. By the end of the war, CAP had flown over eighty-six thousand coastal patrol missions. The Civil Air Patrol still exists today as the Air Force's official civilian auxiliary. Its most robust program is for youth, promoting airmindedness and providing flight training scholarships.

FIRST HUBBLE SERVICING MISSION LAUNCHES

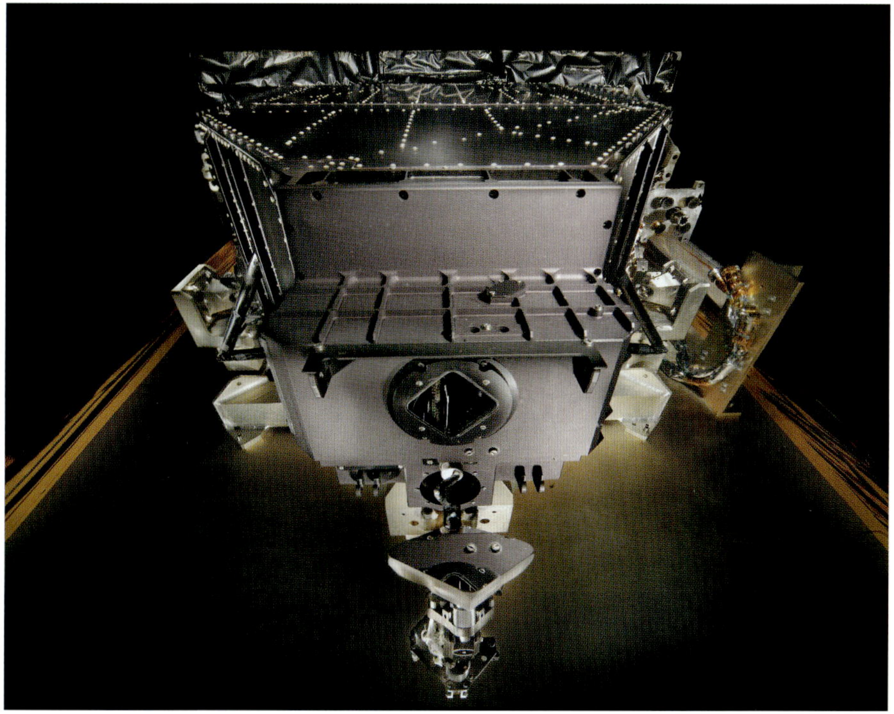

WFPC2, which was installed during the first Hubble servicing mission mission in 1993 and removed during the final Hubble servicing mission in 2009, is now in the collection of the National Air and Space Museum.

Smithsonian's National Air and Space Museum

Soon after the Hubble Space Telescope was launched in 1990 (see page 131), images and data from its instruments revealed that its main mirror was optically flawed. It suffered from a spherical aberration—not all portions of the mirror focused to the same point. The mirror's shape was off by less than 1/50th the thickness of a human hair, but this tiny flaw proved devastating to the quality of Hubble's images and to the efficiency of all of its instruments.

Luckily, Hubble was in low Earth orbit and was designed to be serviced by astronauts visiting it on Space Shuttle orbiters. On December 2, 1993, Space Shuttle *Endeavour* launched on STS-61, the first of five Hubble servicing missions. During the eleven-day mission, the crew conducted five back-to-back spacewalks, working in pairs of two, to repair the telescope. This included replacing the main camera with WFPC2 and installing the COSTAR instrument, which corrected the aberration on the primary mirror using five corrective mirrors.

MARTIN 162A *TADPOLE CLIPPER* MAKES ITS FIRST FLIGHT

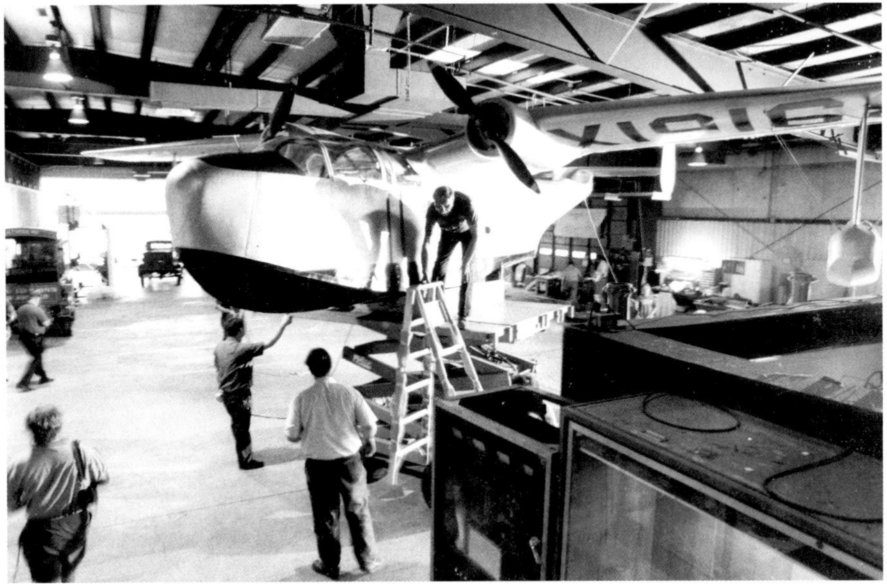

The Martin 162A *Tadpole Clipper* was made of fabric-covered spruce plywood and aluminum. It is now in the collection of the National Air and Space Museum.

Smithsonian's National Air and Space Museum

Also known as the Model 162, the Martin PBM Mariner was one of the most successful naval patrol aircraft of World War II. Manufactured by the Baltimore-based Glenn L. Martin Aircraft Company, the PBM incorporated several novel design elements, including a deep hull mounting a gull wing and an internal bomb bay that enabled higher speeds when the aircraft was loaded with ordnance. Before the Mariner took off for the first time in 1939, however, a 3/8-scale prototype model was flown nearly fifteen months earlier.

Nicknamed the *Tadpole Clipper*, the miniature Martin Model 162A took flight for the first time on December 3, 1937, with test pilot Edward Fennimore at the controls. The nearby Chesapeake Bay offered a wide variety of water conditions to test the scale aircraft's sea-handling qualities, which were essential to the full-size PBM's success as a maritime patrol bomber. While the *Tadpole Clipper* did not accumulate a significant amount of flight time over its useful life, it provided important data that helped engineers refine the hull design of the full-size PBM.

FRANK BORMAN AND JIM LOVELL LAUNCH ON GEMINI VII

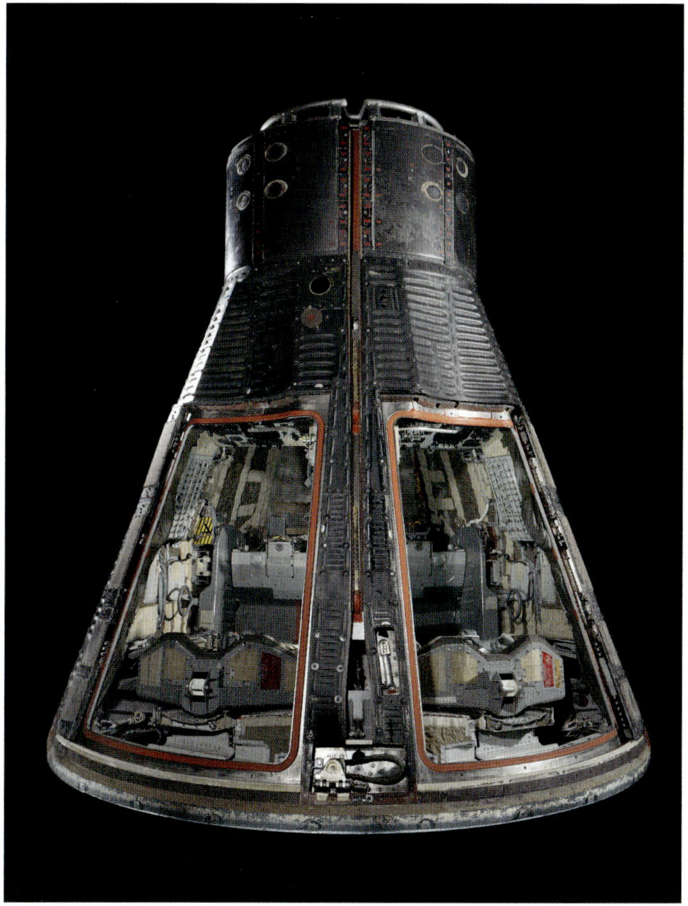

Astronauts Frank Borman and James "Jim" Lovell launched on Gemini VII on December 4, 1965. Their primary mission was to show that humans could live in weightlessness for fourteen days, a record that would stand until 1970. The astronauts each had just one small window to look out and endured experiments regarding food, waste, and sleep.

At 8,000 pounds, the Gemini VII spacecraft was also the heaviest spacecraft launched up to that point, in part because of the extra food and water supplies, but also because the capsule was retrofitted for a transponder to return the radar signal from Gemini VI-A. During the mission, Gemini VII served as the target vehicle for Gemini VI-A, crewed by Walter "Wally" Schirra and Thomas Stafford, who carried out the world's first space rendezvous on December 15. These two achievements were critical steps on the road to the Apollo lunar landing.

Frank Borman and Jim Lovell spent a historic fourteen days in the small Gemini VII spacecraft, on display at the National Air and Space Museum.

Smithsonian's National Air and Space Museum

DECEMBER 5

STAR WARS, BEATLES, AND MORE PLAYED AS WAKE-UP SONGS

HUMAN SPACEFLIGHT

During NASA's first human spaceflight programs, the space agency began a tradition of playing music as wake-up calls for the crews during missions. The songs played by Mission Control in Houston helped build camaraderie and raise the spirits of the astronauts on board the spacecraft. Here is a snapshot of wake-up calls from December 5 through the years:

- STS-27, 1988: *Star Wars* theme music with special satirical song by Darth Vader
- STS-53, 1992: Bagpipe medley by the Houston Highlanders Pipe Band
- STS-61, 1993: "With a Little Help from My Friends" by the Beatles
- STS-80, 1996: "Nobody Does it Better" by Carly Simon
- STS-88, 1998: "Anchors Aweigh" (fight song of the Naval Academy)
- STS-97, 2000: "Fight On" (University of Southern California fight song)
- STS-113, 2002: "Hotel California" by the Eagles

DECEMBER 6

UNITED STATES' FIRST SATELLITE LAUNCH ATTEMPT FAILS

SPACE SCIENCE

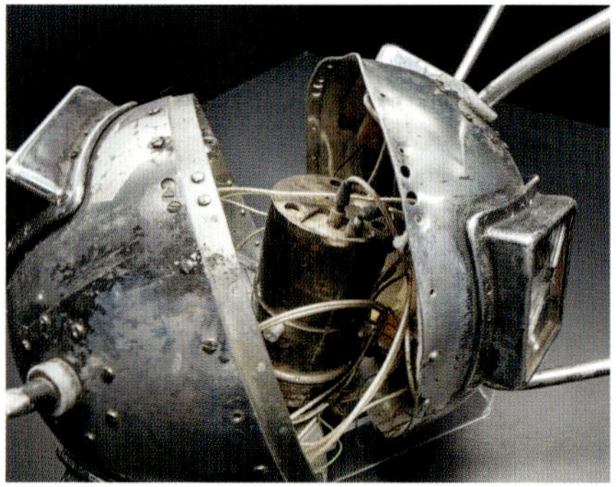

The damaged TV-3 satellite was recovered from the launchpad and is now in the National Air and Space Museum collection.

Smithsonian's National Air and Space Museum

On December 6, 1957, two months after the Soviet Union successfully placed Sputnik in orbit, the United States made its first satellite launch attempt. The Vanguard Test Vehicle-3 (TV-3) failed to reach orbit because its launch vehicle malfunctioned almost immediately after ignition and crashed back onto the launchpad. Newspapers around the world nicknamed the failed TV-3 satellite "Kaputnik," "Flopnik," and "Dudnik." Thankfully, the failure was short-lived, as the United States successfully placed Explorer 1 in orbit two months later (see page 44).

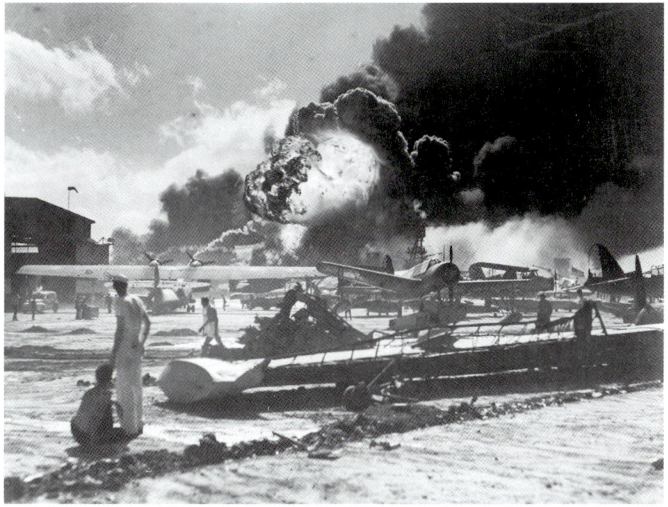

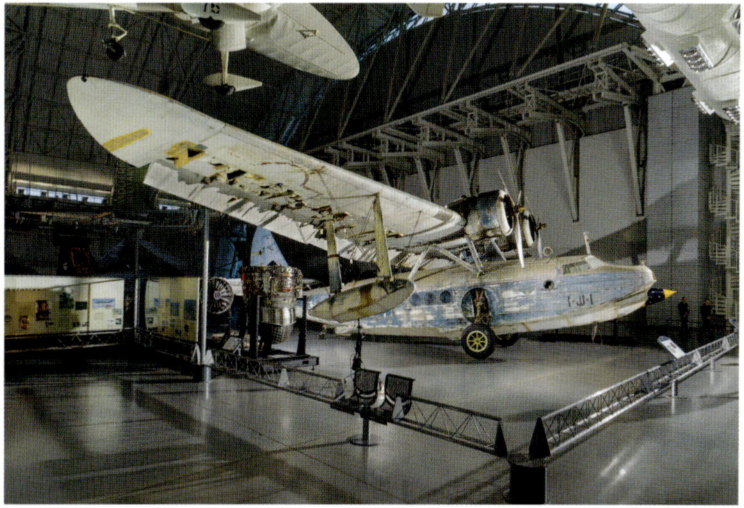

As famously stated by President Franklin D. Roosevelt, December 7, 1941, was "a date which will live in infamy." Recalling how the U.S. "was suddenly and deliberately attacked by naval and air forces of the Empire of Japan," Roosevelt delivered these words as the United States declared war on Japan.

The first wave of 183 Japanese torpedo bombers, dive bombers, and escort fighters attacked Pearl Harbor at 7:48 A.M. on December 7. Shortly before 9 A.M., a second wave of 171 aircraft struck the naval base and airfields. The impact of the attack was devastating: 2,403 Americans were killed, with another 1,143 wounded. The Japanese attack also destroyed 188 U.S. aircraft and sank or damaged all eight of the U.S. Navy's battleships at Pearl Harbor, including the USS *Arizona*; numerous other ships were sunk or damaged as well.

LEFT Service members at the Ford Island seaplane base could see the USS *Shaw* burn after it was hit.

National Archives and Records Administration

RIGHT A Sikorsky JRS-1 is the only survivor of the Japanese attack on Pearl Harbor in the National Air and Space Museum collection.

Smithsonian's National Air and Space Museum

LANGLEY AERODROME A CRASHES ON SECOND ATTEMPTED FLIGHT

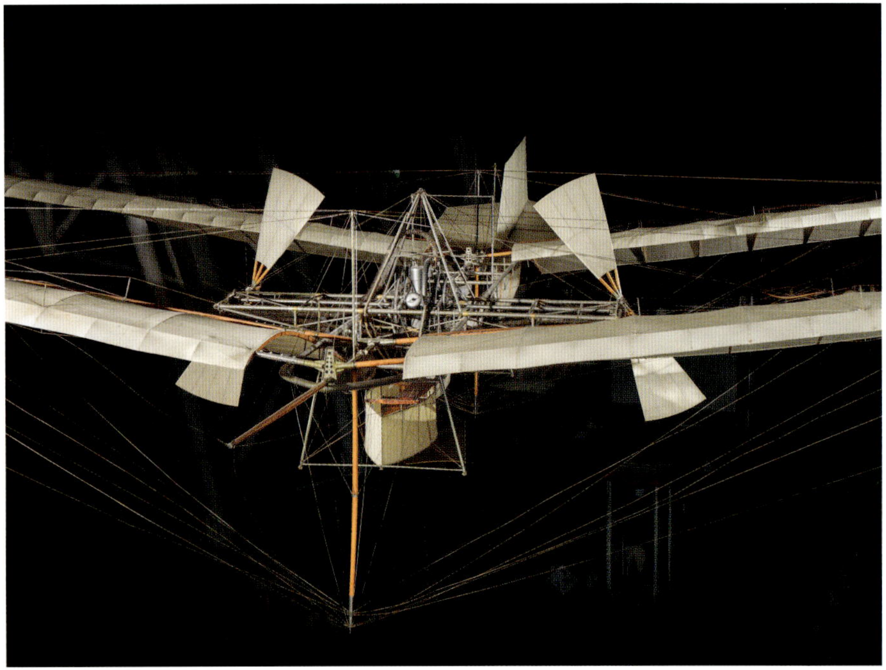

The restored Langley Aerodrome A is on display at the National Air and Space Museum's Steven F. Udvar-Hazy Center.

Smithsonian's National Air and Space Museum

Samuel Pierpont Langley was a leading scientific figure in the United States in the late nineteenth century well known for his astronomical research. Around the time that he was named third Secretary of the Smithsonian Institution in 1887, Langley became fascinated with heavier-than-air flight and began conducting aerodynamic research. Theoretical research gave way to practical experiments in the 1890s as Langley proceeded to build models for testing. Serious work on his first full-size aircraft began in 1898.

Langley made two attempts to catapult-launch his Aerodrome A from the roof of a houseboat on the Potomac River on October 7 and December 8, 1903. Aerodrome A was a scaled-up version of Langley's smaller, uncrewed Aerodromes 5 and 6. The craft was piloted by Langley's assistant, Charles Manly, on both flight attempts. Aerodrome A's structure could not withstand the launch force imposed by the spring-loaded catapult, and both flight attempts resulted in structural failure before the craft left the "launch pad."

BENJAMIN DAVIS JR. IS AWARDED HIS FOURTH STAR

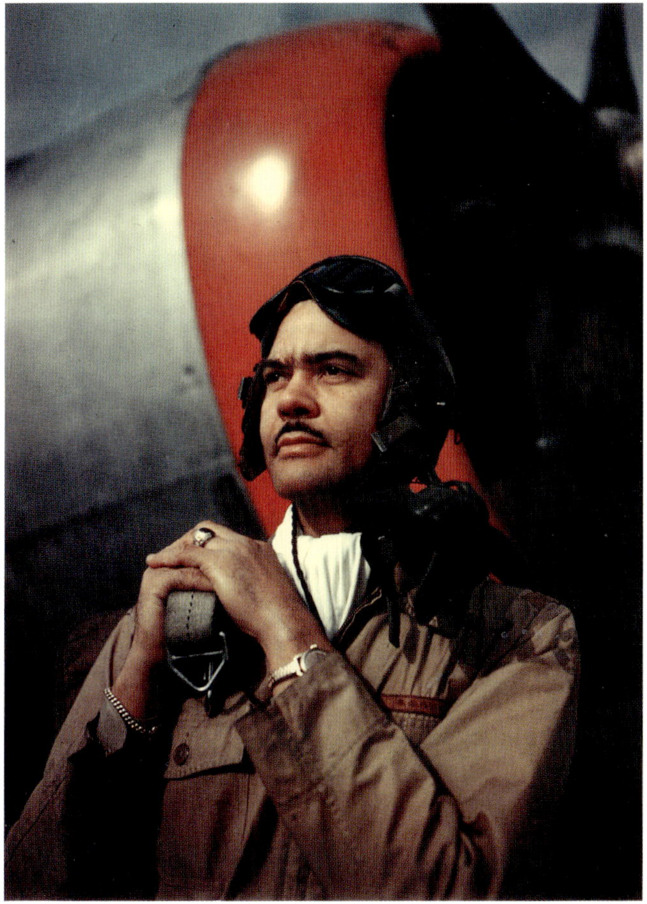

On December 9, 1998, Gen. Benjamin O. Davis Jr. received an honorary promotion to the rank of four-star general in a ceremony at the White House. During the event, President Bill Clinton referred to Davis as a "hero in war, a leader in peace, a pioneer for freedom, opportunity and basic human dignity."

The son of the U.S. Army's first Black brigadier general, Davis graduated from West Point in 1936 and played a major role in the formation and success of the Tuskegee Airmen. He was a member of the first class of cadets to earn their wings at Tuskegee Army Airfield in 1942 and would command each of the units of Black aviators at various times during World War II.

In July 1942, Davis was selected to lead the new 99th Pursuit Squadron, the Army Air Corps' first all-Black air unit. From 1943 to 1945, he led the 332nd Fighter Group, which escorted American bombers and conducted ground attack missions over the Mediterranean and central European theaters, before taking command of the 477th Bombardment Group in 1945. After the war, Davis continued his military career in the newly independent and integrated United States Air Force, becoming the new branch's first Black general.

Benjamin O. Davis Jr. led the Tuskegee Airmen during World War II.

Smithsonian's National Air and Space Museum (NASM 2004-55822)

DECEMBER 10

JOHN STAPP SETS SPEED RECORD IN ROCKET SLED

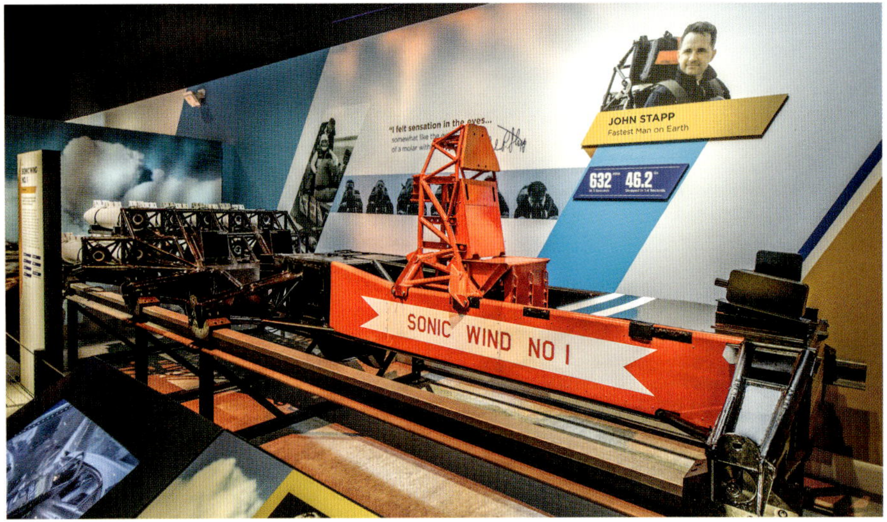

ABOVE The Sonic Wind 1 rocket sled is on display at the National Air and Space Museum.

Smithsonian's National Air and Space Museum

OPPOSITE PAGE John Stapp's rocket sled tests explored the impact of acceleration and deceleration on the human body.

Smithsonian's National Air and Space Museum (NASM 89-4491)

U.S. Air Force flight surgeon Col. John Stapp strapped into the Sonic Wind No. 1 rocket sled for the final time on December 10, 1954. His test rides on the rocket sled at Holloman Air Force Base in New Mexico were part of his research to explore human responses to acceleration, deceleration, and windblast. With new technological advancements in high-speed flight on the horizon, Stapp pushed the limits of the human body at high speeds to improve pilot safety, especially in cases of ejection from disabled aircraft.

On Stapp's final test ride, the rocket sled let loose 40,000 pounds of thrust, propelling the flight surgeon more than 3,000 feet in a few seconds. He came to a stop just as fast and was subjected to a force forty-six times that of gravity (46 gs). Although bruised and badly shaken, Stapp survived without permanent injury and walked away with the world land speed record: 632 miles per hour. He became an international sensation, appearing on magazine covers and TV shows.

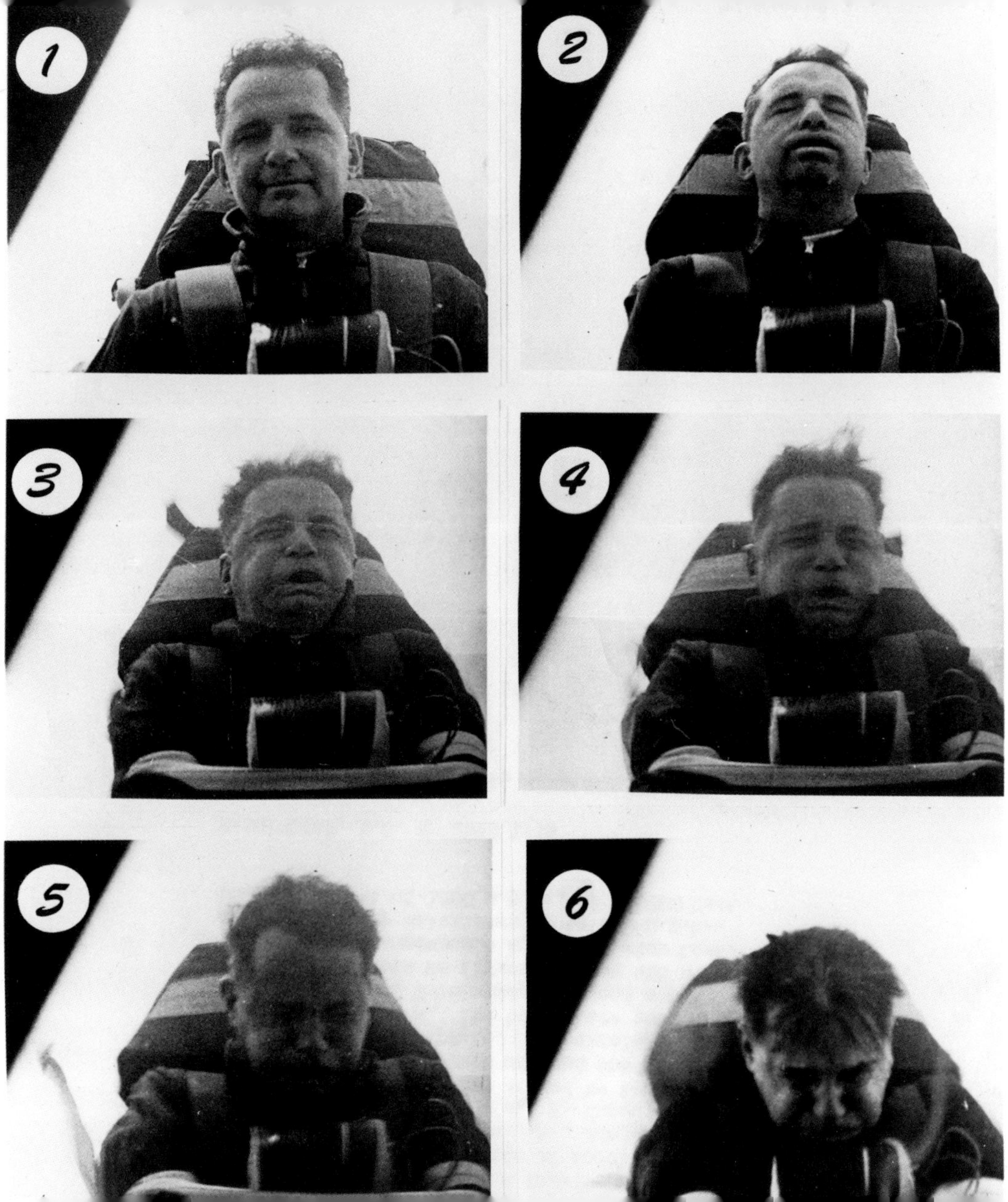
1
2
3
4
5
6

KAMAN K-225 HELICOPTER FLIES WITH BOEING 502-2 ENGINE

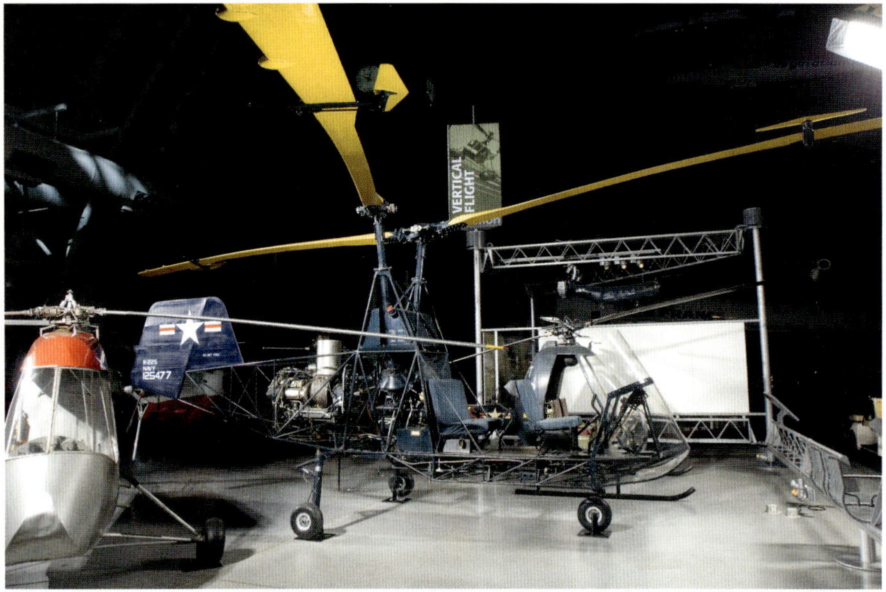

The Kaman K-225 on display at the Steven F. Udvar-Hazy Center was the first helicopter to fly with a gas turbine engine.

Smithsonian's National Air and Space Museum

The Kaman K-225 experimental helicopter was on the verge of fading into distant memory when engineer Charles Kaman accepted a challenge from his Navy colleagues to develop a gas turbine-powered helicopter. Kaman quickly found a naval gas turbine engine, the 175-horsepower Boeing 502-2, to replace the 220-horsepower Lycoming O-435-A2 reciprocating engine that previously powered the K-225.

The first flight of the K-225 with the Boeing engine took place on December 11, 1951, and was a dramatic success. Even though the new turbine engine produced less power than the original reciprocating model, its weight was reduced by more than half and it did not require a heavy cooling fan or clutch assemblies. As a result, the K-225 performed better with the new engine than it ever had before. Kaman's aircraft also made history as the first helicopter to fly with a gas turbine-driven transmission.

APOLLO 17 CREW REPAIR LUNAR ROVER WITH DUCT TAPE

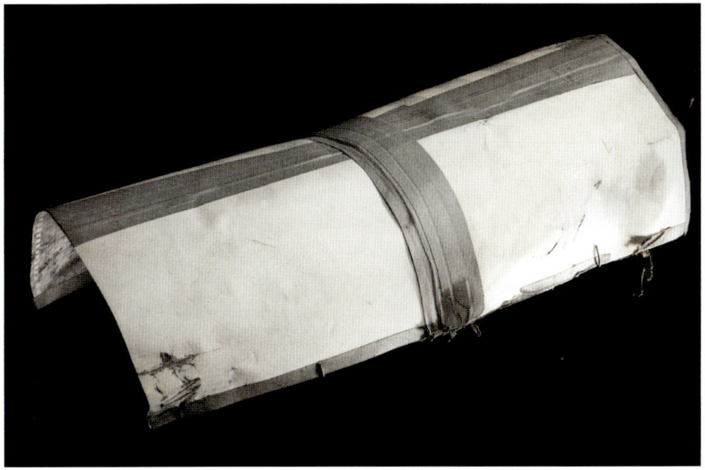

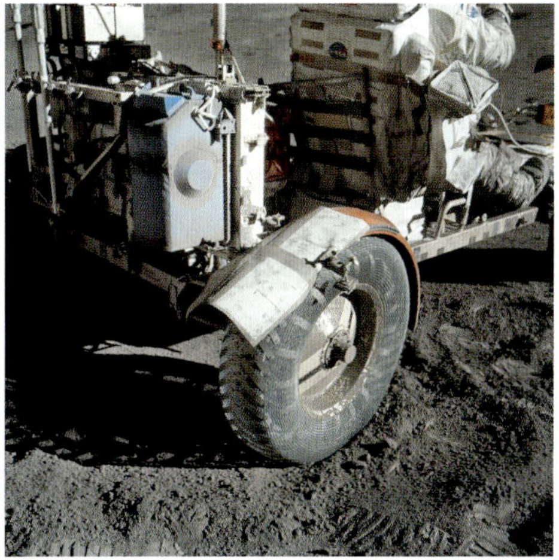

At the end of Eugene Cernan and Harrison Schmitt's first moonwalk of the Apollo 17 mission, the fender extension on the back right tire of the Lunar Roving Vehicle (LRV) came off. Driving the LRV without it caused massive "rooster tails," as the astronauts called them, spreading lunar dust all over their instruments and suits and into every nook and cranny. Between moonwalks, Mission Control back on Earth came up with a solution; they were challenged to devise a replacement fender with only the materials that the astronauts had with them on the Moon.

Their solution was to use duct tape (or as Cernan would later call it, good old-fashioned American gray tape) to connect four of the twenty-eight lunar maps the crew had on board the lunar module. The next day, on December 12, 1972, the astronauts constructed and installed the new fender extension, and it worked. The LRV was back in action, allowing the astronauts to drive another day.

LEFT The makeshift fender extension created by the Apollo 17 astronauts was brought back to Earth and is on display at the National Air and Space Museum.

Smithsonian's National Air and Space Museum

RIGHT The Apollo 17 moonwalkers made a makeshift fender extension out of duct tape and maps.

NASA

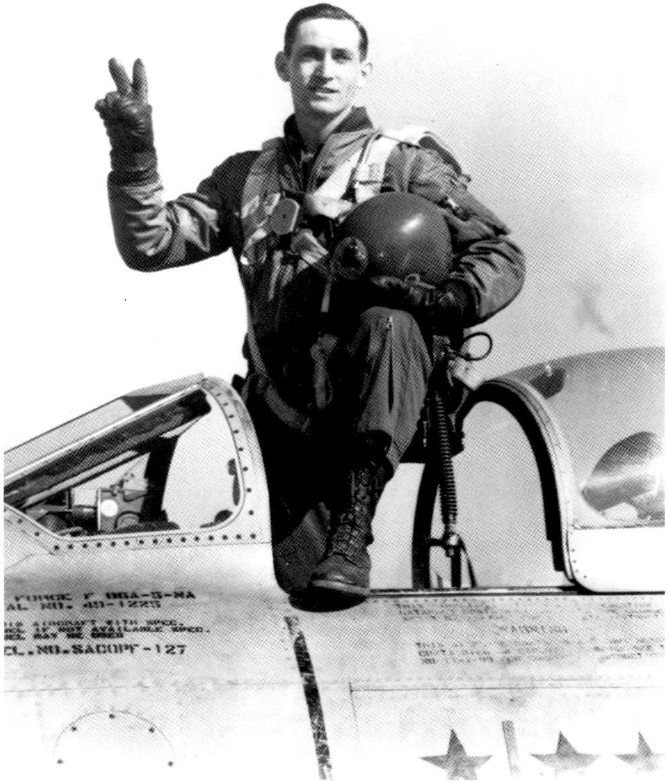

U.S. Air Force Lt. Col. George Davis was one of the highest-scoring American aces of the Korean War, downing fourteen enemy aircraft in less than six months. At the time of his death in February 1952, Davis was the leading American ace of the war.

Four of Davis's victories came during a pair of air battles on December 13, 1951. Davis was leading his unit on a fighter sweep through MiG Alley when the patrol spotted two MiG-15 fighters from the Soviet air force. During the ensuing dogfight, Davis shot down two MiGs, his ninth and tenth victories of the war. These victories made Davis a Korean War double ace.

Later that day, Davis and his unit once again encountered MiG-15s, this time from the Chinese air force. Davis downed two of the aircraft, bringing his aerial victory count for the day up to four. Despite his skill as a fighter pilot, Davis was killed during an aerial battle in which he claimed another two victories. He was posthumously awarded the Medal of Honor for his actions.

Lt. Col. George Davis achieved double ace status in both the Korean War (pictured) and World War II.

U.S. Air Force

DECEMBER 14

LAST HUMANS TO SET FOOT ON THE MOON DEPART THE LUNAR SURFACE

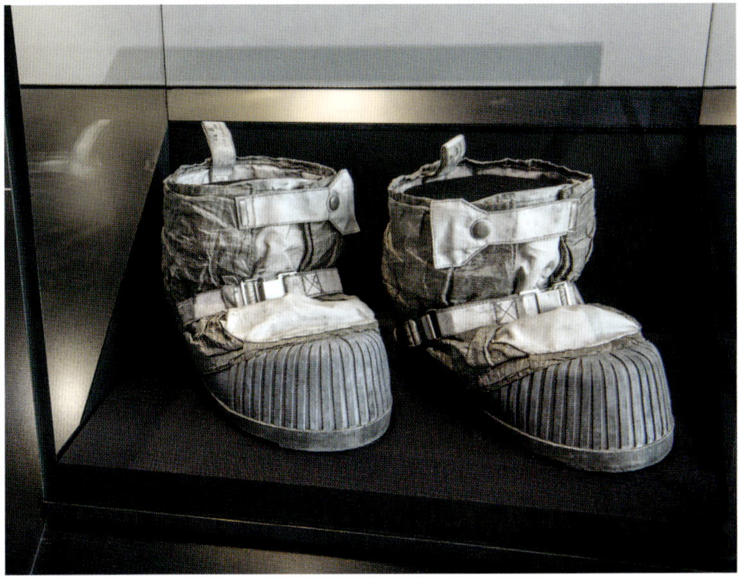

The Moon boots that made the last footprints on the lunar surface are on display at the National Air and Space Museum.

Smithsonian's National Air and Space Museum

The upper stage of the Apollo 17 lunar module *Challenger* departed the Moon on December 14, 1972, with Eugene Cernan and Harrison Schmitt, the last astronauts to walk on the Moon (so far!). Apollo 17 was the sixth and final Apollo mission to land people on the Moon. Compared to previous missions, the Apollo 17 astronauts traversed the greatest distance using the Lunar Roving Vehicle and returned the greatest number of rock and soil samples. Apollo 17 also has the distinction of being the only Apollo mission to carry a trained geologist to walk on the lunar surface: lunar module pilot Schmitt.

Apollo 17 was unique because it was the only Apollo mission that brought the astronauts' Moon boots back to Earth. On previous missions, the boots were left on the Moon to reduce weight in the lunar module for liftoff. In this case, the lunar overshoes that made humanity's final footprints on the Moon returned to Earth and joined the collection of the National Air and Space Museum.

"And, as we leave the Moon at Taurus-Littrow, we leave as we came and, God willing, as we shall return: with peace and hope for all mankind. Godspeed the crew of Apollo 17."

—EUGENE CERNAN

GEMINI VI CREW PLAYS "JINGLE BELLS" IN SPACE

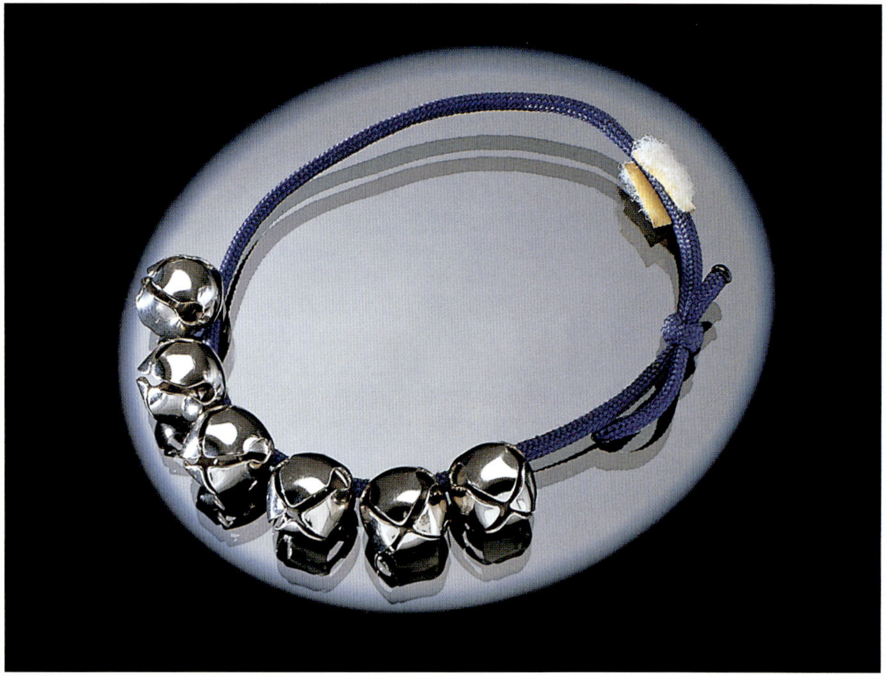

Tom Stafford played a set of bells, now in the collection of the National Air and Space Museum, during the Gemini VI mission in December 1965.

Smithsonian's National Air and Space Museum

On December 15, 1965, during the Gemini VI mission, astronauts Walter "Wally" Schirra and Thomas Stafford treated listeners back home to the first musical interlude from space. Just before Gemini VI reentered Earth's atmosphere, Stafford made a radio transmission: "We have an object, looks like a satellite going from north to south, probably in polar orbit . . . very low, looks like he might be going to reenter soon . . . Standby one, you might just let me try to pick up that thing."

At that point, the sound of a tiny harmonica, accompanied by small sleigh bells, could be heard playing "Jingle Bells." Schirra played the harmonica, while Stafford jingled the bells. According to Stafford, Schirra came up with the idea: "He could play the harmonica, and we practiced two or three times before we took off, but of course we didn't tell the guys on the ground. We never considered singing, since I couldn't carry a tune in a bushel basket," Stafford said.

DECEMBER 16

PAN AM BOEING 314 DEPARTS AUCKLAND FOR SECOND HALF OF ROUND-THE-WORLD FLIGHT

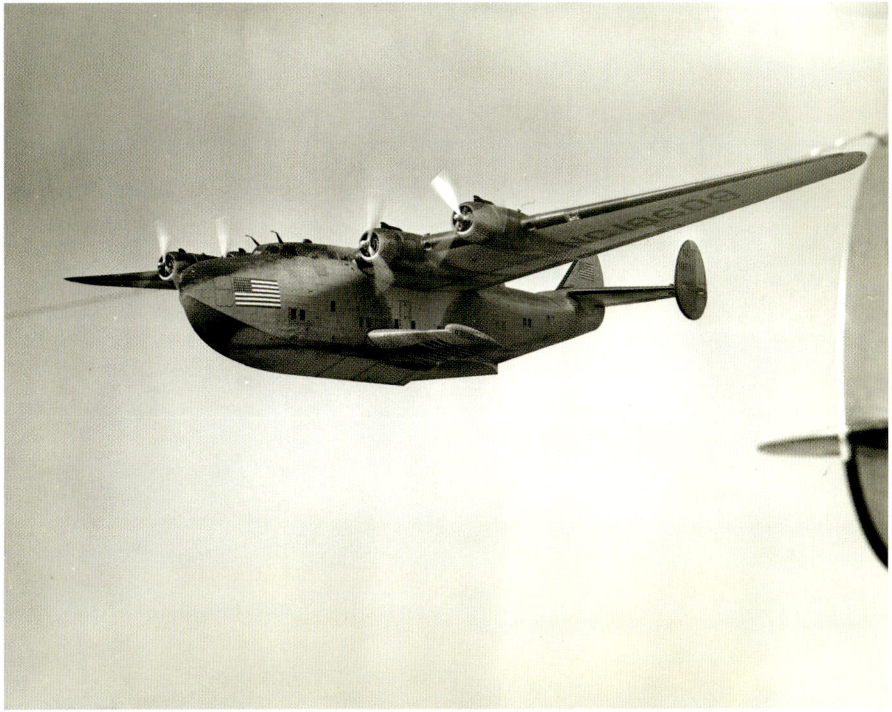

The *Pacific Clipper* flew from New Zealand to New York in December 1941 and January 1942.

Smithsonian's National Air and Space Museum (NASM 75-221)

Pan American Airways' Boeing 314 flying boat *Pacific Clipper* was six days from its home port of San Francisco when the Japanese attacked the U.S. fleet at Pearl Harbor in December 1941 (see page 357). The crew of ten learned of the attack as they were preparing to take off in Auckland, New Zealand. With Pan Am facilities across the Pacific under assault, how was *Pacific Clipper* to get home? The solution: return to the U.S. by flying westward instead of east as originally planned. On their own for gasoline and supplies, the crew would have to fly over unfamiliar land and water.

Pacific Clipper took off from Auckland on December 16, 1941, heading west for Australia and then across 1,400 miles of open ocean to the Dutch East Indies (present-day Indonesia). The rest of their flight required careful navigation as the crew flew across Asia, the Middle East, and Africa. After 209 flying hours and 31,500 miles, the *Pacific Clipper* arrived back in the U.S. at the Marine Air Terminal on Long Island, New York, on January 6, 1942. The successful trip marked the first around-the-world flight by a commercial airliner.

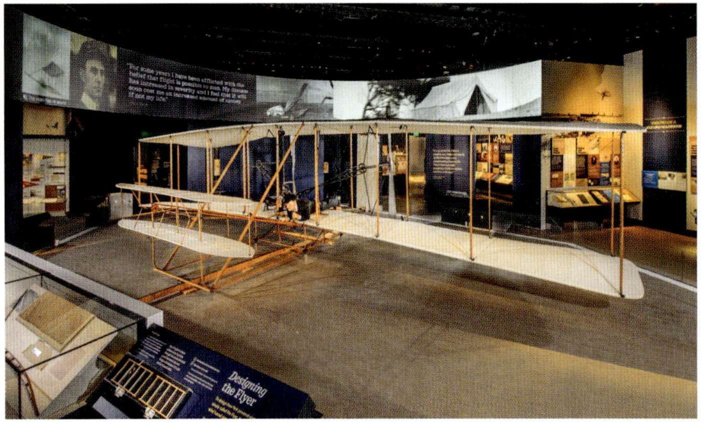

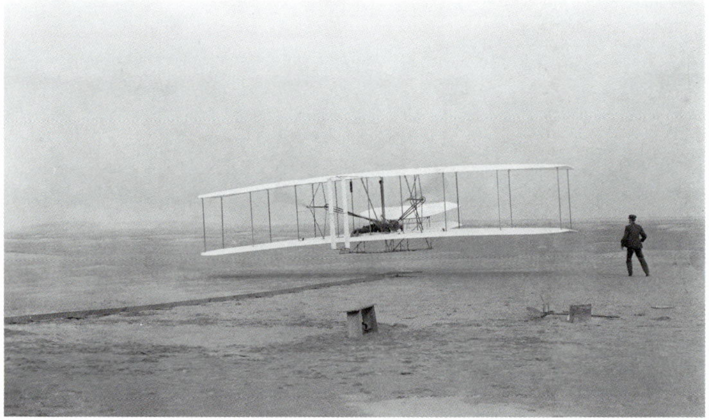

On December 17, 1903, Wilbur and Orville Wright inaugurated the aerial age with the world's first successful flights of a powered airplane. That day, the Wright Flyer became the first powered, heavier-than-air machine to achieve controlled, sustained flight with a pilot. The revolutionary aircraft was the product of a sophisticated four-year program of research and development conducted by the Wright brothers beginning in 1899.

After building and testing three full-size gliders, Orville piloted the Wrights' first powered airplane near Kitty Hawk, North Carolina, making a twelve-second flight and traveling 120 feet. The best flight of the day covered 852 feet in fifty-nine seconds with Wilbur at the controls. The Wrights pioneered many of the basic tenets and techniques of modern aeronautical engineering, such as the use of a wind tunnel and flight testing as design tools.

LEFT The original 1903 Wright Flyer is on display at the National Air and Space Museum.

Smithsonian's National Air and Space Museum

RIGHT John T. Daniels captured Orville Wright making the first flight of a powered airplane in December 1903.

Smithsonian's National Air and Space Museum (NASM 2003-3463)

DECEMBER 18

SCORE SATELLITE LAUNCHES

CIVILIAN APPLICATIONS SATELLITES

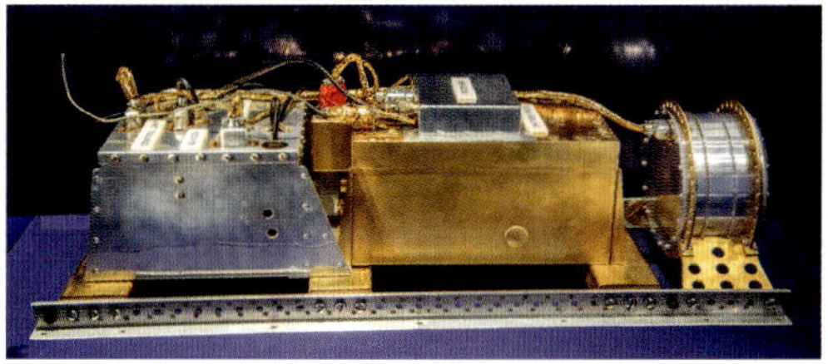

A SCORE satellite backup is on display at the National Air and Space Museum.

Smithsonian's National Air and Space Museum

The first communications satellite, SCORE (Signal Communications by Orbital Relay Equipment), launched aboard an Atlas missile on December 18, 1958. SCORE, which was developed by the U.S. Army Signal Corps, operated for thirty-five days. It proved that satellites could receive signals from one location on Earth and immediately retransmit to another. Its practical application was proven when President Dwight Eisenhower presented a Christmas message of goodwill and peace that was beamed to countries around the world through SCORE.

DECEMBER 19

CHARLES AND ANNE MORROW LINDBERGH COMPLETE 1933 SURVEY FLIGHT

PIONEERS OF FLIGHT

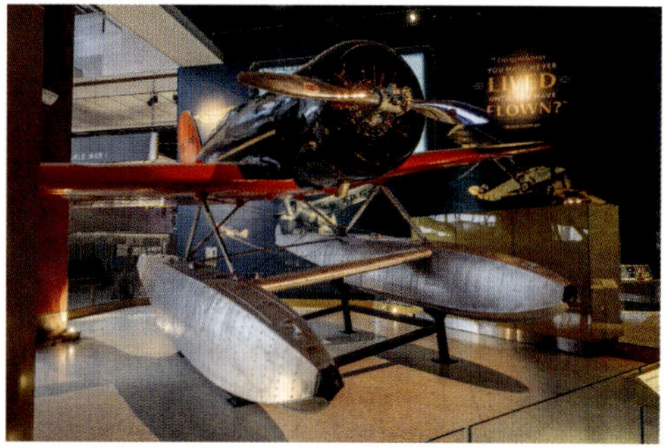

Charles and Anne Morrow Lindbergh flew the Lockheed Sirius *Tingmissartoq* on their 1933 survey flight.

Smithsonian's National Air and Space Museum

In 1931 and 1933, Charles Lindbergh and his wife, Anne Morrow Lindbergh, embarked on two lengthy trips over vast expanses of water and uncharted territory. Their objective was to explore possible air routes across the Atlantic for a cooperative study between Pan American Airways and four other commercial airlines. As Pan Am's technical advisor, Charles was assigned the task of surveying a route from Newfoundland to Europe. The Lindberghs completed their second survey flight on December 19, 1933, providing invaluable information in the pioneering days of international air travel.

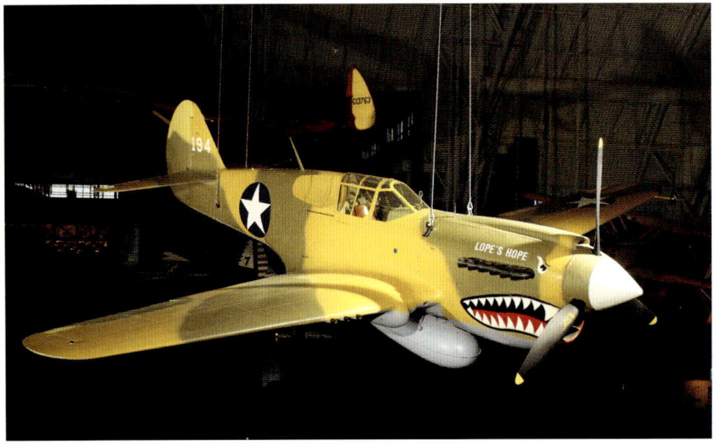

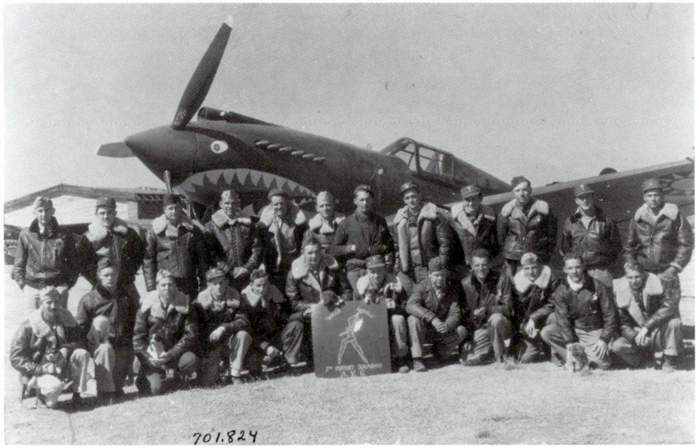

The American Volunteer Group (AVG) was formed in 1941 as part of the Republic of China Air Force to help oppose the Japanese invasion of China. The AVG consisted of pilots and ground crew from the U.S. Army Air Corps, the U.S. Navy, and the U.S. Marine Corps. Recruitment for the AVG began in early 1941, but the Flying Tigers didn't fly their first mission until December 20, 1941, some two weeks after the U.S. entered World War II.

In less than seven months of action, AVG pilots destroyed about 115 Japanese aircraft and lost only eleven planes in air-to-air combat. The AVG disbanded on July 4, 1942, and its assets, including a few pilots, became part of the U.S. Army Air Forces 23rd Fighter Group in the newly activated 14th Air Force. By war's end, the 23rd FG was one of the highest-scoring Army fighter groups.

LEFT The Flying Tigers got their name from the ferocious fangs painted on the nose of their Curtiss P-40s, like the one on display at the Steven F. Udvar-Hazy Center.

Smithsonian's National Air and Space Museum

RIGHT The American Volunteer Group was part of the Republic of China Air Force.

Smithsonian's National Air and Space Museum (NASM 83-4560)

FIVE AIRCRAFT DEPART ON PAN-AMERICAN GOODWILL FLIGHT

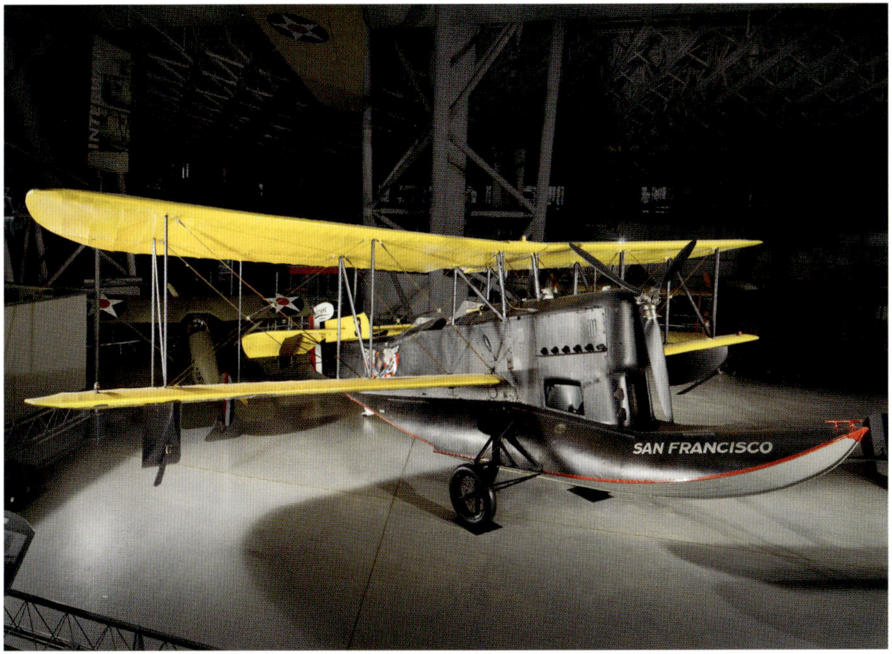

The airplanes used in the Pan-American Goodwill Flight, including the Loening OA-1A *San Francisco* on display at the Steven F. Udvar-Hazy Center, were amphibious aircraft that could operate on land or water.

Smithsonian's National Air and Space Museum

On December 21, 1926, ten pilots departed San Antonio, Texas, in five Loening OA-1A amphibian aircraft for the historic Pan-American Goodwill Flight of 1926 and 1927. The flight through Mexico and Central and South America was intended to improve relations with Latin American countries, encourage commercial aviation, and provide valuable training for U.S. Air Corps personnel. To stimulate public interest, each airplane was named after a major U.S. city: the *New York*, the *San Antonio*, the *San Francisco*, the *Detroit*, and the *St. Louis*.

The journey took 133 days to complete: fifty-nine flying days plus seventy-four days for maintenance, diplomatic meetings, and ceremonies. President Calvin Coolidge greeted the flyers at the conclusion of their trip in Washington, D.C., on May 2, 1927. Although it was eclipsed by Lindbergh's solo transatlantic flight a few weeks later (see page 155), the Goodwill Flight helped pioneer a trail for commercial air transport. When Pan American Airways began South American air service two years later, the company selected its stations in a pattern closely following the route of the Goodwill Flight.

LOCKHEED SR-71 BLACKBIRD FLIES FOR THE FIRST TIME

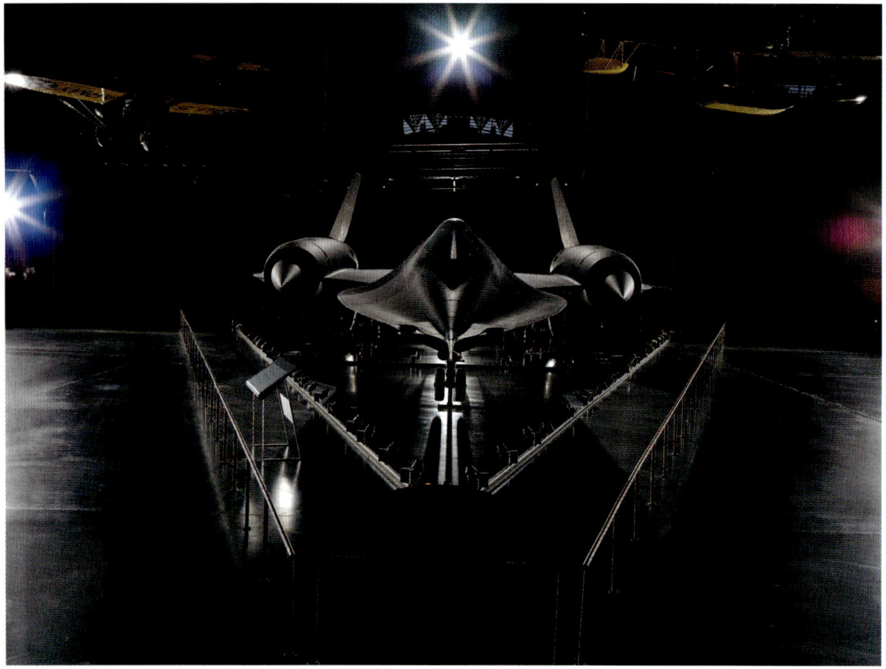

The SR-71 on display at the Steven F. Udvar-Hazy Center accrued some 2,800 hours of flight time during twenty-four years of active service with the U.S. Air Force.

Smithsonian's National Air and Space Museum

No reconnaissance aircraft in history has operated in more hostile airspace or with such complete impunity as the Lockheed SR-71 Blackbird. Flown for the first time on December 22, 1964, the SR-71 is the fastest aircraft propelled by air-breathing engines. The aircraft was designed at Lockheed's Skunk Works by a team led by Clarence "Kelly" Johnson (see page 72) and played a key role in Cold War intelligence gathering for the U.S. Air Force over more than thirty years.

Capable of operating at a maximum speed of Mach 3.3 at an altitude of 85,000 feet, the Blackbird could survey up to 100,000 square miles of territory in a single hour. While stealth features in its design reduced the SR-71's radar signature, the aircraft could also simply accelerate and outfly any surface-to-air missiles fired at it. The SR-71 delivered photographs and other intelligence to U.S. decision-makers at all levels—from military commanders to the White House. If there was a geopolitical crisis between 1968 and 1989, chances are there were Blackbirds flying overhead.

RUTAN VOYAGER COMPLETES FIRST NONSTOP NON-REFUELED FLIGHT AROUND THE WORLD

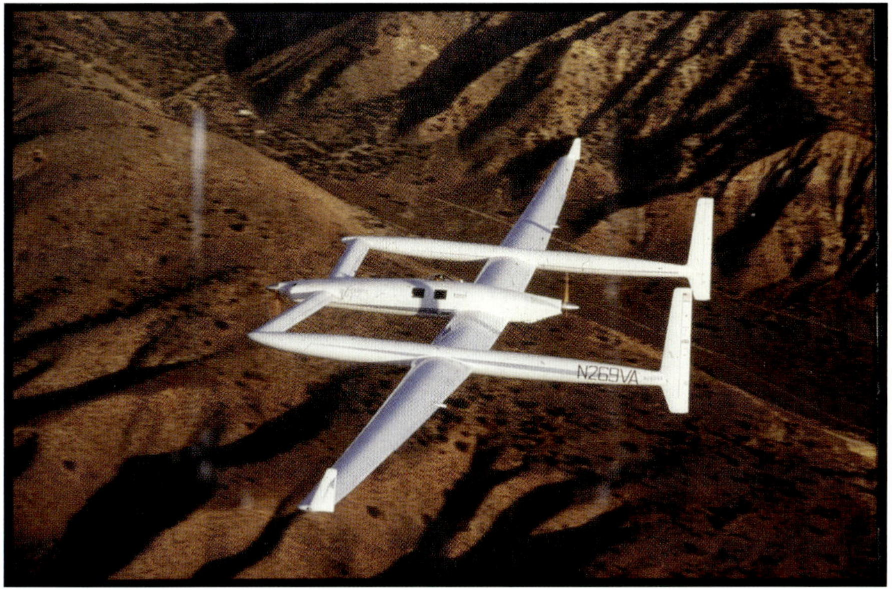

The Rutan Voyager had a wingspan of over 110 feet.

Smithsonian's National Air and Space Museum (NASM 9A16146)

In 1986, the Rutan Voyager demonstrated the strength and efficiency of an all-composite airframe by flying nonstop around the world without refueling. Piloted by Richard "Dick" Rutan and Jeana Yeager, Voyager made the round-the-world flight in just over nine days, completing its journey at Edwards Air Force Base on December 23, 1986.

Aerospace engineer Elbert "Burt" Rutan designed Voyager for maximum fuel efficiency, constructing the aircraft almost entirely from lightweight graphite-honeycomb composite materials. To carry enough fuel for its 25,000-mile journey, Voyager had eight storage tanks on each side of the airplane and a fuel tank in the center, for a total of seventeen tanks. The pilots shifted fuel from tank to tank during the flight to keep the airplane in balance. The 7,000 pounds of fuel aboard at takeoff amounted to nearly 75 percent of Voyager's gross weight, and by the end of the flight, only 106 pounds of fuel remained.

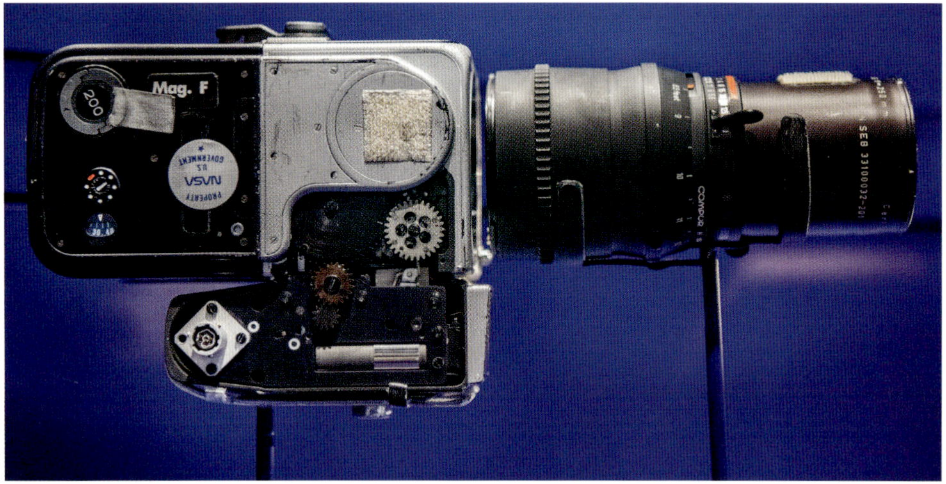

LEFT The camera Bill Anders used to take the Earthrise photo is on display at the National Air and Space Museum.

Smithsonian's National Air and Space Museum

OPPOSITE PAGE Anders took the famous Earthrise photo using a Hasselblad camera.

NASA

In December 1968, all eyes were on the Moon as NASA's Apollo 8 mission took the first astronauts to lunar orbit. While the crew, astronauts Frank Borman, James "Jim" Lovell, and William "Bill" Anders, did not land on the Moon's surface, the flight was an important prelude to a lunar landing, testing the flight trajectory and operations getting there and back.

On December 24, 1968, the Apollo 8 crew delivered a moving TV broadcast to a world audience from lunar orbit, during which they read the first ten verses of the Book of Genesis. That same day, Anders took one of the most iconic photographs of all time when the crew saw Earth rising from behind the Moon's horizon. The image captured the attention of the world when it was published in newspapers globally and provided a new perspective on our home planet. For the fiftieth anniversary of Apollo 8 in 2018, the International Astronomical Union named two of the lunar craters appearing in the Earthrise photo "Anders' Earthrise" and "Eight Homeward."

"Look at that picture over there! There's the Earth coming up. Wow, is that pretty!"

—APOLLO 8 ASTRONAUT BILL ANDERS

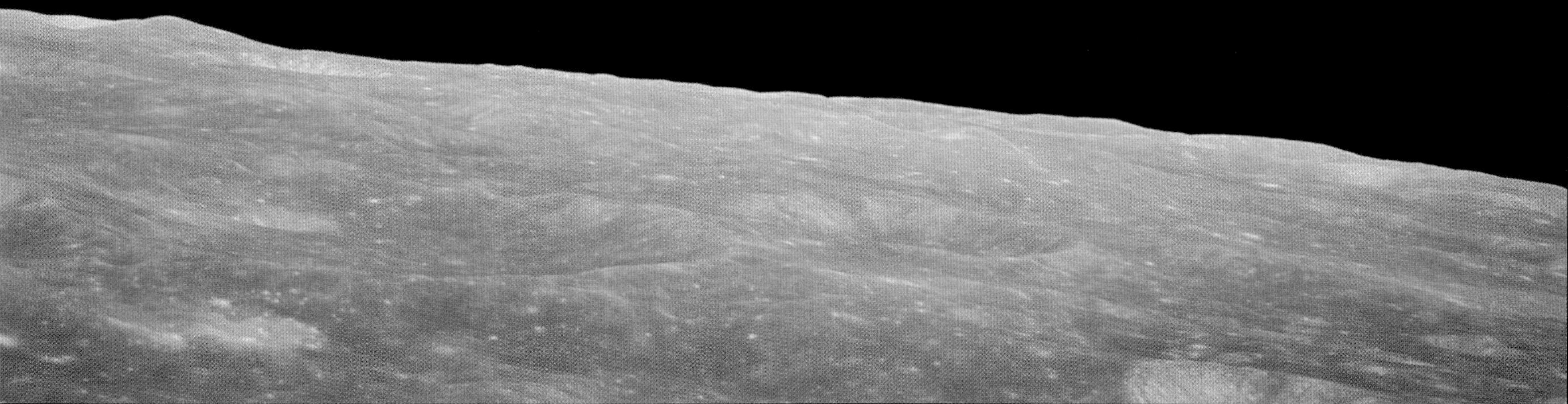

JAMES WEBB SPACE TELESCOPE LAUNCHES

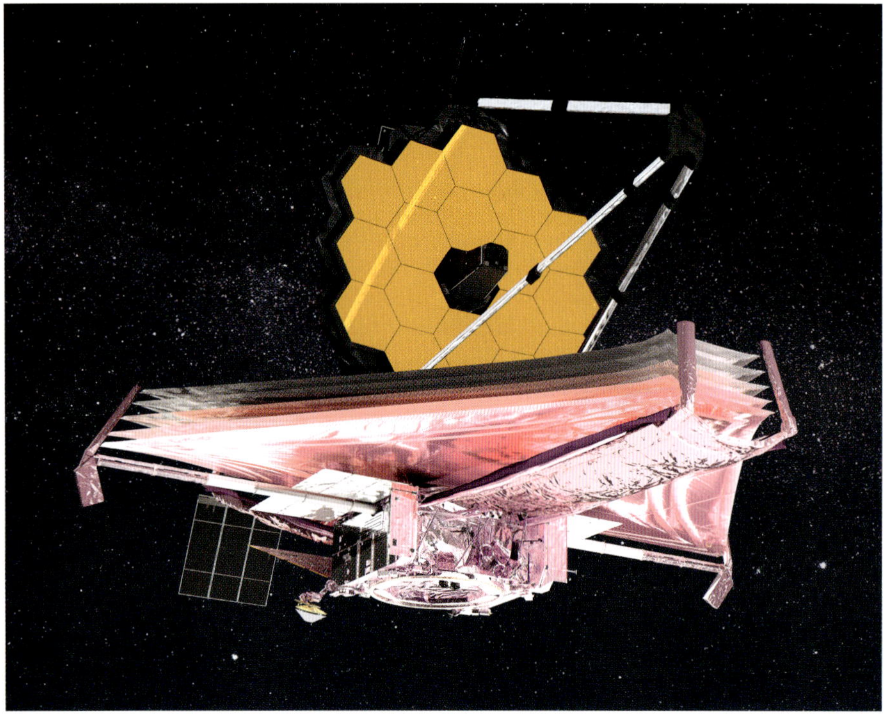

This rendering of the James Webb Space Telescope highlights its iconic hexagonal mirrors.

NASA/CIL/Adriana Manrique Gutierrez

"Liftoff! From a tropical rainforest to the edge of time itself, James Webb begins a voyage back to the birth of the universe." With those words, the James Webb Space Telescope (JWST) was launched from the Guiana Space Centre in French Guiana on December 25, 2021. Once it entered orbit around the Sun at the second Lagrange point (L2) about a million miles from Earth, JWST unfolded to reach its full size, becoming the largest, most powerful space telescope ever deployed. Its primary mirror is twenty-one feet in diameter and its sunshield is about the size of a tennis court.

With Webb's infrared wavelength coverage and extraordinary sensitivity, astronomers are collecting data that complement and extend the discoveries of the Hubble Space Telescope (see page 131). Astronomers use JWST's large, segmented mirror and advanced instrumentation to study nearly every phase of the history of the universe, ranging from the birth of the first galaxies and the formation of planets capable of supporting life to the evolution of our own solar system. The scientific discoveries and implications gleaned from JWST data have already begun to change how astronomers understand the evolution of galaxies and the composition of other planets.

ROBERT GODDARD LAUNCHES HIS HOOPSKIRT ROCKET

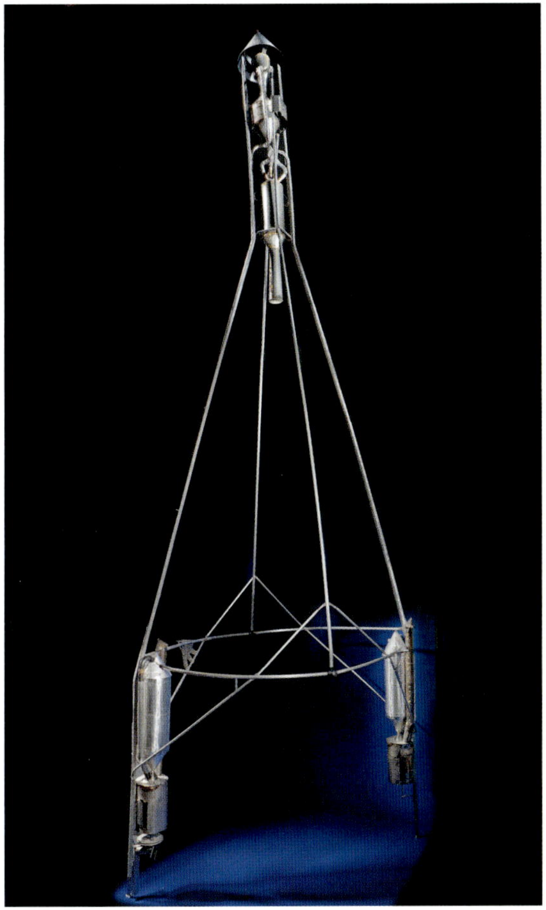

Robert Goddard's work in the late 1920s demonstrated that liquid-fueled rockets could make spaceflight possible. One of his many rocketry experiments was the Hoopskirt rocket. To make it as lightweight as possible, Goddard connected the motor and fuel tanks using a simple hollow frame that resembles a nineteenth-century underskirt, a hoopskirt. He made no effort to build the rocket as a streamlined vehicle, wanting only to test the operation of his rocket motor. The rocket's engine is at the top and pulls the vehicle upward.

Goddard first attempted to launch the rocket in July 1928, but it jammed in the launch tower. Two more failed attempts followed. He was finally successful on December 26, 1928. Goddard launched the Hoopskirt rocket near Worcester, Massachusetts, and it cleared the tower, covering a distance of just over 200 feet in 3.2 seconds.

The Hoopskirt rocket was reconstructed out of the wreckage from its launch and donated to the Smithsonian by Robert Goddard's widow. It is on display at the National Air and Space Museum.

Smithsonian's National Air and Space Museum

DECEMBER 27 ARMY ATTEMPTS TO DIVERT LAVA FLOW WITH AERIAL BOMBARDMENT

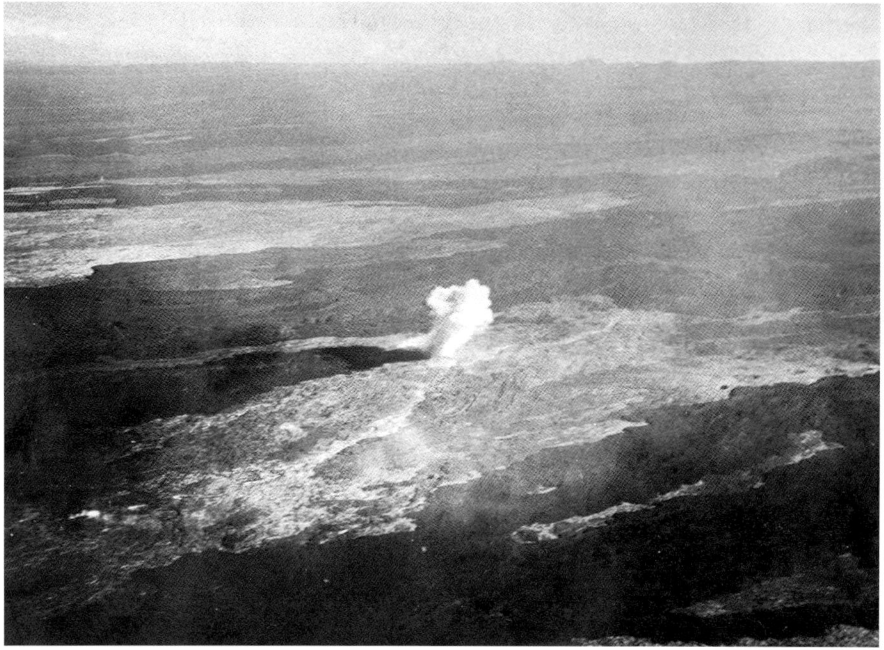

In 1935, the Army dropped twenty bombs on the Mauna Loa volcano.

U.S. Air Force

Pilots are generally advised to avoid volcanic eruptions, but in 1935 a squadron of U.S. bombers took a more aggressive approach. That November, the Mauna Loa volcano in Hawaii erupted and lava began moving toward the town of Hilo at an alarming rate of one mile per day. Hoping to divert the lava flow away from town, volcanologist Thomas Jaggar proposed detonating explosives near Mauna Loa's eruptive vent to collapse the volcano's lava channels—narrow paths of fluid lava with raised rims formed by cooling magma.

On December 27, 1935, Lt. Col. George S. Patton directed six Keystone B-3A bombers and four LB-6 light bombers to begin an assault on Mauna Loa. Flying 4,000 feet above the volcano, the aircraft dropped twenty 600-pound bombs on the lava channels. Fifteen bombs struck the margins, while five others made direct hits, spraying molten rock in all directions. When the eruption ended six days later, Jaggar claimed his idea had helped halt the lava flow, but it is unclear whether the bombing made any difference.

DECEMBER 28

TITAN II CAPTIVE-FIRED FOR THE FIRST TIME

ROCKETS AND MISSILES

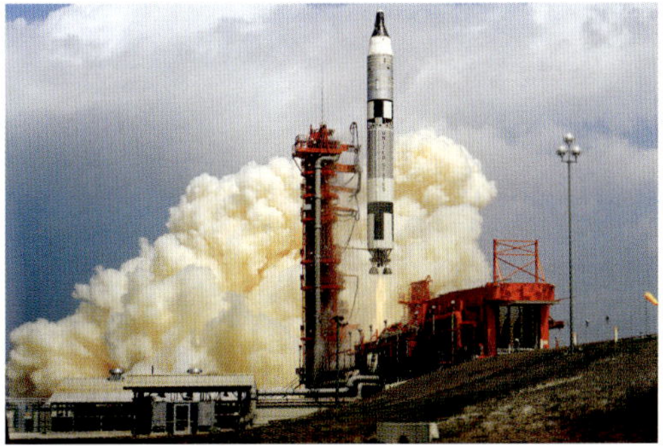

Titan II was NASA's launch vehicle of choice for the Gemini program.

NASA

The missions of NASA's second human spaceflight program, Gemini, were launched using Titan II rockets. Initially developed as an intercontinental ballistic missile (ICBM), Titan II was adapted to be a launch vehicle called Titan II GLV (Gemini Launch Vehicle). Titan II rockets were also used to launch payloads for the U.S. Air Force, NASA, and the National Oceanic and Atmospheric Administration. The Glenn L. Martin Company began work on Titan II in 1960, and the following year, on December 28, 1961, it had its first static ground test as it was captive-fired for the first time.

DECEMBER 29

AERIAL PHOTOGRAPHER MARY LIGHT PHOTOGRAPHS MT. STANLEY

GENERAL AVIATION

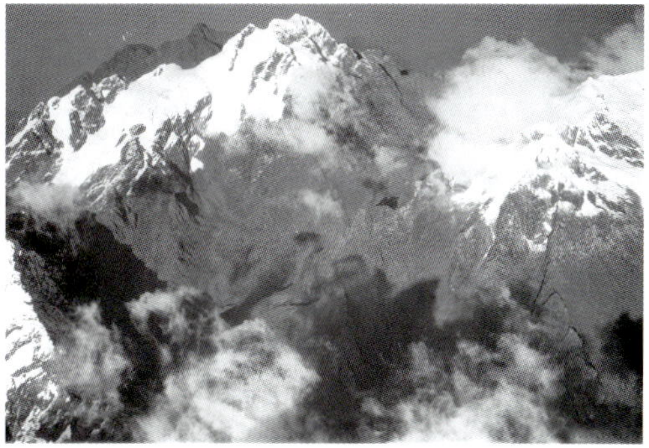

Mary Light took this photo of Mt. Stanley in Uganda in 1937.

University of Wisconsin-Milwaukee Libraries

In 1937, Richard and Mary Light embarked on a scientific expedition for the American Geographical Society to photograph the Ruwenzori mountain range in equatorial Africa. Nearly always shrouded in rain, fog, or snow, the mountains had long thwarted photographic efforts from the ground. On December 29, 1937, Mary successfully photographed the highest peak, Mt. Stanley, from above the clouds at 15,000 feet while Richard piloted their Bellanca CH cabin plane. Their celebration was delayed, however, as Mary suffered from a lack of oxygen and nearly froze to death while photographing from an open window.

GOODYEAR AIRSHIP *PILGRIM* IS RETIRED

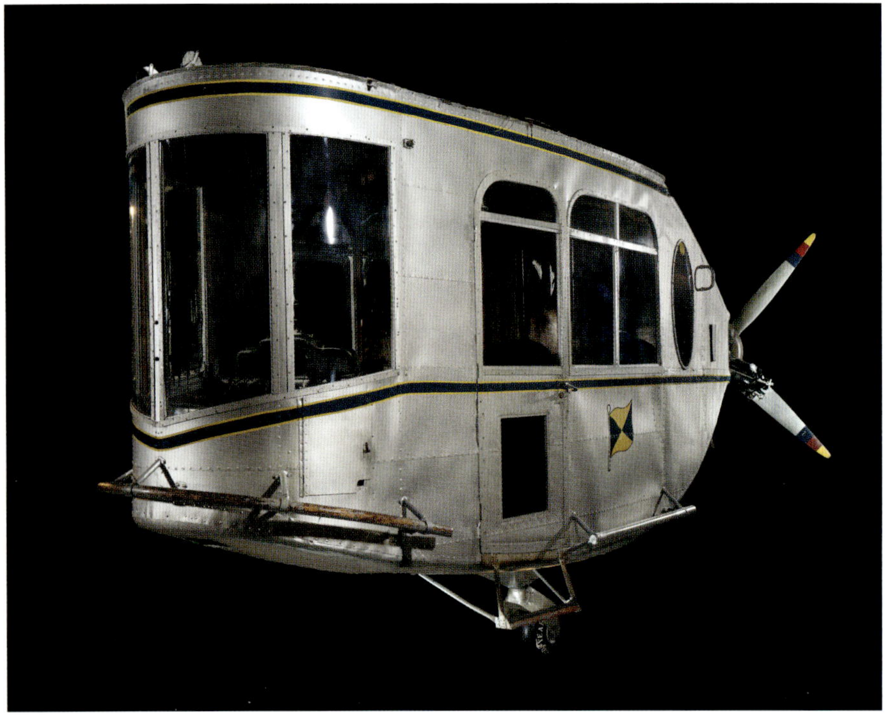

The gondola from Goodyear's *Pilgrim* airship is in the collection of the National Air and Space Museum.

Smithsonian's National Air and Space Museum

In the mid-1920s, the Goodyear Tire and Rubber Company built a fleet of small civil airships to demonstrate the value of lighter-than-air flight and train future pilots. One of these airships—the *Pilgrim*—was Goodyear's first to be inflated with helium, and made its inaugural flight above Akron, Ohio, in 1925. The *Pilgrim* had a gondola, or control car, that could accommodate a pilot and two passengers in the comfort of blue mohair velour–upholstered seats with a mahogany finished veneer.

The *Pilgrim* also came to be an iconic part of Goodyear's advertising. Every December, the airship was transformed into the "Santa Claus Express" and used for toy delivery. By the time it was retired on December 30, 1931, the *Pilgrim* had made 4,765 flights, carried 5,355 passengers, flown a total of 2,880 hours, and covered 95,000 miles.

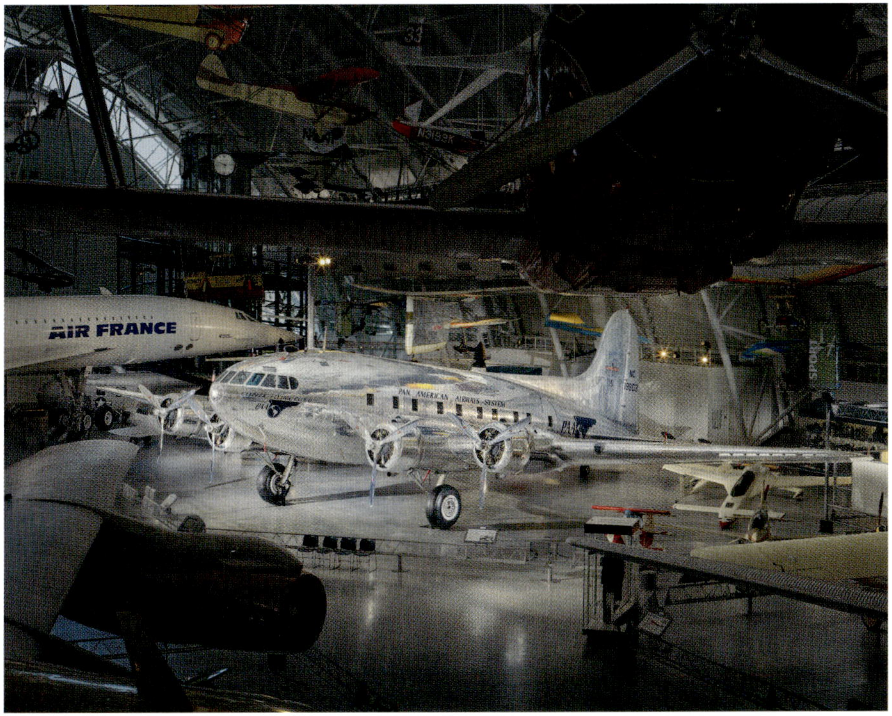

On display at the Steven F. Udvar-Hazy Center, *Clipper Flying Cloud* is the only remaining intact Boeing Stratoliner in the world.

Smithsonian's National Air and Space Museum

When it took off for its inaugural flight on December 31, 1938, the Boeing 307 Stratoliner became the first passenger aircraft with a pressurized cabin. This design feature allowed the Stratoliner to fly above rough weather at unprecedented altitudes for transports of the era. The luxurious aircraft could carry up to thirty-three passengers in great comfort in a wide fuselage fitted with sleeper berths and reclining seats.

Boeing built a total of ten Stratoliners. The first airframe was destroyed in a crash and the remaining nine were purchased by Pan American Airways, Trans World Airlines (TWA), and aviator Howard Hughes. The airlines began operating their 307s in 1940: Pan Am on its southern routes and TWA for transcontinental flights. After the U.S. entered World War II, the military conscripted both companies' Stratoliners and redesignated them as C-75s. The Stratoliners returned to commercial use at the end of the war, and at least three remained in service with various airlines into the 1960s.

HISTORY IS STILL BEING MADE

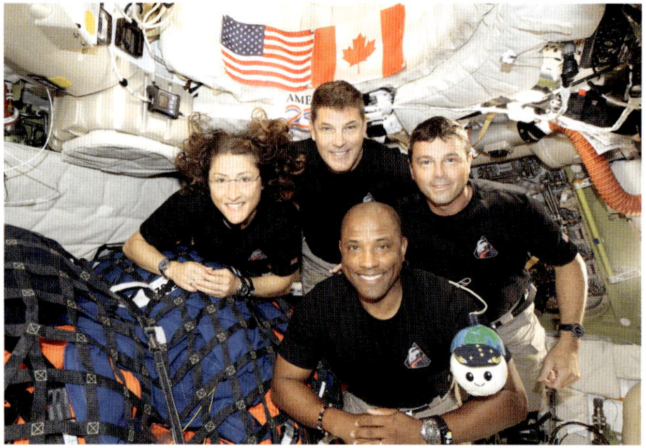

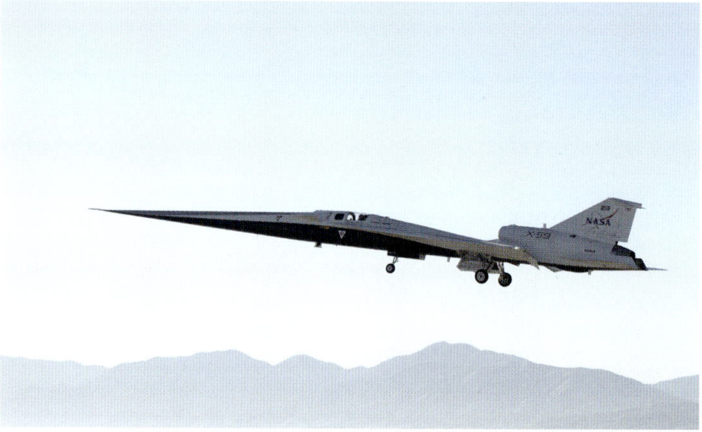

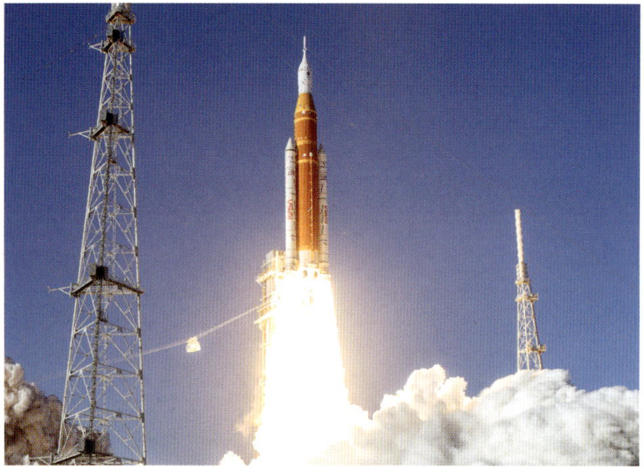

TOP LEFT The mission's zero-G indicator, a plushie named "Rise," pictured here with the crew (clockwise from left: Christina Koch, Jeremy Hansen, Reid Wiseman, and Victor Glover), became quite the mascot for Artemis II.

NASA

TOP RIGHT NASA's X-59 made its first flight on October 28, 2025, from U.S. Air Force Plant 42 in Palmdale, California.

NASA/Carla Thomas

BOTTOM LEFT The Artemis II mission launched on an SLS rocket powered by four RS-25 engines and two solid rocket boosters producing 8.8 million pounds of thrust.

NASA

One of the opportunities—and challenges—of working at the world's most popular aerospace museum is that history is still being made. Our work to chronicle aviation and space history will never be done because there will always be additional stories to tell, milestones to mark, and artifacts to collect.

Even as we look back at the history that got us to where we are today, innovation in aerospace continues. More powerful rockets are tested, new airplanes fly faster and farther, and pioneering missions explore beyond the universe's known horizons.

In just the last year, a number of exciting moments occurred as we worked on this book. One event that future aeronautics curators at the Museum will surely note was the inaugural flight of the experimental quiet supersonic aircraft—better known as the X-59 Quesst—on October 28, 2025. The X-59 is part of a joint research effort between NASA and Lockheed Martin that aims to minimize the noise of supersonic flights over inhabited areas. By turning deafening sonic booms into barely noticeable sonic "thumps," the uniquely shaped X-59 may one day help realize the sought-after dream of supersonic air transportation that is both quiet and affordable.

Our Space History curators have long observed the development of NASA's Artemis program, from initial construction of the spacecraft to the successful launch of Artemis II on April 1, 2026. As the multinational crew of Artemis II astronauts—commander Reid Wiseman, pilot Victor Glover, and mission specialists Christina Koch and Jeremy Hansen—made humanity's first trip around the Moon and back in over fifty years, the world watched the live-streamed mission and was drawn closer than ever to the unfolding history it represented. The Museum was fortunate enough to have a small artifact—a piece of fabric from the 1903 Wright Flyer (page 368)—stowed inside the Artemis II *Integrity* spacecraft. Recognizing this as an important cultural moment, our curators also diligently collected artifacts from people gathered at Kennedy Space Center for the launch. Working together with NASA, we hope to add several Artemis II objects to our extensive collection of human spaceflight artifacts—many of which were featured in this book.

The X-59 and Artemis programs are just two examples of how aerospace history continues to unfold. While we don't know what inspiring achievements the future holds, you can be sure that the National Air and Space Museum will be here to tell those stories and immortalize them for decades to come.

INDEX

C

H

L

M

N

O

P

U

V

W

X

Y

ACKNOWLEDGMENTS

We are grateful to everyone at the Smithsonian's National Air and Space Museum who supported our work on this book.

To the Museum's senior leadership team, including John and Adrienne Mars Director Chris Browne, associate director for external affairs Meg Caulk, and associate director of research and curatorial affairs Jeremy Kinney.

To the chairs of our departments: Russ Lee, Marc Sklar, and Margaret Weitekamp.

To the Museum's curators in the Department of Space History and Aeronautics Department, who provided valuable expertise and feedback: Colleen Anderson, John Anderson, Dorothy Cochrane, Tom Crouch, Roger Connor, Michael Hankins, Peter Jakab, Cathleen Lewis, Michael Neufeld, Emily Margolis, Andrew Meade McGee, Christopher Moore, Teasel Muir-Harmony, Thomas Paone, Carolyn Russo, Matt Shindell, Alex Spencer, Caroline Tapp, Samantha Thompson, and F. Robert van der Linden.

To our colleagues who helped with the images in this book: Museum photographers Mark Avino, Patrick Leonini, Eric Long, Dane Penland, and Jim Preston; the National Air and Space Museum Archives, including Marilyn Graskowiak and Kate Igoe; the Registrar Unit, including Erik Satrum and Rachel Poe; and the Smithsonian Office of General Counsel, including Melissa Wright.

To the Office of Communications, including Amelia Grabowski, Amanda Laughead, Michael Persaud, and Alison Wood.

To the team at Smithsonian Enterprises who helped make this idea a reality, including Elizabeth Bakacs, Jill Corcoran, Brigid Ferraro, and Paige Towler.

To the 2024-2025 cohort of the Smithsonian's Emerging Leaders Development Program, for their encouragement and support.

And to our loved ones, who perhaps know more about what happened each day in the history of aviation and space than they ever wanted to know.

AUTHOR BIOGRAPHIES

Amy Stamm, a digital content strategist in the Office of Communications at the National Air and Space Museum, manages the Museum's social media and works on editorial content, including blogs, videos, newsletters, and other digital projects. She specializes in taking the Museum's artifacts, expertise, and stories and making them relevant and compelling for online audiences.

Dr. Joseph Abel, a curator in the Aeronautics Department at the National Air and Space Museum, oversees the Museum's collection of artifacts related to aeronautical engineering and the aviation industry. His research examines the history of working people and labor unions in the United States, with a particular focus on aircraft manufacturing.

Dr. Jennifer Levasseur, a curator in the Department of Space History at the National Air and Space Museum, oversees the Museum's collection of artifacts related to the Space Shuttle, the International Space Station, astronaut cameras, and chronographs. Her research looks at the cultural impact of astronaut photography and how the material culture of astronaut life helps us connect to their experiences in space.

Editor: Soyolmaa Lkhagvadorj

Designer: Heesang Lee

Managing Editor: Jodi Wong

Production Manager: Larry Pekarek

Library of Congress Control Number: 2026933955

ISBN: 978-1-4197-9139-0

eISBN: 979-8-89684-261-3

Printed and bound in China

10 9 8 7 6 5 4 3 2 1

ABRAMS is represented in the UK and Europe by Abrams & Chronicle Books, 22-24 Ely Place, London EC1N 6TE and Média-Participations, 57 rue Gaston Tessier, 75166 Paris, France.

abramsandchronicle.co.uk and media-participations.com

info@abramsandchronicle.co.uk

ABRAMS The Art of Books
195 Broadway, New York, NY 10007
abramsbooks.com